THE WORLD ECONOMY

THE WORLD ECONOMY
Ted Walther

Bates College

John Wiley & Sons, Inc.
New York • Chichester • Brisbane • Toronto • Singapore • Weinheim

ACQUISITIONS EDITOR   Whitney Blake
MARKETING MANAGER   Wendy Goldner
PRODUCTION EDITOR   Edward Winkleman
COVER DESIGNER   Harry Nolan
INTERIOR DESIGNER   David Levy
MANUFACTURING MANAGER   Mark Cirillo
ILLUSTRATOR   Janet Starosta
ILLUSTRATION COORDINATOR   Rosa Bryant

This book was set in 10/12 Janson by Carlisle Communications and
printed and bound by Hamilton Printing. The cover was printed by Phoenix Color.

Recognizing the importance of preserving what has been written, it is a
policy of John Wiley & Sons, Inc. to have books of enduring value published
in the United States printed on acid-free paper, and we exert our best
efforts to that end.

Library of Congress Cataloging in Publication Data:
Walther, Ted.
   The world economy / by Ted Walther.
      p.   cm.
   Includes bibliographical references (p.).
   ISBN 0-471-13831-2 (cloth : alk. paper)
   1. International economic relations. 2. International trade.
3. Commercial policy. 4. Balance of payments. 5. International
finance. 6. Foreign exchange. 7. Debts, Public. 8. International economic
integration. I. Title.
HF1359.W355 1997
337—DC20   96-35526
                                                                    CIP

Printed in the United States of America
10 9 8 7 6 5 4 3 2 1

To Joan

Preface

This volume is designed to introduce nonspecialists to the workings of the world economy. It is specifically intended for a one-semester introductory survey of international economics for non-economics majors and economics majors who have limited background in economics. It has been written as an alternative to texts in international economics that often presuppose two years of economic analysis and are aimed primarily at economics majors with strong backgrounds in the field. For this reason, many students who have an interest in international trade and finance lack the background to profit from the typical text, and one suspects that they also lack the patience required to master the necessary theoretical tools. What these students want is a guide to help them understand the world economy's basic workings, but at the same time one that does not compel them to jump hurdles erected by high theory.

This book attempts to meet that need. It does this by casting all aspects of international trade and finance into two models suitable for students familiar with nothing beyond a course in principles of economics: market supply and demand and aggregate supply and demand. These models provide a framework to analyze and relate seemingly disparate events so that students are not forced to confront developments in isolation, but rather, are able to understand relations among variables and the economic logic behind series of events.

By no means does the use of these models make the book simplistic or devoid of analysis. Instead, its approach is strongly influenced by the style of *The Economist*, a weekly newspaper that analyzes complex issues with only basic economic tools and yet manages to explain them clearly. The text attempts to describe how the world economy works by employing a mixture of theoretical, institutional, and basic empirical analysis.

Because it is a survey, *The World Economy* does not explain all the postulates of international economics in detail. This may be disappointing, but the cost of adding further rigor at the introductory level is considerable. On the other hand, it *is* assumed that readers have already been introduced to basic economic concepts (the review up front of market supply/demand and aggregate supply/demand is to refresh readers who may have been away from the subject for an extended period).

Features of the Book

The outline of the book is novel. Part 1 outlines fundamentals—market supply/demand and aggregate supply/demand and their relation to international economics, the foreign exchange market, and balance of payments accounting. In particular, the first two chapters emphasize the analytical tools that will be used throughout. This format enables students to move with ease from the micro to the macro effects of a tariff or a currency depreciation. Moreover, by reviewing fundamentals at the outset, a student can immediately begin to understand what transpires, on a day-to-day basis, if the dollar takes a dip on the foreign exchange market or Japan and Europe move from recession to expansion. The underlying assumption, and hence justification, is that world economic events move rapidly in the headlines, and a student should not have to wait until midterm before he or she can begin to use analytical tools to understand and discuss them.

Parts 2 through 5 follow the conventional progression of most courses in international economics through international trade, commercial policy, balance of payments adjustment, and international monetary policy. Part 6 then takes up selected current issues of the world economy, using tools already presented.

There are other features to this text as well. For example, in focusing on a nation's competitive position and its external accounts, the text stresses the differences in impact between investment-led and consumption-led growth. This is an important and recurring theme. In addition, the book develops an absorption schedule, which is used together with aggregate supply and demand schedules to simultaneously show an economy's internal and external positions. With these tools, a student can easily see when a devaluation may lead to an expansion in real output and an improvement in a nation's trade account, and when it may lead to a simultaneous expansion in output and the domestic price level and only modest improvement in the nation's external accounts and perhaps none at all.

Essentially, *The Word Economy* attempts to explain international trade and finance as directly and clearly as possible in order to attract and inform the widest possible audience. Because of the audience toward which it is directed, the book does not employ mathematics in the main body of the text, except for some rudimentary algebra, which students have already confronted in principles of economics.

Pedagogical Tools

The books contains several pedagogical tools which are designed to enhance the learning process.

BOXES

There are 59 boxes in the text. Some are used to further explain certain topics introduced in the text, others present statistics and describe pertinent points, and still others are case studies. In addition, current events are discussed throughout the text in order to illustrate theoretical concepts.

END OF CHAPTER QUESTIONS

There are a number of review questions at the end of each chapter. In most cases, the answers are quite direct; but in others, the answer requires students to look at the question from various perspectives.

GLOSSARY

The extensive glossary describes all the terms highlighted in the text, plus some additional terms that a student may encounter when he or she studies the international economy.

KEY TERMS

Major terms are boldfaced throughout the text and listed together at the end of each chapter. Studying these terms provides students with a quick way to understand some of the key concepts of each chapter.

MARGIN COMMENTS

Running comments are used throughout the text in order to reinforce the students' understanding of key concepts. The margin notes also provide a quick reference for locating central ideas.

SUGGESTED READINGS

Suggested readings are given at the end of most chapters. The readings have been kept at a suitable level. Students are warned in advance if a particular reading is at a more advanced level.

INSTRUCTOR'S RESOURCE GUIDE

The Instructor's Resource Guide that accompanies this text presents an overview of each chapter and points out some chapter topics that students may find difficult. In addition, the guide provides some sample examination questions.

Acknowledgements

In writing this text, I have incurred many debts. My greatest debt is to Paul Nockleby, agent, editor, and friend. Without his guidance and patience, this project would never have got off the ground.

The idea for this text first emerged while I was on leave at the University of Bath. I want to express my appreciation to the faculty of economics at the University of Bath, especially to David Collard, John Cullis, Philip Jones, and Colin Lawson, for their hospitality and kindness. Two of my colleagues at Bates College, David Aschauer and Carl Schwinn helped sweep some cobwebs from my mind on several points. How does one ever adequately thank a colleague?

This book owes a lot to the criticism and advice of the reviewers, some anonymous, who have read and commented on the many drafts of the manuscript. In most instances, their comments were far more than very helpful. Thanks are due to:

Carol Adams, formerly at the University of California at Santa Cruz, Sohrab Behdad of Denison University, Chi-Chur Chao of Oregon State University, Susan Pozo of Western Michigan University, Ronald M. Schramm of Columbia University, Mark Schupack of Brown University, Zeljan E. Suster of the University of New Haven, and Helen Youngelson-Neal of Portland State University.

I am also grateful to Gary Burke, formally associated with Mayfield Publishing Co., who encouraged me to continue on with this project despite some setbacks.

Obviously, I am heavily indebted to many individuals at John Wiley, especially to Whitney Blake, executive editor, to Edward Winkleman, senior production editor, to Shelley Flannery, copyeditor, to Harry Nolan, designer, to Rosa Bryant, illustration coordinator, to Mark Cirillo, manufacturing manager, and to Wendy Goldner, senior marketing manager.

To all of them, thank you. I hardly need to add that I am solely responsible for any errors and omissions.

Ted Walther
Lewiston, Maine

Contents

Part 2: International Trade

Chapter 5: Trade and the International Division of Labor

Chapter 6: Trade and Prices

Part 4: Balance of Payments Policy

Chapter 10: Trade Balance and Income Adjustment

Chapter 11: Exchange Rate Adjustment

Chapter 12: Capital Flows and the Balance of Payments

Chapter 13: Money and the Balance of Payments

Part 5: Exchange Rate Systems, International Reserves, and Economic Policy

Chapter 14: Exchange Rate Systems

Chapter 15: International Liquidity and International Monetary Cooperation

Part 6: Current Economic Issues

Chapter 16: Economic Integration

Chapter 17: The North American Free Trade Agreement

Introduction

L ike all economic phenomena, international trade is a *double-edged sword*: It extends benefits while imposing costs. For many countries, trade is the key to economic growth and employment. But despite ample evidence that the benefits a nation derives from trade swamp the associated costs, surging imports can often hurt certain domestic industries and cause painful dislocations and unemployment.

The Bright Side

Today questions concerning the costs and benefits of international trade have become more compelling because trade has become more important. In the United States, exports and imports as a percentage of *gross domestic product (GDP)* have more than doubled since 1965 (Figure I.1). And rapid rises in exports and imports as a percentage of GDP have occurred in other nations besides the United States. Except in the case of Japan, the export/import ratios of major developed countries have grown substantially—even Italy's ratios have risen 27 percent. Table I.1 compares the export and import ratios of major *Organization for Economic Cooperation and Development (OECD)* countries in 1965 and 1990.

Economic growth and stability have many causes. But an expanding world economy is a sturdy source for economic stability, for trade reduces the magnitude and duration of economic imbalances of individual nations. When a nation's economy slows down due to a drop in domestic demand, as long as the rest of the world economy remains prosperous, trade makes it easier for the country to recover from recession since foreign markets provide opportunities for sustained production and employment.

Trade is, in addition, a powerful catalyst for economic growth. Thus, it is not surprising that an expanding world economy, triggered by international trade, led to rising living standards in the developed world. Economic progress after World War II

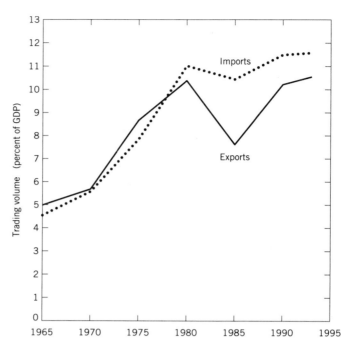

FIGURE 1.1 U.S. exports and imports as a percent of GDP.

In the last 25 years, U.S. exports and imports have more than doubled as a percentage of gross domestic product.

Source: International Monetary Fund, *International Financial Statistics* (various issues).

extended far beyond the boundaries of the major developed countries. In many *less-developed countries (LDCs)* real economic growth, spurred on because the developed world provides markets for burgeoning export industries of the LDCs and the *newly industri-*

TABLE 1.1 Export [X] and Import [M] Ratios for Major OECD Nations

Nation	1965		1990	
	X/GDP	*M/GDP*	*X/GDP*	*M/GDP*
Canada	18.6%	18.8%	25.4%	25.6%
France	12.6	11.6	22.5	22.6
Germany	19.0	18.9	36.5	29.7
Italy	14.9	14.0	19.0	19.4
Japan	10.5	9.1	10.8	10.1
UK	18.3	19.3	24.2	26.8
United States	5.0	4.5	10.1	11.3

Source: Calculated from relevant country pages in International Monetary Fund, *International Financial Statistics Yearbook*, 1993.

alized countries (NICs), outstripped population growth and led to higher living standards. Some LDCs outperformed developed nations. Hong Kong, Taiwan, Singapore, South Korea, and more recently China have had faster rates of economic growth than most OECD countries.

In summary, from the end of World War II to the early 1970s, the world economy grew at a relatively calm and stable rate. Recessions were temporary and countries experiencing trade imbalances returned, after adjustment, to accustomed patterns of growth and, for the most part, low inflation.

The Dark Side

Calmness and stability ended in the early 1970s, when economic growth tailed off in major OECD countries. Spurred by two oil shocks, inflation accelerated, unemployment rose, and the world economy slipped badly. In the late 1970s and the 1980s several problems emerged paradoxically against the backdrop of international trade's growing importance, among them wide fluctuations in exchange rates, staggering international debts, fears about collapse of international capital markets, and new trade restrictions by countries attempting to spur domestic employment by reducing imports. World trade, which had expanded between 6 and 8.5 percent annually from the 1950s through the 1970s, came to a near-standstill between 1980 and 1985 when trade grew at a paltry 1.2 percent annual rate.

Then, between 1985 and 1990, world trade picked up again, growing at an annual rate of 5.6 percent. By 1987, the economies of all seven major OECD nations grew in real terms, inflation was cut, and unemployment declined, though modestly. Improved economic performance of OECD nations in the late 1980s was accompanied by a substantial jump in their exports of goods and services.

The economic situation in the seven major OECD nations declined in the early 1990s, only to rebound in late 1993. In the rest of the world the economic picture has been mixed: Some countries, China for example, have enjoyed solid economic growth, while others have stagnated. In most cases, economic growth has been closely tied to export expansion. When world trade is not expanding, it does not provide a safety valve for domestic economies. Thus, President Clinton's attempts to stimulate the U.S. economy in the early 1990s were handicapped by recessions in Japan and Western Europe, which held down U.S. exports. (See Figure I.2.)

In recent years, the bright hopes of the immediate postwar period which envisioned international trade and finance as a catalyst for securing a better world have been dimmed, as chronic recession plus incessant bickering over trade policy has plagued the international economic scene. Even the hopeful conclusion to the *Uruguay round* of trade negotiations in late 1993 did not completely change the outlook. Negotiators hailed the pact as a breakthrough to foster world trade expansion. Other analysts argued more cautiously that, while the Uruguay round may have halted the slide toward more restricted trade, it did not reverse the trend. One exception was passage of the *North American Free Trade Agreement* in 1993 creating a *free trade area* that includes Canada, Mexico, and the United States.

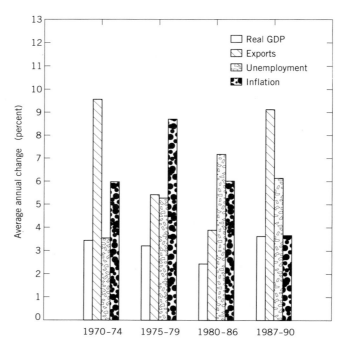

FIGURE 1.2 Average annual changes in major OECD economies.

In the last 20 to 25 years, the growth of exports and the growth of total output in the major OECD nations have moved in the same direction, an increase in the growth rate of one variable being associated with an increase in the rate of growth of the other and a decrease in the rate of growth of one variable being associated with a decrease in the rate of growth of the other.

Source: Organization for Economic Cooperation and Development, *Economic Outlook* (various issues).

Finding the Middle Ground

Economic growth since World War II has not followed from some immutable law of economics. Through careful diplomacy and negotiation, the major Western economic powers have sought to establish an international trading system that would guarantee the prosperity of all countries. Two organizations were founded to help create and maintain economic order: the *International Monetary Fund (IMF)* and the *General Agreement on Tariffs and Trade (GATT)*. The purpose of the IMF is to oversee international monetary policy, and that of its sister organization, the *International Bank for Reconstruction and Development (IBRD)*, more commonly known as the *World Bank*, to funnel capital from the developed to the less-developed world. The GATT was established as a forum for negotiation to assist world leaders who believe that unrestricted or free trade is best for all but who are individually unable on their own to eliminate trade barriers. The GATT was very successful at first. By the time the *Tokyo* round of tariff negotiations concluded in 1979, *tariffs* had been virtually eliminated among the major developed nations that dominated world trade. After 1980, however, *nontariff trade barriers*, such as *voluntary export restraints* and the *multifiber arrangement*, were erected. A voluntary export agreement limited the number of cars Japan could export to the United States, while the multifiber arrangement limited the quantity of textiles that developing countries could export to the developed world. The painfully slow progress of the Uruguay round of trade talks may have further jeopardized international trade, although the conclusion of the talks may have given world trade new life.

Today the world economy stands at a crossroads, and the effects of today's decisions will extend far beyond the world of economists and bankers. *Economic analysis counts.* But the world economy does not operate in a vacuum—it operates in an environment created, for better or worse, in the political arena. In addition to the question of economic feasibility, there are questions of social desirability and political possibility. The international debt problem and the economic difficulties facing Eastern Europe, for example, depend primarily on political will. If the politics of trade and trade barriers are to be resolved, others besides economists must become involved.

References and Suggested Readings

International trade theory includes much analysis which goes over the heads of lay readers. Suggested readings at the ends of chapters are held to those accessible to introductory readers.

Students who wish to take a bigger bite into the theory of international economics should consult some of the more advanced texts available. Three of the better texts are: Richard E. Caves, Jeffrey A. Frankel, and Ronald W. Jones, *World Trade and Payments: An Introduction*, 6th edition (New York: HarperCollins, 1993); Peter B. Kenen, *The International Economy*, 3rd edition (New York: Cambridge University Press, 1994); and Paul R. Krugman and Maurice Obstfeld, *International Economics: Theory and Policy*, 3rd edition (New York: HarperCollins, 1994).

International economic statistics vary in quality and in the methods used to calculate them. The IMF, which attempts to reconcile the statistical approaches of its member states, is the best source of information through its major publications, including *International Financial Statistics*, *Balance of Payments Statistics*, and *The Direction of Trade*. The United Nations *Yearbook of International Trade Statistics* breaks down the exports and imports of many nations into a multitude of categories.

The IMF and the World Bank, respectively, annually publish *The World Economic Outlook* and *The World Development*

Report. Together with the *Annual Report* of the IMF, these volumes provide a wealth of description, analysis, statistics, and projections on pressing issues in world economy. The GATT publishes *International Trade* each year in two volumes, the first of which provides an overview of the world economy plus chapters on international trade, while the second offers a wealth of international trade statistics by region and products.

The Institute for International Economics, a Washington-based research institution, has published many works on the international economy. Its series, *Policy Analysis in International Economics*, includes relatively brief, readable, original essays on current problems. Many of these are cited and recommended throughout this text.

The Economist, a newsweekly published in London, is an invaluable source for information about current developments in the world economy. *The Economist* regularly distills advanced articles and presents them in highly readable form. It also presents surveys on countries and topics on a regular basis—see, for example, its two surveys on "The Global Economy," both written by Pam Woodall, in the October 1, 1994 and the October 7, 1995 issues. Individuals seeking a brief and lucid introduction to economic terms and institutions might consult Ruppert Pennet-Rea and Bill Emmott, *Pocket Economist*, 2nd edition (Oxford: Basil Blackwell/The Economist, 1987).

Fundamentals

Chapter 1

Open Economy Microeconomics: An Overview

Models are an essential tool of scientific analysis as important to economists as they are to meteorologists or aeronautical engineers. At their best, models explain relationships among variables and allow economists to project the impact of specific economic policies on an industry or a whole nation. At a minimum, models provide a framework allowing an individual to analyze and connect seemingly unrelated events and to grasp the logic behind a series of economic developments. Without a model, one is forced to take an ad hoc view of events and is often completely powerless to relate developments in one area to events in another.

The Path Ahead

Models, then, are the starting point for any economic analysis and one needs to spend time understanding how they work and how to use them. Accordingly, Chapter 1 constructs an extremely useful model for analyzing the microeconomics of trade—how trade affects individual markets and industries; then, in Chapter 2, a different model is developed to study the effects of international trade on the total economy. These two models are to the economist what the hammer and saw are to the carpenter—basic equipment. They are the tools required for understanding other dynamics of the field, such as tariffs and currency fluctuations. Chapter 3 follows these two foundations with a brief presentation of the foreign exchange market. Since most international trade and financial transactions go through or are carried out in the foreign exchange market, Chapter 3 is an important foundation to much that follows.

That, then, is an overview of the first three chapters. As for Chapter 1, after briefly reviewing the basics of market supply and demand, we concentrate on three issues:

- How international trade affects the quantity of goods domestic industries produce and the price they receive for their output.

- The impact of international trade on wages, employment opportunities, and returns on invested capital.
- Macro- or economywide economic developments which may benefit or harm an industry when a country begins to trade.

A Review of Market Supply and Demand

A **demand curve** is a graphical representation of demand schedule.

A **demand schedule** shows the quantity of a good, service, or input that will be demanded at various prices providing everything else is constant.

Picking up where we began in principles of economics, we see that the microeconomics of international trade can be analyzed employing market supply and demand schedules and curves. (Microeconomics, again, is the study of economic phenomena as they affect individual markets and, therefore, individuals, households, and firms.) A **demand curve,** such as D or D_1 in Figure 1.1a, is a graphical representation of a **demand schedule.** A demand schedule, such as Table 1.1, shows the quantity of a good demanded at various prices and illustrates that as the price of a commodity drops more of it will be purchased. This means that a demand curve will slope down from left to right, also illustrating the principle that at a lower price some individuals acquire more of the good and others are induced to buy it for the first time.

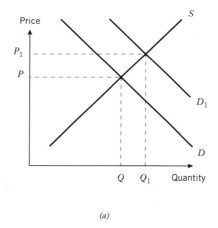

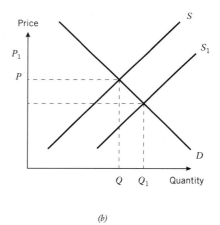

(a)   (b)

FIGURE 1.1 Market supply and demand.

The equilibrium or market-clearing price is established when the quantity demanded equals the quantity supplied, or at the price and quantity where the demand and supply curves intersect. In panel (a), the quantity demanded equals the quantity supplied when the price equals P. The price, P, however, will be the equilibrium price only if other things remain equal. An increase in demand due to an increase in income, for example, will shift the demand curve from D to D_1 and raise the equilibrium price to P_1 and the equilibrium quantity to Q_1. On the supply side, an increase in labor productivity, for example, will shift the supply curve to the right from S to S_1 in panel (b). This means that more units of the commodity will be supplied at all prices. Given the shift in the supply curve, the economy will move down its demand curve until the quantity supplied equals the quantity demanded at the price P_0 and the quantity Q_1.

TABLE 1.1 Hypothetical Demand for Wheat

Price ($ per bushel)	Quantity Demanded (bushels)
$1.45	120
$1.35	160
$1.25	240
$1.15	360

A supply schedule shows the quantity of a good, service, or input that will be supplied at various prices provided everything else is constant.

A supply curve is a graphical representation of a supply schedule.

Some **capital** is mobile (personal computers), but much capital is industry specific. It cannot be shunted between various industries, but can be used only in specific industries. A jackhammer cannot be used to fix rickety teeth.

A **supply schedule,** such as shown in Table 1.2, shows the quantity that will be supplied at various prices providing everything else is held constant. When graphed, a supply schedule becomes a **supply curve** such as S in Figure 1.1a. The supply curve's positive slope indicates that a greater quantity of a good or service will be offered for sale as its price rises. The standard explanation of the upward slope of the supply curve emphasizes rising unit costs of production, that is, it costs more to produce the second unit of output than the first, more to produce the third than the second, and so on.

Why do unit costs of production rise as output expands? In order to produce greater output, the industry will have to hire more labor, purchase additional raw materials, and utilize ever more capital equipment. If the industry is small compared with the total economy, it can purchase an unlimited supply of raw materials and labor at a steady price. Whether it purchases a large or small quantity of labor, one small industry's actions will not dramatically impact the overall wage rate. If the wage rate is $10, a small industry can hire as much labor as it desires at this rate.

On the other hand, if an industry needs to purchase large quantities of specific raw materials that are in relatively short supply in order to expand production, it may have to pay a higher price to obtain them. This demand for specialized inputs can be true for labor as well. Some occupations are specialized and require extended training so that it is impossible for an untrained individual to enter the specialized labor market on short notice; a plumber cannot become a doctor on short notice nor, for that matter, can a doctor become a plumber in the short run. Therefore, when an industry needs to hire specialized labor, it usually has to offer such labor a higher wage in order to obtain its services. But if we can assume that labor is homogeneous, then we can also assume that an industry is able to hire an unlimited quantity of labor at a given wage rate.

Capital equipment, unlike unskilled labor, is not homogeneous and cannot be shunted from one industry to another. Delivery vans, trucks, and computers can be

TABLE 1.2 A Firm's Hypothetical Supply Schedule

Output	Labor	Wages (total)	Output Per Worker	Labor Costs Per Unit of Output
10	1	$10	10	$1.00
18	2	$20	9	$1.11
24	3	$30	8	$1.25
28	4	$40	7	$1.43

transferred from one industry to another with relative ease. But a loom cannot be used for printing a newspaper nor can a printing press be employed to weave cloth. Because a significant proportion of the existing capital stock cannot move between industries in the short run, we can assume for purposes of discussion that capital equipment is immobile.

Given these assumptions plus the assumption that raw materials are relatively unimportant in the production process, Table 1.2 explains the positive slope of the supply curve.

The **law of diminishing returns.** A common-sense idea that states if the quantity of capital is fixed, hiring increasing amounts of labor will, after some point, increase output at a decreasing rate. If the quantity of labor is fixed, utilizing more and more capital will have the same result.

Suppose the demand for wheat increases, raising its price, and that the typical firm attempts to capitalize on the higher demand by expanding its output. As the firm hires additional labor, output increases but at a decreasing rate, or the **law of diminishing returns** holds. Why? With the quantity of capital fixed, the quantity of capital per worker decreases as additional workers are hired. Because each worker combines with less capital, labor productivity, or output per laborer, falls as more are hired as indicated in column 4. Given a constant wage rate, total wages increase by a set amount as each additional worker is hired. Output, however, increases at a decreasing rate and this means that labor costs per unit of output increase as a greater quantity is produced. Higher labor costs per unit of output, in turn, "explain" why the supply curve has a positive slope.

If we assume that there are 10 firms in the wheat industry, all with similar supply schedules, the supply of wheat and the demand for wheat (as presented in Table 1.1) will be equal when the price of wheat is $1.25 per bushel. At this price, the quantity of wheat offered for sale equals the quantity of wheat demanded. Thus, $1.25 is the equilibrium price in the wheat market.

Why Demand and Supply Curves Shift

A demand curve shows the quantity demanded at various prices providing everything else is constant. Economic conditions, however, seldom remain constant and, as they change, supply and demand curves can shift either to the left or to the right.

First consider demand. If incomes rise, people will demand more of a whole multitude of products at every price. For example, given a hefty boost in their income, individuals will demand more travel. Therefore, the demand curve for travel services will shift to the right. If the price of a substitute good goes up, people will demand more of a particular product at all prices. The best known illustration of such substitution relates the price of Coca-Cola and the demand for Pepsi-Cola. If the price of Coca-Cola rises, the demand curve for Pepsi-Cola will shift to the right. In addition to a rise in income or an increase in the price of a substitute commodity, a change in tastes will cause a demand curve to shift. The development of compact discs caused the demand curve for records to shift to the left. In conclusion, any development that increases the demand for a given commodity at all prices shifts the demand curve to the right. This is shown in Figure 1.1a, where the demand curve shifts from D to D_1. Such a shift means that individuals will purchase more of the commodity at every price even though they will still buy less of it at high prices compared with low prices.

Supply curves also shift to the left or to the right for various reasons. If more firms enter a particular industry, the market or industry supply curve will shift to the right from S to S_1 in Figure 1.1b. Even if the number of firms remains constant, but each firm increases its capital stock or the size of its plant and equipment, the industry supply curve will shift to the right. Referring back to Table 1.2, an increase in the amount of capital per worker will raise labor productivity and boost output per worker. As a result, the values in column 1 will increase. In turn, assuming the wage rate is constant, the greater productivity will reduce labor costs per unit of output. A technological breakthrough will also shift the supply curve to the right. The supply curve can also shift to the left. An increase in the price of inputs, for example a higher wage rate in Table 1.2, will raise labor costs per unit of output and shift the supply curve to the left.

Elasticity: Measuring the Impact of a Change in Price

It is important to know why supply curves and demand curves shift. But it is equally important to know how much a change in price will affect the quantity demanded and the quantity supplied. Consider Figure 1.1b again. Suppose the supply curve shifts from S to S_1. As a result, the price drops and the economy moves down along the demand curve to a new equilibrium price and quantity. The question is: How much did the price drop and how much did the quantity demanded increase? Since the slope of the demand curve tells us how much the quantity demanded increases following a decrease in the price, if we measure the slope, we should have the answer.

But there is a problem here. Prices are measured in different units of money, such as nickels, dimes, and dollars, while quantities are computed in bolts of cloth, tons of steel, bushels of wheat, and other units of measurement. We have no way of easily comparing the effect of a $1 decline in price on the demand for steel with its impact on the demand for bananas. Although measuring the slope is a good place to start, it is not in itself sufficient to make a comparison easy.

Price elasticity is the percentage change in the quantity demanded or supplied given a percentage change in the price of the product in question. If the price of a Big Mac changes by 10 percent, elasticity tells us how much the percentage change in the quantity demanded will be.

This difficulty is a major reason why economists employ a measure called **price elasticity** to calculate the effect of a change in the price on the quantity demanded or supplied. Expressed formally, the price elasticity of demand is the percentage change in the quantity demanded divided by the percentage change in price, or:

$$\epsilon_D = \%\Delta Q / \%\Delta P$$

where ϵ_D equals the price elasticity of demand. If the quantity demanded rises by 5 percent following a 1 percent decrease in the price, the price elasticity of demand equals -5. (The negative sign of the price elasticity of demand reflects the inverse relationship between the quantity demanded and the price.) In this case, since the percentage change in quantity demanded exceeds the percentage change in the price and the resulting quotient is greater than 1, measured in absolute terms, it tells us that demand is heavily influenced by price. In such cases, demand is said to be price elastic. If the resulting quotient is less than 1, measured in absolute terms, the quantity demanded is not responsive to changes in price and demand is said to be price inelastic. The price elasticity of supply can be measured in a similar manner. Although it is not strictly

Income elasticity is the percentage change in the quantity demanded divided by the percentage change in income. It tells us how much more (less) of a particular commodity, say champagne, people will demand—measured as a percentage change—when their income increases (decreases)—also measured as a percentage change.

cricket, one can normally get an indication of the elasticity of the demand curve, and the supply curve, by observing the slope of the curve. If it is flat, it is elastic; if it is steep or vertical, it is inelastic.[1]

We have just described how a change in price will, providing other things remain constant, lead to a change in the quantity demand. The impact of a change in income on the demand for a commodity is measured by **income elasticity**, or by the percentage change in the quantity demanded divided by the percentage change in income. This relationship can be expressed as a formula.

$$\epsilon_y = \frac{\%\Delta Q}{\%\Delta Y}$$

The **cross-elasticity** of demand measures the percentage change in the demand for one good, Pepsi-Cola, relative to the percentage change in the price of another, Coca-Cola. Formally, cross-elasticity is written as follows:

$$\epsilon_{AB} = \frac{\%\Delta Q_A}{\%\Delta P_B}$$

If the cross-elasticity of demand is positive, the goods are substitutes—an increase in the price of Coke increases the demand for Pepsi. If the cross-elasticity of demand is negative, the goods are complements—a decrease in the price of ski holiday packages, for example, will increase the demand for ski equipment.

Using Elasticity

Cross-elasticity. Essentially the Whopper effect on the demand for Big Macs, or percentage change in the demand for Big Macs given a change in the price of Whoppers. In this case, the cross-elasticity is most likely positive since the two health foods are substitutes. The cross-elasticity of demand for french fries and Big Macs is probably negative. A decrease in the price of Big Macs will probably be associated with an increase in demand for french fries since french fries and Big Macs are complements.

It is important to know how to compute elasticity, but it is more crucial to grasp how elasticity can be employed as a tool in economic analysis. The success or failure of an economic policy often turns on the question of how responsive the quantity supplied and demanded is to a change in price. For example, in the summer of 1993—and in the summer of 1994, as well—the American authorities attempted to talk down the value of the dollar. Whether or not their lecturing played a role is a moot point, but it so hap-

---

[1]In some cases the slope and elasticity of the demand curve are one and the same. A demand schedule with constant elasticity can take the following form: $P = Q_0 Q_D{}^{-\beta}$, where P equals price, Q_0 equals some constant, Q_D equals the quantity demanded at various prices, and β equals the price elasticity of demand, which is negative because of the inverse relation between the quantity demand and price. When the expression is graphed, it is hyperbolic. However, transforming the values of P and Q into natural logarithms yields: $\ln P = \ln Q_0 - \beta \ln Q_D$. The demand curve is now a straight line; more important, $-\beta$ equals the slope of equation and its reciprocal equals the price elasticity of demand or $(dP/P)/(dQ/Q) = -\beta$, or $\%\Delta P/\%\Delta Q = -\beta$, and $\%\Delta Q/\%\Delta P = 1/-\beta$. Thus if the slope of the equation equals 0, or is a horizontal line so that $\beta = 0$, the elasticity of the demand curve relative to price is infinite. If the slope tends toward infinity or is a vertical line, the elasticity of the curve is zero. And if the slope equals -1, which means that $\beta = -1$, the price elasticity of the demand curve is one or unity. Supply elasticity can be computed in the same manner, although the initial expression would equal $P = Q_0 Q_S{}^{\beta}$.

BOX 1.1 International Elasticities

The price elasticity of demand varies among products. As one might suspect, basic food-stuffs such as onions and potatoes have low demand elasticities, while the demand for sporting goods is highly elastic.

In the world economy, the study of elasticity centers on individual countries rather than individual commodities. Thus we measure the elasticity of demand for a nation's exports and the nation's elasticity of demand for imports. We ask the question: How much will a 5 percent change in price change the volume of a nation's imports, exports, or both? We also ask: Given a 3 percent change in income, how much will imports increase?

Jaime Marquez estimated the price and income elasticities for several nations and groups of nations using quarterly data from 1973 to 1985. His estimates are presented in Table 1.3. (Note once again that the negative sign for the price elasticities reflects the inverse relation between prices and quantities.)

TABLE 1.3 International Elasticities

Country	Import Price Elasticity	Export Price Elasticity	Income Elasticity (Imports)
Canada	−1.02	−.83	1.84
Germany	−.60	−.66	1.88
Japan	−.93	−.93	.35
United Kingdom	−.47	−.44	2.51
United States	−.92	−.99	1.94
ROECD*	−.49	−.83	
Developing countries	−.81	−.63	
OPEC*	−1.14	−.57	

*ROECD equals rest of the OECD countries, a group of developed countries. OPEC stands for Organization of Petroleum Exporting Countries.

Source: Jaime Marquez, "Bilateral Trade Elasticities." *Review of Economics and Statistics* 72 (February 1990) Table 2, p. 75. ©1990 by the President and Fellows of Harvard College.

pens that the yen rose from ¥120/$ to ¥105/$ during this period—a yen appreciation against the dollar of some 13 percent.

Why were American officials so anxious to push down the value of the dollar? In their view, yen appreciation would raise the dollar price of Japanese goods in the United States. And when Americans confronted the higher prices, they would purchase fewer Japanese products. In turn, if Americans spent a lower total sum of dollars on Japanese products, the United States trade deficit with Japan, which was running at a yearly rate of approximately $40 billion at that time, would be reduced.

Elasticity analysis tells us that the policy would be successful only if the percentage change in the quantity of Japanese goods bought exceeded the percentage change in the price, or if the elasticity of demand was greater than one or elastic. Thus, the success of the policy depended in good measure upon the elasticity of demand.

Demand, Supply, and International Trade

The review of the basics of market supply and market demand permits us to ask: How are market supply and demand and output and consumption affected when a formerly closed economy begins to trade? To help us answer these questions, we employ the supply and demand schedules for wheat and textiles which are given in Table 1.4. (To reduce monotony, not all values are listed in the table.)

Figures 1.2a and b depict the effects of international trade on two domestic industries. The figures are bare-boned and avoid complications such as the types of textiles and wheat produced and consumed.

The domestic supply and demand for wheat is shown in Figure 1.2a. Prior to trade, supply equals demand when the price is $6. When the economy begins to trade, the domestic price must be compared with the world or international price since producers can now sell their products in either the domestic or world market and consumers can purchase either domestically produced or foreign-produced commodities. If both the domestic price and the world price are equal, the nation, or more accurately its firms, will neither export nor import the good and, it is assumed, consumers will only purchase domestically produced goods. However, if world and domestic prices are different, trade will take place.

In this example the world price is drawn as a horizontal line because it is assumed that the nation is a **small country,** at least from the economic if not the geographic or physical point of view. Its consumption and production of wheat is such a small proportion of the world's total consumption and production that regardless of the amount of wheat it consumes or produces, the world price of wheat will not be affected. As a result, the world's elasticity of demand and supply of wheat is infinite from the nation's point of view. Given these assumptions plus the assumption that the country is an efficient wheat producer, the world price line, Pw, is also the world's wheat demand curve, Dw, from the nation's point of view.

Because the nation is an efficient wheat producer, the domestic price of wheat is below the world price prior to trade. When trade begins, foreigners purchase domestic wheat because of its low price and, in the process, drive the domestic price up to the assumed world price of $10. Domestic firms pick up production and produce 10 units of wheat. Domestic consumers, confronted with the higher price, reduce their con-

In the case of a **small country,** the world price line is drawn as a horizontal line since regardless of the quantity the nation demands or supplies, the world price does not budge.

TABLE 1.4 Supply and Demand for Wheat and Textiles

	Wheat			Textiles	
Price	Quantity Demanded	Quantity Supplied	Price	Quantity Demanded	Quantity Supplied
$12	0	12	$12	0	12
$10	2	10	$10	2	10
$ 8	4	8	$8	4	8
$ 6	6	6	$6	6	6
$ 4	8	4	$4	8	4
$ 2	10	2	$2	10	2
$ 0	12	0	$0	12	0

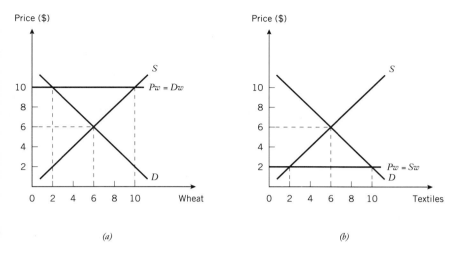

(a)   (b)

FIGURE 1.2 Market supply and demand and exports and imports.

Prior to trade, supply equals demand in the wheat market when the price is $6 and the quantity is 6 units. The same equilibrium conditions hold in the textile market as well prior to trade. With trade, the domestic price of wheat rises to the world price of wheat, $10. As a result, the quantity of wheat supplied jumps from 6 to 10 units, while the quantity of wheat demanded in the domestic market falls from 6 to 2 units. The excess of domestic production over domestic consumption at the world price, or 8 units of wheat, equals domestic exports. In the textile market, international trade drives the domestic price down to the world price, $2. At this price, the domestic consumption of textiles exceeds the domestic production of textiles by 8 units. These 8 units will be imported.

sumption of wheat to 2 units, and the excess of wheat production over domestic consumption, 10 units minus 2 units, is exported.[2] Because exports lead to greater production and presumably higher profits, wheat producers will champion international trade. Wheat consumers, by contrast, will not be pleased with the results of international trade: namely, higher wheat prices.

Figure 1.2b shows the effects of international trade on a domestic industry which, from the global viewpoint, is a high-cost producer. The world price of textiles, $2, is below the domestic price, $6. That means that, in this situation, the world price line is also the world's textile supply curve, Sw. Trade drops the domestic price of textiles, leading to greater domestic consumption and lower domestic production of textiles. The excess of consumption over domestic production, 10 units minus 2 units, represents the

---

[2]If the nation is a large producer (consumer) so that its production (consumption) affects the world price, the Dw line would be drawn with a negative slope and the Sw line with a positive slope. Imagine our country is a large wheat producer and the quantity of wheat it supplies influences the world price; then the world price will decline as the nation produces more wheat. In such a case, the world demand schedule, Dw, will have a negative slope, although presumably it will be flatter, more elastic, than the domestic demand schedule. Given the same initial world price or intercept as in the small country case, the nation will end up producing and exporting less at a lower price. However, except in rare cases, trade still pays for the nation's wheat producers. They will produce more wheat and sell it at a higher price given trade than they would in a no-trade situation. By the same token, the nation's textile producers, as discussed below, will still be hurt by trade but not by as much as in the initial case when the world supply curve is infinitely elastic.

nation's imports. Because domestic production falls, profits decline in the domestic textile industry. Trade brings good news to textile consumers, but bad news to the domestic textile producers.

When viewed in this light, the end results of international trade, its benefits relative to its costs, appear indeterminate. For consumers, the price of textiles has dropped while the price of wheat has increased. Some firms and their owners are better off, while others suffer. The model explains why certain industries are pro-trade while others are antitrade. The model shows why the American aircraft industry favors trade while the U.S. textile industry, for the most part, opposes it.

Trade and Economic Welfare

Consumer surplus is the price an individual would be willing to pay for a good or service minus the price she actually pays. If she would be willing to pay $5 for a Big Mac, but can purchase one for $2, her surplus is $3.

Producer surplus. If MacDonald's would be willing to produce Big Macs for $1, but can sell them for $2, Mr. MacDonald has a producer surplus of $1 per Big Mac.

It can be demonstrated that international trade actually does increase a country's economic welfare. The impact of trade on **consumer surplus** and **producer surplus** tells us why. Consumer surplus is the amount an individual is willing to pay for a good minus the amount she actually pays for it. Consider the demand for wheat and assume for the moment that there is only one consumer. Assume she would be willing to pay $11 for her first unit of wheat consumed, $10 for the second unit of wheat consumed and so on. The idea is that each additional unit of wheat gives her less utility or satisfaction than the previous unit. She is, therefore, willing to pay more for the first unit of wheat than the second, more for the second than the third, and so forth.

How many units of wheat she purchases depends on the market price. If the market price is $6 per unit, she will purchase 6 units of wheat and receive a surplus of $15. Why? The first unit of wheat was worth $11 to her but she only had to pay $6 for it. Clearly she is $5 ahead on the first unit of wheat and just as clearly she is $4 ahead on the second unit of wheat. And she also obtains a surplus on the third, fourth and fifth units of wheat she purchases. She does not, however, receive a surplus on the sixth unit of wheat since she pays $6 for it or exactly what it is worth to her. But it is clear that the greater her consumer surplus the better off she is.

Producer surplus is the other side of the coin. It equals the amount of money a producer receives for selling a product minus the sum needed to induce him to produce it. Suppose there is only one wheat producer and he needs to be paid $1 to produce one unit of wheat, $2 to produce a second unit, and $3 to produce a third—he must be paid higher amounts to produce each additional unit of wheat since the more time he spends producing wheat, the less time he has to do other things. If demand meets supply at a price of $6 and six units of wheat, the producer surplus will equal $15. The wheat producer receives $6 for the first unit of wheat he produced since all units of wheat sell for $6, even though he would have produced that unit of wheat for $1. He, therefore, receives a $5 surplus on this unit of wheat. On the second unit, he receives a surplus of $4 and, therefore, he collects a total surplus of $15 in this example.

Figures 1.3a and b show how consumer and producer surplus can be calculated from a graph and how international trade, by increasing consumer and producer surplus, expands national economic welfare. Figure 1.3a shows the domestic wheat market. Prior to trade, domestic supply and demand are equal at the price $6 and the quantity 6 units. Consumers, however, would have been willing to pay a higher price for each unit of wheat purchased up to the last unit bought. Their surplus, prior to trade, equals the

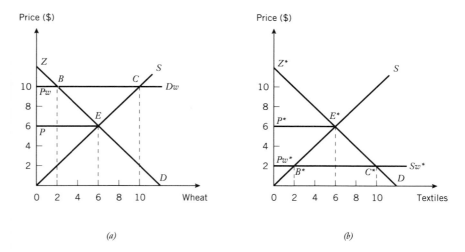

FIGURE 1.3 Trade and economic welfare.

Prior to trade, supply equals demand in the wheat market and in the textile market when the price equals $6 (or P and P^*, respectively), and the quantity supplied and demanded equals 6 units. Given the equilibrium quantity, consumer surplus equals the area under the demand curve minus the amount of money consumers spend to buy the product. In the case of wheat, consumer surplus equals the triangle ZPE; in the textile market, consumer surplus equals $Z^*P^*E^*$. On the other hand, given the equilibrium quantity, producer surplus equals the total revenue the producer receives (price times quantity) minus his costs of production which equals the area under the supply curve at the equilibrium level of output. In the case of wheat, the producer's revenue equals $0PE6$ and his production costs equal the triangle $06E$. Thus, producer surplus equals the triangle $0PE$. By the same reasoning, producer surplus in the textile market equals $0P^*E$. When trade takes place, the price of wheat rises to Pw or $10 and the price of textiles falls to Pw^* or $2. Consumer surplus falls to $ZPwE$ in the wheat market, but rises to ZPw^*C^* in the textile market. Producer surplus rises to $0PwC$ in the wheat market, but falls to $0Pw^*B^*$ in the textile market. In the wheat market, the gain in producer surplus, $PPwCE$, exceeds the loss in consumer surplus, $PPwBE$, by the triangle BCE. And in the textile market, the gain in consumer surplus, $P^*Pw^*C^*E^*$, exceeds the loss in producer surplus, $P^*Pw^*B^*E^*$, by the triangle $B^*C^*E^*$. Overall, what consumers lose in the wheat market is more than compensated for by what they gain in the textile market. And what producers gain in the wheat market exceeds what they lose in the textile market. Thus, trade increases the welfare of both consumers and producers. The net gain in consumer surplus equals the triangle $B^*C^*E^*$ in panel (b); and the net gain in producer surplus equals the triangle BCE in panel (a).

triangle ZPE, or $15 in this case. By similar reasoning, the producer surplus equals the triangle $0PE$, or $15 based on the figures in Table 1.4.

Trade raises the price of wheat and reduces the price of textiles and affects consumer and producer surplus in both markets. In the wheat market, the higher price reduces consumer surplus and increases producer surplus. Given the higher price of wheat, assumed to be $10 as before, the consumer surplus is reduced by the amount $PwBEP$. In fact, consumer surplus is reduced to $1, since the consumer only receives a surplus on the first unit of wheat she purchases. Thus, her loss in consumer surplus equals $14.

The higher price and greater quantity sold raises the producer surplus by $PwCEP$. The gain in producer surplus equals $30, because, given trade, total producer surplus rises to $45 in this example. Since the gain in producer surplus exceeds the loss in consumer surplus by the triangle BCE, the nation is better off. Expressed in figures, the $30 gain in producer surplus exceeds the $14 loss in consumer surplus. The gain of one group exceeds the loss of the other.

Trade drops the domestic price of textiles toward the world price of $2, so consumers gain while domestic textile producers lose. But the gain in consumer surplus, $Pw^*C^*E^*P^*$, exceeds the loss in producer surplus, $Pw^*B^*E^*P^*$, by the triangle $B^*C^*E^*$. Expressed in terms of Table 1.4, the gain in consumer surplus equals $30, while the loss in producer surplus equals $14. Once again, the loss of one group is less than the gain of the other so that the nation's economic welfare is larger. In addition, one can see that gain in consumer surplus resulting from the fall in the price of textiles—$30—exceeds the loss in consumer surplus—$14—following the rise in the price of wheat. The consumer's net gain equals the triangle $B^*C^*E^*$ in the textile market. For producers, their net gain equals the triangle BCE in the wheat market. Since both consumer and producers gain, trade increases the economic welfare of both consumers and producers.

Trade and Income Distribution

If an individual loses a job for a short period of time or takes a temporary job that pays less than his previous wage, he suffers a **transitory loss** of income.

Permanent trade adjustment costs occur if an individual loses her job because of trade and must permanently accept a lower-paying job. However, an expansion of trade may provide her with better employment opportunities, in which case she would enjoy **permanent benefits.**

Consumers and producers as a whole may gain, but the expansion of wheat production and the decrease in textile production means that wheat producers gain from trade while textile producers lose. This puts a different light on the situation. Yet it is quite likely that these gains and losses will be temporary. Over the longer term, higher profits in the wheat sector should induce resources to migrate from the declining and less profitable textile sector to the expanding and more profitable wheat sector. Due to this migration, the wheat supply curve will shift to the right and the textile supply curve to the left. As a result, both exports and imports will expand. But what is more significant is that the expansion and contraction in the industries will tend to level profit rates between them. That means that although there will almost always be short-run **transitory** costs and benefits when an economy begins to trade, there may be no long-run or **permanent trade adjustment costs** or benefits.

Suppose, however, the theoretical story is only partially correct; what happens then? For example, the model assumed that labor was homogeneous and mobile so that the labor supply curve facing an industry was infinitely elastic. When trade was initiated, the demand for domestic wheat increased and so did the demand for labor and other inputs required to produce it. This demand for labor and other inputs on the part of the wheat industry was satisfied quickly and at a constant wage rate as workers moved from the textile to the wheat industry.

The assumption is not realistic. It takes time for individuals to move from one industry to another. In the short run, wages may decline or workers may be let go in the textile industry while workers may receive higher compensation in the wheat industry as they work additional hours at overtime wage rates. As a result, there will be transitory adjustment costs and transitory benefits when trade begins. It is normally assumed that any and all transitory costs and benefits vanish over the intermediate to long run as workers move from one industry to another. Because of this assumption, workers, whether in the wheat or textile industry, will not obtain permanent benefits nor suffer permanent adjustment costs as a result of trade.

But what if all labor is not alike and the supply curves for particular types of labor are not infinitely elastic? In such cases, transitory costs and benefits are certain and it is possible that there will be permanent or extended adjustment costs and benefits as well. Imagine that the wheat industry primarily employs skilled labor while the textile industry employs unskilled labor. Even if both wheat and textiles can be produced by utilizing various combinations of skilled and unskilled labor, it is assumed that the ratio of skilled to unskilled workers employed in wheat production is always higher than the proportion of skilled to unskilled labor employed in the textile industry regardless of the wage rate paid to skilled compared to unskilled workers.

Under these conditions, the demand for skilled labor will increase while the demand for unskilled labor will decline when trade begins. Initially, the wheat industry demands more skilled labor than is released by the textile industry, and the textile industry releases more unskilled labor than is demanded by the wheat industry. As a result, there is an excess demand for skilled labor and an excess supply of unskilled labor at pretrade wage rates. If labor markets are to clear, the wage rate for skilled labor must rise in order to eliminate excess demand and the wage rate for unskilled labor will have to decline to eliminate excess supply. In fact, it is the change in relative wage rates that encourages producers to use more unskilled relative to skilled labor in producing both commodities.

The crucial point is that the wage of skilled labor will rise relative to the wage of unskilled labor. Since it is assumed that trade raises national income, skilled workers will gain both absolutely and relatively to unskilled labor. Unskilled laborers will lose relatively, but may not lose absolutely if the assumed trade-induced increase in national income is sufficiently large. If it is not, the redistribution of income could be permanent or last as long as the supplies of skilled and unskilled labor remain constant.

The presence of transitory and permanent costs is one reason why some groups oppose trade. Even though international trade should raise national income, this will not count for much in the view of those individuals who must bear the transitory and permanent costs associated with trade. For example, suppose an individual who received a wage of $10,000 a year loses her job because imports displace domestic production. If she is able to find another position for, say, two years paying $5,000 per year, she loses $10,000 over the two years. If after two years, she is able to obtain a position paying $10,000 a year, her transitory costs are such that she should be antitrade even though what have been called her permanent costs would be zero. And if she cannot secure a job paying her pretrade salary, but must accept one that pays less and ends up paying a permanent cost due to trade, she will oppose trade vehemently. If, however, she obtains a position in the expanding export sector paying $15,000 per year, either immediately or after working for two years at $5,000 per year, she will be better off in the long run and hence she should be pro-trade since her permanent gains will exceed her transitory losses.

So far the discussion has neglected capital. International trade benefits some owners of capital and harms others. However, unlike the case of labor, losses will be limited in most instances. A loss will last only as long as the capital equipment (such as the wheat combines and looms) in existence when trade commences is still in use or still has the potential to be used.

Imagine a weaver purchases a $100 loom with a productive life of 10 years. Over the 10 years, the weaver anticipates that he will earn sufficient income to cover the cost of replacing the loom and, in addition, obtain a return on his invested capital. Although

BOX 1.2 | Trade and Low-Skilled Labor

Between 1979 and 1993, the wage gap between skilled and unskilled male laborers in the United States widened. The real wages of the top 10 percent of male workers advanced, although only modestly, while the real wages of the bottom 10 percent dropped some 20 percent. The change in relative wages reflected market fundamentals. The demand for skilled workers rose, or at least kept pace with supply, while the demand for unskilled workers declined—at least relative to the supply of unskilled workers.

Such a pattern can be explained by many factors of which international trade is just one. However, Adrian Wood, a British economist, argues that the decline in the demand for unskilled labor in industrialized countries can be explained by their trade with LDCs. Essentially, the greater the imports from LDCs, the greater the decline in the demand for unskilled labor in the developed world. The explanation is simple. If it costs $16 an hour, including fringe benefits, to hire a production worker in the United States, but only $2.50 to hire a worker in Mexico, the price of Mexican-produced goods will be substantially cheaper than American-made products.

Some economists dispute Professor Wood's findings. First, an American worker may receive several times more than the Mexican wage, but if because of her productivity, her output per hour is also a multiple of the Mexican worker's, labor costs per unit of output may be similar in both countries—a topic expanded upon in Chapter 6. Robert Lawrence and Matthew Slaughter believe that there is some common factor other than trade that explains the decline in the demand for unskilled labor. They reason that if trade had displaced unskilled labor and, as a consequence, dropped its price, all firms in the United States would have changed the mix of skilled to unskilled labor they utilized. They would have hired more of the now-cheaper unskilled labor compared to expensive skilled labor. Since they did exactly the opposite, and hired more skilled relative to unskilled labor across the board, trade, Lawrence and Slaughter concluded, is not the culprit.

Figure 1.4 provides a brief look at this question. It compares the decline in employment in several manufacturing industries, which are classified as unskilled, with the net change in the export/import position of the industry. Both exports and imports count since a decline in exports, like an increase in imports, will decrease the demand for labor. To give any change in the net export/import position some basis for comparison, it is computed as a percentage of the value of shipments made by the industry. Thus, a decrease in exports or an increase in imports can lead to a radical change if the value of shipments declines at the same time.

Figure 1.4 shows that there is a relationship between jobs and trade, but the relationship is strongest in specific industries such as apparel and leather, rather than in low-skilled industries as a group. In the leather industry, primarily shoes and handbags, employment fell from 200,000 to 106,000 between 1982 and 1991, or by nearly 50 percent. There is little doubt that trade played a large role in causing unemployment in this sector. Although the industry's exports increased during the period, imports rose at even a faster pace. In 1982, the industry's net export position, exports minus imports, was minus 41 percent of the value of shipments; in 1991, the figure was minus 101 percent, a change of 60 percent.

While the experience of the leather and apparel industries is not necessarily cause for trade restrictions, it indicates that trade can cause economic dislocations.[3]

_____

[3]References are given at the end of the chapter.

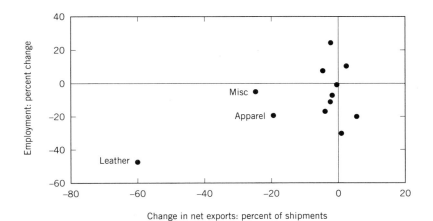

FIGURE 1.4 Employment and trade (low-skill industries: 1982—91).

Except for leather, apparel, and miscellaneous manufacturing, there appears to be little relation between trade and employment in low-skilled industries. In nine of the twelve industries investigated, there was no relation at all between trade and employment opportunities.

Source: United States Bureau of the Census, *Statistical Abstract of the United States,* various issues.

the return is not guaranteed, the weaver must be fairly confident that the return is highly probable if he is to undertake the investment in the first place. Assume, given anticipated sales, that he expects to earn $10 per year, or the current rate of interest—10 percent—times the cost on the loom, on his investment.

If the nation imports textiles, the price and quantity of domestically produced textiles will fall and the weaver's revenue will decline. How much depends on both the fall in the price of textiles and the decrease in his level of production. Assuming he can limp along and produce at his pretrade level but only receives a $5-per-year return on his investment, he will be hurt.

Prior to trade, he required a cash flow of $20 a year (actually just slightly more than $16 a year) in order to replace his loom and obtain a 10 percent rate of return on his investment. Neglecting replacement costs, if the return on his investment is cut in half, the market value of his capital asset, the loom, will decline. Cast in different terms, we can say that since the rate of interest is 10 percent, the price of every capital asset must be such that the return on each asset is, at a minimum, 10 percent. Thus if the dollar return on an asset falls, the asset's price must fall so that the new dollar return on the capital asset equals 10 percent.

Suppose a weaver purchases a loom that costs $100 and that the next day imports flood into the country and cut the return on his investment from $10 to $5. If he attempts to sell his loom, the loom will only fetch $50 since no one will pay $100 for an asset that yields $5 when the interest rate is 10 percent. The weaver will lose.

It is difficult to calculate the weaver's loss exactly since it depends on the interplay of several variables: sales, the price of the product, and the remaining productive life of the loom. For example, if the textile imports enter the country on the last day of the loom's productive life, the weaver will not take a loss. Nevertheless, short of that, it is clear that the weaver will suffer a permanent loss. However, his loss, and the gains of the owner of the wheat combine, will cease once the productive life of the loom or the combine runs its course.

NAFTA and the Gains and Losses from Trade

The possible gains and losses associated with international trade are vital. In 1994, Canada, Mexico, and the United States formed a free-trade area called *NAFTA* (*North American Free Trade Agreement*). Its supporters admit that certain American industries will be hurt as U.S. trade barriers, especially those with Mexico, are either eliminated or substantially reduced. Apparel, furniture, glassware, shoe manufacturing industries, and other low-tech industries will be affected adversely by NAFTA. In addition, despite last-minute maneuvering, citrus producers and vegetable farmers will also most likely suffer because of the agreement.

There is, of course, another side to NAFTA—the opening up of the Mexican market to U.S. industries. American automobile, computer, and telecommunication equipment sales to Mexico will, it is predicted, increase as will sales of other high-tech products. In addition, NAFTA may be a bonanza to the U.S. wheat industry and the American financial services industry. On balance, the majority of economists believe that NAFTA will be a plus rather than a minus for the American economy.

The emphasis on the costs associated with trade tends to obscure the benefits side of the coin—the side that does not receive nearly as much attention as the costs side. If a nation reduces trade, there will be temporary and very likely permanent adjustment costs. Nor should it be forgotten that if trade raises national income, it is at least possible to compensate an individual so that she does not suffer a permanent loss in income. By contrast, if trade restrictions reduce income, it will be impossible to compensate groups for either the transitory or permanent losses they incur.

Macroeconomics, Market Supply and Demand, and International Trade

Up to this point, the macro- or total economy has been ignored, an omission that appears perfectly justifiable at first glance. Macroeconomics, after all, talks about the general price level, the general wage rate, and the total level of output. And so far we have argued that trade takes place because the relative prices of domestically produced wheat and textiles differ from world prices. We have, in other words, talked about differences in relative prices, not differences in general price levels. Therefore, the inclusion of macroeconomic considerations at this stage runs against the traditional grain of closed economy microeconomics where one just assumes that macroeconomic stability exists and lets it go at that. That approach is not warranted in the case of an open economy. In the open economy, international and domestic macroeconomic developments impact individual national markets for better and for worse.

For example, if a closed economy undergoes a bout of inflation, it is often assumed that all prices in all sectors of the economy rise by the same degree so that nothing much happens in one individual market compared to others. An increase in the price level will lead to an increase in wages so that, in the end, price and wages have increased by, say, 10 percent across the board. In graphical terms, higher wages, as suggested in Table 1.2, will cause the supply curves in Figures 1.5a and b to shift from S_0 to S_1. But the higher wages permit workers to consume the same number of real goods as they did prior to the rise in the general price level. Thus, the demand curves for wheat and textiles shift to the right from D_0 to D_1. It turns out that the physical production and consumption of both commodities is exactly the same both prior to and after the inflation.

But in an open economy, inflation raises all domestic prices relative to world prices, a step that reduces the nation's international competitiveness and hurts its ability to compete in world markets. As shown in Figures 1.5a and b, the production of exports and imports contract while the consumption of both commodities goes up. Domestic wheat production, for example, declines from 10 to 8 units, and wheat consumption rises from 2 to 4 units. As a result, wheat exports drop from 8 to 4 units. Textile production also declines, falling to zero units, whereas the consumption of textiles increases by 2 units to 12 units and textile imports increase from 8 to 12 units. Clearly the change in domestic prices relative to world prices is not neutral in terms of output and employment.

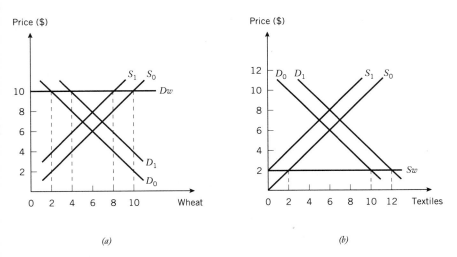

(a)   *(b)*

FIGURE 1.5 The impact of domestic inflation on exports and imports.

Due to domestic inflation, the supply curves in both the wheat and the textile markets shift from S_0 to S_1, and the demand curves shift from D_0 to D_1. The higher domestic price level reduces the domestic economy's competitiveness in both markets. In the wheat market, domestic consumption rises to 4 units and domestic production falls to 8 units. As a result, exports of wheat fall from 8 to 4 units. In the textile market, greater consumption and lower production raises imports from 8 to 12 units.

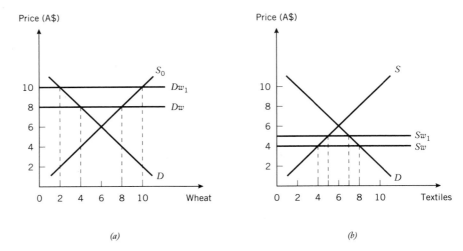

(a) *(b)*

FIGURE 1.6 Currency depreciation and exports and imports.

Assuming that wheat and textiles are priced in U.S. dollars on the world market, a depreciation of the Australian dollar raises the price of both commodities when *expressed* in Australian dollars even though the U.S. dollar price of both commodities remains constant. Assuming a 25 percent depreciation, the price of wheat rises from A$8 to A$10, and the price of textiles rises from A$4 to A$5. The higher wheat price leads to an increase in Australian wheat exports, panel (a), and the higher price of textiles reduces Australia's imports of textiles, panel (b). Exports of wheat increase from 4 to 8 units and imports of textiles drop from 4 to 2 units.

Now consider one last example of a macroeconomic effect, one that can be better understood with the help of Figures 1.6a and b. Suppose the exchange rate, in this case the number of Australian dollars required to purchase an American dollar, climbs from, say, A$1.2/$ to A$1.5/$, or the Australian dollar depreciates.[4] Assume that the price of wheat on world markets is expressed in US dollars, a realistic assumption since many traded commodities are priced in US dollars.

If the world price of wheat is *$6.67* per bushel, not $10 as previously assumed, the Australian price will be $6.67 times the exchange rate, A$1.2/$, or A$8. Now suppose the Australian dollar depreciates to A$1.5/$ and that the world price of wheat, expressed in US dollars, remains constant. Given the depreciation of the Australian dollar, the price of wheat expressed in Australian dollars will climb to A$10. If we assume that the world price of textiles is *$3.33*, the depreciation of the Australian dollar will raise the world price of textiles expressed in the Australian currency from A$4 to A$5. Given the higher Australian price, Australia's wheat production increases from, say, 8 to 10 units and, by the same reasoning, its textile output expands from 4 to 5 units. As shown in Figures 1.6a and b, Australia's consumption of both commodities falls, and its exports rise relative to its imports.

---

[4] Since this example may rush the analysis somewhat, it can be skipped. The effects of depreciation on an economy and its industries are discussed in Chapter 11.

BOX 1.3   Currency Appreciation and the Firm

Because currency appreciations and depreciations affect industries, they also affect individual firms. The Caterpillar company, a manufacturer of earth-moving equipment, was adversely affected by dollar appreciation in the first half of the 1980s. This is not to say that the reduction and ensuing increase in Caterpillar's sales were solely the result of dollar appreciation followed by dollar depreciation, since the world economy experienced first recession and then expansion in the 1980s. (See Table 1.5.)

Nevertheless, there is a strong relation between Caterpillar's sales and the international value of the dollar. As the dollar appreciated, Caterpillar's sales fell off both in the domestic market and in foreign markets. However, the company's external or foreign sales fell more drastically than its domestic sales, measured either in absolute numbers or in percentage terms, in the first half of the 1980s. As the dollar stopped appreciating and actually began to fall, Caterpillar's domestic and foreign sales recovered, especially its foreign sales.

TABLE 1.5   Caterpillar, Inc.: Sales and the Exchange Rate

Year	Total Sales[a]	Foreign Sales[a]	Foreign/ Domestic Sales	Exchange Rate[b]
1980	$8.6	$4.9	53.6%	68.4
1981	$9.2	$5.2	56.6%	76.7
1982	$6.5	$3.7	56.7%	85.5
1983	$5.4	$2.5	46.0%	89.7
1984	$6.6	$2.8	41.2%	96.8
1985	$6.7	$3.0	44.0%	100.0
1986	$7.3	$3.3	45.6%	80.2
1987	$8.2	$3.9	47.5%	70.2

[a] = billions.

[b] 1985 = 100.

Source: Moody's Industrial Manual, 1988, p. 1047 and 1983, p. 1191; and International Monetary Fund, *International Financial Statistics Yearbook*, 1992, p. 717.

Summary

Microeconomic analysis shows that there are both winners and losers when a nation initiates or expands trade. Some industries gain, some lose, and some workers may gain relative to others. But the number of losers should decline as an economy moves from its transitory position to its final or permanent one. While economic analysis recognizes that there are adjustment costs in moving from the temporary to permanent position, it says little in practical terms about how such costs can be reduced.

Even though the costs of restricting trade are larger than those associated with expanding it, if trade is to be expanded, trade proponents still must demonstrate that trade raises national income. Today, the burden of proof is on traders. They must show that all groups benefit from trade, or that trade raises income sufficiently so that those who lose from trade will find other avenues by which to maintain their income or that those who benefit from trade will have sufficient additional income to compensate the losers for bearing both the transitory and possible permanent costs of trade. This is done later; first, it is necessary to extend our examination of the macroeconomics of international trade.

Key Concepts and Terms

consumer surplus

demand curve

demand schedule

derived demand

diminishing returns

elasticity

homogeneous versus nonhomogeneous

labor costs per unit of output

LDCs

market demand and supply

NICs

producer surplus

shifts versus movements along demand (supply) schedules

short- versus long-run supply

supply curve

supply schedule

transitory versus permanent adjustment costs and benefits

Review Questions

1. Assume that the supply and demand schedules for Japanese cars in the American market are as follows and that all Japanese cars are made in Japan.

Price	Quantity Demanded	Quantity Supplied
$20,000	1.5mn	3.5mn
18,000	2.0	3.0
16,000	2.5	2.5
14,000	3.0	2.0
12,000	3.5	1.5

(a) What is the equilibrium price and quantity?

(b) If American income falls and the demand for Japanese cars falls by .5mn units at every price level, what is the new equilibrium price and quantity?

(c) Assume American income recovers to its original level. If the Japanese agree to limit their exports of cars to 2mn units, what is the equilibrium price and quantity?

2. Draw an industry supply schedule. What will help determine the steepness of the schedule? What will happen to the schedule if:

(a) The wage rate rises?

(b) Due to better education and health, labor productivity doubles?

(c) The demand for the industry's product expands?

(d) More firms enter the industry?

3. If the price elasticity of demand for a product is low, what does this mean? For example, what happens to the quantity of widgets demanded if their price falls by 10 percent and the price elasticity of demand for widgets equals .2? What would be your answer if the price elasticity of demand equals 3?

4. Return to question 1. At the equilibrium price and quantity, what is the consumer surplus? What is the producer surplus? If Japanese exports are restricted to 2mn units, what is the level of consumer surplus?

5. While trade expansion and trade contraction both may involve transitory or temporary adjustment costs, why do some individuals claim that only trade contraction will involve permanent adjustment costs? Are such individuals talking about the total economy or all groups within the economy?

6. Draw the market supply and demand for widgets in a particular country. Imagine that the international price exceeds the domestic autarkic equilibrium price of widgets. Describe what will happen to the domestic output of widgets and the nation's exports of widgets if:

(a) There is an increase in the worldwide demand for widgets.

(b) The domestic demand for widgets declines at all price levels.

(c) For some reason, the domestic cost of producing widgets declines.

(d) Domestic inflation rises from 0 to 10 percent.

References and Suggested Readings

Adrian Wood's masterly study is *North–South Trade, Employment and Inequality* (Oxford: Oxford University Press, 1994). The book is nearly 500 pages long, however, Professor Wood presents a helpful summary of his work in the first 25 pages. Robert Z. Lawrence and Matthew J. Slaughter present their findings in their article "Trade and American Wages in the 1980s: Giant Sucking Sound or Small Hiccup," *Brookings Papers on Economic Activity: Microeconomics* (1993, no. 2): pp. 161–211. Jeffrey D. Sachs and Howard J. Shatz present a different view in their article "Trade and Jobs in U.S. Manufacturing," *Brookings Papers on Economic Activity* (1994, no. 2): pp. 1–69. Both articles are long and the analysis is intensive.

Briefer and more accessible treatments of the effects of trade on wages and employment in manufacturing are Paul R. Krugman and Robert Z. Lawrence, "Trade, Jobs, and Wages," *Scientific American* 170 (April 1994): pp. 44–49, and "Schools Brief: Workers of the World Compete," *The Economist* (April 2, 1994): pp. 69–70. The Federal Reserve Bank of New York devoted the January 1995 issue of its *Economic Policy Review* to an analysis of wage trends in the United States. The articles by Robert Z. Lawrence, "U.S. Wage Trends in the 1980s: The Role of International Factors," and by Jagdish Bhagwati, "Trade and Wages: Choosing among Alternative Explanations," investigate the role of trade on wage trends in the United States. The article by David A. Brauer and Susan Hickok, "Explaining the Growing Inequality in Wages across Skill Levels," is outstanding even though it discusses more than the impact of trade on wages and employment.

The theoretical foundations of the current debate on the impact of trade on particular wages is based on a classic article by Wolfgang Stolper and Paul Samuelson, "Protection and Real Wages," *Review of Economic Studies* 9 (November 1941): pp. 58–73.

Chapter 2

The National Economy in the World Economy: An Overview

Chapter 1 focused on the microeconomics of international trade or how international trade affects individual markets. This chapter describes the impact of international economic relations on a nation's total economy. It does this in three steps.

The Path Ahead

Aggregate demand is the total level of expenditures within an economy. It equals the amount that consumers, business firms, and the government spend on goods and services at a given moment.

- First we review the **aggregate demand** and **supply** framework in reference to a closed national economy, an economy which does not trade.
- Then we expand the aggregate demand and supply framework to embrace the international economy by introducing the **export** and **import schedules.**
- Finally, we show how the expanded *AD-AS* framework can be utilized to explain the impact of external developments on the domestic economy.

Aggregate Demand

Aggregate supply is the total amount of goods and services supplied in an economy.

The market supply and demand framework explains the behavior of individual markets. Aggregate demand and supply, on the other hand, describes how the *total* economy works. At this point in the discussion, we concentrate on aggregate demand and, for the sake of simplicity, neglect aggregate supply.

Aggregate demand (AD) in an economy equals the level of *total expenditures* on goods and services at a given moment. In a **closed economy,** one which does not have external economic relations, aggregate demand (*AD*) equals the sum of consumer

The **export schedule** shows the total quantity of goods that a country will export at various national price levels providing everything else is constant.

The **import schedule** shows the total quantity of goods and services that a nation will import at various price levels assuming everything else is constant.

A **closed economy** does not have any economic relations with the rest of the world. It is the opposite of an open economy.

Gross domestic product (GDP) is the single best measure of the total level of economic activity in an economy.

Nominal GDP equals gross domestic product measured at current price levels. Nominal GDP also equals aggregate demand.

expenditures (*C*) plus investment (primarily business) expenditures (*I*) plus government spending on goods and services (*G*), or:

$$AD = C + I + G = \text{GDP}$$

As can be seen from the equation, aggregate demand or the sum of consumption, investment, and government expenditures also equals **gross domestic product (GDP),** the most common measure of the overall level of economic activity.[1] But it is important to stress that aggregate demand equals **nominal** not **real** GDP.

What is the difference between nominal and real GDP? Nominal GDP equals the value of consumption plus investment plus government expenditures at *current* prices. Real GDP equals the total value of expenditures (*C*+*I*+*G*) at *constant* prices. Real GDP strips away the effects of price changes on the value of output and enables us to see how many more cars, boats, airplanes, and so on—all measured in physical units—were actually produced. For example, in the United States, nominal GDP rose from $6,343 billion in 1993 to $6,737 billion in 1994, an increase of 6.2 percent. But the United States was not 6.2 percent richer in real terms because prices rose by 2.1 percent during the year. Therefore, the increase in real GDP was 4.1 percent.

We can therefore see that if the level of nominal GDP (*PQ*) is known, real GDP (*Q*) can be computed by dividing nominal GDP (*PQ*) by the national price index (*P*), $Q = (PQ)/P$. In other words, in order to compute real GDP, one must adjust nominal GDP for changes in the general price level.

Figure 2.1 helps to sort things out. The **aggregate demand curve** in Figure 2.1b shows the sum of consumption, investment, and government expenditures at various national price levels. Real GDP is measured on the horizontal axis (labeled income/output), and the national price level is measured on the vertical axis. At any point along the *AD* curve, aggregate demand equals the national price level (*P*) multiplied by real GDP (*Q*). The price level times output (real GDP) also equals nominal GDP. Therefore, although one can talk of aggregate demand in real terms, the aggregate demand curve equals nominal GDP.

Why the Aggregate Demand Curve Shifts

Real GDP equals nominal GDP adjusted for changes in the national price level. A change in real gross domestic product tells us how much the total level of real economic activity has increased or decreased.

The *AD* curve in Figure 2.1b assumes that other things remain equal. In the real world, however, other things do not remain constant and various forces will cause an aggregate demand curve to shift to the left or to the right. Given a constant price level, the *AD* curve will shift to the right if consumers decide to spend a greater proportion of their income, or if business firms choose to purchase more equipment or add to their plant capacity, or if the government raises its expenditures on goods and services. In addition, a tax cut that raises disposable income may lead to higher consumption expenditures and shift the *AD* curve to the right. And an increase in the money supply may also lead to greater consumption and investment expenditures and shift the *AD* curve to the right.

---

[1]GDP can be computed either by adding the flow of expenditures (as here) or by adding sources of income such as wages, rents, profits, etc.

The **aggregate demand curve** shows the amount of real output that will be demanded in the total economy at various national price levels assuming everything else is constant.

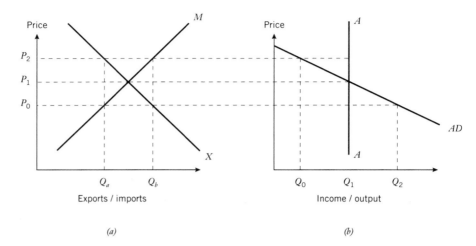

(a)   *(b)*

FIGURE 2.1 Exports, imports, and aggregate demand.

As shown in panel (a), the level of exports and imports depends on the general price level. If the general price level declines, exports increase and imports decline. Because aggregate demand depends on net exports (exports minus imports), in addition to other variables, the aggregate demand curve is a function of the domestic price level. As the price level falls from P_2 to P_1 to P_0, net exports increase, which in turn increases aggregate demand. Thus the aggregate demand curve, AD, in panel (b) has a negative slope, or aggregate demand is inversely related to the price level. In a closed economy, one without trade, aggregate demand depends solely on absorption. If the level of absorption is independent of the price level, the aggregate demand curve will be a vertical line such as A. (See pages 34–35 for a more complete discussion.)

None of these events describes why the AD curve has a negative slope. The schedule, and the resulting curve, assumes that the government's budget or fiscal policy, the central bank's monetary policy, business investment plans, and discretionary consumer expenditures are set.

The Real Balance Effect and the Slope of the AD Curve

There is, in fact, no reason for the AD curve to slope down to the right at all. Recall that nominal GDP or aggregate demand can be computed either as a flow of expenditures, $C+I+G$, or as a flow of income receipts (wages, interest, rents, and profits). Assume that all expenditures are consumption expenditures and that all income receipts are wages. Naturally, if prices drop while wages remain constant, real expenditures will rise and real output will increase. But if prices and wages move in tandem, a drop in prices accompanied by a drop in wages will have no effect on real output.

Let's show this with a hypothetical example. Suppose there is only one worker and consumer in the society and that she is paid $100 for producing widgets which she spends entirely on widgets, the only good available.[2] She will purchase 100 widgets if

---

[2]A widget is a composite good of unheard-of qualities. You can eat it, wear it, drive around town in it, and even put it under your pillow at night to scare away evil spirits. A widget can also clean your clothes and fix

the price is $1. Suppose her wage drops to $50, but, at the same instant, the price of widgets falls to $.50. In this new environment, she will, as before, purchase 100 widgets. Therefore, despite the fall in the general price level, her demand for widgets in real terms and real GDP will remain constant. If her demand for widgets is the same at every price level, because we assume that price and wages rise and fall together, the *AD* curve will be a vertical line. Thus, the negative slope of the *AD* curve must be explained by other forces.

The **real balance effect** and the **trade effect** are two forces which help explain why the *AD* curve has a negative slope.[3] In its simplest form, the real balance effect asserts that individuals want to hold a **money balance** with constant purchasing power. Suppose an individual starts out with a nominal money balance of $100 and the price level is 1. Given this setting, the real and nominal values of the money balance are equal since the real balance equals the nominal balance divided by the price level. Now imagine that the price level doubles. The value of the nominal balance will remain constant at $100, but its purchasing power will be cut in half which is the same as saying that the value of the real balance is reduced by 50 percent. If an individual wants to maintain a money balance with constant purchasing power, she will have to increase her nominal money balance by $100 to $200.

Given this background, it is possible to examine how the real balance effect influences the slope of the aggregate demand curve. If an individual receives a wage income of $100 per month and spends it all on widgets which, as before, sell for $1, her income and expenditures will equal $100 per month and 100 widgets will be produced and consumed. Now assume also she starts and ends the month with a money balance of $100. The money balance equals 100 percent of her income which is assumed to be the money/income ratio she desires to maintain.

If both her wages and the price of widgets fall by 50 percent, nothing happens in real terms. Her wage income of $50 is used to purchase 100 widgets that now cost $.50 each. However, since she started out with a money balance equal to $100, its value or purchasing power has doubled and is now twice her income. Measured either way, she clearly has an excess money balance. Advocates of the real balance effect argue that she will spend her excess money balance in the attempt to restore her original money/income ratio or real balance. In the process, she will spend an additional $50 and purchase 100 additional widgets.

What are the implications of the real balance effect for the economy? The nominal money supply equals $100 at both the initial and second price level. When the price level equals 1, 100 widgets are demanded. If the price level drops to .5, the demand for widgets rises to 200 units. Thus, given a constant nominal money balance, a decrease (increase) in the price level leads to greater (lower) demand. Aggregate demand and the price level, therefore, are inversely related.

The **real balance effect** describes how a fall in the national price level can lead to an increase in expenditures.

The **trade effect** shows how a decrease in the price level, by increasing exports and decreasing imports, leads to an increase in total expenditures.

Money balance. As the name implies, the amount of money an individual has on hand at any given moment. A desired money balance equals the amount of money an individual wants to hold relative to her income.

The **interest rate effect** shows how a change in the interest rate will either raise or lower aggregate demand. In this sense, the interest rate effect helps to determine the slope of the aggregate demand curve.

---

your rickety teeth. Moreover, widgets can be used to produce a whole array of goods. A widget, then, is a good, it is a service, and it is an input. This last quality of a widget is important. Much trade consists of sending finished products between countries, but much trade also consists of sending inputs for final products between countries.

[3]The slope of the aggregate demand curve is also determined by the **interest rate effect.** This effect is explained in greater detail later. Essentially, the interest rate effect argues that given a higher price level, individuals will demand more money to carry out transactions. This increased demand for money will raise interest rates. And in turn, higher interest rates will curtail investment expenditures and some consumption expenditures. If the price level and interest rates are correlated or move together, a higher price level will raise interest rates and contract aggregate expenditures. Some economists claim that the higher interest rates that follow an increase in the price level are sufficient by themselves to contract aggregate expenditures.

The relationship can be spelled out formally.

$$MS = kPQ$$

MS equals the money supply and k equals the proportion of nominal income, PQ, that one desires to hold in the form of money. If k equals 1, the relationship can be rewritten as $MSP/P = Q$. If it is also assumed that the money supply is constant, the last equation shows the inverse relationship between a change in the price level and a change in the level of real output demanded.

The slope of the AD curve, therefore, is affected by the strength of the real balance effect. If the real balance effect is strong, the AD curve is flat or flatter; if it is nonexistent, the AD curve is a vertical line and a change in the price level will not, other things remaining equal, affect the level of real demand.

Trade and the Slope of the AD Curve

An **open economy** trades goods and services and, in some cases, financial assets with the rest of the world.

Regardless of whether the real balance effect is strong or weak, the foreign trade effect leads to a flatter AD curve. Indeed, even if the real balance effect is nonexistent, the AD curve will slope down from left to right due to the trade effect. A first step toward understanding why this is the case is to compare the aggregate demand equation for an **open economy** with the aggregate demand equation for a closed economy. In an open economy, aggregate demand equals:

$$AD = C + I + G + X - M$$

C, I, and G were previously defined. X and M equal exports and imports respectively. Consumption, investment, and government expenditures on goods and services may not be directly influenced by a change in the price level, but exports and imports are. An increase in the domestic price level will raise the price of the nation's exports and reduce the quantity sold. Higher domestic prices will also encourage domestic consumers to purchase foreign-made products in place of domestic brands. For these two reasons, a change in the domestic price level will increase or decrease aggregate demand in an open economy.

Import curve. A graphical representation of an import schedule. It shows the quantity of goods and services that will be imported at various national price levels.

All these relationships can be seen in Table 2.1 and in Figure 2.1a (page 32). Table 2.1 shows that as the price level drops from P_2 to P_1, exports rise from 10 to 20, and imports fall from 30 to 20. In Figure 2.1a, which reflects the export and import schedules of Table 2.1, the **import curve** slopes up from left to right and the **export curve**

When an export schedule is graphed, it is called an **export curve.** It shows the quantity exported at various national price levels when other things remain equal.

TABLE 2.1 Export and Import Schedules

Price	Exports	Imports
P_2	10	30
P_1	20	20
P_0	30	10

TABLE 2.2 Exports, Imports, and Aggregate Demand

Price Level	Exports	Imports	C+I+G	Aggregate Demand
P_2	$10	$30	$100	$80
P_1	20	20	100	100
P_0	30	10	100	120

slopes down from left to right. Given the open economy aggregate demand equation, we see that an increase in the general price level will reduce aggregate demand since exports will contract and imports will increase. Because the aggregate demand curve is drawn as a function of the price level, a change in the price level will not shift the aggregate demand curve. Rather, the economy will move along a given aggregate demand curve in response to the change in the price level.

Imagine that the real balance effect equals zero and that the sum of $C+I+G$ equals $100 at all price levels. Now assume that exports and imports each equal $20 when the domestic price level is P_1. The equation, and Table 2.2, show that aggregate demand will equal $100 at this price level. If the domestic price level drops to P_0 and, as a result, imports fall to $10 while exports expand to $30, aggregate demand will climb to $120.

Figures 2.1a and b show how changes in the domestic price level affect exports and imports, and help determine the slope of the AD curve. In Figure 21.b, it is assumed that the sum of $C+I+G$ is constant and equals the quantity Q_1 at all price levels. ($C+I+G$ equals the curve or line A in Figure 2.1b.) Figure 2.1a shows the relationship between exports, imports, and the price level. When the domestic price level declines, the nation's exports become cheaper and foreigners purchase more of them; imports, however, become relatively more expensive and decrease as citizens substitute domestic goods for foreign goods. When the price level is P_1, exports equal imports and aggregate demand equals Q_1. If the price level falls to P_0, exports exceed imports by Q_A–Q_B in Figure 2.1a and by Q_1–Q_2 in Figure 2.1b. Because net exports are now positive, real aggregate demand equals Q_2. On the other hand, if the nation's price level rises to P_2, some exports are priced out of the world market so that total exports fall off. Moreover, domestic consumers discover that some foreign goods are cheaper than comparable domestic products and, as a result, purchase foreign goods in place of domestic products. The country runs a trade deficit which, in this example, *exactly* corresponds to the surplus *it* ran when the price level fell to P_0. However, and this is the important point, output falls to Q_0 at the higher price level.

Why the Export and Import Curves Shift

Export and import curves shift about for many reasons. When they do shift, the aggregate demand curve also shifts in most instances. For example, an increase in world income shifts the export curve and the aggregate demand curve to the right. An increase in the world price level will increase the nation's exports at all domestic price levels and the export and aggregate demand curves will move to the right. The same result occurs if the foreign rate of inflation exceeds the domestic rate of inflation. Currency depreciation will also shift the export curve to the right and lead to a shift in the aggregate demand curve as shown in Figure 2.2.

How does the import curve react to similar developments? An increase in the foreign price level or a depreciation of the dollar shifts the U.S. import curve to the left. If imports drop at all price levels, and other things remain constant, the U.S. aggregate demand curve shifts right. However, an increase in aggregate demand that shifts the aggregate demand curve to the right also shifts the import curve in the same direction. An expansionary fiscal policy, for example, raises the level of aggregate demand at all price levels and the AD curve shifts to the right. Given a higher income, Americans spend a portion of their additional income on imports so that imports rise at all price levels. The import curve, therefore, shifts right.

Figures 2.2a and b clarify how shifts in the export and import curves affect the AD curve. During the summers of 1993 and 1994, the United States encouraged the depreciation of the dollar relative to the yen in order to close its trade imbalance with Japan. How can the hoped-for results of that policy be explained in terms of the AS-AD framework?

Figure 2.2a shows the export and import curves of the United States. Dollar depreciation, which reduces the price foreigners must pay for U.S.-made goods and services, will presumably raise U.S. exports at all domestic price levels causing the export curve to shift from X_0 to X_1. Dollar depreciation or yen appreciation will raise the dollar price of Japanese goods in the United States. As a result, the U.S. import curve will shift to the left from M_0 to M_1. Given the price level, the U.S. export-import picture will clearly improve as exports expand and imports contract. However, as the aggregate demand equation for an open economy makes clear, the rise in exports and fall in imports will raise U.S. aggregate demand and shift the AD curve to the right in Figure 2.2b. In turn, the increase in U.S. income will cause some Americans to demand more

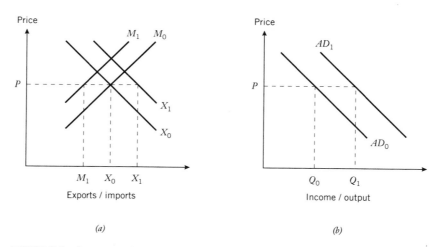

(a)   (b)

FIGURE 2.2 Currency depreciation and aggregate demand.

When a currency depreciates, the export curve shifts from X_0 to X_1 at all price levels and the import curve shifts from M_0 to M_1 at all price levels. The resulting increase in net exports at all price levels shifts the aggregate demand curve from AD_0 to AD_1 in panel (b), which, assuming the general price level remains constant, increases output and employment.

foreign goods and the import curve will shift back toward M_1. Yet, as can be seen, dollar depreciation has been successful in American eyes. The U.S. trade position, exports minus imports, improves, although not as much as originally indicated.

Exports Minus Imports Equals Lending or Borrowing

Trade balance. Exports minus imports. A country has a **trade surplus** when its exports exceed its imports.

Absorption equals the total sum of expenditures on goods and services, produced either at home or abroad, for use within the domestic economy. It is equal to the sum $C + I + G$. In a closed economy, absorption always equals domestic output. In an open economy, absorption can be greater than, equal to, or less than domestic output.

Because exports and imports are affected by so many forces, it would be surprising if a nation's exports and imports were balanced for an extended period. In reality, the majority of nations run either trade surpluses or trade deficits most of the time.

In fact, Figures 2.1a and b indicate that there is only one price level and one level of real GDP, other things considered equal, at which exports equal imports at a given point in time, namely at a price level of P_1 and a real GDP of Q_1. If, given the level of income, the price level rises, the nation's **trade balance (TB)**, exports minus imports, will be negative. If the price level falls, exports will exceed its imports and the nation will have a **trade surplus.** Of course, if the export and import curves shift for any of the reasons described above, there will be a new price and income level at which exports will equal imports.

There are advantages and disadvantages in running a trade deficit. When a nation's imports race ahead of its exports, it is able to absorb more goods and services than it produces. **Absorption** equals the total sum of expenditures on goods and services, both domestic and foreign produced, for use within the domestic economy. (In Table 2.2, absorption equals the sum of $C+I+G$.) The definition applies to both open and closed economies, but there is a fundamental difference between the two cases. In a closed economy, total expenditures cannot exceed domestic production or a nation can only absorb what it produces. In an open economy, absorption can exceed domestic production. If the domestic production of personal computers is limited to 100 units, citizens can absorb more of them by purchasing them abroad. The relationship can be defined more precisely. In an open economy output, Y, equals absorption, A, plus the trade balance, TB, or in symbols:

$$Y = A + TB$$

Thus it is possible for absorption, A, to exceed domestic output, Y, if the trade balance, TB, is negative or imports, M, exceed exports, X.

However, if a nation absorbs more than it produces or imports more than it exports, it must run down any cash reserve on hand or borrow funds to finance its deficit. A nation is no different than a private citizen. If an individual's expenditures exceed his income, he must somehow finance the gap. In a two-country world, if the United States is to run a trade deficit with Japan, America must either borrow yen from the Japanese or induce the Japanese to accept dollar-denominated IOUs. Simply put, in a two-country world, if the United States must borrow, the Japanese must lend.

There is a major drawback to such a lending-borrowing arrangement. In the future, the United States will have to reduce its absorption relative to its output and run a trade surplus in order to repay the principal and interest charges on the debt or service the debt. The Japanese, in turn, will have to absorb more than they produce and run a trade deficit in order for the United States to service the debt.

The Japanese, however, will obtain future benefits if they produce more today than they absorb today. Due to its current trade surplus and requisite lending, Japan will be able to absorb more tomorrow than would have been possible if their present trade position were balanced. How much more depends on two factors: its current level of lending and real rate of return it receives on such lending.[4]

Will the Japanese gain or lose from this arrangement? If the Japanese prefer future consumption to current consumption, their current lending makes sense. If they are indifferent to future versus present consumption or if they prefer current consumption, they should not run a trade surplus today.

What of the United States? Borrowing abroad and running a trade deficit is not necessarily a step on the road to ruin. Families, after all, borrow to purchase houses, cars, and college educations. In fact, there are times when a nation, like an individual, may want to borrow external funds to finance an import surplus or to absorb more than it produces. Such a surplus when used prudently, for example, to import badly needed investment goods, may lead to an expansion in income not only sufficient to pay off both the principal and interest charges of the loan, but to raise national income as well.

In the 1960s, South Korea ran trade deficits and financed them by borrowing abroad. It used the import surplus to build up basic industries such as steel, cement, petrochemicals, and shipbuilding. Once these and other industries had been built up, South Korean exports expanded dramatically. And although the country is still paying off its external debts, its export surpluses have been deployed to reduce its international indebtedness and the country has enjoyed a rapid rate of economic growth—some 8.7 percent per annum between 1970 and 1990.

On the other hand, not much can be said in favor of external borrowing that is used to finance current consumption. A country that devotes its import surplus to raising its level of consumption will increase its external debt but not its capacity to repay it. Such unwise borrowing took place in the 1970s and 1980s when many South American countries ran up hefty external debts; many experts feel that this same pattern is occurring in the United States at the present time. In the last decade, the United States has shifted from being the world's largest creditor nation to being the world's largest debtor and it does not have too much to show for it.

Aggregate Supply

The **aggregate supply curve** shows the total quantity of goods and services that will be provided within an economy at various national price levels. If other things do not remain equal, a supply curve will shift to the left or to the right.

The price of an individual commodity is determined by market demand and supply. In a similar manner, the general price level is determined by the interplay of aggregate demand and **aggregate supply.** For example, an increase in aggregate demand at all price levels shifts the *AD* curve to the right. What proportion of the increase in nominal income will show up as an increase in the price level and how much will reflect an increase in real GDP depends on the slope of the aggregate supply curve. If it is flat, the increase in aggregate demand leads to an increase in real income and output; if the aggregate supply curve is vertical, the increase in aggregate demand leads to a higher price level alone. Thus if the aggregate supply curve is somewhere between a horizon-

[4]All this assumes that the ¥/$ exchange rate remains constant over the borrowing-repaying cycle.

tal or vertical line, a shift in the *AD* curve leads to an increase in both output and the price level.

What determines the slope of the aggregate supply curve? Figure 2.3 shows a series of aggregate supply (*AS*) curves. All have positive slopes which indicates that more goods and services are supplied as the general price level rises. As we said in Chapter 1, the slope of a supply curve depends on the increase in labor costs per unit of output that takes place as production expands. In turn, labor costs per unit of output are explained by the wage rate, the number of workers employed, and the level of **labor productivity.** An increase in the wage rate raises labor costs per unit of output while an increase in labor productivity reduces labor costs per unit of output.

Labor productivity measures *output per unit of labor,* and is normally reckoned as either output per worker or output per worker hour. Labor productivity depends on a whole host of elements such as levels of health and education, public infrastructure investment, the business climate, the speed of technological innovation, and so on. Economists tend to emphasize the quantity of capital per worker as a primary determinant of labor productivity. Give a worker more and better capital equipment to work with and her output per hour will rise.

In the short run, the quantity of capital and other determinants of productivity are pretty much set. Therefore, as additional laborers are employed, capital per worker declines and output per worker on average and at the margin decreases—illustrating once again the law of diminishing returns. Since the wage rate is assumed constant, output per worker declines as more workers are employed, which means that labor costs per unit of output increase.

Columns 1 and 5 of Table 2.3 together describe an individual aggregate supply curve such as AS_1 in Figure 2.3, which assumes that the wage rate, W_1, the capital stock, K_1, and the state of technology, T, are constant. (The assumptions are denoted by the symbols in the parentheses.)

As with aggregate demand, aggregate supply curves can shift in either direction. AS_0 and AS_2, for example, are drawn under different assumptions. In the case of AS_0, the

Labor productivity. How much a worker produces. Normally measured either as output per worker or output per worker hour.

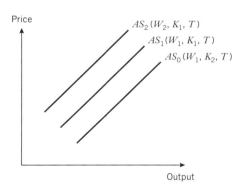

FIGURE 2.3 Aggregate supply schedules.

The figure shows the relation between aggregate supply and the price level. As the price level increases, the quantity supplied also increases. The aggregate supply schedule can shift to the left or to the right. A higher wage rate, say W_2 rather than W_1, shifts the aggregate supply curve to the left, from AS_1 to AS_2. On the other hand, an increase in the capital stock from K_1 to K_2 raises output per laborer, which causes the aggregate supply curve to shift to the right, from AS_1 to AS_0.

		TABLE 2.3 Computing Aggregate Supply		
Output	*Labor*	*Wages (total)*	*Output per Worker*	*Labor Costs per Unit of Output*
10	1	$10	10	$1.00
18	2	$20	9	$1.11
24	3	$30	8	$1.25
28	4	$40	7	$1.43

wage rate rises from W_1 to W_2 while the capital stock and productivity remain constant. Labor costs per unit of output increase at every price level and the aggregate supply curve shifts to the left. In terms of Table 2.3, the wage rate would rise to $20 and total wage payments would double at every level of output. In the case of AS_2, the wage rate is constant at W_1, but the capital stock increases to K_2, raising output per worker. With a constant money wage rate but higher productivity, labor costs per unit of output fall and the aggregate supply curve shifts to the right. In addition, an increase in state of technology, T, would also shift the aggregate supply curve to the right by increasing worker productivity.

Other factors could cause the aggregate supply curve to shift to the left or to the right. For example, if the price of a foreign-produced input such as oil drops, the AS curve shifts to the right. And if the value of the domestic currency appreciates, the price of foreign inputs will fall in terms of the domestic currency and shift the curve to the right. Japan, for example, benefited from this double whammy in the 1980s when the price of a barrel of oil fell some 45 percent from $31.38 to $14.14 per barrel between 1982 and 1988, while the yen appreciated by 50 percent from ¥249/$ to ¥128/$ during the same period. Since oil is normally priced in dollars, falling oil prices and yen appreciation had a powerful impact on the Japanese economy. Indeed, employing the figures already cited, the yen price of a barrel of oil fell from roughly ¥7900 in 1982 to roughly ¥1800 in 1988. In turn, the decline in the price of this essential input shifted Japanese industry supply curves and Japan's aggregate supply curve to the right, and powerfully so in the case of Japan because of the importance of oil in the production process.

Market supply and aggregate supply curves are similar in only some respects. If there is a change in relative commodity prices within an economy, industry supply curves shift to the right and to the left as labor and capital migrate from one industry to another in the wake of the change in relative profit opportunities. However, the aggregate AS curve will not shift as a result of change in relative prices. If the price of textiles rises while the price of wheat declines, the composition of an aggregate supply curve may change but the curve itself will not shift.

Potential Output in the Short Run

A nation's economy cannot expand indefinitely along a given aggregate supply curve, as it can produce only so much output with a fixed capital stock and a finite labor force. Moreover, as it moves toward the point where all existing capital and labor are

The **potential level of output** measures how much physical output a nation can produce given the state of technology and the full employment of all its existing resources.

The **nominal wage rate** is the amount of money a worker gets paid in current dollars.

The **real wage rate** equals the nominal wage rate adjusted for any change in the general price level or the cost of living.

employed, the economy moves toward what is called its **potential level of output.** When it arrives at this point, a nation will be unable to increase real output for an extended period. Under such conditions, an increase in aggregate demand must ultimately lead to a higher price level alone or what is sometimes called pure inflation.

One can trace the dynamics of aggregate supply and demand using Figure 2.4. The aggregate demand curve, AD_0, and the short-run aggregate supply curve, AS_0, intersect at the general price level, P_0. Output, at that point, equals Qn. Imagine that Qn corresponds to the economy's potential level of output. Now, suppose aggregate demand shifts to AD_1. The economy moves along AS_0, output expands to Q_1, and the price level rises to P_1. However, the economy can move along AS_0 only if the **nominal wage rate** remains at W_0. But since the price level is now higher than P_0, a constant nominal wage rate means that **real wages** have declined, or $W_0/P_1 < W_0/P_0$. Workers react to this decline by demanding higher nominal wages to protect their standard of living. Wage rates then climb to W_1 and the aggregate supply curve shifts up and to the left to AS_1. As can be seen, the price level rises to P_2 and output ends up between Qn and Q_1. Since output still exceeds potential output, further adjustments take place until the economy settles at a point where the price level is P_n, output Qn, and the wage rate W_n, and the equilibrium short-run aggregate supply curve is AS_n.

Ultimately, the initial shift in aggregate demand leads to pure inflation since real output remains constant. Most economists agree that if a closed economy is operating at its potential this inflationary pattern will occur. They disagree as to whether an economy is always close to its potential output and how close it must be to its potential output

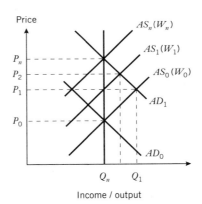

FIGURE 2.4 Potential output.

If an economy is operating at its potential level of output or at Qn, any increase in aggregate demand will lead to pure inflation in the long run. Initially the aggregate supply and demand curves intersect at P_0 and Qn. If the government attempts to raise output, it will push the aggregate demand curve from AD_0 to AD_1. At first, the policy is a success. Although the price level rises to P_1, the level of real GDP rises to Q_1. However since money wages are constant, real wages will fall when the price level rises. In order to protect their real wages, workers raise their money wages to W_1. But that step shifts the aggregate supply curve to AS_1. As a result, the price level goes up to P_2 and the level of output falls to some level between Qn and Q_1. Yet at P_2, real wages have once again declined. Once more workers react, raise wages, and the AS curve shifts to the left again. This process, a price-wage spiral, continues until the final aggregate supply curve, AS_n, intersects AD_1 at the price level P_n. At this price level, real output, once again, equals Qn.

before wages respond to an increase in the price level. When an economy is operating near its potential and the labor market is tight, labor responds quickly to an increase in the price level, especially if there has been a recent history of inflation. But if there is slack in the economy, an increase in aggregate demand should lead to only a minor rise in the price level, if any at all. Previously unemployed workers who are hired at the prevailing wage rate will be happy to be employed. And while previously employed workers will not like the higher price level and the decline in real wages, they may not be able to do much about it given the slack demand for labor and the pool of unemployed workers searching for work. In such a situation, the economy expands along its initial *AS* curve.

In what follows, it is assumed that wages do not respond to a slight increase in the price level, especially when the economy is performing below its potential. But it is assumed that wages do rise when the *AS* and *AD* curves intersect to the right of the *Qn* line or curve or, as it is often called, the long-run supply curve. Hence, there is a limit to the degree an economy can expand before an increase in aggregate demand will lead to pure inflation.

But this does not mean that potential income is fixed. Both GDP and GDP per capita are higher today than they were 50 years ago. Thus, potential output curves must have shifted to the right. An increase in productivity, for example, will shift the *AS* and the *Qn* curves to the right simultaneously and potential output will be higher. It may be that the new *AS* curve will intersect the new *Qn* curve at the original price level since both curves may shift by the same amount. On the other hand, an increase in productivity combined with a lower wage rate will lead to an increase in potential output plus a lower price level.

Higher labor productivity is the major source of an increase in potential output. But an increase in the size of the labor force will also raise potential output. There is, however, a crucial difference between an increase in productivity and an increase in the labor force alone. If the size of the labor force doubles, it is doubtful that output will double. As previously emphasized, as more workers combine with the same quantity of capital, output per worker will decline. Thus whether or not potential output increases depends on the interplay of the increase in the labor force and the decline in labor productivity. If the former exceeds the latter, potential output will rise.

Equilibrium: Demand Meets Supply

By combining aggregate supply and demand curves, as in Figure 2.5, it is possible to show the equilibrium position of an economy. But there is nothing sacrosanct about this position. An internal or external shock to the system may cause the aggregate demand, aggregate supply, and the import and export curves to interact and move the economy away from one equilibrium position toward another. Exactly how much and in what direction the economy moves will depend on the state of the economy and the shock or shocks that take place. For example, an export boom will push the aggregate demand curve to the right and the economy will end up with a higher level of output and a higher price level.

The aggregate demand and supply framework can be utilized to trace out the possible implications of selected economic policies for both a nation and the world

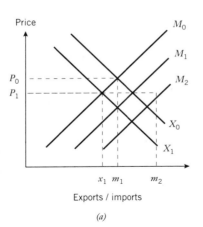

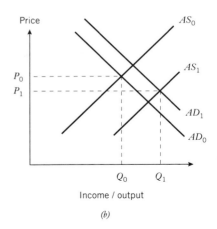

(a)   (b)

FIGURE 2.5 Fiscal expansion and currency appreciation.

Assume, as in panel (b), that AS_0 equals AD_0 at the price level P_0 and at the output level Q_0. Also assume that at this price and income level, exports equal imports, or they both equal m_1 in panel (a). An easy fiscal policy will shift the AD curve to the right, but currency appreciation will shift it to the left. Suppose that the impact of fiscal expansion on aggregate demand is greater than the effect of currency appreciation on aggregate demand. The aggregate demand curve will then shift from AD_0 to AD_1. Income and output are boosted further because currency appreciation shifts the aggregate supply curve to the right from AS_0 to AS_1, which drops the domestic price level from P_0 to P_1. But while the combination of fiscal expansion and currency appreciation helps the domestic economy, it exacerbates the economy's export/import position. Currency appreciation shifts the export curve to the left or to X_1, and decreases exports at all price levels. The effect of currency appreciation on exports is offset, to some degree, by the lower price level. The import curve shifts to the right for two reasons. First, currency appreciation means that foreign goods are now relatively less expensive. The import curve, therefore, shifts from M_0 to M_1, and it shifts even further to the right, to M_2, as a consequence of the higher level of domestic output. In the end, domestic output is higher, the domestic price level is lower, but the nation's external trade position has deteriorated. Imports, m_2, exceed exports, x_1.

BOX 2.1 Using the Aggregate Demand and Supply Framework

Between 1982 and 1985, the U.S. federal government ran robust budget deficits measured either in dollars or as a percentage of GDP; the U.S. economy also ran record trade deficits, again measured either in dollars or as a percentage of GDP. Yet the U.S. economy enjoyed relative prosperity during most of the 1980s, with modest growth in real GDP combined with relatively low unemployment and a declining rate of inflation.

Table 2.4 presents some basic data on the U.S. economy during 1982–1985. Column 1 shows the annual growth in nominal GDP and column 2 presents the annual rate of increase in the general price level ($\Delta P/P$). Thus, the rate of growth of real GDP equals column 1 minus column 2. Columns 3 and 4 respectively show the federal budget deficit (B/GDP) and exports minus imports ($X-M$/GDP) as a percent of nominal GDP. Column 5 measures the annual percentage change in the value of the dollar relative to other major international currencies ($\Delta\$/\$$). Finally columns 6 and 7 present the yearly percentage change in exports and imports ($\Delta X/X$) and ($\Delta M/M$).

How does the aggregate demand and supply model explain these developments? Look first at Figure 2.5b. Fiscal expansion, due to a combination of tax cuts and a rapid increase in government expenditures, shifted the *AD* curve to the right. The easy fiscal policy was supplemented by the introduction of an easier monetary policy in 1983, which further shifted the *AD* curve to the right. Together these forces overpowered the impact of dollar appreciation, which, by reducing U.S. exports and increasing U.S. imports, pushed the *AD* curve back to the left. (The budget deficit, which totaled some $736 billion over the period, was stronger than the trade deficit of roughly $330 billion.)[5] In addition to the shift in the *AD* curve, the aggregate supply curve shifted to the right due to falling oil prices and, up until early fall 1985, the appreciation of the dollar, which reduced the price of imported inputs.

During the period 1982–1985, shifts in the aggregate demand and supply curves raised income and led to greater imports, as shown in Figure 2.5a where the import curve shifts from M_0 to M_1 as a result of the higher national income. By itself, the fall in the U.S. price level or the decrease in its rate of inflation, due in part to the fall in the international price of oil, should have made the United States more competitive in international markets and raised its exports and cut its imports. However, since the price of oil fell worldwide, an individual oil importing country did not obtain a competitive advantage relative to other oil importing nations. Actually, the U.S. competitive position declined when the dollar appreciated between 1980 and 1985. Dollar appreciation shifted America's export curve to the left to X_1 and its import curve further to the right to M_2 and led to a large trade deficit. The economy ended up in a position similar to one outlined in Figure 2.5b with the price level at P_1, real income at Q_1, and a trade imbalance equal to the difference between M_2 and X_1 at the price level P_1.

TABLE 2.4 Selected Macroeconomic Data of the United States: 1982–85 [percentage change or proportion]

Year	(1) ΔGDP/ GDP	(2) $\Delta P/P$	(3) B/ GDP	(4) X−M/ GDP	(5) $\Delta\$/\$$	(6) $\Delta X/X$	(7) $\Delta M/M$
1982	3.9%	6.2%	4.1%	−.6%	12.2%	−6.6%	4.7%
1983	8.1	4.1	6.3	−1.5	7.5	−2.1	8.2
1984	10.9	4.4	5.0	−2.7	10.3	9.0	23.5
1985	6.9	3.7	5.4	−2.9	3.5	0.0	3.2

ΔGDP/GDP equals the annual rate of growth of GDP; $\Delta P/P$ equals the annual rate of growth of the GDP price deflator, a measure of inflation; B/GDP equals the budget *deficit* as a percentage of GDP; (X−M)/GDP equals net exports of goods and services as a percentage of GDP; $\Delta\$/\$$ equals the annual rate of appreciation of the dollar relative to a group of other currencies, what is called a *multilateral exchange rate*; $\Delta X/X$ and $\Delta M/M$ equals the annual percentage rate of growth, relative to the previous year, of exports and imports of goods and services.

Source: Economic Report of the President, 1995, pp. 274, 275, 279, 366, and 402.

---

[5]Actually the trade deficit was the result of two forces: dollar appreciation and income expansion. As the income equation in the second part of the chapter demonstrates, an increase in imports resulting from an increase in aggregate demand will not shift the *AD* schedule to the left. Currency appreciation is a different story. It will shift the aggregate demand schedule to the left.

economy. For example, in early 1995, Republicans advanced legislation to reduce the federal government budget deficit to zero by the year 2002 through a combination of budget cuts and a reduction in the rate of increase in selected government programs.

There are several possible scenarios if the U.S. budget does move toward balance. Lower government expenditures combined with a steady growth in tax receipts should shift the aggregate demand curve to the left with a resulting slowdown in the U.S. economy. Since the import curve would also shift to the left, the U.S. trade deficit would be reduced. Declining U.S. imports would reduce exports and the level of economic activity in the rest of the world, provided other things remain constant. Of course, other things are not likely to remain constant. If the narrowing of the U.S. trade deficit leads to dollar appreciation, economic activity will be further curtailed in America. The export curve would shift left but the import curve could, ultimately, shift either to the left or to the right. It will shift to the left due to the decline in economic activity and to the right as a result of dollar appreciation. This means that some of the improvement in the U.S. export-import picture that results from reduced domestic economic activity would be lost as a result of dollar appreciation.

The *AS-AD* framework can be employed to explain economic developments in other countries as well. The Japanese economy, for example, grew by less than 1 percent in 1994, and some economists have projected that it would not do much better in 1995. There are many explanations of the slow-down in the rate of Japanese economic growth. One explanation points to the effect of the rapid rise in the value of the yen on the Japanese economy. According to the *AS-AD* framework, yen appreciation will shift the Japanese export curve to the left and its import curve to the right. These developments will, after a lag, reduce Japan's staggering trade surplus. More important, the decline in Japan's net exports will shift the aggregate demand curve to the left. As a result, Japan's rate of economic growth will be curbed. For the rest of the world, the impact of yen appreciation and Japan's slower economic growth will be mixed. Yen appreciation will make other countries more competitive with Japan, which should boost their exports, cut their imports, and push their aggregate demand curves to the right— all a plus for the rest of the world. But a slow-down in Japanese economic growth will reduce the market for the rest of the world's exports. From the perspective of the rest of the world, yen appreciation combined with economic expansion in Japan would be the preferred choice.

Extending the AS-AD Framework

Autonomous consumption. Consumption that does not depend on the level of income. The arrival of a child may lead a family to increase its consumption even though its income remains constant.

National income can be more formally derived. Recall that in an open economy, the equilibrium level of nominal income is attained when output (Y) equals aggregate demand or when $Y = C + I + G + X - M$.

The consumption function is often written in the following form: $C = C_0 + c(Y - T)$. Consumption, therefore, is composed of two parts: an **autonomous** element, C_0, which does not depend on the level of income, and another component, $c(Y - T)$, which does. If C_0 equals $10, it will equal $10 regardless of whether income is $0 or $1000. The second or **income-induced** component of the consumption function depends on the level of income or, more correctly, on the level of disposable income. Given an increase

Income-induced consumption. The increase or decrease in consumption due to an increase or decrease in disposable income.

The **marginal propensity to consume (mpc)** tells us how much consumption will increase given an increase in income, more specifically, the increment in consumption given an increment in income.

The **marginal propensity to save (mps)** equals the increment in savings given an increment in income.

The **marginal propensity to import** equals the increment in imports given an increment in income.

The **multiplier** tells how much income will change given an increase or decrease in some autonomous expenditure such as investment, government expenditures, exports, etc. In an open economy, the simple multiplier equals the reciprocal of the sum of the marginal propensity to save plus the marginal propensity to import.

in her disposable income, an individual will spend some of it to purchase additional goods and services.

Disposable income equals income minus taxes, or $Y - T$. In this example, it is assumed that taxes, T, are a given sum of money such as \$10. Taxes, therefore, are similar to a poll or head tax and not an income tax.[6] Lowercase c in the consumption function represents the **marginal propensity to consume (mpc)**. The *mpc* describes the increase in consumption resulting from an increase in disposable income. In most examples, it is assumed that *mpc* is greater than zero and less than one or that $0 < mpc < 1$. Since the *mpc* is less than 1, if an individual receives an additional dollar of income, she will not spend all of it purchasing goods and services, but will save some of it. How much of this additional income she saves depends on her *mpc*. If it is .9 and her disposable income increases by \$50, she will spend \$45 purchasing additional consumption goods and save the remaining \$5. Her additional savings can also be computed by multiplying the increase in her disposable income by her **marginal propensity to save (mps)**. Since the sum of the *mpc* and the *mps* equals one, or $mpc + mps = 1$, her *mps*, s, equals .1 in this example. Thus if an individual's disposable income increases by \$50, her additional savings, S, is computed by the following formula: $\Delta S = s\Delta Y$.

Like consumption, imports are divided into two parts. One, M_0, is autonomous and does not depend on income. It will increase regardless of the level of income when the domestic price level rises or when the domestic currency appreciates. A second portion of imports, mY, does depend on income. These rise or fall as income expands or contracts. Lowercase m equals the **marginal propensity to import (mpm)**. Like the *mpc* and the *mps*, the *mpm*, symbolized by the letter m, is assumed to be greater than zero but less than one, or $0 < m < 1$.

Finally, it is assumed that investment (I), government spending on goods and services (G), and exports (X) are given or not determined by income. Given these definitions and relationships, the national income equation is written as follows:

$$Y = C_0 + c(Y - T) + I + G + X - M_0 - mY$$

$$Y = C_0 + cY - cT + I + G + X - M_0 - mY$$

$$Y - cY - mY = C_0 + I + G - cT + X - M_0$$

$$Y(1 - c + m) = C_0 + I + G - cT + X - M_0$$

since $1 - c = s$,

$$Y(s + m) = C_0 + I + G - cT - M_0$$

$$Y = (1/s + m)C_0 + I + G - cT + X - M_0$$

If the *mps* and the *mpm* each equal .1, then the value of the open economy **multiplier**, $(1/s + m)$, equals 5. The multiplier tells us how much income will change when any of the autonomous elements in the income equation rise or fall.

---

[6]Most countries employ income rather than head taxes. Given an income tax, induced consumption equals $c(Y - tY)$, where t is the income tax rate. Total tax collections would equal the tax rate times the level of income or tY. Employing an income tax would change some of the formulas given below. However, variations in the consumption function are not a major thrust of this text.

Suppose a business firm decides to spend $10 to expand its plant. In adding to its capacity, the firm must hire and pay labor a wage to carry out the construction. This expenditure shows up as an increase in investment and, with it, an increase in aggregate demand. The workers will, in turn, spend at least a portion of their wages on various goods and services, further raising aggregate demand. As a result, the final increase in income will be some multiple of the initial investment expenditure. In this case, the $10 increase in investment (ΔI) will raise nominal income (ΔY) by $50, or:

$$\Delta Y = (1/s + m)\Delta I$$

The $50 increase in income leads to a $45 increase in consumption, .9($50), and a $5 increase in imports, $m\Delta Y$ or .1($50). The breakdown of the increase in income is given below.

$$\Delta Y = \Delta C + \Delta I - \Delta M$$
$$\$50 = \$45 + \$10 - \$5$$

Income will also change by $50 if either C_0, G, X, or M_0 changes by $10, only a $10 increase in autonomous imports will decrease income by $50 (note the negative sign). However, if taxes are cut by $10, income will rise by only $45 since individuals will spend only $9 of the tax cut, or $c\Delta T$, and save the remaining $1. The initial $9 of expenditures generated by the tax cut will be multiplied through the economy and raise income by a multiple of 5, or to $45. The increase in income is given below.

$$\Delta Y = (1s + m)c\Delta T$$
$$\Delta Y = (5).9(10)$$
$$\Delta Y = 45$$
$$\Delta Y = \Delta C - \Delta M$$
$$45 = (c\Delta Y + c\Delta T) - m\Delta Y$$
$$45 = (40.5 + 9) - 4.5$$
$$45 = 49.5 - 4.5$$

Shifts in Aggregate Supply and Exports and Imports

A shift in the aggregate supply curve will affect exports and the imports; exactly how is not clear cut since there is a range of possibilities. First, assuming that everything else remains constant, including the AD curve, a shift in the AS curve to the right will drop the national price level. As a result, the economy will move down its existing export and import curves. Given this movement, exports will increase and imports will decrease and the economy's balance of trade will improve.

Second, an increase in productivity which drops labor costs per unit of output will shift the export curve to the right and the import curve to the left. The shift in the export curve follows logically from the drop in labor costs per unit of output. The shift in the import curve results from the increase in labor productivity and the drop in unit costs of production in import substitute industries. As a result, the increased competitiveness in the import substitute industries reduces the demand for imports at all price levels and causes the import curve to shift to the left. Thus an increase in productivity that shifts the *AS* curve to the right improves a nation's export-import balance because it (1) drops the price level and (2) reduces unit costs of production in the export and import substitute industries.

Let's run through these cases. Suppose there is an increase in investment that raises labor productivity and shifts the *AS* curve to the right. Also assume that the increase in investment comes at the expense of consumption. Investment rises and consumption falls, so that the shift in the *AS* curve is unaccompanied by a shift in the *AD* curve.

As shown in Figure 2.6, the shift in the *AS* curve causes the domestic price level to fall from P_0 to P_1. How will this fall in the general price level affect exports and imports? A lower price level will stimulate exports and reduce imports as the economy moves down along the existing export and import curves. As shown on the horizontal axis of Figure 2.6a, exports increase and imports decrease.

Since in this example investment increases as a percentage of output, labor productivity should rise. Given the higher labor productivity, the nation should be able to produce exports at a lower cost since labor cost per unit of output declines in the export industry. Under such conditions, the export curve should shift to the right. In addition, the decrease in labor costs per unit of output across the economy means that domestic

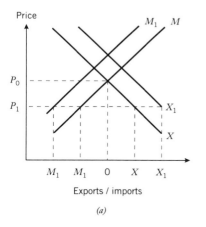
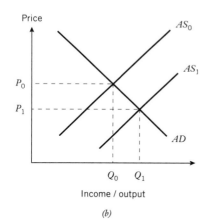

(a)   (b)

FIGURE 2.6 Aggregate supply, exports, and imports: I.

An increase in investment shifts the aggregate supply curve from AS_0 to AS_1. Since we assume that higher investment is offset by lower consumption, the aggregate demand curve does not shift. The domestic price level, however, falls to P_1 and the level of output rises to Q_1, as in panel (b). Higher productivity should also increase the economy's international competitiveness, which, in turn, shifts the export curve to the right from X_0 to X_1 and the import curve to the left from M_0 to M_1 in panel (a). By itself, the productivity effect leads to an export surplus. But, in addition, higher productivity also leads to a lower price level. Thus, exports increase and imports decrease for two reasons: the competitiveness effect of higher productivity and the price effect.

industries should be able to produce import substitutes at a lower price. Thus, the import curve should shift to the left. In the final analysis, the economy will run a trade surplus for two reasons: The increase in productivity will shift the export curve to the right and the import curve to the left; and the shift in the aggregate supply curve will lower the domestic price level which will stimulate exports and reduce imports.

This latter possibility is sketched out in Figure 2.6. As before, the shift in the AS curve drops the price level from P_0 to P_1. In addition, higher labor productivity shifts the export curve from X to X_1 and the import curve from M to M_1. Compared with the previous example, the nation's trade balance improves more dramatically. On the horizontal axis of Figure 2.6a, exports now equal X_1 and imports equal M_1.

BOX 2.2 Investment and Exports

Some evidence of the relation between investment and export expansion is presented in Table 2.5. The table shows the average growth of the volume of exports and the investment/GDP ratios of several countries. The volume rather than the value of exports was selected since an increase in the price of exports, although certainly good for the exporting country, could be the result of an abnormal state of affairs. The rise in the value of oil exports in the two oil shocks of the 1970s is an example.

The relationship described is not perfect, partly because the volume of exports depends upon a multitude of factors that will be described in later chapters. On the other hand, the relationship is far from imperfect. The three nations with the highest average investment/GDP ratios—Singapore, Japan, and South Korea—had the fastest average rates of export expansion while the three countries with the lowest investment/GDP ratios—Belgium, the UK, and the United States—had the slowest rate of export expansion.

TABLE 2.5 Investment and Exports: Investment/GDP and Percentage Increase in the Volume of Exports (period average 1970–1990)

Nation	I/GDP	%ΔExports
Singapore	38.4%	11.2%
Japan	31.4	7.2
South Korea	27.8	17.2
Italy	22.6	5.2
France	22.3	5.4
Canada	22.0	5.0
Germany	21.5	5.4
Netherlands	21.1	5.2
Belgium	19.2	4.9
UK	18.1	4.4
US[a]	16.5	4.5

[a] = 1970–1988.

Source: Calculated from relevant country pages in International Monetary Fund, *International Financial Statistics Yearbook*, 1993. Investment is calculated as private gross fixed capital formation.

However, although it is not shown in the graph, the shifts in the export and import curves will shift the AD curve to the right. Recall the income formula previously given where an increase in exports or a decrease in autonomous imports raised aggregate demand. An increase in aggregate demand will stimulate induced imports so that the import curve will shift back to the right. In the end, the nation's income will be higher and its trade balance lower than previously indicated.

It is unlikely that an increase in investment will be offset by a decline in consumption and thus it is improbable that the AD curve will remain fixed following an increase in investment. We've seen that an increase in investment will normally lead to an increase in consumption and imports via the multiplier process. Suppose the increase in investment does not displace consumption, but rather that it is a net addition to aggregate demand. Both the AS and AD curves shift to the right. If they shift by the same degree, output rises and the price level remains constant.

In this example, the import curve is buffeted by two forces. Higher productivity leads to lower unit labor costs and shifts the curve to the left, but higher aggregate demand shifts it to the right. If these two forces offset each other, the curve will not shift. Nevertheless, the export curve will shift due to the productivity effect and the nation's trade balance position will improve, although not to the degree in the previous example. Since the price level remains constant, the price effect on exports and imports will not take place. The case is summarized in Figure 2.7, where the AS, AD, and X curves shift to the right.

Economic theory usually assumes that an increase in investment will shift the aggregate demand curve to greater degree than it shifts the aggregate supply curve, particularly in the short run. An increase in investment increases consumption, and ag-

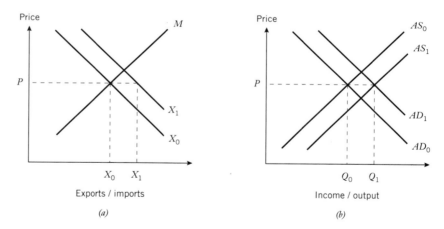

FIGURE 2.7 Aggregate supply, exports, and imports: II.

An increase in investment shifts the aggregate supply curve from AS_0 to AS_1 and the aggregate demand curve from AD_0 to AD_1. Although the level of output is higher at Q_1, the price level remains constant, panel (b). The export curve shifts to the right due to the enhanced competitiveness that follows the greater investment. The import curve remains constant because improved competitiveness, which shifts the curve to the left, is offset by an increase in income, which shifts the curve to the right. In the end, the economy ends up with a higher level of income and, of some importance, a surplus of exports over imports.

gregate demand, by some multiple of the expansion in investment. Thus a $10 increase in investment raises aggregate demand by $50 at all price levels. However, the additional $10 investment will *not* necessarily shift the aggregate supply curve by $10 at all price levels. The degree of the shift of the *AS* curve depends on how much the additional investment increases productivity. The greater the increase in productivity, the greater the shift in the *AS* curve.

On the other hand, if the *AD* curve shifts further to the right than the *AS* curve, the domestic price level will rise. A higher price level will reduce exports and increase imports as the economy moves along its given export and import curves and cause a net trade deficit. In addition, the import curve will shift to the right at all price levels as income climbs, further increasing the nation's trade deficit. These forces, however, will be countered by the productivity or competitiveness effect resulting from greater investment. The competitive effect will shift the export curve to the right and the import curve to the left. The interaction of all these factors means that it will be difficult to spell out exactly the nation's ultimate trade balance position.

Given all the possibilities, what do you suppose would be the final trade position of economy given a shift in its *AS* curve? Empirical evidence is mixed and depends on the time period under observation. In the short run, it is likely that an increase in economic growth will lead to a trade deficit as imports initially outrace exports. But there is little doubt that the combination of high investment, price stability, and strong economic growth leads to trade surpluses and appreciating currencies over the longer run. Clearly the answer to the question as to whether investment-led economic growth leads to a trade surplus or a trade deficit depends on the time frame analyzed.

Summary

In this chapter we reviewed the aggregate supply and aggregate demand framework. In addition to describing why the aggregate supply curve slopes up from left to right, we saw why the curve may shift either to the left or to the right due to domestic or international economic developments. We also saw why the aggregate demand curve slopes down from left to right—the real balance effect and the foreign trade effect—and why it too can shift either to the left or to the right as a result of domestic economic policy or external economic developments.

We developed the import and export curves in order to show the relationship between the domestic price level and the levels of either imports or exports, assuming all other economic variables are constant. Since all other economic variables will not remain constant except in the very short run, we described how changes in such variables cause the export and import curves to shift about, and how, in turn, shifts in the export and import curves may lead to shifts in the aggregate demand curve.

Introducing the export and import schedules and curves enabled us to look at other aspects of international economics. We saw that regardless of domestic income, a country may have a trade surplus or a trade deficit. If a country has a trade deficit, it is absorbing more than it is producing and will have to borrow abroad to finance its excess absorption or the trade deficit, which are one and the same. Likewise, if a country has a trade surplus, if it is producing more than it is absorbing, it will have to lend abroad.

We concluded with a discussion of the potential effects of an increase in investment on a nation's trade position. We saw that under certain conditions an increase in investment will lead to both a higher level of national income and a trade surplus, although the country may actually run a trade deficit before the trade surplus appears.

The aggregate demand and supply model has been criticized. Some complain about its construction, some about its never ending assumptions, and others about its failure to come to clear-cut conclusions. But before castigating the model, one should consider its merits. Recall the questions the model implicitly posed when describing the possible economic consequences of a reduction in the U.S. budget deficit combined with an appreciation of the dollar.

1. How much will a reduction in the budget deficit reduce American income?
2. How much will U.S. imports and foreign exports contract as a result of the fall in American income?
3. How much will dollar appreciation offset the initial decline in American imports? This is certainly an important question from the foreign point of view.
4. Since dollar appreciation will shift the U.S. aggregate supply curve to the right, how much will the U.S. price level decline or the U.S. rate of inflation be reduced? To what degree will the lower rate of inflation offset the effects of dollar appreciation on U.S. exports and imports?
5. What are the consequences of U.S. economic policy on foreign nations, and how will they react?

Only with luck will one be able to answer these questions precisely. However, given the *AS-AD* model, one can a get grip on what questions should be asked. More important, one can get a hold on the range of possible answers.

Key Concepts and Terms

absorption

aggregate demand

aggregate supply

AD schedule

AS schedule

autonomous expenditures

closed economy

export schedule

gross domestic product (GDP)

import schedule

induced expenditures

labor productivity

marginal propensity to consume

marginal propensity to import

marginal propensity to save

nominal GDP

price level versus individual price

open economy

potential output

price index

real balance effect

real GDP

real money balance

total expenditures

trade balance

trade effect

trade surplus (deficit)

Review Questions

1. Draw a nation's import curve. What will most likely happen to this curve if:
   (a) The domestic price level rises?
   (b) The domestic currency depreciates?
   (c) Domestic income falls?

If (a), (b), and (c) occur simultaneously, what do you think will happen to the value of the nation's imports? Explain your answer.

2. What will happen to a nation's export schedule if:
   (a) The domestic price level rises?
   (b) The domestic currency depreciates?
   (c) Domestic income declines?

3. What is the difference between absorption and aggregate demand (a) in a closed economy and (b) in an open economy?

4. Draw an aggregate supply schedule. What will happen to this schedule if (a) there is an increase in the nation's capital stock, and (b) nominal wages rise within the economy?

5. Draw the aggregate demand and supply and the export and import schedules for an economy. Show and describe how these schedules will most likely be affected if:

    (a) The demand for domestic exports increases.

    (b) There is an inflationary increase in the domestic money supply.

    (c) Production and output decline in the rest of the world.

6. Imagine an effective OPEC emerges and raises the price of petroleum by 100 percent. Describe how this might affect the output, exports, imports, and price level of an oil importer such as Japan.

7. The income equation tells us that $Y = C_0 + mpcY + I + G - mpcT + X - M_0 - mpmY$. Suppose that: $C_0 = 20$, $I = 20$, $G = 20$, $T = 20$, $X = 30$, and $M_0 = 6$. If the *mps* and the *mpm* each equal .2, what is the level of income? What is the level of total imports?

Now if investment rises by $10, what is the new level of income and what is the new level of total imports?

References and Suggested Readings

All principles of economics texts contain an extended discussion of income determination. For example, see William J. Baumol and Alan S. Blinder, *Economics: Principles and Policy*, 6th edition (New York: Dryden Press, 1994). Chapter 25, Appendix B, and Chapter 26, Appendix A, run through the simple algebra of income determination. For those desiring to take a bigger bite from macroeconomic theory, a good starting point is Rupert Pennant-Rea and Clive Crook, *The Economist Economics* (London: Penguin, 1985). This book is readable and short—only 178 pages of text—and contains an outstanding list of additional readings.

Chapter 3

The Foreign Exchange Market

In 1965, a dollar was worth 360 yen (¥) and 4 Deutschemark (DM). Thirty years later, in late 1995, a dollar was worth ¥104 and DM1.42.[1] This means that in the last 30 years, the yen and DM appreciated 4 percent and 3.6 percent annually against the dollar. Moreover, in the last 10 years, the yen and DM rose at annual rates of 8.1 percent and 7.7 percent respectively against the dollar. The record begs two questions: What explains the fall of the once-almighty dollar and what of the future? Will the dollar continue to slide against the mark and the yen and, if so, will it fall at recent rates?

The Composition of the Foreign Exchange Market

In order to answer these questions, we need to know how exchange rates are established and why they rise and fall. The answers are multifaceted. Many factors, from economic fundamentals to expectations, interact to determine an exchange rate at a particular moment and push it up or down over time. And not only are there many factors, there are also many players in the foreign exchange markets. The foreign exchange market is the largest financial market in the world with more than $1.2 trillion in transactions each day. This number is more than 100 times larger than the volume of transactions on the New York Stock Exchange, which in 1994 was approximately $10 billion per day.

Unlike the New York Stock Exchange, whose main trading center is in New York, the foreign exchange market is a worldwide market. The major trading centers are in

---

[1]In the 1960s, Arthur Frommer wrote a best-selling travel guide entitled *Europe on $5 a Day*. Today the title of the book is *Europe on $50 a Day*. While not the only cause, the sinking dollar is one reason for the new title.

Located in Basel, Switzerland, the **Bank for International Settlements (BIS)** is the central bankers' bank.

London, New York, and Tokyo. A survey conducted by the **Bank for International Settlements (BIS)** concluded that roughly 30 percent, 16 percent, and 10 percent of the average daily volume of foreign exchange trading took place in the United Kingdom, the United States, and Japan respectively in 1995. (Singapore, Switzerland, and Hong Kong each accounted for approximately 6 percent of the daily volume.) The actual trades are carried out by large commercial banks such as Citibank, Chemical, Deutsche Bank, JP Morgan, and HSBC/Midland, to name the top five foreign exchange dealers in 1993.[2]

Even though all currencies are traded on the foreign exchanges, 83 percent of the transactions involved the dollar and some other currency, 37 percent involved the mark and other currencies, and 24 percent involved the yen and other currencies. (Every transaction involves two currencies, because if one currency is bought, another must be sold. For example, in 1992, 25 percent of the transactions involved the dollar and the mark, 20 percent the dollar and the yen, and 9.5 percent the dollar and the pound.)

There are other dimensions to the foreign exchanges that tend to be overlooked because of the daily drama played out in that market. The overwhelming majority of international transactions, both the trading of goods and services and the purchase and sale of foreign financial assets, pass through this market. Without effective foreign exchange markets, it is highly probable that international trade and investment would be distorted since individuals would be unable to buy and sell the goods and financial assets they wanted to, and the level of such transactions would be reduced which would diminish national and world economic welfare.

Moreover, the exchange rate is arguably the most important price for many nations since an increase or decrease in the price of a nation's currency has a direct bearing on their economic fortunes. It helps to determine whether or not a nation can export certain commodities and how much it will cost its citizens to purchase foreign-made goods, a point of some concern in open economies where exports and imports may constitute 50 percent of GDP.

The Path Ahead

This chapter examines the foreign exchange market and concentrates on four issues:

- How exchange rates are determined.
- How exchange rates are tied to and affected by fluctuations in economic growth, inflation, interest rates, and expectations.
- How and why governments attempt to control or influence the exchange rate.
- Technical details on the day-to-day operations of money managers and international traders in the foreign exchanges.

---

[2]Rosemary Bennet, "Foreign Exchange: Universal Banks Play the Investor Card," *Euromoney* (May 1993). p. 71; HSBC/Midland = Hongkong Bank and Midland.

How Exchange Rates Are Established

An **exchange rate** equals the value of one currency in terms of another. A dollar, for example, equals DM1.4.

Exchange rates for each currency are established minute-by-minute by the interplay of the demand and supply of one currency relative to another. Because the demand for and supply of a currency is influenced by a multitude of factors, we will use a hypothetical example to begin our analysis of the foreign exchanges. If, for example, a German firm wants to buy an American product, it will need dollars just as an American who wants to visit Paris will need francs since dollars are not accepted when you purchase a ticket for the metro. The German firm obtains the needed dollars by selling marks and buying dollars on the foreign exchange market. The increase in the demand for dollars and the increase in the supply of marks will raise the price of the dollar in terms of the mark.

Table 3.1 presents hypothetical demand and supply schedules for both dollars and marks at various exchange rates, or the dollar-mark market since it is a single market viewed from different angles. This means that the $/DM rate is the reciprocal of the DM/$ rate. Thus if the exchange rate stands at DM4/$ in the dollar market, the corresponding exchange rate is $.25/DM in the mark market. As can be seen, the demand schedule in the dollar market shows the quantity of dollars demanded at various prices providing other things are held constant and the supply schedule shows the quantity of dollars supplied at various prices providing everything else is constant.

Given supply and demand schedules, one can derive supply and demand curves. This is done in Figure 3.1a, which shows the supply and demand curves for dollars expressed as marks per dollar, or more simply, the dollar market, and in Figure 3.1b, which shows the market for marks expressed in dollars, or dollars per mark. In both cases, the demand curve slopes down from left to right and the supply curve slopes up from left to right.[3]

What determines the slope of the demand curve or how much will the quantity of currency demanded change with a change in the exchange rate? Suppose a German desires to buy U.S.-made compact discs that, for ease of exposition, we assume cost $1 per unit in the United States. It stands to reason that the German will buy more U.S.-made CDs as their mark price declines. It is at this point that the exchange rate comes into play. For even if the dollar price of an American-made CD remains constant, its mark price will vary with changes in the exchange rate. Suppose the exchange rate stands at DM4/$. At this exchange rate, the corresponding mark price of the American-made CD is DM4. If the German wants to buy two CDs at this price, he will purchase $2 on the foreign exchange market by selling DM8 since the exchange rate tells us that he must give up DM4 for every dollar he wants.

---

[3]This creates a problem: Is the dollar exchange rate DM2/$ or $.5/DM? Both answers are correct. In the academy, the tradition is to quote the exchange rate as the number of units of domestic currency per one unit of foreign currency, or the dollar as $.5/DM. This means that in order to find out the price of the dollar, one has to look at the market for German marks. Thus, an increase in the demand for dollars shows up as an increase in the supply of marks. This practice seems at odds with what one has learned about markets in principles of economics. It is also at variance with how exchange rates are quoted on CNN and on the Internet. There exchange rates are quoted as so many marks, French francs, and so on per dollar—the exception being the dollar-pound exchange rate, which is quoted as $/£. (One never sees the dollar quoted as .0002142 dollars per ruble; rather the exchange rate is given as 4,677 rubles per dollar.) In this text, we will follow the practice of the Internet, and as much as possible quote exchange rates in terms of dollars except when we are looking at the supply and demand for a particular currency. If we want to discover how an economic policy affects the French franc, we will look at the franc market.

TABLE 3.1 Supply and Demand for Dollars and Marks

Dollar Market

Price DM/$	Demand for Dollars	Supply of Dollars
4	2	16
3	4	10
2	8	8
1	20	4

Mark Market

Price $/DM	Demand for Marks	Supply of Marks
1.00	4	20
.50	16	16
.33	30	12
.25	64	8

Now imagine that the price of the dollar falls to DM3/$. Even though the dollar price of the CD is constant, its mark price will fall to DM3. If the German now wants to buy four CDs because their mark price is now lower, he will sell DM12 in exchange for $4. Therefore, with everything else held constant, the demand for dollars increases as its price declines and the supply of marks increases as its price rises.

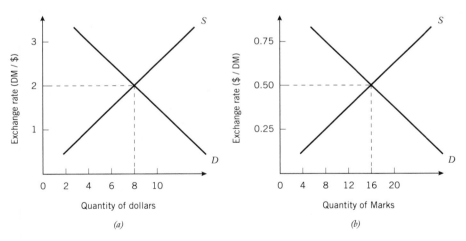

(a)   *(b)*

FIGURE 3.1 The dollar market and the mark market.

The equilibrium exchange rate for any currency, including the dollar and the mark, is established when the quantity of the currency supplied equals the quantity of the currency demanded at a particular exchange rate or price. In a two-currency world, if Germans decide to purchase more American goods at every exchange rate, the demand curve for dollars in panel (a) will shift to the right and the supply curve of marks in panel (b) will shift to the right as well. As a result, the price of the dollar will rise and the price of the mark will decline. An increase in the German rate of inflation relative to the U.S. rate of inflation will also increase the demand for dollars and the supply of marks. In addition, it will reduce the supply of dollars and the demand for marks.

The **equilibrium price** or exchange rate is established when the demand for one currency, dollars, in terms of another, marks, equals the supply of that currency, dollars, in terms of the other currency, marks.

Since the German sold marks in order to buy dollars, there is a direct relation between the demand for dollars and the supply of marks. Indeed, if the demand schedule for dollars is known, the supply of marks can be calculated and vice-versa. In a similar manner, in a two-currency world, if the demand for marks is given, the supply of dollars can be computed.

Given the tendency of supply and demand to find equilibrium, the foreign exchange market will move toward an **equilibrium price** at which the quantity of a currency demanded equals the quantity supplied. In the example, when the price of the dollar is DM2, the supply and demand for dollars each equals 8 units or $8; and at this price, since DM2/$ is the same as $.5/DM, the supply and demand for marks equals 16 units or DM16. The market, therefore, is in equilibrium whether looked at from the dollar or mark side.

Economic Fundamentals and Exchange Rates

Equilibrium prices, of course, are not constant. They fluctuate as the quantities supplied and demanded adjust to a multitude of factors. The same is true of exchange rates. They rise and fall as the supply and demand for currencies are buffeted about by changing expectations and economic fundamentals, such as inflation and economic growth.

For example, if the American rate of inflation exceeds the German rate of inflation, the price of U.S. goods will increase relative to the price of German products, and as a result, the demand for German commodities will rise relative to the demand for American products. In the foreign exchange markets, the difference in the relative rates of inflation will lead to an increased demand for marks and a decreased demand for dollars, and, at the same time, an increased supply of dollars and a lower supply of marks. In terms of Figure 3.1a, the supply curve of dollars will shift to the right as Americans purchase more German goods and the demand curve for dollars will shift to the left as Germans purchase fewer American products at every exchange rate. As the exchange rate adjusts to these shifts in supply and demand, the dollar will fall in terms of marks.

While it is relatively simple to come to a firm conclusion regarding the impact of inflation on an exchange rate, this is not the case when there is a change in real income. Economic growth impacts the exchange rate differently depending on the time frame and whether economic growth is based on increased consumption or increased investment. In the short run if higher consumption is the primary cause of faster growth, domestic citizens will demand more foreign goods. Thus the supply curve of the domestic currency and the demand curve for the foreign currency will shift to the right. As a result, the value of the domestic currency will fall on the foreign exchanges. For example, the dollar fell against the yen and the mark in 1994 because higher U.S. income increased Americans' demand for foreign products.

Investment-led growth takes place when investment is the major reason for economic expansion—a common occurrence in parts of Asia.

But there is little evidence that **investment-led growth** causes currency depreciation over the long run. When investment leads to lower production costs and new product development, demand for domestic products worldwide may swamp the domestic demand for imports. Although the supply curve of dollars in Figure 3.1a will shift to the right as increased American income stimulates demand for imports, the demand curve for dollars may shift even further to the right as Germans demand new and cheaper American-made products. In Japan, as in Germany, income expansion and currency appreciation have been almost inseparable.

Yet there is a problem here. Even if growth and inflation differentials lead to exchange rate adjustments, one can ask how much adjustment should take place. If growth and inflation differentials between the major economies of the world are not that far apart, why have the ¥/$ and DM/$ rates jumped about so much in the last 15

BOX 3.1 Economic Fundamentals and Exchange Rates in Practice

Table 3.2 presents some rough data on the impact of inflation and economic growth on the yen/dollar exchange rate in the 1980s and the early 1990s. In theory, if the U.S. rate of inflation exceeds the Japanese rate of inflation or if the Japanese economy grows at a faster rate than the American economy, the dollar should depreciate unless Japanese growth is consumption led.

The evidence casts doubt on the theory. Between 1980 and 1985, the growth and inflation differentials implied that the yen should have appreciated against the dollar, but it actually fell. Even if it is claimed that the potential impact of economic growth on the exchange rate is so muddled that it is impossible to discover any clear-cut relationship between the two variables, the relatively higher rate of inflation in the United States should have led to yen appreciation, not depreciation. Nor does the exchange rate experience of 1985–90 offer much comfort. According to the theory the yen should have appreciated, but not at a 9.5 percent annual rate. The exchange rate moved in the right direction, but its appreciation was excessive. And the appreciation was, according to this analysis, even more excessive in the 1990 to 1994 period.

Over the total period, economic fundamentals provide a better explanation of changes in the ¥/$ rate. Economic fundamentals suggest that the yen should have appreciated at a 4.2 percent annual rate; in actuality, it appreciated at a 5.6 percent annual rate—a rate close to that predicted. The evidence suggests that economic fundamentals explain exchange rate movements in the long run, but that, in the all-important short run, exchange rate variation depends on other forces.

TABLE 3.2 Inflation, Growth, and Exchange Rate (annual percentage change)

	1980–85	1985–90	1990–94	1980–94
Growth				
USA	2.5%	2.6%	2.3%	2.5%
Japan	4.8	4.5	1.6	3.4
Difference	−1.3	−1.9	.7	−.9
Inflation[a]				
Japan	0.0	−1.9	−1.7	−1.2
USA	2.8	2.4	.9	2.1
Difference	−2.8	−4.3	−2.6	−3.3
¥$	1.0	−9.4	−8.4	−5.6

[a]Measured by the wholesale price index.

Source: The figures were computed from data in International Monetary Fund, *International Financial Statistics Yearbook*, 1995, pp. 469, 471, 779, 781.

years? The evidence presented in Box 3.1 indicates that other variables must explain exchange rate fluctuations in the short run.

Capital Flows and Exchange Rates

Capital flows occur when individuals buy and sell foreign financial assets. Capital flows swamp trade flows by a factor of 60.

Most economists agree that **capital flows** are the primary cause of short-run variations in major exchange rates. Capital flows are indeed important. Recall that the daily volume of transactions on the foreign exchange markets is roughly $1.2 trillion a day. But the total value of trade in goods and services is at best around $10 trillion a year. If trade were the sole determinant of foreign exchange transactions, the foreign exchange markets would have to be open for only two weeks in the year. They are open all year since the value of capital transactions swamps trade transactions by at least 40 to 1. (Some individuals estimate the multiple to be 60 to 1.)

Capital movements complicate our analysis of foreign exchange markets. Consider Figure 3.2. Given capital flows, the price of the dollar is influenced both by trade flows and by capital transactions. The total supply of dollars equals those supplied in order to purchase foreign-produced products, S_m in Figure 3.2, plus those sold in order to

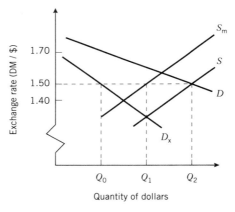

FIGURE 3.2 The exchange rate: trade and financial transactions.

The demand for dollars can be separated into two parts: first, the foreign demand for the dollars needed to purchase U.S. goods and services, and second, the foreign demand for the dollars needed to buy U.S. financial assets. In Figure 3.2, the total demand for and supply of dollars at various exchange rates is shown by the demand curve, D, and the supply curve, S. The foreign demand for dollars to purchase the U.S. goods and services is shown by the demand curve D_x and the American supply of dollars offered for sale in order to buy foreign goods and services is shown by the supply curve S_m. Thus S minus S_m equals American demand for foreign financial assets and D minus D_x equals the foreign demand for U.S. financial assets. At the equilibrium exchange rate, 1.50, U.S. imports of goods and services exceed its exports of goods and services by Q_0 to Q_1. But U.S. export of financial assets exceeds its import of financial assets by Q_1 to Q_2. An increase in the demand for the nation's goods and services alone will shift both the D_x and D curves to the right. An increase in the foreign demand for U.S. financial assets at all exchange rates will shift the D schedule alone to the right.

purchase foreign financial assets, S minus S_m. The demand for dollars is also split into two parts. The demand curve D_x equals the foreign demand for dollars due to trade, while D represents the total demand for dollars. Thus D minus D_x equals the demand for dollars generated by the demand for American financial assets.

At the exchange rate of DM1.5/\$1, the total demand for dollars equals the total supply of dollars. But notice that at that exchange rate, S_m exceeds D_x. The excess supply of dollars at the exchange rate indicates that the United States is spending more on imports of good and services than foreigners are spending to purchase U.S. goods and services, or that the quantity of dollars supplied to purchase German goods, Q_1, exceeds the quantity of dollars demanded by Germans to purchase U.S.-made good and services, Q_0. Thus, at the exchange rate DM1.5/\$1, the United States is running a deficit on its trade or current account even though the total demand for dollars equals the total supply of dollars at this exchange rate. It follows, therefore, that foreigners are demanding more dollars to purchase U.S. securities than American citizens are supplying in order to buy foreign financial assets. At the equilibrium exchange rate, the United States is running a capital account surplus which exactly offsets its trade, or goods, deficit. In terms of Figure 3.2, the U.S. trade deficit equals the amount Q_0 to Q_1, and this amount also equals the U.S. capital account surplus.

If an exchange rate is **overvalued,** the supply of the currency exceeds the demand for the currency at that exchange rate. If the equilibrium exchange rate is \$1.5/£ while the actual exchange rate is \$1/£, the dollar is overvalued.

If the dollar is overvalued, the pound is **undervalued.**

Viewed solely from the perspective of trade in goods and services, the dollar in Figure 3.2 is **overvalued** since the value of imports of goods and services exceeds the value of exports of goods and services. Put another way, the United States is spending, or supplying, more dollars to purchase imports than it is earning by exporting goods and services. If United States trade in goods and services is to be balanced, the exchange rate, or the price of the dollar, would have to fall to DM1.4/\$ in Figure 3.2. Exactly the opposite holds true for trade in financial assets. The dollar is relatively **undervalued.** At the exchange rate DM1.5/\$, foreigners are more eager to purchase U.S. financial assets than Americans are to buy foreign financial assets. Only if the exchange rate rises to DM1.70/\$, a step that would reduce the dollar price of foreign financial assets and raise the foreign price of U.S. financial assets, would the capital account be balanced.

The Mainsprings of Capital Flows

Speculation. Briefly, an attempt to make a quick buck. A speculator hopes to obey the first and most enduring principle of economics: *buy low, sell high.*

Capital flows, the offspring of the rapid development of international capital markets, occur for many reasons and are viewed with mixed emotions. Most everyone agrees that certain capital movements, such as the flow of funds from the capital-rich north to the capital-starved south, are desirable, but several individuals question the desirability of others. Among these are capital flows induced by the search for speculative profits based on variations in exchange rates. If an individual expects that the French franc will depreciate 25 percent in the near future, selling francs today for marks or dollars makes sense. If she sells francs for dollars at an exchange rate of, say FFr4/\$, and the franc falls to FFr5/\$, she can make a profit of 25 percent when she converts her dollars back into francs.

In some circles such **speculation** is deemed immoral and any profits derived from it are described as theft. Such sentiments, however, may be misplaced. Many so-called gnomes of Zurich are not speculators attempting to make a quick profit; rather, they are firms trying to avoid a loss. A large multinational corporation normally holds a

Multiple exchange rates. A system of two or more exchange rates, each one of which is used for different types of transactions on the foreign exchanges.

BOX 3.2 Dual Exchange Rates in South Africa

Many countries employ dual or **multiple exchange rate** systems in order to discriminate between trade flows and capital flows and between various types of trade and capital flows. Until recently, the Union of South Africa had such a system. There was one exchange rate, the commercial rate, for the export and import of goods and services and another for the purchase and sale of South African financial assets by foreigners, the financial rand. At times, the financial rand was at a 25 percent discount relative to the commercial rand.

What was the purpose of the dual exchange rate system and why was it introduced in the first place? Suppose the commercial rand stood at R3.65/$ ($.274/R) while the financial rand was at R4/$ ($.25/R), a discount of roughly 10 percent. The lower value of the financial rand meant that a foreigner could purchase R100,000 of South African securities for $25,000 rather than $27,400. The lower price was designed to induce foreigners to purchase South African securities and cause capital to flow into South Africa. From a foreign perspective, the downside of the dual exchange rate system was that if they attempted to sell previously purchased South African securities to a South African and ship the proceeds home, the lower value of the financial rand would penalize such a transaction. Of course, if a foreigner could purchase South African securities using the financial rand, sell them to someone in South Africa, and ship the proceeds of the sale home at the commercial rate, she would make a huge profit. The ability to carry out such get-rich-quick schemes was outlawed by the South African government. It became easy to put funds into South Africa, but difficult to get them out.

The dual exchange rate system was introduced in the mid-1980s as a result of the political turmoil which swept the country at that time. Due to external political and social pressures resulting from apartheid plus the risks associated with investing in South Africa, most foreigners wanted to ship funds out of the country rather than invest in the country. The financial rand was designed to attract foreign capital and to prevent it from fleeing.

Although the system may have been a modest success, the South African authorities were aware that the free movement of capital was and is in the best interest of their country. The chance to eliminate the dual exchange rate system arrived in early 1995 following the democratic elections of 1994 and the generally conservative economic policies undertaken by the African National Congress–led government of national unity.

The rand actually appreciated by some 4 percent in the second half of 1994. In addition, a R3.5 billion capital outflow in the first half of 1994 turned into a R9 billion inflow in the second half of the year. As a result, South Africa enjoyed a net capital inflow in 1994 in contrast to the capital outflow that had taken place in the preceding two years. Moreover, South Africa's international reserves rose by R12.5 in 1994. While not large by international standards, the international reserve position of the country showed a marked improvement. Given these developments, the South African government merged the two exchange rates by dropping the financial rate on March 13, 1995.

South Africa's currency experience is not unique. Many countries have employed dual exchange rate systems. Typically, countries have attempted to fix the commercial exchange rate, or maintain it within a narrow range, but have allowed the financial rate to float or be set by market forces. As shown in Figure 3.2, an influx of short-term capital can push the international price of the domestic currency so high that the nation's exports are impeded. To overcome this bind, many countries have introduced dual exchange rate systems or capital controls to prevent capital inflows and outflows from affecting the commercial exchange rate.

Sources: Mark Suzman, "Economic Strength Spurs End of Finrand: . . . " *Financial Times* (March 11, 1995): p. 4, and "After the Finrand," *Financial Times* (March 13, 1995): p. 27.

portfolio of many currencies to facilitate its worldwide operations. If the comptroller of such a company believes that the dollar is going to decline relative to other currencies, she will sell dollars and buy competing currencies in order to maintain the international purchasing power of the firm's portfolio.

Indeed, if she ignored the warning signs and failed to move the firm's funds out of the dollar, she might be fired. Let's assume a situation in which, for simplicity, there are only two currencies: the mark and the dollar. Imagine that the exchange rate stands at DM2/$ and that the firm holds DM200 and $100. Since the firm is readily able to convert one currency into the other, the firm can hold either DM400 or $200. If the firm happens to hold only dollars and exchange rate moves to DM1/$, the purchasing power of the firm's currency holdings will be $200 expressed in dollars, but only DM200 expressed in marks. Thus, the purchasing power of its currency holdings expressed in marks will be cut in half. By comparison, if the firm held all of its funds in marks and the mark appreciated as before, the purchasing power of the firm's currency holdings would remain constant in terms of marks, but double in terms of dollars. A comptroller, therefore, has a strong incentive to get out of a weak currency and into a strong one if she anticipates that the exchange rate will change. One would be hard-pressed to find fault with such self-protective behavior.

Because short-run exchange rate variation is keyed to capital flows, two questions arise: *What* causes capital movements to start in the first place and *why* have exchange rates been driven up and down to the degree observed? While there is no solid agreement on what initiates capital flows in every instance, there is abundant evidence of what causes capital to flow in this or that direction on specific occasions.

Interest Rates and Exchange Rates

The **interest differential** is the difference between interest rates in one financial center relative to those in another financial center.

Exchange rates and interest rates are closely linked in financial markets. An alert firm will maintain its cash reserve in the currency which gives it the highest yield. If interest rates are higher in New York than in London, the firm will hold dollars. (Firms actually hold their dollar assets in such instruments as U.S. Treasury bonds or in certificates of deposits, CDs, that have short maturities and pay interest). But if British interest rates should rise above U.S. rates and the **interest differential** moves in favor of London, firms will switch out of dollar assets and into short-term British financial assets. In order to convert from American to British financial assets, the firm will sell its American financial assets for dollars. It will then go to the foreign exchange market, actually to its bank, and sell dollars and buy pounds. Pounds in hand, the firm will purchase British financial assets and the switch will be complete.

On the foreign exchanges, the transaction will drive down the value of the dollar in terms of pounds. In Figure 3.1, the supply curve of dollars shifts to the right as U.S. investors sell dollars in order to buy pounds and the demand curve for pounds shifts to the right as Americans demand more pounds in order to purchase more British financial assets.

Like most postulates in economics, the interest rate effect holds only if other things, including expectations, remain constant. If the interest rate on a one-year British CD is 10 percent while the comparable U.S. return is 4 percent, an American money manager should purchase British CDs. But suppose that an American money manager gazes into his crystal ball and comes to the conclusion that the pound will depreciate by 8 percent over the year. Given his expectations, he will purchase British financial assets and buy the pounds required to carry out the transaction only if the British interest rate exceeds the comparable American rate by at least 8 percent. True, if he purchases a U.S. Treasury bill yielding 4 percent, he will lose 6 percent if the British interest rate is 10 percent and the pound does not depreciate. However, if the pound drops by 8 percent as anticipated, his net gain, measured in dollars, will be only 2 percent if he buys a British Treasury bill and converts the proceeds into dollars following the depreciation of the pound. Thus, given his expectations and current interest rates, he will invest in a U.S. Treasury bill.

Even a British money manager, who ultimately wants to hold pounds rather than dollars, will place her funds in New York under these conditions. For although she loses 6 percent on the interest differential, she gains 8 percent when she converts the dollars back into pounds. Assuming that the exchange rate initially stands at $1/£, her initial £100 will grow to £110 if she stays in sterling. If she buys a $100 U.S. Treasury bill paying 4 percent interest, she will have $104 at the end of the year. Assuming the pound drops by 8 percent to $.92/£, she can convert her dollar holdings into £113.04, a net gain of £3.04.

Interest Rate Expectations and Exchange Rates

Just as changes in *actual* interest rates can lead to capital flows and to raising or lowering a particular exchange rate, so too can changes in interest rate *expectations*. What follows is a brief nontechnical glimpse at the impact of expectations on exchange rates.

We've seen that if interest rates rise in Germany and fall in the United States, funds will move from New York to Frankfurt and the mark will appreciate relative to the dollar. But if an international money manager expects that the value of the mark will rise tomorrow, she will buy marks today. Or if she expects German interest rates will rise tomorrow and lead to an appreciation of the mark, she will buy marks today as well.

Or will she? If she buys marks today, she faces a trade-off since if interest rates rise, the prices of financial assets fall. Suppose she purchases a DM100,000 six-month Treasury bill today prior to the rise in German interest rates and that the current interest rate is 5 percent. Since the price of the Treasury bill is given by the following formula,

$$\text{Price} = \frac{\text{DM100,00}}{(1.05)^{1/2}}$$

it will cost her DM97,590 to purchase it. Now if the German interest rate rises to 6 percent, the price of the bill will fall to DM97,128. That means that if she sells the bill immediately after buying it, she will take a capital loss of close to 1 percent on an annual basis. This seems to suggest that the money manager will shift into marks only after German interest rates and the price of the mark itself have gone up.

However, if the mark appreciates by 2 percent, the money manager is a winner even if she buys marks before the appreciation since although she might take a 1 percent capital loss on the Treasury bill if she sells it immediately, she will gain 2 percent on the appreciation of the mark. If she holds the Treasury bill to maturity and the mark appreciates as before and the previous interest differential in favor of New York was just ½ percent, she is most definitely a winner.

Expectations about interest rate changes make a big difference in day-to-day exchange rates. Many analysts believe that interest rate expectations in the winter of 1994–1995 were a major cause of the appreciation of the mark relative to the dollar. Although the Federal Reserve had raised U.S. interest rates repeatedly from 3 to 6 percent in the previous year, the slowdown in the pace of U.S. economic activity created the feeling that the Fed might cut U.S. interest rates. At the same time, an increase in German economic activity led to the belief that the Bundesbank might boost German rates. Given these expectations about interest rates, the demand curve for marks shifted to the right while the supply curve of marks shifted to the left. Both shifts led to an increase in the price of the mark.

"News" and the Foreign Exchanges

If the supply and demand for a currency were determined solely by inflation, income expansion, and interest rates, foreign exchange dealers would have far less stressful jobs and, one suspects, would not receive such handsome salaries. But exchange rates are influenced by more than the hard, objective factors just mentioned. Like tomorrow's weather, all sorts of elements influence exchange rates, most of which are easier to explain *after* the fact than *before* it.

How does one explain the depreciation of the pound relative to the dollar in the fall of 1986, especially in light of the appreciation of the pound during the winter of 1987? Let's examine the economic indicators available from that period, shown in Table 3.3.

On balance, the numbers tell us that the pound should have *appreciated*, not depreciated, relative to the dollar. Britain's economic growth outstripped that of the United States. Since economic growth was consumption-led in both countries, growth should have put downward pressure on the pound. However, in other regards, the relative economic performance of Britain should have strengthened the pound. The rate of British

TABLE 3.3 Economic Indicators: United Kingdom and United States (third quarter, 1986; percent change over previous period, ratio, and rate).

	UK	U.S.
ΔGDP/GDP	4.3%	.3%
ΔP/P	−5.1%	−4.3%
TB/GDP	−1.8%	−3.5%
Interest rate[a]	10.9%	6.2%

P = wholesale price index.
TB = trade balance (exports − imports).
[a]6-month treasury bill rate.

Source: Calculated from the relevant country pages in International Monetary Fund, *International Financial Statistics* (December 1987).

deflation, measured by the wholesale price index, was higher; and, although both nations were running trade deficits, the British trade deficit, measured as a proportion of GDP, was smaller than the comparable United States trade deficit. Finally, British interest rates were some 4 to 4½ percent higher than those in the United States. While the figures suggested that the pound should have appreciated or at least not have depreciated against the dollar, it fell by 5 percent in the fall of 1986 or at more than a 20 percent annual rate.

What may appear surprising, especially since it contradicts some of the previous analysis, was that high British interest rates were looked upon as a sign of the pound's weakness. Britain, it was claimed, needed high interest rates in order to prop up the pound. However, even high interest rates did not halt the pound's slide in the early autumn of 1986, and the Bank of England was forced to intervene in the foreign exchange markets to support the pound.

Some analysts felt that the pound's decline was best explained by a combination of economics and politics, with the economics tied to the falling price of oil. Since North Sea oil was a prime foreign-exchange earner for Britain, the drop in oil prices forewarned the British of future trade deficits and a weaker pound. The political explanation was based on party politics and the upcoming general election of that time. The Labour Party claimed that the then Thatcher government had presided over the deindustrialization of Britain, which had crippled the nation's ability to compete in world markets. Thus, but for high interest rates, the pound would have collapsed according to Labour. The Conservatives responded that a Labour victory would mean greater government spending, higher taxes, inflation, and, perhaps, exchange controls. Thus, even the slightest prospect of a Labour victory would send the pound reeling.

What was an international money manager to do in this situation? Clearly, her best course of action was to get out of the pound until she acquired solid information regarding the future price of oil and the likely outcome of the general election. Economics alone would not have been enough; she needed to pay attention to the political sphere as well. Political events often foretell future economic developments and explain current economic behavior. The pound began to recover against the dollar in late 1986, and later rose relative to all European currencies, as the standing of the Conservative Party moved from strength to strength in political opinion polls.

A more recent example of the impact of politics on expectations and exchange rates took place in Canada in the fall of 1993 when the Liberals, led by Jean Chretien, absolutely demolished Prime Minister Kim Campbell and the Progressive Conservatives at the polls. As it became increasingly evident that the Liberals were going to win the election, many individuals sold Canadian dollars and the Canadian dollar slid against the U.S. dollar by close to 6 percent. Many people believed that the Liberals would follow an expansionary fiscal policy in an attempt to reduce unemployment despite their pledge to reduce the budget deficit from 5.2 to 3 percent of GDP. Fiscal expansion, it was felt, would lead to inflation and, hence, a depreciation of the Canadian dollar. Thus it made sense to sell the currency.

As a matter of fact, the Canadian dollar recovered just before the election, when the mood swung toward the view that a strong Liberal party would be better for the Canadian dollar than a weak Conservative one. The Canadian dollar, however, took another hit, and the Bank of Canada was forced to intervene to prop up the Canadian dollar, when the Bloc Quebecois and the Reform Party, both of which have separatist leanings, captured second and third place in the election.

These are just two examples of how "news" influences exchange rates. Certainly political developments and their implications for business conditions are "news." Yet even if such "news" does affect exchange rates, it does not indicate why international currency values have varied to the degree observed. Perhaps the dollar should have recovered with the election of President Reagan, but should it have recovered so much? And if there was reason for the increase in the value of the dollar in the early 1980s, what explains its slide from 1985 on against major currencies?

Explaining Exchange Rate Variability

Overshooting is a term used to describe the tendency of exchange rates to move more than is necessary to attain a new equilibrium exchange rate.

Economists have mulled these questions over and have developed theories about exchange rate determination in which exchange rates, moving from one position to another, **overshoot** their ultimate value. These theories are very complicated. But their basic message is that given rational behavior on the part of individuals and firms in the foreign exchange market, it is not at all surprising that exchange rates shoot up and down more than a bystander would expect.

But it is likely that the recent magnitude of exchange rate variability is beyond what such theories would envision. And even if there are sound explanations why exchange rates rise above or fall below their ultimate position, this does not tell us why such overshooting is more prevalent today than it was in the past.

One explanation for exchange variability is that international financial markets are far larger today and communications among them much better. Economics usually assumes that an increase in the number of market participants combined with better lines of communication and superior information leads to more stable markets. But it is hard to square this traditional assumption about market behavior with the recent performance of foreign exchange markets. For example, the yen appreciated some 20 percent against the dollar in the first quarter of 1995, an annual rate of appreciation of over 100 percent. Yet the yen fell 7 percent against the dollar in the early spring of 1995, only to advance 2½ percent against the dollar in May 1995. Exchange rate volatility clearly appears to be the *rule* rather than the exception.

Price volatility, however, is not limited to the foreign exchange markets since many financial markets, or segments of them, show wide price swings. These wide gyrations may be difficult to understand. Explaining the stock market booms of early 1987, *The Economist* wrote:

> Because it is in the nature of markets to test extremes, the share boom will go on until the market reaches ridiculous and untenable levels. Market cycles usually end in a climactic crescendo. Herd behavior dominates. This is because markets are emotional places made up of flesh and blood, which is why rational intellectuals are so bad at making money in them.
>
> *The Economist* (January 23, 1987): p. 15.

Such behavior may be the nuts and bolts of foreign exchange markets in the short run. Currency values shoot up and down based not so much on fundamentals as on the idea that if a currency is rising, one had better buy it to make a profit and, at the same instant, sell another currency to avoid a loss. Combined with the growth of

A speculative bubble
occurs when people buy
a financial asset today
because they believe its
price will be higher
tomorrow regardless
of economic
"fundamentals."

market participants, who if they do not seek speculative profits attempt to avoid losses, it is not surprising that when a currency starts to move in one direction, it is carried on a **speculative bubble** and the currency rises or falls further than dictated by fundamentals.[4]

BOX 3.3 The Future of the Dollar

Wither the dollar? Many observers believe that it will continue to slide against major currencies for several reasons. First, the structure of the world economy is changing. *The Economist* estimates that one-half of the world's private financial wealth is held in dollars or in dollar-denominated assets, that 67 percent of world trade is invoiced in dollars, that 75 percent of international bank lending is done in dollars, and that 61 percent of international reserves are held in dollars. Yet America's stake in the world economy has waned. Unlike the immediate post–World War II period when the United States produced 50 percent of the world's output, America today accounts for only 20 percent of world output and 14 percent of world trade.

In light of America's relative decline internationally, it is surprising that the dollar is still in such heavy demand. We may expect the worldwide role of the dollar to decline if America's relative position in the world economy continues to slide. If Asian countries trade with each other, why should they invoice their exports in dollars? And how many banks will denominate their loans in dollars if trade is invoiced in other currencies? If, from an Asian perspective, the important exchange rate is the yen-to-won or yen-to-yuan rate, why should we expect them to hold dollars as international reserves? In fact, why would anyone hold dollars as international reserves at all if the dollar continually depreciates against the mark and yen? (Recently, China reduced the proportion of its international reserves held as dollars from 90 to 75 percent.) In sum, the worldwide demand for dollars will, at best, increase at a *decreasing* rate.

On the other hand, the quantity of dollars supplied may increase at an *increasing* rate. American pension and mutual funds have discovered emerging financial markets offering higher returns than domestic markets. At present, Americans hold a mere *3 percent* of their financial assets in foreign securities, far below the 25 percent held by the British. Despite the setback that emerging financial markets took in 1994 and 1995 as a result of the peso crisis, Americans and Europeans will no doubt invest more heavily in these higher return markets in the future. Indeed, it has been predicted that emerging markets may account for some 40 percent of global stock market capitalization by 2010, up from their present 15 percent. For the United States, this means that fewer long-term funds will invest in American financial assets and more American funds will seek investment opportunities overseas. In terms of the foreign exchange market, there will likely be a relative *decrease* in the demand for the dollar and a relative *increase* in its supply.

But this outlook on the dollar's future may be too pessimistic. It is possible that the dollar will slip over the long run, but not necessarily at its present rate. Some analysts believe that its recent skid is due to special circumstances. In late 1994, for example, the United States committed $20 billion of its international reserves, roughly half of its foreign exchange reserves, to help stabilize the Mexican peso. If the stabilization plan fails, $20 billion of America's reserves will go down the drain with dire consequences for the dollar. Given that possibility, some money managers sold dollars. Moreover, some critics of U.S.

---

[4]Joseph Stiglitz defines a bubble in the following terms: "If the reason that the price is high today is *only* because investors believe that the selling price will be high tomorrow—when "fundamental" factors do not seem to justify such a price—then a bubble exists." Joseph Stiglitz, "Symposium on Bubbles," *Journal of Economic Perspectives* 4 (Spring, 1990): p. 13.

international economic policy asserted that the U.S. pledge to guarantee the Mexican peso impeded its (America's), desire to stabilize the dollar. At the time, they believed that the United States should have raised its interest rates to bolster the dollar. But these critics felt that the United States would not take that needed but difficult step since higher U.S. interest rates, rates that Mexico would have to pay if it borrowed from the United States, could very well have jeopardized the possible success of the Mexican stabilization program.

The peso crisis no doubt contributed to the weakness of the dollar in 1995. But that implies that if the peso weathers the storm, the dollar will recover. A second reason for the dollar's slippage in recent years (according to optimists, anyway) is that its current doldrums have been exacerbated by the business cycle. The U.S. economy grew rapidly in 1994, which raised its imports. In comparison, the German economy was relatively flat and the Japanese economy was absolutely flat. However, the rate of U.S. economic expansion slowed in early 1995 and there were indications that the German economy would move ahead at a faster clip in the next few years, although Japan's prospects looked bleak. But regardless of Japan's economic prospects, slower growth in the United States and faster growth in Germany should decrease and increase the rate of imports respectively into these two countries. These anticipated income movements plus the hefty depreciation of the dollar led many economists to forecast dollar rejuvenation.

In fact, Michael Prowse of the *Financial Times* argued that "the era of the hard dollar may be dawning." He cited three reasons: the restructuring and increased efficiency in the manufacturing sector; the strong efforts being undertaken to raise productivity in the service industries; and steps being taken to reduce the size and improve the efficiency of the public sector. If these measures are combined with a move toward a balanced budget and tax reforms designed to encourage savings, the U.S. economy will attain microefficiency and macrostability with a higher savings rate.

By most accounts, increasing microefficiency is no longer a problem in the United States. However, balancing the budget and raising the savings ratio still face their share of difficulties. If they can be overcome and the budget balanced and the savings ratio increased, the dollar could begin to recover, according to the optimists. However, if the United States cannot raise its national savings rate it will probably continue to absorb more than it produces. In that event, unless Germany and Japan begin to absorb more than they produce, the long-term prognosis is that the dollar will continue to fall against the major currencies of the world, although not quite at its 1994–1995 rate.

Sources: The Economist, "The Yen, the Dollar and All That" (April 5, 1995): pp. 67–68, "Economic Focus: The Dollar" (November 12, 1994): p. 88, and "Market Focus: Dollar Woes" (October 29, 1994): p. 96; Michael Prowse, "We're All for Balanced Budgets Now," *Financial Times* (June 19, 1995): p. 15.

The Forward Market

If an individual will need a foreign currency six months from now, but does not buy that currency today in the forward market, he is taking an **open position.** If the individual buys the foreign currency in the forward market, he is taking a **covered position.**

Given exchange rate variability, it is difficult to predict future exchange rates accurately and this inability creates a problem for both traders and international investors. Suppose interest rates are 10 percent in New York and 5 percent in London. Previously it was argued that a British investor would place her funds in New York providing she was sure that the dollar would not depreciate by over 5 percent. The trouble is she has no way of knowing what the exchange rate will be six months or a year from now. If she has nerves of steel, she can take what is called an **open position** by buying dollars on the spot market and purchasing a one-year U.S. treasury bill today. When the treasury bill matures in one year, she can convert dollars back into pounds. Providing the dollar has not depreciated during the year, her investment will make sense. But she has taken a risk. If the dollar did happen to depreciate during the year, that could wipe out her potential profit and also lead to a capital loss.

Most individuals are unwilling to take such chances because they are risk averse. Prior to moving funds from London to New York, they will want to purchase an insurance policy in order to hedge their bet and make sure that the value of their funds will not be adversely affected by exchange rate fluctuations. Buying such an insurance policy is called taking a **covered position** and is carried out in the **forward exchange market.**

The forward exchange market allows individuals, for a fee, to buy or sell a currency for future or forward delivery. The British investor, knowing that she will want to convert so many dollars into pounds a year from now, can enter into a contract today that will permit her to sell the dollars for pounds at a fixed price at that time. That price is called the **forward exchange rate.**

The forward rate is normally quoted as a percentage of the current or spot rate. This means that the forward premium or discount equals $(\pounds_f - \pounds_s)/\pounds_s$, where the subscripts f and s stand for the forward and spot exchange rates, respectively. For example, if the current or spot rate is \$1.50/£ and the six-month forward rate is \$1.45/£, the pound is at 3.4 percent **forward discount,** which means that the dollar is at 3.4 percent **forward premium.** However, since forward premiums and discounts are normally measured on an annual basis, the forward discount would be approximately 6.8 percent. If the forward rate is \$1.60/£, the forward pound is at 13.33 percent forward premium when measured on an annual basis.

Traders as well as money managers utilize the forward market. For example, suppose the current exchange rate is \$1.50/£ and that an American automobile dealer purchases 100 Jaguars at a price of £40,000 per car and agrees to pay the Jaguar company £4 million, the value of the total purchase, in three months' time. To meet his obligations, the automobile dealer must sell all the cars within three months at an average price of \$60,000—actually the price would have to be higher to cover his operating costs and yield a profit. If all goes as planned and the exchange rate still stands at \$1.50/£ when all the cars have been sold, he can convert his \$6 million into £4 million and pay his obligations to the Jaguar company.

But suppose that the pound appreciates and the exchange rate moves to \$2/£ over the three months. For the automobile dealer, pound appreciation or dollar depreciation is a catastrophe. He converts his \$6 million into £3 million, pays the automobile manufacturer every last dime he made from the sales, but still owes £1 million. If the dealer had purchased pounds three months forward at \$1.50/£, he would not lose any money if the pound appreciated.[5]

> The **forward exchange market** is the market where currencies are bought and sold for delivery at some specified date in the future.
>
> The **forward exchange rate** is the price of one currency in terms of another in the forward market.
>
> Forward exchange rates are quoted as a percentage of the present current exchange rate. If the forward price of a currency is less than its current price, the currency is said to be at a **forward discount.** If the forward exchange rate is higher than the current exchange rate, the forward rate is at a **forward premium.**

Covered Interest Arbitrage and Capital Movements

Return to the example of the British investor.[6] Suppose as before the interest rate is 10 percent in New York and 5 percent in London. Also assume that both the spot and forward exchange rates equal \$1.50/£. In this situation, the British investor will obviously

---

[5]If the pound happened to be at a three-months-forward premium when he agreed to purchase the Jaguars, he would have to adjust his retail price to take this into account.

[6]The operations discussed in the following apply only to major currencies for which there is an active forward exchange market.

Options confer the right (but not an obligation) to buy (call) or sell (put) a currency at a specified exchange rate at some agreed-upon date in the future.

BOX 3.4 The Options Market

The automobile dealer could also cover himself by utilizing the **options** market. An **option** is the right, not the obligation, to purchase or sell a currency at some designated date at a specified price. An individual does not have to exercise his option, but this can be expensive since it costs something to buy or sell, "call" or "put," the option in the first place. Suppose the American automobile dealer purchases a number of Jaguars, invoiced in sterling and to be paid for in three months, and the current exchange rate stands at $1.5/£. His real concern is how to protect himself from the effects of pound appreciation. He could purchase sterling three months forward at, say, $1.5/£. But if the pound falls to $1.4/£ during the period, he will not be able to take advantage of this 6.7 annual percent depreciation of the pound since he has signed a binding contract. If, instead, he purchased an option to buy pounds three months forward and the pound fell as before, he would simply not exercise his option. He would take a loss on the purchase price of the option, but gain on the 6.7 percent depreciation of the pound. If, however, the pound appreciated, he would exercise his option and purchase sterling at $1.50/£. Which financial instrument he purchases will depend on the relative costs of traditional forward cover versus options.

move her funds to New York. But just as obviously, everyone else will smell out this opportunity and send their funds to New York as well. In the process, investors will sell pounds spot and buy them forward. This will drop the pound on the spot market to say $1.47/£ or by 2 percent. However, on the forward market, the pound will rise to $1.545/£ or by 3 percent. As a result, the pound will move to a 5 percent forward premium and funds will not move between the financial centers. The interest differential in favor of New York, 5 percent, will be exactly offset by the cost of the cover measured by the 5 percent forward premium on the pound.

But until this happens, funds will move between London and New York based on interest differentials and forward premiums and discounts. Figure 3.3 describes the conditions under which funds will flow between financial centers. The vertical axis shows the interest differential between London and New York, which can be positive or negative. The horizontal axis measures the forward discount or premium on the dollar. The diagonal line, labeled parity, shows the combination of interest differentials and forward rates at which, excluding transactions costs, funds will not shift between the financial centers. Along this line, the interest differential, positive or negative, equals the forward premium or discount on the dollar. To the left of the diagonal line, funds move to London; to the right they move to New York. For example, at point A in Figure 3.3 the interest differential is 4 percent in favor of London and the dollar is at a 1 percent forward premium. In this case, funds move to London. By contrast, consider point B in Figure 3.3. Under these conditions, funds will move to New York. Although the interest differential is 1 percent in favor of London, the dollar is at 3 percent forward premium. If an Englishwoman purchases a U.S. treasury bill she will lose 1 percent on the interest rate but gain 3 percent when she converts the dollars back into pounds.

Covered interest arbitrage is the buying and selling of financial assets to take advantage of interest differentials while at the same time covering yourself for the exchange rate risk in the forward market.

As indicated, the flow of funds between financial centers will be limited for several reasons. Buying a currency spot and selling it forward pushes it to a forward discount, and **covered interest arbitrage** falls to zero. In addition, the movement of funds from, say, London to New York may cause interest rates in New York to drop as the supply of loanable funds increases in this market while the supply of loanable funds declines in London raising interest rates in that financial center.

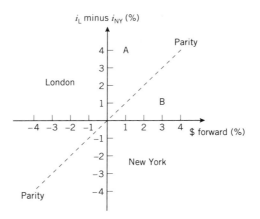

FIGURE 3.3 Covered interest arbitrage.

An arbitrager exploits differences in prices, such as interest rates, in order to make money. Covered interest arbitrage involves taking advantage of differences in interest rates between financial centers, which use different currencies, but also protecting yourself from any unforeseen fluctuations in foreign exchange rates by simultaneously buying a currency spot and selling it forward. At point *A* in the graph, an American will move funds to London to take advantage of the higher interest rates. To do this, she must buy pounds on the spot market. At the same time, she will sell pounds forward in order to protect herself from the effects of pound depreciation. If the interest differential in favor of London exceeds the forward premium on the dollar, funds move to London. As the figure shows, if the interest differential in favor of New York is less than the forward discount on the dollar, funds also move to London.

Speculation and the Forward Market

The abundance or scarcity of forward cover is not important to speculators who want to take open or uncovered positions in a currency in either the spot or forward market, or in the options market. Essentially, these speculators are betting that an exchange rate will move up or down. To them, the direction and magnitude of the change in the exchange rate—not its stability—is the important thing.

Suppose the three-month forward rate is $1.50/£ and a speculator believes that three months from now the spot rate will be $1.70/£. He will, say, sell $1 million forward today. If three months hence the exchange rate is indeed $1.70/£, he will be in clover. He will sell $1 million at the agreed price of $1.50/£ and obtain £666,667. He will then turn around and buy dollars at the new spot rate of $1.70/£ and obtain $1.13 million. At the end of the process, he will have made $.13 million on a three-month investment of $1 million, which works out to be an annual return in excess of 50 percent. His return will even be greater if he had borrowed the initial $1 million on a 10 percent margin. In that case, his gain would be over the moon. Of course, disaster could strike. If the exchange rate moved from $1.50/£ to $1.30/£, rope might be his only answer.

The Uncovered Interest Rate Parity Theorem

Investors are not speculators. To them, forward cover or an insurance policy is important. But while it is easy to obtain short-term cover, purchasing long-term cover is more difficult due to the narrowness of the long-term forward market. That means that it is often difficult and expensive for long-term investors to obtain exchange rate insurance. Yet most individuals do not want to invest blindly in foreign bonds, hoping that providence will be on their side and that the price of the foreign currency does not plummet. Therefore, they need some guidelines to help them estimate future exchange rates.

The **uncovered interest rate parity theorem** provides one such guideline. According to this theorem, the future DM/$ rate equals the difference between German and American nominal interest rates.

Suppose the German long-term interest rate is 10 percent, while the comparable U.S. interest rate is 6 percent. Assuming the risk of default on both German and U.S. bonds equals zero, it make sense for an American to buy German bonds and gain an extra 4 percent per annum providing the mark does not fall 4 percent or more.

How does she decide whether to purchase a German or U.S. bond? The uncovered interest parity theorem argues that arbitrage ensures that **real interest rates,** the nominal rate of interest rates minus the expected rate of inflation, are equal across all financial centers.[7] If the real rate is 4 percent in Frankfurt, it will be 4 percent in New York, London, Tokyo, Paris, and so on. And if the real rate of interest rises to 6 percent in Frankfurt, funds will flow from, say, New York to Frankfurt. The flow of funds will, in theory, drop the real rate to, say 5 percent in Frankfurt and raise it to 5 percent in New York and all other financial centers.

The flow of funds, however, will not necessarily equalize nominal interest rates in Frankfurt and New York since nominal rates depend on the real rate plus the expected rate of inflation. If the expected rates of inflation in Germany and the United States are different, national nominal interest rates will reflect this difference. Suppose that the real rate of interest is 4 percent. If the nominal rate of interest is 10 percent in Germany and 6 percent in the United States, it means that the expected rate of inflation is 6 percent in Germany and 2 percent in the United States.

According to the uncovered interest rate parity theorem, exchange rates move with inflation differentials. Because the expected rate of inflation in Germany is 4 percent higher than the expected rate in the United States, the market will anticipate that the mark will drop 4 percent per annum against the dollar. Under these conditions, an American will not gain by purchasing German bonds since the additional 4 percent in interest will be wiped out by the 4 percent depreciation of the mark.

These relationships can be expressed as a formula where i and i^* are the U.S. and German nominal interest rates, r, which equals r^*, is the real rate of interest, and p^e and p^{*e} are the expected rates of inflation in America and Germany. The expected

The **uncovered interest rate parity theorem** holds that future exchange rates can be predicted by current interest differentials between nations. If the current six-month interest rate in Frankfurt is 4 percent higher than the corresponding interest rate in New York, the theorem argues that the mark will depreciate at a 4 percent annual rate against the dollar over the next six months.

The **real rate of interest** equals the nominal rate of interest plus the expected rate of inflation.

---

[7]The assumption is that lenders want to receive a nominal rate of interest which equals a certain real return plus an additional return to cover any inflation. If a lender knows that the rate of inflation will be 6 percent, he will demand a return equal to 6 percent, the inflation premium, plus a certain real return. The only trouble is that the lender does not know today what the rate of inflation will be tomorrow. The lender will, therefore, have to estimate the future rate of inflation based on all information at his disposal.

percentage change of DM/$ exchange rate, $(e^e - e)/e$ (where e^e equals the expected exchange rate), equals $p^{*e} - p^e$. Thus, if $i^* - p^{*e} = r^*$, and $i - p^e = r \equiv r^*$, then:

$$i^* - p^{*e} = i - p^e$$
$$i^* - i = p^{*e} - p^e$$
$$i^* - i = (e^e - e)/e$$

The conclusion is that the expected percentage change in the exchange rate equals the difference between national nominal interest rates. Does the theorem hold all the time? In a perfect world—one of complete financial integration where all bonds have the same degree of risk, all individuals have the same inflationary expectations, and nominal interest rates accurately reflect inflationary expectations—the answer would be *yes*. But in the imperfect real world, the answer is *not all the time*.

In early 1991, German short-term interest rates were 2½ percentage points higher than U.S. short-term rates, and long-term German rates were roughly one-half percentage point higher than comparable U.S. rates. Assuming the real rate of interest was similar in Germany and the United States, and that nominal interest rate differentials reflected different rates of expected inflation, the figures suggested that the mark should have depreciated against the dollar in 1991 and 1992, although at a decreasing rate. However, a poll of 170 economists conducted by Consensus Economics estimated that inflation would be roughly 1 percent higher in the United States than in Germany in 1991 and ½ percent higher in the United States in 1992.[8] Based on expected rates of inflation, the mark should thus have appreciated against the dollar at a decreasing rate. Obviously, both conclusions could not be correct. It turns out that the dollar appreciated against the mark by 2.7 percent in 1991, but fell by 4.8 percent relative to the mark in 1992.

The crucial point is that real interest rates are not necessarily identical between nations. Suppose the nominal interest rises to 10 percent in the United States while all other values remain constant. Under these assumptions, the real rate of interest would rise to 8 percent in the United States and investors would have an incentive to purchase American securities. A German could purchase a U.S. bond yielding 10 percent and also obtain an additional 4 percent on the appreciation of the dollar. Since the expected rate of inflation in Germany is 6 percent, the German investor would receive a real return of 8 percent expressed in marks, which is far better than 4 percent.

While market forces should or may work to equalize real interest rates between financial centers, real interest rate differentials may last for a protracted period and generate capital flows which push an exchange rate up or down. Several economists claim that high American real rates of interest were the major reason why the dollar appreciated in the early 1980s. In turn, the high real rates were due to an increase in nominal rates without a corresponding increase in the expected and the actual rate of inflation in the United States. U.S. experience suggests that if inflation differentials between major countries are minor, any wide divergence in nominal interest rates between the countries can lead to large capital flows and marked swings in exchange rates.

In short, in its rudimentary form, the uncovered interest rate parity theory works only some of the time in predicting future exchange rates.

---

[8]*The Economist*, March 23, 1991, p. 111.

Stabilizing Exchange Rates

A **political exchange rate** is one that is selected by a government. Quite often when an exchange rate is selected for political reasons, the currency ends up being overvalued.

So far the discussion has concentrated on analyzing what causes a currency to rise and fall on the foreign exchanges. Not much has been said about the impact of exchange rate variation on the economy—that is, whether it is beneficial or whether it hampers economic activity and, accordingly, should be reduced. The question at hand is not whether an exchange rate should be allowed to fluctuate, but rather whether its *degree* of variation should be reduced. (There are, of course, some countries or groups of countries that believe that exchange rates should be fixed and permitted to fluctuate only 2 percent, for example, above and below the fixed rate. See the discussion of the European Union's exchange rate mechanism in Chapter 16.)

Economists have agreed to disagree on this question. Some insist that the market should be the sole arbiter of exchange rates because inevitably governments will seek to maintain a **political exchange rate** instead of an "economic" one. Given the opportunity to set exchange rates, many governments would opt for an *overvalued* rather than an *equilibrium* exchange rate. An overvalued exchange rate helps hold down the price of imports and minimizes any increase in the cost of living. Even though such a policy hampers the expansion and development of export industries and a country's long-run economic potential, most governments live in a short time frame in which political popularity rather than long-run economic potential is the major criterion of success.

Even if a well-meaning government simply wants to stabilize an exchange rate at its economic equilibrium, it faces a daunting task. The funds that any government has at its disposal to carry out such exchange rate stabilization are puny compared to the resources of the private sector. If the private sector believes that a currency is overvalued and sells it off, governments do not have the resources available to match the private sector dollar for dollar. The argument against stabilization boils down to three points: (1) The market, not the government, is the best judge of the proper level of an exchange rate; (2) governments cannot be trusted; and (3) governments do not have the resources necessary to carry out a stabilization policy.

Other economists insist that not only should exchange rates be stabilized but that governments have the obligation and capacity to do it. Markets can make mistakes. Spooked by rumors and carried on by bandwagon effects, exchange rates can move away from an equilibrium dictated by economic fundamentals. Thus, to overcome such market failures, governments should attempt to stabilize exchange rates.

To stabilize an exchange rate, a government has two policy options: it can either raise or lower domestic interest rates or it can intervene in the foreign exchange market by buying or selling foreign currencies. There is a third option. A government can also introduce exchange controls that arbitrarily limit the ability of citizens to buy and sell foreign currencies. That option, rarely if ever attempted in the developed world, is not considered here

Interest Rates and Exchange Rate Stabilization

Let's look at stabilization policy through a hypothetical example. Suppose the British pound comes under selling pressure and its price begins to slip on international currency markets. Assume that to halt the slide, the Bank of England raises British interest rates. A higher interest rate should depress British aggregate demand and reduce Britain's demand for imports. As a result, the supply curve of pounds will shift to the left in the foreign exchange market and, providing everything else remains constant, raise the price of the pound. In addition, a higher British interest rate, providing everything else remains constant, could induce foreigners to invest their funds in London. Put differently, the high interest policy would increase the demand for pounds and raise its price on the foreign exchanges. Obviously if other things do not remain equal, if money managers believe that the pound is weak, they may view the increase in the British interest rate as a confirmation of their suspicions and sell pounds.

Notwithstanding that possibility, there is a downside to raising interest rates in order to sustain an exchange rate. Depressing British demand will lead to unemployment so that the cost of stabilizing the pound will be paid for by unemployed workers. In addition, higher interest rates may depress aggregate demand by curtailing investment more than consumption. A reduction in the level of investment will reduce the rate of productivity growth and render Britain less competitive in the future. These are some of the trade-offs in using interest rates to stabilize an exchange rate.

Central Bank Intervention in the Foreign Exchange Market

A **central bank intervenes** in the foreign exchange market by buying and selling foreign currencies in order to preserve or smooth out fluctuations around a target exchange rate.

International reserves consist of foreign exchange holdings at the central bank. Holdings of international reserves can be supplemented by lines of credit provided by other central banks or international organizations such as the International Monetary Fund.

Many economists feel that a nation's first line of defense should be **central bank intervention** in the foreign exchange market. Most central banks hold **international reserves** or deposits of foreign currencies—primarily marks, dollars, and yen—and can use such funds to stabilize the price of their currency. If the pound comes under pressure, for example, the Bank of England can sell its foreign exchange reserves, say marks, and use the proceeds of the sale to purchase pounds. If all goes well, the increased demand for pounds coupled with the increase in the supply of marks will raise the value of the pound relative to the mark.

Exchange rate intervention and stabilization can be understood better with the help of Figure 3.4. Figure 3.4a shows the supply and demand for pounds in terms of marks, and Figure 3.4b presents the mark market. As the pound comes under selling pressure, the supply curve of pounds in Figure 3.4a shifts to the right from S_0 to S_1 and the demand for marks shifts from D_0 to D_1 in Figure 3.4b. As a result, the pound falls relative to the mark. To preserve the initial exchange rate, the Bank of England can sell some of its international reserves, assumed to be marks, on the mark market. The sales will shift the supply curve of marks from S_0 to S_1 in Figure 3.4b. In turn, the Bank of England will use the proceeds of the sales to purchase sterling, which will shift the demand for pounds from D_0 to D_1 in Figure 3.4a. If all goes as planned, the price of the pound moves back to its initial level and the policy is a success.

Any central bank's ability to intervene in the foreign exchange market is circumscribed by its holdings of international reserves. The Bank of England, for example, can supplement its reserves by borrowing marks from the Bundesbank today and agreeing to repay the Bundesbank at a later date, a so-called **swap agreement,** or Britain can draw on its line of credit or **drawing rights** at the International Monetary Fund. But in the final analysis, Britain's level of international reserves, owned plus borrowed, is limited.

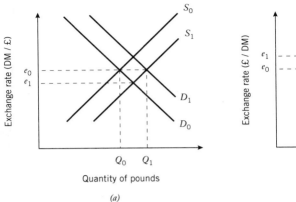
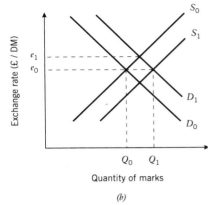

(a)

(b)

FIGURE 3.4 Intervention in the foreign exchange market.

Assume that initially the supply and demand for pounds and marks are given by the supply and demand curves S_0 and D_0 in panels (a) and (b). The exchange rate equals e_0. Suppose British citizens demand more marks and supply more pounds in order to purchase them. The demand curve for marks shifts from D_0 to D_1 in panel (b) and the supply curve of pounds shifts from S_0 to S_1 in panel (a). Because of these shifts, the price of the mark rises from e_0 to e_1 in the mark market and the price of the pound falls from e_0 to e_1 in the pound market. If the Bank of England wants to maintain the initial exchange rate, it must sell some of its international reserves, assumed to be marks, on the mark market and use the proceeds of the sale to purchase pounds in the sterling market. Together, the sale of marks and the purchase of pounds will push the supply curve of marks from S_0 to S_1 and the demand curve for pounds from D_0 to D_1. In the end, the exchange rate will be established where the supply curves, S_1 in both panels, intersect the demand curves, D_1 in both panels. Due to the Bank of England's intervention the original price of the pound (and the mark), e_0, is restored.

A **swap agreement,** as defined here, is an agreement whereby, for example, the Bundesbank loans the Bank of England some Deutschemarks for a specified period of time.

IMF drawing rights are a member nation's line of credit at the International Monetary Fund.

In addition, a central bank can lose on a swap. Suppose the Bank of England borrows DM5 billion, or roughly £2.13 billion, from the Bundesbank when the exchange rate stands at DM2.35/£. Now assume that the Bank of England sells the borrowed marks on the foreign exchange market in an attempt to prop up the pound, but that the pound falls to DM2.2/£ despite the Bank's efforts. In order to repay Bundesbank, as it must under the swap agreement, the Bank of England will have to spend £2.27 billion to purchase DM5 billion on the foreign exchanges. The failed operation will cost the Bank of England £140 million or some 6.6 percent on a one-year swap and nearly 30 percent on a three-month swap measured at an annual rate.

Central Bank Cooperation and Exchange Rate Stabilization

Once the Bank of England has employed all its international reserves, owned and borrowed, it will be powerless to stop the slide in the pound short of raising interest rates, introducing exchange controls, and the like. At this stage, only one party can maintain the value of the pound: the Bundesbank. The Bundesbank cannot create pounds, but it can create marks. If it turns on the spigot and creates an unlimited supply of marks and buys an unlimited amount of pounds, a stable DM/£ exchange rate will be maintained.

It is unlikely that any country would be willing to expand its money supply without limit in order to help another country stabilize the international value of its currency. International monetary cooperation may be essential if exchange rates are to be stabilized, but it is asking much of a strong currency country's central bank to, in effect, purchase unlimited supplies of a presently weak currency and risk being caught holding the bag if the weak currency depreciates still further. One can talk of the need and desire for international monetary cooperation, but the gritty question of how much cooperation one can expect cannot be pinned down.

The Target Exchange Rate

Under a system of modified floating exchange rates, nations often attempt to maintain a **target exchange rate.** Countries often disagree as to what the rate should be.

Even if international monetary cooperation is forthcoming, there is the additional question of the level or **target** at which the exchange rate should be stabilized. On this score, there is bound to be disagreement. In the winter of 1994–95, for example, the Mexican peso fell from approximately 3 pesos per dollar to 6 to 7 pesos per dollar. Both the United States and Mexico agreed that the peso should be stabilized, but the question was at what level. Mexico proposed that a 6-peso-per-dollar rate would be best, while the United States responded that a 5-peso-per-dollar rate would be preferable. The first rate would help Mexican exporters while the second rate would be better for U.S. exporters.

Disagreement over the level of exchange rates is not limited to the two countries directly concerned. U.S. firms were happy while their counterparts in Japan were decidedly unhappy when the yen rose relative to the dollar, while South Koreans were both happy and sad as the won/$ exchange rate remained relatively constant while the ¥/$ rate fell. Yen appreciation gave the South Korean car, semiconductor, and machinery sectors a competitive advantage vis-a-vis the Japanese. The downside was that yen appreciation raised the cost of essential Japanese-made capital equipment and spare parts.

Advocating exchange rate stabilization is not an argument for supporting a currency come hell or high water. If a currency is under pressure and overvalued, it should not be supported. However, it does not make much sense to allow exchange rates to gyrate wildly about. The erratic swings of the dollar during the 1980s did not increase the wealth of nations worldwide. Excessive dollar appreciation from the early-to-mid-1980s reduced U.S. competitiveness which, in turn, helped foster domestic protectionism in the United States, something that hurt all countries.

Summary

This chapter covered a lot of ground and did not come to a firm answer to the question: What determines the level of an exchange rate at a particular period? One answer, held by a large number of economists, contends that exchange rates are determined by fundamentals such as inflation and economic growth over the long run, but that in the short run, exchange rates bounce around their trend values due to financial forces and expectations.

But a word of caution: In the autumn of 1993, many international money managers were bullish on the dollar because they felt the U.S. economy would enjoy the most rapid rate of economic growth among the major OECD economies. Income expansion, of course, can lead to a surge of imports and currency depreciation. Dollar bulls, however, expected that rapid growth would lead to higher interest rates in America and generate a heavy capital flow to the United States. That, in turn, would cause the dollar to appreciate. In the end, it so happens that the dollar bulls were wrong and they were dispatched.

Key Concepts and Terms

central bank swaps

commercial versus financial rand

covered interest arbitrage

covered versus open or uncovered position in the market

dual exchange rate systems

exchange rate

exchange rate intervention

exchange rate stabilization

foreign exchange market

forward discount or premium

forward exchange rate

hedging

income effects on exchange rates

inflationary effect on exchange rates

interest arbitrage

interest rate effect on exchange rates

interest rate expectations

international purchasing power of a portfolio

international reserves

options

overvalued exchange rates

puts and calls

real and nominal interest rates

speculative bubble

spot exchange rate

target exchange rate

Review Questions

1. Draw the supply and demand curves for dollars as determined by the exchange rate, or the number of marks per dollar. Explain what will most likely happen in this market, which curve shifts in which direction, and why, if each of the following events takes place:

   (a) If tax reductions lead to an increase in U.S. consumption.

   (b) If U.S. beer drinkers start to purchase German rather than domestic beer.

   (c) If the U.S. inflation rate rises to 10 percent per annum.

   (d) If U.S. interest rates increase and other things remain equal.

2. Suppose there is a sudden rush of foreign capital into a developing country. What would happen to the nation's exchange rate? What might happen to its exports and imports? Why might such a nation want to introduce a dual exchange rate?

3. If the nation in question 2 does introduce a dual exchange rate system, which exchange rate do you believe will have the higher value expressed in terms of a foreign currency? What will this mean for the country's exports of goods and services?

4. What is meant by the forward exchange rate? If the current spot exchange rate is $2/£ and the 12-month forward rate is $2.20/£, is the dollar at a forward premium or discount and by how much?

5. Explain how the forward exchange market can be used to hedge or to speculate.

6. What is the difference between the forward exchange market and the foreign currency options market?

7. What is meant by the term *covered interest arbitrage?* Suppose the current spot rate is $2/£ and the 12-month forward rate is $2.10/£. If the U.S. interest rate is 8 percent, what interest must prevail in London to prevent funds from flowing either to London or New York?

8. Given your answer to question 7, imagine the New York interest rate climbs to 12 percent. What will happen initially? Which way will funds flow? Why will the flow of funds between financial centers be eliminated?

9. Suppose the pound comes under selling pressure and its value starts to decline on the foreign exchanges. If the British government wants to maintain the external value of the pound, what steps can it take?

Exchange Market Activity in April 1995 (Geneva: Bank for International Settlements, 1996). Pam Woodall wrote a highly informative and readable survey of international financial markets. See Pam Woodall, "A Survey of the World Economy," *The Economist* (October 7, 1995).

There are many publications on the mechanics of the foreign exchange market. Michael Melvin, *International Money and Finance*, 4th edition (New York: HarperCollins, 1995). Chapters 4 and 5 of Melvin's book extend the discussion of some of the topics in this text. An outstanding article on the foreign exchange market is K. Alec Chrystal, "A Guide to the Foreign Exchange Market," Federal Reserve Bank of St. Louis, *Review* 66 (March 1984): pp. 5–18. Gregory P. Hooper wrote a brief, readable essay on currency options. See Gregory P. Hooper, "A Primer on Currency Derivatives," Federal Reserve Bank of Philadelphia, *Business Review* (May–June 1995): pp. 3–14.

Stephan Schulmeister gives another explanation of the path of the dollar in recent years in his article, "Currency Speculation and Dollar Fluctuations," Banca Nazionale del Lavoro, *Quarterly Review* (December 1988): pp. 343–365. Charles Engel and Craig S. Hakkio, "Exchange Rate Regimes and Volatility," Federal Reserve Bank of Kansas City, *Economic Review* 78 (Third Quarter 1993): pp. 43–58, contains examples of recent exchange volatility and an excellent, concise discussion of the impact of economic fundamentals and expectations on exchange rate determination.

Each issue of *The Quarterly Report of the Federal Reserve Bank of New York* contains an article entitled "Treasury and Federal Reserve Foreign Exchange Operations." These articles analyze current developments in the foreign exchange markets.

References and Suggested Readings

The figures on the level of foreign exchange transactions and the currencies involved are reported in the Bank for International Settlements, *Central Bank Survey of Foreign*

Chapter 4

The Balance of Payments

With few exceptions, all international trade and capital transactions pass through the foreign exchange market and are recorded in the balance payments accounts. But the public has remarkably different attitudes toward the foreign exchanges on the one hand and the balance of payments on the other. Given a foreign exchange crisis, people sit glued to their television sets as commentators discuss, analyze, and proclaim the *whys* and *wherefores* of the crisis and its implications for the present and for the future. By comparison, if people are told that the U.S. merchandise account improved by $1 billion in the second quarter compared with the first quarter of the year, or by $2 billion over the year, they can hardly stifle a yawn. In short, despite their seemingly equal importance, the public's interest drops like a stone when the discussion turns from the foreign exchanges to the balance of payments.

This lack of interest in balance of payments statistics is unfortunate, since these numbers, like a school report card, provide a record of how a country's economic relations with the rest of the world are moving and can be used to foresee a looming foreign exchange crisis. In retrospect, *everyone* is aware that the Mexican peso crisis of 1994–1995 was the result of Mexico's trade imbalance. But if economic policy movers and shakers had paid more attention in 1992–1993 to Mexico's deteriorating balance of trade position, the peso crisis might have been avoided.

The usefulness of information provided by balance of payments statistics is not limited to crisis management. Observed over time, they show emerging trends in international trade and investment patterns, or who trades what with whom and who is investing where and why. Moreover, a nation's external accounts often reflect domestic economic imbalances, a point emphasized at the end of the chapter when the twin deficit hypothesis is discussed. When one looks beyond the figures, beyond the pluses and minuses to the overall patterns and historic trends, the balance of payments statistics can be very enlightening indeed.

The Path Ahead

This chapter concentrates on four topics:

- It investigates the balance of payments, which provides a record of a country's international transactions with the rest of the world over a given period, normally a year.

- It defines and describes a nation's net international investment position, that is, whether the nation is a debtor or creditor nation.

- It describes the present trading patterns of the United States, which foreign nations are the largest buyers of U.S. goods and services, and from whom America purchases its imports.

- It analyzes the relationship between a nation's external accounts and its economy.

The Balance of Payments Balances or Credits Equal Debits

Every nation's balance of payments should sum up to zero. This is because balance of payments accounting is based on double-entry bookkeeping—a technique that some people have called the greatest invention since the wheel. It means that a credit item on the balance of payments should be offset by a corresponding debit item. When an American travels to London, she is purchasing or importing a British service. That means that the British are exporting a service and so they earn dollars. Since one can assume they will not eat them, the British will have to spend the dollars on something.

There are several possibilities. The British could buy an American-made personal computer (PC), take a vacation in Florida, buy a building in Chicago, purchase some IBM stock, or build up a dollar deposit at Citibank. What do all these transactions have in common? In each case, Americans receive the dollars. Therefore, all of the transactions would be recorded as a credit item or an export on the U.S. balance of payments and as a debit item or an import on the British balance of payments. If the value of the British purchases equals the value of the American's trip to London, the balance of payments of both nations will balance, or credits minus debits will equal zero for both countries.

British citizens might decide they do not want an American-made PC, IBM stock and so on. In this case, they would sell the dollars to the Bank of England in exchange for pounds. The Bank of England could then use the dollars it purchased to bolster Britain's international reserves. What does this mean for the U.S. balance of payments? The United States would import a service from Britain, the trip to London, and export international reserves to Great Britain. The British balance of payments would show the export of a service and the import of international reserves.

There is, however, a distinct difference between America paying for its imports by exporting PCs, vacations, stocks, and so on, and paying for its imports by exporting international reserves. In the first case, the U.S. balance of payments is in good shape. It imports a service and pays for it by exporting goods or services, such as the trip the British took to Florida, or by exporting financial assets. In the second case, America imports, but the British are unwilling to purchase any American goods, services, or financial assets. The United States must rely on the desire of the British government to increase its holdings of international reserves in order to balance its external accounts.

Imagine that the silent old lady of Threadneedle Street, as the Bank of England is known, does not want to build up its international reserves. What happens then? Assuming that the Fed, acting as an agent for the U.S. government, has a reserve of pounds on hand, the British exporter will sell the dollars he or she earned to the Fed in exchange for pounds. In other words, the United States will pay for its imports, the trip to London, by exporting some of its international reserves—surely not a good sign for the United States or for the international value of the dollar.

Because this discussion covered the balance of payments at the speed of light, it should be viewed as a prologue to what follows. But it will be easier to work through balance of payments accounting if one always remembers that credits must equal debits so that the balance of payments always balances. Nevertheless, it is far better for a country to attain this balance by exporting goods, services, and financial assets than by exporting international reserves.

The Current Account

A nation's **balance of payments** consists of two accounts: the current account and the capital account. By definition, the sum of the two accounts must equal zero.

The **current account** includes four parts: the merchandise account, the service account, the income account, and unilateral transfers.

The **capital or financial account** shows the flows of capital, the purchase and sale of capital assets, between nations.

The **merchandise account** adds up exports and imports of goods. Often it is called the trade balance, but not here.

The first step in getting acquainted with the structure of the **balance of payments** is to slog through the components of the balance of payments accounts. Table 4.1 presents the U.S. external accounts for 1991–1994. Two subtotals in the accounts receive the most attention: the **current account,** which essentially records exchanges in goods and services, and the **capital or financial account,** which chronicles capital flows between nations.

The current account, the immediate focus of our attention, is split into four parts, two of which are major: the **merchandise account** and the **service account.** In the past, primary attention was focused on the merchandise or goods account while the service account was treated as a poor relative. That disparity is no longer the case due to the rapid growth and increasing importance of trade in services. (In early 1994, the U.S. Department of Commerce began to report the merchandise balance and the service balance on a monthly basis. Previously, the merchandise balance was reported monthly while the service balance was reported quarterly. The change reflects the official recognition of the importance of the service balance.)

As shown in Table 4.1, U.S. exports of services equaled 40 percent of its merchandise exports between 1991 and 1994, hardly an insignificant amount, and a marked increase compared with an 18 percent ratio in 1980. Most everyone understands what is involved in the export or import of a good. When an American anglophile strolls down the street in his Burberry raincoat with a copy of the *Financial Times* tucked under his arm, people are aware that the chap has imported British goods and that the British have received dollars in payment. If this same individual buys a ticket and boards a British Airways jet and flies to London, once again he has imported a British product since the British will receive the dollars. But in this case, the American has purchased British services, not goods.

TABLE 4.1 United States Balance of Payments: 1991—94 (billions of dollars)

	1991	1992	1993	1994
A. Current Account	−8	−62	−100	−151
Merchandise exports	417	440	459	505
Merchandise imports	−491	−536	−590	−669
Service exports	164	178	186	197
Service imports	−118	−121	−128	−137
Trade Balance	−28	−39	−73	−104
Income (net)	14	9	7	−10
Unilateral transfers (net)	7	−33	−34	−35
B. Capital or Financial Account (net)	14	39	−3	121
Direct investment (net)	−9	−25	−32	0
Portfolio investment (net)	7	16	−39	42
Other investment	16	49	67	78
C. Net Errors and Omissions	−29	−26	36	−14
Official Reserve Balance	−22	−49	−67	−45
D. Reserves	22	49	67	45
Official reserves	6	4	−1	5
Foreign official reserves	16	45	68	40
Basic Balance (modified)	−17	−89	−132	−151
Basic Balance	10	−82	−153	na

Source: The figures, which are rounded and will not sum up to required values, were computed from International Monetary Fund, *Balance of Payments Statistics Yearbook,* 1995, p. 822.

The **service account** shows a nation's exports and imports of services, for example, tourism.

The **trade balance** or the **balance of trade** equals the sum of the merchandise account and the service account.

The **income account,** normally shown on a net basis, consists of interest payments and the repatriation of profits on overseas investments. Such payments move both toward the domestic country and to the rest of the world.

The growing importance of the service account can be gleaned from the external accounts of other countries. In 1991 and 1992, Spain ran merchandise deficits of $31 billion each year. However, Spain's net tourism account, a service item, rang up surpluses of $14.5 and $16 billion in these years, offsetting Spain's negative merchandise balances by roughly 50 percent. Tourism is important for Spain, but it is also important for the United States. (As indicated in Table 4.4, travel and related passenger fares are the most important service export and service import of the United States.)

Officially, the sum of exports of goods and services minus the sum of imports of goods and services equals the balance on goods and services. However, in what follows, this balance is called the **trade balance** or the **balance of trade.**

Notice that income payments and unilateral or current transfers are listed after the merchandise and service figures in the current account. The **income account** measures the earnings of Americans on overseas investments and payments made to foreigners on investments they hold in the United States. For example, if an American holds shares in Royal Dutch Shell and a long-term British bond, she will receive dividends and interest payments which are recorded as a positive item on the U.S. balance of payments. In addition, an American firm that operates overseas may repatriate or send some of its profits earned overseas back to the United States, again a positive item on the U.S. balance of payments. Obviously, foreign nationals receive interest payments and dividends on shares of American firms they own, and foreign firms operating in the United States ship some of their profits home. Such payments to foreigners are debit items on the U.S. balance of payments since foreigners get the dollars. The income account is recorded on a net basis—credits minus debits. This means that the total actual payments are substantially larger than indicated in Table 4.1. In 1994, the United States earned $138 billion on this account and paid out $148 billion in interest and repatriated profits for a net debit of $10 billion.

Unilateral transfers, often called net transfers, are payments made by private citizens and governments of one country to another. If the United States sends so many dollars to Somalia to help fight hunger in that country, it is listed as an official unilateral transfer on the U.S. balance of payments.

Unilateral transfers, the final item on the current account, are comprised of both private and official transfers. Recall our example of the American who visited Britain. It could be that one of the British citizens, say an innkeeper, who provided a portion of Britain's exports and received a portion of the dollars has a relative in the United States. If he sends her $1,000 as a graduation present, it would be recorded as a unilateral or net transfer. Private transfers are important for countries such as Egypt, Mexico, and Turkey, where domestic nationals work overseas and ship some of their earnings back home.

Official transfers reflect interest payments on official debt and contributions to or receipts from international organizations. Normally, this item is not too important for the U.S. external accounts. However, between 1990 and 1991, the net change in official unilateral transfers had a hefty impact on the U.S. balance of payments position. In 1990, official unilateral transfers were −$21 billion. In 1991, they were +$21 billion—a swing of $42 billion. The swing coincided with the financing of the Persian Gulf war when foreign countries paid substantial sums to the United States to cover the cost of the war. With the end of the war and special financing, official unilateral transfers returned to a $19 billion deficit in 1992. As can be seen in Table 4.1, the total transfer account of the United States moved from a $7 billion surplus in 1991 to a $33 billion deficit in 1992—a swing of $40 billion.

The current account can be expressed as an equation. The current account, *CA*, equals the trade balance, *X−M*, plus the income account, *iK*, and net transfers (unilateral transfers), *NT*, or:

$$CA = X - M + iK + NT$$

As indicated, the net income and net transfer accounts can be either positive or negative. Traditionally, America's net income account has been positive and its net transfer account negative.[1]

The Capital Account

What is normally called a **capital export** is actually a debit item on the balance of payments; when you buy a freshly minted German bond, the Germans get the dollars.

Besides the merchandise and services accounts, capital flows are the other major item in the balance of payments. Capital flows or the capital account are usually computed as a net figure even though this method conceals their magnitude. One technical note must be stressed. When a U.S. firm builds a plant overseas or an American "buys" a Swiss bank deposit, it may be called a **capital export,** but it counts as a debit item in

---

[1] In the income account, iK, K equals the net value of overseas investments and i measures the rate of return on such investment. The account can also be written $i^*_{-1}K_{-1} - i_{-1}K^*_{-1}$. In this case, K^* equals the stock of foreign investment in the home country and i^* equals the rate of return in the foreign country. It is assumed that the income earned by a nation depends on the stock of financial assets and physical investment in existence at the end of the previous year and the interest rate and profit rate prevailing at that time. In other words, the flow of income in 1994, for example, is governed by the stock of domestic-owned overseas assets in 1993 and the rate of interest and profits they generated in 1993. Both interest earnings and profits are captured by i and i^*. (In all cases, * indicates foreign.)

the balance of payments. Recall that whether an item is a credit or a debit depends on who gets the dollars. If an American takes a trip to London and flies via British Airways, it is a U.S. import because the British get the dollars.[2] Likewise, if an American purchases a bond issued by a Japanese firm, the Japanese firm receives the dollars, and the American's "capital export" is listed as a debit item or import on the U.S. balance of payments.

Foreign Direct Investment

Foreign direct investment consists of building a plant overseas or acquiring what is deemed to be a "controlling" or important interest in an established overseas firm.

Portfolio investment. The purchase of stocks of a foreign firm.

Capital flows used to be divided into long- and short-term capital movements. Long-term capital flows were defined as **foreign direct investment (FDI),** such as occurs when an American firm constructs or purchases a plant overseas, plus **portfolio investment** and long-term loans. (While it is easy to obtain figures on direct investment and portfolio investment, obtaining figures on long-term versus short-term loans is quite difficult at the present time.)

The difference between direct and portfolio investment is somewhat arbitrary. If you purchase some foreign stocks, whether your purchase is classified as direct or portfolio investment depends on how much of the total outstanding stock you buy. If you buy 10 percent or more, it is considered a direct investment. The assumption is that you will gain a controlling interest in the firm. If you acquire less than 10 percent of the outstanding stock, the capital export is tallied as portfolio investment. Thus, if an American purchases $1 million worth of a foreign stock, it may be listed as a portfolio investment, whereas if the same individual buys a $50,000 chalet in the Algarve in southern Portugal, it is listed as a direct investment.

Historically, foreign direct investment has been politically unpopular in most countries. A major complaint in most countries is that FDI involves foreigners, who, according to local opinion, cannot be trusted. It is feared that foreigners will take over vital sectors of the economy and run them for their own personal benefit, not for the welfare of the host country. Traditionally, this nationalistic criticism was voiced within third world countries, although lately, some American politicians and interest groups have become critical of foreign investment in the United States. Of course, there is no doubt that some foreign investors do behave badly, running their affairs mindless of the needs of the host country. But today the overwhelming majority of foreign direct investment is aimed at establishing facilities within a country in order to serve that country's domestic market. The reason to invest in the European Union is to sell to Europeans, in America to sell to Americans, or in China to sell to the Chinese. Moreover, today multinational companies come in many stripes and under different flags, and actively compete with each other to get a toehold in the host country. In a

---

[2]If the same American flew to London by Delta Airlines and stayed at the Hilton in London it would be a different story. But not as different as one might at first think. Some of the flight to London would be an import since Delta must pay various fees to land at Heathrow and would also purchase various British goods and services while the plane was in London. The payment to Hilton would definitely be an American import. The London Hilton would get the dollars and hire British people to work the hotel and purchase goods and services from British suppliers. If the Hilton makes a profit and sends it back to the United States, the profits would count as a credit for the United States on income account of the current account.

BOX 4.1 U.S. Foreign Direct Investment and Foreign Direct Investment in the United States

Which countries have the largest direct investments in the United States and where, in turn, do Americans tend to invest? Table 4.2 provides the answers. For the most part, U.S. firms invest in developed countries. Nearly 50 percent of U.S. overseas direct investment is in Europe where the United Kingdom is the prime host country. European nations have the largest investment position in the United States. In dollar terms, the United Kingdom has more direct investment in the United States than any other country, but Japan is a close second. Nearly half of all U.S. FDI is in manufacturing, and 31 percent is in banking, finance, insurance and real estate. In fact, almost all American direct investments in Bermuda, Panama, and Switzerland fall into this latter category.

Approximately 60 percent of foreign direct investment in the United States is in manufacturing and roughly 25 percent is in financial services and real estate. British investment in the United States is spread among a host of industries, but manufacturing, 42 percent; insurance, 9.8 percent; and petroleum, 9.6 percent, are the three most important. Japanese investment is primarily in the areas of trade, 33 percent; manufacturing, 20 percent; and real estate, 12.5 percent.

TABLE 4.2 U.S. Direct Investment Abroad and Foreign Direct Investment in the United States: 1994 (major countries, historical costs in billions of dollars)

U.S. Direct Investment		Foreign Direct Investment in the United States	
Total	$612.1	Total	$504.4
Canada	72.8	Canada	42.2
Europe	300.2	Europe	312.9
United Kingdom	102.2	United Kingdom	113.5
Germany	39.9	Netherlands	70.6
Switzerland	34.5	Germany	39.6
France	27.9	France	33.5
Netherlands	24.1	Switzerland	25.3
Latin America	115.0	Japan	103.1
Bermuda	29.3		
Brazil	19.0		
Mexico	16.4		
Panama	13.8		
Japan	37.0		
Australia	20.5		
Hong Kong	12.0		
Singapore	11.0		

Because historical costs are different than current costs, the values of total foreign direct investment given in Table 4.7 do not equal the values given in this table.

Source: Department of Commerce, *Survey of Current Business* (June 1995); pp. 63, 67.

competitive world, it is difficult for one company to behave badly if several others are lined up, so to speak, to get their foot in the door.

Perhaps the best proof of this proposition is the changing attitude toward FDI prevalent in most LDCs. Compared with, say, the 1950s and 1960s, when the phrase "Yanqui Go Home" was seen on posters throughout much of Latin America, attitudes have swung 180 degrees. Today, few LDCs complain that they are being invaded by avaricious foreigners. Rather, their lament is that multinationals appear strikingly uninterested in their economies.

This is not to say that all the sources of political opposition to foreign direct investment have vanished. But it is nonetheless incongruous that at the same time certain national politicians are inveighing against foreign direct investment in the United

---

The crawling peg is an officially fixed exchange rate that depreciates at some predetermined rate.

BOX 4.2 The Fall of the Peso

The fall of the peso in 1994–1995 illustrates the dangers of financing a trade imbalance through portfolio investment and short-term capital.

Prior to the peso crisis, Mexico had been considered an economic success, a role model for the third world. Mexico had battled back from the debt crisis of the 1980s, and together with Canada and the United States had signed a free trade agreement, the North American Free Trade Agreement, or NAFTA. That act gave Mexico access to one of the largest markets in the world. In terms of macroeconomic policy, moreover, the Mexican government had been accorded high marks. Mexico's budget deficit was 1 percent of GDP and the internal public debt/GDP ratio, at 40 percent, was lower than the U.S. debt/GDP ratio and lower than the average country debt/GDP ratio in the European Union. (See Table 16.2.) The Mexican rate of inflation was only 4 to 5 percent higher than the rate of inflation in the United States, and Mexican short-term interest rates were roughly 10 percent higher than comparable U.S. interest rates. Moreover, Mexico had adopted a **crawling peg** exchange rate which permitted the peso to depreciate 4 percent per year against the dollar. And at the beginning of 1994, Mexico's international reserves stood at roughly $30 billion.

In short, there was little reason to suspect that the Mexican peso would collapse. An annual rate of peso depreciation of 4 percent would just about cover the inflation differential between Mexico and the United States. And the 10 percent interest differential in favor of Mexico meant that even if the peso depreciated by 4 or 5 percent per year, an investor would get a better return in Mexico than in the United States. In addition, it was felt that Mexico had ample international reserves to overcome any hiccup in the peso/dollar market.

But Mexico had a problem. It was running a current account of deficit and the imbalance was becoming larger. In 1990, the deficit was $7.4 billion. By 1993, the deficit had grown to $23 billion and reached roughly $14 billion in just the first half of 1994. These current account deficits had been financed by a large capital inflow. But an estimated 80 percent of the capital inflow consisted of portfolio investment and short-term capital.

Mexico faced a dilemma. Its rising current account deficit called for a depreciation of the peso. Yet even the slightest hint of peso depreciation would halt the capital inflow and induce a flight of short-term capital out of the country. If Mexico was unable to finance its trade deficit, it would have to depress domestic income in order to reduce its imports. But depressing income would lead to unemployment. Mexico realized its situation and attempted to overcome downward pressure on the peso through central bank intervention hoping that it was indeed dealing with a mere hiccup. But it was far more than a hiccup and Mexico's reserve position, which had appeared so robust in 1993, quickly deteriorated. Reserves dropped from roughly $30 billion at the beginning of 1994 to an estimated $7 billion by December 1994. And the peso crisis hit the headlines.

Sources: Robert L. Bartley, "The Challenge of Capital Inflows," *Wall Street Journal* (May 17, 1995): p. A20; "The Lessons from Mexico," *The Economist* (March 18, 1995): pp. 73–75.

States, individual state governments try their hardest to woo foreign firms to build plants in their states by offering tax breaks and other inducements.

Patriotic bombast against foreign direct investment misses an important point: FDI investment yields benefits. FDI is a prime conduit for transferring modern technology between countries. When a foreign firm establishes operations in the host country, it will in all likelihood utilize the productive and managerial techniques it employs at home. It will not take host country firms long to emulate these techniques—the example of American car manufacturers copying Japanese management strategies comes immediately to mind. While it can be argued that the Americans would have eventually copied the Japanese in any event, their ability to initiate lean production was greatly speeded up by the relocation of Japanese companies and managers to the United States.

Another reason for viewing FDI more favorably has to do with its positive impact on the host countries' balance of payments. If the host country's economy runs into a recession, foreign direct investors will most likely suffer along with the host country. Their profits will be sliced and they will have little to send home, or repatriate. Consider the alternatives. If a host country takes out foreign loans, it will have to service them, pay interest, and repay the principal, regardless of the state of its economy. And if the host country borrows short-term, it is indeed courting danger since short-term foreign investors can pull their funds out of the country at a moment's notice. That does not mean that a nation should never borrow long-term or rely exclusively upon FDI as the sole source of external finance. It implies that there may be an optimum mix of external financing, which may include FDI and portfolio investment as well as long-term loans.

Short-Term Capital and the Balance of Payments

Short-term capital flows are also part of the balance of payments story. These occur when a citizen of one country builds up a bank account in a foreign currency, purchases short-term foreign financial assets, or acquires a foreign government bond of, surprisingly, any maturity.

As we shall see, short-term capital flows are the subject of a debate when it comes to calculating a country's balance of payment "surplus" or "deficit." Some people believe that short-term capital flows are simply flows of "hot money" that fly between financial centers based on interest differentials and rumors of impending exchange rate fluctuations. Because of their transitory and volatile nature, some economists believe that short-term capital movements should be overlooked in computing a nation's external "surplus" or "deficit."

Summing Up: The Basic Balance of Payments

The fluidity of short-term capital flows is one reason why many economists believe that the **basic balance of payments** is the best measure of a country's external accounts. The basic balance is computed by summing up the current and long-term

The **basic balance of payments** equals the current account plus the long-term capital account. If the sum of these two accounts is positive, the basic balance is in a surplus.

capital accounts period. (Given the changes in the IMF's accounting procedures, which fails to distinguish between long-term and short-term capital flows, it is no longer possible to compute the basic balance of payments as originally formulated.) If the current account plus the long-term capital account are in surplus, implying that short-term capital movements are in deficit, the balance of payments is in surplus. As pointed out, the total balance of payments is always balanced since, given double-entry bookkeeping, credits always equal debits. Thus, if an individual talks of an external deficit, he is arbitrarily saying that some items are what is called *above the line* (read *important*), and that the sum of these items, positive or negative, equals the balance of payments surplus or deficit.

Not everyone agrees with this method of toting up a country's external position. Many economists believe that long-term capital flows, especially portfolio investment, can be just as volatile as short-term capital movements. Investors, after all, do move into and out of stocks quickly. Critics conclude that either the basic balance concept should be scrapped or it should be amended to include only the current account and foreign direct investment. An attempt to follow such suggestions has been made in Table 4.1 where the **modified basic balance of payments**, which includes the current account plus net foreign direct investment, is listed.

The **modified basic balance of payments** equals the current account plus foreign direct investment.

Summing Up: The Official Reserve Balance

The **official reserve balance** equals the current account plus all, both long and short, private capital accounts and net error and omissions. Whether a nation has an official reserve surplus can be computed by adding up the movements in official reserves, both domestic and foreign.

The balance of payments surplus or deficit on an **official reserve** basis equals the current account and the capital account plus net error and omissions. (The inclusion of net errors and omissions shows that not all items in the balance of payments are accurately counted. In certain countries, the figure reflects smuggling and other illicit activities. Drug dealers can hardly be expected to admit to exporting or importing so many tons of cocaine with a street value of a zillion dollars.)

The official reserves surplus or deficit can be computed by two methods. First, rows A–C of Table 4.1 can be summed up. Alternatively, one can take the difference between the change, increase or decrease, in U.S. official reserves and the change in foreign official, central bank, holdings of dollars to compute the U.S. official reserve balance of payments position. Neglecting rounding errors, we see that the United States had official reserve deficits of $22, $49, $67, and $45 billion between 1991 and 1994.

The official reserves method places all items except row D above the line, simply meaning that they are autonomous items, while changes in official reserves, both domestic and foreign, are the financing elements. In 1993, the $67 billion U.S. deficit was financed by foreign central banks building up their reserves by $68 billion, a credit item for the United States, and the United States *adding* $1 billion to its foreign exchange reserves, a *debit* item for the United States. In 1994, America's $45 billion deficit was financed by foreigners adding $40 billion to their official dollar reserves, again a credit item for the United States, and by the United States *selling* off $5 billion of its international reserves, a *credit* item for the United States.

The signs associated with a change in official reserves, foreign and domestic, appear incorrect. For example, in 1994 when the United States lost or sold $5 billion of reserves, this was counted as a credit or a plus even though foreigners received the funds. And when the U.S. built up its reserves in 1993 by $1 billion, the transaction was recorded as a deficit. In addition, if foreign central banks build up their dollar holdings

BOX 4.3 The Balance of Payments Among Nations: An Illustration

The following example demonstrates how the balance of payments is balanced if trade and payments are extended to cover three countries. (All figures are listed in dollars to avoid the complexity of currency conversions.)

United States		Japan	
Long-term capital (LTC)	−$10	Long-term capital (LTC)	+$10
Short-term capital (STC)	+$10	Short-term capital (STC)	−$10

Initially, let's suppose that the Mitsubishi Corporation of Japan floats or sells a $10 bond in the United States, reckoned as a long-term capital "export" for the United States and a long-term capital "import" for the Japanese. The United States has a debit and Japan a credit. Suppose that Mitsubishi builds up a dollar bank balance at Citibank in New York. This short-term deposit is listed as a credit for the United States and a debit for the Japanese. According to original definitions, the United States has a basic balance of payments deficit of $10 and Japan a basic surplus of $10. On an official reserve basis, the balance of payments of both nations is balanced.

United States		Japan		Germany	
LTC	−$10	Imports	−$10	Exports	+$10
STC (Germany)	+$10	LTC	+$10	STC	−$10

In the second stage, Mitsubishi draws on its bank account at Citibank in order to pay for some equipment it purchases from Daimler-Benz. The Japanese balance of payments now shows a credit from sale of a long-term bond in the United States and a debit based on its imports from Germany. Let us assume that Daimler-Benz receives payment from Mitsubishi in dollars and elects to keep these funds on deposit at Citibank. The German balance of payments then shows a credit of $10 for exports, and a debit of $10, the bank deposit in the United States. Nothing has happened to the U.S. external accounts, except that the bank deposit once owned by Mitsubishi is now owned by Daimler-Benz.

At this stage, the United States still has a basic balance of payments deficit, while Germany has a basic surplus and Japan's basic balance is balanced. On an official reserve basis, all three countries are in balance.

United States		Japan		Germany	
LTC	−$10	Imports	−$10	Exports	+$10
Reserves*	+$10	LTC	+$10	Reserves	−$10

In the final stage, Daimler-Benz closes its bank deposit at Citibank and sells the dollars to the Bundesbank for marks. The Bundesbank then holds the dollars as official or foreign exchange reserves. Recall from the previous discussion that changes in official reserves are a balancing item and, therefore, take on the opposite sign that one would normally expect. For the United States, Germany's increase in its dollar reserves counts as a credit. (Reserves* indicates foreign official holdings of dollars.)

Once again, the total balance of payments of the three nations sums to zero. However, judged by the basic balance of payments, the United States has a deficit of $10, Japan is

> balanced, and Germany has a $10 surplus. The figures are exactly the same on an official reserve basis: The United States has a deficit of $10, Germany a surplus of $10, and Japan is balanced.
>
> The example was rudimentary: Things are normally more complicated. Nevertheless, if all nations' exports and imports of goods, services, and capital plus any changes in official reserves are accurately recorded, every credit in every country should have an offsetting debit and the total balance of payments of all countries will be balanced.

or receive dollars, it is recorded as a credit item on the U.S. balance of payments. This paradox is explained by the fact that a change in a nation's international reserves is the last item and, therefore, the *balancing item* on the balance of payments. (Recall that the balance of payments must sum to zero.)

The official reserve position can be understood and computed more easily if it is written as an equation. Start with the fact that the balance of payments must equal zero and recall the definition of the current account.

$$X - M + i^*K - iK^* + NT + k^* - k + \Delta FX^* - \Delta FX = 0$$

In the equation, k^* and k equal capital flows, and ΔFX^* equals the change in the rest of the world's official holdings of the domestic currency and ΔFX equals the change in the nation's official holdings of foreign exchange.[3]

The equation can be rearranged to yield.

$$CA + k^* - k = -\Delta FX^* + \Delta FX$$

The official reserve balance of payments position can now be calculated by looking at the right-hand side of the equation. And in this case, unlike the previous equation, the change in the home and foreign country's official international reserves takes on the sign one would expect. If the final sum is positive, the country has a surplus; if it is negative, the nation has a deficit. In 1993, foreign official dollar holdings rose by $68 billion and the United States added $1 billion to its international reserves. The net change in international reserves, minus $68 billion plus $1 billion, equals the official reserve deficit of $67 billion in that year.

The Structure and Direction of U.S. Trade

Trade can be broken down by product and destination. A broad breakdown of U.S. merchandise trade in the early 1990s shows that the United States ran surpluses in capital goods and foods, feeds, and beverages and trade deficits in industrial supplies and raw materials, automotive goods, and in consumer goods (Table 4.3).

---

[3]The flow of capital in a given period will equal the change in the capital stock over the period or $k = K - K_{-1}$. If a country or its citizens own $100 of foreign securities at the beginning of 1992 and they purchase an additional $20 of such securities during the year, they will start 1993 with a stock of foreign securities equal to $120. The capital flows could be, and are in the actual statistics, subdivided into various categories such as direct investment, portfolio investment, other long-term capital flows, and short-term capital movements.

Table 4.4, which presents the major components of the American service account, shows that the United States ran substantial surpluses in travel and royalties and license fees. In fact, the United States is by far the world's largest exporter of services and has the world's largest surplus in services.

Table 4.5 lists the major trading partners of the United States in 1994. The figures include exports and imports of both goods and services. Table 4.6, on the other hand, covers only merchandise trade. Canada is far and away the most important market for U.S. merchandise exports while Japan and Mexico rank second and third respectively. Canada, Japan, and what are called the "little tigers," Hong Kong, Korea, Singapore,

TABLE 4.3 U.S. Merchandise Trade by End Use
(billions of dollars)

	1991	1992	1993	1994
Exports	**$416**	**$440**	**$457**	**$503**
Foods, feeds, & beverages	36	40	40	42
Industrial supplies & materials	110	110	112	121
Capital goods	167	177	183	206
Automotive goods	40	47	52	57
Consumer goods	46	50	53	60
Other exports	17	16	15	16
Imports	**489**	**536**	**589**	**669**
Foods, feeds, & beverages	27	28	28	31
Industrial supplies & materials	132	140	152	165
Capital goods	121	134	152	184
Automotive goods	86	86	102	119
Consumer goods	108	123	134	146
Other imports	19	19	20	24

Source: U.S. Department of Commerce, *Survey of Current Business* (March 1995); p. 64. The figures have been rounded and may not sum to the total figure. The *Survey of Current Business* also gives a more detailed account of U.S. exports and imports.

TABLE 4.4 U.S. Balance of Services: Major Components
(billions of dollars)

	1991	1992	1993	1994
Total Service Exports	**$164**	**$178**	**$186**	**$197**
Travel	48	54	58	60
Passenger Fares	16	17	17	17
Other Transportation	22	23	24	26
Royalties and License Fees	18	20	21	22
Total Service Imports	**$118**	**$121**	**$128**	**$137**
Travel	35	40	40	44
Passenger Fares	10	11	11	13
Other Transportation	23	24	27	28
Royalties and License Fees	4	5	5	6

Source: International Monetary Fund, *Balance of Payments Statistics Yearbook*, 1995, p. 822; and U.S. Department of Commerce, *Survey of Current Business* (June 1995): p. 85.

TABLE 4.5 Major Trading Partners of the United States: 1994 (goods and services in billions of dollars)

	Exports	*Imports*
Canada	$132.3	$143.0
Japan	82.2	134.2
Mexico	59.6	58.6
United Kingdom	44.2	42.5
Germany	30.5*	39.6*

*Excludes military services.

Source: U.S. Department of Commerce, *Survey of Current Business* (June 1995): pp. 92–94.

TABLE 4.6 U.S. Merchandise Trade by Region: 1994 (billions of dollars)

	Exports	*Imports*
Western Europe	$115.4	$132.9
Canada	114.9	131.1
Japan	51.8	107.3
Latin America	92.0	88.5
(Mexico)	(50.7)	(50.0)
Asia—excluding Japan	104.0	173.5
(Hong Kong, Korea,		
Taiwan, Singapore)	(56.7)	(72.4)
(China)	(9.2)	(38.9)
OPEC	17.1	31.7

Source: U.S. Department of Commerce, *Survey of Current Business* (June 1995): pp. 92–94.

and Taiwan, were the major suppliers of U.S. merchandise imports although U.S. imports from China have increased dramatically. Surprisingly, Japan was the largest importer of U.S. services in 1994 as it consumed $34.4 billion of U.S. services that year. Canada and the United Kingdom were the other major players on the service side. They imported $17.4 and $18.2 billion of U.S. services in 1994. For its part, the United States imported $17.6 billion and $15.1 billion of British and Japanese services in 1994.

International Investment and the Balance of Indebtedness

If a family's expenditures exceed its income, it must borrow funds to cover the imbalance. In the same manner, if a country imports more than it exports, it must either run down its financial assets or borrow the funds to finance its trade imbalance. Just as a family keeps a record of its investment position, placing assets on one side of the ledger and liabilities on the other, so does a country. This national record is called a country's **international investment position.**

The **international investment position** shows whether a country is a **creditor** or a **debtor.** It does this by adding up the physical and financial assets that a country holds abroad and subtracting the physical and financial assets that foreigners hold in the domestic country.

In accounting terms, the balance of payments is analogous to the profit and loss statement of a corporation; it is a record of how a country has done over a year. Its international investment position records its financial position at a particular point in time and is equivalent to a corporation's balance sheet. It shows whether a nation is a **creditor** or **debtor** and, when viewed over time, it discloses how its creditor/debtor position has changed.

Table 4.7 is an abbreviated picture of the international investment position of the United States from the end of 1991 to the end of 1994. We can see that over the four years covered, America's investment position with the rest of the world worsened by $333 billion.

TABLE 4.7 International Investment Position of the United States: 1990–1994 (billions of dollars)

	1991	1992	1993	1994
U.S. assets abroad[1]	2039	2055	2291	2378
U.S. official reserves[1]	67	60	62	63
Other U.S. official assets	79	81	81	81
U.S. private assets abroad	1893	1914	2148	2233
Direct foreign investment[2]	644	658	707	761
Foreign bonds	144	156	245	245
Foreign corporate stocks	159	178	298	314
U.S. claims on foreigners' reports by U.S. banks and nonbanks	256	254	250	287
Foreign assets in the United States	2487	2658	2939	3159
Foreign official assets	402	443	517	545
Private foreign assets in the United States	2085	2215	2422	2613
Direct foreign investment[2]	492	499	535	580
U.S. treasury securities	189	225	253	266
Corporate and other bonds	287	320	392	418
Corporate stocks	272	300	340	338
U.S. liabilities to foreigners reported by U.S. banks and nonbanks	844	872	971	1011
Net U.S. international investment position	−448	−603	−648	−781
U.S. balance of indebtedness	−600	−762	−820	−962

[1]U.S. official reserves do not include U.S. gold holdings, which were valued at $93, $87, $103, and $100 billion in 1990 through 1993. Gold is no longer actively employed as a reserve asset, but the exclusion of gold holdings depresses the U.S. foreign asset position relative to official statistics.

[2]Direct foreign investment is calculated on a current cost basis. All figures are rounded.

Source: U.S. Department of Commerce, *Survey of Current Business* (June 1995): p. 60.

BOX 4.4 The International Investment Position of the United States

The net international investment position of the United States has changed dramatically since 1980. In 1981, the U.S. net investment position was plus $268 billion, but by 1994, it was negative $781 billion. In thirteen years, the U.S. position deteriorated by over a tril-

The **balance of indebt-edness** computes the net financial position of a nation within the world economy. It equals the net international investment account minus foreign direct investment overseas and in the domestic country.

lion dollars. The same trend took place in the U.S. balance of indebtedness, which measures a country's net financial position—all items in Table 4.7 minus direct foreign investment. The U.S. **balance of indebtedness** in 1981 stood at $16 billion and it rose to $70 billion in 1983, which means that from the financial side alone, the United States was a net creditor in 1983. But after that date, the U.S. balance of indebtedness declined sharply and turned negative as a result of persistent trade deficits. At the end of 1994, America's balance of indebtedness stood at −$962 billion and the United States had become the world's largest debtor.

The United States fared better in the area of net foreign direct investment (Figure 4.1). Its net position was $252 billion in 1981, and at the end of 1994 it was $181 billion. The picture is not as bright if one looks at rates of growth. Foreign FDI rose at a 10 percent annual rate while U.S. FDI grew at a 3 percent annual rate over the period.

What all the figures tell us is that the United States, due to persistent trade deficits, built up its external debts and that foreigners have used their trade surpluses with the United States to expand their investment positions in America. The full impact of the change in the U.S. debtor position has not been felt in America yet. For a large portion of the twentieth century the United States has been a creditor country, meaning that the income account of the United States has always been positive. Given the growing external debt of the United States, the day is fast approaching when this account will turn negative. Foreigners will earn more interest on their financial investments and have more profits to repatriate or ship back home than the United States. As a result, the United States will have to export more goods and services in order to pay for its imports plus to pay out on the income account.

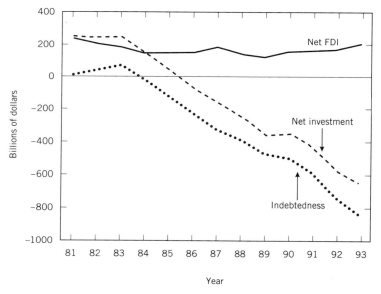

FIGURE 4.1 Measures of the net foreign investment position of the United States: 1981–1993.

Net FDI means *net foreign direct investment;* net investment stands for *net international investment;* and indebtedness means the *balance of indebtedness.*

Source: U.S. Department of Commerce, *Survey of Current Business* (June 1994): p. 71.

The Twin Deficit Hypothesis

So far the discussion has concentrated exclusively on the external accounts. Nothing has been said about their relationship to the domestic economy. But the external accounts are tied to the domestic economy. In the 1980s, the United States federal government ran massive budget deficits and America became the world's largest international debtor. Many economists believe that the budget deficits were the direct cause of the balance of payments deficits, a causal relationship summed up in the **twin deficit hypothesis.**

In its rudimentary form, the **twin deficit hypothesis** claims that trade deficits are the result of budget deficits not offset by private savings.

The twin deficit hypothesis does not argue that a country's external accounts will be balanced only if its government's accounts are balanced. A government can run a budget deficit without the nation adding to its international debt, providing the level of domestic savings is sufficient to finance both the government's deficit plus the level of domestic investment. When this is not the case, the country in question will have to borrow abroad to finance its budget deficit.

These relationships can be shown by adjusting the national income equation introduced in Chapter 2. Recall that GDP equals the sum of consumption and investment expenditures, government expenditures on goods and services, plus exports minus imports:

$$Y = C + I + G + X - M$$

Since consumption equals income minus taxes and savings, or $C = Y - T - S$, the income equation can be written as:

$$Y = Y - T - S + I + G + X - M$$

Rearranging the equation and dividing the result by Y or GDP yields the following:

$$(s - i) + (t - g) = (x - m)$$

Here, the lowercase letters represent the savings-to-income ratio, S/Y, the investment ratio, I/Y, and so on. *In this case only*, lowercase s and m do not equal the marginal propensity to save and the marginal propensity to import; rather they are the savings-to-income and imports-to-income ratios.

Expressed in terms of levels rather than ratios, the equation explains that if government expenditures exceed taxes by, say, $100, exports will equal imports providing domestic savings exceed domestic investment by $100; or in terms of ratios, if $(s - i)$ is positive but greater than a negative $(t - g)$, $(x - m)$ will be positive or $(x - m) > 0$. However, if the budget deficit, $100, exceeds the excess of domestic savings over domestic investment by, say $50, imports will exceed exports and the nation will have a trade deficit; or if $(t - g)$ is negative but in absolute terms exceeds $(s - i)$, which is positive, $(x - m)$ will be negative or $(x - m) < 0$.

For example, in 1990, American families saved $179 billion, the business sector saved $605 billion, and gross investment hit $745 billion. Therefore, gross private savings, $784 billion, exceeded gross investment by $39 billion. However, government expenditures exceeded government tax receipts by $161 billion at the federal level. So even though state and local governments had a $35 billion surplus, government units combined ran a $126 billion deficit. The United States, by itself, was unable to finance domestic investment plus the government deficit and had to turn toward foreign sources to cover the shortfall. The United States borrowed $90 billion, a sum equal to its trade deficit. One can say that the sum of consumption, investment, and government expenditures exceeded current output and that the excess absorption (see Chapter 2) was satisfied by an import surplus.

The American experience does not prove that budget deficits automatically lead to current account deficits, or even that current account deficits are bad. In 1988, the United Kingdom ran a current account deficit equal to 3.4 percent of its GDP and the British government had a budget surplus equal to 1 percent of GDP. The equation just given reveals that Britain's investment ratio exceeded its savings ratio by 4.4 percent. Britain borrowed in order to raise its investment/GDP ratio and expand its capital stock. Presumably this would have raised British productivity and have given it the ability to repay its external borrowing. By contrast, the United States had a current account and budget deficits that equaled -1.6 percent and -2.5 percent respectively of its GDP in 1990. This meant that although the gross domestic saving ratio exceeded the gross domestic investment ratio by .9 percent the excess was not sufficient to cover the negative budget/GDP ratio.

Because of the difference, the British trade deficit was dubbed **benign,** while the American deficit was considered **malign.** Britain borrowed in order to increase its investment ratio, raise its capital stock, and increase it productivity. In contrast, the United States borrowed to expand consumption and did not, therefore, increase its productive capacity and, hence, its ability to service its debts.

The twin deficit hypothesis framework is one tool that helps us to explore the relationship between domestic savings and investment, the budget position, and exports and imports. For example, during the last decade, Japan ran strong trade surpluses even though its high (over 30 percent) investment-to-GDP ratio exceeded its savings-to-GDP ratio (also over 30 percent). How did Japan do it? Japan ran budget surpluses that more than covered for the relative shortage of private savings and enabled Japan to run trade surpluses, lend abroad, and maintain a high investment-to-GDP ratio simultaneously. The Japanese experience suggests that if the United States wants to stop running trade deficits (and raise its investment-to-GDP ratio), it must balance its budget and raise its private savings-to-GDP ratio.

Summary

We have reviewed the various components of the balance of payments and have also showed two ways—the basic balance, modified and original, and the official reserve balance—that a balance of payments surplus or deficit can be computed. We have also showed how surpluses or deficits are added up over time in the form of the net international investment position or in the form of the balance of indebtedness. We have seen that if a country runs continual balance of payments deficits, its net international investment position will deteriorate, as the recent experience of the United States shows. Finally, through the twin deficit hypothesis, we have demonstrated how the private sector's decisions to save and invest and the government's decisions to tax and spend impact a nation's external accounts.

Key Concepts and Terms

balance of indebtedness

balance of trade or the trade balance

basic balance of payments (original versus modified)

capital account

capital export or import

current account

foreign direct investment

income account

merchandise trade balance

net creditor or debtor

net international investment position

official reserve balance

portfolio investment

repatriated profits

services account

twin deficit hypothesis

unilateral transfers

Review Questions

1. Consider the following items listed below. In each case, indicate under which category it would be listed in the U.S. balance of payments, and whether it would be a credit or debit item from the point of view of the United States. (Recall that the categories are: exports and imports of goods and services, the income account, unilateral or net transfers, and long-term and short-term capital. Long-term capital consists of foreign direct investment, portfolio investment, and long-term investments or loans.)

(a) Air France purchases twelve Boeing 747s.

(b) An American student spends at year studying in Britain.

(c) A U.S. businesswoman builds up her dollar account at a Swiss Bank.

(d) A Japanese consortium purchases the World Trade Center in New York.

(e) IBM sells some mainframe computers to Japan and uses the proceeds to build a factory in Germany.

(f) A Mexican citizen works in the United States and sends his wages back to his family in Mexico.

(g) A Mexican company successfully floats a bond on the U.S. market.

2. Explain what happens to the balance of payments of both countries given the following:

(a) The United States grants Somalia $1 million so that it can purchase U.S. wheat.

(b) A U.S. citizen contributes $100 to an international relief agency, which then purchases some drugs in Switzerland and gives them to Rwanda.

(c) A German firm purchases a factory for DM2 million in the Czech Republic and in the following year stocks it with DM2 million worth of German-made machine tools.

3. Suppose you purchase some shares of stock in Great Metropolitan, the British firm that owns Burger King. Is your purchase listed as foreign direct investment or as portfolio investment on the balance of payments accounts?

4. Many economists believe that the basic balance of payments is the best measure of a nation's balance of payments. Why? How is the basic balance of payments computed? How is the modified basic balance of payments computed?

5. What is the difference between the basic balance of payments and the official reserve balance of payments? How can one calculate the official reserve balance? If a Japanese corporation purchases U.S. Treasury bonds, how would this affect the basic balance and the official reserve balance of the United States? If the Bank of Japan purchased the same U.S. Treasury bonds, how would this affect the basic balance and the official reserve balance of the United States?

6. What is meant by the *balance of indebtedness?* How does it differ from the net international investment position of a country?

7. What is the difference between a malign and a benign deficit?

References and Suggested Readings

International Trade, an annual publication of the General Agreement on Tariffs and Trade, presents international trade statistics for many nations and world regions.

Allen Lenz wrote an excellent article which outlines where and how the U.S. trade balance went into the red. See Allen Lenz, "A Sectorial Assessment of the U.S. Current Account Deficit: Performance and Prospects," *International Adjustment and Financing: The Lessons of 1985–1991*, edited by C. Fred Bergsten (Washington, DC: Institute for International Economics, 1991). William Emmott wrote a sparkling essay, "The Limits of Japanese Power," on the present and potential Japanese savings ratio. It is included in *International Economics and Financial Markets*, edited by Richard O'Brien and Tapan Datta (Oxford: Oxford University Press, 1989).

Edward Graham and Paul Krugman investigate the impact of foreign investment in America in their book, *Foreign Direct Investment in the United States*, 3rd edition (Washington, DC: Institute for International Economics, 1994).

The discussion of malign versus benign deficits suggests that all government expenditures are consumption oriented. This is not necessarily the case. David A. Aschauer has persuasively argued that the United States has neglected its public capital stock or infrastructure to its detriment in his article, "Infrastructure: America's Third Deficit," *Challenge* 34 (March/April 1991); pp. 39–45. *The Economist* attempts to put the issue of trade deficits into perspective in "Schools Brief: In defense of deficits," *The Economist* (December 16, 1995); pp. 68–69.

PART 2

International Trade

Chapter 5

Trade and the International Division of Labor

Our earlier analysis of the potential gains from trade centered on consumer and producer surplus. Here we take the analysis a step further and illustrate the gains from trade through the theory of comparative advantage, which explains why trade makes sense. Then we present an informal discussion of the relationship between international trade and economic growth. Finally, although the law of comparative advantage shows that all parties gain from trade, some gain more than others; hence we need to address the distribution of the gains from trade, what is called the *terms of trade*.

The Path Ahead

In short, the objectives of the chapter are first to discuss the theories of absolute and comparative advantage, then to move on to an informal description of the relationship between trade and growth, and then to conclude with an analysis of the division of the gains from trade.

Absolute Advantage

Absolute advantage. The ability of a nation to produce a good with fewer inputs than any other nation.

A core assumption of economics is that *trade benefits both parties*. Adam Smith developed the theory of **absolute advantage** to show why trade is a win/win proposition. Suppose, Smith would argue, that the United States or Canada can produce either wheat or textiles. If the United States devotes all its resources—assumed to be labor only at this point—to producing wheat, it can produce 10 units, and if all its resources are committed to producing textiles, it can produce 20 units. Within these limits, the

United States can produce an additional one-half unit of wheat for every unit of textiles it is willing to forego. Imagine the opposite conditions hold true in Canada. If all of Canada's resources are used to produce wheat, it can produce 20 units; or if all its resources are devoted to producing textiles, it can produce 10 units. In other words, Canada can produce 2 units of wheat for every unit of textiles not produced.

The various possible production mixes for the United States and Canada are given by their **production possibility schedules** as in Table 5.1. A production possibility schedule shows the combinations of two goods that a nation can produce assuming that all its productive resources are employed given the existing state of technology. In the United States, assuming five inputs of labor, at combination A, all inputs are used to produce wheat; at combination B, one input is used to produce textiles and four inputs are devoted to producing wheat, and so on. As additional inputs are used to produce either textiles or wheat in either country, output increases by a constant amount. In the United States, when an additional input is devoted to producing textiles, the output of textiles rises by four units. The same pattern, although not necessarily the same number, holds for wheat production in the United States and for textile and for wheat production in Canada.

This means that the production of both textiles and wheat in both the United States and Canada displays **constant returns to scale.** Thus, in Canada, as an additional laborer is shifted from the wheat to the textile industry, the output of textiles rises by two units.

Because the production of textiles and wheat in both Canada and the United States occurs under conditions of constant returns to scale, the **opportunity cost** of producing either commodity in either country is constant as well. The opportunity cost of producing an additional unit of textiles in the United States equals one-half unit of wheat, since that is the amount of wheat that it must forego in order to produce an additional unit of textiles. In Canada, the opportunity cost of each additional textile is 2 units of wheat. On the other hand, the opportunity cost of producing an extra unit of wheat is 2 units of textiles in the United States and one-half unit of textiles in Canada.

Opportunity costs tell us that a unit of textiles will exchange for 2 units of wheat in the United States and for one-half unit of wheat in Canada. And it is the difference in domestic exchange ratios, which in turn are based on differences in opportunity costs, that opens up the possibility of profitable trade for both parties.

If, operating separately or without regard to the other country, both nations devote half their resources to manufacturing textiles and half to producing wheat, the United States will produce 10 units of textiles and 5 units of wheat. Canada will produce ex-

A **production possibility schedule** shows the combination of goods an economy can produce given its existing resources and the present state of technology.

Constant returns to scale. If all inputs are doubled, output doubles.

Opportunity costs measures the costs of what must be given up to consume or produce a commodity, for example, how many compact discs must be foregone in order to purchase a VCR.

TABLE 5.1 Production Possibility Schedules for United States and Canada

| Combination | United States | | Canada | |
	Textiles	*Wheat*	*Textiles*	*Wheat*
A	0	10	0	20
B	4	8	2	16
C	8	6	4	12
D	12	4	6	8
E	16	2	8	4
F	20	0	10	0

actly the opposite, 10 units of wheat and 5 units of textiles. Under these conditions, the world will produce 15 units of each product as shown in Table 5.2.

One can see that each country will be better off if it concentrates on producing the commodity in which it has the absolute advantage. Since the United States can produce textiles more efficiently than Canada, the United States has an absolute advantage in manufacturing textiles, while Canada has an absolute advantage in producing wheat. If the countries specialize and the United States produces 20 units of textiles and Canada produces 20 units of wheat, world production will expand, which by itself shows the advantages of trade.

The **international exchange ratio** (commonly called the **terms of trade**) tells us, for example, how many compact discs will exchange for a VCR in the world economy.

Moreover, if we assume that Canada and United States trade textiles and wheat at a 1:1 ratio, each country will be better off. Why? Without trade, the United States must forego a unit of textiles to obtain one-half unit of wheat. But with trade, it can obtain one unit of wheat by foregoing a unit of textiles. The **international exchange ratio** (more commonly called the **terms of trade**) of wheat to textiles, one unit per one unit, is superior to the **domestic exchange ratio,** one-half unit of wheat per unit of textiles. The same is true for Canada. Without trade, it gains one-half unit of textiles for every unit of wheat it sacrifices. With trade, Canada obtains a unit of textiles for every unit of wheat it sacrifices. Because the international exchange ratio of textiles for wheat or wheat for textiles lies between the two domestic exchange ratios, both countries will be better off if they trade with each other.

The **domestic exchange ratio** tells us how many compact discs exchange for a VCR within a closed economy.

Suppose the United States produces 20 units of textiles and sells 8 of them to Canada in return for 8 units of wheat. U.S. consumers now consume an additional 2 units of textiles, plus an additional 3 units of wheat. Clearly, they are better off. With trade, Canadians consume an additional 2 units of wheat and an additional 3 units of textiles. Equally important, because trade allows both countries to specialize in production, world production of textiles and wheat rises by 5 units each, as shown in Table 5.2.

A **production possibility curve** is a graphical representation of a production possibility schedule.

The discussion is summarized in Figure 5.1. The solid lines in panels (a) and (b) represent the **production possibility curves** of the United States and of Canada. Prior to trade, both countries produce and consume at points A and A^* on their respective production possibility curves. With trade, the countries specialize completely in production, Canada in wheat and the United States in textiles, and produce at points P and P^*

TABLE 5.2 Hypothetical Gains from Trade: I (pretrade)

	Production		Consumption	
	Textiles	Wheat	Textiles	Wheat
United States	10	5	10	5
Canada	5	10	5	10
World	15	15	15	15

(posttrade)

	Production		Consumption	
United States	20	0	12	8
Canada	0	20	8	12
World	20	20	20	20

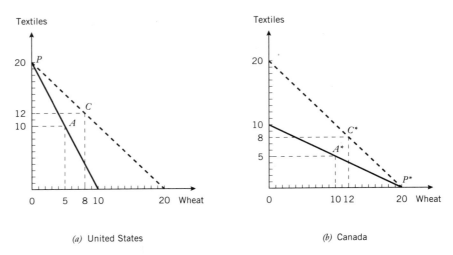

(a) United States   *(b)* Canada

FIGURE 5.1 Absolute advantage.

Suppose that prior to trade, the United States consumes and produces at point *A* on its production possibility curve, or 10 units of textiles and 5 units of wheat. Suppose also that prior to trade, Canada produces at point *A** on its production possibility curve, or 5 units of textiles and 10 units of wheat. With trade, both countries specialize completely in production and produce at points *P* and *P** respectively on their production possibility curves and consume at points *C* and *C** respectively on their consumption possibility lines. The United States produces 20 units of textiles and consumes 12 units of textiles and sends 8 units of textiles to Canada in exchange for 8 units of wheat. Canada produces 20 units of wheat and consumes 12 units of wheat and exports 8 units of wheat to the United States in exchange for 8 units of textiles, which it consumes. Thus, trade allows both countries to consume larger amounts of both commodities.

The **consumption possibility line** shows the various combinations of two goods that can be consumed at a given terms of trade or international exchange ratio.

on their production possibility curves. (One can note that the slope of the U.S. production possibility curve equals 2—measured in absolute terms. This line also equals the domestic exchange ratio between textiles and wheat in the United States prior to trade. For Canada, the slope of its production possibility curve is one-half.)

However, we have assumed that trade takes place at an exchange ratio, or terms of trade, of one unit of textiles per one unit of wheat. Accordingly, the terms of trade line, the *dotted line*, has a slope of one—in absolute terms. The terms of trade line equals the **consumption possibility line**, which shows us the possible combinations—how much wheat and how many textiles—that can be consumed given trade. Here, we assume that the United States consumes 12 units of textiles and 8 units of wheat, or point *C* on its consumption possibility line, and that Canada consumes 8 units of textiles and 12 units of wheat, or point *C** on its consumption possibility line.

Since U.S. production of textiles exceeds its consumption of textiles—20 minus 12, the United States exports 8 units of textiles to Canada. And since its consumption of wheat, 8 units, exceeds its production of wheat, zero units, it imports 8 units of wheat from Canada. (The production, consumption, exports, and imports for Canada can be computed in exactly the same manner in Figure 5.1b.)

Comparative Advantage

The United States has a **comparative advantage** in textiles if it can produce both wheat and textiles with fewer inputs than Canada, but needs fewer relative inputs compared to Canada to produce textiles than to produce wheat.

But if we suppose that one nation is more efficient in producing *both* wheat and textiles, should the Canada and United States still trade? The answer is *yes*, and David Ricardo's theory of **comparative advantage** demonstrates why. Suppose that the United States can produce 40 units of textiles if it devotes all its resources to producing textiles, but that if it devotes all its resources to producing wheat, it can produce 20 units. (We assume, therefore, that the productivity of American resources or labor has doubled.) Within these limits, the United States can produce textiles and wheat in a ratio of 1 unit of textiles to one-half unit of wheat. Suppose, as before, that Canada can produce either 10 units of textiles or 20 units of wheat or, within its production limits, some combination of the commodities in the ratio of 1 textile to 2 units of wheat. An abbreviated list of the possible production combinations of both nations is given in Table 5.3.

While the United States can produce more of both commodities—just slightly in the case of wheat, a difference that will be ignored from this point on—it is twice as productive as Canada in textiles, 40 to 20, and equally productive in wheat, 20.5 to 20. The United States, therefore, has an *absolute advantage* in producing both commodities, but a *comparative advantage* in producing textiles since it is relatively more efficient in that industry. Canada, while at an absolute disadvantage in producing either commodity, has a comparative advantage in wheat production since 20/20.5 > 20/40.

Because the nations in this example have different relative productive capacities, wheat and textiles trade at different exchange ratios within each country prior to trade. In the United States, 1 unit of textiles exchanges for one-half unit of wheat, while a textile commands 2 units of wheat in Canada. Just as in the case of absolute advantage, it is the differences in domestic exchange ratios that form the basis for trade. If the United States can sell a unit of textiles for more than one-half a unit of wheat, it will gain from trade; and if Canada can obtain 1 unit of textiles by giving up anything less than 2 units of wheat it will profit as well. Thus, trade will benefit both countries if the international terms of exchange or trade settle anywhere within the range of 1 unit of textiles to one-half units to 2 units of wheat.

(If domestic exchange ratios are equal, trade will not take place. Imagine the United States can produce either 40 units of wheat or 80 units of textiles. In that event, both the Canadian and American domestic exchange ratios would equal 1 wheat to 2 textiles

TABLE 5.3 Production Possibilities

Combination	United States		Canada	
	Textiles	Wheat	Textiles	Wheat
A	40	0	10	0
B	32	4.1	8	4
C	24	8.2	6	8
D	16	12.3	4	12
E	8	16.4	2	16
F	0	20.5	0	20

and nothing could be gained from trade unless demand patterns in the two nations were strikingly different. It is the dissimilarity in relative production capabilities which leads to differences in domestic exchange ratios that, in turn, generates the possible gains from trade. A butcher trades with a cobbler, not with another butcher.)

Suppose that, prior to trade, the United States uses 3.5 units of its 5 units of labor to produce wheat and 1.5 units of labor to produce textiles, that is, it produces half-way between points B and C on its production possibility schedule. This means that the United States will produce 28 units of textiles and 6 units of wheat. As before, let's assume that Canada utilizes one-half of its inputs to produce textiles and one-half to produce wheat. Canada, therefore, produces 5 units of textiles and 10 units of wheat. (Canada would produce at a point half-way between combinations C and D on its production possibility schedule.)

Now, suppose trade opens up and each country specializes completely in producing the commodity in which it has the comparative advantage and that the terms of trade settle at 1 unit of textiles for 1 unit of wheat. Thus, the United States produces 40 units of textiles and Canada produces 20 units of wheat. If the United States exchanges 8 units of textiles for 8 units of wheat, its consumption of textiles will go up to 32 units, an additional 4 units, and its consumption of wheat will rise to 8 units, a gain of 2 units. Because of trade, Canada will be able to consume 3 additional units of textiles and 2 additional units of wheat. In other words, both countries are able to consume more of both products due to trade. In addition, the worldwide production of textiles rises from 33 to 40 units and the worldwide production of wheat rises from 16 to 20 units. Table 5.4 summarizes the results.

Figure 5.2, which is similar to Figure 5.1, shows the benefits of trade. Prior to trade, both countries produce and consume textiles and wheat at points A and A^* on their respective production possibility curves. With trade, they produce at points P and P^* on their production possibility curves, but consume at points C and C^* on their respective consumption possibility curves. U.S. production of textiles, 40 units, exceeds its consumption of textiles, 32 units. This difference equals its exports. Since its consumption of wheat, 8 units, exceeds its production of wheat, 0 units, this difference equals its imports. Once again, Canadian production, consumption, exports, and imports can be calculated in a similar manner.

TABLE 5.4 The Hypothetical Gains from Trade: II
(pretrade)

	Production		Consumption	
	Textiles	*Wheat*	*Textiles*	*Wheat*
United States	28	6	28	6
Canada	5	10	5	10
World	33	16	33	16

(posttrade)

	Production		Consumption	
United States	40	0	32	8
Canada	0	20	8	12
World	40	20	40	20

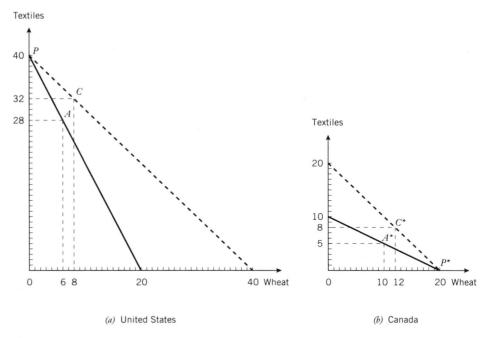

FIGURE 5.2 Comparative advantage.

Prior to trade, the United States produces and consumes 28 units of textiles and 8 units of wheat; Canada produces and consumes 5 units of textiles and 10 units of wheat—point *A* and *A** on their respective production possibility curves. With trade, the United States devotes all its resources to producing 40 units of textiles (point *P*), and Canada devotes all its resources to producing 20 units of wheat (point *P**). The United States sells Canada 8 units of textiles for 8 units of wheat. After trade, both nations consume at points *C* and *C** on their respective consumption possibility lines. Canada consumes 8 units of textiles and 12 units of wheat; the United States consumes 32 units of textiles and 8 units of wheat. Due to trade, both countries are able to consume more of both commodities.

Trade and Relative Price Ratios

A relative price ratio equals the price of a VCR compared to the price of a compact disc.

The gains from trade can be cast in terms of **relative price ratios.** Assume that the price of textiles is constant at $1 and that the C$/US$ exchange rate is one-to-one. In this case, prior to trade, the price of wheat would be $.50 in Canada and $2 in the United States. (Since Canadians exchange 2 units of wheat for 1 unit of textiles, the price of wheat must be half the price of textiles in Canada or $.50 per unit. By the same reasoning, the price of wheat is $2 per unit in the United States.)

Given the relative price ratios, Canadians will consume a relatively high proportion of wheat while Americans will consume a relatively high proportion of clothes. When trade is initiated, the price of wheat rises to $1 in Canada and falls to $1 in the United States—recall that the price of textiles is assumed to remain constant at $1. In Canada, the relative increase in the price of wheat encourages Canadians to produce wheat, while the relative decline in the price of textiles induces them to consume more textiles. In the United States, the relative price of wheat falls. America produces more textiles and less wheat and Americans consume more wheat.

BOX 5.1 Trade Under Increasing Opportunity Costs

So far, when we have discussed the theory of comparative advantage, we have assumed that both Canada and the United States face constant opportunity costs in production, meaning that if either nation gives up consecutive equal amounts of textiles, it will get so much wheat in return. Yet, in reality, it is more likely that one or both nations will face *increasing* opportunity costs, and that it will have to forego, for example, increasing quantities of textiles in order to obtain the same number of additional units of wheat.

Table 5.5 shows a hypothetical production possibilities schedule for the United States. Given five laborers, as each laborer moves from the textile to the wheat industry the output of wheat rises by 4 units—or constant returns to scale hold. However, as each additional laborer is moved from the wheat to the textile industry the output of textiles increases, but at a decreasing rate. Thus, there are **decreasing returns to scale** in the textile industry.

Decreasing returns to scale. If all inputs are doubled, output increases by *less* than 100 percent.

Due to decreasing returns to scale in the textile industry, the opportunity costs of producing either more textiles or more wheat increase as the nation produces more of either commodity. Start at combination F, where the United States produces 20 units of wheat and 0 units of textiles. As resources are steadily moved from producing wheat to producing textiles or as the economy moves from combination F to combination A, the production of wheat declines by 4 units with each move. But the production of textiles increases at a decreasing rate. If the United States moves from combination F to combination E, it gives up 4 units of wheat but gains 12 units of textiles. However when it moves from combination B to combination A, it gives up 4 units of wheat, but gains only 4 units of textiles. Likewise, if the United States moves from combination A to combination F, it gains 4 additional units of wheat with each move, but at each consecutive step it must sacrifice increasing quantities of textiles to obtain each additional 4 units of wheat.

Now we can ask: What is the impact of increasing opportunity costs on trade? Increasing opportunity costs do not refute the law of comparative advantage nor diminish the fact that countries and the world gain from international trade. Nor, given the assumed Canadian production possibility schedule, will increasing opportunity costs change the U.S. comparative advantage. The United States will still export textiles and import wheat. What will happen is that the United States will not specialize completely in the production of textiles—except in the rarest of circumstances. Thus, the gains from specialization, one of the benefits of trade, will be reduced. As a result, one could argue, the potential benefits to be derived from trade will be lower—at least for the U.S.

Figure 5.3 shows the impact of trade on domestic production and consumption when increasing opportunity costs are the rule of the day. Due to increasing opportunity costs, the production possibility curve is bowed-out, reflecting the fact that as the United States gives up increasing amounts of wheat, it obtains diminishing additional amounts of textiles. Suppose that, prior to trade, the United States produces and consumes at point A where the terms of trade line, TOT_0, is tangent to its production possibility curve. The terms-of-trade

TABLE 5.5 Production Possibilities for the United States

Combination	Textiles	Wheat
A	40	0
B	36	4
C	30	8
D	22	12
E	12	16
F	0	20

line shows the relative exchange ratio between textiles and wheat given the relative demands for the two commodities.

Given trade, it is reasonable to assume that the price of U.S.-made textiles will rise relative to the price of U.S.-produced wheat, since the U.S. demand for textiles is now supplemented by the Canadian demand for textiles and the U.S. supply of wheat is now supplemented by the Canadian supply of wheat. Because of the change in the relative price ratio, its reciprocal, the relative physical exchange ratio, will change as well, and, in the United States, a unit of textiles will be worth more units of wheat.

The change in the relative exchange ratio shows up as a change in the slope of the terms-of-trade line. Given trade, the relevant terms-of-trade line is TOT_1, a line that is flatter than the initial terms of trade line, which demonstrates that a given quantity of textiles now exchanges for more units of wheat. The United States now produces at the point where TOT_1 is tangent to the production possibility schedule, or at point P, and consumes at some point along TOT_1, its consumption possibility schedule. We assume that the United States consumes at point C.

We can see that the United States has gained from trade since point C involves both more textiles and more wheat than point A. But we can also see that the United States does not produce only textiles; it produces some wheat as well. U.S. textile exports can be measured along the vertical axis. Since the point P represents a higher quantity of textiles than point C, the excess of U.S. textile production over textile consumption equals U.S. textile exports. U.S. imports can be measured along the horizontal axis. Since the quantity of wheat consumed, given by point C, exceeds the amount of wheat produced, given by point P, the United States imports the difference.

As suggested, increasing opportunity costs do not change the basic propositions of the theory of comparative advantage. They do, however, indicate that most countries will not specialize completely. Increasing opportunity costs also suggest that the more a country specializes, the more it will benefit from trade. First, it will move more of its resources to the industry where they are most productive, and, second, in order for a country to specialize, the terms of trade must move in favor of its export good.

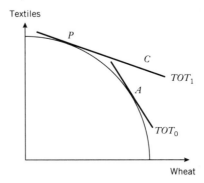

FIGURE 5.3 Trade under increasing opportunity costs.

In isolation, the economy produces and consumes at point A where the terms-of-trade line, TOT_0, is tangent to its production possibility curve. Trade raises the price of textiles relative to the price of wheat as shown by the new terms-of-trade line TOT_1. Given international trade, the country produces at point P where TOT_1 is tangent to the production possibility curve. After trade begins, the nation consumes at point C on the terms-of-trade line TOT_1. As can be seen, point C represents a greater quantity of both textiles and wheat than point A. As in the case of constant opportunity costs, the nation consumes greater quantities of wheat and textiles with trade than without trade.

Trade and Micro and Macro Models

The production and consumption effects flowing from international trade can be related to the micro and macro models described in Chapters 1 and 2. In Chapter 1, with the inception of trade, a nation produces more and consumes fewer exportable goods because their prices rise and it consumes more but produces fewer importable goods because their prices decline. Thus, a key difference between the present example and the previous results is that the consumption of exportable goods increases whereas previously it contracted.

The consumption of both wheat and textiles in both countries increases because world production is higher. Since we assume that full employment prevails both before and after trade, greater production at all price levels means that the world's aggregate supply curve has shifted to the right. But if all resources were fully employed in Canada and the United States prior to trade, how could they possibly produce a greater output given trade? The answer is that *the world economy has one potential income without trade and another, higher one with trade.* (Conversely, the world operates below its potential when international trade is restricted.) By encouraging the world's labor force and other resources to specialize, international trade leads to an increase in productivity, which reduces labor costs per unit of output and shifts the world's aggregate supply (*AS*) curve to the right.

Because the world's aggregate supply curve is the sum of national *AS* curves, if it shifts to the right, national aggregate supply curves will also shift to the right. Common sense may suggest that the *AS* curves of some nations could shift to the right while those of other nations could shift to the left. In this case, trade would actually "beggar" or "immiserize" certain nations. But the theory of comparative advantage demonstrates exactly the opposite: Trade benefits *all* nations. And no country would tolerate international trade if doing so caused harm to its economic welfare.

Trade and Country Size

The theory of comparative advantage asserts that the more a country specializes in its production, other things considered, the more it will benefit from international trade. It can be seen intuitively that if the United States can produce either 100 units of textiles or 60 units of wheat while Canada can produce 10 units of textiles and 20 units of wheat, then Canada may specialize completely in the production of wheat while the United States will continue to produce both commodities. Since a relatively greater proportion of Canada's resources will shift to producing in an area where they have greater productivity, Canada will gain the most from trade.

Canada or a small country will obtain relatively greater benefits from trade for an additional reason: The larger nation's export supply and import demand will dominate international markets and, as a result, the international terms of trade will settle closer to the larger nation's than to the smaller nation's pretrade terms of trade. The terms of trade improve for both countries, but more for the smaller country (Canada) than for the larger country (the United States).

TABLE 5.6 Country Size and Trade
(pop = population, X/GDP = exports/GDP)

Nation	GDP	Pop	X/GDP
United States	1	1	8.7
Japan	2	2	12.1
Germany	3	3	23.9
France	4	6	18.0
UK	5	5	21.0
Italy	6	4	21.2
Canada	7	7	25.7
Netherlands	8	8	44.6
Sweden	9	10	25.3
Belgium	10	9	54.4

Source: International Monetary Fund, *International Financial Statistics* (various issues). Population and GDP are 1980 figures and exports/GDP are the average of 1979–1981.

There is, however, a downside to increasing specialization. Greater specialization often means greater transitory adjustment costs such as the costs of liquidating textile mills and retraining workers. In the example, 30 percent of U.S. resources or inputs moved from the wheat to the textile industry. In Canada, 50 percent of its resources shifted from textile to wheat production. Obviously, Canada bears greater transitory adjustment costs.

A practical consequence of this analysis is that in the years ahead, Mexico may have to endure greater adjustment costs as a result of NAFTA than the United States. Nevertheless, the theory of comparative advantage also implies that Mexico will gain more from NAFTA than the United States. Is there any truth to this hypothesis? If small nations gain the most from trade—the so-called **importance of being unimportant**—then, other things remaining equal, trade as a proportion of total output or GDP should be larger in small countries compared with large countries.

Table 5.6 ranks nations by gross domestic product (GDP), population, and exports as a proportion of GDP.

The relationship between country size and trade as a percent of GDP is not perfect. But with the exceptions of Germany and Sweden, Table 5.6 indicates that trade is *inversely* related to country size, just as trade theory suggests. Moreover, since all these nations have high and similar per-capita incomes, the data suggests that smaller nations can overcome the limitations imposed by a small domestic market through trade and specialization.

The **importance of being unimportant** describes why when smaller countries trade with larger countries the smaller countries are likely to enjoy a larger portion of the mutual gains from trade.

Trade and Economic Growth

The figures in Table 5.6 may vouch for the importance of trade for smaller nations, but they do not demonstrate the importance of trade and specialization in raising living standards—a matter of critical importance for all nations. Table 5.7 shows the relation

TABLE 5.7 Annual Rates of Growth of Real GDP and the Volume of Exports: 1970–90

Nation	GDP	Exports
South Korea	8.7%	17.2%
Singapore	8.0	11.2
Japan	4.6	7.2
Philippines	3.8	6.7
Canada	3.8	5.0
Italy	3.0	5.2
France	2.8	5.4
US[a]	2.8	4.5
Germany	2.4	5.4
Netherlands	2.4	5.2
Belgium	2.4	4.9
UK	2.1	4.4

[a] = 1970–1988.

Source: Computed from relevant country pages in International Monetary Fund, *International Financial Statistics Yearbook*, 1992.

between the growth in real gross domestic product and the growth in the volume of exports for the major OECD countries as well as three developing countries.

Once again, the relationship is not perfect since the relative position of the United States is out of line. Yet the data show that economic growth and export expansion are closely related. This is true regardless of the time period, as the link between economic growth and export expansion held between 1970 and 1980 and also between 1980 and 1990 even though not all nations maintained their relative rank over these years. For example, between 1970 and 1980, Philippine exports grew at an average rate of 8.6 percent per year and its GDP advanced at a 6.1 percent rate, while during the 1980s, the rate of growth of its exports fell off to 4.9 percent and its GDP advanced at a sluggish 1.6 percent per annum.

The correlation of export growth and income expansion is especially important for LDCs. Without open trade and an expanding world economy, many small LDCs would be trapped in poverty. Over two centuries ago, Adam Smith pointed out that specialization, what he called the division of labor, was limited by the size of the market. The implication of Smith's observation is that many, even most, LDCs will not be able to specialize and raise their living standards unless they have access to markets in the developed world. Domestic markets of LDCs are often too small and incomes per capita too low to provide the incentives for production on a scale sufficient to achieve and sustain high economic growth. One would hardly expect a small market to support car production. Volvo, for example, is a going concern because it sells cars worldwide, not just in the Swedish market even though Swedish income per capita is high, not low.

International trade's crucial role in fostering development has been studied by the **International Bank for Reconstruction and Development** or, as it is more commonly known, the **World Bank,** which compared the performance of outward-looking versus inward-looking economies in terms of economic growth, increase in income per capita, export performance, and income distribution. The World Bank's study concluded that the performance of outward-looking economies was superior (see Table 5.8).

The **World Bank,** officially the **International Bank for Reconstruction and Development,** attempts to assist economic development by extending loans to developing countries.

TABLE 5.8 Inward- and Outward-Looking Economics and Economic Performance (average percentage change)

	Growth: GNP		Growth: Mfd Exports	
	1963–73	1973–85	1965–73	1973–85
Outward-Looking	9.5%	7.7%	14.8%	14.2%
Inward-Looking	4.1	2.5	5.7	3.7

Mfd = manufactured.

Source: World Bank, *World Development Report: 1987* (New York: Oxford University Press, 1987); p. 85.

What distinguishes outward-looking from inward-looking economies? Outward-looking economies have low import barriers and provide incentives to offset any import barrier that might impinge upon the production of potential exports. In addition, outward-looking economies usually attempt to maintain realistic exchange rates or ones that do not punish exporters. By comparison, inward-looking economies follow policies devised to promote the creation of domestic industries designed to serve the domestic market alone. Therefore, they impose high trade barriers to protect such industries from foreign competition and maintain overvalued exchange rates that discourage exporting, further inducing firms to produce for the domestic market. Even though an overvalued exchange rate tends to encourage, not restrict, imports, the previously mentioned trade barriers hold back imports and secure domestic markets for domestic producers.

Who Benefits Most from International Trade?

International trade raises national economic welfare, but by how much? Two forces are crucial in answering that question: the level of national exports and the price of exports relative to the price of imports.

The price of exports relative to the price of imports is called the terms of trade, or more accurately the **commodity terms of trade.** The terms of trade are affected by everything that affects the supply and demand for exports on the one hand and imports on the other. If the price of oil doubles while everything else remains constant including the quantity of oil demanded, an oil-producing nation will obtain additional benefits from trade as each barrel of oil will now purchase twice as many personal computers as before. Likewise, if the price of imports, say, personal computers, falls by 50 percent while the price of oil and everything else remains constant, the OPEC nations would obtain greater benefits from trade.

Doubling the volume of exports will also raise national income providing other things remain constant. But if a doubling of the volume of exports leads to a decrease in the price of exports, the country may be better off or worse off. If Canada, for example, expands its production of wheat and offers it for sale on the international market, the greater supply could push down the price. Whether Canada will gain or lose in this situation depends on the elasticity of the demand for wheat. Given an elastic

The **commodity terms of trade** equals the price of exports divided by the price of imports.

demand for wheat, Canada will gain; but if the demand for wheat is inelastic, Canada may actually lose—more on this topic and its implications later.

Canada, however, is a large wheat producer. Therefore, if it produces more wheat and sells it on the world market, the price of wheat will decline. But if a *small* country, say Uruguay, doubles its production of wool and sells it all on the world market, its additional exports will not affect the world price of wool nor, it follows, Uruguay's terms of trade. This may lead us to conclude that only large countries have to worry about what are called the terms-of-trade effects of international trade.

But, alas, small countries are also vulnerable to changes in the terms of trade. Swings in the world's demand for and supply of wool, regardless of Uruguay's contribution, will raise and lower its price and cause Uruguay's terms of trade either to improve or deteriorate. Over the years, raw material producers, both large and small, have seen the price and volume of their exports buffeted by worldwide market forces with predictable effects on their terms of trade.

When a nation's terms of trade rise or fall due to bouts of worldwide expansion or contraction, there is probably little it can do about it. A **buffer stock** arrangement (see Box 5.2) may help, although, to date, such organizations have not been an overwhelming success.

A **buffer stock** scheme is a method employed to stabilize the price of raw materials. If the price of the commodity in question is too low compared to some target price, the buffer stock manager buys the commodity. If the price is too high, the manager sells some of the commodity from her stocks of the commodity.

BOX 5.2 Buffer Stocks

Commodity prices can be stabilized through a buffer stock system. Under such an arrangement, the manager of the buffer stock, with a sum of cash in one hand and a supply of the commodity, say tin, in the other, stands ready to buy and sell the commodity at a target price. The workings of a buffer stock arrangement are illustrated in Figure 5.4.

Consider Figure 5.4a. Suppose the target price of tin is P_t and that the demand curve equals D_1. Since the demand for tin equals the supply of tin at the target price, the buffer stock manager has neither to buy nor sell tin in order to sustain the target price. If, however, the demand for tin increases at all price levels so that the demand curve for tin shifts to the right to D_2, demand will exceed supply at the target price of P_t. The buffer stock manager will sell Q_1–Q_2 of tin from his inventory of the commodity in order to maintain the target price. If demand decreases and the demand curve shifts to the left, to D_0, the manager will purchase Q_0–Q_1 of tin on the market in order to maintain the target price.

When run in this manner, a buffer stock places all the burden of maintaining the target price on the demand side of the market. Some commodity price stabilization schemes, however, have attempted to introduce the supply side into the picture by establishing production or marketing quotas. This effort is illustrated in Figure 5.4b. Production quotas for all members of the buffer stock arrangement are represented by the vertical supply curves S_0, S_1, and S_2. Assume initially that the demand and supply curves are D_1 and S_1 so that demand equals supply at the target price.

If, however, the demand for tin drops and the demand curve for tin shifts to D_0, the manager must spring into action since supply exceeds demand by Q_0–Q_1 at the target price. But rather than just purchasing the excess supply of tin as in the previous example, the manager now cuts production quotas, which reduces the supply tin from S_1 to S_0. As a result, the manager has to purchase only half the amount of tin previously purchased in order to maintain the target price. The buffer stock thus has to hold only one-half of the amounts of cash and stocks of tin that it previously held.

Buffer stocks have run into many snags. When production or marketing quotas are cut, there usually is a fight over how much each member of the arrangement must cut its production. Even in good times, aggressive low-cost producers often want to displace more passive high-cost producers. Finally, fundamental changes in supply and demand cause problems in maintaining the target price and disagreements tend to erupt over what the new target price should be.

With all these destabilizing pressures, it is understandable why buffer stock arrangements have not worked well. The international tin agreement, one of the more successful arrangements, came crashing down in 1986 when the buffer stock manager ran out of cash and the sponsoring nations refused to provide additional funds.

Despite their poor performance, buffer stocks have political appeal and many politicians have called for reestablishing such arrangements. Many LDCs' foreign exchange earnings are tied to one or a few commodities: Bolivia's foreign exchange earnings are tied to tin, Ghana's to cocoa, and Zambia's to copper, for example. And it is assumed that stable export earnings will assist such nations' economic development. This is why the IMF created its **Compensatory and Contingency Financing Facility,** which helps countries offset swings in their foreign exchange earnings caused by variations in commodity prices.

Compensatory and Contingency Financing Facility. An arm of the IMF, which, by lending, helps countries to offset the effects of wide swings in their export earnings caused by variations in commodity prices. A nation can also borrow funds from this facility in order to finance its contributions to buffer stock schemes.

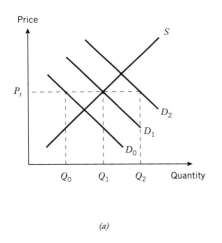
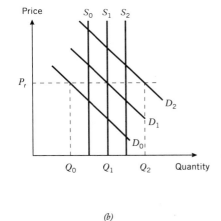

(a)   *(b)*

FIGURE 5.4 Buffer stock operations.

A buffer stock scheme attempts to stabilize the price of some commodity, normally a raw material, at some prescribed level. In panel (a), the target price is P_t. If the demand curve shifts from D_1 to D_2, the price of the commodity would rise above the target level. In this situation, the buffer stock manager would sell some of her inventory of the commodity, increasing the supply, and bring the price down to its target level. If the demand curve shifts from D_1 to D_0, the price of the good would fall below the target level. The buffer stock manager would then use her cash reserve to buy the commodity on the market and increase its price. Panel (b) shows how a buffer stock scheme works if the normal buying and selling of the commodity is supplemented by a system of export quotas. Under these conditions if the price of the commodity falls below the target level, the buffer stock manager would purchase the commodity on the open market. In addition, the total amount of the product sold on the market by all members of the buffer stock scheme would be cut from S_1 to S_0.

Measuring the Terms of Trade

A nation's **income terms of trade** equals its commodity terms of trade times the quantity of its exports and measures the nation's capacity to import.

There are several measures of the terms of trade, but two measures stand out: the commodity terms of trade, and the **income terms of trade.** The commodity terms of trade, the most common definition of the terms of trade, is computed by dividing the price of exports by the price of imports.

$$TOT_C = \frac{P_X}{P_M}$$

where P_X equals the price of exports and P_M is the price of imports. Using the wheat/textile example, Canada's commodity terms of trade would be measured by the price of wheat divided by the price of textiles. If the price of its exports rises from $1 in 1995 to $2 in 1996 while the price of its imports remains constant, its commodity terms of trade will double. Normally the terms of trade are calculated as an index number. If 1995 is the base year, the index number, P_X/P_M, would rise from 100 or $1/$1 times 100, to 200 or $2/$1 times 100.

The income terms of trade, which determines a nation's capacity to import, is also used to calculate a nation's gains from trade. It equals the commodity terms of trade times the quantity of exports.

$$TOT_Y = (TOT_C)\, Q_X = \frac{P_X}{P_M}\, Q_X$$

An understanding of these two concepts of the terms of trade tells us under what conditions a nation will maximize its gains from trade. If the price of a country's imports decline, and the price and demand for its exports rise, the nation will be a clear winner and portraits of Adam Smith and David Ricardo will adorn the walls of the presidential mansion.

The Commodity and Income Terms of Trade

Such a happy chain of events may not transpire. Reconsider the original example, that of a large country. Imagine that Canadian wheat production doubles and the international price of wheat in terms of textiles drops from 1 unit of wheat to 1 unit of textiles to 1 unit of wheat to .5 unit of textiles or that 1 unit of textiles now exchanges for 2 units of wheat instead of 1 unit of wheat. If the original commodity terms of trade equaled 100, or $P_X/P_M = 100$, the new terms of trade will be 50, a sharp fall in Canada's commodity terms of trade.

Because the new international terms of trade equals the initial Canadian domestic terms of trade, 2W = 1T, it is tempting to conclude that Canada will gain nothing from trade. But this conclusion would be incorrect. After the doubling of wheat production, Canada's domestic exchange ratio will move from 2 units of wheat per textile to 4 units of wheat per textile. Thus to calculate whether Canada should trade, one must look at the new, not the old, domestic exchange ratio. It still pays Canada to trade because the

BOX 5.3 **Fair Trade**

Although the commodity terms of trade of most LDCs did not deteriorate sharply in the period 1976–1993 (see Box 5.4), exporters of some commodities such as coffee, tea, and honey have been hurt. For example, the price a farmer receives for growing a pound of coffee is roughly 20 percent of its final selling price, which is often not enough to cover costs of production, to say nothing of improving living standards.

The plight of such people has sparked attempts to foster what is called **fair trade** under which, for example, a coffee producer receives a price sufficient to cover his production costs and also to improve his standard of living. The main organizers behind fair trade are groups called **alternative trading organizations** (ATOs). In order to attain their objectives, ATOs either import the products themselves—paying a higher price for the coffee—or bargain with importers to pay producers an *ethical* or *fair price*. How can such a "fair trade" arrangement possibly help an importer? If an importer pays a premium for coffee, economic theory tells us that his profits must decline, assuming competition establishes a certain retail price for coffee. Paying more for coffee may enhance his "feel-good index," but it will play havoc with his bottom line.

To overcome this problem, ATOs stamp the packages of coffee with their seal of approval. Thus if the coffee is sold in stores other than ATO outlets, consumers will know which brands of coffee are, in a sense, "ethically correct." ATOs believe that some people are willing to pay a little more for coffee and other products if they are aware of what the extra money is going for. And given the growth in the sales of ATO products, there is an indication that they are correct.

ATOs are most prominent in Switzerland and Germany, home of GEPA,[1] Europe's largest ATO. GEPA, whose sales doubled between 1991 and 1994, sells its products in over 600 "Third-World stores" and GEPA-approved products are sold in some 3,600 supermarkets. Members of the German Bundestag, in fact, have been drinking ATO-approved coffee for the last few years.

Source: Raymond Colitt, "The Growing Force Behind Fair Trade," *Financial Times* (May 5, 1995); p. 4.

Advocates of **fair trade** believe that certain individuals, especially farmers in less-developed countries, do not receive a fair price for their products and, thus, for their efforts. **Alternative trading organizations** are associations that attempt to see that such individuals receive a just or socially ethical return on their labor.

---

international terms of trade, 2 units of wheat per textile, are superior to its new domestic exchange ratio of 4 units of wheat per textile.

The important point is that the gains from trade should be computed by comparing the *current domestic exchange ratio* with the *current international exchange ratio*, not by comparing the current domestic exchange ratio with some ideal international exchange ratio.

Moreover, the Canadian commodity terms of trade may not fall as drastically as first indicated in this example. If the foreign demand for Canadian wheat is elastic, the fall in the price of wheat will lead to an increase in the quantity of wheat demanded. Let's say that as the price of wheat falls from $1 to $.80 per bushel, the quantity of Canadian wheat demanded jumps from 100 to 200 bushels. In this situation, the slide in Canada's terms of trade will be restrained by two developments. First, the price of wheat will not fall as much as one would expect if the demand for Canadian wheat was completely inelastic since the price-induced increase in the quantity of wheat demanded brakes the decline in the price. Second, given the elasticity of demand for Canada's exports, the

---

[1]GEPA, Gesellschaft zur Foerderung der Partnerschaft mit der Dritten Welt, is a public company owned, primarily, by Catholic and Protestant churches.

volume of Canadian exports expands. In fact, even though Canada's commodity terms of trade decline by 20 percent, its income terms of trade improve by 60 percent—(80/100) 200 = 160. Therefore, by one measure Canada is worse off; by another it is better off.

Other scenarios can occur. At one extreme, the demand for Canadian wheat could be completely inelastic so that the quantity of wheat demanded would remain the same regardless of the change in price. In that event, the decline in the commodity terms of trade and the income terms of trade would be equal and depend solely on Canadian production—the greater Canada's production, the more the deterioration in its commodity and income terms of trade.

In the small-country case, the demand for the nation's export is infinitely elastic and all the nation's exports, whatever the amount, can be sold at a given dollar price. Doubling wheat production would have no effect on the commodity terms of trade. And because the commodity terms of trade are constant, a small nation's income terms of trade will double when its production doubles—small is beautiful.

Although the magnitudes of the Canadian example are out of line—a nation's export volume never doubles in a year—the basic thrust of the example is borne out by experience. Box 5.4 shows the commodity and income terms of trade for selected nations and groups of nations. The commodity terms of trade moved both in favor and against all nations during the period—Japan is almost a clear exception to the pattern. And yet, except for developing-country fuel exporters and Germany in the two years following reunification, the income terms of trade of all nations and groups improved.

A Graphical Representation of the Terms of Trade

Figure 5.5 illustrates much of this discussion. Figure 5.5a shows the rest of the world's (ROW) supply and demand for wheat while Figure 5.5b shows the domestic supply and demand for wheat. Initially, the domestic supply, S_0, exceeds domestic demand, D_0, at the world price P_0. Canada, therefore, exports the quantity of q_0–q_2 in Figure 5.5b to the rest of the world. At the initial world price, P_0, the ROW's demand exceeds its supply by the quantity Q_1–Q_2. This amount equals the ROW's imports of wheat from Canada.

Now imagine that Canada's supply curve of wheat shifts to the right, or to S_1, as shown in Figure 5.5b. Due to the increase in the quantity supplied at all price levels, the price of wheat drops to P_1. At the new price, Canada's demand for wheat equals q_1 in Figure 5.5b and quantity supplied by Canadian producers is q_3. Canada now attempts to sell the quantity q_1–q_3 to the ROW. The lower price has two effects: Wheat consumption in the ROW expands to Q_3 and the amount of wheat sold by ROW producers drops to Q_0 since some of these producers cannot compete at the lower price. As a result, the ROW now imports Q_0–Q_3 of wheat from Canada. All these developments are shown in Figure 5.5a. Is Canada better off? The answer depends on what happens to its terms of trade.

Assuming the price of Canada's imports is constant, the Canadian commodity terms of trade fall as the price of exports drops from P_0 to P_1. But Canada's income terms of trade improve because the increase in the quantity sold exceeds the drop in the price so that the dollar volume of exports increases. This can be seen by comparing the

BOX 5.4 The Commodity and Income Terms of Trade

Table 5.9 shows the movement of the commodity and income terms of trade of the three major economies and groups of nations over the last 18 years.

The statistics tell us that the commodity terms of trade of developing countries in general declined over the last two decades while those of the industrialized world improved. These movements in the commodity terms of trade appear to verify the thesis that international trade immiserizes the developing world to the benefit of the developed. But if the performance of fuel and non–fuel exporters is looked at separately, a different picture emerges. The commodity terms of trade of developing country non–fuel exporters remained fairly constant over the period. The drop in their commodity terms of trade in 1976–85 was exactly mirrored by a similar decline in the commodity terms of trade of the industrialized countries. When, however, the income terms of trade are considered, a different picture emerges. The income terms of trade of developing-country non–fuel exporters rose faster than the income terms of trade of any other individual country or group of countries cited. What is the conclusion? Far from immiserizing the developing world, trade has been a positive stimulus for growth.

TABLE 5.9 Commodity Terms of Trade
(annual percentage change)

	1976–85 average	1986–90 average	1991	1992	1993
United States	.4	−1.5	1.7	−.3	.7
Japan	−1.9	5.5	10.2	7.3	8.5
Germany	−1.6	3.5	−2.3	2.5	.8
Industrialized countries	−.3	2.4	1.2	1.5	1.6
Developing countries	2.4	−3.0	−3.0	.0	−1.5
Fuel exporters	5.0	−6.2	−10.9	−1.0	−5.3
Non–fuel exporters	−.3	.0	.1	.2	−.3

Income Terms of Trade
(annual percentage change)

	1976–85 average	1986–90 average	1991	1992	1993
United States	2.7	9.0	9.3	7.5	6.5
Japan	6.6	8.3	12.6	8.9	7.4
Germany	4.0	8.2	−1.1	4.1	−.3
Industrialized countries	4.8	7.8	4.1	5.7	4.0
Developing countries	3.1	6.0	4.4	7.8	7.4
Fuel exporters	.7	1.2	−9.4	1.1	−.4
Non–fuel exporters	6.1	9.7	9.6	10.0	9.8

Source: International Monetary Fund, *World Economic Outlook* (October 1994); pp. 144–145. The income terms of trade were computed from data appearing on these pages.

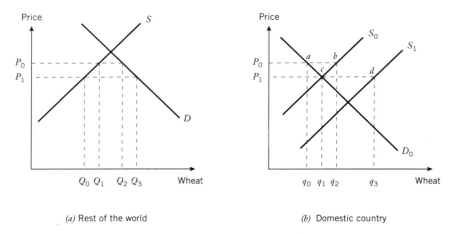

(a) Rest of the world   (b) Domestic country

FIGURE 5.5 The terms of trade: Large country case.

An increase in domestic output of wheat shifts the supply curve of wheat from S_0 to S_1, and reduces the price of wheat from P_0 to P_1. Assuming the price of imports is constant, the commodity terms of trade of the domestic nation will decline. However, the increase in exports, from $q_0–q_2$ to $q_1–q_3$ in panel (b), more than offsets the drop in the price. The nation's income terms of trade will rise since the value of its exports increases from q_0abq_2 to q_1cdq_3.

movement along the vertical axis with the movement along the horizontal axis. It also can be seen by comparing the initial value (price times quantity) of exports with their value following the shift in the domestic supply curve. In the first case, the value of exports equals the rectangle q_0abq_2; in the second, the value of exports equals the rectangle q_1cdq_3. Since the second rectangle is larger than the first, Canada is better off.

The Terms of Trade, Aggregate Demand, and Aggregate Supply

A change in the terms of trade affects aggregate supply and demand, and, thus, the total economy. Suppose worldwide economic expansion raises the price of raw materials throughout the world. How will this affect the commodity and income terms of trade of Uruguay? The possible results are shown in Figure 5.6. On the microlevel, Figure 5.6a, the greater demand for wool raises its worldwide price to Pw_1. Uruguay's commodity and income terms of trade improve. In addition, greater demand shifts Uruguay's export curve to the right, Figure 5.6b, so that Uruguay receives a higher price for any quantity of wool exported. The shift in Uruguay's export curve shifts its aggregate demand curve to the right to AD_1. In addition, Uruguay's aggregate supply curve shifts to AS_1 and its potential income rises from Qn to Qn_1.

Why does Uruguay's aggregate supply curve shift to the right and its potential level of income increase? Recall from Chapter 2 that when the price of imported inputs increased, the domestic aggregate supply curve shifted to the left. Such a shift will reduce any nation's potential level of output. For example, when the OPEC nations raised the

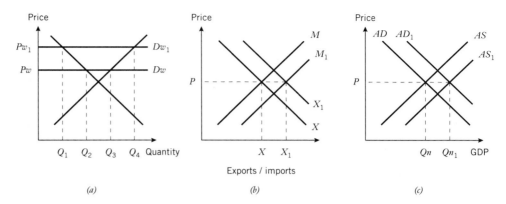

FIGURE 5.6 Export demand and the terms of trade: Small country case.

In the case of a small country, an increase in the demand for its export will raise the price of the export from Pw to Pw_1 in panel (a). From the country's point of view, both measures of the terms of trade improve. In addition, the export curve shifts to the right at all price levels in panel (b). Since the country can obtain more imports from a given amount of resources, or more goods from the same amount of inputs, its potential income rises from Qn to Qn_1 in panel (c) and its aggregate supply curve shifts to the right. The increased purchasing power of exports shifts the aggregate demand curve, in panel (c), to the right and the country's import curve shifts to the right given the higher level of national income, in panel (b).

price of oil in the 1970s, oil importers, in effect, had to work more hours to pay for oil. As a result, they had less time available to devote toward satisfying domestic consumption and investment. If Uruguay, for example, had produced 100 units of wool and had exchanged 10 units of wool for 10 units of oil prior to the increase in the price of oil, it would have ended up with 10 units of oil and 90 units of wool. When, however, the price of oil doubled, Uruguay had to exchange 20 units of wool in order to obtain 10 units of oil. Uruguay was left with only 80 units of wool and 10 units of oil. The people of Uruguay would have worked just as hard but received less.

The argument could be cast in terms of inputs. Imagine that Uruguay had 100 inputs. Prior to the change in the terms of trade, it used, at least indirectly, 10 inputs to purchase oil and the remaining 90 to produce wool for domestic consumption. After the change in the terms of trade, it had only 80 inputs that could be used to produce wool for domestic consumption since 20 units had to be employed producing the wool needed to import 10 units of oil.

The argument can be reversed. We can assume that the price of wool rises or that the price of oil falls or both. If 5 units of wool now exchange for 10 units of oil, Uruguay obtains all the oil it wants with 5 inputs. As a result, 5 inputs are released from producing oil—at least indirectly—and can be used to produce additional goods. Uruguay is quite obviously better off. Given a fixed amount of inputs, it is now able to absorb more goods without running a trade deficit, which means that Uruguay's potential output has risen to a higher level.

Summary

We can see that the more open an economy and the more concentrated its exports, the greater will be the economywide effects of a change in the commodity terms of trade. If exports are concentrated, swings in the world economy from expansion to contraction and back can pull and push the nation's commodity and income terms up and down like a yo-yo. A rough estimate of the maximum effect of a change in the commodity terms of trade can be calculated by multiplying the change in the terms of trade by the trade/GDP ratio. If trade constitutes 30 percent of GDP and the commodity terms of trade deteriorate or improve by 10 percent, a nation could possibly lose or gain 3 percent on its potential GDP. The impact of a change in the income terms of trade, which includes the commodity terms of trade, can be calculated in much the same manner.

We have also seen that nations gain from international trade, whether small or large. And while some nations gain more from trade than others, a nation gives up even its modest gains if it decides to end trade, go it alone, and drop out of the world economy. The theory of comparative advantage demonstrates that international trade raises a nation's productivity, and empirical evidence confirms that trade is an engine of growth. This is important. A majority of the world's population lives in LDCs and often in a state of wretched poverty. But those LDCs that have been outward looking, that have attempted to ride trade and the world economy toward prosperity, have improved themselves markedly more than those countries that have turned inward and their backs on the world economy.

Key Concepts and Terms

absolute advantage

alternative trading organizations and fair trade

buffer stocks

commodity terms of trade

comparative advantage

Compensatory and Contingency Financing Facility

constant and decreasing returns to scale

consumption possibility line

country size and trade

exports and economic growth

importance of being unimportant

income terms of trade

international exchange ratio

inward- versus outward-looking economies

opportunity costs

production possibilities schedules and curves

relative price ratios

Review Questions

1. What is the difference between absolute and comparative advantage?

2. The theory of comparative advantage is a major explanation of international trade. Think of examples of how the theory can be employed to explain trade between individuals who through trade are able to raise their income.

3. The table below shows how many videos and compact discs can be produced in either Canada or the United States if each nation devotes all its resources to producing just one product.

	Videos	*Compact Discs*
Canada	10	15
United States	40	30

(a) In what product does Canada have the comparative advantage?

(b) What are the domestic exchange ratios in each country?

(c) What is the possible range of the international terms of trade?

4. Why would one expect Canada to gain more from trade than the United States? What principle summarizes this result?

5. What is a buffer stock arrangement? What is its purpose? How does it attempt to achieve its end?

6. What is the difference between the commodity terms of trade and the income terms of trade?

7. Consider Figure 5.6. Draw a comparable figure and explain what would happen to a nation's exports, imports, and output if the price of its exports drops.

Suggested Readings and References

References and suggested readings are given at the end of Chapter 6.

Chapter 6

Trade and Prices

Very little international trade is carried out by swapping one product for another. Firms sell goods and services for dollars, marks, yen, and other currencies—not for wheat, textiles, and computer chips. Comparative advantage is still the underlying motive for trade, but exporters and importers are concerned with money prices, not barter arrangements.

The Path Ahead

This chapter starts out by bringing economic theory down to earth, showing how comparative advantage can be translated into money prices, and continues with an explanation of refinements in the theory and practice of international trade that have taken place over the years. Two of these refinements have special relevance in the present world economy: the growth of trade between developed countries and the emergence of several Asian countries as major players in the international economic arena.

We begin with how one converts comparative advantage into money prices and then turn to the implications of developments in international trade theory for trading patterns and countries.

Trade and Money Prices

Imagine that comparative advantage dictates that the United States should export textiles to Canada in exchange for wheat. But if a ton of Canadian wheat costs US $20 while a ton of U.S. wheat costs US $10, *no one* will purchase Canadian wheat regard-

126

less of the potential advantages of such an exchange. But comparative advantage is not an abstraction; it can be illustrated in terms of money costs and prices as in Table 6.1, where the production of bikes and cars in the United States and France is computed in money costs.

Suppose that to produce either a bike or a car in the United States 10 hours of labor are needed, while 15 hours of labor are required in France to produce a bike and 30 are needed to manufacture a car. The United States has an *absolute advantage* in producing *both* commodities, since it needs fewer labor hours to manufacture either commodity. But the United States has a *comparative advantage* in producing cars since the United States requires only one-third of the labor inputs required to make a car in France compared with two-thirds of the inputs needed to construct a bike in France. The theory of comparative advantage tells us that the United States should export cars and import bikes. But Americans will purchase French bikes only if their price is less than the price of the American-made bikes.

Since prices depend primarily on labor costs per unit of output, the wage rate in both countries is crucial. We assume the wage rate is $10 per hour in the United States and FFr20 per hour in France, and that labor costs equal 80 percent of the costs incurred in producing either product, while the remaining 20 percent is payment to capital and other inputs. Thus, it costs $125 in the United States to produce either a bike or a car. Ten units of labor are each paid $10 so that labor costs equal $100, which is 80 percent of the total cost of $125. In France, it costs FFr375 to produce a bike and FFr750 to manufacture a car.

Now, if the exchange rate is FFr4/$ or, equivalently, $.25/FFr, the dollar cost of a French-made bike is $93.75. This is $31.25 less than its American-made counterpart. In France, the cost of an American-made car is FFr500, or FFr250 less than the cost of a comparable French-made automobile. If trade takes place, France will export bikes and import cars.

If either wages or exchange rates fall out of line, trade may become unbalanced and the world may be unable to reap the benefits of comparative advantage. For example, if the U.S. wage rate rises above $15 an hour, it will cost more to produce a car in the United States than in France, and France will export both goods to the United States. If the French wage rate rises over FFr26.67, the French will purchase U.S.-made bikes. If wages and productivity remain constant and the exchange rate of the dollar climbs to FFr6/$ or higher, France will export both goods. On the other hand, if the dollar falls to FFr3/$, the United States will become the sole exporter.

TABLE 6.1 Production Costs: France and the United States

	France		USA	
	Bikes	*Cars*	*Bikes*	*Cars*
Labor Inputs	15	30	10	10
Wage Rate	FFr20	FFr20	$10	$10
Labor Costs	FFr300	FFr600	$100	$100
Total Costs	FFr375	FFr750	$125	$125
Exchange Rate	$.25/FFr		4FFr/$	
Franc Costs	FFr375	FFr750	FFr500	FFr500
Dollar Costs	$93.75	$187.50	$125	$125

Testing the Ricardian Theory

The Ricardian theory of comparative advantage, named after its founder David Ricardo, argues that comparative advantage is based on differences in labor productivity between countries.

This explanation of comparative advantage that is based on labor productivity is normally called the **Ricardian theory of comparative advantage,** after its founder David Ricardo. The British economist Donald MacDougal was among the first to test its validity. MacDougal examined 25 industries and postulated that since U.S. wages were double British wages, U.S. productivity would have to be double the corresponding UK productivity in a particular industry if America was to be the dominant exporter of that product. If U.S. productivity was four times the British level in a certain industry, U.S. exports would be, say, double British exports in third markets. If U.S. productivity were double the British level in a second industry, the ratio of U.S. to UK exports in third markets would be, say, one. MacDougal adjusted the productivity figures for relative wage rates since differences in productivity may be offset by differences in relative wage rates. Some of MacDougal's findings are presented in Table 6.2.

The last two columns of Table 6.2 are the more important ones. Column 2 measures exchange-rate-adjusted relative labor costs per unit of output and, together with column 3, shows the relationship between labor costs per unit of output and relative shares of exports. Although the labor cost/export relationship is not perfect (glass containers are substantially out of line), the correlation is strong enough to show that labor costs per unit of output are important in determining trade patterns.

A Multiproduct Model

MacDougal's approach and findings can be illustrated by adding a third industry to the France/United States example. If 10 labor hours are required to produce a moped in the United States while 25 hours are required to manufacture one in France, the dollar price of a moped would be $125 and the franc price would be either FFr625 or, considering the given exchange rate, $156.25. Under these assumptions, the United States would export mopeds. MacDougal's study suggests that the ratio of U.S. exports/French exports to Latin America would be greater in the case of cars than in the case of mopeds. The greater relative productivity of the United States in automobiles compared with mopeds would translate into a larger price differential in favor of cars for the United States.

Which nation will export a particular commodity or be the dominant exporter in third markets depends on the following relationship:

$$(L)(W) = (L^*)(W^*)(e)$$

L and L^* represent the number of labor hours required to produce a particular good in the United States and France, W and W^* equal American and French wage rates, and e is the exchange rate, assumed to be $.25/FFr. The equation can be rearranged:

$$L/L^* = (W^*)(e)/W$$

TABLE 6.2 Ratio of U.S. to UK Exports in Third Markets

Industry	(1) Output per Worker US/UK	(2) Unit Costs US/UK	(3) Exports US/UK
Pig iron	3.6	0.4	5.100
Cars	3.1	0.6	4.300
Machinery	2.7	0.7	1.500
Glass containers	2.4	0.8	3.500
Paper	2.2	0.9	1.000
Cigarettes	1.7	0.9	0.470
Leather footwear	1.4	1.1	0.320
Hosiery	1.8	1.1	0.320
Cotton spinning and weaving	1.5	1.1	0.110
Beer	2.0	1.3	0.060
Cement	1.1	1.5	0.100
Woollen and worsted	1.4	1.5	0.004
Male outer wool clothing	1.2	1.8	0.040

Source: G.D.A. MacDougal, "British and American Exports: A Study Suggested by the Theory of Comparative Costs," *Economic Journal* 61 (December 1951); Table III, p. 707. Reprinted with permission from Blackwell Publishers Ltd. on behalf of the Royal Economic Society. Unit costs refer to labor costs per unit of output. The figures have been rounded.

If $L/L^* < (W^*)(e)/W$, the United States will export the good. Consider the case of cars. Placing the assumed values into the previous equation yields the following result, which indicates that the United States will export cars:

$$10/30 < (20)(.25)/10$$
$$1/3 < 1/2$$

If the right-hand side of the equation is less than the left-hand side, France will export cars. If the two sides of the equation are equal, France and the United States will neither export nor import cars to each other and their export shares in third markets will be roughly equal.

If $(W^*)(e)/W$ equals .5, American productivity in a given industry must be at least double the comparable level in France if the United States is to export the good, or since labor productivity was calculated as the number of labor inputs needed to produce a commodity, the number of U.S. labor inputs required must be less than half the number required in France. The U.S./French ratio of labor inputs for cars, mopeds, and bikes are .33, .4, and .67 respectively. The United States, therefore, should export the first two products to France and import the last one from France. In third markets, the ratio of American to French exports might be something like 4, 1.5, and .25 respectively.

The model can be extended to encompass many products. Assume there are five products: A, B, C, D, and E. Each product can be compared to other products according to labor inputs required to produce a given unit. Thus $L_A/L^*_A < L_B/L^*_B < L_C/L^*_C < L_D/L^*_D < L_E/L^*_E$, meaning that, relatively speaking, the United States needs less labor inputs compared to France to produce product A compared to product B, less for B than C, and so forth. If it turns out that the United States exports products A through

C, the final equation would look like this: $L_A/L^*_A < L_B/L^*_B < L_C/L^*_C < [(W^*)(e)/W] < L_D/L^*_D < L_E/L^*_E$. The American comparative advantage would decline as one moved from product A to C and the French comparative advantage would increase as one moved from product D to E. Any changes in W^*, e, or W would change the exports of both countries, but not their relative rates of productivity and their comparative advantages.

Expanding the Number of Countries

The model can also be extended to include more than two countries, although why this is so is not readily apparent. The previous example argued that if fewer inputs are required to produce a certain product in the United States than are needed to produce it in France, the United States will export the good. Why then should any country purchase the French product?

If the product is produced under conditions of increasing costs, a greater demand for the product will lead to higher production costs in the United States and U.S. firms will have to charge a higher price. The effect of increasing production costs and relative export shares is shown in Figure 6.1. Country A is clearly the low-cost producer and Country C is just as clearly the high-cost producer. Country B lies somewhere between these two extremes.

Assuming trade takes place, Country A, the low-cost producer, will begin to step up its production. But as it does, its production costs will begin to rise. There comes a point when Country A's higher costs of production will equal production costs in Country B. If Country C still has an excess demand for the product at the higher price, both countries A and B will expand their production to meet Country C's demand. In equilibrium, the world price will settle at Pw and the excess demand of Country C will be satisfied by the excess supply of Country A plus the excess supply of Country B. Both A and B export the good to C.

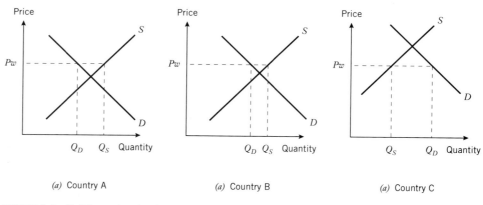

(a) Country A   (a) Country B   (a) Country C

FIGURE 6.1 Multicountry trade.

At the world price Pw, Country C's demand for personal computers exceeds its supply. The country satisfies its excess demand for personal computers at the world price by importing them. The bulk of its imports come from Country A, and a smaller amount comes from Country B.

Competitiveness and Exports

Economists have questioned some of the example's assumptions. Labor costs as a percent of total costs vary among industries and wages are not similar across industries in each country. However, if one uses labor costs per unit of output, the second problem is eliminated. Third, the example assumed that the exchange rate was fixed, but exchange rates have varied markedly over the last decade-plus. Prices, however, can be adjusted for variations in exchange rates.

Despite shortcomings, the Ricardian framework has been employed to measure relative competitive positions of nations in the world economy, especially for international trade in manufacturing. Table 6.3 shows the compound rate of growth of manufacturing exports for several nations measured in physical units from 1980 to 1990. It also shows the compound rate of growth of labor costs per unit of output in manufacturing and changes in trade-weighted exchange rates.

Table 6.3 does not contain specific figures on labor productivity and wage rates, but their effects are captured by the figures on labor costs per unit of output. If labor productivity advances at a faster rate than the increase in wage rates, as in the case of Japan, then labor costs per unit of output will decline.

Competitiveness also depends on the exchange rate or, more specifically, the trade-weighted or multilateral exchange rate—this concept is spelled out in detail in Chapter 11. A change in a nation's competitive position is computed by adding the percentage change in its labor costs per unit of output and the percentage change in its multilateral exchange rate. The resulting figure is then multiplied by -1 so that a positive sum of changes in labor costs and the exchange rate indicates a decrease in competitiveness. Between 1985 and 1990, Japanese labor costs per unit of output fell by .2 percent per

TABLE 6.3   Unit Labor Costs, Exchange Rate, Competitiveness (Competitive), and Manufactured (Mfrd) Exports
(compound annual rates of growth: 1980–85, 1985–90)

	Labor Costs		Exchange Rate		Competitive		Mfrd Exports	
	1980–85 (1)	1985–90 (2)	1980–85 (3)	1985–90 (4)	1980–85 (5)	1985–90 (6)	1980–85 (7)	1985–90 (8)
Canada	6.3%	4.5%	−.7%	.6%	−5.6%	−5.1%	8.6%	5.0%
France	8.3	.4	−5.1	.9	−3.2	−1.3	1.7	6.9
Germany	2.7	2.6	3.2	3.6	−2.7	−6.2	3.8	4.3
Italy	10.9	4.2	−6.1	0.0	−4.8	−4.2	4.9	2.4
Japan	−.9	−.2	5.6	4.7	−4.7	−4.5	7.6	2.6
Sweden	5.7	7.0	−4.7	−1.2	−1.0	−5.8	6.0	2.6
UK	3.1	3.5	−3.2	−1.1	.1	−2.4	1.2	6.0
US	1.8	0.0	9.3	−9.2	−11.1	9.2	−3.9	10.5

Sources: Labor costs per unit of output were computed from data presented in U.S. Department of Labor, *Monthly Labor Review* (November 1991). Manufactured exports were calculated from the United Nations' *Monthly Statistical Bulletin* (December 1991). Exchange rate variations are based on data presented in the International Monetary Fund, *International Financial Statistics Yearbook*, 1991.

annum, but the yen appreciated by 4.7 percent per year. Simply summing the two figures would lead to the conclusion that Japan's competitiveness increased 4.5 percent per annum when it actually fell by that amount.

Table 6.3 shows the change in the competitive position of some major countries. Between 1980 and 1985, Canada's labor costs rose 6.3 percent per year, which decreased its competitiveness by that amount. However, the decline in Canadian competitiveness was partially offset by the depreciation of the Canadian dollar, so the net decrease in Canada's competitiveness was 5.6 percent per year. In France and Italy, wage expansion was countered by hefty depreciations of the franc and the lira. In the same period, U.S. labor costs per unit of output in manufacturing rose at a modest rate of 1.8 percent per year. Yet the combination of productivity growth and wage restraint in the United States was swamped by the appreciation of the dollar and, as a result, America's competitiveness fell at an annual rate of 11.1 percent.

If the Ricardian theory is correct, there should be a relation between a nation's export performance and its competitiveness. Table 6.4 ranks nations by competitiveness (CR) and exports (XR) and attempts, crudely, to see if exports and competitiveness are linked.

The figures are discouraging, especially those for 1980 to 1985, and in particular the rankings of Canada, Japan, and the United Kingdom. The figures for 1985–90 are better but far from outstanding. The fit is perfect as regards the United States in both periods and the Japanese fit is much improved in the second period. Since the international value of the dollar fluctuated more widely than other currencies in both periods and the yen appreciated more than any other currency in the second period—even including a sharp depreciation of the yen in 1990—the figures confirm the importance of the exchange rate in determining a nation's international competitiveness in the short run.

Because a country's export performance depends on many factors, it is a mistake to pinpoint just three. For example, the decrease in the rate of growth of Japan's exports was not due solely to the appreciation of the yen. Many countries erected trade barriers with the sole purpose of restricting Japanese exports into their domestic markets. Canada's robust export performance in the first period, despite the relative deterioration in its competitive position, is explained partly by the strong economic performance of its major trading partner, the United States. Nevertheless, competitiveness is still important since an increase in labor costs per unit of output, for example, will hurt a nation's trade position even if other factors are improving it.

TABLE 6.4 Competitive Rank [CR] and Export Rank [XR]

	1980–85		1985–90	
	CR	**XR**	**CR**	**XR**
Canada	7	1	8	4
France	4	6	2	2
Germany	3	4	7	5
Italy	6	5	4	8
Japan	5	2	5	6/7
Sweden	2	3	6	6/7
UK	1	7	3	3
US	8	8	1	1

Source: Computed from Table 6.3.

BOX 6.1 The Exchange Rate and Competitiveness

In the early 1990s, U.S. car producers made a strong comeback in the American car market. Japanese car makers lost about 4 percent of their share of the American market between 1991 and 1993 while the Big Three American car makers boosted their market share to 70 percent. Much has been made of the American car companies' ability to emulate Japanese production techniques and produce a better-quality car more efficiently—an often-overlooked benefit of international trade. Less attention has been paid to the effect of yen appreciation.

The cost differential between American and Japanese car manufacturers has markedly narrowed. In 1982, Japanese production costs were approximately 60 percent of U.S. production costs; in 1992, production costs were almost equal when measured in dollars (Table 6.5). The number of direct labor hours needed to produce a car in the United States declined roughly 24 percent over the same 10 years. However, the Japanese did not stand still. The number of labor hours required to produce a car in Japan fell roughly 18 percent, a gain for U.S. producers but hardly a breakthrough. (Labor costs include wages and benefits paid to workers within the firm and wages paid to workers outside the firm to produce materials needed to build a car. The latter costs are not calculated but are included under such items as components and materials purchased.)

The big gain in the cost advantage of American car producers came from the appreciation of the yen, which rose 61 percent over the period. To be exact, 90 percent of the 68 percent increase in the dollar cost of producing a car in Japan can be attributed to the appreciation of the yen. The yen has continued to appreciate against the dollar since that time.

TABLE 6.5 U.S. and Japanese Automobile Production Costs (production costs for small cars)

1982: Exchange rate Y240/$

	US	Japan
Labor Compensation	$23.31	$11.91
Labor Hours per Car	84	51
Labor Costs	$1950.00	$603.00
Components & Materials	$3548.00	$2858.00
Total Costs*	$7285.00	$4363.00

1992: Exchange rate Y130/$

	US	Japan
Labor Compensation	$31.97	$25.78
Labor Hours per Car	64	42
Labor Costs	$2057.00	$1071.00
Components & Materials	$4202.00	$4818.00
Total Costs	$7436.00	$7313.00

Source: Clyde V. Prestowitz, Jr. and Paul S. Willen, *The Future of the Auto Industry: It Can Compete, Can It Survive?* (Washington, DC: Economic Strategy Institute, 1992), Tables 1.8 and 1.9, pp. 15–16. Total costs in 1982 are adjusted for the rate of capacity utilization and certain costs have not been listed.

The Heckscher-Ohlin Theorem

Factor intensity measures the relative use of a factor of production in producing a product. Electrical generation, for example, requires a lot of capital and, relatively speaking, little labor. By comparison, textiles production requires relatively more labor than capital.

The **Heckscher-Ohlin theorem,** named after Eli Heckscher and Bertil Ohlin, claims that trade is based on differences in relative factor endowments.

Because international trade is based on more than just the distribution of natural resources and labor productivity, other economists have come forward to explain the existence of comparative advantage. An elaborate theory of international trade was developed by Swedish economists Eli Heckscher and Bertil Ohlin. Heckscher and Ohlin postulated that various commodities are produced with different relative quantities of land, labor, and capital—known as **factor intensity.** For example, if the ratio of land to labor used to produce wheat is higher than the ratio of land to labor used to produce textiles, as is the case, wheat production is relatively land intensive when compared with textile production.

According to the **Heckscher-Ohlin (H-O) theorem,** wheat will tend to be produced in countries where land, when measured by world standards, is *relatively* abundant, that is, in those nations where the quantity of land relative to labor is high when compared with other nations—the United States compared to the Netherlands, for example. Given the relative abundance of land in one country compared with another, the *relative* price of land compared with the price of labor will be lower in the first country than in the second.

In fact, wheat is produced in countries such as Australia, Canada, and the United States where land is relatively abundant and the population density is low. By contrast, poultry production tends to be labor intensive rather than land intensive. Thus, poultry products should be produced where labor is relatively abundant and relatively cheap rather than where labor is relatively scarce and relatively expensive. Denmark, for example, should produce poultry, not wheat.

The United States, of course, produces both wheat and poultry and may be more efficient than Denmark in producing both commodities. Nevertheless, its comparative advantage would lie in wheat production due to its high land/labor ratio and the resulting relatively low price of land compared with labor in the United States. The low price of land means that it is cheaper to produce wheat in the United States.

Most expositions of the Heckscher-Ohlin theorem utilize capital/labor ratios and the relative prices of capital and labor to explain trade. Steel production, for example, normally requires substantial amounts of capital relative to labor, while, by comparison, the manufacture of textiles requires less capital and more labor. This does not mean that a unit of steel can only be produced with 5 parts capital to 1 part labor since steel can be produced by many combinations of capital and labor (for political and psychological reasons the Chinese produced, or attempted to produce, steel in backyard furnaces in the hinterland). But with the exception noted in the footnote to this discussion most expositions of the H-O theorem suggest that regardless of the level of output and the relative price of capital to labor, steel production will require a higher capital/labor ratio than textile production. It follows that steel should be produced in a country where capital is abundant and relatively cheap rather than in a country where capital is scarce and relatively expensive.*

---

*It is possible that the initial capital/labor ratio utilized in producing a good may change as production expands, what is called **factor reversal.** For example, steel production may start out employing labor-intensive techniques of production but change to capital-intensive production techniques as output expands. If such factor reversals are common, it will be difficult to determine which country will export (import) what good based on relative factor endowments.

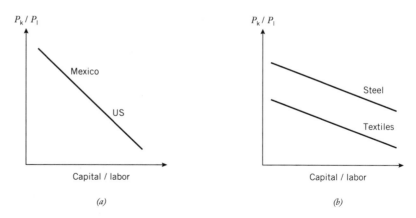

FIGURE 6.2 Factor price ratios, factor proportions, and production.

Regardless of the relative price of capital compared to labor, *Pk/Pl* in panel (b), steel production requires a relatively higher capital-to-labor ratio than textile production. The relative price of capital-to-labor, *Pk/Pl* in panel (a), depends on the relative amounts of capital and labor available. If we assume that the United States is heavily endowed with capital relative to labor compared with Mexico, the relative price of capital will be cheaper in the United States than in Mexico. This means, other things remaining equal, that it will be relatively cheaper to produce steel in the United States compared to Mexico.

The basic thesis of the Heckscher-Ohlin (H-O) theorem can be understood with the help of Figure 6.2. Figure 6.2a shows the relative price of capital and labor on the vertical axis and quantities of capital and labor on the horizontal axis. The relative price of capital declines as the quantity of capital increases relative to the quantity of labor. Thus, the relative price of capital will be low in the United States (point U.S.) compared to the price in Mexico (point Mex), because the United States is a relatively capital-abundant nation and Mexico is a relatively labor-abundant nation.

Now consider Figure 6.2b. It shows the capital/labor ratios that will be employed to produce certain quantities of steel and textiles given the relative price ratio of capital to labor. The relative price of capital is measured on the vertical axis and the potential capital/labor ratios for producing units of steel and units of textiles on the horizontal axis. As the relative price of capital falls, both steel and textiles will be produced by more capital-intensive methods. The point to be stressed is that at all relative prices of capital and labor, steel production is *more capital intensive* than textile production. This can be shown by drawing a horizontal line, representing a certain capital/labor price ratio, from any point on the vertical axis and then reading off the capital/labor ratios used to produce both textiles and steel on the horizontal axis. The implication is that given national endowments of capital and labor and their relative prices, the capital-abundant nation will produce steel while the labor-abundant nation will manufacture textiles.

In sum, the Heckscher-Ohlin theorem asserts that nations will export commodities produced with large proportional amounts of their abundant factor and import goods produced with high proportional amounts of their scarce factor. According to the theory, the United States, heavily endowed with capital relative to labor, will export capital-intensive goods and import labor-intensive goods. Through trade, the United States will exchange what it has a lot of (capital) for what it has little of (labor).

The Leontief Paradox

The **Leontief paradox** emerged when Wassily Leontief discovered that the production of U.S. exports was relatively labor intensive compared to the production of U.S. import substitutes. Leontief's findings refuted the Heckscher-Ohlin theorem—at least in the case of the United States.

The **third factor of production** has been used to explain the Leontief paradox. Thus, trade is based on more than just capital and labor. Raw materials and all types of skills of labor plus other factors can explain trade.

The Heckscher-Ohlin theorem has become the dominant theory of international trade, and much analysis has been cast in terms of the H-O model. But a study by Wassily Leontief raised questions about the theory, at least in its rudimentary form. Leontief's study of U.S. trade patterns revealed that the capital/labor ratio of domestically produced importable goods was higher than the capital/labor ratio of exports. In other words, the U.S. exported goods with a relatively low capital/labor ratio and imported commodities which, when produced in the United States, had a relatively high capital/labor ratio.

The **Leontief paradox** has not completely undermined the H-O framework since other studies have verified its relevance in other instances. Instead, the Leontief paradox led to extensions and refinements of the basic H-O model. One of these refinements is **the third factor of production.** For example, if all U.S. imports have a high raw material content, or absorb raw materials which are scarce and expensive in the United States, then American imports would depend primarily on raw materials and not on capital/labor ratios. In fact, the United States is short of raw materials compared with capital and labor, and imports goods with a high raw material content regardless of capital/labor intensities.

The third factor explanation has been extended to include items such as skilled labor and research and development (R&D) expenditures. Since the United States has an abundant supply of skilled labor, it exports scientific and professional equipment. Lacking unskilled labor, it imports products such as textiles, shoes, and many traditional manufactures.

Research and development expenditures also explain trade patterns. Studies indicate that U.S. exports have a high R&D component—the chemical, drug, aircraft, and computer industries, for example. In fact, the share of these industries in total U.S. manufacturing exports is greater than their proportion of total U.S. manufactured output. In industries with a low R&D profile, measured either by research and development expenditures as a percentage of total expenditures or the proportion of scientists employed to total employees, their percentage of national production is greater than their percentage of national exports.

Some observers have also cited managerial talent to explain trade patterns. For example, managers in the U.S. food-processing industry are cited as being better than their foreign competitors, while Japanese car managers are listed as being the best in the world. Given free trade (decidedly not the case regarding cars), one would expect the Japanese to export cars and the United States to export processed foods, which, in fact, is the case.

If international trade depends solely on labor costs per unit of output, a noninflationary economic policy alone would help a nation maintain its competitive position. But if a nation's competitive position is based on labor skills, R&D, and the like, other policies are necessary to enhance its competitiveness. If a nation's exports depend on a skilled labor force, then the nation should be sure to foster its educational system. To the extent that its exports are based on R&D, a nation needs to train scientists and, through the tax code, encourage expenditures in that area. In other words, the theory of comparative advantage helps to establish the foundations for public policy. If a nation has no raw materials, it cannot create them from thin air. It can, however, develop other talents or resources which will otherwise give it an edge and then use this comparative advantage to import raw materials.

Recent Developments in Trade Theory

Intraindustry trade occurs if a country both exports and imports the same commodity.

Trade theory has taken new twists in recent decades due to the growth of **intraindustry** trade and the export performance of several Asian nations. Intraindustry trade defies traditional trade theory: The H-O theorem, for example, is hard-pressed to explain why the major OECD nations should trade among themselves and simultaneously export and import the same products. And yet these countries do just that and on a grand scale, as Tables 6.6 and 6.8 attest.

The theory of comparative advantage tells us that trade between developed countries (DCs) and less-developed countries (LDCs) should have grown over time as a proportion of total trade. Yet from 1965–1990 there was only a *slight* tendency for DCs to increase their imports from LDCs, with only a modest expansion in the early 1990s. The substantial expansion of LDC exports to developed nations from the middle 1970s to the early 1980s can be accounted for by the hefty increase in the price of oil. As the price of oil eased, the value of trade between developed and less-developed nations fell back toward its 1970 position. Hence, there is little evidence that trade is grounded exclusively on relative endowments of capital and labor, skilled and unskilled labor, and so forth.

The figures in Table 6.6 mask the second development which though it fits the mold of traditional trade theory, modified the way economists look at trade and alarmed policy makers: namely, the export performance of Hong Kong, Korea, Singapore, Taiwan and China, and other Asian countries. Granted their *share* of the world's exports of manufactures is dwarfed by those of the big three—United States (12.2 percent),

TABLE 6.6 Developed Nations' Export and Import Shares: 1965–1990

	Exports to			Imports from	
Year	DCs	LDCs		DCs	LDCs
1965	74.4%	21.0%		73.7%	22.6
1970	67.3	18.8		69.5	20.2
1975	65.3	27.9		66.5	29.6
1980	67.5	27.3		63.9	32.1
1985	72.5	24.1		70.1	27.4
1990	76.0	21.5		74.0	23.9

Sources: Figures were computed from International Monetary Fund, *Direction of Trade Statistics Yearbook*, various issues. Former communist bloc nations are not included in either category.

TABLE 6.7 Merchandise Exports: Selected Countries

Country	Share 1994	Rank 1980	Rank 1994
Hong Kong	3.6%	24	9
China	2.9	31	11
Singapore	2.3	26	12
Korea	2.3	32	13
Taiwan	2.2	23	15

Source: World Trade Organization, *International Trade: Trends and Statistics*, 1995 (Geneva: World Trade Organization 1995); p. 12.

Germany (10.5 percent), and Japan (9.4 percent)—nevertheless their relative *ranking* improved at a rapid clip (Table 6.7).

The rise in rank of these five countries is coupled with the fact that a large percentage of the exports of these five countries is directed toward developed countries. For example, the value of China's manufactured exports to the United States jumped from $1.1 billion in 1980 to $31.5 billion in 1993, an annual growth rate of 29 percent. The explanations and implications of these nations' export expansion are discussed later. Now it is time to look at intraindustry trade more closely.

Intraindustry Trade

Trade among developed countries is dominated by intraindustry trade. In 1994, the United States *exported* $252 billion of machinery and transport equipment, but it also *imported* $315 billion of machinery and transport equipment. Thus, its degree of intraindustry trade in these products was roughly 89 percent (how the degree of intraindustry trade is measured is taken up in Box 6.2). By comparison, the United States imported $38.6 billion of clothing in 1994, but exported only $5.6 billion of clothing in the same year, an intraindustry trade ratio of 25.3 percent. However, U.S. imports of machinery and equipment were 8 times larger than its imports of clothing and the ratio of U.S. exports of machinery and equipment to clothing was even larger. The data illustrate the relative importance of intraindustry trade for the United States and also the relative importance of trade among developed countries. The United States exported and imported machinery and transport equipment to and from developed countries while it imported clothing primarily from LDCs.

Table 6.8 indicates the degree of intraindustry trade by listing the six leading exporters and importers of machinery and transport equipment, office machines and telecommunications equipment, and automotive products. By themselves, the tables do not show the degree of intraindustry trade for a given country in a particular industry, although it can be calculated from the tables in most instances.

One would expect larger countries to dominate the rankings of exporters and importers. However, according to both the H-O model and the Ricardian framework, na-

TABLE 6.8 Major Exporters/Importers in Selected Product Groups, 1994 (billions of dollars)

Machinery and Transport Equipment

Exporters		Importers	
Japan	$284.6	United States	$314.6
United States	252.3	Germany	127.3
Germany	208.1	UK	90.6
France	91.9	France	80.5
UK	83.0	Canada	76.2
Italy	69.9	Japan	52.7

Office Machines and Telecommunications Equipment

Exporters		Importers	
Japan	$94.5	United States	$113.7
United States	79.0	Germany	35.8
Singapore	32.3	UK	29.2
UK	27.7	Japan	22.8
Germany	24.8	France	19.8
Malaysia	24.5	Singapore	19.0

Automotive Products

Exporters		Importers	
Japan	$82.4	United States	$102.8
Germany	70.5	Germany	35.3
United States	49.6	Canada	32.0
Canada	40.9	UK	24.7
France	28.4	France	22.2
Belgium	21.7	Italy	14.8

Source: World Trade Organization, *International Trade: Trends and Statistics,* 1995 (Geneva: World Trade Organization 1995); pp. 102, 106, 112. Because figures for Hong Kong include significant re-exports and imports for re-export, they have not been listed. Singapore's figures are for domestic exports and retained imports only. Belgium = Belgium-Luxembourg.

tions may produce and consume a whole range of products, but a given nation should not be a major exporter and importer of a particular product at the same time. Only one nation, Japan, fits the traditional mold; it is a major exporter and, at best, a weak importer of the products listed. But it should be noted that the Japanese record, its lack of intraindustry trade, is viewed by many of its trading partners as proof that Japan unfairly restricts its markets.

Consider Table 6.9, listing clothing exports and imports. Trade in clothing follows the pattern of comparative advantage. Clothing production tends to be labor intensive, so it is produced and exported by nations having an abundance of unskilled labor. Clothing is imported primarily by countries well endowed with capital and skilled labor but short of unskilled labor.

TABLE 6.9 Major Exporters/Importers of Clothing: 1994 (billions of dollars)

Exporters		Importers	
China	$23.7	United States	$38.6
Italy	12.5	Germany	22.4
Hong Kong	9.5	Japan	15.3
Germany	6.6	France	9.1
Korea	5.6	UK	7.3
United States	5.6	Netherlands	5.0

Source: World Trade Organization, *International Trade: Trends and Statistics*, 1995 (Geneva: World Trade Organization 1995); p. 124. Hong Kong's exports do not include re-exports.

BOX 6.2   Measuring Intradindustry Trade

Table 6.10 is a replica of Table 4.3. The data contained in the table can be used to construct a crude index of intraindustry trade for the United States in 1994.

TABLE 6.10   U.S. Merchandise Trade by End Use: 1994 (billions of dollars)

Exports	**$502**
Foods, feeds, & beverages	42
Industrial supplies & materials	121
Capital goods	206
Automotive goods	57
Consumer goods	603
Other goods	16
Imports	**$669**
Foods, feeds, & beverages	31
Industrial supplies & materials	165
Capital goods	184
Automotive goods	119
Consumer goods	146
Other goods	24

Source: U.S. Department of Commerce, *Survey of Current Business* (March 1995): p. 64.

There are various methods of constructing an intraindustry trade index. The method employed here is true to the more traditional methods of computing the degree of international trade and provides an introduction to how an index number is constructed. (Since exports and imports of other goods, taken together, are a catchall item, they are ignored in what follows.)

The first step in constructing an index of intraindustry trade is to compute the degree of intraindustry trade in each category of exports and imports using the following formula:

$$IT_i = 1 - \frac{|X_i - M_i|}{X_i + M_i}$$

In the formula, IT_i equals the degree of international trade in a particular industry, i; $|X_i - M_i|$ equals the absolute value of the difference between exports and imports in the industry; and $X_i + M_i$ equals the total value of exports and imports in the industry. For example, American exports and imports of foods, feeds, and beverages were \$42 and \$31 billion respectively in 1994. The degree of intraindustry trade in this group was $1 - [(42 - 31)/(42 + 31)]$ or $1 - (11/73)$ or .85, a relatively high degree of international trade.

In Table 6.11, the intraindustry trade index for each product group is placed in the column headed IT Index. The values in the column labeled Weight measure the relative importance of each product group. Thus the weight for foods, feeds, and beverages equals the sum of the exports and imports in this group divided by the sum of total exports and imports, or $73/1030 = .0646$—recall that other goods have been dropped from the calculations. The last column, Weight times Index, is the product of the first two columns. A nation's intraindustry trade index equals the sum of the last column. The index of .78 indicates that the United States has a high degree of intraindustry trade.

Using the figures in Table 6.8, intraindustry trade indexes consisting of the three produce groups listed can be constructed for three major countries: United States .83, Germany .75, and Japan .31.

TABLE 6.11 Degree of Intraindustry Trade: Major Product Groups; 1994

Product Groups	IT Index	Weight	Weight times Index
Foods, feeds, & beverages	.85	.06	.05
Industrial supplies & materials	.85	.25	.21
Capital goods	.94	.34	.32
Automotive goods	.65	.16	.10
Consumer goods	.58	.18	.10
IT Index for the nation			.78

Source: Computed from Table 6.10. The figures have been rounded.

Representative Demand and Intraindustry Trade

Staffan Linder attempted to explain the prevalence of intraindustry trade through the theory of **representative demand.** Representative demand is comprised of several elements, the major one being *income per capita.* Linder hypothesized that nations with similar incomes per capita will trade with each other. Why? Most products are developed for domestic markets, which means that a U.S. manufacturer will concentrate on the American market first before looking toward overseas markets. Commodities generated for the American market tend to be labor-saving and sophisticated due to the relative shortage of labor in the United States and the high American

Representative demand is a concept introduced by Staffan Linder to explain intraindustry trade. While it is composed of many elements, the representative demand of any country, what it will buy, depends on income per capita.

Quite often the benefits of mass production are described by the terms **scale economies** or **decreasing costs.** Due to high startup costs, unit costs of production decline as output expands. However, after some point, unit costs will start to rise. But the assumption of scale economies is that this point will not be reached until output has substantially increased.

per capita income that permits its citizens to purchase expensive, sophisticated products. (A sizable proportion of intraindustry trade consists of trade in intermediate goods such as semiconductors, fuel injectors, and parts of all types in addition to trade in final products.)

Most capital goods produced in the United States and other developed nations are noted for their labor-saving and raw-material-saving characteristics. But how does trade evolve if manufacturers innovate and introduce new products for the domestic market? Many products are produced under what are called **scale economies** or **decreasing costs,** which means that a firm's average unit costs of production will fall as output expands. For example, a motorcycle manufacturer may have high startup costs due to the need for high capital investment, large R&D expenditures, and the cost of setting up marketing channels. The firm must pay these fixed costs whether it produces one or one million motorcycles. As the firm produces more motorcycles, the fixed costs can be distributed over a larger number of them. As a result, average costs per unit of output decline as production expands. If fixed costs are $1 million, they will average $10,000 per unit when 100 motorcycles are produced, $1,000 per unit if 1000 motorcycles are made, and $100 per unit if 10,000 are produced.

If the key to higher profits is greater production, the key to greater production is a larger market. Foreign markets, therefore, could be vital to the firm's success. But not just any foreign market will do. A firm needs to direct its production toward effective markets, one in which consumers are willing and able to purchase the product. A microwave oven designed to satisfy demand in the United States, for example, will probably find more customers in Germany than in Bangladesh. Honda builds station wagons in the United States, its major market for the vehicle, but exports them to Japan and Europe, which have high GDP per capita like the United States. Products with a high R&D content, such as pharmaceuticals, are another example. A higher volume of sales will reduce the level of R&D expenditures per unit sold and build up the firm's potential profits. Effective markets for pharmaceuticals are greatest in developed nations.

The New Theory of International Trade

The implications of the theory of effective demand have been extended by what is often called the **new theory of international trade,** associated with the pioneering work of Paul Krugman and others. The new theory does not argue that traditional trade theory should be abandoned, but rather that trade need not be based exclusively on relative factor endowments or even on comparative advantage as commonly defined. Scale economies or decreasing costs of production may be the crucial factor in determining a nation's trading patterns.

Differentiated products. A car is a car, but a Ford is different from a Chevy.

The new theory argues that most intraindustry trade, and therefore most trade between developed countries, is carried out by monopolistic producers. Because such firms manufacture **differentiated products,** they are able to avoid some of the rigors normally associated with a competitive market, although by no means can they sit back on their haunches, charge whatever they want for their products, and still maintain their market shares. It implies that rather than being strict price takers, they have some latitude in setting prices and may sell their product at different prices in various markets in order to gain a bigger share of the world market (a point investigated further in the discussion of dumping in Chapter 8).

What are the important implications of the new theory of trade? If the majority of intraindustry trade is conducted by monopolistic or oligopolistic firms it does not mean that trade is bad for a society. On the contrary, monopolistic competition is a compelling reason to *promote trade*. There are only three domestic automobile manufacturers in the United States and without trade they would monopolize car production in the United States. And given that monopoly position, it is a safe bet that they would raise their prices and might let the quality of their products slip. (For example, after Japan agreed to restrict exports of Japanese cars to the United States in 1981, the price of new cars in the United States increased 49 percent between 1981 and 1984 while the consumer price index rose 26 percent.) Due to trade, there are in effect a multitude of automobile producers in the United States. Competition, although restrained by government intervention, is keen and the rate of product development is rapid.

Increasing returns to scale occur if output more than doubles when all inputs are doubled.

A key feature of the new theory is the importance it places on **increasing returns to scale** and their effect upon the gains from trade. Increasing returns to scale means that output more than doubles when all inputs, capital and labor for example, are doubled. Increasing returns to scale are a close cousin to decreasing production costs, sometimes called scale economies. The difference between decreasing costs or scale economies and increasing returns to scale, here at least, is that increasing returns to scale occur when output *more than doubles* when all inputs are doubled so that average units of cost of production fall. In scale economies, high startup costs lead to decreasing average unit costs as production expands even if some inputs, for example, plant and machinery, are held constant.

Figure 6.3 helps to explain the basic ideas of the new theory. Imagine there are two nations, both of which have five car companies that produce and sell a million cars each. Each car that rolls off the assembly line is produced either under increasing returns to scale or decreasing costs so that each firm's unit costs of production decline as it produces more cars. But the more firms there are, the less each firm is able to enjoy economies of scale. As a result, unit costs of production rise as the number of firms in the industry increases, as shown in Figure 6.3.

Figure 6.3a shows the price, output, and average unit costs of automobile production in one national economy prior to trade. The more firms there are in the industry, the higher are average unit costs of production, but also the greater the degree of competition and the lower the price of the product. This last relationship is captured in the schedule *P* in the figures. It shows that the price of a car falls as the number of car producers and the level of competition increase. Prior to trade, the average unit costs schedule and the *P* schedule intersect at the price level *Pn* in the national market.

International trade offers many benefits in this situation. First, it expands the market and enables more efficient firms to capture further economies of scale. Second, the global market increases competition and brings down the price of cars in both countries. This is shown in Figure 6.3b. With trade, eight rather than ten firms compete in the world market, which displaces the two national markets. Although two firms fall by the wayside, the eight remaining firms are able to capture additional economies of scale because they each now produce 1.25 million cars instead of 1 million cars. For this reason, the average unit costs schedule is lower in Figure 6.2b than it is in Figure 6.3a.

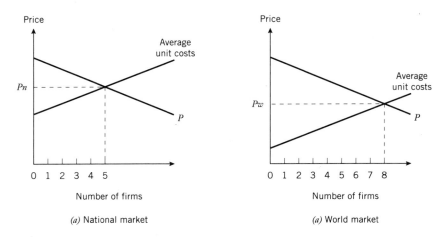

FIGURE 6.3 International trade under monopolistic competition.

Prior to trade, five firms produce cars in each of two national markets, panel (a). With trade, average unit costs of production decline as the market expands and firms are able to capture economies of scale—note that the average unit cost line in panel (b) is lower than the average unit cost line in panel (a). However, line P, which shows the relationship between the number of firms, the degree of competition, and the price that can be charged for cars is the same in both panels. That means that although firms are able to capture economies of scale as the market expands from national markets to a world market, increased competition reduces the price of cars, Pn in panel (a) compared to Pw in panel (b). As a result, the number of firms able to survive in the highly competitive world market is less than the total number of firms that can survive when there are two separate national markets and the degree of competition is not as keen. Some, two in this case, car makers are crowded out of the market.

At the same time, greater competition, the result of trade and the increase in the number of firms operating in both national markets that together are the world market—8 instead of 5—means that the P or price schedule, which does not shift, now intersects the average unit costs schedule at a lower price level, namely at the world price Pw. Trade, therefore, benefits consumers as well as the eight remaining firms.

The theory does not tell us which country will gain the most from trade or whether one country's gain will be another country's loss. Recall that two car producers are driven out of business when trade begins. If the two defunct car producers came from the same nation, that nation's car production will fall to 3.75 million units. Viewed solely from the production side, the country will probably lose rather than gain from trade. In the other country, car production will increase from 5 million to 6.25 million units. Clearly, this country will gain from trade unless the price of cars falls steeply due to increased competition.

Because one country may gain from intraindustry trade while the other loses, the new theory of international trade argues that government policy may help national firms gain a toehold in various industries or enable a firm to expand its production and be the first to capitalize on economies of scale. These topics are discussed in Chapter 9, where the case for and against a national industrial policy is analyzed.

Offshore Production and Factor Mobility

The Heckscher-Ohlin theorem assumes that factors of production are immobile, since, for example, one can hardly move a steel plant from Homestead, Pennsylvania to Monterrey, Mexico. Ohlin, in fact, argued that international trade would be reduced to a trickle if labor and capital were mobile. Labor, he argued, would emigrate from labor-abundant to labor-scarce regions, and, if all factors followed this pattern, regional factor proportions would become similar throughout the world. In this event, trade could not be based on differences in relative factor proportions. It is, however, highly doubtful that perfect labor mobility will come to pass in the near future.

But capital is another case—it is highly mobile. Given an influx of foreign capital, a capital-scarce country may become capital abundant and technologically proficient in one or more sectors of its economy. In such a case, a low-wage country will have a distinct advantage over a high-wage country. Given the construction of factories and transfer of technology to Spain, physical output per worker could be similar in Germany and Spain. The lower Spanish wage rate would then assure that a Spanish factory would be more cost-efficient.

As a matter of fact, many observers in the early 1970s felt that Spain, Portugal, and North Africa would become the automobile producers of Europe for exactly these reasons. Car manufacturers, lured by inexpensive labor, would rush to establish production facilities in these regions. As it turned out, Spanish car production and exports *did* expand remarkably in the 1980s.

But the implications of the growth of the Spanish car industry can be taken too far. Carla Hills, a former U.S. Trade Representative, pointed out that if labor costs were the only determinant of plant location, the LDCs would be the rich countries of the world. Low wages can be offset by the introduction of robotics and other forms of advanced technology, and this could be the case even though such technology was transferred to LDCs and newly industrialized countries (NICs). If greater capital intensity cuts labor costs to 20 percent of total production costs and labor costs are 50 percent lower in the "typical" LDC compared with the "typical" developed nation, the cost advantage of producing a car in a developing country will be 10 percent. However, if transportation and other costs associated with manufacturing an automobile in an LDC for sale in a developed country exceed 10 percent of the total production cost, it would be cheaper to produce the car in the developed nation. That is why Japanese automobile manufacturers have not established major plants in developing nations, although they no doubt will do so in the future to serve growing Asian markets.

Nevertheless, capital mobility is important in explaining emerging trade patterns. Because most final products consist of numerous parts—the figures presented in Table 6.5 show that the cost of materials is the major cost of producing a car—a nation can gain a competitive advantage in a particular segment of a selected industry provided it has the capital and technology required to produce the good. And capital mobility and the transfer of technology may make this possible.

The Product Cycle

Product cycle theory.
The idea that the production of a particular product becomes simpler over time as product developments and improvements grind to a halt. The application of product cycle theory to international trade theory was the result of the efforts of Raymond Vernon.

The potential effects of capital mobility have been combined with Raymond Vernon's **product cycle theory** of international trade to explain the rapid expansion of exports in some LDCs and NICs. In his original model, Vernon argued that some products follow a life cycle that can be divided into three phases.

1. Initially, a product is produced for the domestic market and is continually modified and improved. Since product modification is continuous, the product will be manufactured in the domestic economy close to sources of innovation, even if it is sold in external markets.

2. As the product matures and foreign sales become more important, the firm must at least establish marketing facilities overseas in order to promote such sales. Over time, the firm may discover that it is cheaper to manufacture all or some of the product overseas in order to satisfy sales in the foreign market.

3. In the final stage, innovation and modifications grind to a halt; if overseas production costs are cheaper, the product will be manufactured abroad and exported back to the domestic country.

Vernon and others extended the product cycle theory to take the emergence of multinational corporations into account. The product is still initially produced and improved in a developed nation. But once the technology matures, mass production at the cheapest cost becomes the order of the day. Rather than produce in another developed nation because of proximity to markets, production may take place in an NIC and be exported to the rest of the world, especially if labor costs are a large percentage of total costs and transportation costs are low. The majority of what are called American-made television sets are actually manufactured and assembled overseas in U.S.-owned plants and then exported back to the United States.

Recent versions of the product cycle theory have been employed to explain the export performance of Hong Kong, Singapore, and Taiwan, and increasingly such countries as China, Malaysia, and Thailand. The previously cited export performance of some of these countries has led to a gloomy assessment of the future path of world trade—at least in Western countries. Pessimistic forecasters have concluded that before long the majority of manufactured tradable goods will be produced in newly industrialized countries. If most or even a sizable proportion of such production takes place in NICs, it would certainly jolt production patterns in developed countries.

How likely is it that such a shift in production will occur? The answer, of course, will be determined industry by industry. But a recent analysis of semiconductor manufacturers in Europe by Michiyo Nakamota came to a surprising conclusion: plant location decisions, even for products that have a high value and low weight (and thus low shipping costs), are not based on labor costs alone.[2] For example, labor costs in the semiconductor industry are significantly lower in the Asia/Pacific area and in Mexico than in Europe, Japan or the United States—some 30–45 percent lower in the Asia/Pacific area and 40–58 percent lower in Mexico.

---

[2]Michiyo Nakamota, "Leading Players Weigh Up Costs of an EC Base," *Financial Times*, November 16, 1992, p. 4.

Why then should a firm decide to maintain its production facilities in Europe, Japan, or the United States, or transfer its production from Europe to Japan and the United States rather than to Mexico and the Asia/Pacific? Proximity to markets is one reason. If a firm sets up shop near its customers, it will be able to maintain regular contact with them and more readily adapt products to their needs. Moreover, if research and development and production take place at the same location, a firm can quickly integrate new developments into the production process. Finally, although it is more a question of politics than economics, **domestic** or **local content rules,** the requirement that a certain proportion of the value of a product be manufactured within an area, may make local production imperative.

Domestic or **local content rules.** A government decree that a certain amount of the value of product must be locally produced if the product is to be sold in the domestic market.

Other forces as well help to determine plant location. One is the availability of inputs, especially machinery, needed to make the product. Others are the state of the economic infrastructure and the supply of repair persons who can quickly service equipment when it breaks down. Such reasons bode well for establishing production facilities in Japan or the United States even if not in Western Europe. When measured by proximity to market, R&D operations, infrastructure, supply of inputs, and servicing facilities, Japan and the United States have an advantage over the typical NIC. Thus, where a plant is located, in Japan or the United States or in Thailand, depends on many factors, not just labor costs.

Because plant location decisions are complex, the fear is overdrawn that NICs will become the factories of the world and that trade will become lopsided, forcing developed nations to reduce real wages or real exchange rates in order to remain

---

BOX 6.3 South Korean Investment in the United States

Proximity to market and ready access to the fruits of advanced research and technology are some of the reasons why Hyundai and Samsung, both South Korean firms, want to build $1.3 billion semiconductor plants in Eugene, Oregon and Austin, Texas respectively. According to the plans, the Hyundai plant, for example, will be the world's largest memory chip factory, capable of producing 30,000 wafers a month.

A major reason for Hyundai's decision to build a plant in Oregon is that the United States is the major buyer of South Korean semiconductor chips. In addition, a presence in the United States will avoid possible U.S. trade barriers and enable Hyundai to gain access to advanced chip technology. Hyundai plans to conduct research at its new plant to spur the development of more advanced chips.

The plans ran into a snag in late 1995 after the South Korean government imposed new restraints on foreign investment by South Korean firms. The curbs are designed to curtail foreign borrowing by South Korean firms, which the government claims is contributing to the rise in the country's foreign debt. (South Korea's external debt rose from $48 billion in June 1994 to $70 billion in June 1995.) Under the new rules, South Korean firms must finance at least 20 percent of the foreign investment with domestic funds. Both Hyundai and Samsung had planned to raise the needed investment funds, through their U.S. subsidiaries, on the U.S. capital market since U.S. interest rates were some 5 to 6 percent lower than South Korean interest rates. Given their profits, both companies can easily raise 20 percent of the needed investment funds in South Korea and plan to go ahead with the investments. Nevertheless, the regulations will raise the cost of foreign investment.

Source: John Burton, "South Korean Groups Hit by Foreign Investment Curbs," *Financial Times* (October 12, 1995); p. 1; and John Burton, "Hyundai Builds Global Role with $1.3bn U.S. Chip Plant," *Financial Times* (May 24, 1995); p. 4.

TABLE 6.12 Merchandise Exports/Imports: Rank and Value 1994 (billions of dollars)

Country	Exports		Imports	
	Rank	Value	Rank	Value
Hong Kong	9	$151.5	7	$165.9
China	11	121.0	11	115.7
Singapore	12	96.8	12	102.7
Korea	13	96.0	13	102.3
Taiwan	14	92.9	15	85.5

Source: World Trade Organization, *International Trade: Trends and Statistics*, 1995 (Geneva: World Trade Organization, 1995); p. 13. The figures for Hong Kong and Singapore include significant re-exports and imports for re-export.

competitive. Moreover, although the exports of Korea and other Asian countries have grown dramatically, so have their imports. Table 6.12 shows that some of these nations have had merchandise surpluses while others have had deficits.

Greater exports and higher incomes have led Koreans and other Asians to demand more foreign goods, some of which have been produced in OECD nations. In addition, it is simply *not* the case that the trade positions of all developed nations markedly deteriorated in the last few decades, especially when trade in services is considered; like the NICs, some DCs had trade surpluses while others had trade deficits. Trade patterns have not been static, nor will they be in the future. Product cycle theory suggests that the composition of the typical developed nation's exports and imports will change over time as more and more LDCs are brought into the world economy. Such an evolution is not new. The composition of the developed countries' exports and imports has changed over the years but there is no evidence that such changes have reduced their standards of living.

Summary

We have shown how to convert a commodity exchange into money costs and have demonstrated the importance of productivity, wage rates, and exchange rates in determining a nation's competitiveness. We then surveyed some recent and not-so-recent developments in trade theory, including the Heckscher-Ohlin theory of international trade. Unlike the Ricardian theory of international trade, which talks in terms of labor only, the H-O theorem argues that what a country exports and imports is determined by its *relative* endowment of capital and labor. Given this theorem, it is not much of a step to suggest that a nation's trade will depend on its relative endowments of capital, skilled labor, unskilled labor, raw materials, managerial capacities, research and development expenditures, and so on.

Many recent developments in trade theory have not been based solely on logical extensions of economic models. Some have been grounded on actual world developments. The theory of intraindustry trade emerged because of the observed fact that developed countries do trade with each other. Linder's theory of representative demand is one attempt to explain why. Intraindustry trade also paved the way for the new theory of international trade in which economies of scale play a major role in determining which country exports a good and, in turn, which countries import it. One feature of the new theory of international trade is that, first, it is not easy to predict which nation will actually export a good, and, second, it is possible for some countries to lose from trade in the sense that some of their firms may lose their competitive positions and be forced to the wall. The new theory stresses that such a country will not automatically gain a competitive advantage in another industry (that is, if its computer industry suffers a loss, its telecommunications industry will automatically take up the slack). What is even worse, the demise of a country's computer industry may even lead to the demise or the loss of competitiveness of its telecommunications industry. Because such developments are possible, the new theory leads to the case for initiating an industrial policy, a topic to be discussed in Chapter 9.

We then surveyed another phenomenon, the growing export potential of many LDCs, and discussed how international trade theory has been modified to explain this pattern. The explanations are based on two elements: the ability of firms to set up factories and shift technology from developed to less developed countries, and the product cycle.

Key Concepts and Terms

capital mobility

decreasing costs/scale economies

differentiated products

factor intensity

factor proportions in production, (capital/labor ratios)

fixed costs of production

Heckscher-Ohlin theorem

increasing returns to scale

intraindustry trade

Leontief paradox

local content rule

monopolistic competition

new theory of international trade

plant location decisions

product cycle (Vernon)

relative factor endowment

relative factor prices

representative demand (Linder)

Ricardian theory of comparative advantage

technological transfer

third factor of production

Review Questions

1. Describe what a nation can do to improve its international competitiveness. What longer-run measures might help a nation improve its competitiveness? If you wanted to improve the competitiveness of the U.S. economy, what government policies might you advocate?

2. Explain the Heckscher-Ohlin theorem of international trade. According to this theorem, what types of goods do you believe Canada, Mexico, and the United States should export to and import from each other?

3. What is the Leontief paradox? Given the paradox, how has the third factor of production theory been used to salvage the Heckscher-Ohlin theorem?

4. What is meant by representative demand? How do representative demand and economies of scale help explain intraindustry trade?

5. Below are figures for a nation's exports and imports. Compute an intraindustry trade index for the country. In which commodity is the degree of intraindustry trade the highest?

Commodity	Exports	Imports
A	100	200
B	300	200
C	400	200

6. The product cycle theory explains why some LDCs or NICs sell to the developed world. But only some, not all, LDCs export hefty amounts to the developed world. Can you think of why this is the case?

References and Suggested Readings

For a highly readable description of the theory of comparative advantage see: "Schools Brief: The Miracle of Trade," *The Economist* (January 27, 1996): pp. 61–62.

G.D.A. MacDougal's article, "British and American Exports: A Study Suggested by the Theory of Comparative Costs," and Wassily Leontief's "Domestic Production and Foreign Trade: The American Capital Position Re-Examined," are reprinted in *AEA Readings in International Economics* (Homewood, Il: Richard D. Irwin, 1968), edited by Richard Caves and Harry D. Johnson.

Donald Keesing, "Labor Skills and Comparative Advantage," *American Economic Review* 56 (May 1966): pp. 249–58, was the first to stress labor skills as a source of comparative advantage. Staffan B. Linder introduced the theory of representative demand in his book, *An Essay on Trade and Transformation* (New York: Wiley, 1961). The product cycle was first explained by Raymond Vernon, "International Investment and International Trade," *Quarterly Journal of Economics* 80 (May 1966): pp. 190–207; Vernon later modified his article, "The Product Cycle Hypothesis in a New Environment," *Oxford Bulletin of Economics and Statistics* 41 (November 1979): pp. 255–267.

Many economists have empirically tested the validity of various trade theories. Some of this work makes for heavy reading. Robert E. Baldwin wrote a pathbreaking article that estimated the importance of various elements in explaining U.S. exports. Entitled "Determinants of the Commodity Structure of U.S. Trade," it was published in the *American Economic Review* 61 (March 1971): pp. 126–46. A more current and briefer explanation on how to determine comparative advantage is Robert E. Baldwin and R. Spencer Hilton, "A Technique for Indicating Comparative Costs and Predicting Changes in Trade Ratios," *Review of Economics and Statistics* 66 (February 1984): pp. 105–110.

For a discussion on the relation between trade and economic development, see the International Bank for Reconstruction and Development, *World Development Report 1987* (New York: Oxford University Press, 1987), Chapter 5. Three articles on the U.S. competitive position and its consequences appeared in *Science* 241 (July 15, 1988): George N. Hatsopoulos, Paul R. Krugman, and Lawrence H. Summers, "U.S. Competitiveness: Beyond the Trade Deficit"; Lawrence R. Klein, "Components of Competitiveness"; and John A. Young, "Technology and Competitiveness: A Key to the Economic Future of the United States." One should also read Paul Krugman's article, "Competitiveness: A Dangerous Obsession," *Foreign Affairs* 73 (March/April 1994): pp. 28–44.

A more comprehensive introduction to the new theory of international trade can be found in Paul R. Krugman and Maurice Obstfeld, *International Economics: Theory and Policy*, 3rd edition (New York: HarperCollins, 1993), Chapter 6, and in the introduction to Krugman's book, *Rethinking International Trade* (Cambridge: MIT Press, 1990). Krugman also edited a series of essays that discuss the policy implications of the new theory of international trade: *Strategic Trade Policy and the New International Economics* (Cambridge: MIT Press, 1986).

Pam Woodall wrote a stimulating article discussing the potential impact of the newly emerging economic giants, primarily Asian, on the world economy over the next 25 years. See Pam Woodall, "The Global Economy," *The Economist* (October 1, 1994).

Tariffs and
Commercial Policy

Chapter 7

Tariffs and Quotas

One of the enduring struggles in every economy is between economic logic and political expediency. Despite ample evidence that international trade "lifts all boats," politicians never tire of talking about restricting trade by imposing tariffs and erecting nontariff barriers (NTBs).

The Path Ahead

This chapter is the first of three that analyze the effects of trade restriction policies on specific industries as well as the whole economy. We concentrate on the three themes:

- The microeconomics of a tariff and the difference between revenue and protective tariffs.
- Quotas and how they differ from tariffs.
- The costs of trade protection.

A First Look at Trade Restrictions

A **tariff** is a tax on imports. It can either be levied at a flat rate or as a percentage, ad valorem, of the landed value of the import.

A **tariff** is a tax on imports. It can be levied at a flat rate, such as $1,000 per car chassis or 10 percent of the unit's landed value or price when it enters the country. Tariffs levied as a percentage of the value of the import are called ad valorem tariffs. Since a tariff is a tax, it works via the price mechanism. **Nontariff barriers,** on the other hand, are not a "hurdle" but a "gate." They establish a physical limit on the number of units

Nontariff barriers consist of a wide range of government policies that limit the physical quantity of goods that can be imported.

of a good that can be imported (for example, only 10,000 Toyota Camrys produced in Japan can be sold in Australia).

Worldwide tariffs have been reduced steadily since 1945. The same cannot be said of nontariff barriers (NTBs), which became popular in the late 1970s and show little sign of fading away. By one count, the percentage of U.S. imports subject to NTBs increased from 8 percent in 1975 to 25 percent in the late 1980s while the percentage of all developed countries' imports affected by NTBs is estimated by Sam Laird and Alexander Yeats to have risen from 25 to 48 percent between 1966 and 1986.

Table 7.1 shows that NTBs grew across product groups and countries, especially for foods and manufactures, with the major exception being fuel imports affected by NTBs in Japan and the United States. By contrast, the percentage of textiles and clothing imports and of ferrous metal imports affected by NTBs rose rapidly from 30 to 89 percent and from 24 to 83 percent respectively. The percentage of imports affected by NTBs rose least in the transport equipment sector, from 56 to 65 percent.

The Many Varieties of NTBs

Quotas are nontariff barriers that limit the quantity of, say, sugar that can be imported.

Since the 1970s, the world has witnessed not only the growth in NTBs, but a burgeoning in the types of NTBs employed. Here is a brief list of the types. A **quota** is the most common nontariff barrier and most NTBs behave as a quota. But because quotas are not permitted under current international trade rules many countries have gone to great lengths to establish different varieties of trade restrictions that are functionally identical to quotas.

Under a **voluntary export restraint (VER)**, a foreign industry, such as the Japanese car industry, agrees to limit the quantity of cars it exports to a particular country such as the United States.

In the early 1980s, the United States negotiated a **voluntary export restraint (VER)** with the Japanese car industry that limited the number of Japanese cars which could be exported from Japan to the United States. Thus, on the face of it, a quota and a VER are similar. However, in terms of trade diplomacy, they are different. Since a VER is undertaken "voluntarily," the initiating country cannot be accused of unilaterally introducing trade restrictions—although there is always the nagging question of how much arm-twisting is necessary to get the exporting country or industry to volunteer to restrict its exports to a certain country. Moreover, most VERs are introduced

TABLE 7.1 Percentage of Trade Affected by NTBs in Developed Countries

Product Group	US 1966	US 1986	EU 1966	EU 1986	Japan 1966	Japan 1986	All Countries 1966	All Countries 1986
All foods	32	74	61	100	73	99	56	92
Agr. raw materials	14	45	4	28	0	59	4	41
Fuels	92	0	11	37	33	28	27	27
Ores and metals	0	16	0	40	2	31	1	29
Manufactures	39	71	10	56	48	50	19	58
All commodities	36	45	21	33	31	43	25	48

Source: Sam Laird and Alexander Yeats, "Trends in Nontariff Barriers in Developing Countries, 1965–1986," *Weltwirtschaftliches Archive* (1990, No. 2); p. 312.

as temporary measures that presumably will be lifted once the current problem, however defined, subsides. Because they are voluntary and temporary, they are permitted under current international trade guidelines. The final point in favor of VERs is that, unlike a tariff, which applies, for example, to all car imports, a VER can and has been used to restrict imports from a particular country.

This is important. Unlike a quota—which is often directed at the exports of specific countries—a 10 percent tariff on car imports into the United States would apply to all car imports regardless of where the cars were produced. But in the early 1980s, America was not being inundated by a flood of BMWs and Volvos; rather, it was Japanese car producers that were grabbing an increasing share of the American market. In order to protect its domestic auto industry, the United States needed to discriminate against Japanese car producers and this is why it opted for a VER.

An **orderly marketing agreement (OMA)** is a close cousin to a VER. The difference is a technical legal one. OMAs are agreements negotiated between two or more governments, while a VER, as stated, is negotiated between a country and the particular export industry of another country.

The **multifiber arrangement (MFA),** which was signed by roughly 50 countries in 1974 and has gone through several rounds of negotiations, is one example of an OMA. Ostensibly, the MFA attempts to manage international trade in textiles; in reality, it

An **orderly marketing agreement (OMA)** is an arrangement under which two or more countries agree to limit the quantity of exports going from one or more countries to other nations.

The **multifiber arrangement (MFA)** is a worldwide orderly marketing agreement which restricts the quantity of textiles that can be exported by LDCs to the industrialized world. The arrangement is due to be phased out by 2004.

BOX 7.1 Voluntary Export Restraint Agreements

Table 7.2 presents the number of voluntary export restraints in existence in 1989. Textiles, steel, and agricultural products were the three products most subject to VERs, and the European Union imposed the most VERs. "Europe" includes the European Union (EU) plus European Free Trade Association (EFTA).

As might be expected, Japanese products were subject to the most VERs (70) and Korean products were next (38). Other restrained exporters were classified as other developing countries (83), other industrial countries (57), and Eastern European countries (41). The figures exclude restrictions under the multifiber arrangement, which is discussed above.

TABLE 7.2 Voluntary Export Restraints by Country and Product: 1989

Industry	U.S.	Europe	Japan	Others*	Total
Textiles	13	39	6	8	66
Agriculture	2	40	5	4	51
Steel	35	15	0	0	50
Electronics	3	25	0	0	28
Cars	1	18	0	1	20
Footwear	1	15	0	2	18
Machine tools	10	4	0	0	14
Other	4	36	2	0	42
Total	69	192	13	15	289

*Canada imposed 12 VERs.

Source: General Agreement on Tariffs and Trade, *Review of Developments in the Trading System* (1989).

BOX 7.2 **Invisible Nontariff Barriers**

Certain NTBs have the same effect as a quota, but it is difficult to measure exactly how much they restrict imports. Many border controls and health and safety standards fit into this mold. If rules and regulations are changed suddenly and capriciously, it is fair to suspect that one of their chief functions is to hold down imports. Ruppert Pennant-Rea and Bill Emmott gave a classical example of such behavior:

> Perhaps the most blatant example (of NTBs) in the 1980s came from . . . France. In 1982, the French government announced that all imports of video tape recorders would have to pass through Poitiers, a tiny customs post in central France with only a handful of customs officers. Being methodical chaps, they were able to okay only 2,000 recorders a week; before that about 15,000 a week had been coming into France, mainly from Japan. . . . But touché: in 1986, Japanese authorities suddenly decided that Japanese snow is different from European and American varieties, and introduced new regulations for ski equipment, forcing importers to change their products or pull out. Surprise, surprise: before the rule change, European manufacturers held about half the Japanese ski market.

Ruppert Pennant-Rea and Bill Emmott, *The Pocket Economist*, 2nd edition (Oxford: Basil Blackwell; and London: *The Economist Publications*, 1987); p. 163.

Government procurement policies are governmental purchasing procedures that discriminate in favor of domestic producers and against foreign producers when the government purchases goods and services. For example, a government may only purchase foreign-made goods if they are 10 percent cheaper than domestic-made goods.

A **subsidy** is, normally, a government payment to domestic producers to encourage domestic output. A subsidy may keep the price of domestic products below actual production costs.

restricts textile exports of LDCs and NICs to the developed world through a bewildering array of quotas. Under the arrangement, a textile and apparel importer, such as the United States, reaches bilateral agreements with individual textile and apparel exporters, such as Hong Kong, Taiwan, and Korea, that limit the amount of textiles, by categories, that these nations can export to the United States. (As pointed out in the next chapter, the MFA is on its last legs.)

Government procurement policies and **subsidies** are normally placed under the nontariff barrier rubric as well, but, for the most part, that is a mistake. If a government, for example, will purchase foreign-made products only if they are 12 percent cheaper than comparable domestic goods, its procurement policy is based on *price differentials* and, hence, should be regarded as a *tariff*. Likewise, government subsidies such as tax rebates on exports or the funding of R&D expenditures differ significantly from a VER. For this reason, a VER should be regarded as a quota and a subsidy as a subsidy.

The Microeconomics of Tariffs

The **consumption effect** of a tariff measures the impact of the tariff on the consumption of the good in question.

Trade restrictions affect households and firms as well as the whole economy. But the *microeconomics* of trade restrictions receive the most media attention since trade restrictions are usually introduced to shield a *particular* domestic industry, not the total economy, from foreign competition. The microeconomic effects of a tariff have four dimensions: consumption, protective, revenue, and redistribution effects. The **consumption effect** refers to the impact of the tariff on the consumption of the commodity in question, which can be large or small. The **protective effect** measures the degree to which a tariff encourages domestic production, while the **revenue effect** de-

The **protective effect** of a tariff measures the increase in the domestic production of, say, luggage that occurs as a result of the imposition of a tariff on imported luggage.

The **revenue effect** of a tariff describes how much tax revenue the government collects by imposing a tariff.

scribes how much tariff revenue a government will receive when a tariff is imposed. The **redistribution effect** measures the amount that a tariff redistributes income away from consumers toward domestic producers—in other words, the change in producer surplus.

Most tariffs contain all four elements to varying degrees. Indeed, they may be self-canceling in that they may undermine the ultimate objective of the tariff. For example, a **revenue tariff** is supposed to raise tax revenue and not restrict imports. Dampening or completely shutting out imports destroys the tax base, the thing that is taxed, and reduces potential revenues. By comparison, a **protective tariff** is designed to protect a domestic industry by keeping imports out, not to raise revenue.

A tariff, in any case, *raises the domestic price* of the imported good. If the higher price causes all consumers to stop consuming the product on the spot, the tariff will neither raise revenue nor provide a protected market or any market at all for domestic producers. Whether a tariff is designed to protect a domestic industry or raise revenue, a tariff will do a better job if it has a *negligible consumption effect*—that is, if it does not reduce domestic consumption of the product by large amounts. That is why the consumption effect is essential in determining the effectiveness of an import duty.

The Microeconomics of a Tariff in a Small Nation

A tariff tends to redistribute income from consumers to producers. The **redistribution effect** of a tariff measures this magnitude. The redistribution effect equals the gain in producer surplus that results from imposing a tariff.

A **revenue tariff** is used to raise revenue. Ideally, it should not restrict imports.

A **protective tariff** is designed to protect a domestic industry. If effective, it will keep all imports out of a country so that domestic producers will not face competition from foreign-made products.

Figure 7.1 shows the microeconomic effects of a tariff in a small nation. Prior to the tariff, given the world price of Pw, domestic demand equals Q_4 and domestic supply equals Q_1. Imports, therefore, equal Q_1–Q_4. Now suppose the nation introduces a tariff equal to Pw–Pw_t, which raises the domestic price of the commodity to Pw_t. The new price of imports now equals the initial price, Pw, plus the tariff, Pw–Pw_t. Given the higher price, domestic demand falls to Q_3, and domestic production expands to Q_2. Accordingly, imports fall to Q_2–Q_3. The expansion in domestic production, which in this case equals Q_1–Q_2, is the protective effect of a tariff since it shows how much production expands as a result of the tariff.

All tariffs involve costs. In Figure 7.1, the tariff raises the domestic price of the product and this leads to a reduction in consumer surplus equal to the sum of the areas of the rectangles and triangles A, B, C, and D. But what the consumers lose, other parties may gain. If the reduction in consumer surplus is totally offset by an increase in producer surplus plus government revenue, the economy as a whole does not lose. Consumers, to be sure, are worse off, but producers and the government are better off. Given the loss in consumer surplus, therefore, the question is, how much does producer surplus increase and how much additional revenue does the government receive as a result of the tariff?

In Figure 7.1, the producer surplus expands by the rectangle A following the imposition of the tariff and the added government revenue equals the tax or tariff rate, Pw–Pw_t, times imports, Q_2–Q_3, or the area C. This leaves the triangles B and D, the protective (production) effect and the consumption effect respectively. Their sum equals the **dead-weight loss** of a tariff, since it is the loss in consumer surplus *not* offset by a gain in either producer surplus or government revenue. Of these two triangles, the protective or production effect is the most important since it measures the additional cost of expanding domestic output and, hence, the economic inefficiency of the tariff.

Most taxes, including tariffs, involve a **dead-weight loss.** The dead-weight loss of a tariff equals the loss in consumer surplus not offset by the gain in tax revenue plus the gain in producer surplus. Thus, the dead-weight loss of a tariff equals the sum of the protective and consumption effects of a tariff.

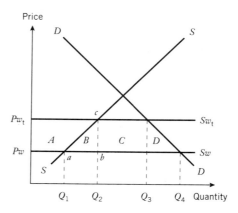

FIGURE 7.1 Microeconomic effects of a tariff: Small country.

Prior to the imposition of a tariff, the domestic price equals the world price, Pw. At that price, the domestic demand for personal computers equals Q_4 and the quantity of PCs supplied by domestic producers equals Q_1. As a result, imports equal the distance between Q_1 and Q_4. When the country imposes a tariff equal to Pw to Pw_t, domestic price of personal computers rises to Pw_t. Due to the higher price, domestic production jumps to Q_2 and domestic consumption of PCs falls to Q_3. Imports, therefore, drop to Q_2–Q_3. The tariff-related loss in consumer surplus equals the areas A, B, C, and D. However, area A is transferred to producers, which raises the level of producer surplus. Moreover, the government collects additional revenue equal to the tariff rate, Pw–Pw_t, times the quantity of imports, Q_2–Q_3, or area C in the diagram. Nevertheless, the sum of the revenue collected by the government plus the increase in producer surplus is less than the loss in consumer surplus. The tariff, therefore, involves a dead-weight loss which equals the protective effect, triangle B, plus the consumption effect, triangle D. The larger the triangles, are, the greater dead-weight loss associated with the tariff.

Prior to the tariff, the country's imports equal Q_1–Q_4, which can be subdivided into three parts, Q_1–Q_2, Q_2–Q_3, and Q_3–Q_4. With the imposition of the tariff, the first quantity, Q_1–Q_2 is produced domestically, but only at a higher cost/lower efficiency. With trade, the domestic resource cost of the goods acquired is equivalent to Q_1acQ_2; but with the tariff, the cost is Q_1abQ_2 or an additional domestic resource cost equal to abc which equals the triangle B.

The higher production costs can be described more directly. Imagine that under free trade a nation employs 10 workers to produce a certain number of compact discs that it exchanges for 20 foreign-produced bottles of wine. If when trade is restricted the nation must employ 12 workers to produce the 20 bottles of wine, 20 percent more resources are required to obtain the same output. Obviously, the tariff has generated inefficiency.

Traditional tariff theory probably underestimates the dead-weight loss of a tariff, because it normally assumes that any increase in producer surplus, area A, will be spent wisely or at least not unproductively. Indeed, some proponents of tariffs claim that while a tariff may impose short-run costs, it will generate long-run benefits. A protective tariff should increase the profitability of domestic firms, and, given such profits, the firms should be able to expand their productive capacity, which will shift the domestic supply curve of the product to the right. The theory implies that as domestic firms become more competitive, the need for the tariff will disappear. In brief, the claim is that a tariff will initiate a chain of events that will render it unnecessary in the long run.

The argument is flawed on two grounds. Expansion in one industry, unless it is the result of technological innovation, requires contraction in another since resources or inputs are limited. A nation cannot devote more resources to producing more wine unless it takes them from another sector of the economy. In addition, because resources are being used less efficiently, the economy will not reach its free-trade level of potential output.

But there are other implications regarding a tariff. Suppose the tariff does generate a $100 increase in producer surplus. Because this is a government-sponsored "gift" to producers, one can ask how much producers will be willing to pay to obtain it. If they pay $50, they gain $50. If they pay $99, their net gain will be cut to $1, but it will still be positive. It seems logical that producers will be willing, perhaps even eager, to bribe, via political contributions, government officials to enact tariff legislation in order to fatten their purses. But such actions will not enhance the productive capacity of the economy—if anything, they will reduce it. Therefore, the costs of trade restrictions are probably larger than traditional tariff theory suggests.

Protective Tariffs

Because most tariffs are designed to protect domestic industries from foreign competition, it is well to ask under what conditions they will be successful in fostering domestic production. First and foremost, the elasticity of domestic supply should be large so that a small price increase, implying a low tariff, induces a dramatic expansion in domestic output. Put simply, if the domestic supply is inelastic, there is really nothing to protect and a protective tariff will fail. Second, and of less practical importance, the demand for the product should be price inelastic. If a small price increase dramatically reduces the demand for the product, the posttariff demand for the product could be so small that the newly protected domestic industry will face a constricted market. (To see why, redraw the demand curve in Figure 7.1 so that it crosses the point where the original demand curve intersects the Sw curve, but also intersects the price axis half-way between Pw_t and Pw. Given such a demand curve, a tariff will still have a protective effect, but it will induce far less domestic production than in the initial case.) Thus, as in much of economics, the elasticity of supply and demand are the prime determinants of the potential success of a particular economic policy.

The Microeconomics of a Tariff in a Large Country

If a tariff is imposed by a *large* country, its microeconomic effects will be similar to the effects just described with one notable addition. Whenever a large country *supplies more* or *demands less* of a particular commodity, the world price of that commodity will fall or rise. So when a large country imposes a tariff, the world price of the commodity in question will decline. In turn, the fall in the world price means that foreign supply and demand elasticities as well as national elasticities must be taken into account when analyzing the potential microeconomic impact of a tariff.

Figure 7.2 shows the foreign and the national supply and demand curves. Together, the foreign and national markets make up the world market for the commodity. Given free trade, the world price is P_0. Foreign consumption and production, Figure 7.1a,

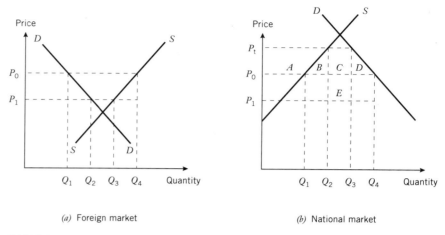

(a) Foreign market   (b) National market

FIGURE 7.2 Microeconomic effects of a tariff: large country

With a notable exception, the microeconomic effects of a tariff on a large country are similar as those in a small country. The tariff raises the price of, say, personal computers in the domestic economy from P_0 to P_t. The higher price stimulates domestic output of PCs, which rises from Q_1 to Q_2, and reduces the quantity of PCs demanded from Q_4 to Q_3. Imports, therefore, decline to Q_2–Q_3 from Q_1–Q_4—panel (b). However, because the domestic country is large, the decrease in its demand for PCs causes the price of personal computers to fall to P_1 from P_0 in the foreign country as shown in panel (a). Thus, when the large country imposes a tariff equal to P_1–P_t, the domestic price rises by only 50 percent of the tariff rate in this example. The foreigner, therefore, pays 50 percent of the duty, or area E—the so-called terms-of-trade effect. In *this* example, the tariff does not involve a dead-weight loss. The areas of triangles B and D, the dead-weight loss of the tariff, exactly equal the area of the rectangle E, the terms-of-trade effect of the tariff.

equal Q_1 and Q_4. National, or domestic, consumption and production equal Q_4 and Q_1. The excess of domestic consumption over production equals the excess of foreign production over consumption. In this case, the large country will import $Q_1 - Q_4$ from the rest of the world.

Now suppose the nation introduces a tariff equivalent to the vertical distance $P_t - P_1$ in Figure 7.2b. Given the large-country assumption, the world price falls to P_1. In the foreign market, production slides back to Q_3 and demand rises to Q_2. Although the world price declines, the domestic or national price, which equals the world price plus the tariff, rises to P_t. Given the higher price, domestic consumption falls back to Q_3, but domestic supply expands to Q_2. Since domestic demand still exceeds domestic supply despite the higher price, the large country continues to import the commodity, albeit a smaller amount, from the rest of the world. But, as can be seen, the tariff rate exceeds the rise in the national price, or $P_t - P_1 > P_t - P_0$. This means that foreign exporters end up paying a proportion of the tariff. Put differently, the exporters are willing to absorb or pay some of the duty in order to retain a share of the nation's market. Therefore, the **incidence** of the tariff, who *actually pays* the tax, is partly borne by foreign exporters. The more *inelastic* the foreign supply curve, the more the incidence of the tariff rests on the shoulders of the foreign exporters.

A large-country tariff has all the effects previously described for a small country: the redistribution, protective, revenue, and consumption effects, which are labeled A, B, C,

The **incidence** of taxation measures the ultimate distribution of the burden of a tax. In the case of an excise tax or a tariff, it determines who, the consumer or the producer, pays the tax.

When a large country imposes a tariff and its demand for the import declines, the world price of the import may also decline. If this happens and the price of the large nation's exports stays constant, the country's terms of trade improves. This is called the **terms-of-trade effect** of a tariff.

and *D* in Figure 7.2b. In the case of a large country, there is an added effect, however—area *E* in the Figure 7.2b, which represents the amount of the tariff paid by foreign exporters. Area *E* is often referred to as the **terms-of-trade effect** of a tariff. Because the importing country is now able to purchase imports at a lower price, its terms-of-trade—the price of exports divided by the price of imports—increases.

The *larger* area *E* is relative to area *C*, the more the foreigner pays the duty. If foreign exporters pay a portion (or even *all*) of the import duty, the large country gains by collecting taxes from foreigners. So in computing the dead-weight loss of a tariff for a large nation, area *E* must be subtracted from the sum of the areas *B* and *D*. In Figure 7.2b, the tariff does not entail a net dead-weight loss nor does the country gain as a result of the tariff. However, there are conditions under which area *E* might actually exceed the dead-weight loss associated with areas B and D. Then it would be possible to argue that the nation's economic welfare actually *improves* as a result of the tariff.

The question at hand, however, is not that of national welfare, but rather under what conditions a large nation can impose a tariff with some confidence that it will have the intended protective effect. The previously cited domestic elasticity conditions still hold, but, in addition, foreign supply and demand elasticities also come into play. The more *inelastic* the foreign supply curve, the greater the proportion of the tariff paid by foreign suppliers but (and this is the downside) the less the decline in imports. At the extreme, if the foreign supply curve is *completely inelastic*, foreign suppliers will pay all the tariff and the level of imports will remain constant. The domestic nation will raise much tax revenue, but the tariff will not protect its domestic industry.

Alfred Marshall observed that, just as both blades of the scissors are needed to cut paper, foreign demand elasticity as well as the foreign supply elasticity are needed to determine a tariff's effectiveness in the large-country case. If foreign demand is elastic, a protective tariff has a better chance of achieving its goal. Imagine a tariff is introduced and as a result the domestic demand for the product falls, which, in turn, causes the world price of the commodity to decline. If foreign demand is elastic, foreigners will absorb a portion of the former domestic demand. By comparison, if foreign demand elasticity is so low, so *inelastic* that a lower world price does not stimulate foreign demand at all, the world price will probably drop in step with the increase in the tariff. In that case, foreign suppliers will pay the import duty and the level of domestic imports will remain high.

While foreign demand elasticity is essential in determining the protective effect of a large country's tariff, it is not vital in calculating the revenue effect of the tariff. Foreign demand elasticity helps tell us *who pays the tax*, but not about the success of the policy. If foreign demand elasticity is high, domestic consumers pay the tariff through higher prices; if it is low, foreign producers "eat" the duty through lower sales receipts.

Table 7.3 summarizes the effects of supply and demand elasticities, domestic and foreign, on the revenue-raising and protective capacities of a tariff, although one should bear in mind that foreign elasticities are relevant only in the case of a large country. What does the chart tell us? Look at the line marked Demand right under the line marked Domestic Elasticities. If domestic demand elasticity is high (the second column), a tariff will have neither a protective effect nor a revenue effect. A tariff-induced increase in the price of the product will sharply curtail the domestic demand for the product. Thus, the tariff will not help a domestic supplier since the higher price will contract her or his market, nor will it raise much revenue since the quantity of goods imported will fall with the higher price. If, however, the domestic demand for the product is inelastic, a higher price will not curtail the demand for the product. Thus, depending upon other elasticities, a tariff will either raise a lot of revenue or provide a market for domestic suppliers.

TABLE 7.3 Supply and Demand Elasticities: Protection and Revenue Effects

Domestic Elasticities	High	Low
Demand	Neither	Both
Supply	Protective	Revenue
Foreign/World Elasticities		
Demand	Both	Neither
Supply	Both	Revenue

While the choices in real life are not as clear cut as pictured here, the chart does describe the conditions required if a tariff is to hit its objective. Thus a would-be protective tariff in a small country will be more successful if the domestic demand is inelastic and the domestic supply is elastic. Moreover, since world demand elasticities tend to be higher than their domestic counterparts, the ability of a tariff to protect domestic industry depends in most instances on domestic rather than world conditions.

Quotas

If a country is confronted by an inelastic foreign supply curve, a tariff will raise a hefty sum of money, most or all of it paid by the foreigner, but it will not protect a domestic industry. Under such conditions, the nation will have to impose a quota if it wants to shield the domestic industry from foreign competition. Since only large nations can face an inelastic foreign supply schedule, we can see why they might need quotas to protect a domestic industry from foreign competition, and why they have been keen to cut tariffs but have dragged their feet on eliminating NTBs. On the other hand, we can see why small nations can obtain protection through tariffs, but why they will not obtain any additional protection if they employ a quota. Thus, for the most part, quotas are only applicable in the large-country case.

Figure 7.3 shows the impact of a quota which, it is assumed, has exactly the same protective effect as the tariff in Figure 7.2. Under a quota, the quantity of imports permitted is set at Q_2-Q_3, shown by the horizontal difference between domestic supply, S_d, and the total supply S, the domestic plus foreign supply. (Under a quota, the foreign supply schedule is a vertical line since only a fixed quantity of imports is permitted to enter the domestic economy irrespective of price. However, since the foreign supply schedule is added to the domestic supply schedule to obtain the total supply schedule, the total supply schedule has the same slope as the domestic supply schedule.) With the imposition of a quota, the price of imports rises from Pw to Pw_q, domestic production expands from Q_1 to Q_2, demand drops to Q_3, and imports decline from Q_1-Q_4 to Q_2-Q_3.

With one exception, the costs of a quota are similar to those of a tariff. The revenue derived from the quota, area C, may end up in the hands of the government, of domestic firms which import the good, of foreign exporters, or a combination of all three.

We can see one reason why a quota is considered inferior to a tariff. Under a tariff, the government gets the revenue, which it may spend on projects benefiting the soci-

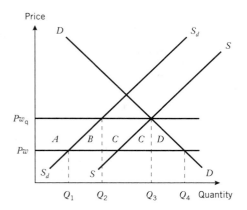

FIGURE 7.3 Microeconomic effects of a quota.

A quota can have exactly the same protective effect as a tariff. If the world price of personal computers is Pw, a tariff equal to Pw_t–Pw raises the domestic price to Pw_t and leads to the effects outlined in Figure 7.1. If a nation introduces a quota equal to the horizontal difference between S_d and S, the number of foreign-made PCs permitted to enter the country equals Q_2–Q_3. S_d is the domestic supply curve and S is the total supply of personal computers available to domestic consumers at various price levels, domestic production plus imports, at any price level. The quota will have the same effects as a tariff. Domestic production expands, domestic consumption contracts, income is redistributed, and the dead-weight loss of the quota equals the triangles B and D. A key difference between tariffs and quotas concerns the question of who collects the revenue or rent that results from the quota. If the government auctions off the import permits, it will gain the revenue. If the government gives the import permits free of charge to selected importers, the importers can purchase the permitted PCs at the world price of Pw and sell them in the domestic market for Pw_q and pocket the difference. In certain cases, foreign exporters may be able to raise the export price of the PCs to Pw_q. If that happens, foreign exporters will gain the quota rent.

Quota rent arises because a quota raises the domestic price of an import. An alert individual can walk away with the rent if she purchases the import at the world price and turns around and sells it at the higher domestic price. The quota rent may be grabbed by domestic importers, the home country government, or by foreign producers.

ety in general or which it may use to reduce overall tax rates. In contrast, if the quota revenue, or *rent* as it is called by economists, ends up in the hands of the importers, the government will subsidize a lucky few at the expense of all citizens. If foreign firms end up with the **quota rent,** the government will, in effect, have taxed its citizens in order to transfer wealth to foreigners.

The government may be unable to prevent foreign firms from expropriating the quota revenue, but it *can* prevent unwarranted transfers of income from domestic consumers to domestic importers from taking place. Under a quota system, one needs a permit in order to import the specified goods. If the government auctions off the permits, importers would bid the price of the permits up to Pw_q and the government would collect the same amount of revenue as under a tariff. Unfortunately, it is more likely in practice that the government will hand out the import permits on a random basis or to traditional importers. These fortunate individuals, permits in hand, then purchase the goods at the world price of Pw and sell them at the domestic price of Pw_q and pocket the difference (area C).

Foreign exporters are more likely to appropriate all or some of the quota rent if their products are differentiated. When the VER which restricted the export of Japanese cars to the United States was initiated, Japanese firms altered the product mix they exported to the United States. They still shipped a full line of cars to the United States, although many people felt they skewed their exports to more expensive top-of-the-line models. Many of the cars entered the United States loaded with compulsory options and Americans had to choose between purchasing deluxe models or not consuming Japanese cars at all. They chose to purchase the cars and the Japanese sold the maximum number of cars permitted under the agreement. Because profit margins on top-of-the-line models and optional equipment are greater than margins on conventional cars, Japanese car makers walked away with most of the quota's revenue effects, demonstrating why some foreign suppliers do not object strenuously to a VER.

But it should be noted that even if foreign exporters expropriate the quota rent, not all foreign exporters will be better off given the introduction of the quota. If a foreign car exporter can sell 200,000 units at $10,000 per unit without a quota, she will not necessarily be better off if she can export only 100,000 cars under a quota even though she may receive $15,000 per unit exported.

Quotas versus Tariffs

Suppose the government decides to auction import permits to the highest bidders and that foreign supply is inelastic. It might first appear that tariffs and quotas would be equivalent in this case since the government gains all the quota's revenue or rent. This is not true since the effects of tariffs and quotas are not similar over the longer run.

For example, if a country were to impose a tariff on automobile tires, this would raise the domestic price of tires and presumably increase the profits of domestic tire producers. But the domestic producers' ability to ignore market forces is limited. Imagine the international price of tires is $50 and that the country introduces a tariff of $10 per tire. Assuming the domestic demand for tires is inelastic, domestic firms would be able to charge $60 per tire. However, if they charge, say, $65 a tire, consumers will purchase foreign rather than domestic tires. The result would be different under a quota, since a quota by definition would limit the number of foreign tires that can be imported; hence, a domestic producer can raise her price without fear of foreign competition.

A tariff protects an economy over the business cycle better than a quota. A quota does not offset variations in demand and may, in addition, encourage wide swings in prices and offer little protection to domestic firms in periods of slack demand. For example, during an economic boom when demand for and price of steel are rising, a quota blocks additional imports of steel and domestic prices may race ahead. Domestic producers are overjoyed, but domestic consumers are dismayed. Foreign consumers, on the other hand, benefit from the quota. If the United States restricts imports of Swedish steel, a greater portion of the world supply can go to satisfy demand in Peru and Colombia and hold down price increases in those countries.

In a recession, by contrast, a quota may actually *hurt* rather than help domestic producers. Assume that the domestic demand for tires equals 100 units. If a quota restricts tire imports to 50 units, domestic producers will supply one-half of the market. If demand drops to 75 units and foreign firms are the low-cost producers, 50 units will still be imported, which means that domestic production will contract by 25 units. If instead of a quota a flat-rate tariff of, say, $10 on imported tires was enacted, the contraction of demand associated with a recession might actually *raise* the rate of protection. Suppose as demand shrinks, the world price of a tire falls from $50 to $40, the flat-rate tariff measured as a proportion of price will rise from 20 to 25 percent and yield a greater rate of protection.

The effects of tariffs and quotas on the total economy can be graphically illustrated by shifting the demand curve for the product in Figure 7.3 either to the right or to the left. Economic expansion raises the demand for all commodities and shifts the demand curve to the right; a recession shifts the schedule to the left. The impact of a tariff versus a quota, given a shift in the demand curve, can be seen from this exercise.

The Costs of Protection

Protection, whatever its form, has a price tag. Consumers pay more for goods because they are forced to purchase domestically produced commodities in place of cheaper foreign ones. How much have American consumers paid for selected trade restrictions? Table 7.4 presents some of the findings of Gary Clyde Hufbauer and Kimberly Ann Elliott. The industries in question are divided into four categories: those protected by high tariffs, those protected by quotas, those protected by VERs, and those protected by special arrangements, such as the semiconductor and the steel industries, which have been protected by an international agreement and by a combination of antidumping and countervailing duties respectively.

One thing is readily apparent from the table. In most cases, the *cost per job saved*, not only to the consumer but also to the economy, exceeds the wages of the workers whose jobs were being saved. Assuming it were politically possible to do so, it would be

TABLE 7.4 Estimated Costs of Protection
(total number and millions of dollars)

Industry	Jobs	Cost to Consumer per Job	Net Welfare Costs per Job
Benzoid chemicals	216	$1,000,000	$46,296
Canned tuna	390	$187,179	$25,641
Orange juice	609	$461,412	$57,471
Luggage	226	$933,628	$115,044
Polyethylene resins	298	$590,604	$67,114
Dairy products	2,378	$497,897	$43,734
Peanuts	397	$136,020	$55,416
Sugar	2,261	$600,177	$256,696
Apparel	152,583	$138,666	$50,543
Textiles	16,203	$202,061	$55,175
Machine tools	1,556	$348,329	$247,429
Steel	1,239	$835,351	$47,619
Semiconductors	2,342	$525,619	$415,844

Source: Gary Clyde Hufbauer and Kimberly Ann Elliott, *Measuring the Costs of Protection in the United States* (Washington, DC: Institute for International Economics), Copyright © 1994 by the Institute for International Economics. All rights reserved. Tables 1.3 and 1.5, pp. 12–13, 20. *Note:* The jobs involved in the cases of dairy products and sugar are processing jobs only.

BOX 7.3   Calculating the Costs of Protection

Protection, in terms of consumers' costs per job saved, can be computed by the loss in consumer surplus divided by the number of jobs saved. In the case of a tariff, net welfare costs are computed by summing up the protective and consumption effects, or the dead-weight loss of a tariff, divided by the number of jobs saved. In the case of a quota, one must add the triangles *B* and *D* in Figure 7.1 plus that portion of the quota rent, area *C*, obtained by foreigners and divide that sum by the number of jobs saved.

    Hufbauer and Elliott conclude that the costs of protection in the semiconductor and steel industries have been steep (Table 7.5). The costs to consumers per job saved equals row 1 divided by row 7, or $1,231 million divided by 2,342 in the case of semiconductors; and $1,035 million divided by 1,239 in the case of steel. The net welfare loss per job is computed by dividing row 6 by row 7.

TABLE 7.5   Calculating the costs of protection [in millions of dollars except for jobs saved]

		Semiconductors	*Steel*
(1)	Consumer surplus loss	$1,231	$1,035
(2)	Producer surplus gain	257	657
(3)	Tariff revenue gain	na	318
(4)	Quota rent loss	835	na
(5)	Efficiency loss	139	59
(6)	Net welfare loss	974	59
(7)	Jobs saved	2,342	1,239

Source: Gary Clyde Hufbauer and Kimberly Ann Elliott, *op. cit.*, p. 20.

cheaper for the economy to pay these workers the average wage and scrap the trade restrictions.

    American consumers paid a high price to protect a handful of jobs, with the apparel and textile industries being the exceptions. But even there, the costs to consumers per job saved were staggering. Although the net welfare costs of trade restrictions are less than the costs to consumers, that is no consolation to consumers since the lower net welfare costs simply reflect the transfer of income from consumers to producers—not a harbinger of good times to consumers.

The Macroeconomic Effects of Protection

So far the macroeconomic effects of trade restrictions have been ignored. At the national level, protectionists often argue that trade restrictions will boost domestic employment and improve the trade balance—especially if the economy is operating below its potential. There is a kernel of truth in this argument provided other things remain equal. Suppose Canada imposes a tariff on machine tools and other things remain constant. The higher costs for imports should shift the import curve to the left while the export curve remains constant as in Figure 7.4a. It follows that the improvement in the trade balance should shift the aggregate demand curve to the right as in Figure 7.4b. According to the figures, domestic employment rises and the nation's trade account improves.

But since a tariff raises the costs of imported machine tools and the price of domestic-made machine tools, the aggregate supply curve may shift up to the left, damping any improvement in real income. Yet if the economy is suffering from high unemployment so that the aggregate supply curve in Figure 7.4b is a horizontal line, AS_0, the higher costs associated with the tariff may be barely noticeable and output and employment effects will swamp any price effects. However, if the economy is near full employment so that the supply curve is more vertical than horizontal, AS_1 in Figure 7.4b, a protective tariff will lead to pure inflation and the economy will end up with a higher price level. Moreover, since the aggregate supply curve will shift to the left (not shown), the economy may end up with lower income and a lower potential income since trade restrictions will, as pointed out, reduce worker productivity.

There is a very high probability that other things will not remain equal. Foreign retaliation, for example, is a real possibility. In terms of Figure 7.4a, foreign retaliation will shift the export curve to the left and adversely affect any possibility of a net expansion in domestic income and employment. Even if the rest of the world is stoic and does not retaliate, the initial improvement in the nation's trade balance, income, and

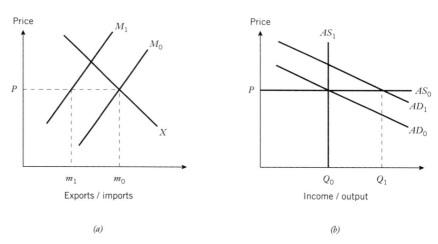

(a) (b)

FIGURE 7.4 Macroeconomic effects of a tariff.

A tariff on machine tools shifts the import curve to the left from M_0 to M_1 in panel (a). If exports and the domestic price level remain constant, the improvement in the trade balance should shift the aggregate demand curve from AD_0 to AD_1 in panel (b), and raise the domestic level of income from Q_0 to Q_1. The success of the policy depends on the slope of the aggregate supply curve; if it is flat, implying that the country's economy is operating below its potential, the policy *may* work. If, however, the aggregate supply curve is a vertical line, such as AS_1 in panel (b), indicating that the economy is operating at its potential, the increase in aggregate demand will lead to higher prices, or pure inflation. In the end, the level of real income will remain constant and, in this example, trade will be balanced.

employment will probably decrease over time. Steady exports and a declining demand for foreign-made machine tools means that on the foreign exchanges the demand for the domestic currency would remain constant while the supply of the domestic currency contracts. As a result, the exchange rate would rise, contracting exports, stimulating imports, and decreasing aggregate demand.

Even if the exchange rate remains constant, foreign income should fall as foreign exports of machine tools decline following the imposition of the tariff. And it is just for this reason that foreign retaliation, with its predictable results, is quite probable. Even if foreign nations remain impassive, any drop in their incomes will reduce their demand for Canadian products.

All these possibilities—currency appreciation, shrinking export markets, and foreign retaliation—have led most economists to conclude that unemployment is solved better by domestic policy measures rather than trade restrictions, and that trade imbalances are better corrected by currency appreciation or depreciation than by trade restrictions.

Effective Protection

A nation's **tariff structure** measures how it taxes various imports. Typically, industrial countries place higher tariffs on finished products than on raw materials.

The **effective rate of protection** is the amount of protection the domestic industry actually gets. It is computed by dividing the nominal rate of protection on a particular product by the domestic content or value added of the product.

Value added. If you purchase some materials for $10, work on them, and sell them for $40, you have added $30 to the value of the ultimate product.

Tariffs and quotas are not uniformly applied across all product categories. Some imports face a stiff tariff, while others are waived into the country with a customs agent giving them only a perfunctory nod.

Thus, an average tariff rate of 5 percent on all imports may include tariff rates of zero on some imports and 50 percent on others. The LDCs have long felt that the **tariff structure** of developed countries discriminated against their *potential* manufactured exports to the industrialized world. This is because although nominal tariff rates have always been low in the developed world, their **effective rates of protection** have been much higher.

Effective rates of protection measure the *actual rate of protection* granted a domestic industry, such as the shoe industry. Suppose a nation places a 50 percent tariff on all imported shoes, but at the same time allows the raw materials (leather) needed to make them to enter the nation duty-free. Suppose, further, that the cost of leather equals 50 percent of the total cost of producing a pair of shoes, so that if a pair of shoes sells for $60 in the domestic market, the cost of the leather required to produce them is $30. Assuming the shoe industry imports leather, the domestic **value added** to a pair of shoes is $30. (Value added can be computed quite directly. If a lumberjack sells a cabinetmaker some lumber for $100, and the cabinetmaker then constructs a cabinet out of the wood and sells it for $300, the value added by the cabinetmaker equals $200.) And it is the value added, the jobs of domestic workers, that the country wants to protect.

The effective rate of protection, the one that counts from the point of view of the domestic industry, can be calculated from the following formula.

$$T_{\text{eff}} = \frac{T_j - T_i I_{ij}}{1 - I_{ij}}$$

T_{eff}, the rate of effective protection, equals the tariff rate on the final product, T_j, minus the tariff rate on the inputs used to produce it, T_i, multiplied by the proportion of the input relative to the total product, I_{ij}, all divided by the proportion of the value added domestically. Assume T_j, the tariff on finished shoes, equals .5; T_i, the tariff on leather, equals zero; and I_{ij}, the proportionate value of leather in producing a pair of shoes, equals .5. Although the nominal tariff rate is 50 percent, the effective rate of protection, what the shoe industry actually obtains, is 100 percent, which means that the actual tariff barrier on shoes is *twice as high* as listed.

$$T_{eff} = \frac{.5 - (0)(.5)}{1 - .5} = \frac{.5}{.5} = 1 = 100\%$$

If both shoes and leather faced a 50 percent tariff, the effective rate of protection would be 50 percent or $(.5 - .25)/.5$ equals .5. If shoes faced a 50 percent tariff while leather imports were taxed at 100 percent, the effective rate of protection would equal zero. In such a case, the nominal tariff rate would be higher than the effective rate.

Most countries impose higher tariffs on *final products* than on inputs so that effective rates are normally higher than nominal rates of protection. Such tariff structures make it more difficult for outsiders, including LDCs, to penetrate markets within the industrialized world. However, quotas, not effective rates of protection, are probably the biggest commercial stumbling block hindering LDC exports to the developed world. Furthermore, it is worth noting that LDCs, not DCs, have the highest rates of effective protection.

BOX 7.4   Flat Panel Displays

It may seem incredible that any nation would introduce a tariff or a nontariff barrier that, in effect, creates a negative effective rate of protection. Yet, this is precisely what occurred in 1991, when the United States accused Japanese firms of dumping (selling below production costs) flat panel displays (FPDs) in the United States and retaliated by imposing a 63 percent duty on the Japanese products even though virtually all FPDs were manufactured in Japan at that time. (FPDs are an important component in laptop and notebook computers now and may be used in television screens in the future.)

U.S. laptop computer and notebook manufacturers vigorously fought the U.S. government's action and threatened to move their manufacturing activities offshore. From their perspective, the U.S. government had raised the price of an essential foreign-made input, one for which there was no domestic substitute. Since the government's action put them at a competitive disadvantage, they claimed that their only recourse was to set up shop overseas where they could obtain the essential input at a competitive price.

The duty was suspended in the summer of 1993 when a fledgling American FPD manufacturer, Optical Imaging Systems, was taken over by Guardian Industries. Guardian, which did substantial business with U.S. laptop and notebook producers, realized that raising laptop and notebook production costs and, in effect, driving laptop producers overseas was not in their best interest. Therefore, they successfully petitioned the U.S. Department of Commerce to suspend the import duty on FPDs.

Source: "U.S. Backs Down on Computer Displays," *Financial Times* (June 24, 1993); p. 3.

BOX 7.5　Effective Rates of Protection

Alan Deardorff and Robert Stern computed nominal and effective rates of protection in the European Union, Japan, and the United States in the 1980s (see Table 7.6). Even though only the *top five* effective rates of protection are presented in the present table, we can see that nominal and effective rates of protection have been highly correlated. Industries that received a high nominal rate of protection also received a high effective rate of protection.

On average, effective rates of protection were higher in Japan than in the United States, which, in turn, were higher than in the European Union. Note that certain industries, wearing apparel and footwear, for example, had high effective rates of protection in all three regions.

TABLE 7.6　Nominal and Effective Rates of Protection

	Nominal Rate	Effective Rate
European Union		
Footwear	11.1%	20.1%
Wearing apparel	13.4%	19.3%
Food, beverages & tobacco	10.1%	17.8%
Transportation equipment	8.0%	12.3%
Glass and glass products	7.7%	12.2%
average for 22 industries	6.1%	8.8%
Japan		
Food, beverages & tobacco	25.4%	50.3%
Footwear	15.7%	50.2%
Wearing apparel	13.8%	42.2%
Agr., forestry & fisheries*	18.4%	21.4%
Furniture and fixtures	5.1%	10.3%
average for 22 industries	8.3%	10.9%
United States		
Wearing apparel	22.7%	43.3%
Textiles	9.2%	18.0%
Footwear	8.8%	15.4%
Food, beverages, & tobacco	4.7%	10.2%
Glass and glass products	6.2%	9.8%
average for 22 industries	3.6%	5.8%

*Agriculture, forestry, and fisheries.

Source: Alan V. Deardorff and Robert M. Stern, *The Michigan Model of World Production and Trade: Theory and Applications* (Cambridge, MA: MIT Press 1985); pp. 103–108. © by Massachusetts Institute of Technology 1986.

Summary

Because most economists believe that free trade raises national economic welfare, the majority of economists advocate unrestricted trade except in very special circumstances. However, in the real world, there is always tension between expanding and restricting international trade and often the political case for restricting trade wins the day despite the economic case for free trade.

Two of the major weapons employed to restrict trade are tariffs and quotas. Since a tariff is a tax, it restricts trade by raising the price of imported goods. A quota is a "gate." It allows only so many pairs of shoes, for example, to be imported into a country. In recent decades, quotas by other names, such as voluntary export restraints and orderly marketing agreements, have been used to limit the quantity of specific goods that can enter a country.

Although some tariffs are used to raise revenue, most tariffs are designed to protect domestic industries from the rigors of foreign competition. Because a tariff is a tax which raises the price of imports, the effectiveness of a tariff in protecting a domestic industry depends on the domestic elasticity of supply and demand in the small-country case. In the large-country case, the success of the tariff depends on the elasticities of foreign demand and supply in addition to the domestic elasticities of demand and supply.

Since a tariff raises the price of the imported good, it reduces the domestic demand for the product (the consumption effect) and increases the production of domestic substitutes (the production or protective effect). The sum of these two effects equals the dead-weight loss of a tariff and also equals the net loss in national economic welfare that results when a tariff is introduced.

In the large-country case, it is possible that the foreign supplier will end up paying the tariff. This means that it may actually be possible for a nation to increase its net national economic welfare via a tariff.

A quota is formally equivalent to a tariff, with one exception. The revenue effect, what is called the quota-rent, may be snatched by either the government, domestic importers, or foreign exporters.

Tariffs and quotas, however, do not have the same effects over time. During an economic boom, a tariff will raise the price of imports but not limit the quantity of imports. A quota, however, will both raise the price and limit the quantity of imports. Thus, a quota has a greater inflationary bias than a tariff. As described in the chapter, a quota's protective effect is less than a tariff's during a recession.

Empirical studies suggest that trade restrictions are a very expensive way to protect domestic industries. The costs per job saved, whether measured in terms of consumer surplus or in terms of net national economic welfare, most often exceed the wages of workers working in the protected industry.

Key Concepts and Terms

ad valorem tariff

consumption effect of a tariff

dead-weight loss

effective protection

flat-rate tariff

incidence of a tax or tariff

multifiber arrangement

net welfare effect of trade restrictions

nominal tariff rate

nontariff barriers

orderly marketing agreement

protective effect of a tariff

protective tariff

quota

quota tariff

redistribution effect of a tariff

revenue effect of a tariff

revenue tariff

terms-of-trade effect of a tariff

value added

voluntary export restraint

Review Questions

1. Draw the market supply and demand curves for bottled water in Hong Kong. Assume that the world price of bottled water is $1 below the domestic price of $2 per bottle. Assuming free trade, show the domestic nation's production, consumption, and imports of bottled water. Now suppose the country imposes a flat rate tariff of 50 cents per bottle of water imported. What happens to domestic production, consumption, and to imports?

2. Now, employing the same diagram, explain the redistribution and revenue effect of the tariff. What is the dead-weight loss of the tariff? Why do some economists believe that the customary way of measuring the dead-weight loss of a tariff underestimates its true value?

3. If the domestic supply schedule becomes more inelastic, how will this affect your answer to question 1?

4. Explain the elasticity conditions essential for the success of a protective tariff.

5. Under what conditions and with what objectives will a country select a quota in place of a tariff?

6. What reasons do economists employ in arguing that tariffs are superior to quotas?

7. Consider the following. In order to produce a purse which sells for $100 in the United States, American firms must import $50 worth of leather.

(a) If a 10 percent tariff is placed on imported handbags, what is the effective rate of protection for domestic purses?

(b) If a 10 percent tariff is placed on both imported purses and imported leather, what is the effective rate of protection on domestic purses?

(c) If the 10 percent tariff is placed on imported leather alone, what is the effective rate of protection on domestically produced purses?

8. Assuming no foreign retaliation, what is the effect of a tariff on national income and employment in the short run? If foreigners do indeed retaliate, what may be the impact of a tariff on domestic income and employment?

References and Suggested Readings

Robert Crandall wrote two excellent articles on VERs and their impacts: "Import Quotas and the Automobile Industry: The Costs of Protectionism," *Brookings Review* 2 (Summer 1984): pp. 8–16; and "The Effects of U.S. Trade Protection for Autos and Steel," *Brookings Papers on Economic Activity* 1 (1987): pp. 271–288. Michael Kostecki discusses export restraints in his article "Export-restraint Arrangements and Trade Liberalization," *World Economy* 10 (December 1987): pp. 426–453.

Anne O. Krueger has written several articles on this subject; one of her better-known articles is "The Political Economy of a Rent Seeking Society," *American Economic Review* 64 (June 1974); pp. 291–303. It is a classic, though advanced, article.

Gary Clyde Hufbauer and Kimberly Ann Elliott wrote an outstanding study of the costs of trade protection and trade liberalization in United States entitled *Measuring the Costs of Protection in the United States* (Washington, DC: Institute for International Economics, 1994). This study is the starting point for analyzing the impact of trade restrictions on the U.S. economy.

Chapter 8

The Political Economy
of Trade Policy

In this chapter we explore some models of political economy for clues as to why trade becomes restricted in the first place. Then we take a look at existing U.S. trade legislation and describe the workings of the **General Agreement on Tariffs and Trade (GATT),** which since 1948 has been an institutional catalyst for reducing trade barriers throughout the world. Then we look at the accomplishments of the **Uruguay Round** of trade negotiations, during which the GATT evolved into the **World Trade Organization (WTO).** Hence, the chapter is more descriptive than theoretical and is focused more on institutions than on theory.

The Political Economy of Trade Restrictions

The **General Agreement on Tariffs and Trade (GATT)** is an international organization of over 100 countries that establishes rules of trade for all members. Through various rounds of negotiations, such as the **Uruguay Round,** which was completed in 1994, the GATT has attempted to reduce impediments to trade worldwide.

Given the benefits of free trade and the demonstrated costs of trade restrictions, why is trade restricted? One explanation is that the benefits derived from trade restrictions go to specific groups while their costs are dispersed across the total population. For years the United States has limited sugar imports in order to protect domestic producers. (Sugar is protected by a hybrid form of protection called a **tariff rate quota (TRQ).** Under a TRQ imports in excess of a certain amount, the quota, can be imported, but are subject to a tariff which is often steep). The price of sugar has been kept artificially high and consumers have been compelled to pay tribute to producers—according to Table 7.4 (Chapter 7) roughly $5.5 per year per person. Yet, U.S. consumers have not gone to the barricades to protest the tax even though almost everyone consumes sugar either directly or indirectly. Why the inaction? Most Americans are unaware of the quota and, in any event, spend only a small proportion of their income on sugar. Therefore, even if they are aware of the tax, consumers have concluded that it is not worth the effort to mount a campaign against the quota. The characteristics of the sugar market may tell us why industries are able to secure trade restrictions, but they do not tell us why industry X is successful in obtaining protection while industry Y is not.

BOX 8.1 Who Pays for Trade Restrictions?

So far, the costs of trade restrictions have been calculated either as a cost to consumers or as a net cost to the society per job saved. So if the *costs* to consumers per job saved is multiplied by the *number* of jobs saved and then divided by the *population*, the per-capita cost of saving a job in the apparel industry can be expressed in dollar terms—roughly $85, in terms of the data from Table 7.4.

However, this approach does not tell us who really bears the burden of the trade restriction. To a family of four, $340 a year would be meaningful or trifling depending on the family's income. But since low-income groups need a full set of clothes just like anyone else, they end up parting with a greater percentage of their income in order to pay the costs imposed by the restriction than do higher income groups. In short, most trade restrictions, like most sales taxes, are *regressive*.

How regressive? Susan Hickok, using a different methodology than Hufbauer and Elliott, measured the effects of trade restrictions on various income groups in 1984. She calculated the costs of trade restrictions on clothing, sugar, and cars as a percent of income and as a percent of the income tax they paid or as an income tax surcharge—a tax on a tax (Table 8.1).

The figures tell us one reason why President Clinton limited the proposed punitive 100 percent tariff to luxury cars during the 1995 car imbroglio between Japan and the United States—an individual with a less-than-average income does not buy a Lexus. Trade restrictions, then, help some workers, but all workers pay for them and some pay a disproportionate amount.

TABLE 8.1 Trade Restrictions and Income: 1984

Income Range	Costs as a Percent of Income	Income Tax Surcharge
$7,000–$ 9,350	4.53	66%
$9,350–$11,700	3.98	47%
$11,700–$14,050	3.80	39%
$14,050–$16,400	3.53	33%
$16,400–$18,700	3.26	28%
$18,700–$23,400	3.06	24%
$23,400–$28,050	2.92	20%
$28,050–$35,100	2.79	17%
$35,100–$46,800	2.52	13%
$46,800–$58,500	2.33	10%
$58,500 and over	1.68	5%

Source: Susan Hickok, "The Consumer Cost of U.S. Trade Restraints," Federal Reserve Bank of New York, *Quarterly Review*, 10 (Summer 1985): p. 11.

The **World Trade Organization (WTO)** is the new (1994) version of the GATT.

Under a **tariff rate quota (TRQ),** a certain quantity of, say, semiconductors can be imported duty free. After that quantity has been reached, all other imports of semiconductors pay a tariff.

Economic analysis can help answer that question. Economics argues that individuals, either alone or in concert with others, will attempt to maximize their economic welfare. It follows that if trade restrictions increase a group's economic welfare, it will push to limit trade. How much pushing will be done? Obviously, the efforts will be limited because the group does not have unlimited resources and any that are dedicated to promoting trade restrictions will not be available to satisfy other desires. To the group, pushing for trade restrictions is a question of costs versus benefits. That means that the trade restrictions must raise the income of firms or the wages of workers affected sufficiently so that the group can cover the costs of lobbying for the protection. This premise can be viewed in another light. One can argue that the costs of not pressing for protection, measured by the impact of import penetration, must exceed the costs of pursuing it. In the first case, the group's income actually goes up. In the second case, its income may actually fall, but, by taking action, the group will be able to limit the extent of the decline.

Common Interests and Actions

A **common interest group** is a group of firms (people) who band together to press for trade restrictions.

The political economy of trade restrictions can be understood through the **common interest group** model, which specifies the characteristics most apt to facilitate the creation of an industrywide organization to protect domestic markets from foreign competition: (1) if there are few firms in the industry, (2) if capital and labor are industry specific, (3) if the industry is nondiversified, and (4) if import penetration is high.

A high degree of industrial concentration—for example, the top 8 industry firms grab the lion's share of industrywide sales—makes it easier for an industry to establish a central organization that can lobby for protection through "public education" and campaign contributions. Moreover, a concentrated industry is more likely to be able to overcome the problems associated with **free riders**—individuals or firms who want trade restrictions passed, but who sit on the sideline because they believe others will wage the campaign without their political or financial support. If trade restrictions are enacted, free riders will enjoy the benefits since they are a **public good,** meaning that everyone has the ability to consume them. In sum, the free rider will get something for nothing. If the legislation is rejected, he will not have wasted his time or money. The possibility of free riding means that a few committed individuals will always be more effective than a larger number of half-hearted participants.

As the name implies, a **free rider** is a firm or person who obtains the benefits that result from the efforts of other individuals without having to pay for them. If one group cleans up the environment, others (the free riders in this case) enjoy the benefits.

A **public good** is a good or service which if it is provided to one person can be used by other individuals at no additional cost (for example, a lighthouse or a cleaner environment).

Capital and labor which cannot easily move from one industry to another are often strongly motivated to defend the domestic market against foreign goods. Moreover, the *higher* the wage level of the workers, the greater the pressure to limit imports. Older workers are often resistant to foreign competition, because they have often invested many years acquiring job-related skills (commonly referred to as human capital) and it may be difficult to find new jobs where such skills are demanded. Transferring to a new job—a difficult process for any worker—may mean accepting a lower wage, and this prospect creates a strong political lobby for trade restrictions. Finally, if a company produces only one product—magnetic tape, let's say—import penetration can pose serious problems. And such a firm, compared with a multiproduct firm, will be more eager to restrict actual or potential imports.

Adding Machine Model

The **adding machine model** takes a different tack than the common interest group model. It starts with a candidate wanting to get elected, not with a group wanting to

BOX 8.2   Influencing Policy: How Much Is Enough?

The political economy of commercial policy tells us more than who will tend to seek protection from foreign-produced products. It also describes the economic strategy a group should follow in attempting to win such protection. Assume there is a tight electoral race between two political candidates both of whom have said they support tariff legislation favored by the group. But one of the two candidates favors a 20 percent tariff while the other supports a 10 percent tariff. Should the alliance cover all bases and support both candidates, perhaps backing Mr. 20 percent more than Ms. 10 percent? William Brock and Stephen Magee say *no*—the group *only* should support the candidate who backs the 20 percent tariff since if the second candidate is elected, the group will see a 10 percent tariff enacted anyway. The only possible reason for supporting the second candidate is to try to make sure she does not change her mind and *lower* her tariff proposal.

How much money, then, should the group give the *first* candidate, the chap who promises to support a 20 percent tariff? If the group expects to gain an additional $50,000 due to the passage of his tariff proposal compared with the 10 percent proposal, they should not contribute more than $49,999 to the campaign. But such a contribution is far too much. The group should use the following method as a guide. Suppose contributions can be accepted only in increments of $1,000. Imagine also that each contribution increases the candidate's probability of being elected but at a decreasing rate. With the first contribution, the candidate's probability of winning jumps 3 percent; for the second contribution, the probability increases by 2 percent; and for the third contribution, the increase is 1 percent.

Under these assumptions, the group should contribute $2,000 to the candidate's campaign fund. Here is why: The first $1,000 contribution increases the probability of the candidate winning by 3 percent and since his victory is worth $50,000 to the group, the expected gain to the group is .03 times $50,000, or $1,500. The second contribution increases his probability of winning by an additional 2 percent, .02 times $50,000, or $1,000. Hence, the group breaks even on its second contribution. But since the third $1,000 would yield an expected gain of just $500, or 1 percent of $50,000 (.01 times $50,000), the third contribution does not make sense.

If the first candidate wanted to "shake the tree" for additional funding, he might *raise* his tariff proposal from 20 percent to, say, 50 percent since it would raise the interest group's expected gain and make the group more willing to give money to his campaign chest. The second candidate, on the other hand, would not cut her tariff proposal to, say, 5 percent, since this would cause campaign contributions flowing to her opponent to increase. In fact, all things considered, she would *raise* her tariff proposal in order to *reduce* the magnitude of campaign contributions going to her opponent. If she did so, the pressure group would win advantage politically since the two candidates would become more and more alike.

In sum, the election must pit *polar opposites* in the same contest and must be considered *extremely close* if the pressure group is to justify throwing its weight to one candidate and thus try to tip the scales of the election. The group should *save its money* if both candidates are committed to a similar level of tariff protection or if a free trader is running against a protectionist and one of the two is heavily favored.

However, even if the victory of a free trader in one election is inevitable, the interest group need not sit out other elections. For example, the group can turn its attention toward a Senate race since, according to Robert Baldwin, U.S. Senators are more effective in pushing trade restrictions than are members of the House of Representatives. Should the group fail to obtain a majority in the Senate, it can lobby the Department of Commerce (DOC) and other agencies and departments of the executive branch such as the International Trade Commission (ITC). It could also attempt to gain the favor of the American public with a national advertising or information campaign. The point is that a well-organized common interest group can gain maximum clout through the intelligent use of economic leverage.

Source: This example is based on an article by William Brock and Stephen Magee, "The Economics of Special Interest Politics," *American Economic Review* 68 (May 1978): pp. 246–250.

The **adding machine model** describes how, for example, a Congressperson will support legislation, including trade legislation, depending upon whether it will help or hurt his or her reelection prospects. The Congressperson adds up the votes he or she may obtain by supporting or rejecting proposed legislation and acts accordingly.

plead its case. A candidate who wants to maximize her chances of being elected should support the trade legislation that will bring her the largest number of votes. Since organized labor represents lots of votes, trade legislation which seems to benefit labor-intensive industries should be popular. Thus, trade restrictions that assist the textile and shoe industries appear rational from this perspective. But are they? Since consumers lose by trade restrictions, the candidate must go through a balancing act before making her decision.

Up to this point, it appears that consumer interests are always sacrificed when a commercial policy is established. This is not always the case. Industries have opposed trade restrictions on inputs, thereby representing the consumer's point of view on many occasions. Attempts to restrict the import of foreign-made shoes have been fought by the large retail chains that distribute them. Moreover, trade policy in the United States is made by the Congress but carried out by the president. Members of Congress, some of whom have to stand for election every two years and are from districts of a few hundred thousand voters (often heavily dependent on a single manufacturer or industry), are likely to feel the political heat that results from import penetration and act accordingly. The president, on the other hand, is elected at large every four years and must give voice to the general interest. The president is thus more likely than the Congress to advocate a more global and coherent trade policy reflecting the general interest of *all* citizens.

The **status quo model** of political economy argues that a country will not reduce trade restrictions if such a step would radically alter income distribution within a country or seriously hurt particular groups.

Additional models have been developed to explain the political economy of tariffs. The **status quo model** contends that a country will not reduce trade restrictions if it is felt that a heavy surge of imports would seriously alter the distribution of income within a country or impose heavy adjustment costs on particular groups. This implies that developed countries will protect low-skilled industries because such workers are generally paid less than the average wage and can least afford the burdens associated with the transitory and permanent adjustment costs of trade.

The **bargaining framework model** describes how nations bargain with each other and why a nation chooses to grant or not grant trade concessions to another country. A nation with hefty investments in another country will tend to treat that country favorably partly from fear that, otherwise, its investment income might be subject to controls or expropriation. The model also explains why nation A may accuse nation B of dumping or subsidizing its exports if it feels that B unfairly restricts its (A's) potential exports.

The **bargaining framework model** describes how nations bargain with each over trade and other matters. In the case of trade, the model describes why a country might or might not give trade concessions to another country.

The ever-widening scope of the models allows one to explain the rationale of trade restrictions and demonstrates the richness of the political economy of trade restrictions. Unfortunately, there is a disadvantage to the richness. If each and every trade restriction can be explained by one or more models, it is difficult to say which model is most relevant. It turns out that every case of trade protection can be explained by one or more models, but not all of them can be explained by one model alone.

Current Commercial Policy Provisions in the United States

At the present time, U.S. commercial policy rests on four pillars: the **escape clause provision** (section 201 of the Tariff Act of 1974); **super 301** (section 301 of the Tariff Act of 1988); **antidumping duties;** and **countervailing duties,** plus a host of nontariff barriers. The escape clause provision gives industries temporary protection. Initially, the provision was similar to article XIX of the General Agreement on Tariffs

The **escape clause provision** gives an industry *temporary* protection from imports when it is judged that imports have caused serious injury to the industry.

and Trade, under which a nation is permitted to introduce a temporary tariff to protect an industry injured by previous trade concessions. The GATT guidelines, however, also stipulate that the restricting nation must offset this restriction by reducing other tariffs. Should a nation refuse to do so, then the exporting nation is permitted to introduce countervailing trade restrictions.

The Trade Act of 1974 broadened the definition of injury and the ability of domestic industries to obtain temporary protection. Prior to the legislation, an industry needed to prove that imports were the major cause of the injury in order to obtain assistance. An industry now must establish only that imports are a substantial cause of the injury as demonstrated by either an absolute or relative increase in imports. The new legislation does not *guarantee* relief or permanent protection to an industry. In fact, even if the industry obtains protection under this provision of the tariff code, relief is limited to five years with the possibility of a three-year extension. Moreover, under the Trade Act of 1988, and under previous acts as well, industries seeking protection are also expected to develop plans for modernization, downsizing, and the like that should eliminate the need for import restrictions.

Super 301 has been described as a crowbar used to pry open foreign markets that shut out U.S. exports. The ultimate objective of super 301 is to open foreign markets and expand trade by threatening to close domestic markets to imports if a foreign country discriminates against the domestic country's potential exports.

Because the escape clause provides only temporary assistance, many industries prefer to obtain relief under VERs (voluntary export restraints) or VRAs (voluntary restraint agreements) that are easier to renew and, therefore, give longer periods of protection. In addition, a growing number of appeals for protection are filed under antidumping and countervailing duty provisions. Unlike escape clause provisions, where the injury may be caused by more efficient foreign producers, antidumping and countervailing duty appeals are based on the claim that foreign firms are cheating by either selling below costs (dumping) or gaining a low-cost advantage through government subsidies. **Countervailing duties** are used to offset the cost-reducing effects of such government assistance.

Dumping

Firms can gain a competitive advantage if their production is subsidized by the government. Due to a subsidy, a foreign firm may become the low-cost producer and grab a large share of the domestic market. A **countervailing duty** is a tariff that offsets the foreign subsidy.

Dumping involves selling an item below **full costs** or selling a good at one price in one market and at a lower price in another. Dumping, therefore, is one form of price discrimination, and is most apt to occur when markets are **segmented,** that is, when what happens in one market only partially influences what takes place in another. If markets are segmented, an imperfect competitor, a firm which has some liberty in setting its prices, can charge different prices for the same product in various markets. Most cases of dumping are linked with intraindustry trade. Thus, every developed nation seems to complain that foreign-made steel is dumped in their domestic market. It is, therefore, not surprising that the overwhelming majority of dumping charges are brought by developed nations against other developed nations or NICs.

What motivates a firm to dump in the first place? Suppose a firm can produce up to 100 videos and has **fixed costs** of $1,000. That means that the firm will have a cost of $1,000 whether it produces zero or 100 videos. However, it also means that fixed costs per unit of output will decline as production expands. In addition to fixed costs, the firm has **variable costs,** such as those associated with hiring labor and purchasing raw materials. These costs rise and fall as production expands or contracts. Suppose these variables costs equal $10 per unit produced.

Dumping is selling below costs. **Antidumping duties** attempt to offset such practices by imposing a tariff on goods that allegedly have been dumped.

Full costs are the total costs of producing a commodity, including a "reasonable" profit.

When two markets are **segmented,** a producer can sell at one price in one market and at another price in the other market.

Fixed costs are set and do not vary with the level of output.

Variable costs are those costs, such as labor and raw material costs, which vary with the level of output.

Sporadic dumping occurs when a nation sells below costs in foreign markets at periodic intervals.

A **predatory dumper** sells a product below costs and drives competitors out of a market. Freed from the constraints of competition, the dumper then raises the price of the product and rakes in a hefty profit.

Under these assumptions, a firm is better off if it can produce at full capacity since its unit costs will decline as production expands. Imagine the firm is able to sell 50 videos in the domestic market at $30 per unit. Its fixed costs are $1,000 or $20 per unit and its total variable costs are $500, or 50 times $10. Since total revenue equals total costs, the firm does not make a profit.

If the firm can sell 50 videos at $15 per unit in a foreign market, in addition to its sales in the domestic market, it is clearly better off. It sells 50 videos at $30 apiece in the domestic market and another 50 videos at $15 each in the foreign market, and thus earns $2,250. Its total fixed costs equal $1,000 or $10 per unit and its total variable costs also equal $1,000. The bottom line is that the firm makes a profit of $250, and it makes this profit even though its average costs are $20 per unit and it is selling videos for $15 each in the foreign market.

Under such conditions, the firm is not only selling at different prices in different markets—tantamount to dumping in the opinion of many observers—but it is not covering its full costs of production on foreign sales—another sign of dumping. Nevertheless, the pricing policy makes sense from the firm's point of view.

The example is rudimentary, but it illustrates the tension. The firm could charge $20 per video in the foreign market, cut the domestic price to $25 and sell more of its output in its domestic market. However, its ability to follow this or other strategies is based on its capacity to sell the product in foreign markets; and it is assumed that in order to do this, it must charge a lower price in the foreign than in the domestic market. Expressed differently, the demand for its product is inelastic in the domestic market, which allows the firm to follow a high-price policy at home. In comparison, the firm is not well-known in the foreign market and faces an elastic demand. To sell videos in the foreign market, it must follow a more aggressive pricing policy.

What is wrong with this policy from the perspective of the importing country? Obviously, domestic firms will be distressed, but what about the nation as a whole: Should it be upset or not? If the dumping is **sporadic,** such as when Swedish firms, for example, dump steel in the American market when the Swedish market is weak but stop the practice when the Swedish market recovers, the U.S. steel industry could be placed on a rollercoaster. The demand for its output would depend upon the state of the Swedish market and could very well involve sporadic adjustment costs in the United States. From a national point of view, this is intolerable.

A second complaint is that the Swedish dumping of steel in the United States could be **predatory.** If by selling steel at cut-rate prices Swedish firms can drive American steel firms into bankruptcy, the Swedish firms could then have the market to themselves. Blessed with a monopoly position, they could charge monopoly prices and make a monopoly profit. But predatory dumping is highly unlikely since we live in a competitive world economy where many firms from many countries produce steel.

Suppose that rather than being sporadic or predatory, the dumping is continuous and leads to permanently lower prices. It can be argued that it does not make much sense for the United States to stop it. As in the case of the alleged Japanese dumping of flat panel displays, the imposition of antidumping duties could raise the price of an essential input and increase the production costs of domestic firms, rendering them less competitive in the world economy.

In the spring of 1993, the *Financial Times* reported that John Norquist, Mayor of Milwaukee, became upset with the antidumping and countervailing duties imposed on imports of foreign steel by the U.S. Department of Commerce. In addition to costing some Milwaukee longshoremen their jobs, a local business firm, the Milwaukee Paper Machinery Company, had to absorb the 10 to 20 percent increase in steel prices which

---

BOX 8.3 | **Antidumping Actions and Countervailing Duties**

Countervailing duty and antidumping appeals have grown markedly in the United States. When an industry seeks antidumping or countervailing duties, the Department of Commerce (DOC) determines whether its complaint is justified and the ITC attempts to discover the extent of the damages. If the DOC concludes that the claim is warranted, it imposes duties in line with the estimated damages.

While the United States appears to be predominant in imposing countervailing duties, many countries institute antidumping actions. The recent rise in antidumping cases in the United States is related to the demise of an orderly marketing agreement in steel which had kept imports at bay. Although the countries or the areas listed in Table 8.2 were the most likely to utilize antidumping actions, Mexico and New Zealand instituted 25 and 13 antidumping actions respectively in 1992.

TABLE 8.2 Antidumping and Countervailing Duty Cases Initiated

	1981–84 Average	1985–88 Average	1989	1990	1991	1992
Countervailing duties						
Australia	4	1.5	2	7	10	8
Canada	1.5	3.5	1	2	1	0
European Union	2.25	.5	0	1	0	0
United States	60.25	20.5	8	6	8	15
Antidumping actions						
Australia	65.5	39.5	19	23	46	76
Canada	40.5	65	14	14	12	16
European Union	46.75	35	29	16	15	23
United States	49.5	47.25	25	24	52	62

Sources: P. A. Messerlin, "Antidumping," in *Completing the Uruguay Round*, edited by Jeffrey J. Schott (Washington, DC: Institute for International Economics). Copyright © 1990 by the Intstitute for International Economics. All rights reserved. Table 6.1, pp. 110–111; and General Agreement on Tariffs and Trade, *Basic Instruments and Selected Documents*, various issues.

---

resulted from the temporary tariffs. Because the firm was in competition with German and French companies, the additional costs put the firm at a relative competitive disadvantage. Mr. Norquist was quoted as saying: "If someone wants to set prices under their costs of production, say thank you. The high value products are those which use steel. If they do subsidize steel, that makes our other products more competitive."[1]

However, as emphasized in the discussion of commercial policy, most national tariff and quota policies are designed to *protect* selected domestic firms from foreign competition *regardless of the consequences* for the nation. It is not surprising, therefore, that all nations prohibit dumping, at least in their home markets. The number of cases of alleged dumping has increased dramatically since 1980. Under GATT rules, nations are permitted to slap on antidumping duties against the offending goods. The real question is *what* constitutes dumping, especially in an age of imperfect competition and segmented markets.

---

[1]Nancy Dunne, "The 'Plain Folks' Kantor Risks Alienating," *Financial Times* (May 11, 1993): p. 5.

Because cases of dumping are complex, they are adjudicated by GATT panels, national trade commissions, or both. One test for dumping is to compare the price at which the product, say Swedish steel, is sold with the production costs of an efficient steel-producing nation, say Japan. If the selling price of Swedish steel is below the Japanese production costs, it is taken as evidence of dumping; should the price of Swedish steel equal Japanese production costs, Swedish firms might be accepting lower profits, but, by this standard, it would be hard to prove they are dumping. Dumping can also be measured by calculating production costs and tacking on a certain profit markup to obtain a "legitimate" price. If a firm sells its product below such a price in a foreign market, it will be accused of dumping.

The growth of antidumping and countervailing duties in the 1980s and early 1990s led to a raft of charges and countercharges as some nations were accused of dumping and unfairly subsidizing selected industries while other nations were charged with using dumping and subsidy allegations as a ruse for introducing trade restrictions. This was the background as the Uruguay Round attempted to sort out the issues. To their credit, the participants established clearer rules and more precise criteria for investigating dumping allegations.

For example, under the new rules, antidumping investigations must be terminated if the dumping margin is less than 2 percent of the export product's price or if the quantity of goods allegedly sold below true value is less than 3 percent of the imports of the product in the importing country. In addition, a *sunset clause* was instituted under which antidumping measures are automatically terminated after five years unless it can be demonstrated that doing so will cause the original injury to recur.

Section 301 and the Hit List

Together with escape clause provisions, antidumping duties, and countervailing duties, the fourth pillar of American commercial policy is *section 301* of the Trade Act of 1974, as amended by the Trade Act of 1988, which created what is called *super 301*. Section 301 attempts to answer a different problem. It is designed to overcome foreign impediments that stifle potential American exports. Under the Trade Act of 1988, the *U.S. Trade Representative (USTR)* has the power to investigate and cite instances of foreign restrictions and practices that hamper U.S. exports in general.

Hit list. Under super 301, countries that are found to discriminate the most against potential U.S. exports are placed on the hit list and subject to U.S. actions.

In 1989, the United States accused Brazil, India, and Japan of policies that unfairly hindered American exports and placed them on the super 301 **hit list,** a list reserved for the "worst offenders." Japan, for example, was accused of inhibiting U.S. exports of satellites, telecommunications, and forest products, and was threatened with reprisals unless it eased these restrictive practices. The threatened action was canceled when Japan agreed to reduce the trade impediments in question. Proponents of super 301 legislation cite this example, plus cases involving Taiwan and South Korea, as evidence that the policy has teeth.

Super 301, and legislation like it, runs against conventional trade theory. The traditional view holds that since trade benefits a nation, a country should not shoot itself in the foot by introducing trade restrictions regardless of what other countries do. If foreigners decide to restrict trade and reduce their standard of living, that is their option, but the home country should not follow suit. Advocates of super 301 believe this view is myopic. If the United States, or any country for that matter, believes that Japan or

---

BOX 8.4 The Bomb That Did Not Explode _____

In May 1995, Japan and the United States got into a trade dispute over cars and car parts which threatened to torpedo the WTO before it was launched. The immediate cause of the friction was the American contention that, through a system of official policies and business practices, the Japanese market was effectively closed to American car and car parts manufacturers whereas Japanese firms enjoyed free and unencumbered access to the American market. The unequal access to markets, or lopsided playing field, was a chief reason for America's 1994 $30 billion trade deficit with Japan in the automotive sector, according to U.S. officials.

To right the balance and level the playing field, the United States, under section 301, threatened to impose a 100 percent tariff on all Japanese luxury cars landed in the United States unless the Japanese opened up their market to U.S. cars and, especially, car parts. It was estimated that the tariff would completely decimate sales of Japanese luxury cars in the United States and cost Japanese auto producers close to $6 billion.

At the eleventh hour, a deal was struck averting execution of what would have been a painful penalty indeed. Both sides claimed victory. But the *real* winner was not the United States or Japan but world trade and the World Trade Organization. If a deal had not been struck, the dispute could have spread to other sectors and started a much larger trade war.

In some nations' eyes, the American ultimatum was especially galling notwithstanding the dampening effect of Japan's system of car safety inspections, which effectively closed much of the Japanese car-parts market to foreign products. Critics contend that the United States should have first taken its case to the WTO and its dispute-settlement system. They believe that by ignoring this machinery, or considering it only after announcing the tariff, the United States kicked the WTO in the teeth.

Second, the United States clearly broke the letter and spirit of WTO rules, which state that members should treat all trading partners alike and not raise tariffs above agreed-upon levels—2.5 percent in the case of cars. For such critics of U.S. behavior the crucial question is: How many more times will nations flout the WTO if they find its rules inconvenient or believe its disputes-settlement procedures too ponderous? And what does this mean for the future of the WTO?

Source: Helene Cooper and Valerie Reitman, "Back on the Road," *Wall Street Journal* (June 29, 1995); p. A1, A6; *The Economist,* "Mr. Kantor's Outrageous Gamble" (May 20, 1995); p. 59; John Jackson, "US Threat to New World Trade Order," *Financial Times* (May 23, 1995); p. 13.

---

any nation discriminates against its exports, it should threaten to retaliate. If the Japanese persist in restricting potential U.S. exports and section 301 is invoked, trade will most definitely drop. The United States will be hurt, but its pain will be mild compared with that suffered by Japan. Since the Japanese are astute and aware of this, they will eliminate the restrictions. In the end trade will expand, benefiting all parties.

Super 301 created an uproar around the world. Most economists vilified the act, yet some Europeans argued that the European Union should forge its own crowbar similar to super 301. Regardless of how that debate is resolved, two results of the American legislation are especially pernicious. The hit list has been dominated by nations who have had bilateral trade surpluses with the United States. Some observers are suspicious that super 301 is being used to eliminate or improve bilateral trade imbalances. The concern is that if all nations insisted on balanced trade with each and every trading partner and developed hit lists in the attempt to attain that objective, trade would shrink.

Balanced trade does not require a nation to balance its external accounts with each and every trading partner. The nation can have a trade surplus with some partners and deficits with others. But what is of more concern is a question of attitudes. Any nation that adopts a super 301–like crowbar sends out a message that it is quite willing to take unilateral action against presumed offenders rather than attempt to rectify the situation through multilateral negotiations. Historical evidence suggests that unilateral action taken by one nation will most likely generate counteraction by others. And, in the end, not only will no one gain, but all will lose. That is why proponents of free trade believe that there is a clear need for all nations to promote multilateral trade under the auspices of the WTO.

The General Agreement on Tariffs and Trade

The GATT/WTO is a half-century old. In 1947, when the world was attempting recover from the ravages of World War II and the legacy of the depressed 1930s, 23 countries signed the General Agreement on Tariffs and Trade. The signatories believed that trade restrictions, which had reduced international trade to a trickle, had fostered and accentuated the Great Depression of the 1930s. Looking forward, the nations felt that free trade would benefit them, their trading partners, and the world. The problem was that with all nations sitting behind tariff walls, who was going to take the first step toward trade liberalization? Economic theory may argue that a nation should take advantage of any opportunities that present themselves regardless of what others do. But practical politics precluded any country from taking the first step by itself. Enter the GATT. It became a forum where nations bargained and hammered out codes governing international trade.

Since its inception the GATT/WTO has been guided by two principles: **reciprocity** and **nondiscrimination.** Reciprocity means that if a country gives up something, it gets something in return. Country A agrees to cut its tariff on coal by 15 percent if country B reduces its tariff on clothing by 10 percent. But there is a difference in the GATT negotiations. Trade concessions granted one member are automatically extended to all other members under the nondiscrimination or **most-favored-nation (MFN)** clause.

The GATT has been successful, although many people felt it was getting decidedly wobbly toward the end of its existence and some of its critics even felt that its time and relevance had passed. Yet, consider some of the following facts. Tariffs on merchandise trade were brought down from an industrial-country average of 40 percent in 1947 to roughly 3 percent in 1994. Nor is it coincidence that trade expanded rapidly during the period even though it would be incorrect to attribute all of the spectacular growth in trade since post–World War II to the GATT. However, by establishing a level playing field, the GATT created an environment which opened up the opportunities that helped trade reach its high levels. The volume of world merchandise exports, for example, expanded roughly elevenfold between 1950 and 1990, a growth rate of approximately 8.3 percent per year.

The GATT's popularity grew over the years. Today, it has close to 100 members and more countries are waiting in the wings to join its successor, the WTO. Many of them are LDCs and Eastern European nations who have concluded that import substitution does not lead to economic development and have decided to attempt export-led growth instead. In order to follow this path, GATT/WTO membership is essential

Under the rules of the GATT, **reciprocity** means that if a country grants a trade concession it gets one in return.

Under the GATT, **nondiscrimination** and **most-favored-nation** status means that if a GATT member grants a trade concession to one member, it automatically grants it to all members.

since even if a nonmember nation establishes a free trade agreement with a GATT member, it will not necessarily be treated as a most favored nation by the other signatory nations.

GATT/WTO membership has obligations. A prospective member must agree not to raise its tariffs, eliminate certain practices such as requiring important licenses, and reduce export subsidies. For smaller member nations, affiliation provides them with an avenue to defend their positions in trade disputes with larger countries. When Mexico, together with Canada and the EU, took the United States before a GATT panel over what is considered to be a discriminatory oil import levy, Mexico won. One would hardly expect Mexico to emerge victorious if it battled one-on-one with the colossus to its north.

Less-developed countries have benefited from GATT membership in other ways. They have been granted most-favored-nation status without having to cut their own tariffs. In fact, under the **generalized system of preferences (GSP),** some LDC exports were afforded preferential treatment in world markets. An LDC export to, say, Europe might have faced a zero tariff while a similar U.S. export might have confronted a 10 percent tariff at the European border. The GSP, however, has become less important as tariff rates have been cut across the board.

Where, according to friendly critics, has the GATT come up short? One area concerns its treatment of regional trading blocs. Under the GATT, regional free trade areas such as the EU and NAFTA have been permitted to cut tariffs within the region but not necessarily extend the reductions to other GATT members. Other shortcomings relate to trade policy regarding textiles and agriculture. The GATT stood by when the multifiber arrangement was instituted and its regulations concerning trade in agricultural products were either lacking or, at best, cloudy. But these shortcomings were corrected, at least partially, at the Uruguay Round.

Notwithstanding these complaints, the GATT has bolstered international trade in other ways. Since trade disputes are bound to occur, the GATT has attempted to prevent minor disagreements from blowing up into a full-scale conflict by establishing dispute-panels to adjudicate complaints. If a panel finds that one party has violated GATT statutes, the guilty party is ordered to correct its behavior. In theory, the injured party may request compensation. In practice, injured nations are allowed to introduce countervailing duties to offset the effects of initial action. However, under GATT/WTO rules, no country can take unilateral action regardless of the circumstances, unless the dispute is not covered by GATT/WTO law.

This does not mean that all trade disputes brought before a GATT panel are solved quickly or smoothly. In 1990, a GATT panel ruled that the European Union was discriminating against U.S. exports of oilseeds, such as soybean and rapeseed oils. The confrontation arose when the EU adopted a system of price supports that led to an increase in the European production of oilseeds. When the greater production was coupled with a series of EU import duties, U.S. oilseed exports to the EU fell from roughly 12 million tons in 1982 to approximately 6 million tons in 1990 and cost American farmers $1 billion a year according to the U.S. government. The GATT panel found that the EU had violated a commitment it had made in the early 1960s to permit U.S. soybean exports duty-free access to European markets.

Despite two GATT rulings in favor of the United States, a solution was not reached until late 1992, and, then, only after the United States threatened to introduce punitive duties on EU exports, wine for example, to the United States. Under a joint EU-U.S. accord, the EU agreed to limit the amount of land devoted to oilseed production. According to projections, the limit will lead to a fall in EU oilseed production from 13 million to 9.5 million tons.

Under the **generalized system of preferences (GSP),** industrialized countries permit the exports of less-developed countries to enter their country at a lower than normal tariff rate.

The oilseed controversy, the growth of NTBs, and other disputes led a number of individuals to conclude that the GATT was at a crossroads at the beginning of the 1990s. While granting that it played a vital role in eliminating quotas and dropping tariff rates across the board, some observers contended that it had been helpless to halt the growth in nontariff barriers in the previous decade. It was estimated that there were approximately 250 voluntary export restraint agreements in force at the beginning of the 1990s. Critics found the GATT had only partially addressed the thorny questions of subsidies, countervailing duties, and antidumping actions.

The Uruguay Round

It was against the background of rising trade restrictions that the latest round of GATT negotiations began in Uruguay in 1986. (Previous GATT rounds were the Kennedy Round, concluded in 1967, and the Tokyo Round, signed in 1979.) The talks were concluded at the end of 1993 after bitter wrangling between the United States and the European Union and achieved some noteworthy results.

In the next 10 years or by 2004—the proposed period for implementing the agreement—tariffs on industrial goods in advanced economies will be cut from an average of 4 percent to 3 percent and the percent of tariff-free-traded commodities will increase from 20 to 44 percent (Table 8.3). Major traders scrapped duties on items such

TABLE 8.3 Pre- and Post-Uruguay Round Tariffs: Industrial Products

		Imports	
		Percentage of Total	
Tariffs by Group	Value*	Pre-UR	Post-UR
Advanced Economies			
Total	763.9	100	100
Duty free		20	44
0.1–5.0%		41	32
5.1–10.0%		24	15
over 10.1%		14	10
Developing Countries			
Total	350.5	100	100
Duty free		39	42
0.1–5.0%		6	5
5.1–10.0%		8	10
over 10.1%		47	43
Transitional Economies			
Total	34.7	100	100
Duty free		13	16
0.1–5.0%		27	37
5.1–10.0%		27	35
over 10.1%		32	11

*Billions of U.S. dollars.

Source: General Agreement on Tariffs and Trade, *The Results of the Uruguay Round of Multilateral Trade Negotiations: Market Access for Goods and Services* (Geneva: GATT 1994); p. 11.

as construction, farm, and medical equipment, and pharmaceuticals. Because most tariffs were already low, further cuts, while good in principle, will not lead to a substantial increase in trade.

At the Uruguay Round, the advanced economies also agreed to cut their tariffs on imports from developing countries, although tariffs on finished products are still higher than those applied to raw materials (Table 8.4). The difference—5.4 percent—is not enormous and it has been reduced. But, as stressed previously, nontariff barriers are the primary tool employed by developed countries to restrict imports from developing countries at the present time.

For the first time in GATT history, a framework covering trade in services was created, a step that was long overdue since trade in services equals approximately 30 percent of merchandise trade at the present time and is growing rapidly. Bringing trade in services under the WTO umbrella is no doubt more important for the future of world trade than the projected cuts in tariffs. It is especially important for the United States, which is the world's largest exporter of services, $190 billion, and had the world's largest service surplus, roughly $60 billion, in 1994.

No agreement, however, was reached covering trade in financial services and in telecommunications at the negotiations. Trade in financial services in particular remains a sore point even though the European Union sponsored such an agreement in 1995, a year after the conclusion of the Uruguay Round. However, the United States, which is quite adamant that it will not grant a WTO member most-favored-nation status in this area if the nation unduly restricts the ability of U.S. financial institutions to operate within its borders, declined to join these negotiations. What is at stake is whether developing countries should be given special treatment, a generalized system of preferences for financial services. The United States says no. Unfortunately, if no agreement that includes the United States is reached, it could be a serious blow to the WTO.

The Uruguay Round talks reached an extensive agreement on intellectual property rights, including payments for licensing patents and rules protecting copyrights on items such as microchip designs, computer software, and pharmaceuticals. The United States pushed hard on this issue because Americans, it claimed, were losing $60 billion a year due to the pirating of intellectual property rights. For example, American officials claimed that pirated Chinese compact discs cost American recording artists and firms roughly $1 billion a year.

TABLE 8.4 Tariffs on Advanced Economies' Imports of Industrial Products from Developing Countries

	Raw Materials	*Semimanufactures*	*Finished Products*
Imports			
Billions of U.S. Dollars*	36.7	36.5	96.5
Percent of Total	22	21	57
Tariff (percent)			
Pre-Uruguay	2.1	5.4	9.1
Post-Uruguay	.8	2.8	6.2

*Excludes petroleum.

Source: General Agreement on Tariffs and Trade, *The Results of the Uruguay Round of Multilateral Trade Negotiations: Market Access for Goods and Services* (Geneva: GATT 1994); p. 11.

The rationale for protecting intellectual property rights is straightforward. The up-front costs of making a recording and the research costs of inventing a new drug are far more expensive than the subsequent costs of printing a CD or of producing and putting some pills into a bottle. In order for firms to cover up-front and research costs, it is generally agreed that the producers and inventors of the products should have a monopoly position on selling, or licensing others to sell, the products for a given period of time. Under the provisions of the Uruguay Round, WTO members are obliged to grant and *enforce* patents for 20 years and copyrights for 50 years. Rich countries were to start enforcing intellectual property rights within the year. Poorer countries were given a grace period of 5 years and the poorest countries a grace period of 10 years.

But what is good for some Americans, and other first-world firms, may not be good for some LDCs, who will have to pay higher prices for medicines and seeds because of the agreement. Because third-world countries had an incentive *not* to enforce intellectual property rights, since they benefit from pirating drugs, seeds, computer programs, and so on, the protection of intellectual property rights was a controversial topic at the Uruguay Round and will probably be a sticky issue in the future.

If the LDCs lost with respect to intellectual property rights, they gained from the scrapping of the multifiber arrangement, which is to be phased out over ten years. However, it is worth noting that roughly half the trade covered by quotas will not be eliminated until 2004. Nevertheless, the gains should be real since approximately 35 percent of world trade in clothing, and 11 percent of world trade in textiles, have been covered by the MFA in recent years. While the major beneficiaries of this step will be LDC clothing and textile producers, some high-price LDC producers may actually lose out. Under the legislation, all countries, both developed and less developed, must open their markets to clothing and textile imports. Thus, high-cost producers, regardless of their state of development, will become net importers even if they previously had been net exporters. Quotas such as the multifiber arrangement, which states that one country can export X amount of a good, another country Y, and a third Z, promote inefficiency. When such arrangements are terminated, the least-efficient producers are likely to lose out.

Guidelines on dumping and subsidies and the use of antidumping actions and countervailing duties were also instituted at the Uruguay Round. However, it is a safe bet that the last word on these new regulations has not been heard. The new rules do not prevent or even seriously discourage a country from taking antidumping actions if it feels that a foreign country is selling a good below its fair value in its domestic markets. But the new rules, as outlined before, should moderate antidumping initiatives.

Steps were also taken to simplify custom valuation and import licensing procedures and to harmonize technical norms, testing, and certification to prevent such measures from being used to impede trade. This may seem like simple stuff, but environmentalists are afraid that harmonizing product standards will discourage nations from raising their product standards above the norm and, thereby damage the environment.

Agriculture and the Uruguay Round

The crowning achievement of the Uruguay Round was in agriculture, a sector previously not covered by the GATT. In fact, some observers project that 90 percent of the gains in world trade due to the Uruguay Round will be in agriculture, where the agreement calls for reforms in subsidies and import restrictions over six years. Quotas will be converted into equivalent tariffs and reduced by one-third.

The accord on export subsidies, a topic which had pitted the United States against the farmers and governments of the European Union and had brought negotiations to a standstill, was one highlight of the Uruguay Round. The question of subsidies had been tied to the European Union's **common agricultural policy (CAP)**, a price-support system which, although it supported farm income within the EU, led to excess production—mountains of butter and lakes of wine as some have put it.

Figure 8.1 highlights the former CAP policy. Prior to the formation of the EU and the introduction of the CAP, Europe was a net importer of foods. The European supply and demand for, say, wheat intersected at a point above the world price, Pw. Because the European demand for wheat, Q_2, exceeded its production of wheat, Q_1, by the quantity Q_1–Q_2, Europe imported this quantity in order to satisfy its excess demand.

The EU was unhappy with this situation, one in which increases in world output would depress both the world price of wheat and European farm income as well—all EU members had farm income support programs prior to the inception of the CAP. To counter this possibility, the EU had introduced a communitywide program to prop up farm income. The heart of the program was guaranteed minimum prices for agricultural products and a series of import duties. Obviously, the EU could not raise the price of union farm products and make the policy stick if EU consumers were permitted to purchase foreign foods products at world prices. That's why their governments implemented a system of variable import duties that kept potential imports at bay and established minimum or support prices, such as Ps in Figure 8.1, for selected agricultural commodities. In practice, this meant that if EU farmers were unable to find buyers for their output at the support price, the European Union would purchase their excess production.

The **common agricultural policy (CAP)** is the European Union's vehicle for supporting farm income within the EU. Until recently, it attempted to attain that objective through a system of agricultural price supports.

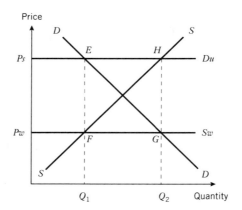

FIGURE 8.1 Supply and demand under the CAP.

Prior to instituting a support price, the European Union (EU) imported Q_1 to Q_2 units of wheat at the world price Pw. The support price raises the price of wheat within the EU to Ps. As a result, the quantity of wheat supplied within the EU rises from Q_1 to Q_2, while the quantity of wheat demanded falls from Q_2 to Q_1. The value of the excess supply of wheat, which the CAP is required to purchase in order to maintain the support price of wheat, equals EQ_1Q_2H. If the EU sells the excess supply of wheat at the world price, Pw, it receives revenues equal to FQ_1Q_2G. Thus, subsidized wheat sales reduce the cost of maintaining the price-support system.

Due to the higher price, European food consumption fell to Q_1 while its food production rose to Q_2, leading to an excess supply of Q_1–Q_2 at the price Ps. The European Union ended up with surplus food with a total value equal to Q_1EHQ_2; it also ended up with the problem of what to do with the excess food production. Some of the surplus was distributed to the needy, some of it warehoused, but the majority was exported. The EU was, of course, unable to sell the food at the support price, Ps, since it was above the world price, Pw. But they could sell the surplus at the world price and, as a result, receive revenue equal to the rectangle Q_1FGQ_2. As can be seen, the revenue the EU received was less than the sum it paid for the product in the first place, the difference equaling the rectangle $EFGH$. This last amount equaled the export subsidy or what the authorities paid out. Of this amount, EFH was an addition to producer surplus. Therefore, the dead-weight loss of the subsidy equaled the triangle FGH, which, it turns out, also equaled the net cost of the subsidy and the income maintenance program. The important point is that although the EU took a loss on its exports, subsidized sales reduced the net cost of its program.

Subsidized export sales, as expected, hurt other agricultural producers. The more the EU subsidized its exports and dumped its products on the market, the more the world price for agricultural products declined and the more the exports of other nations were crowded out of the market. Table 8.5 shows that the EU's percent of total cereal exports climbed continuously during the period, while the exports of the other nations either stood still or declined. Since total cereal exports were approximately 200 million tons per year, any decline in the percent of market sales meant a decline in the physical quantity of exports. It was the external consequences of EU's agricultural program that led to an impasse at the GATT negotiations.

The European Union revamped its agricultural policy in the summer of 1992 with the objective of bringing its agricultural prices down to world levels in three years. Under the revisions, support prices for grains and beef were cut by 29 and 15 percent respectively over a three-year period. Ostensibly, lower support prices would reduce EU production, but it would also reduce farm income. And if farmers reacted to their lower income by expanding output—shifting the EU supply curve in Figure 8.1 to the right—the EU could end up with a larger surplus despite the lower support price. To counter this possibility, the EU imposed production quotas, at least via the back door, as farmers were paid to take land out of production. In one step, the EU solved two problems. It reduced supply and sustained farm income with direct payments.

The EU also hammered out an agreement with the United States regarding agricultural exports—the so-called Blair House Agreement of 1992. Under the terms of

TABLE 8.5 Cereal Exports (percent of world total)

	1978–83	1983–87	1987–91
Australia	6.8	10.0	7.1
Canada	11.4	12.7	11.4
European Union	8.7	11.6	13.7
United States	53.4	42.0	48.4
Other Europe	2.0	4.6	3.5
Developing countries	14.6	18.4	14.5
(Argentina)	7.7	8.5	4.5

Source: Margaret Kelly and Anne Kenny McGuirk, *Issues and Developments in International Trade Policy* (Washington, DC: International Monetary Fund), Table A26, p. 133.

the accord, the EU agreed to reduce the value of its export subsidies by 36 percent, and decrease the volume of its subsidized exports by 21 percent over 6 years. The result of the Blair House Agreement was to cut the value and volume of export subsidies, reduce production subsidies, and form the basis for the export subsidy reforms contained in the final version of the Uruguay Round.

Global Impact of the Uruguay Round

Several studies estimate that due to the Uruguay Round world GDP will rise $230 billion (GATT) to $275 billion (OECD) per year by the turn of the century, which is approximately .75 percent of projected world GDP. This appears to be a small payoff given the stress of seven years of negotiations. However, the increase will be permanent, not a onetime bump, and it is hard to think of any nation that would not gladly accept a permanent .75 percent boost in its GDP.

There is, however, a downside to the Uruguay Round. According to projections, the gains from the round will not be spread evenly across the world. The EU and China will be big winners, but, unfortunately, some LDCs will actually lose from the agreement. It is estimated, for example, that Africa south of the Sahara will lose $2.8 billion per year as a result of the treaty. Some analysts, however, disagree with this assessment. They feel that the dynamic effects resulting from increased trade and greater worldwide investment will offset some of the negative effects of trade liberalization. Given greater trade and growth in the world economy, the demand for minerals—the major export of the majority of African nations—will increase, raising African exports and income.

How can a country lose from trade liberalization? As pointed out, some LDCs' exports have received preferential tariff treatment under the generalized system of preferences. But preferential treatment becomes less meaningful as tariff rates are reduced. Nations that gained from high tariffs lose when they are cut. In addition, the phasing out of the multifiber arrangement will hurt high-cost textile producers, and new laws protecting intellectual property rights will most likely raise the prices of pharmaceuticals and seeds in some LDCs. Finally, the elimination of export subsidies will probably cause agricultural production to decline and, hence, raise food prices. Food importers, especially low-income food importers, will be hit by such a development. Thus, any high-cost textile producer that imports food and must now pay royalties could be hurt.

Assessing the Uruguay Round

If some poor nations become poorer because of the Uruguay Round, should the agreement have been negotiated? Most economists would say yes. The possibility that some nations may lose as a result of trade liberalization while the world as a whole gains is reason to consider introducing an international compensation policy similar to the national compensation policy discussed in Chapter 1—it is *not* a case for backtracking or halting trade liberalization.

Outright rejection of the Uruguay Round, on the other hand, could have ushered in a worsening international scene: trade restrictions under the guise of managed trade and attempts to control or shape other areas of the economy. Second, even though curtailing trade might not have crippled the developed world (although it would have made it poorer), it would have been a disaster for many LDCs, which have relied upon an expanding world economy to help lift them out of poverty.

It has been suggested that the success of the Uruguay Round can be gauged more by the trends it appears to have halted than by the proposals actually enacted. Prior to the Round, trade was tending to become increasingly restricted. So, even though the talks did not solve all international trade problems on the initial agenda, they established a base from which the world can move on to further liberalize trade, and of some importance, reduced the pressures on governments to restrict trade.

Summary

We have seen that a large number of political-economic models, such as the common interest group and adding machine models, by stressing the characteristics of industries, explain why industries are able to protect their domestic markets from foreign imports. These models are not mutually exclusive. Two or more models, for example, may explain why the domestic sugar industry has been successful in keeping foreign sugar out of the United States.

We then looked at four pillars of current U.S. commercial policy: the escape clause provision of section 201 of the Tariff Act of 1974; antidumping duties; countervailing duties; and section 301 of the Tariff Act of 1988. The first three pillars are designed to keep foreign imports out of the United States. The escape clause provision provides temporary relief to domestic producers who have been injured by a stream of imports. Thus, this provision does not claim that foreign exporters have grabbed a share of an American market by underhanded methods—foreign exporters are simply too competitive. Antidumping and countervailing duties are different. Here, the claim is that foreigners have seized a share of an American market by devious methods: They have either sold below reasonable production costs, including a profit, or they have become low-cost producers due to government subsidies.

By contrast, the objective of super 301 is not to keep imports out; its goal is to open foreign markets to U.S. exports. If foreign imports are restricted under this act, it is only because foreign markets, in the opinion of the U.S. government, are closed to U.S. exporters. In fact,

the hope is that the threat of action under super 301 is sufficient to open foreign markets and prevent the need to impose important restrictions. Indeed, it can be argued that if imports are restricted under this act, the act has been a failure.

Finally, we looked at international institutions and international trade negotiations by describing the GATT and the results of the Uruguay round of trade negotiations.

Key Concepts and Terms

adding machine model

antidumping actions

bargaining framework model

common agricultural policy

common interest groups

countervailing duties

escape clause provision (section 201)

fixed costs

free riders

full costs

General Agreement on Tariffs and Trade (GATT)

generalized system of preferences

hit list (section 301)

most-favored-nation status

nondiscrimination

predatory dumping

public goods

reciprocity

segmented markets

sporadic dumping

status quo model

super 301

U.S. International Trade Commission

U.S. Trade Representative

variable costs

World Trade Organization

Review Questions

1. What are the characteristics of a common interest group that will lead them to seek protection from foreign competition?

2. What is meant by a free rider? Free riders exist in all types of economic activity. Give some examples of free riders not related to international economics.

3. Two candidates are running for elective office and seek your moral and, more important, material support. As a consumer, how do you decide which candidate to back and how much you will "support" her? Imagine both candidates favor restricting trade.

4. Proponents of super 301 argue that vigorous use of this provision will actually expand trade. Thus, they claim, the act will benefit the United States and foreign countries as well. Explain the proponents' position.

5. Describe the following concepts:
    (a) Escape clause provisions.
    (b) Countervailing duties.
    (c) Most favored nation.
    (d) The CAP.

6. Imagine that *all* agricultural support programs are eliminated. Who do you think would be the winners? Who do you suspect would be the losers?

7. Describe how you would measure whether a firm is dumping products in a market. Is all dumping bad? From whose point of view did you answer the question?

References and Suggested Readings

Mancur Olsen initiated much of the modern discussion of political economy. His major work in this regard is *The Logic of Collective Action: Public Goods and the Theory of Groups* (Cambridge, MA: Harvard University Press, 1965). The example of optimum political contributions is based on an article by William Brock and Stephen Magee, "The Economics of Special Interest Politics," *American Economic Review* 68 (May 1978): pp. 246–250. An excellent survey of the literature on trade restrictions and politics is Robert E. Baldwin's "The Political Economy of Trade Policy," *Journal of Economic Perspectives* 3 (Fall 1989): pp. 119–135. Anyone interested in this topic should read at least the first chapter of Baldwin's book, *The Political Economy of U.S. Import Policy* (Cambridge, MA: MIT Press, 1985).

The basic features of the 1988 Trade Act are described in Elizabeth Wehr, "Senate Clears Trade Bill by Lopsided Vote," *Congressional Quarterly* (August 6, 1988); pp. 2215–2222. The *Economic Report of the President* (1987); pp. 131–136 describes various cases initiated under Section 301 of the Trade Act of 1984, while the 1989 *Report*, pp. 176–179, discusses Section 301 of the Trade Act of 1988. Ronald A. Cass discusses the Trade Act of 1988 in "Velvet Fist in an Iron Glove: The Omnibus Trade and Competitiveness Act of 1988," *Regulation* 14 (Winter 1991); pp. 50–56.

The case for and against super 301 is debated in two articles that appeared in *International Economic Insights* 2 (November–December 1991); pp. 22–28: Richard A. Gephardt, "Super 301: It's Time for Teeth!"; and S. Linn Williams, "The Case Against Gephardt II."

Some individuals believe that the GATT has outlived its usefulness. Clyde V. Prestowitz, Jr., Alan Tonelson, and Robert W. Jerome present this case lucidly in their article, "The Last Gasp of GATTism," *Harvard Business Review* 69 (March–April 1991): pp. 130–138.

Jeffrey J. Schott, assisted by Johanna W. Burman, *The Uruguay Round: An Assessment* (Washington, DC: Institute for International Economics, 1994), is a readable and detailed review of the Uruguay Round. A briefer survey of the

Uruguay Round is Norman S. Fieleke, "The Uruguay Round of Trade Negotiations: An Overview," Federal Reserve Bank of Boston, *New England Economic Review* (May–June 1995): pp. 3–14. Ian Goldin, Odlin Knudsen, and Dominique van der Mensbrugghe estimated the gains from the Uruguay Round in *Trade Liberalization, Global Economic Implications* (Washington, DC: OECD and The World Bank, 1993). Also see *An Analysis of the Proposed Uruguay Agreement with Particular Emphasis on Aspects of Interest to Developing Countries* (Geneva: GATT, 1993). For a brief review of these studies, see "Economic Focus: For richer, for Poorer," *The Economist* (December 18, 1993); p. 66. For a discussion on intellectual property rights, see "Economic Focus: Trade Tripwires," *The Economist* (August 27, 1994); p. 61.

Finally, *The Year in Trade: Operations of the Trade Agreements Program*, published every year by the United States International Trade Commission, presents a rundown of trade developments during the year as they pertain to the United States.

Chapter 9

Trade Restrictions
and the Macroeconomy

This chapter discusses trade and economic policies with a very different character from those discussed in Chapter 7. There we looked at trade restrictions from the point of view of a *particular industry*. Some trade barriers, however, are designed to serve the *national* interest. Here, we examine national defense, infant industry, optimum tariffs and export duties, managed trade, and industrial policy for their effects on the value of exports and the cost of imports, and their impact on national economic welfare.

National Defense

The **national defense** argument for trade restrictions is based on the claim that a nation will require certain supplies, and the industries needed to supply them, in case of armed conflict.

National defense is often a persuasive argument for tariff protection since a nation must have the capacity to arm itself in times of war. But ensuring a nation's ability to produce war-related goods is not an argument for protecting a whole industry; it is a case for subsidizing a few firms which are critical to national survival. Thus, Boeing and General Dynamics shipbuilding should be protected, but not Cessna and Evinrude. A **national defense tariff** is imposed on imports of strategic consequence (for example, airplanes, or uranium, or even food). It is imposed for *political*, not economic reasons, since a national-defense tariff, like any tariff, *restricts trade and reduces national income.*

Infant-Industry Protection

The **infant-industry** argument is one of the oldest arguments for protection. Alexander Hamilton, in the 1780s and 1790s, proposed that the newly independent United States enact such a tariff so as to promote domestic industrialization. In its

The **infant-industry** argument for protection claims that new industries need protection until the domestic market expands sufficiently so that domestic firms can take advantage of economies of scale and become competitive both at home and abroad.

classic form, infant-industry measures seek to improve a nation's productive capacities. For example, an infant-industry tariff today might be imposed by the government of Nigeria on semiconductors in order to encourage domestic production of computer chips.

The traditional argument for infant-industry protection runs along the following lines. Suppose the Nigerian semiconductor industry has high startup costs due to either large initial capital outlays or heavy R&D expenditures. Imagine these costs equal $1 billion. As production expands, the $1 billion outlay is distributed over greater output and, assuming other costs of production are negligible, unit costs of production drop until some optimum point, Q_{opt} in Figure 9.1a, where unit costs are at a minimum, is reached. However, the optimum-size production run, the one that leads to the lowest average costs per unit of output, may be very large. Put more succinctly: Bigger is better.

According to the theory of the **learning curve,** industries learn by doing and, as a result, production costs decline over time.

Decreasing per-unit costs of production can be based on increasing returns to scale and the **learning curve.** Under increasing returns to scale, output *more than doubles* when all inputs are doubled. The learning curve hypothesis argues that unit costs of production decline, not necessarily over a specific production run, but rather *over time*

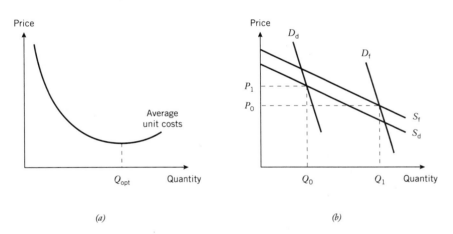

(a)   *(b)*

FIGURE 9.1 | Infant-industry protection.

Panel (a) shows us that if an industry faces high startup costs due to large initial capital outlays or hefty up-front R&D expenditures, average unit costs of production will decline as output expands until some optimum point of production, Q_{opt}, is attained. But to reach such a point, there must be a strong demand for product. Panel (b) shows that if the production of semiconductors is subject to increasing returns to scale under which output more than doubles when inputs double, unit costs of production will continuously decline. This means that the first country (or firm) to produce semiconductors will enjoy a cost advantage over newcomers. The same holds true in the case of the *learning curve*. Unit costs of production are lower in those countries that have spent more time producing semiconductors and thus have learned from doing. Thus, timing and the size of the market, not productive efficiency, can be key to whether a country will be competitive. In panel (b), the domestic industry would be competitive if given a chance. But domestic demand is so low relative to foreign demand that the domestic semiconductor industry will never get off the ground even though, compared to foreign firms, it would be more efficient.

as producers learn by doing. For example, the more computer chips produced in Nigeria, the fewer mistakes, and this reduces production costs. But then technical improvements occur in the production process itself and this raises output per unit of input. Thus, in Figure 9.1b, the value on the horizontal axis could measure either output (increasing returns), or cumulative output (the learning curve).

If unit costs of production decline for whatever reason as output expands, established firms hold a decided advantage over newcomers. Consider two firms: one an established company operating in Japan, the second a new firm attempting to get started in Nigeria—the home country in this example. Due to decreasing costs, the relative cost of producing semiconductors depends heavily on demand, namely, the greater the demand, the greater production and the lower unit costs. Since a firm operating in Nigeria faces a limited domestic market, one that has not reached its potential, it will be a high-cost producer. An established company operating in Japan will have achieved economies of scale in its operations and, therefore, will be the low-cost producer.

This situation is presented graphically in Figure 9.1b. Nigerian production costs, P_1, exceed foreign production costs, P_0, because foreign demand, D_f, is greater than domestic demand, D_d. The Japanese can produce and sell the quantity Q_1 in its domestic market while the Nigerian firm can sell only Q_0 of semiconductors in its domestic market. However, if Nigerian firms are actually the potential low-cost producers—their representative cost curve, S_d, lies below the foreign cost curve, S_f, at all levels of output—Japanese firms have a present-day cost advantage only because they are established and operate in a developed market, not because they are the potential low-cost producers. Given the development of the Nigerian market, domestic firms will become the more efficient producers.

Domestic Production in a Limited Market

Most consumers, however, live in the present. If Japanese semiconductors are cheaper than Nigerian semiconductors, people everywhere (including Nigerians) will purchase the Japanese brands. As a result, any incipient Nigerian demand will enlarge the demand for Japanese products and give foreign firms even greater opportunities to capture economies of scale or move down along their learning curves. Infant Nigerian firms will, therefore, be effectively shut out of the domestic market and never be able to reach their potential.

What is the economics minister of Nigeria to do? He hears from local producers that if domestic firms are given protection today, they will become competitive and profitable tomorrow as the domestic economy expands. Cast in these terms, the infant-industry argument for protection is weak. If potential profits actually exist, one would expect that domestic producers will establish productive facilities today, accepting short-run losses in order to obtain long-run gains.

There is an even more serious drawback to the argument. If Nigerian producers are indeed the world's low-cost producers, their relevant market is the world market, not the national market. Domestic production devoted to satisfying domestic demand may be restricted by the size of the domestic market, but domestic production is certainly not restricted by the size of the world market. In fact, the world market would be the catalyst for expanded domestic production.

A **market failure** exists when private markets cannot provide a good or service at some optimum level. In such cases, the government should, either directly or indirectly through taxes and subsidies, step in to fill the void.

The **United Nations Conference on Trade and Development (UNCTAD)** was formed in 1964 and is a permanent agency of the United Nations' General Assembly. It is generally regarded as an advocate for developing countries.

For this reason, many infant-industry advocates base their case on what are called **market failures.** What does this mean? Suppose domestic entrepreneurs are aware of the long-run profit potential and are willing to make the necessary investment today but lack the funds to carry it out. They must borrow at least a portion of the required investment funds on the capital market. If there is no domestic capital market or domestic lenders are unwilling to lend long-term, the investment will not take place unless the domestic entrepreneurs can tap international capital markets. If that path is blocked as well, the investment will be short-circuited and a profitable opportunity forgone.

What can a government do to overcome the financial constraint? It might step in and fill the gap by creating a domestic capital market, subsidizing the firm, or protecting it from foreign competition. The first two options are superior to the third—as described later. But if it is impossible to either create capital markets or raise revenue needed to fund a subsidy, trade restrictions are the only option.

But this may not be the case today. In the last few years, foreign direct investment has flowed from the developed to the developing world. The **United Nations Conference on Trade and Development (UNCTAD)** estimates that foreign direct investment inflows to the developed world equaled $80 billion or 47 percent of the total inflows of FDI in 1993. As Table 9.1 indicates, the inflow of FDI toward developing countries has more than doubled relative to the 1986–90 average while the inflow of FDI toward developed countries has actually declined during the period. Moreover, there has been a net inflow toward developing countries and a net outflow from developed countries.

Many Western firms—for example, the Ford Motor Company—have established production facilities in Asia in order to position themselves in that growing market. Other Western firms have entered into joint ventures with domestic firms in the LDCs. Such firms, once established in a developing country, will no doubt export some of their output back to developed countries. That, after all, is just what the amended product cycle theory of trade predicts.

Even in the absence of inflows of foreign capital, which itself might signal to Nigeria's minister of economics that something is amiss, one should be wary of

TABLE 9.1 Inflows and Outflows of Foreign Direct Investment (billions of dollars)

	1986–90 annual average	1991	1992	1993*
Developed countries				
Inflows	$130	$121	$102	$109
Outflows	163	185	162	181
Developing countries				
Inflows	25	39	51	80
Outflows	6	7	9	14

*Estimated.

Source: United Nations Conference on Trade and Development, *World Investment Report 1994: Transnational Corporations, Employment and the Workplace* (New York: United Nations 1995); Table I.4, p. 12.

recommending trade restrictions. It is one thing for a central government to establish a development bank, but quite another to protect a handful of firms and, in the process, give them a monopoly position. Trade restrictions which create a domestic monopoly or cartel may *hurt* the country more than the creation of the industry helps it, especially if the commodity in question is produced by several foreign firms who actively compete in an attempt to gain larger market shares throughout the world.

External Economies and Protection

Externalities occur when production by one party impacts another party. A classic example of a beneficial externality is a beekeeper who provides pollination services to neighboring farmers. Externalities can be negative and generate what are called *diseconomies*, which adversely affect neighboring parties (either raising their costs of production or reducing their welfare). All forms of environmental pollution are an example of diseconomies.

A tariff yields **side benefits** when the protection of industry A yields benefits or positive externalities to industry B.

Despite its weakness, the infant-industry argument for protection has many advocates around the world. One reason for its attractiveness is that it is said to create *external economies of production*, also called **externalities.** These are **side benefits** to the tariff— certain domestic industries reduce production costs in other sectors of the economy. For example, greater aluminum production may lead to lower unit costs of production and reduce the cost of producing a car, farm equipment, home appliances, and so forth. Moreover, when a particular firm adapts existing technology to domestic conditions (all types of engines adapted to the desert, let's say in Israel), its experience will benefit those firms that follow in its footsteps by reducing their startup costs. In both cases, the **social benefits** derived from the first firm's production may exceed the **private benefits** it receives when it sells its product.

Put another way, since a firm is driven by the quest for private profits, it will produce only up to the point where private benefits equal private costs. Argentina will not produce microprocessors if the world price is $100 and its production costs are $120 per unit. But if the social benefits derived from producing a microprocessor are $200 while the social costs of producing it are $120, Argentina as a whole will benefit if microprocessor production is subsidized. For Nigeria's minister of economics, then, the creation and protection of a national semiconductor industry can be defended not only because that industry may become efficient and competitive some time in the future, but also because the social benefits derived from the industry will exceed its social costs.

If this infant-industry argument is valid, the case for protection is not limited to LDCs, but is applicable to any industry in any country where social benefits exceed social costs and social costs and benefits diverge from private costs and benefits.

Qualifications

Social benefits are what society as a whole gains from, for example, the production of a particular good. Such benefits may exceed the **private benefits,** which are what the firm gains from producing the good.

Government intervention in cases of market failure are best solved by *subsidies* rather than tariffs and quotas, since the judicious use of subsidies, including the possibility of termination, can help prevent an infant industry from becoming an unproductive and expensive drain on the economy. But trade restrictions are justified only if the externalities flow from the creation of the industry and not from its final product. For example, if computers themselves create externalities but can be imported from a multitude of competitive foreign firms, externalities can be obtained through trade itself. Creating a relatively high-cost infant industry behind tariff walls might actually *reduce*

BOX 9.1   Infant-Industry Protection in South Korea

Many nations have sought to establish new industries and promote industrialization. By and large, these efforts have not been very successful; while they have benefited the chosen few, they have not done much for the economy as a whole. The economic success of South Korea, where the government actively promoted the creation and expansion of particular industries, shows that such a policy is feasible. It so happens that the influence of the South Korean government is declining because the growing financial strength of private firms has reduced the government's leverage over them. Yet the effects of the government's policy since the 1970s should not be overlooked.

South Korea employed a wide array of policies to promote industrialization. Favored industries received tax breaks and easy access to credit at favorable interest rates. And some firms, especially those starting up, received direct subsidies from the government. Normally, the subsidies were awarded on a declining basis so that the amount of the subsidy fell over time.

Trade restrictions were utilized to protect infant industries and to shield the domestic markets of exporting firms from foreign competition. The logic behind this last measure was simple. Imagine a firm produces multiple products—shoes for the domestic market and memory chips for foreign markets. If the firm is protected from foreign competition in the home market, it can charge a high price for shoes, a relatively lower price for chips, and still remain profitable. The profits, in turn, enable the firm to expand its productive facilities and export potential.

South Korea's development policy has been export-dominated since the country was acutely aware that its limited domestic market was unable to sustain large-scale manufacturing facilities by itself. That meant that if South Korean industries were to attain economies of scale and generate externalities, they required the larger markets of the world economy. The government also recognized early on that if its industries were to remain competitive, the won, the South Korean currency, could not be overvalued; it could not exchange for, say, $5 if a realistic competitive exchange rate was $1 per won. South Korea did not make this mistake; if anything, the won was kept undervalued.

Indicative planning attempts to boost output in particular sectors of the economy. Under indicative planning, a government provides economic forecasting and information to an industry and attempts to show the industry why it is in its best interests to expand production in certain sectors.

To assure export expansion, the government and firms mutually established export targets, a process called **indicative planning.** Firms were not compelled to meet the targeted goals, but it was certainly in their interest to do so. Government assistance was tied to performance, especially export performance. If firms did not hit the goals or targets, government assistance could be cut, subsidies canceled, access to cheap credit blocked, and import protection eliminated. Since firms surpassed export targets in the overwhelming majority of cases, government assistance was never curtailed.

Will the South Korean experience serve as a model for other LDCs? Some economists think not. Japan and South Korea built up their own industries by their own bootstraps, effectively shutting foreigners out of the process. But times have changed. The other "tigers" of Asia—Hong Kong, Singapore, Taiwan, Thailand, and Malaysia—have welcomed foreign investment, a good portion of it from Japan. Evidently, they have concluded that it is cheaper to utilize foreign investment and finance to assist in the development project than to carry the whole burden of development on their backs alone. Times have changed in other ways as well. As *The Economist* points out, a stable and prosperous Japan and South Korea were important to the Western World during the cold war. Given that need, many Western countries were more willing to put up with nationalistic economic policies than they are today in the post–cold war era.

Sources: Larry E. Westphal, "Industrial Policy in an Export-Propelled Economy: The Lessons from South Korea's Experience," *The Journal of Economic Perspectives* 4 (Summer 1990): 41–59; Sebastian Mallaby, "A Survey of South Korea," *The Economist* (June 3, 1995); and "Asia's Competing Capitalisms," *The Economist* (June 24, 1995): p. 16.

domestic welfare since the resources devoted to manufacturing computers might be employed more productively elsewhere, let's say in building 300 new elementary and secondary schools in the poorest part of the country. On the other hand, if the process of manufacturing computers leads to positive externalities—for example, by training segments of the labor force—then there is greater justification for initiating an infant-industry tariff.

Moreover, if infant-industry protection does produce externalities, the world as a whole may gain when a given nation imposes such a tariff, especially if the nation is the potential low-cost producer. Foreign firms that exported computers will suffer, but if externalities raise productivity and income in the protecting nation and expand its demand for other imports, world exporters may very well gain.

Tariffs and the Terms of Trade

A large country may have the ability to raise its welfare by imposing a tariff. Even though the tariff will reduce the volume of imports, if it reduces the international price of the import by a greater percentage, it is claimed that the country will be better off. In simpler terms, it can be argued that an **optimum tariff** will maximize a country's income terms of trade for a particular commodity.

An **optimum export duty** will maximize a country's, or a cartel's, revenue from exporting a particular commodity. If the demand for the product is inelastic, imposing an export duty will raise the price of the commodity by a greater percentage than it will reduce the quantity demanded.

In most instances, trade restrictions raise the domestic price of imports. Assuming the price of exports remains constant, the ratio of the price of exports to import prices falls, and the *domestic* commodity terms of trade move against the nation. Even if the world price ratio, Px/Pm, remains constant, the domestic price ratio, Px/Pm_t, where Pm_t equals the domestic price of the import after the imposition of the duty, will decline. Because the domestic price of imports rises, domestic consumers have to work harder, export more, in order to purchase the same number of imports. In the majority of cases, trade restrictions have this effect and the country as a whole loses.

But there are times when a tariff makes sense, when introducing trade restrictions may actually raise a nation's economic welfare. For example, if a nation enjoys a monopoly buyer or seller position, it can utilize a tariff or export duty to increase its economic welfare by turning the commodity terms of trade in its favor. Such tariffs and export duties are called **optimum tariffs** and **optimum export duties.**

Consider the pricing and production policy of OPEC. In 1973 and 1974, on the heels of the six-day war, the OPEC nations placed an export duty on oil exports that raised the price of their oil exports from under $3 per barrel to almost $12 per barrel. The tax raised the price of oil relative to the price of imports and improved the OPEC members' commodity terms of trade. Given the inelastic demand for oil, the decline in the volume of OPEC exports was more than offset by the higher price so that both the commodity and income terms of trade of OPEC members improved. They were richer even though they exported fewer barrels of oil.

The OPEC policy was an example of an optimum export duty. Together with an optimum tariff, it is one case, almost the singular one, where economists agree that free trade is not best for a nation. But before one rushes to judgment and concludes that all nations should adopt optimum export and import duties, the history of most OPEC members should be considered. That history suggests that the conditions required for introducing and preserving an optimum export duty are restricted.

Figure 9.2a demonstrates how an optimum export duty can be chosen. The demand curve, DD^*, represents the world's demand for the nation's export or one of its exports. Between the points D and B, demand is elastic; between points B and D^*, it is inelastic. If the nation, or a small number of nations acting in concert, is the sole producer of the commodity and production costs are trivial, it will select the price that will maximize

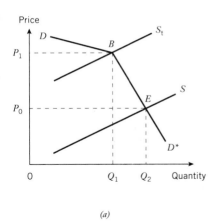

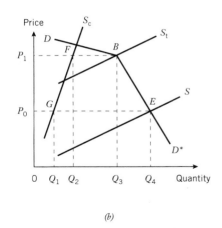

(a)   (b)

FIGURE 9.2 Optimum export duty.

In panel (a), a cartel imposes an export duty that raises the price of, say, oil, from P_0 to P_1. If the price elasticity of demand for oil is inelastic, as between the points B and D^* on the demand curve, the cartel members are sitting pretty. They can raise the price of oil knowing that the higher price will more than offset the price-related decline in the quantity of oil demanded. As can be seen, despite the drop in the quantity of oil sold, the total export earnings of the cartel rise from $0P_0EQ_2$ to $0P_1BQ_1$. If, however, competitors exist, then the export duty may help the competitors more than it helps the cartel members. In panel (b), prior to the imposition of the export duty, the price of oil is P_0 and the quantity demanded equals Q_4. The competitors supply 0–Q_1 of oil and the cartel members supply Q_1 to Q_4. Thus, the total revenue earned by the cartel members equals Q_1GEQ_4. The export tax raises the price of oil to P_1, but the quantity of oil exported by the cartel members falls to Q_2–Q_3 and their export earnings are now Q_2FBQ_3. Although the cartel members may earn additional revenue by imposing the export duty, the clear winners are the competitors, whose earnings jump from $0P_0GQ_1$ to $0P_1FQ_2$.

its total earnings. Assume that initially the supply curve, S, intersects the worldwide demand curve at the price P_0 and that the quantity supplied and demanded equals Q_2.

Now imagine that the nation introduces an export duty equal to the vertical difference between the curves S and S_t. The export duty shifts the supply curve from S to S_t. As a result, the price of the commodity climbs to P_1 while the quantity demanded falls to Q_1. The country ends up earning more revenue since the increase in price swamps the fall in the quantity sold. Prior to the imposition of the duty, the total export earnings of the nation equal $0P_0EQ_2$; after the duty is applied, export earnings equal $0P_1BQ_1$.

It turns out that the optimum duty in this example is equal to S–S_t. A higher or lower tax rate will be inferior from the nation's point of view. A higher duty will cut demand to such a degree that the nation's total export earnings will decline. A lower tax, and thus a lower price, will not allow the nation to maximize its export earnings because the increase in the quantity sold will be more than offset by the decline in the price. This means that an optimum export duty can be computed by looking at the nation's income terms of trade, $(Px/Pm)Qx$. As long as the income terms of trade improve, the country should keep raising the export duty.

Selecting an optimum tariff is similar to picking an optimum export duty. The idea is to maximize $(Px/Pm)Qm$, or the commodity terms of trade times the volume of imports. Consider the following example: Suppose a country's demand for CDs is elastic while the foreign export supply is highly inelastic. Prior to introducing a tariff, the nation imports 100 CDs at a cost of $1 per unit. Now assume the nation imposes a $.50 tariff on CDs and that the domestic price of CDs rises 10 percent to $1.10, and that the domestic demand for CDs falls by 10 percent to 90 units. Given these assumptions, the foreign supplier pays a $.40 tax on every CD she exports. Put more succinctly, the foreign exporter pays 80 percent of the duty.

As a result, the tariff-imposing nation imports CDs at $.60 per unit. And although domestic consumers pay $1.10 per CD, the government gains $.50 per CD imported, or $45 in this example, which it can use to lower domestic income taxes or raise government expenditures. The tariff-imposing nation benefits since its commodity terms of trade improve by a greater proportion than its imports decline. (Figure 7.2 gives some indication of the conditions under which an optimum tariff can be imposed.)

An Optimum Export Duty and National Income

An optimum export duty improves the imposing nation's terms of trade and raises its income. Indeed, this is the reason for introducing the policy in the first place. How it raises domestic income can be seen with the help of Figure 9.3.

The export duty shifts the export curve from X_0 to X_1 in Figure 9.3a. The vertical distance between X_1 and X_0, which is the same as the vertical distance between P_1 and P_0, equals the level of the export duty. For simplicity, it is assumed that the physical quantity of exports remains constant so that the value of exports equals the rectangle $0P_1EX$. The increase in the value of exports will shift the aggregate demand curve to the right, providing the government spends the tax receipts either by increasing its expenditures or cutting other taxes.

In either case, the AD curve shifts to the right in Figure 9.3b. The higher level of income causes the import curve to shift from M_0 to M_1. The physical volume of imports rises so that even though the price of imports remains constant, the value of imports now equals $0P_0ZM_1$, which equals the value of exports. In the end, domestic real income is higher and trade is balanced. As indicated, the country's terms of trade improve so that the national aggregate supply curve shifts to the right, and its potential level of income increases. The magnitude of the increase in potential income depends on the improvement in the terms of trade and the trade/GDP ratio. Back-of-envelope figures suggest that a 10 percent increase in the price of exports relative to the price of imports will raise national income by 3 percent if the trade/GDP ratio is 30 percent. (The calculation neglects the effect of the higher price on the demand for the nation's exports; thus the actual increase in potential income is less than indicated.)

An optimum import tariff has similar macroeconomic results. In both cases (either an optimum export duty or an optimum tariff), the tariff-imposing nation can choose to expand aggregate demand or build up its international financial position, or both.

Given the potential benefits of optimum export and import duties, why have so few nations attempted to introduce them? First, a nation seldom enjoys monopoly buying

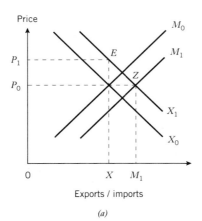
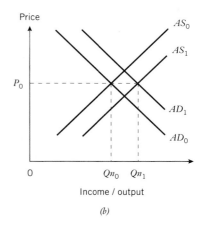

(a)   *(b)*

FIGURE 9.3   Optimum export duty and the economy.

An optimum export duty may raise a country's national income. Prior to imposing the export duty, exports equal imports when the price level is P_0, as shown in panel (a). And given the price level P_0, AS_0 equals AD_0 when the level of real GDP is Qn_0, panel (b). The export duty shifts the export curve from X_0 to X_1 and raises the price of exports to P_1 in panel (a). The improvement in the terms of trade shifts the aggregate supply curve from AS_0 to AS_1 and the potential level of income from Qn_0 to Qn_1. The trade surplus also shifts the aggregate demand curve to AD_1. The higher level of aggregate demand raises the demand for imports, and the import curve in panel (a) shifts from M_0 to M_1. Despite the greater physical quantity of imports, $0m_1$, the value of imports $0P_0ZM_1$ equals the value of exports $0P_1EX$ even though the physical quantity of exports remains constant. In other words, the price of exports increases while the price of imports remains constant, or the terms of trade improve.

power. And even if it does, such power would be restricted to a few imports at most. The message is that an optimum tariff policy must be selective. Some imports should enter the country duty-free, while others should be taxed to the hilt.

Even in the best of circumstances, it is unlikely that a nation can impose and maintain an optimum tariff over the long run. If people are taxed for the privilege of selling you a running shoe, some of them will stop producing shoes and start producing other goods instead. Supply curves, in other words, become more elastic over time and that reduces the possibility of carrying out a successful optimum tariff policy over the longer run.

Instituting an Optimum Export Duty: A Historical Example

Attempts to establish and sustain optimum export duties have not fared well. OPEC is an example. Initially, the oil cartel was successful. The price of oil rose dramatically and the member states' commodity and income terms of trade improved markedly, so much so that they became awash with dollars in the late 1970s, which they used to purchase capital assets in Europe and the United States. But the OPEC buying spree came to an abrupt halt because higher oil prices had other effects that ultimately drove the price of oil down. Consumers reduced their consumption of oil and, lured by the high price, non-OPEC oil producers stepped up production. Decreased demand and an increase in supply caused the price of oil and the earnings of the OPEC members to plummet.

Figure 9.2b illustrates just some of the difficulties involved in conducting an optimum export duty policy. Figure 9.2b is almost a duplicate of Figure 9.2a with one crucial difference: The line labeled S_c is the supply curve of a competitor or a non-OPEC oil producer. That means that the supply curve S now equals the sum of the competitor's supply and the OPEC supply. The quantity supplied by OPEC equals the total supply, S, minus the competitor's supply, S_c, at all price levels. Thus, the market is in equilibrium initially when the price equals P_0 and the quantity supplied and demanded

BOX 9.2   Semiconductors and International Trade

The semiconductor case of the mid-1980s is an example of the complications associated with economies of scale, dumping, subsidies, and even industrial policy. Semiconductors are essential for operating computers, telephones, laser printers, and all types of other equipment. Because they are so critical, it has been asserted that every nation should have a semiconductor industry. (Of course, if all nations promote, develop, and foster a particular industry, any potential benefits associated with comparative advantage will most likely fall by the wayside.)

Semiconductor production involves expensive up-front research costs and learning by doing (the learning curve). Production, therefore, is subject to increasing returns to scale. In turn, due to increasing returns to scale, **forward pricing** is the norm. Firms price the product, chips in this case, below average production costs at the outset when the market is limited in order to stimulate demand and create a market for the commodity. As demand expands, firms are able to capture economies of scale and make a handsome profit.

However, in order to be able to take advantage of an expanding market, a firm must have excess capacity standing at the ready to meet the projected demand. There is, therefore, a reward for being the first firm to build such productive capacity.

In the 1980s, U.S. semiconductor producers watched as Japanese producers grabbed an increasing share of the U.S. semiconductor market, especially the market for dynamic random access memory chips (DRAMs). For U.S. manufacturers, the problem of shrinking market shares came to a head in 1986 when the demand for chips nosedived as the sales of personal computers sharply dropped. Japanese firms responded to the contracting market by slashing prices, a policy that enabled them to sell more chips in foreign, including European, markets. The Japanese initiative forced U.S. firms to cut their prices, which hurt their profitability.

Faced with contracting markets and lower prices, U.S. producers cried foul claiming that the Japanese firms were dumping their products in foreign markets and restricting access to the Japanese market. The Department of Commerce (DOC) investigated the pricing policy of Japanese firms and concluded that they were indeed selling chips below average production costs, including a profit markup.

Based on the findings of the DOC, the American government imposed tariffs on Japanese chips as well as laptop computers and TV sets. The U.S. action and threat of further action led to the semiconductor agreement of 1986, which was renewed in 1991. Under the terms of the agreement, quarterly price floors were set for Japanese-produced memory chips and the Japanese government agreed to monitor the export prices of Japanese-made chips sold in the United States and the rest of the world. In addition, the Japanese government agreed to push Japanese firms to purchase more U.S.- and

Forward pricing is tied to product development and scale economies. When a product is introduced and demand is low, a company is unable to capture economies of scale. The firm will price the product on the basis of future demand. The lower price will enable the firm to induce a growing demand and capture economies of scale and higher profits at a later date.

foreign-made chips. In fact, an import target of 20 percent of the Japanese market was established. (To the surprise of many observers, foreign firms actually captured 20 percent of the Japanese chip market in the fourth quarter of 1992, up from 15 percent in the preceding quarter. And although the foreign share dropped to roughly 18 percent of the Japanese market in the first three quarters of 1993, it rose to close to 21 percent in the final quarter of that year and averaged 22.4 percent in 1994 and hit a record 26.2 percent in the third quarter of 1995.)

Under pressure from their own government, Japanese chip makers cut production and raised their prices in the mid-1980s. No sooner had these steps been taken than the market for chips expanded. Japanese chip producers who had been stuck with excess capacity and a dormant market were overjoyed as the price of chips tripled. The U.S.-sponsored cartel plus expanding demand bailed out Japanese firms. U.S. firms, such as laptop producers, were the obvious losers.

At this stage, several European countries, chip importers, took the issue of Japanese pricing policy before the GATT. The GATT found that Japan's attempts to police the price of chips violated international trade laws. And then came the Koreans, who rapidly expanded their production of chips, which further increased supply. The end result was that the price of 1-megabyte DRAMs fell from slightly below $50 in late 1986 to roughly $10 by the end of 1989, and to $6.60 in the middle of 1990. And 4-megabyte chips, which sold for $20 in 1991, sold for $12 in mid-1992. The attempt to stabilize the price of chips crashed.

What can be gleaned from this experience? In the case of DRAMs, there are several Japanese, Korean, and Taiwanese producers. Providing they are competitive and charge low prices, the United States might be better off letting the foreign firms dominate the production of DRAMs which, by most accounts, yields very modest profits. The example also illustrates the wide scope of antidumping legislation. In this case, dumping in third markets led the United States to take action.

In 1995, the international semiconductor market was in flux. Non-American firms had a lock on the production of DRAMs. However, in what might be called the upscale part of the market, microprocessors, for example, U.S. firms were the powerhouse. And it appeared that their lead over Japanese firms in this area was increasing. U.S. firms, led by Intel, controlled 90 percent of the market for "flash" memory chips.

Moreover, American-Japanese rivalry in semiconductors seemed to be subsiding in the early and mid-1990s as U.S. and Japanese firms signed a series of joint ventures to design and manufacture chips. For example, Intel signed an agreement with Sharp to produce flash chips, and IBM, Toshiba, and Siemens, a German firm, agreed to cooperate to design and build new memory chips. What led to the recent spat of marriages between American designing and Japanese production? According to industry experts, it is far cheaper to design and produce a chip jointly than for a firm to go it alone. In addition, the theory of comparative advantage suggests that if the designers, Americans, and the producers, Japanese, come together, they will both benefit.

The joint ventures have their critics. American skeptics believe that Japanese firms will dominate the agreements and exploit the American firms. Even more important, perhaps, is the question of *where* the chips will be produced and *which* nation will gain the most jobs. These questions cannot be answered at the present time. But if the joint ventures stick, the semiconductor agreements of 1986 and 1991 may very well become moot. The semiconductor agreements may become moot for another reason. In the fall of 1995, the Japanese government announced it had no intention of extending the accord when it expires in July 1996.

Sources: Brink Lindsey, "Don't Renew the Semiconductor Cartel," *Wall Street Journal* (May 20, 1991): p. 18A; "America Chips Away at Japan," *The Economist* (March 27, 1993): pp. 65–66; "Chip Diplomacy," *The Economist* (July 18, 1992): p. 65 ff; "South Korea Chip Exports Soar," *Financial Times* (October 25, 1994): p. 5; "Foreign Chip Sales Up in Japan," *Financial Times* (December 16, 1994): p. 6; Laura Tyson, "Higher Yen Boosts Taiwan's Chip Prospects," *Financial Times* (June 15, 1995): p. 4; and William Dawkins, "Japan to Scrap Chip Market Access Accord," *Financial Times* (October 21–22, 1995): p. 3.

equals Q_4. At equilibrium, the export earnings of the competitor equals $0P_0GQ_1$ and the export earnings of the cartel equals Q_1GEQ_4.

Suppose OPEC imposes an export duty as before. The price of oil climbs to P_1 and the quantity demanded falls from Q_4 to Q_3. However, the higher price causes the competitor to increase the quantity it supplies from Q_1 to Q_2. That means that OPEC exports drop from Q_1–Q_4 to Q_2–Q_3. Does the export duty make sense from OPEC's viewpoint? The answer depends on what happens to its total export earnings. Prior to introducing the export duty, OPEC's export earnings equaled Q_1GEQ_4; after imposing the export duty, its earnings equal Q_2FBQ_3. OPEC's export earnings rise, but only by a very modest amount. Who is the big winner? The competitor. Its export earnings jump from $0P_0GQ_1$ to $0P_1FQ_2$; it exports more oil and at a higher price, giving true meaning to the term *free rider*.

Subsidies: Static and Dynamic

A subsidy is a cash payment made in order to induce greater production.

Subsidies are money payments made in order to keep prices below what they would be in a free market. In the context of international economics, subsidies can be used to restrict imports, much like a tariff, or they can be employed to expand exports. First, we will consider subsidies as a substitute for a tariff. In the next section, we look at subsidies in a more dynamic light, as a tool for expanding exports.

It is generally agreed that if a nation wants to protect an industry facing fierce foreign competition, a **subsidy,** such as a cash grant (e.g., $10 per unit produced), is superior to a tariff. For one, a subsidy involves a lower dead-weight loss than a tariff. Furthermore, because it is a cash grant, a subsidy shows up as a budget expenditure and can be reviewed, and perhaps reduced or eliminated, at budget time. Since a tariff is not an expenditure, and may even raise revenue, it is not subject to the same degree of scrutiny.

In many respects, a subsidy is similar to a tariff. The microeconomic effects of a subsidy are illustrated in Figure 9.4, where the world price, domestic production and consumption, and imports are analogous to those in Figure 7.1. Since a subsidy reduces production costs, it induces greater production by domestic firms.

This chain of events is shown in Figure 9.4, where a subsidy rate equal to vertical distance between S_1 and S_2 or EZ shifts the domestic supply curve to the right from S_1 to S_2. Domestic production expands from Q_1 to Q_2 and imports drop from Q_1–Q_4 to Q_2–Q_4. Consumption, however, remains constant at Q_4 because the domestic price, which equals the world price, does not change. A subsidy, therefore, avoids the consumption effect associated with a tariff and imposes a lower dead-weight loss than a tariff.[1]

To get a better grip on this argument, a price line, Pw_t, is drawn through point E. This makes it possible to compare the results of subsidies and tariffs. The rate of subsidy is EZ, the quantity of production subsidized is O–Q_2, so that the total subsidy equals the area $PwEZPw_t$. The subsidy can be divided into two parts: A, the redistri-

---

[1]A common complaint is that this analysis is incomplete since in order to pay a subsidy, a government must raise taxes, such as the income tax. Thus, although the relative price of the subsidized good does not increase and, therefore, its consumption should not decline, higher taxes may decrease the general consumption among those individuals who pay the tax to finance the subsidy. However, the general consumption of those who receive the subsidy should increase.

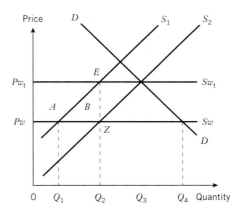

FIGURE 9.4 The cost of a subsidy versus the cost of a tariff.

In order to expand domestic production from Q_1 to Q_2, a tariff would need to raise the domestic price of the product from Pw to Pw_t. A production subsidy of the same magnitude has the same protective effect, but it is less expensive. A subsidy of EZ per unit of output, exactly the same rate as the required tariff, cuts the cost of producing a personal computer. As a result, the domestic supply schedule shifts to the right from S_1 to S_2 and domestic output rises to Q_2. Since the subsidy does not raise the domestic price of PCs, nor does it raise any revenue, the consumption and revenue effects of a tariff are avoided. However, the total subsidy payment to producers equals the subsidy rate times the number of units produced, or $PwPw_tEZ$, and someone must pay it—namely, the domestic consumers of PCs. Some of the subsidy, area A, represents the redistribution of income from consumers to producers; and some of the subsidy, area B, represents the protective effect and is also the dead-weight loss of the subsidy. But the dead-weight loss of a subsidy (area B) is lower than the dead-weight loss associated with a tariff: areas B and D in Figure 7.1.

bution effect; and B, the protective effect. Because a subsidy does not have a consumption effect, its superiority over a tariff depends on the domestic elasticity of demand. If it is completely inelastic, the dead-weight loss of a tariff and subsidy are equal. As demand becomes more elastic, the superiority of a subsidy increases and a nation achieves the same protective effect at a lower cost.

While superior to a tariff, a subsidy still costs. Under a tariff, consumers indirectly subsidize an industry through a higher price. In the case of a subsidy, they pay taxes directly to the government, which then transfers the funds to producers. It is this feature of a subsidy—visible higher taxes—that encourages people to believe that, unlike a tariff, a subsidy will not become permanent, although the long history of agricultural subsidies throughout the world should put a damper on such optimism.

Subsidies, Subsidy Wars, and Trade Wars

Since subsidies restrict international trade, there is a danger in employing them: namely, the outbreak of a subsidy war. If nation A grants subsidies and country B is unable to match them step for step because of budget constraints, it might resort to quotas as a countermeasure. In fact, countries have increasingly introduced countervailing duties in order to offset the effects of foreign subsidies on the price of imports, actual and potential. This practice is just one indication that a subsidy war can be transformed into a tariff or quota war.

To prevent such tariff or quota wars from occurring, subsidy guidelines were established at the Uruguay Round. Under the agreement, regional and to some degree research subsidies were exempted from the guidelines. But rules were instituted in other cases, especially in those where one nation's subsidy harmed its competitors. For specific products, subsidies were limited to 50 percent of basic research expenditures and 75 percent of the cost of building prototypes. LDCs were exempted to some degree from these guidelines. But given the sorry state of most LDC budgets, this concession is probably of little value.

Questions regarding subsidies and countervailing duties still remain murky. The ability of the world economy to reach an agreement on these issues will depend on the capacity of the WTO and its dispute panels to establish recognizable guidelines and enforce them. The WTO will have to ensure that countervailing duties are not employed as a stratagem for erecting trade barriers; it will also have to ensure that trade-distorting subsidies are not introduced in the first place.

Strategic Trade Policy

Fighting tariffs and subsidies by the WTO may be easier said than done. Subsidies take many forms such as direct grants, low-interest-rate loans, preferential tax treatment, government procurement policies, and even indirect subsidies in the form of research contracts for government projects with commercial applications. The recent hurling of charges and countercharges by American and European officials over who subsidizes their particular jetliner industry most is an example. Few deny that Airbus Industrie, a jetliner consortium owned almost exclusively by Britain, France, and Germany, is subsidized. The Europeans claim the subsidies do not violate rules laid down by GATT/WTO and that the United States, through military contracts and space research, subsidizes its aircraft industry.

Presumably, the United States and the European Union reached an accommodation regarding the level of aircraft industry subsidies. Under the terms of the agreement, the EU agreed to eliminate production subsidies and limit funding for aircraft development to 30 percent. In addition, the agreement imposed strict terms and conditions for repayment of development funds advanced to Airbus Industrie by the various governments. For example, any loan extended to Airbus Industrie must bear a realistic or market rate of interest, not an artificially low or subsidized rate. The agreement, negotiated by the Bush administration in 1992, appeared to be in trouble in 1995, when it appeared that the United States wanted to renegotiate the bilateral agreement in order to reduce the ceiling for direct government subsidies for new aircraft development from 33 percent to 20 percent.

A **strategic trade policy** explains how, under special conditions, a nation may gain at the expense of its trading partners by employing subsidies.

Another complication concerning subsidies has arisen. Based on the work of James Brander and Barbara Spencer, economists have developed theoretical models that justify the use of subsidies and have led to the development of the theory of **strategic trade policy.** Strategic trade policy has startling implications. It demonstrates that under certain conditions a free trade policy may not be best for a nation. By employing subsidies and encouraging industrial development in specific sectors, a nation can gain at the expense of its trading partners. Thus, as in the case of an optimum tariff or export duty, a free trade policy may not benefit both parties, a violation of one of the basic tenets of comparative advantage.

Under what conditions does this occur? Suppose, due to high startup costs, an industry operates under conditions of decreasing costs or increasing returns to scale. This means that as production expands, fewer and fewer firms will be able to survive, but those that do endure will earn excess returns due to a lack of competition. If the market is so limited that it can support only one firm, a strategic trade policy may be a nation's best option.

Consider the classic example of Paul Krugman given in Figure 9.5. Both Boeing and Airbus can produce enough airplanes to satisfy the world market. In fact, the world market can profitably support only one firm. What happens if both firms produce planes? The first payoff matrix shows that if both companies produce planes, they will both lose $5. But if one company produces while the other does not, it will earn $100. If Boeing has the edge and is first off the mark, it will earn $100. Aware that it would lose $5 if it produced airplanes, Airbus will not produce. The two companies, therefore, end up in the top-right cell on the chart. (Boeing's profit or loss is indicated in the lower left-hand corner of each cell.)

Now suppose the European Union grants Airbus a $10 subsidy. This radically changes the payoff matrix. Boeing will still gain $100 if Airbus does not produce and will lose $5 if Airbus enters the business; but Airbus will gain whether or not Boeing produces. If Boeing produces, Airbus gains $5—the $10 subsidy minus the $5 loss; if

Payoff matrix, no subsidy

		Airbus	
		Produces	Does not produce
Boeing	Produces	−5 −5	0 100
	Does not produce	100 0	0 0

Payoff matrix, Airbus subsidy

		Airbus	
		Produces	Does not produce
Boeing	Produces	−5 −5	0 100
	Does not produce	100 0	0 0

FIGURE 9.5 Krugman diagram.

The first payoff matrix demonstrates that the first company off the mark, Airbus or Boeing, will capture the market, since the latecomer will lose money if it produces planes. The second payoff matrix shows why, given a subsidy, only Airbus will produce planes.

Source: Paul R. Krugman, "Is Free Trade Passé?", *Journal of Economic Perspectives*, (Fall 1987): p. 136.

Boeing does not produce, Airbus obtains $110—the $100 profit plus the $10 subsidy. Clearly, under these conditions Airbus will produce and, just as clearly, Boeing, aware of Airbus's decision and the subsidy, will not. The companies end up in the lower-left cell. Airbus produces the plane and because its profits exceed the subsidy by a large margin, it is able to repay the government and everyone in the EU will be happy. If one tacks on the assumption that Airbus learns by doing (the learning curve), and that its production generates positive externalities, the case for a subsidy becomes compelling.

The subsidy pays. Indeed, even if the subsidy were higher, its benefits would still exceed its costs. But the subsidy's "profitability" can introduce complications. If the EU is willing to grant a subsidy to Airbus, what happens if the United States grants a subsidy to Boeing? Both companies would produce airplanes and, given the subsidy, might actually make a profit or cover costs. In the example, each firm's, but not each country's, $5 loss would be offset by a $10 subsidy.

If production engenders positive externalities on both sides of the Atlantic, both areas may end up in a better position—although inferior to the position each would hold as a monopolist. And even if external economies do not exist, one nation, say the United States, may be better off despite the money lost as a result of the countersubsidy. With a subsidy, America loses $5 but maintains at least a portion of its jetliner industry and its resulting employment. Without a subsidy, it will transfer a substantial sum of money and jobs to the EU.

Given various assumptions, several outcomes are possible. For example, the EU could "up the ante" by paying out a higher subsidy. Airbus could use a portion of the subsidy to drop the price of its planes and capture a larger share of the market. In that event, some of the EU subsidy would be transferred to jetliner consumers. Moreover, since subsidies take resources away from other areas of the economy, ever higher subsidies would diminish the net benefits of the program to the EU.

Many individuals have serious reservations regarding the effectiveness of strategic trade policies. Not only is there the possibility of a subsidy war breaking out and leading to a trade war, the political economy of commercial policy suggests that often government assistance is directed toward selected interest groups, not toward the national interest. Critics are dubious that a well-thought-out and logical strategic trade policy can be carried out.

Nevertheless, despite such criticism, there is a growing interest in strategic trade policy. And regardless of one's view of whether a government should introduce such a policy, the implications of strategic trade policy still hold. As Paul Krugman has put it:

> It is possible, then, both to believe that comparative advantage is an incomplete model of trade and to believe that free trade is nevertheless the right policy. . . . So free trade is not passé—but it is not what it once was.
>
> "Is Free Trade Passé?", *Journal of Economic Perspectives* 1 (Fall 1987): p. 143.

Industrial Policy

Industrial policy is one of the more popular Washington, D.C.–based phrases of the 1990s. An industrial policy is designed, among other things, to promote strategic industries. Therefore, not only will it complement a strategic trade policy, it may even be a prerequisite for such a policy. An industrial policy is based on the assumption that

An **industrial policy** attempts, by various measures such as subsidies, favorable tax treatment, and cheap credit, to develop what are called leading-edge industries. These industries are normally hi-tech and are presumed to generate all sorts of externalities.

certain industries are crucial for a country's economic welfare and its international competitiveness. Typically, the industries are high-tech and require large R&D expenditures. Thus, the manufacture of computer chips is felt to be more important for the long-run economic welfare of the society than the production of potato chips. Because of the growing demand for high-tech products, the nations that produce them will enjoy expanding export markets and dominate the world economy. In addition, the production of high-tech items generates positive economywide externalities. Thus, regardless of its impact on foreign trade, an industrial policy will enrich a nation. Given the benefits derived from an industrial policy, advocates argue that governments should undertake policies to help expand output in such strategic sectors to the point where the industry-generated social benefits, including externalities, equal the social costs of production.

There are diverse views over exactly what an industrial policy should entail. Most observers agree that if an industrial policy is designed to enhance a nation's overall international competitiveness, it will need to include certain macro- as well as micromeasures. The relationship among high savings, high investment ratios, and international competitiveness is not perfect, but it is certainly too strong to be neglected. This means that an effective industrial policy may very well need to include measures that will raise national investment-to-GDP and savings-to-GDP ratios. An industrial policy, therefore, could involve revising the tax system so that it rewards savings and investment and penalizes consumption. Other non–industry- or non–firm-specific policies could include developing labor skills and expanding the stock of the public infrastructure.

There is little evidence that firm-specific policies alone can improve a nation's overall competitiveness. The former Soviet Union was a technological leader in designing and producing armaments, and modern military arms are the epitome of high-tech. Yet Soviet proficiency in this area did not make the Soviet economy internationally competitive or even place it in the top ten nations when measured by per-capita GDP.

While there is a surprising degree of unanimity among economists regarding the macro side of an industrial policy, the unanimity breaks down when the question of the degree of direct public assistance to specific industries is raised. Some individuals believe that the government should take an active role and subsidize—through cheap loans, trade protection, tax relief, and subsidies—those firms that it believes will be the technological leaders of tomorrow and that it should also sponsor joint public-private research consortiums such as Sematech. Others are more wary of using public funds to promote private developments. They are concerned that governments have subsidized too many white elephants, such as the supersonic transport project, in the past. The major thrust of the critics is that it is one thing to talk about social benefits, social costs, externalities, and the like, and another to calculate them. Does the government, for example, have enough information to make such calculations? The critics say no. And, lacking information, the authorities will have to fly by the seat of their pants picking winners and avoiding losers, something at which, in the opinion of critics of industrial policy, governments have been inept.

Moreover, industry-specific subsidies run headlong into questions of countervailing duties, GATT guidelines, and potential subsidy wars. And even barring all of the above, there is always the question of who is going to subsidize what and what will be its impact on international trade. Americans who demand that the United States launch an industrial policy to counter unfair trade advantages obtained by Japan and to secure the positive externalities that result from the development and growth of strategic industries seldom consider that Brazil, China, Germany, India, Russia,

BOX 9.3 Industrial Policy in Japan: The Record

Richard Beason and David Weinstein tallied up Japanese industries that received the major share of government assistance between 1955 and 1990 and compared *assistance* to *performance*. Performance was measured by the annual percentage growth in output. Assistance was also measured in relative terms. Cheap loans were computed by adding up the loans an industry received from the Japan Development Bank and dividing this figure by the total loans the industry received. Trade protection was calculated by the degree of effective protection applied to an industry's products. In the end, all sectors were ranked by performance and specific types of assistance. The industry that received the most relative aid in a category was ranked first; the industry that received the least was ranked thirteenth. Mining, for example, received the most cheap loans, the most net transfers, and the most tax relief, but the least amount of trade protection.

The figures are not a ringing endorsement of Japan's industrial policy, and in fact it appears the Japanese government has backed many losers. In every category, the correlation between an industry's growth and the amount of assistance it received was negative. Hence, the Japanese government gave more support to *laggard* industries than to *rapidly expanding* ones.

TABLE 9.2 Growth and Government Assistance in Japan: 1955–1990

Industry	Growth	Cheap Loans	Net Transfers	Trade Protection	Tax Relief
Electrical machinery	1	8	9	8	8
General machinery	2	12	4	11	8
Transport equipment	3	7	11	4	8
Fabricated metal	4	10	6	12	7
Oil and coal	5	2	13	7	3
Precision instruments	6	13	10	6	8
Ceramics, stone, and glass	7	5	8	9	3
Pulp and paper	8	6	5	10	13
Chemicals	9	3	7	5	3
Basic metals	10	4	2	3	6
Processed foods	11	9	12	1	12
Mining	12	1	1	13	1
Textiles	13	11	3	2	2

Source: Richard Beason and David E. Weinstein, *Growth, Economies of Scale, and Targeting in Japan (1955–1990)* (Cambridge, MA: Harvard Institute of Economic Research 1993), Discussion Paper 1644, Table 1, p. 18. Forthcoming as Richard Beason and David E. Weinstein, "Growth, Economies of Scale and Targeting in Japan, 1955–1990," *Review of Economics and Statistics,* Vol. 78 #2 (May 1966), pp. 286–295. © by the President and Fellows of Harvard College and the Massachusetts Institute of Technology.

Mexico, the Nordic countries, and so on may also embark on such a policy now or in the future. Yet, if every nation has a subsidized and protected computer industry, semiconductor industry, and telecommunications industry, trade in such products may come to a halt.

Japan is always cited as an example of how an industrial policy can stimulate growth. Certainly Japan has enjoyed rapid growth in the post–World War II period and much has been written regarding the role of the Ministry of International Trade and Industry and the Bank of Japan in fostering this growth. Critics of industrial policy, especially in the United States, argue that Japan got its macroeconomic policy right and that is the major reason for Japan's economic expansion since 1960. Japan has had a high investment-to-GDP ratio that has been made possible by its high savings-to-GDP ratio. Given normal market incentives plus a high investment ratio, it is only natural, they claim, that Japan has prospered. In addition, they cite a recent study by Richard Beason and David Weinstein (see Box 9.3, Table 9.2) that claims that Japan's industrial policy may be overrated.

Beason's and Weinstein's study gives pause to the idea that economic growth was due in large part to the government selecting and nurturing rapidly growing industries. The Japanese government appears to have supported more than its share of lemons.

One study, however, does not necessarily prove that industrial policies are ineffective. Governments help industries for various reasons and more often they help the weak rather than the strong in order to maintain some sort of social equilibrium—recall the *status quo model* of Chapter 8. Indeed, tariff theory and practice suggests that governments often protect noncompetitive domestic industries from the effects of international competition. That's why industrial policy proponents argue that one should separate out those government activities designed to protect weak industries from those devised to promote dynamic ones. Evidence suggests that governments will always assist weak industries. Thus, the real question is whether governments should, in addition, assist newer, more dynamic industries. Viewed in this light, an industrial policy, despite admitted shortcomings, looks more viable.

Summary

Generally, free trade is superior to restricted trade, a subsidy is superior to a tariff, and a tariff is better than a quota. Cases can be made for three types of trade restrictions: an optimum tariff, an extended infant-industry tariff, and a strategic subsidy. But the prerequisites for a successful optimum tariff or export duty seldom exist even in the short run; and when they do, they decline over time. For a developed nation, a subsidy is the superior method of assisting an infant industry; in the special case of LDCs, it may be impossible for a government to raise the revenue to finance a subsidy, so that the LDC will have to rely on a tariff. However, this justification for a tariff is often overplayed. And as South Korean experience illustrates, infant-industry protection requires a cohesive set of polices and the willingness of the government to take away assistance as well as to give it. Finally, although a promising theoretical development, a strategic trade policy, and an industrial policy as well, must overcome obstacles such as uncertainty over what will be the leading-edge industries a generation from now.

Key Concepts and Terms

externalities

forward pricing

indicative planning

industrial policy

infant-industry argument for protection

learning curve

market failures

national-defense argument for a tariff

optimum export duty

optimum tariff

social versus private costs and benefits

strategic trade policy

subsidies

Review Questions

1. Explain the arguments for infant-industry protection, taking care to differentiate between cases based on decreasing costs or increasing returns to scale and those based on external economies.

2. Assuming a nation successfully introduces an infant-industry tariff, what may be the impacts of this tariff on the rest of the world?

3. Under what conditions might a nation introduce an optimum tariff?

4. What is the rationale for introducing an optimum export duty? Why do many observers believe that an optimum export duty loses its potency over time?

5. Explain what is meant by the learning curve and by forward pricing.

6. Many, indeed most, economists argue that a subsidy is better than a tariff. What explains their position?

7. Strategic trade policy suggests that under certain conditions a nation may discover that a free trade policy is not best from its point of view. Explain when a nation may find it advantageous to restrict trade.

8. Many members of the Clinton administration claim that the United States should introduce an industrial policy. What is meant by the term "industrial policy"? What are the macro- and microeconomics of such a policy? In light of the study by Richard Beason and David Weinstein, what is your view regarding the introduction and implementation of an industrial policy?

References and Suggested Readings

The whole question of U.S.-Japanese economic relationships is examined by C. Fred Bergsten and Marcus Noland in *Reconcilable Differences? United States–Japan Economic Conflict* (Washington, DC: Institute for International Economics, 1993). On this subject, one should also consult Clyde Prestowitz, *Trading Places: How We Allowed Japan to Take the Lead* (New York: Basic Books, 1988).

A seminal article on strategic policy was written by James A. Brander and Barbara J. Spencer, "International R&D Rivalry and Industrial Strategy," *Review of Economic Studies* 50 (October 1983): pp. 707–722. However, a more accessible and outstanding description of strategic trade is Paul R. Krugman, "Is Free Trade Passé?", *Journal of Economic Perspectives* 1 (Fall 1987): pp. 131–144. Paul Krugman also edited a collection of essays on strategic trade policy, *Strategic Trade Policy and the New International Economics* (Cambridge: MIT Press, 1986). The essays, for the most part, are accessible to the general public, especially Professor Krugman's introduction. Laura D'Andrea Tyson, former Chair of the Council of Economic Advisors, has long been an advocate of industrial policy. See Laura D'Andrea Tyson, *Who's Bashing Whom? Trade Conflict in High-Technology Industries* (Washington, DC: Institute for International Economics, 1992). Paul R. Krugman and Maurice Obstfeld, in *International Economics: Theory and Policy*, 3rd edition (New York: HarperCollins, 1994), pp. 284–287, demonstrate that altering the figures in the payoff matrix illustrated in Figure 9.5 can change the results.

A series of short articles by Peter A. Petri, Otto Graf Lambsdorff, Michael Borrus, David Stout, I. J. Singh, and Daniel Malkin appeared in *International Economic Insights* IV (March–April 1993) under the title "Industrial Policy Revisited."

In this regard, one might also consult Anne O. Krueger, "Government Failures in Development," Mrinal Datta-Chaudhuri, "Market Failure and Government Failure," and Albert Fishlow, "The Latin American State," all in the *Journal of Economic Perspectives* 4 (Summer 1990).

Balance of Payments Policy

Chapter 10

Trade Balance
and Income Adjustment

Trade theory most often assumes that a nation's exports equal its imports. But in reality, countries usually have either a positive or negative trade position. Consider Table 10.1 which shows the trade balances and current accounts of the G7 countries in 1994. Not one nation's external accounts, regardless of how measured, equaled zero. All had either surpluses or deficits.

Even though the surplus of one country will equal the deficit of one or more other countries, the question of deficits is most pressing. In the overwhelming majority of cases and notwithstanding capital flows, if a country's external accounts go into the red, it must eventually take steps to eliminate the excess of imports over exports since no nation can run a trade deficit indefinitely. Such steps can prove costly. And if they impose a heavy burden, a nation may reduce its commitment to free trade in order to avoid them. So, while the *logic* for trade primarily hinges on the benefits derived from

TABLE 10.1   Trade and Current Account Positions: 1994
(billions of dollars)

Country	Trade Account	Current Account
Canada	12.2	−17.4
France	9.1	8.8
Germany	51.0	−20.9
Italy	35.5	14.6
Japan	144.1	122.9
United Kingdom	−16.0	0.0
United States	−166.5	−156.2

The trade account equals the merchandise account.

Source: Computed from the relevant country pages of International Monetary Fund, *International Financial Statistics Yearbook,* 1995.

comparative advantage, the *level* of trade is conditioned by the ability of nations to overcome trade imbalances without imposing heavy burdens on the society.

The Path Ahead

This chapter is the first of three that discuss what is called the *adjustment mechanism*, or how a country can right its trade balance. The present chapter concentrates on income changes and how they affect the external accounts. It does this in four steps:

- A review of the relationship between external and internal equilibrium.
- An explanation of the relationship between output and absorption and a nation's trade balance, followed by development of the *Absorption Schedule* or *Curve*, an important tool for analyzing the external position of an economy given its internal position.
- A discussion of how a change in income can affect the trade balance assuming that the general price level is stable.
- Analysis of the impact of a change in income on the trade balance assuming a rise in the general price level.

External and Internal Equilibrium

An **expenditure-switching** policy, such as currency depreciation, causes individuals to reduce their purchases of foreign products and to increase their expenditures on domestic products.

An **expenditure-reducing** policy, such as an increase in tax rates, will reduce total expenditures. Since the policy is reversible, it can be **expenditure increasing** as well.

An over-riding concern of closed-economy macroeconomics is what must be done to guarantee that an economy attains full employment and stable prices simultaneously. The over-riding concern of open-economy macroeconomics is what steps must be taken to assure that an economy operates at full employment with price stability (internal equilibrium) while, at the same time, its external accounts are balanced (external equilibrium). An open economy may attain internal equilibrium but, at the same time, fall short of realizing external equilibrium. The reverse can occur. A country's external accounts may be balanced while the country suffers from unemployment or inflation. And there is also the possibility that a country may be trapped in one of the so-called zones of misery, listed here, and attain neither internal nor external equilibrium.

Zone I: unemployment surplus
Zone II: inflationary surplus
Zone III: inflationary deficit
Zone IV: unemployment deficit

If a nation finds itself in one of these four zones, it can, in fact, restore both internal and external equilibrium by introducing either **expenditure-switching** policies or **expenditure-reducing** or **increasing** policies. In most cases when an economy is in disequilibrium, both expenditure-switching (such as exchange rate depreciation or appreciation) and expenditure-reducing policies (such as cutting or raising government expenditures) are required if an economy is to simultaneously attain external and internal equilibrium.

An Inflationary Deficit

Many countries have run up against the combination of inflation and a trade deficit (Zone III); there are fewer examples of countries that have faced unemployment with a trade surplus (Zone I). In the 1930s, the United States suffered from a crushing depression, but nevertheless had a trade surplus. And at the end of 1995, Japan, despite a stagnant economy, still managed to run a trade surplus, although a dwindling one.

Figure 10.1 presents the case of an economy which faces an inflationary deficit. (Since an unemployment surplus is the mirror image of an inflationary deficit, it is not described.) Suppose an economy is operating at a point where, as in Figure 10.1b, AD_0 intersects AS at the price level P, considered noninflationary, and output level Qn, the potential level of output. At this price and income level, exports equal imports as shown in Figure 10.1a.

Now, if there is an increase in aggregate demand which pushes the aggregate demand curve to the right from AD_0 to AD_1, the price level will rise to P_1 and the economy will move into an inflationary position. At the same time, as the AD curve shifts to the right, the import schedule will move from M_0 to M_1, and the country will run a

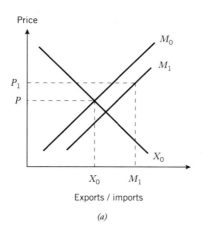

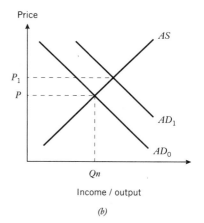

(a) (b)

FIGURE 10.1 Inflationary trade deficit.

If the aggregate supply curve, AS in panel (b), intersects the aggregate demand curve, AD_1, at the price level, P_1, the economy will be in an inflationary situation since it will be operating above its potential level of income, Qn. If at the same time, imports exceed exports, or the import curve, M_1, lies to the right of the export curve, X_0, at the price level P_1, the economy will have a trade deficit. An expenditure-reducing policy will help to restore internal and external equilibrium. The policy will shift the aggregate demand curve to the right to AD_0, reduce the level of GDP, and drop the domestic price level to P. Given the decline in income, the import curve will shift from M_1 to M_0. Together with decline in income, the drop in the price level will eliminate the trade deficit.

trade deficit for two reasons. First, the higher level of aggregate demand will stimulate the demand for more imports, and second, the higher price level will increase imports and decrease exports. The way out of this bind is quite direct. The country, through an expenditure-reducing policy, should shift its aggregate demand curve to the left.

An Inflationary Surplus

Many countries have simultaneously faced unemployment and a trade deficit. In fact, some European Union nations were in that position during most of the 1990s. Countries that have suffered from inflation, or potential inflation, while running a trade surplus are a rarer breed, although some analysts suggest that Germany has faced such a dilemma from time to time since 1960. Figure 10.2 helps explain why.

Imagine that the aggregate demand and aggregate supply schedules intersect at points to the right of Qn and above P, as in Figure 10.2b. From the preceding discussion, we might conclude that the country should follow an expenditure-reducing policy, one that would shift the AD schedule back to the left in order to reduce inflation. But notice that in Figure 10.2a, the nation has a trade surplus at the price level P_1.

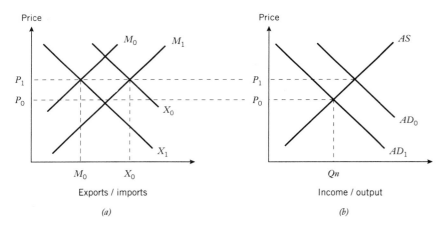

FIGURE 10.2 Inflationary surplus.
If an economy faces an inflationary surplus, an expenditure-reducing policy alone will not restore internal and external equilibrium. Such a policy may reduce domestic inflation, but it will exacerbate the trade imbalance. In panel (b), AS intersects AD_0 at the price level P_1, and the economy faces inflation. However, at the price level P_1, the export curve, X_0, lies to the right of the import curve, M_0, so that the economy has a trade surplus. Simply reducing aggregate demand, shifting the aggregate demand curve from AD_0 to AD_1, will reduce inflationary pressures, but a lower level of aggregate demand combined with a lower price level will increase exports and reduce imports. The trade surplus, therefore, will grow. Currency appreciation, however, will damp down inflation plus eliminate, or reduce, the trade surplus. With an appreciation of the currency, the export curve shifts to X_1, and the import curve shifts to M_1. The elimination of the trade surplus shifts the aggregate demand curve from AD_0 to AD_1, drops the price level to P_0, and reduces the actual level of income to the potential level of income, Qn.

Thus, while pushing the aggregate demand to the left through an expenditure-reducing policy may help to eliminate domestic inflationary pressures, it will increase the trade surplus since the import schedule will shift to the left and the price level will fall.

If the country employs an expenditure-switching policy, currency appreciation in this case, it may be able to simultaneously attain internal and external equilibrium. Appreciation of the Deutschemark (DM) will shift Germany's export schedule to the left, from X_0 to X_1, and its import curve to the right, from M_0 to M_1. The drop in German exports and increase in German imports at all price levels will shift the aggregate demand schedule from AD_0 to AD_1. In the end, inflationary pressures within Germany will be stamped out and the German trade surplus will evaporate.

Absorption Schedule and Curve

The **absorption schedule (curve)** shows the level of absorption at various price levels. The stronger the *real balance effect*, the flatter the absorption curve.

Before discussing the impact of income (or expenditure) changes on the trade balance, it will be helpful to derive the **absorption schedule**, since, together with the aggregate demand schedule, it shows the magnitude of a nation's trade surplus or deficit given the general price level and the level of national income. Employing the **absorption curve,** which shows the level of absorption at various national price levels other things considered equal, enables us to dispense with the export and import curves and to show the external and internal position of an economy in a single graph.

As a first step toward deriving the absorption schedule, we briefly review the national income relationships initially presented in Chapter 2. They are summarized in Table 10.2. As before, Y equals income and output, AD equals aggregate demand, and A equals absorption, and C, I, G, X, and M equal consumption, investment, government expenditures, exports, and imports.

Domestic production or output equals aggregate demand in both closed and open economies. However, in an open economy, unlike a closed economy, absorption, which equals the total expenditure on domestic and foreign output for use in the domestic economy or the sum of $C + I + G$, may be greater or less than aggregate demand and, concurrently, greater or less than domestic output. This is the case because citizens cannot purchase foreign goods in a closed economy, but they can in an open economy.

The relationship between income (aggregate demand) and absorption in an open economy can be seen by bringing the trade balance into the picture. If absorption exceeds domestic output, or $A > Y$, the trade balance is negative or $TB < 0$. For example, suppose at a given price level a country produces 100 supercomputers, but universities, business firms, and the government want to buy 150 of them. The excess of

TABLE 10.2 National Income Relations: Closed and Open Economies

Closed Economy	*Open Economy*
$Y = AD$	$Y = AD$
$AD = C + I + G$	$AD = C + I + G + X - M$
$A = C + I + G$	$A = C + I + G$
$Y = AD = A$	$TB = X - M$
	$Y = AD = A + TB$
	$A = AD - TB$

TABLE 10.3 Exports, Imports, Aggregate Demand, and Absorption

Price Level	Exports	Imports$_1$	Imports$_2$	Aggregate Demand	Absorption
P_2	$50	$30	$30	$150	$160
P_1	$60	$20	$40	$200	$200
P_0	$70	$10	$50	$250	$240

absorption over domestic output must be imported, so the trade balance here is negative 50 supercomputers.

Because aggregate demand equals absorption *plus* the trade balance, and absorption equals aggregate demand *minus* the trade balance, the trade balance and aggregate demand are the keys to deriving the absorption schedule. Table 10.3 shows how, given the level of aggregate demand and the trade balance, the absorption schedule can be derived. (The exact derivation of aggregate demand is done shortly. At this point, we assume that it is given.)

The trade balance equals the difference between exports and imports. In Table 10.3, it is assumed that exports depend solely on the domestic price level, rising as the price level falls. When the price level is P_2, for example, exports are $50. On the other hand, imports depend on the price level *plus* the level of domestic income or aggregate demand. Imports$_1$, or M_0, depend only on the domestic price level in this example, while imports$_2$, or mY, equal 20 percent of income regardless of the domestic price level, that is, imports$_2$ are a function of income. Thus, when the price level equals P_2 and aggregate demand equals $150, total imports equal $30 plus $30 or $60. Absorption, therefore, equals aggregate demand, $150, minus the trade balance, $-$10, or $140. (The rest of the absorption schedule can be derived following this procedure.)

As Table 10.3 points out, both the *AD* schedule and *A* (absorption) schedule slope down from left to right. However, because the absolute value of the slope of the aggregate demand curve is less than the absolute value of the slope of the absorption curve, the *AD* curve is flatter than the *A* curve. Because of their different slopes, the *AD* and the *A* curves will intersect at some price level—a point of some importance, as we will see later.

Measuring the Trade Balance Graphically

The *AD* and *A* curves will not, however, intersect at all price levels. When they do not intersect, the nation will have either a trade surplus or a trade deficit at a given price level. As shown in Figure 10.3, the trade surplus (or deficit) equals the horizontal distance between the *AD* and *A* curves at various price levels. When absorption exceeds aggregate demand at a given price level, the trade balance is negative and the absorption curve lies to the right of the aggregate demand curve. Conversely, if absorption is less than aggregate demand (as in the case of a trade surplus), the absorption curve lies to the left of the aggregate demand curve at the current price level.

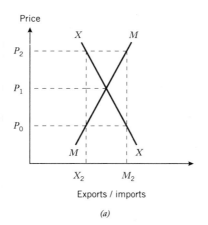

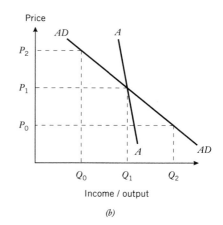

(a)   *(b)*

FIGURE 10.3   The absorption curve.

Since absorption equals aggregate demand minus the trade balance, the absorption schedule can be derived from the aggregate demand curve and the export and import curves. At the price level P_1, exports equal imports in panel (a), which means that absorption equals aggregate demand at that price level. (They both equal Q_1 at the price level P_1, as shown in panel (b).) However, at the price level P_2, imports exceed exports. Thus, absorption exceeds aggregate demand at that price level as well. And when the price level is P_0, exports are greater than imports, and aggregate demand is greater than absorption.

Income and the Trade Balance

With the absorption curve or schedule in mind, we move on to the central question of the chapter: namely, how does a change in income affect the trade balance, or how does an expenditure-increasing or -decreasing policy work? The effects of change in domestic income on the trade balance can be analyzed under the assumption either that the price level is fixed or that it is flexible, that is, that the aggregate supply curve is either flat (horizontal) or upward sloping. First, assume the aggregate supply curve is flat or infinitely elastic.

To begin the analysis, we assume that $Q = Y = C + I + G + X - M$, where the symbols have the usual meanings, and that $\Delta Q = \Delta Y$ because the price level remains constant regardless of any change in the level of output. Since the analysis seeks to explain the effect of changes in income, and income alone, on the trade balance, some modifications can be made to the national income equations previously employed in Chapter 2. Consumption, C, is assumed to depend only on income, but imports are assumed to depend on both income and the price level—although at this point, we assume that the price level is constant. In addition, the government sector, G and T, is neglected. Given these adjustments, the income equation is written as follows, in which c and m equal the marginal propensity to consume and the marginal propensity to import, respectively.

$$Y = cY + I + X - M_0 - mY$$
$$Y - cY + mY = I + X - M_0$$

$$Y(1 - c + m) = I + X$$

$$Y = (1/(s + m))(I + X - M_0)$$

The expression, $(1/(s + m))$, is the **foreign trade** or **open economy multiplier.** It tells us how much income will rise or fall if there is an increase or decrease in investment or exports or non–income-determined imports. In the equation, M_0 represents those imports not determined by the level of income, or imports$_1$ in Table 10.3. As before, the symbols c and m represent the marginal propensity to consume and the marginal propensity to import, respectively, and describe how much consumption or imports change as income rises or falls. Since 1 minus the marginal propensity to consume equals the marginal propensity to save, or $1 - c = s$, the marginal propensity to save is employed in the final equation.

The framework allows us to determine the level of income, the trade balance, and level of absorption given the level of investment, exports, autonomous imports, and the marginal propensities to save and import. Suppose that investment equals $40, exports equal $60, autonomous imports equal $20—price level P_1 in Table 10.3—and that the mps and the mpm each equal .2. Using the previous equation, we find that income equals $200 and that the trade balance equals zero, which tells us that absorption also equals $200. The level of income is computed from the following formula:

$$Y = (1/(s + m))(I + X - M_0)$$

$$Y = (1/(2 + .2))(40 + 60 - 20)$$

$$Y = 2.5(80)$$

$$Y = 200$$

With income known, the trade balance can be computed. The trade balance equals exports minus imports or:

$$TB = X - M_0\, mY$$

$$TB = \$60 - \$20 - .2(\$200) = 0$$

Since absorption equals the level of income minus the trade balance, it can be computed from the income and trade balance equations, or $A = Y - TB$. In this example, since the trade balance is zero, absorption equals income or $200.

$$A = Y - TB$$

$$\$200 = \$200 - \$0$$

A Change in Investment and the Trade Balance

Now, if investment increases, the changes in income, absorption, and the trade balance can be computed. The change in income is given by the following formula:

$$\Delta Y = (1/(s + m))\, \Delta I$$

BOX 10.1 Computing the Marginal Propensity to Import

Computing the marginal propensity to import can be difficult. A researcher must calculate the change in imports, ΔM, given a change in income, ΔY, while holding everything else constant—not an easy task. Because of the difficulties involved, most economists compute the marginal propensity to import by first calculating a nation's income elasticity of demand for imports, $(\Delta M/M)/(\Delta Y/Y)$. The last equation equals $(\Delta M/\Delta Y)/(M/Y)$, or the marginal propensity to import divided by the average propensity to import. Thus if one multiplies the income elasticity of demand for imports by the average propensity to import, or $[(\Delta M/\Delta Y)/(M/Y)]\,[M/Y]$, one can arrive at an estimate of the marginal propensity to import.

In this example, the marginal propensity to import of each nation was calculated by first computing the import-to-GDP ratio for each nation over the last ten years and then using the average of those ten years as the average propensity to import. The average propensity to import (apm) was then multiplied by the income elasticity of demand for imports to obtain the marginal propensity to import (mpm).

Table 10.4 gives two estimates of each nation's marginal propensity to import, because the table uses two different estimates of a nation's income elasticity of the demand for imports. Since Jaime Marquez's estimates are more recent, there is a natural tendency to employ them in computing marginal propensities to import rather than the estimates of Houthakker and Magee. But it is more important to note the differences between the national marginal propensities to import. What the figures tell us is that income expansion in Japan will not lead to a sharp increase in Japanese imports, whereas income growth in Germany and the United Kingdom will generate a sizable increase in their imports. More on this important point later.

TABLE 10.4 The marginal propensity to import

Country	apm	Income Elasticity[1]	Income Elasticity[2]	mpm[1]	mpm[2]
Canada	.261	1.84	1.20	.48	.31
Germany	.292	1.88	1.80	.55	.53
Japan	.088	0.35	1.23	.03	.11
UK	.267	2.51	1.66	.67	.44
United States	.110	1.94	1.51	.21	.16

[1]Income elasticities from Jaime Marquez, "Bilateral Trade Elasticities," *Review of Economics and Statistics* 72 (February 1990); Table 2, p. 75. © 1990 by the President and Fellows of Harvard College.

[2]Income elasticities from Hendrik Houthakker and Steven Magee, "Income and Price Elasticities in World Trade," *Review of Economics and Statistics* 51 (May 1969); Table 1, p. 113. © 1969 by the President and Fellows of Harvard College.

Average propensities to import were computed from International Monetary Fund, *International Financial Statistics Yearbook*, 1994.

If s and m each equal .2, the open economy multiplier equals 2.5. Now, if investment rises by $10, income will increase by $25. As income rises, imports increase and the trade balance deteriorates because absorption increases at a faster pace than output. In the example, since X and M_0 are assumed constant, the change in trade balance equals[1]:

---

[1]The change in the trade balance resulting from a change in investment is computed from the following formula: $\Delta TB/\Delta I = \Delta X/\Delta I - m(Y/\Delta I)$. Since we know that $\Delta Y/\Delta I$ equals $1/s + m$, $\Delta TB/\Delta I = -(m/s + m)$. This last equation describes the **trade balance multiplier**—or how much the trade balance will change given a

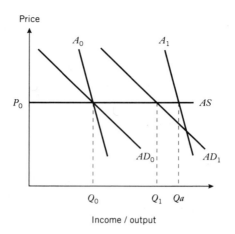

Price

A_0 A_1

P_0 AS

AD_0 AD_1

Q_0 Q_1 Q_a

Income / output

FIGURE 10.4 Income expansion and the trade balance: I.

When the level of GDP or income/output is Q_0 and the price level is P_0, absorption equals aggregate demand. An increase in investment will shift both the AD curve and A curve to the right, but it will shift the A curve by more than the AD curve. At the new equilibrium level of income, Q_1, where AD_1 equals AS, the country has a trade deficit equal to the difference between Q_a and Q_1.

$$\Delta TB = (X - M_0 - m\Delta Y)$$
$$\Delta TB = -m\Delta Y$$

The trade balance deteriorates by $5 or .2($25). Since the change in absorption equals the change in income minus the change in the trade balance, it is a simple matter to compute it:

$$\Delta A = \Delta Y - \Delta TB$$

The following columns sum up the changes in income, the trade balance, and the level of absorption, given a $10 change in investment:

$\Delta Y = (1/(s + m))\Delta I$	$\Delta TB = \Delta X - \Delta M - m\Delta Y$	$\Delta A = \Delta Y - \Delta TB$
$\Delta Y = 2.5($10)$	$\Delta TB = 0 - 0 - .2($25)$	$\Delta A = $25 - (-$5)$
$\Delta Y = 25	$\Delta TB = -$5$	$\Delta A = 30

The **trade balance multiplier** describes the change in the trade balance given a change in autonomous expenditures such as investment, exports, or government expenditures. The **absorption multiplier** does exactly the same thing for absorption.

The changes in income, absorption, and the trade balance are graphed in Figure 10.4. Following the increase in investment, both the aggregate demand and the absorption curves shift to the right, but the absorption curve shifts by more than the aggregate demand curve. (Q_a is greater than Q_1 at the price level P_1). Since absorption exceeds aggregate demand, imports exceed exports.

change, in this case, of investment. The **absorption multiplier** equals the income multiplier minus the trade balance multiplier: $\Delta A/\Delta I = (\Delta Y/\Delta I) - (\Delta TB/\Delta I)$, or $\Delta A/\Delta I = (1/s + m) - (-m/s + m)$, so that $\Delta A/\Delta I = (1 + m)/(s + m)$. It is worth noting that because the trade balance multiplier is not the same in every case, the absorption multiplier will not be the same in every case.

The analysis just presented outlines the effect of an expenditure-increasing policy on the trade balance. An easy monetary policy which drops interest rates and encourages investment will lead to a trade deficit. An increase in government expenditures would have the same effects as an increase in investment and a *decrease* in tax rates would also have roughly the same effects (see Chapter 2). Thus, an easy fiscal policy will raise income and imports. An expenditure-reducing policy, a tight monetary and/or fiscal policy, will have the opposite effects outlined here. It will drop income and decrease imports. Thus, a country which faces the twin problems of inflation and a trade deficit (Zone III) can overcome them by introducing an expenditure-reducing policy.

Export Expansion and the Trade Balance

An increase in income does not necessarily lead to a deterioration in the trade balance. Suppose that instead of an increase in investment, exports climb from \$60 to \$70, or increase by \$10. Income rises by \$25 as before, but the trade balance improves since aggregate demand, which equals output, grows at a faster rate than absorption. The value of the income multiplier remains the same so that the change in income equals:

$$\Delta Y = (1/(s + m)) \, \Delta X$$

But in this case, the trade balance improves since the increase in exports will exceed the income-induced increase in imports.[2]

$$\Delta TB = \Delta X - \Delta M_0 - m\Delta Y$$

or,

$$\$5 = \$10 - 0 - .2(\$25)$$

This means that the increase in absorption, \$20, is less than the increase in income. The columns below summarize the changes in income, the trade balance, and the level of absorption given an increase in exports, and Figure 10.5 graphically depicts what has taken place.

$\Delta Y = (1/(s + m)) \, \Delta X$	$\Delta TB = \Delta X - \Delta M - m\Delta Y$	$\Delta A = \Delta Y - \Delta TB$
$\Delta Y = 2.5 \ (\$10)$	$\Delta TB = \$10 - 0 - .2(\$25)$	$\Delta A = \$25 - \$5$
$\Delta Y = \$25$	$\Delta TB = \$5$	$\Delta A = \$20$

---

[2]In this case, the trade balance multiplier is calculated as follows: $\Delta TB/\Delta X = \Delta X/\Delta X - m(\Delta Y/\Delta X)$. Recalling that $\Delta Y/\Delta X = 1/s + m$, the equation can be rewritten: $\Delta TB/\Delta X = 1 - (m/s + m) = (s + m/s + m) - (m/s + m) = (s + m - m)/(s + m) = s/s + m$. Because the trade balance multiplier is different when the stimulus comes from exports rather than investment, the absorption multiplier will also be different. Under these conditions, the change in absorption given a change in exports is given by the following relationship: $\Delta A/\Delta X = (1/s + m) - (s/s + m)$, which equals $(1 - s)/(s + m)$.

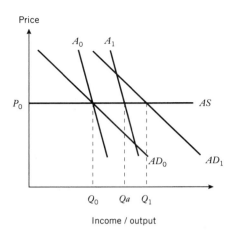

FIGURE 10.5 Income expansion and the trade balance: II.

An increase in exports shifts the aggregate demand curve from AD_0 to AD_1 and the absorption curve from A_0 to A_1. Since the price level is assumed constant and aggregate demand shifts by more than absorption, the nation runs a trade surplus equal to $Qa-Q_1$.

In Figure 10.5, the increase in exports shifts the AD and A curves to the right, but the AD curve shifts further to the right than the A curve, or the rise in income, Q_1, is greater than the rise in absorption, Q_a. Higher income does induce an increase in imports. However, the economy still runs a trade surplus because the increase in exports, $10, exceeds the income-induced increase in imports, $5.

The analysis just given does not explain the impact of an expenditure-increasing or -reducing policy, but it does provide a glimpse of the effects of an expenditure-switching policy. As discussed in the next chapter, currency depreciation will *raise* exports and *reduce* non–income-induced imports, or M_0. Thus, if a nation faces unemployment and a trade deficit, currency depreciation will raise income and also improve the trade balance.

An Increase in Investment and the Trade Balance: A Second Look

The traditional view that an increase in investment will lead to a trade deficit contradicts the notion, presented in Chapter 2, that investment-led economic growth may generate a trade surplus. There are too many examples of high-investment countries that have run trade surpluses and not trade deficits to ignore that possibility. The model can be modified to take the presumed relationship between investment and exports into account. For now we will suppose that an increase in investment leads to an increase in exports equal to one-half the rise in investment. In a previous example, a $10 increase in investment led to a $25 jump in income and a trade deficit of $5. Given the present assumptions, income rises by $32.50 and the trade balance goes into the red by $1.50. The following equations tell us why:

$$\Delta Y = (1/(s + m))\Delta I + \Delta X \quad \Delta TB = \Delta X - m\Delta Y \quad \Delta A = \Delta Y - \Delta TB$$
$$\Delta Y = 2.5(\$10 + \$5) \qquad \Delta TB = \$5 - .2(\$32.50) \quad \Delta A = \$32.50 - (-\$1.50)$$
$$\Delta Y = \$32.50 \qquad\qquad \Delta TB = -\$1.50 \qquad\quad \Delta A = \$34.00$$

In terms of the macroeconomic model, the increase in income is larger since investment leads to higher exports. And because exports are higher, the trade deficit is smaller.

Cast differently, investment-led growth will shift the aggregate demand curve to the right, but it will also shift the aggregate supply curve to the right. The shift in the aggregate supply curve means that, given a shift in the aggregate demand curve, a greater proportion of any increase in absorption can be satisfied by domestic production, and any excess absorption, which equals the trade deficit, will be lower.

Foreign Repercussions and the Foreign Trade Multiplier

Foreign repercussions measures the impact of the change in the level of economic activity in one country on the level of economic activity in another country or on the rest of the world.

In a world economy, economic developments in one country affect economic activity in other countries. Economic expansion in the United States will create a larger market for, say, German exports. But an increase in German exports, in turn, will raise German income and create a market for American exports. What does this mean for the United States? Given foreign repercussions as just described, any economic expansion in the United States will lead to a higher level of income in the United States and a lower American trade deficit since the rise in German income will generate a demand for U.S. exports. This is an example of the foreign trade multiplier with **foreign repercussions.**

Implications of the Foreign Trade Multiplier

Foreign-trade multiplier analysis has several implications. First, the larger a nation's marginal propensity to import, the more its trade balance will deteriorate given an increase in its income and the more its trade balance will improve following a decline in its income. Multiplier analysis also suggests that it would be unwise for a country with a low marginal propensity to import, the United States for example, to attempt to reduce its trade deficit by curtailing domestic income alone. There is the other side of the coin. A relatively closed economy can expand its aggregate demand more than an open economy before it runs into a given trade deficit.

The foreign trade multiplier also allows us to see more clearly the extent to which domestic economic policy is affected by the world economy. Starting in late 1992 and early 1993, the United States began to recover from recession, but the economies of Japan and Western Europe remained in the doldrums. In these circumstances, stagnant foreign demand combined with American economic expansion led to a widening U.S. trade deficit, just as the foreign trade multiplier tells us. The deficit was larger and U.S. economic growth slower because slack demand in foreign economies restrained U.S. exports.

BOX 10.2 Springboards for Recovery

If the world economy is in a recession, it is quite apparent that large economies need to take the lead and provide a springboard for worldwide economic recovery. The larger the nation the better the springboard, providing other things remain equal. Thus, economic recovery in Western Europe does more for the world economy than economic expansion in Central America. But one can ask which large country will be the best springboard? The quick answer is the country with the highest marginal propensity to import. Given a high mpm, its economic expansion will spill over and help the rest of the world. If in addition to a high mpm, the country has a low propensity to save, it will be the ideal choice. The lower a nation's propensity to save, the more a given economic stimulus will raise income in that country and induce greater imports and raise the exports of the rest of the world.

Which country will best fill the role of engineer or leader is shown in Table 10.5, where mpm stands for the marginal propensity to import and aps equals the average propensity to save, which is used as a proxy for the marginal propensity to save; $1/s + m$, where s equals the mps and m equals the mpm, is the foreign trade or open economy multiplier; and ΔM tells us how much a nation's imports will increase given a $10 increase in domestic expenditures.

According to Table 10.5, the United Kingdom, followed by Germany and Canada, is best suited to serve as a springboard. The UK ranks fist because it has a high mpm and a low mps. Japan is not suited for the role at all. Its high propensity to save plus its low propensity to import mean that an increase in Japanese expenditures will not generate a hefty increase in Japanese income and little of whatever expansion that takes place will spill over to the rest of the world. Thus, calls for Japan to introduce a fiscal stimulus in order to raise its income and cut its trade surplus may be questioned. That does not mean that a high propensity to save automatically eliminates the possibility that a nation may serve as a springboard. Consider Germany. Its relatively high mps is countered by its relatively high mpm. Given the size of its economy, it may be the best springboard of the five countries listed.

TABLE 10.5 Springboards for Economic Recovery

Country	mpm	aps	$1/s + m$	ΔM
Canada	.31	.14	2.22	$6.89
Germany	.53	.22	1.33	$7.06
Japan	.11	.34	2.22	$2.44
UK	.44	.13	1.75	$7.70
United States	.16	.15	3.22	$5.16

Sources: The mpm's were calculated from Houthakker and Magee's estimates of income elasticities cited in Table 10.4. The average propensities to save, which have been used in place of marginal propensities to save, equal the average of the savings-to-GDP ratio from 1990 to 1993. They were computed from the Organization for Economic Cooperation and Development, *Economic Outlook* , © OECD, (May 1995); p. A30.

Aggregate Supply and Demand, Absorption, Output, and Inflation

So far the discussion has assumed that the aggregate supply curve is infinitely elastic. This is not a realistic assumption unless an economy is operating below its potential. As the economy moves toward its potential level of output, the aggregate supply curve will slope up from left to right and the domestic price level will rise given a shift in the aggregate demand curve to the right. Under these conditions, earlier conclusions describing the relationship between income expansion and the balance of trade need to be modified.

Consider Figure 10.6. Initially, the aggregate supply, aggregate demand, and absorption curves intersect at the price level P_0 and the income level Q_0. Suppose that an increase in government expenditures causes the AD curve to shift to the right, to AD_1, and the absorption curve to shift to A_1. If the supply curve is infinitely elastic, the price level will remain at P_0. The rise in income will increase imports and the country will end up with a balance of trade deficit equal to the horizontal difference between A_1 and AD_1 at the price level P_0, or the difference between Q_3 and Q_2 on the income/output axis.

The aggregate supply curve, however, is *not* a horizontal line. When the aggregate demand shifts to AD_1, the price level rises to P_1. The higher price level will increase imports and decrease exports. The trade balance will deteriorate as exports drop due to the price effect and imports rise as a result of both the price and income effects. The more inelastic the aggregate supply curve, the larger the trade deficit and the smaller the expansion in real income.

The results are graphically explained in Figure 10.6. The price level rises to P_1, given the increase in aggregate demand and absorption, and the level of real output

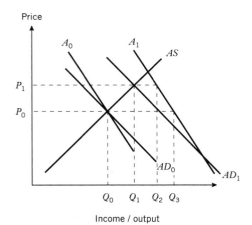

FIGURE 10.6 Income expansion and the trade balance: III.

An increase in investment shifts the aggregate demand curve to AD_1 and the absorption curve to A_1. If the price level remains constant, the trade deficit equals Q_2–Q_3. But since the aggregate supply curve is upward sloping, the price level rises to P_1 with the increase in aggregate demand. And at the higher price level, the trade deficit equals Q_1–Q_2.

climbs to Q_1, not to Q_2. The trade deficit equals the difference between absorption and aggregate demand at the price level P_1, or the difference between Q_2 and Q_1 on the income/output axis.

An upward-sloping aggregate supply curve has further implications for the relationship between income expansion and the trade balance. Recall in Figure 10.5 that an increase in exports raised income and led to a trade surplus. This conclusion needs to be revised in light of an upward-sloping aggregate supply curve.

In Figure 10.7, as in Figure 10.5, an increase in exports shifts the aggregate demand curve further to the right than it shifts the absorption curve to the right, or output expands more rapidly than absorption at the initial price level, P_0. Providing the price level remains constant, a nation will run a trade surplus equal to the difference between Q_3 and Q_2 on the horizontal axis. However, if the AS curve slopes up from left to right as depicted, an increase in aggregate demand will cause the price level to rise from P_0 to P_1. The rise in the general price level will have the previously described effects on exports and imports. As a consequence, real output will rise to Q_1, not Q_3, and, in this example, the trade will be balanced since the absorption and aggregate demand curves intersect at the price P_1. If the price level does not rise to P_1, the nation will have a trade surplus since output will exceed absorption; if the price level rises above P_1, absorption will exceed output and the nation will have a trade deficit.

The so-called **Dutch disease** occurs when the demand for one of a country's exports rises to such dizzying heights that production costs rise throughout the economy. As a result, export expansion in one sector of the economy hinders exports in others.

Can such a string of events actually occur? Experience with the so-called **Dutch disease** says they can. In the 1970s and early 1980s, oil shocks created a hefty demand for oil substitutes such as natural gas, a Dutch export. The demand for natural gas rose along with the demand for the inputs needed to produce it, labor for example. Because wage rates and the price of other inputs rose substantially, nongas exports were adversely affected. That is, the higher demand for natural gas led to higher Dutch prices,

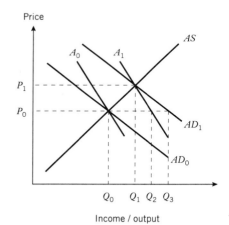

FIGURE 10.7 Income expansion and the trade balance: IV.

An increase in exports shifts the aggregate demand curve from AD_0 to AD_1 and the absorption curve from A_0 to A_1. The country will run a trade surplus equal to Q_2 to Q_3 providing the price level remains constant. But given the slope of the aggregate supply curve, the expansion in aggregate demand raises the price level to P_1. The higher price level reduces exports and increases imports and, as a result, A_1 and AD_1 intersect at the higher price level. In the final analysis, the level of real GDP equals Q_1 and trade is balanced despite the initial increase in exports.

which made other Dutch exports less competitive. This is not to say that an increase in the demand for a particular Canadian export will automatically generate such a rate of inflation within Canada that Canada's trade balance will turn negative. Indeed, most evidence suggests that higher exports lead to trade surpluses. However, the phenomenon of the "Dutch disease" points out the need to consider the supply side of the equation when computing the impact of income expansion on the trade balance.

There is perhaps one bright spot in the relationship between income expansion and the trade balance under conditions of increasing costs. In a closed economy, where aggregate demand equals absorption, any attempt to raise absorption will stimulate inflation. Consider Figure 10.6 once again. The attempt to increase absorption, shown by the shift in the absorption curve from A_0 to A_1, will almost immediately raise the price level to the point where the AS curve intersects the A_1 curve at a price level above P_1. Since this implies that real wages will have declined, one can expect that workers will seek higher nominal wages in order to maintain their real wages. Effort by workers to preserve their real wages will shift the AS curve to the left and the economy will end up with a still higher level of prices and, following the argument in Chapter 2, the same initial level of income, Q_0.

In an open economy, an import surplus enables a nation to repress potential inflation. The demand for additional output is satisfied by an inflow of foreign goods. (In Figure 10.6 both the aggregate demand and the absorption curves shifted to the right. The price level rose to P_1 and real income climbed to Q_1. Since absorption, Q_2, exceeded output, the nation ran a trade deficit. But the trade deficit permitted it to avoid some of the inflationary consequences of the increase in absorption.) Of course, except in exceptional circumstances, a nation cannot run continual trade deficits and continually expand its external debt. The time will arrive when the nation must repay its obligations and when it does, it will need to cut its absorption. It so happens that curtailing absorption in this case will neither reduce the price level nor reduce employment. In terms of Figure 10.6, the absorption curve will move back to, say, A_0 and the aggregate demand curve will remain constant at AD_1. The country can then use its excess of output over absorption to service its external obligations.

Summary

We have seen how an increase or decrease in investment, and by implication an increase or decrease in government expenditures and tax rates, can raise or lower income while at the same time reducing or improving a nation's trade balance. This is the guts of an expenditure-increasing or -reducing policy, showing how such policies work through and affect the level of income and the trade balance.

We also saw how an increase in exports, and by implication a reduction in non–income-induced imports, can raise income and improve the trade balance, or how an expenditure-switching policy will affect income and the trade balance.

At the same time, we showed that if a nation's economy expands, its trade balance may deteriorate. Yet we argued that there can be a significant difference between the effects of consumption-led versus investment-led growth on the trade balance since consumption-led growth will definitely lead to trade deficit, while investment-led income expansion may lead to an improvement in the trade balance. Such a pattern may take place with a lag, since investment-led growth can push the current growth rate of income above its trend rate and lead to a surge of imports. However, given time, investment will generate higher output and expand exports as previously described.

The discussion of income effects has important implications for worldwide economic policy. As pointed out in Box 10.2, if the world economy is in a recession, large, open economies with low propensities to save should play the role of locomotive in pulling the world economy out of a recession. If the world is symmetrical, these same countries should contract their level of economic activity when the world economy faces inflation. Yet one can also argue that the last thing the world economy should want or needs is a large open economy, or several of them, that goes through periods of economic expansion and contraction. Thus, perhaps the best policy would be for such an economy to strive for economic stability and let other countries do the adjusting to inflation and recession noting that if the large economies of the world are stable, the world economy will be more stable.

There is an additional implication of the analysis, covered in detail in Chapter 11. If a nation has a low marginal propensity to import, it will require a large drop in its income in order to rectify a trade deficit and a large increase in its income to close a trade surplus. The country will have to be willing to accept substantial unemployment or a sharp rise in its price level to attain external equilibrium by income changes alone. Such countries, therefore, will have to utilize different adjustment mechanisms to realize external balance. One such adjustment mechanism, exchange-rate depreciation or appreciation, is discussed in the next chapter.

Key Concepts and Terms

absorption schedule and curve

Dutch disease

expenditure-increasing policy

expenditure-switching policy

foreign reactions or repercussions

foreign trade multiplier

induced imports

marginal propensity to import

Swan's zones of misery

Review Questions

1. Consider two nations. The first nation has an inflationary surplus, and the second faces unemployment but has a trade surplus. Describe what the first nation should do to attain internal and external equilibria. How might its policies affect the second nation? Now imagine the second nation faces unemployment but has a trade deficit. How might the policies of the first nation affect the second nation?

2. Explain the difference between expenditure-reducing (-increasing) and expenditure-switching policies.

3. Employing aggregate demand and absorption schedules, plus any other schedules needed, demonstrate how a trade deficit allows a nation to repress inflation.

4. Why is the income multiplier lower in an open economy than in a closed economy? What does this suggest regarding the impact of economic policy on the level of economic activity in open compared to closed economies?

5. Imagine the marginal propensity to save is .2 and the marginal propensity to import is .3 in a given country. What will happen to this nation's level of aggregate demand, absorption, and trade balance, if:

(a) The income of a foreign nation with a propensity to import of .5 advances by $100?

(b) Government expenditures are increased by $50?

References and Suggested Readings

Trevor Swan was one of the first economists to develop a specific framework for the simultaneous analysis of an economy's external and internal positions. His framework and an analysis of the zones of misery are contained in his article, "Longer-run Problems of the Balance of Payments," *The Australian Economy: A Volume of Readings*, edited by H. W.

Arndt and M. W. Corden (Melbourne: Chesire Press, 1963): pp. 383–395. The article is reprinted in *American Economic Association Readings in International Economics*, edited by Richard Caves and Harry D. Johnson (Homewood, Il: Richard D. Irwin, 1968): pp. 455–464. Well worth reading is an article by Paul R. Krugman and Richard E. Baldwin, "The Persistence of the U.S. Trade Deficit," *Brookings Papers on Economic Activity* (1987 #1): pp. 1–43. Two classic articles on the division of adjustment costs are Robert A. Mundell, "The Proper Division of the Burden of International Adjustment," reprinted as Chapter 13 of his book, *International Economics* (New York: Macmillan, 1968): pp. 187–198; and James Tobin, "Adjustment Responsibilities of Surplus and Deficit Countries," in William Fellner et al., *Maintaining and Restoring Balance in International Payments* (Princeton, NJ: Princeton University Press, 1966): pp. 201–211.

Chapter 11

Exchange Rate Adjustment

There are several ways a healthy economy can balance its external accounts. In Chapter 10 we described how expenditure-reducing and expenditure-increasing policies can be used to influence a country's external accounts as well as its level of output and inflation. We also suggested how a country can attain internal and external equilibrium by employing such macroeconomic policies. The options are more limited if a country is confronted with unemployment since an expenditure-increasing policy works only if the economy in question has a trade surplus. Fiscal and monetary expansion will increase aggregate demand and cut unemployment; in turn, the increase in aggregate demand will stimulate the demand for imports and diminish the country's trade surplus. Thus, given unemployment, an expenditure-increasing policy works providing the economy has a trade surplus.

But when an economy is "really sick" and has both unemployment and a trade deficit, an expenditure-increasing policy will reduce unemployment but will lead to an even greater trade imbalance. In this situation, the country will need to initiate an *expenditure-switching policy*, one that causes domestic and foreign consumers to purchase domestic products in place of foreign ones. In short, the nation must improve its competitive position; often this means that the ailing economy will have to devalue or depreciate its currency.[1]

How will currency depreciation simultaneously restore the nation's external position and improve its internal position? Depreciation raises the price of tradable goods (exports and imports) relative to the price of nontraded goods. On the supply side, depreciation should encourage domestic firms to produce more exports and import substitutes. On the demand side, the change in relative prices should move domestic demand away from foreign goods toward domestically produced substitute goods and shift foreign demand toward domestic exports. As pointed out in Figure 10.2, depreciation shifts the export curve to the right and import curve to the left and improves the trade balance. Improvement in the trade balance, in turn, causes the aggregate demand curve to shift to the right, which reduces unemployment.

---

[1]A fixed exchange rate is "devalued"; a flexible or floating rate "depreciates." Since the difference is semantic, the word "depreciation" is employed to cover both.

Yet if everything were so easy to operate, why did the United States continue to run a trade deficit in 1995 despite the almost continual depreciation of the dollar since 1985? And why have other countries discovered that currency depreciation alone did not improve their external balances in certain instances and, indeed, appears to have contributed to a further deterioration in their external accounts?

The Path Ahead

This chapter attempts to shed some light on that puzzle. It does so by focusing on an analysis and understanding of three topics:

- Under what conditions a depreciation will switch expenditures sufficiently so that a nation's trade balance will improve.
- How macroeconomic developments help determine the success or failure of a depreciation.
- The costs of a depreciation and how they compare with the costs of an expenditure-reducing policy.

Marshall-Lerner-Robinson Conditions

The **Marshall-Lerner-Robinson (MLR) conditions** describe the necessary, although not the sufficient, conditions for a successful depreciation. In its simplest form, the MLR conditions state that the sum of the domestic import demand price elasticity and the foreign import demand price elasticity must exceed unity if a depreciation of the domestic currency is to improve the domestic trade balance.

A depreciation involves a change in relative prices. But a change in relative prices will be successful only if supply and demand respond to the change, that is, if their elasticities are sufficiently large. *Elasticity is the key* in all markets regardless of whether they involve foreign trade.

Hence, for depreciation to work as an external account-balancing tool, the elasticities of supply and demand for both exports and imports must be sufficiently high. The required magnitude of the elasticities was formulated separately by Alfred Marshall, Abba Lerner, and Joan Robinson and is collectively credited to the three of them as the **Marshall-Lerner-Robinson (MLR) conditions.**

MLR conditions can be understood with the help of Figure 11.1 Normally we assume that both the export supply and import supply curves are infinitely elastic. The assumption applied to Brazil means that the domestic or Real[2] price of Brazil's exports remains *constant* regardless of the foreign demand for Brazil's exports and that the dollar price of Brazil's imports remains *constant* regardless of the level of Brazil's demand for imports.

However, a 10 percent depreciation of the Real will *raise* the Real price of Brazil's imports by a full 10 percent. Why? If the import supply curve is infinitely elastic, Brazil's demand for imports must be an insignificant amount of the worldwide demand

---

[2]The *Real* is the Brazilian currency. Actually, the Real/$ exchange rate was closer to one-to-one than two-to-one—the exchange rate used in this chapter—during most of 1995.

BOX 11.1 Dollar Depreciation and the U.S. Trade Position

Despite misgivings about the efficacy of depreciation as a policy tool, dollar depreciation did help reduce the U.S. trade deficit in the second half of the 1980s and the early 1990s. This is borne out by the figures in Table 11.1, which show that the U.S. trade balance improved following the depreciation of the dollar. The volume of exports and imports both rose, but exports rose 143 percent while imports increased by 97 percent. The deficit fell both in dollar terms and as a percentage of GDP. The U.S. performance is even more striking if one excludes the years 1993 and 1994, when American imports rose 23 percent due to a rise in U.S. income and the growth in American exports, which rose 13.5 percent, was held down by the recession that prevailed in most OECD countries.

TABLE 11.1 Value of the Dollar and the U.S. Trade Position: 1985–93 (1985 = 100, billions of dollars, and percent)

Year	Dollar[1]	Exports	Imports	X-M[2]	X-M/GDP[3]
1985	100	100	100	−$122	−3.02%
1986	78	107	109	−$140	−3.28
1987	69	120	122	−$154	−3.39
1988	62	149	132	−$115	−2.35
1989	71	169	133	−$61	−1.17
1990	64	185	150	−$80	−1.44
1991	65	201	148	−$30	−.52
1992	63	214	160	−$39	−.65
1993	68	223	175	−$75	−1.18
1994	67	243	197	−$107	−1.59

[1]The value of the dollar equals its real multilateral or trade weighted value as computed by the Board of Governors of the Federal Reserve System.

[2]X-M equals the value of exports minus the value of imports.

[3]X-M/GDP equals the value of exports divided by the value of GDP

Sources: Economic Report of the President, 1995; pp. 274, 402. US Department of Commerce, *Survey of Current Business,* June, 1995; p. 85. Exports, imports, and the value of the dollar are presented as index numbers. All figures have been rounded.

---

for the products in question. Thus, if the dollar price of imports remains *constant* and the Real depreciates by 10 percent, the Real price of the imports will *increase* by 10 percent.

Similarly, even though a 10 percent depreciation of the Real may increase the demand for Brazil's exports, it will not affect the Real price of Brazil's exports, because the supply of its exports is infinitely elastic. Depreciation will, however, *reduce* the dollar price of Brazil's exports by 10 percent since a dollar will command more Reals than previously. It is these changes in prices and their impact on demand that determine the success of the depreciation.

The relationships are captured in Figure 11.1, where it is assumed that supply elasticities are infinite and that the demand elasticities each equal one, that is, the percentage change in the quantity demanded equals the percentage change in the price.

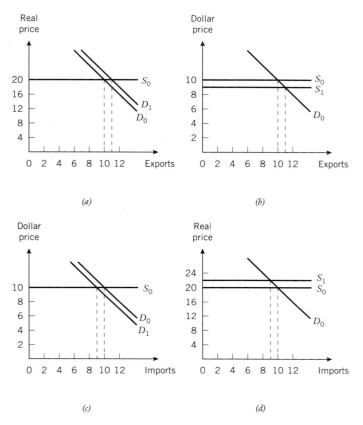

FIGURE 11.1 Depreciation with infinite supply elasticities.

Panels (a) and (d) show Brazil's exports and imports expressed in Reals while panels (b) and (c) show them expressed in dollars. If supply elasticities are infinite and demand elasticities equal unity, a 10 percent depreciation of the Real will increase Brazil's exports from 10 to 11 units. In panel (a), the depreciation shifts the demand curve for Brazil exports to the right. In panel (b), depreciation shifts the supply curve from S_0 to S_1 and reduces the dollar price of Brazil's exports from \$10 to \$9. In panel (d) the Real price of Brazil's imports rises by 10 percent following the depreciation of the Real since the supply curve shifts from S_0 to S_1. As a result, Brazil's demand for imports falls from 10 to 9 units. In panel (c), depreciation causes the demand curve to shift to the left since the dollar price of Brazil's imports do not change. As can be seen in panel (a), Brazil's export earnings expressed in Reals rise from R200 to R220, while its expenditures on imports, panel (d), remain almost constant. One can also see that Brazil's export earnings expressed in dollars, panel (b), remain constant at roughly \$100, while its expenditures on imports expressed in dollars fall from \$100 to \$90.

Initially the price of Brazilian exports and imports equals Reals 20 or \$10 since it is assumed that the exchange rate is Real2/\$. Figures 11.1a and 11.1b depict the supply and demand for Brazil's exports expressed first in terms of Reals and then in terms of dollars. Figures 11.1d and 11.1c show the supply and demand for Brazil's imports expressed first in Reals and then in dollars.

A 10 percent depreciation of the Real *raises* the domestic price of imports even though their dollar price remains *constant*. In Figure 11.1d, the supply curve shifts up or to the left since imports are now more expensive when purchased in the domestic currency. The dollar price of imports remains constant, as indicated in Figure 11.1c, but the demand curve shifts to the left. Why? When the domestic price of imports goes from R20 to R22, the demand for imports falls from 10 to 9 units. And regardless of the currency in which imports are priced, the quantity of imports demanded is the same—specifically, 9 units. Similarly, the quantity of exports must also be the same regardless of the currency employed. But as the dollar price of exports declines, foreign or non-Brazilian demand for Brazil's exports increases from 10 to 11 units and the demand curve shifts to the right as indicated in Figure 11.1a.

Under such conditions, the depreciation can be considered a success. The Brazilian trade balance improves whether it is measured in Reals or in dollars. Prior to depreciation, the exchange rate was R2/$, so following a 10 percent depreciation of the Real, the new exchange rate is R2.2/$. Prior to depreciation, the value of exports and imports was balanced at R200 or $100. After the depreciation, the value of exports expressed in dollars is $99 while the value of imports expressed in dollars is $90; in terms of Reals, the value of exports equals R222 (R20 times 11) and the value of imports is R198 (R20 times 9).

What are the implications of the example? If export supply elasticities are *infinite*, a depreciation improves the trade balance providing the sum of the import demand price elasticities, both foreign and domestic, exceeds one. This is the fundamental proposition of the Marshall-Lerner-Robinson thesis. In the example, depreciation is a success because the sum of the import demand elasticities equals 2.

BOX 11.2 The MLR Conditions Extended

The MLR conditions can be summarized as a formula. The formula allows us to work through the impact of a depreciation or devaluation on a nation's trade balance under different assumptions regarding export and import supply and demand elasticities.

$$\frac{\Delta TB}{\Delta e} = -\left[X\frac{\acute{\eta}_x(\sigma_x + 1)}{(\acute{\eta}_x + \sigma_x)} + M\frac{\sigma_m(\acute{\eta}_m - 1)}{(\acute{\eta}_m + \sigma_m)} \right]$$

where:

ΔTB = the change in the trade balance

Δe = the change in the exchange rate

X = the original amount of exports

M = the original amount of imports

$\acute{\eta}_x$ = the foreign elasticity of demand for Brazil's exports

σ_x = the elasticity of supply of Brazil's exports

$\acute{\eta}_m$ = the elasticty of demand for Brazil's imports, or Brazil's elasticity of demand for imports

σ_m = the foreign elasticity of supply of Brazil's imports

(Note that the change in the trade balance, ΔTB, and the change in the exchange rate, Δe, are inversely related—$\Delta TB/\Delta e$ is negative. Thus if $\Delta TB/\Delta e = -10$, the trade balance improves with a depreciation; if $\Delta TB/\Delta e = +10$, the trade balance deteriorates following currency depreciation.)

If both supply elasticities are infinite and exports initially equal imports (as in our original example), then $\sigma_x + \acute{\eta}_x = \sigma_x$ and $\sigma_m + \acute{\eta}_m = \sigma_m$ since infinity plus any number equals infinity. Under these assumptions, and with a little manipulation, the equation is as follows:

$$\frac{\Delta TB}{\Delta e} = -X\left[\frac{\acute{\eta}_x \sigma_x}{\sigma_x} + \frac{\acute{\eta}_x}{\sigma_x} + \frac{\sigma_m \acute{\eta}_m}{\sigma_m} - \frac{\sigma_m}{\sigma_m}\right]$$

which in turn equals:

$$\Delta TB/\Delta e = -X[\acute{\eta}_x + \acute{\eta}_m - 1]$$

That means that Brazil's trade balance will improve by R20 if the Real depreciates by 10 percent. (This figure does not agree with the one previously given. The disparity is due to the rough-and-ready way the figures were initially computed.)

$$\Delta TB/\Delta e = -200 (1 + 1 - 1)$$
$$\Delta TB/\Delta e = -200$$
$$\Delta TB = -200 \, \Delta e$$
$$\Delta TB = -200 \, (-.1)$$
$$\Delta TB = 20$$

In sum, the MLR conditions argue that a depreciation will improve a nation's trade balance providing supply and demand elasticities are "high," which is another way of stating that market forces will do the job if supply and demand respond sufficiently to change in prices.

An interesting question is whether depreciation will be successful in the case of an LDC. The normal assumption is that the demand elasticity for an LDC's exports and the supply elasticity of its imports are infinitely elastic because the typical LDC is a small country. If $\acute{\eta}_x + \sigma_m$ are infinitely elastic, the equation just given breaks down to the following:

$$\frac{\Delta TB}{\Delta e} = -X\left[\frac{\acute{\eta}_x \sigma_x}{\acute{\eta}_x} + \frac{\acute{\eta}_x}{\acute{\eta}_x} + \frac{\sigma_m \acute{\eta}_m}{\sigma_x} - \frac{\sigma_m}{\sigma_m}\right]$$

which, in turn, equals $\Delta TB/\Delta e = \sigma_x + \acute{\eta}_m$. The final equation tells us that a depreciation will be successful providing $\sigma_x + \acute{\eta}_m > 0$, which suggests that for most LDCs depreciation will indeed be a successful strategy.

Elasticity Pessimism

Elasticity pessimism is the belief that import demand price elasticities, both domestic and foreign, are so low that a depreciation will not improve a nation's trade balance.

But economists differ on the question of elasticities. Some believe that elasticities are high, while other economists are convinced that export and import elasticities are so low that, more often than not, currency depreciation hurts rather than improves a trade balance.

Elasticity pessimism, the belief that elasticities are so low that a depreciation cannot benefit but will actually hurt a nation, is often dismissed on theoretical grounds. Empirical evidence presents a mixed picture, however, and is a major reason for the

---

TABLE 11.2 Multilateral Trade Price Elasticities

Country	Exports[1]	Imports[1]	Exports[2]	Imports[2]
Canada	−.59	−1.46	−.83	−1.02
Germany	−1.25	−.24	−.66	−.60
Japan	−.80	−.72	−.93	−.93
United Kingdom	−1.24	−.21	−.44	−.47
United States	−1.51	−1.03	−.99	−.92
ROECD			−.83	−.49
LDCs			−.63	−.81

---

[1]Estimates of Houthakker and Magee.

[2]Estimates of Marquez.

ROECD = Rest of the Organization for Economic Cooperation and Development.

Sources: Hendrik S. Houthakker and Stephen P. Magee, "Income and Price Elasticities in World Trade," *Review of Economics and Statistics* 51 (May 1969); Table 1, p. 113, ©1969 by the President and Fellows of Harvard College; and Jaime Marquez, "Bilateral Trade Elasticities," *Review of Economics and Statistics* 72 (February 1990); Table 2, p. 75, ©1990 by the President and Fellows of Harvard College.

pessimism. Whether demand elasticities are low or high depends on the countries investigated, when the study was made, and the estimating techniques employed. The general consensus is that the sum of the import demand elasticities exceed unity for major trading nations and that they are higher in the long run compared with the short run.

Table 11.2 presents some of the results of studies on trade elasticities by Hendrik Houthakker and Stephen Magee and by Jaime Marquez. Only the elasticities of the UK in Marquez's study are less than unity, which suggests that while the MLR conditions may not be met in the case of the UK, they hold in all the other nations investigated. (The negative signs of the elasticity coefficients reflect the inverse relation between price and quantity.)

Depreciation: Real versus Nominal

A **nominal depreciation** describes how much a currency, say, the dollar, falls against another currency, say, the mark. If the exchange rate goes from DM4/$ to DM2/$, the dollar has fallen by 50 percent against the mark.

Assuming the elasticities are sufficiently high, depreciation will improve the trade balance providing other things remain equal. But other things hardly ever remain the same. Any depreciation is potentially inflationary because it will raise the price of selected inputs such as oil. And without an effective stabilization policy, there is a strong likelihood that this inflationary impetus will ripple through the rest of the economy and, given price and wage reactions, raise the general price level.

The end result of a depreciation could thus be that the aggregate supply curve will shift to the left so that the general price level will be higher at all levels of output. A higher price level will thus hinder the positive effects of a depreciation. If a 10 percent **nominal depreciation** is followed by a 6 percent rise in the domestic price level, the **real depreciation** is 4 percent. And it is the *real*, not the nominal, rate of depreciation that counts.

The **real rate of depreciation** measures how much a currency has depreciated in real terms. Thus if the dollar depreciates by 50 percent in nominal terms against the mark, but the U.S. rate of inflation exceeded the German rate of inflation by 20 percent, the real depreciation of the dollar against the mark would be 30 percent.

BOX 11.3 Real versus Nominal Exchange Rates

If a nation's currency depreciates by 10 percent, no one will purchase more of its exports if its domestic price level rises by 10 percent. But if the domestic price level falls by 10 percent while the exchange rate remains constant, the relative price of the nation's exports will fall and, presumably, its exports will increase. This gives us some idea of how to compute the real exchange rate.

Table 11.3 presents the nominal and real ¥/$ and DM/$ rates over the last decade. The real exchange rate is computed by multiplying the nominal exchange rate, ¥/$, by the quotient of the U.S. price index divided by the Japanese price index, P_{US}/P_J, or,

$$\left(\frac{¥}{$}\right)_R = \frac{¥}{$}\frac{P_{US}}{P_J}$$

The statistics point to two facts. First, nominal and real exchange rates normally move in the same direction, as did the dollar when it recovered in both real and nominal terms against the yen in 1989 and 1990. Second, the yen and the mark appreciated more in nominal than in real terms between 1985 and 1993. The yen rose at annual rates of 9 and 6.4 percent in nominal and real terms and the mark at annual rates of 6.5 and 5.1 percent in nominal and real terms respectively over these years. This means that nominal rates overestimated the improved competitiveness of the United States—especially in the case of Japan—or they showed that the yen and mark appreciated more than was actually the case.

TABLE 11.3 Nominal and Real Exchange Rates: 1985–94

Year	¥/$	(¥/$)$_R$	DM/$	(DM/$)$_R$
1985	238.6	238.6	2.94	2.94
1986	168.5	179.9	2.17	2.16
1987	144.6	164.8	1.80	1.88
1988	128.2	153.4	1.76	1.89
1989	138.2	178.4	1.88	2.06
1990	144.8	197.8	1.62	1.80
1991	134.5	187.5	1.66	1.84
1992	126.7	180.2	1.56	1.72
1993	111.2	164.4	1.65	1.85
1994	101.8	155.4	1.61	1.81

Source: Computed from International Monetary Fund, *International Financial Statistics Yearbook*, 1995; pp. 387, 389, 469, 471. (¥/$)$_R$ and (DM/$)$_R$ equal real exchange rates.

The Trade-Weighted Exchange Rate

A depreciation against one currency does not necessarily mean a depreciation against all currencies. The dollar depreciated sharply against the yen and the mark in early 1995 while it rose against the Mexican peso. Did the dollar *depreciate, appreciate,* or *remain stable*?

The answer is important. If the dollar, for example, falls against some currencies but rises against others, we have no way knowing if the U.S. trade balance will improve, deteriorate, or remain the same by looking at one bilateral exchange rate alone. If the dollar falls against the yen, the U.S. trade position relative to Japan may improve; but if the dollar rises relative to the South Korean won, its trade position against South Korea will deteriorate. And if now-cheaper South Korean products displace now-more-expensive Japanese products as U.S. imports, the total U.S. trade position could improve, deteriorate, or remain constant.

Because market forces can push *all* exchange rates in various directions, a nation's **trade-weighted** or **multilateral exchange rate**—which is often called the effective exchange rate—is the important one. A country's multilateral or trade-weighted exchange rate measures how its currency stands relative to the currencies of its major trading partners and is computed by taking the weighted average of the domestic currency against the currencies of its major trading partners. (See Box 11.4.) But even in this event, the computed multilateral or trade-weighted exchange rate may be biased. As trading patterns change due to emerging markets, technological change, capital transfers, and so forth and one country becomes a more important trading partner than another country at all exchange rates, the weights assigned to various currencies should change. Although currency weights are adjusted to reflect trading patterns, such adjustments are not undertaken on a yearly basis. For example, given the growth of Chinese-American trade, the yuan/dollar exchange rate should be considered when determining the trade-weighted value of the dollar. As a matter of fact, the yuan depreciated at an annual rate of 12.3 percent against the dollar between 1985 and 1994, but also, as a matter of fact, the yuan was not included in the basket of currencies that determined the trade-weighted value of the dollar.

A **trade-weighted** or **multilateral exchange rate** is a composite exchange rate normally expressed as an index number. It equals the value of a country's currency against the trade-weighted value of the currencies of its major trading partners—each currency is weighted by the particular country's importance in trade with the domestic country. Thus if the dollar falls against the yen, but appreciates relative to the Canadian dollar and the Mexican peso, the trade-weighted or multilateral value of the dollar may *rise, fall*, or *remain constant*. A trade-weighted currency can be measured in either nominal or real terms.

BOX 11.4 Computing a Multilateral or Trade-Weighted Exchange Rate

A multilateral or trade-weighted exchange rate is constructed as an index number in which the base year equals 100 and the other years are computed relative to that base year. There are essentially two steps involved in constructing a trade-weighted exchange rate. The first is to compute the weight or relative importance of each currency that is to be included in the exchange rate. These weights are computed by weighing the importance of each foreign nation in the nation's foreign trade. Table 4.5 showed that Canada, Japan, Mexico, the United Kingdom, and Germany were America's most important trade partners in 1994. Table 11.4 ranks these nations by the sum of their exports and imports to and from the United States. To obtain an individual nation's weight, we divide the value of its exports and imports to and from the United States by the total value of U.S. exports and imports. For example, the total value of U.S. trade with Canada equaled $275 billion in 1994 and the total value of U.S. exports to and imports from the five countries listed was $766 billion. Dividing 275 by 766 yields .36, which is the weight of the Canadian dollar in the U.S. multilateral exchange rate. The other weights in this abbreviated example are computed in the same manner.

Given the weights, the next step is to calculate the various exchange rates as index numbers. In this example, 1988 is the base year. In that year, the average exchange rate of the Canadian dollar expressed in U.S. dollars was C$1.23. This exchange rate is set equal to 100. In 1994, the exchange rate was C$1.36/$. In order to compute the relative exchange rate, we divide the 1994 exchange rate by the 1988 exchange rate and multiply the result by 100 or (1.36/1.12) times 100. Our answer is 111, which tells us that the Canadian dollar depreciated some 11 percent against the U.S. dollar over the period. In a similar manner, we can obtain the relative exchange rates for the other countries and, if desired, we could do it for a series of years.

The last step is to multiply each weight by the corresponding exchange rate, such as 111(.36), and sum up the resulting products. Following that procedure we find that the trade-weighted dollar exchange rate was 100 in 1988 and that it rose to 105.6 in 1994. Thus, on a trade-weighted basis the dollar appreciated some 5.6 percent over the period despite its rapid fall relative to the yen and, to lesser degree, against the mark.

One can also compute a *real multilateral or real trade-weighted exchange rate*. In computing this index, we would employ real exchange rates (see Box 11.3) rather than nominal exchange rates. Measured by the real trade-weighted exchange rate, the dollar fell from 100 in 1988 to 96.3 in 1994, or depreciated by close to 4 percent. Most of the change can be explained by the real appreciation of the Mexican peso during the period. In nominal terms, the Peso/$ rate rose from 2.28 to 3.33, a sharp depreciation in the peso. However, in real terms, the Peso/$ rate fell to roughly 1.7, or a sharp appreciation of the peso in real terms.

TABLE 11.4 Computing a Trade-Weighted Exchange Rate

Country	Exports plus Imports	Weight	Relative Exchange Rate 1988	Relative Exchange Rate 1994
Canada	$275bn	.35	100	111
Japan	$216bn	.28	100	80
Mexico	$118bn	.15	100	149
UK	$87bn	.11	100	116
Germany	$70bn	.09	100	92
Total	$766bn	1.00		

$$\text{TWER}_{94} = (.36)(111) + (.28)(80) + (.15)(149) + (.11)(116) + (.09)(90) = 105.6.$$

Sources: Table 4.5; and relevant country pages in International Monetary Fund, *International Financial Statistics Yearbook*, 1995.

The J Curve

J curve analysis explains why a nation's trade balance will first deteriorate before it improves following a depreciation. The basic explanation for the J curve is that price elasticities become larger over time.

Murphy's Law asserts that whatever can go wrong will go wrong. **J curve analysis** is not as pessimistic as Murphy's Law. Rather, it asserts that a trade balance deteriorates before it improves following a depreciation. Thus even though the dollar started to depreciate in late 1985, it took nearly two years before the U.S. trade position began to improve. The lesson of the J curve is this: A depreciation will work, but only after a lapse of some 1.5 to 2 years (Figure 11.2).

The primary reason for the delayed response to depreciation is that individuals do not immediately adjust to price changes. This is another way of saying that elasticities become *larger* over time. Thus, unlike the case of elasticity pessimism, which argues that a depreciation will not correct a trade balance regardless of the time period, the J curve claims that given sufficient time a depreciation will work. According to the MLR conditions, given infinite supply elasticities and assuming Brazil's exports and imports each equal R100, a 10 percent Real depreciation will lead to a R12 deterioration in Brazil's trade balance if the import demand elasticities each equal .2. If, however, the import demand elasticities increase over time so that their sum exceeds unity, the depreciation will improve Brazil's external accounts.

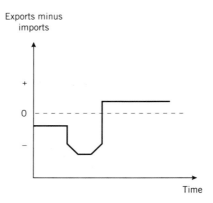

FIGURE 11.2 The J curve.

The J-curve shows that a nation's balance of trade deteriorates after its currency depreciates, but improves over time.

The movement of Brazil's trade balance position resembles the letter J, hence the name J curve. Initially, following the depreciation, when elasticities are low, Brazil's trade balance moves down toward the base of the J curve. After a period, Brazilians adjust more completely to the increase in the Real price of foreign products and foreigners to the lower price of Brazilian products. In terms of the J curve, Brazil's trade balance moves from the bottom of the base up past its initial position and the depreciation is successful.

Depreciation and Imperfect Competition

Tariff theory argues that in the case of a large country a protective tariff will not be successful if the elasticity of the foreign supply is zero, implying that the domestic market is vital for foreign suppliers. Despite the tariff, foreign firms will pay the duty and imports will still flood the domestic market under such conditions. This same type of analysis can be applied to the effects of currency depreciation.

Imagine that the U.S. market is important for German exporters—that sales in the U.S. market can spell the difference between a profitable and an unprofitable year for German exporters. In such a situation, German exporters may set the dollar price for their products based on developments in the U.S. market and pay limited attention to either tariffs or the exchange rate, especially if they expect the DM/$ rate to oscillate back and forth around a certain value over time.

Given their confidence, how will German firms react to currency fluctuations? When the DM/$ rate is high, let's say DM4/$, the Germans could reduce their dollar prices in an attempt to expand their market share. But if they feel they have already attained their potential market share, they will not cut their prices since such a step

The **pass-through-co-efficient,** or the **pass-through-effect,** measures the extent to which a depreciation is passed through onto domestic prices. If, given a 10 percent depreciation of the domestic currency, foreign suppliers only raise the domestic price of their products sold in the domestic market by 5 percent, the pass-through coefficient will equal one-half.

would reduce their profits. As the dollar appreciates, therefore, German firms will fatten their profit margins. On the other hand, as the dollar depreciates, they may maintain the dollar price of their products, even though this cuts into their profit margins, in order to retain their market share in the United States. The end result is that the depreciation, or some of it, is not **passed through** to prices.

Several studies by Catherine Mann support this contention. In her initial investigation of the relationship between profits and exchange rates, Mann discovered that foreign exporters boost profit margins when the dollar appreciates and cut them when the dollar is weak. For example, Japanese construction machinery exporters took a 9 percent drop in their profits when the dollar depreciated between 1977 and 1980, and fattened margins by some 11 percent when the dollar appreciated from 1980 to 1985. Interestingly, U.S. exporters, according to Mann's study, did not, for the most part, follow this pricing pattern.

The impact of such discretionary pricing on the effectiveness of a depreciation can be grasped by recalling the impact of depreciation on Brazil's external accounts. There we assumed that demand elasticities equal 1, that both the export and the import supply elasticities were infinite, and that trade was initially balanced. Under those conditions, a 10 percent depreciation led to a 20 percent improvement in Brazil's trade balance. If one assumes that everything remains constant except that the import supply elasticity equals zero, the MLR formula tells us that a 10 percent depreciation will lead to a 10 percent improvement in Brazil's trade balance. In other words, the depreciation will be only half as effective.

Pricing to market is the idea that firms will set prices at different levels in different markets in order to maintain, or expand, their share of a specific market.

This type of pricing policy, called **pricing to market,** cannot be practiced indefinitely given a large and permanent depreciation of the dollar. German firms pay their workers in marks. If they are confronted with a constant wage bill and falling sales receipts due to dollar depreciation, their profits will be squeezed. The point will come when German firms will find it is no longer possible to cut mark prices and accept losses in order to maintain a position in an increasingly unprofitable market.

There is another reason why pricing to market may not work: the threat of antidumping action. Imagine that the price of a BMW is DM100,000 in Germany and that the exchange rate is DM4/\$. The dollar price of a BMW sold in the United States should be \$25,000. Now suppose the dollar depreciates and the new exchange rate is DM2/\$. Given the new exchange rate, if the mark price of a BMW is constant, its dollar price should double. If the Germans maintain the mark price of the car in Germany and its dollar price in the United States, they could be accused of selling their products at different prices in different markets.

Large firms are aware of this possibility. (For example, in the summer of 1994, Toyota raised the price on some of its cars that were produced in Japan but sold in the United States by 5.5 percent to reflect the appreciation of the yen. In comparison, it raised the price of its U.S.-built Camry by just 1.7 percent.) And to get around this bind, many firms have maintained their market share in the foreign markets by setting up shop overseas. The United States gloated at the end of the June 1995 car war when it was able to announce that Japanese car manufacturers were planning to build or assemble an additional .5 million cars a year in North America. Most analysts attributed this decision to the appreciation of the yen rather than to American diplomacy. Regardless of the impetus, the decision of Japanese firms to build more cars in North America means that dollar depreciation has worked. Even if building cars in the United States does not generate additional U.S. exports, it certainly will cut U.S. imports.

Depreciation and the Economy

So far we have assumed that national income remains constant given depreciation. This assumption is not realistic. Depreciation, if successful, will increase exports and curtail imports and shift the nation's aggregate demand curve to the right from AD_0 to AD_1 and the absorption curve from A_0 to A_1, as in Figure 11.3. Even if it is assumed that the general price level remains constant, depreciation will not improve the trade balance by the magnitude previously indicated.

Recall that Brazil's trade balance improved by R20 following a 10 percent depreciation of the Real. But the increase in Brazil's net exports raised Brazilian income, and assuming that Brazil's marginal propensity to save and its marginal propensity to import each equal .2, the analysis of the last chapter tells us that Brazil's income will increase by R50 and its absorption by R40. The final betterment of Brazil's trade balance, therefore, will be R10, not R20.

But that assumes, however, that Brazil's domestic price level remains constant. If the Brazilian economy is close to full employment, its AS curve will have a positive slope—such as AS_0 in Figure 11.3. Depreciation shifts the AD and A curves as previously described but, given the slope of the AS curve, the price level rises to P_1. In this example, the higher domestic price level shrinks exports and expands imports to such an extent that the trade balance remains balanced despite the depreciation. In other words, cur-

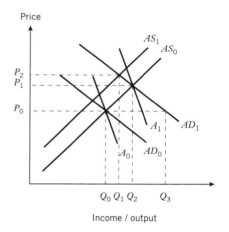

FIGURE 11.3 Depreciation and the economy.

Currency depreciation shifts the aggregate demand curve from AD_0 to AD_1 and the absorption curve from A_0 to A_1. If the price level remains constant at P_0, which implies that the supply curve is infinitely elastic, the nation runs a trade surplus equal to the difference between AD_1 and A_1 at the price level P_0. However, given the supply curve AS_0, the aggregate supply curve intersects AD_1 at the price level P_1. At that price level, absorption will equal aggregate demand and the country's trade balance will be balanced despite the depreciation of its currency. If the higher price level causes workers to push up their nominal wage rate in an attempt to maintain their real wage rate, the aggregate supply curve will shift from AS_0 to AS_1, and raise the price level to P_2. As a result, the country will run a trade deficit equal to the horizontal difference between A_1 and AD_1 at the price level P_2. This pattern of depreciation followed by inflation leads to a vicious circle.

rency depreciation leads to an increase in income and price levels sufficient to wipe out the initial depreciation-induced improvement in the trade balance.

Moreover, depreciation may unleash inflationary pressures in the form of higher input prices and higher wages that will shift the aggregate supply curve to the left, such as from AS_0 to AS_1 in Figure 11.3. Such a shift further complicates the analysis. If the supply curve shifts as indicated, the price level will rise to P_2. At the equilibrium price and income levels, absorption now exceeds aggregate demand and, according to the graph, the nation's trade balance actually deteriorates following currency depreciation.

The last case is more than a theoretical curiosity. In many LDCs, depreciations have unleashed inflationary pressures that have wiped out the initial effects of the currency realignment and left the nation's external accounts in worse, not better, shape. That record led to the development of the **vicious circle** hypothesis, which explains why a currency depreciation causes inflation that generates a greater trade imbalance that leads to further depreciation, higher inflation, and so on. In the end, according to the hypothesis, a nation depreciating its currency will have a higher rate of inflation and a larger trade deficit.

> A **vicious circle** occurs when one event leads to another and the second, or nth, event offsets the positive effects of the first event. A depreciation, introduced to improve the trade balance, may lead to domestic inflation, which negates the trade-improving effect of the depreciation.

All this does not mean that depreciation is useless as a policy tool. It does mean that if an economy is close to full employment, an expenditure-reducing policy will have to be employed in tandem with an expenditure-switching policy so as to simultaneously obtain internal and external equilibrium. (Depreciation may lead to a higher domestic price level for reasons that have not been discussed so far. A trade deficit permits a nation to absorb more than it produces and thereby repress domestic inflation. If depreciation corrects the trade balance, it eliminates the possibility of financing excess absorption at a constant price level. What was once a repressed inflation now becomes open.)

The absorption approach, $TB = Y - A$, emphasizes the point. An expenditure-switching policy restores the trade balance providing real output grows at a faster rate than absorption; or, assuming an economy is producing at full capacity, absorption is *reduced*. Thus, an expenditure-reducing policy that either reduces absorption or holds down its rate of growth is an essential part of a depreciation policy.

Measuring the Costs of a Depreciation

Any economic policy entails costs, and a depreciation is no different. In most circumstances, a depreciation will lead to a *deterioration* in a nation's terms of trade. The degree of the deterioration is inversely related to the sum of the import demand elasticities, or the higher they are, the lower the terms-of-trade cost of a depreciation.[5] Using our Brazil example, if each demand elasticity equals 2, and supply elasticities are infinite, and Brazil desires to improve its trade balance by R20, according to the MLR formula, Brazil will have to devalue the Real by 3.33 percent to hit this target. Since the price of its imports will rise by 3.33 percent, the Brazilian terms of trade will fall from 100 to 96.67.

---

[5]The derivation of the terms-of-trade cost of a depreciation can be found in H. Robert Heller, *International Monetary Economics* (Englewood Cliffs, NJ: Prentice-Hall, 1974); pp. 102–104.

> ### BOX 11.5 Calculating the Effects of a Depreciation _____
>
> In 1994, the United States had a balance of trade deficit of $102 billion; exports of goods and services equaled $716 billion while imports of goods and services totaled $818 billion. How much would a 10 percent depreciation affect the U.S. balance of trade? Recall Marquez's estimate that the U.S. export demand elasticity is .99 and its import demand elasticity is .92. Stephen Magee estimated that the supply elasticity of U.S. exports is 10 and the supply elasticity for U.S. imports is 8.5.[3]
>
> These values can be plugged into the MLR equation previously given:
>
> $$\frac{\Delta TB}{\Delta e} = -\left[\$176 \, \frac{.99(10.0 + 1)}{.99 + 10.0} + \$818 \, \frac{8.5(.92 - 1)}{.92 + 8.5} \right]$$
>
> or $\Delta TB = (\$651) \, \Delta e$.
>
> With this calculation performed, we can estimate that a 10 percent depreciation of the dollar will lead to a $65 billion improvement in the U.S. balance of trade. Once again, however, that conclusion assumes that everything else remains constant—specifically, that the price level and the income level are fixed. But an increase in net exports will raise income and boost imports unless an expenditure-reducing policy is undertaken at the time of the depreciation. Recall from Chapter 10 that the basic trade balance equals:
>
> $$TB = X - M_0 - mY$$
>
> In our example, depreciation raises net autonomous exports, $X - M_0$, by $65 billion. In turn, the increase in net autonomous exports will increase U.S. income by $65 billion $(1/.21 + .15)$ or by $181 billion—where .21 equals Marquez's estimate of the U.S. marginal propensity to import, and .15 is our previous estimate of the U.S. marginal propensity to save. Since the mpm equals .21, the income-induced rise in imports equals $38 billion. That means that the final improvement in the U.S. trade balance following a 10 percent depreciation will be $65 billion minus $38 billion, or $27 billion.[4]
>
> _____
>
> [3]Stephen P. Magee, "A Theoretical and Empirical Examination of Supply and Demand Relationships in U.S. International Trade," mimeo, *Council of Economic Advisors* (1970), as cited in H. Robert Heller, *International Monetary Economics* (Englewood Cliffs, NJ: Prentice-Hall, 1974); p. 29.
>
> [4]If there is a depreciation, X and M_0 will depend on the MLR conditions and as will the increase in income since it will rise by some multiple of the net increase in the trade balance. Thus we write:
>
> $$\Delta TB/\Delta e = -[MLR - (m/s + m) \, MLR]$$
>
> $$\Delta TB/\Delta e = -MLR[1 - (m/s + m)]$$
>
> $$\Delta TB/\Delta e = -MLR \, (s/s + m)$$
>
> where MLR represents the Marshall-Lerner-Robinson conditions.

The change in the terms of trade is palpable. The country is indeed poorer, although it can be argued that the country has been living beyond its means and that the change in the terms of trade simply brings about a needed correction. The last point is important. Previously, it was argued that an adverse movement in the terms of trade reduces a nation's potential level of output depending on the openness of its economy. In terms of the macroeconomic graphs, an adverse movement in the terms of trade shifts the potential output curve or line to the left. If a depreciation generates inflation and reduces potential output, there is not much to be said for it—although there is a lot to be said for currency appreciation and for economic policies that prevent the need for a depreciation.

The terms-of-trade cost of a depreciation, however, should be looked at in a different light. If a country is absorbing more than it is producing, that country's international terms of trade are likely in disequilibrium. Given the relative price of exports to imports, the demand for imports exceeds the supply of exports. One way to eliminate the excess demand is to raise the price of imports or demand relative to the price of exports or supply. Thus in Brazil, depreciation corrects a disequilibrium price. It does not so much reduce potential output as it reduces potential absorption and brings it back into line with potential output.

Depreciation versus Income Changes

Even if the terms-of-trade effect of a depreciation is simply the cost a nation must pay to bring its absorption into line with its potential production, it still is a *cost*. Nevertheless, it may be cheaper for a country to eliminate a trade deficit by depreciating its currency rather than by depressing its income. Which policy—exchange rate depreciation or income changes—is cheapest depends on the import demand elasticities and the marginal propensity to import.

If an economy is fairly closed, its marginal propensity to import will likely be quite low. If so, the income contraction required to eliminate a trade deficit will be large. By contrast, if the nation and its trading partners have high import-demand price elasticities, a small depreciation should right the trade balance at a minimal terms-of-trade cost.

Suppose, for example, that export supply elasticities are infinite, import demand elasticities are each 2, national income is \$1000, exports equal \$50, and imports equal \$100 so that the trade deficit is \$50. Assuming that domestic income, the domestic price level, and foreign income remain constant (big assumptions), a 25 percent depreciation will eliminate the trade deficit.

$$\Delta TB/\Delta e = -[X(Dx) + M_0(Dm - 1)]$$
$$\$50/\Delta e = -[\$50(2) + \$100(2 - 1)]$$
$$\$50/\Delta e = -[\$100 + \$100]$$
$$\Delta e = -[\$50/\$200]$$
$$\Delta e = -.25$$

The cost of depreciation, measured by the terms-of-trade effect, equals the change in the trade balance times the reciprocal of the sum of the import demand elasticities minus one, or $\Delta TB(1/Dx + Dm - 1)$. In the example, the cost equals \$50(1/3) or \$16.67, which is 1.67 percent of national income. Thus, if export supply and import demand elasticities are large, depreciation will not only work but becomes a relatively inexpensive way to close a trade deficit, especially when compared with the cost of correcting a trade deficit via income adjustment.

BOX 11.6 Estimating Adjustment Costs

Table 11.5 lists alternative estimates of the costs of adjustment for five countries. According to Marquez's estimates, Canada, Japan, and the United States should not use an expenditure-reducing or -increasing policy to correct an external imbalance; rather they should rely on an expenditure-switching policy. Germany, on the other hand, should rely on expenditure-increasing or -decreasing policies. Since the sum of the elasticities is less than one in the case of the United Kingdom, the UK also should use expenditure-reducing or -increasing policies if it faces an external imbalance.

Houthakker's and Magee's estimates lead to the same results. Canada, Japan, and the United States should use expenditure-switching policies while Germany should employ expenditure-increasing or -decreasing policies to correct external imbalances. According to Houthakker and Magee, the costs of depreciation and income adjustment are almost the same for the United Kingdom. Thus it has the option of using either policy to correct a trade imbalance.

TABLE 11.5 Alternative Estimates of the Cost of Adjustment

Cost of Adjusting to a $1 Deficit (Marquez)

Country	Sum of Elasticities	Terms of Trade Cost	mpm	Income Costs
Canada	−1.85	−$1.17	.48	$2.08
Germany	−1.26	−$3.85	.55	$1.89
Japan	−1.86	−$1.16	.03	$33.33
UK	−0.91	—	.67	$1.49
United States	−1.91	−$1.09	.21	$6.25

Cost of Adjusting to a $1 Deficit (Houthakker and Magee)

Country	Sum of Elasticities	Terms of Trade Cost	mpm	Income Costs
Canada	−2.05	−$.95	.31	$3.22
Germany	−1.49	−$2.04	.53	$1.89
Japan	−2.52	−$1.92	.11	$9.09
UK	−1.45	−$2.22	.44	$2.27
United States	−2.54	−$.64	.16	$6.25

Sources: H. Houthakker and S. Magee, and J. Marquez, as previously cited.

What will be the income adjustment costs in such a case? If the marginal propensity to import is .10, income would have to fall by $500, $50 = .10Y, to eliminate a $50 trade deficit. It is apparent in this case that depreciation is the least costly method of attaining external equilibrium. But it is also evident that if the sum of the import demand elasticities is *low* and the marginal propensity to import is *high*, the reverse is true. Imagine the sum of the import demand elasticities equals 1.1 and supply elasticities are infinite as before; the cost of eliminating a $50 trade deficit by depreciation is $50(1/1.1 − 1) or $500. By comparison, if the marginal propensity to import equals .5, the cost of eliminating the deficit is $100. The best policy, therefore, depends on the structure of the economy.

Summary

Currency depreciation is an important tool of economic policy. An exchange rate can be adjusted either by a country establishing a new official exchange rate—assuming a system of fixed exchange rates exists—or by simply stating that it will no longer seek to maintain an existing exchange rate and allow the exchange rate to float, as Britain did in the fall of 1992. In either case, the ability of a depreciation to correct a trade imbalance depends on technical factors plus the willingness of a nation to introduce complementary economic policies to assure its success.

A depreciation will not be successful if the Marshall-Lerner-Robinson conditions do not hold. However, in most cases elasticities are sufficiently high that the MLR conditions do not impose a barrier that cannot be overcome. The same is true of the J curve and the pass-through coefficient, the partial failure of a depreciation to be passed onto prices. If they exist, it will take a longer period of time for a depreciation to work, but they will not stop a depreciation in its tracks.

There are, however, economic developments engendered by the depreciation itself that may hamper its success. In most cases, a depreciation will raise the price of some vital inputs. And if these higher prices ripple through the economy, shifting the aggregate supply curve to the left, the success of the depreciation may be placed in jeopardy. In addition, a depreciation leads to economic expansion because it improves the country's net export position. If the country is already pressing against its capacity limits, economic expansion will most likely lead to inflation, which if it is sufficiently high will wipe out the positive effects of the depreciation. This means that in the majority of cases it is absolutely essential that a depreciation be accompanied by an expenditure-reducing policy.

All along we have assumed, for the most part, that a nation will choose to let the international value of its currency decline. In many cases, there is no such choice. If the rate of domestic inflation is high relative to the rate of external or worldwide inflation, depreciation becomes inevitable. Any attempt to forestall the required exchange rate adjustment will make matters worse and increase the costs of the depreciation that, ultimately, must take place. If the costs of depreciation are high, the best course of action is to follow economic policies which prevent it from becoming an imperative. This is important since a depreciation, by itself, is hardly ever a cure-all. It is usually a part of an economic package and the failure to carry out other parts of it will render depreciation, or appreciation, useless. On a more positive note, exchange rate adjustment can give a nation breathing space, enabling it to introduce needed macroeconomic policies.

Key Concepts and Terms

costs of depreciation

costs of income adjustment

depreciation and the terms of trade

elasticity pessimism

J curve

Marshall-Lerner-Robinson (MLR) conditions

multilateral or trade-weighted or effective exchange rate

nominal depreciation

nominal versus real exchange rate

pass-through effect

pricing-to-market

real depreciation

vicious circle

Review Questions

1. Describe the Marshall-Lerner-Robinson conditions. Are they sufficient to assure a successful currency depreciation?

2. What is the difference between a real and a nominal depreciation? Why would one suspect that when a country depreciates its currency, the nominal depreciation will be greater than the real depreciation?

3. Explain the following terms:
   (a) Pass-through effect.
   (b) J Curve.
   (c) Elasticity pessimism.

4. Suppose that a country is confronted with unemployment and a trade deficit. Will currency depreciation alone move the nation toward internal and external equilibrium? Imagine that another country is faced with inflation, and a trade deficit. Explain whether and why currency depreciation will or will not be successful in this case.

5. If the first nation in the question above does depreciate its currency, what would be the impact of this policy on the rest of the world?

6. Why would it be more likely for a relatively closed economy than for a relatively open economy to employ depreciation or appreciation as a policy tool?

References and Suggested Readings

Most texts on international economics formally derive the Marshall-Robinson-Lerner conditions and the terms-of-trade effect of a depreciation.

Catherine L. Mann's study on the pass-through effects of depreciation was published as "Prices, Profits Margins, and Exchange Rates," *Federal Reserve Bulletin* 72 (June 1986); pp. 366–379. Subramanian Rangan and Robert Z. Lawrence, "The Responses of U.S. Firms to Exchange Rate Fluctuations: Piercing the Corporate Veil," *Brookings Papers on Economic Activity* 1 (1993); pp. 341–369, take a different view on the pricing patterns of U.S. firms following dollar depreciation. The articles are relatively advanced.

Michael T. Belongia describes how exchange rate indexes are constructed in "Estimating Exchange Rate Effects on Exports: A Cautionary Note," Federal Reserve Bank of St. Louis, *Review* 68 (January 1986); pp. 5–15. B. Diane Pauls does the same thing in her article, "Measuring the Foreign Exchange Value of the Dollar," *Federal Reserve Bulletin* 73 (June 1987); pp. 411–421, and shows how much the dollar appreciated and depreciated according to various exchange rate indexes.

There is always the pressing question of whether a depreciation will be successful. Steven Kamin summarizes past studies on the efficacy of depreciation and makes his own estimates in *Devaluation, External Balance and Macroeconomic Performance: A Look at the Numbers*, Princeton Studies in International Finance no. 62 (Princeton, NJ: International Finance Section, Princeton University, 1988). Jacques Artus and Ann K. McGuirk provide estimates of the impact of a depreciation on the domestic price level and the trade balance in "A Revised Version of the Multilateral Exchange Rate Model," *International Monetary Fund Staff Papers* 28 (June 1981); pp. 275–309. (This is an advanced article.)

Paul R. Krugman appraises the adjustment mechanism in his short book *Has the Adjustment Process Worked?* (Washington, DC: Institute for International Economics, 1991). Richard N. Cooper wrote a classic essay on the consequences of depreciation in LDCs, *Currency Devaluation in Developing Countries*, Princeton Essays in International Finance no. 86 (Princeton, NJ: International Finance Section, Princeton University, 1971). One might also consult Riccardo Faini and Jaime de Melo, "Adjustment, Investment, and the Real Exchange Rate in Developing Countries," *Economic Policy* 5 (October 1990). Thomas Klitgaard wrote a brief article explaining the Japanese trade surplus, "In Brief: Understanding the Rising Japanese Trade Surplus," Federal Reserve Bank of New York, *Quarterly Review* 19 (Spring 1994). "Economic Focus: A Much Devalued Idea," *The Economist* (March 25, 1995); p. 86, analyzes the results of recent currency devaluations in Europe, and "Schools Brief: A Much Devalued Theory," *The Economist* (January 20, 1996); pp. 70–71, presents a brief, but spirited, analysis of devaluation.

Chapter 12

Capital Flows and the Balance of Payments

U p to this point our discussion of external equilibrium has concentrated on how a country deals with its trade balance alone; we have skirted questions of how capital movements to and from other countries may influence a nation's external position. We have assumed, for example, that if a nation has a $100 trade imbalance, it must either reduce its income or depreciate its currency in order to attain external equilibrium. But if a nation receives a capital inflow of $100, it can run a $100 trade deficit and not have to introduce either an expenditure-reducing or -switching policy since the capital inflow will finance its trade deficit.

Capital movements are important. In the early 1980s, the United States ran persistent trade deficits and especially bilateral trade deficits with Germany and Japan. Since Germany and Japan ran overall trade surpluses, it was reasonable to assume that the mark and yen would appreciate in terms of the dollar and that the ratio of German and Japanese international reserves to American reserves would rise. But the data presented in Table 12.1 show that this did not happen. The dollar soared on the foreign exchanges and, relatively speaking, U.S. international reserves rose dramatically.

The Path Ahead

What we need is a framework that helps explain the impact of capital flows on a nation's external equilibrium. This chapter provides such a framework by first deriving the trade balance and the balance of payments schedules and curves and then developing the capital flow schedule. These are the essential tools for showing the effects of capital flows on a nation's external accounts. Capital flows are determined in part by interest rates. This chapter discusses what determines the interest rate, and also investigates how a nation may be able to utilize monetary and fiscal policy to induce an inflow of capital in the short run.

TABLE 12.1 Export Surplus, Exchange Rates, and International Reserves: Japan and Germany Relative to the United States: 1979—85 (billions of $, 1979 = 100)

Year	Japan/United States			Germany/United States		
	(1)	*(2)*	*(3)*	*(4)*	*(5)*	*(6)*
1979	$37	100	100	$27	100	100
1980	37	104	63	11	99	46
1981	45	100	60	13	120	34
1982	47	114	41	26	131	29
1983	50	108	43	34	139	28
1984	61	108	44	49	155	25
1985	69	109	33	58	161	20

(1) Japan's trade surplus with the United States.

(2) ¥/$.

(3) Japan's international reserves relative to U.S. international reserves.

(4) Germany's trade surplus with the United States.

(5) DM/$.

(6) Germany's international reserves relative to U.S. international reserves.

Sources: Calculated from data in International Monetary Fund, *Direction of Trades Statistics Yearbook*, 1986, pp. 187, 241; and International Monetary Fund, *International Financial Statistics*, December, 1986, pp. 220, 290, 508.

The Trade Balance Schedule

The **trade balance schedule** or **curve** shows the domestic price and income levels at which exports will equal imports.

The first step in understanding the impact of capital flows on a nation's external position is to derive the **trade balance schedule** and **curve.** The trade balance schedule and curve show the domestic price and income levels at which exports equal imports. A hypothetical trade balance schedule is given in Table 12.2.

Table 12.2 is a close cousin to Table 10.3; exports are still a function of the domestic price level and imports depend on the domestic price level plus the level of national income. But there is a difference. Given the price level, Table 10.3 showed what the income level will *actually* be, while Table 12.2 shows what the income level *must* be if exports are to equal imports. When graphed out, columns (1) and (5) of Table 12.2 define

TABLE 12.2 Trade Balance Schedule

Price Level *(1)*	Exports *(2)*	Imports$_1$ *(3)*	Imports$_2$ *(4)*	Income *(5)*
P_2	$50	$30	$20	$100
P_1	60	20	40	200
P_0	70	10	60	300

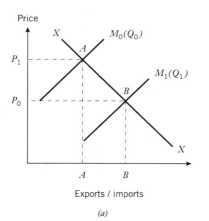

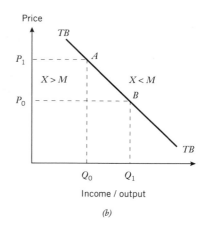

FIGURE 12.1 The trade balance schedule.

The trade balance curve, *TB* in panel (b), shows the price and income levels at which exports equal imports. If the economy lies to the right of this curve, imports exceed exports; if it lies to the left of the curve, exports exceed imports. The *TB* curve is derived in panel (a). The export curve, *X*, slopes down from left to right, which shows that exports *increase* as the price level *decreases*. Imports depend on (i) the price level and (ii) the level of income. When the price level is P_1, exports equal imports providing that the level of income is Q_0. If the price level falls to P_0, exports will increase and imports will decrease *providing* the income level is constant. However, a higher income will induce more imports and restore external equilibrium. Therefore, when the price level is P_0, exports will equal imports providing the income level is Q_1. The points of equilibrium between exports and imports at various price and income levels are then graphed out in panel (b) to arrive at the trade balance curve.

the trade balance curve, since it is only at these combinations of price and income levels that exports equal imports. For example, if the price level is P_2 and the income level is $300, exports will equal $50, but imports will equal $30 plus 20 percent of income, $60, so that total imports will equal $90. As a result, the economy will have a trade deficit. Hence, the *AS* and *AD* curves would lie to the right of the *TB* curve. (If an economy lies to the left of the *TB* schedule or curve, it has a trade surplus.)

One can construct a trade balance curve, as in Figure 12.1b, by combining the export curve with a series of import curves. At points *A* and *B*, where the export curve intersects the import curves, exports equal imports. For example, when the domestic price level is P_1 and domestic income stands at Q_0, exports and imports are each, say, $60. If domestic income rises to Q_1 while the price level remains constant, imports rise to, say, $80 but exports remain at $60. The resulting trade deficit can be eliminated if the domestic price level falls to P_0. The lower price level will reduce imports and stimulate exports. Thus, exports equal imports at higher income levels provided the domestic price level falls at a pace sufficient that the *increase* in imports generated by the higher level of income is *offset* by the rise in exports and decrease in imports brought about by the fall in the domestic price level.

Shifts in the Trade Balance Curve

It is hard to imagine that the trade balance curve will remain constant. Most likely, it will shift to the right over time; but in the short run it may shift in either direction. An increase in foreign income, a fall in foreign competitiveness, or a depreciation of the domestic currency shifts the export curve and, therefore, the trade balance curve to the right. A fall in foreign competitiveness or a depreciation of the domestic currency also causes the import curve to shift to the left, further moving the *TB* curve to the right. If one assumes currency appreciation rather than depreciation, the *TB* curve would shift to the left. The *TB* curve, however, will not shift if imports rise due to an increase in income caused by a change in government expenditures, tax rates, or by an increase or decrease in investment because the *TB* curve includes the impact of a change in domestic income on imports.

This means that an *expenditure-switching* policy will shift the trade balance curve to the left or to the right depending on whether the domestic currency appreciates or depreciates. But *expenditure-reducing* or *expenditure-increasing* policies—such as fiscal and monetary policy, which will shift the aggregate demand curve to the left or to the right—will not shift the trade balance curve.

The Balance of Payments Schedule

The **balance of payments schedule** shows the domestic price and income levels at which the balance of payments is balanced on an official reserve basis.

The two major components of the balance of payments, as pointed out in Chapter 4, are the *current account* and the *capital account*. If we assume that the current account equals the balance of trade, the **balance of payments schedule** can be derived with the help of the trade balance schedule. Table 12.3 shows how this can be done.

Table 12.3 resembles Table 12.2 with one exception. Table 12.2 showed the combination of price and income levels at which exports and imports would be balanced. Table 12.3 shows the price and income levels at which the balance of payments—*trade plus capital flows*—will be balanced. In the table, we assume that there is a positive capital inflow, *K* flow, of $10. Because of the capital inflow, the nation can move to a higher level of income at *every* price level and still maintain external equilibrium compared with the case in Table 12.2. For example, when the price level is P_1 in Table 12.3, exports plus the net capital inflow equal imports when the income level is $250. In Table 12.2, when the price level is P_1, trade is balanced when the level of income is $200. The difference is due to the $10 capital inflow. Assuming that the marginal propensity to import is .2, a nation's income can be $50 higher and income-induced

TABLE 12.3 Balance of Payments Schedule

Price Level (1)	Exports (2)	Imports$_1$ (3)	Imports$_2$ (4)	K Flow (5)	Income (6)
P_2	$50	$30	$30	$10	$150
P_1	60	20	50	10	250
P_0	70	10	70	10	350

imports (imports$_2$) $10 higher at every price level and the nation will still be in external equilibrium—its official reserve balance will equal zero.

The relationship can be graphed. When columns 1 and 6 of Table 12.3 are plotted out, they depict the **balance of payments curve (line).** At any point along this line, or at the corresponding price and income levels, the balance of payments equals zero. If a country's economy lies to the left of the *BP* curve, the nation has a balance of payments surplus; if the economy lies to the right of the *BP* curve, the nation has a balance of payments deficit.

The **balance of payments curve** is a graphical presentation of the balance of payments schedule.

Capital Flows and the Balance of Payments: A Graphical Exposition

Figure 12.2 explains how capital flows affect the balance of payments and what leads to capital flows in the first place. Figure 12.2a demonstrates how the domestic interest rate is determined, Figure 12.2b presents the capital flow curve, and Figure 12.2c displays two balance of payments (*BP*) curves.

It must be emphasized that the *TB* and *BP* curves show the price and income levels at which trade and the balance of payments will be balanced and not the actual magnitude of the surplus or deficit. If an economy lies either to the left or to the right of the *TB* or *BP* curves, neither curve shows the *actual* trade or balance of payments surplus or deficit. However at any price level, the further an economy is away from the schedules, the *greater* the surplus or deficit.

How are the *BP* and the *TB* curves related? Consider the two *BP* curves drawn in Figure 12.2c. In one case, the *BP* curve lies astride the *TB* curve, so that $BP_0 = TB_0$. In this case, net capital flows equal zero and external equilibrium depends solely on the trade balance. (One could return to Table 12.3 and substitute $0 for $10 under capital flows and see how much income would have to decline in order to bring the balance of payments into equilibrium at any given price level. Column 1 and the new column 6 together would then trace out a new *BP* curve.)

In the second example, the *BP* curve, BP_1, lies to the right of the *TB* curve. In this example, capital flows are positive. Given the domestic price level, there is one income level at which exports will equal imports and a higher level of income at which capital inflows will finance an excess of imports over exports. (If the *BP* curve lies to the left of the *TB* curve, capital flows are negative.)

Suppose that BP_1 is the relevant balance of payments curve and that the nation's aggregate supply and demand curves intersect at the combination P_0Q_0 or at point *a* in Figure 12.2c. Because the economy lies on the *TB* curve, its exports equal its imports. But since the economy lies to the *left* of the BP_1 curve, capital flows toward the country and its balance of payments on an official reserve basis is *positive*. If the country's aggregate supply and demand curves intersected at point *b* in Figure 12.2c, the country would lie to the *right* of its *TB* curve and it would have a *negative* trade balance. But the deficit would be more than financed by capital inflows so that the nation's balance of payments would be *positive*.

Table 12.4 summarizes four *possible* positions for a given economy. In each case, the country has a positive capital account regardless of its trade or balance of payments positions. This is true because the *BP* curve lies to the right of the *TB* curve.

Because the *BP* curve equals the *TB* curve plus or minus capital flows, it will shift in tandem with any shift in the *TB* curve. An increase in exports will shift the *TB* curve to

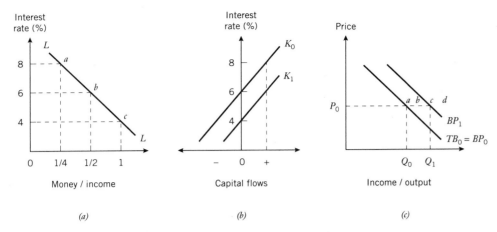

FIGURE 12.2 Interest rates, capital flows, and the balance of payments: I.

Panel (a) shows that the interest rate depends on the money-to-real-income ratio, assuming everything else, including the price level, is constant. An increase in this ratio will lead to a lower interest rate. Panel (b) shows the capital flow curve, K_0. It assumes that capital flows between countries depend upon the interest rate differential prevailing between the domestic nation and the rest of the world. If the domestic and foreign interest rates are both 6 percent, capital will not flow between the countries, providing everything else remains constant. However, if the domestic interest rate rises to 8 percent while the foreign interest rate remains constant, capital will flow toward the domestic country. It is unlikely that other things will remain constant. If the foreign interest rate falls to 4 percent, the capital flow schedule will shift from K_0 to K_1. That means that if the domestic interest remains at 6 percent while the foreign interest rate drops to 4 percent, the domestic nation will enjoy a positive capital inflow. Panel (c) shows the TB curve and the balance of payments curve (BP). The balance of payments curve tells us the price and income levels at which the *balance of payments*, on an official reserve basis, is balanced. If an economy lies to the right of its BP curve, it will have a balance of payments deficit. If it lies to the left of the BP curve, it will have a balance of payments surplus. Finally, if capital flows are *zero*, the TB and BP curves are one and the same. The following example spells out the relationships. Assume the domestic and foreign interest rates equal 6 percent. Given the capital flow schedule K_0, capital does not flow into or out of the nation, panel (b). Since capital flows are nonexistent, the balance of payments curve, BP_0, equals the trade balance curve, TB_0, in panel (c). Now suppose the domestic money supply/GDP ratio falls from one-half to one-quarter. As a result the domestic interest rate rises to 8 percent. Given the higher interest rate, capital flows into the nation, panel (b). The capital inflow causes the balance of payments curve to shift from BP_0 to BP_1 in panel (c).

TABLE 12.4 Trade Balance, Capital Flows and the Balance of Payments Position

Position	Trade Account	Capital Account	Balance of Payments
a	$X = M$	inflow	surplus
b	$X < M$	inflow	surplus
c	$X < M$	inflow	balanced
d	$X < M$	inflow	deficit

the right causing the *BP* curve to also shift to the right regardless of whether it lay initially to the left, right, or astride the *TB* curve. The *BP* curve can, however, shift for reasons of its own. Anything that expands or contracts capital flows will cause the *BP* curve to shift even if the *TB* curve does not budge. Higher domestic interest rates, lower foreign interest rates, or improved investment opportunities in the domestic economy cause the *BP* curve to shift to the right. Because it can move to right or to the left, each *BP* curve is drawn under the assumption that all shift variables, such as those just cited, are constant.

The Capital Flow Curve and the Balance of Payments

The **capital flow curve** shows the level of the flow of capital either into or out of the domestic country at various domestic interest rates providing other things, including foreign interest rates, are constant.

The international **capital flow curve** (K) is drawn in Figure 12.2b. Its positive slope indicates that capital flows to and from a country depend on the level of the domestic interest rates compared with foreign interest rates. Curve K_0, for example, is drawn under the assumption that the foreign interest rate is 6 percent. Thus, if the domestic interest rate is also 6 percent, we can assume that capital flows are nil. However, if the domestic interest rate rises to 8 percent, capital, measured along the horizontal axis, will flow toward the country. The greater the differential between domestic and foreign interest rates, the larger the capital flows will be.

If the foreign interest rate falls to 4 percent, the capital flow curve will shift down and to the right to K_1. Since the foreign interest rate is now lower, capital will flow toward the country, if the domestic interest rate remains at 6 percent. Additionally, given the drop in the foreign interest rate, the domestic rate could be cut to 4 percent without this generating a capital outflow.

The relationship between domestic interest rates, capital flows, and the balance of payments can be spelled out even further. Suppose the initial capital flow and balance of payments curves are K_0 and BP_0 in Figures 12.2b and 12.2c. Suppose, as well, that both the foreign and domestic interest rates are 6 percent so that capital flows are nil.

Now, with other things held constant, assume the domestic interest rate rises to 8 percent. Given the higher domestic interest rate, capital will flow toward the domestic economy. This positive capital flow shifts the *BP* curve from BP_0 to BP_1 in Figure 12.2c. Thus, a higher domestic interest rate leads to a capital inflow, which shifts the *BP* curve to the right. The shift in the *BP* curve depends, at least partly, on the responsiveness of capital flows to a change in the interest rates. If capital flows are highly elastic to interest differentials, the capital flow curve will be flatter and a small rise in the domestic interest rate will cause a large shift in the balance of payments curve.

Why Capital Moves Between Nations

Capital flows are determined by many factors as discussed previously in Chapter 3. Changes in domestic and foreign interest rates are the most obvious reasons why capital flows across international boundaries and time zones 24 hours a day. But there are other reasons, and as these reasons change, the capital flow curve, and most likely the *BP* curve, shifts either to the left or to the right.

An improving domestic investment climate due to domestic economic expansion, lower taxes on capital, and so on will lead to a capital inflow even if only temporarily. But the inflow will shift the K and BP curves to the right, again even if only temporarily.

A more complicated case can arise if international money managers expect that a particular foreign currency will depreciate. In that case, the capital flow and balance of payments curves will shift to the right even though both the domestic and foreign interest rate remain at 6 percent. Why? If money managers expect that the foreign currency will depreciate by 2 percent, they will want an additional 2 percent interest on foreign funds to cover for that possibility. In their eyes, the effective foreign interest rate is not 6 percent but 4 percent, or an adjusted 4 percent. That means that if the domestic interest rate stays at 6 percent, capital will flow toward the domestic economy. This is shown by shifting the capital flow curve from K_0 to K_1 in Figure 12.2b.

Determining the Domestic Interest Rate

When graphed, the *money/income ratio* becomes the **money/income curve** which shows the relationship between domestic interest rates and the money/income ratio. An increase in the money/income ratio will lead to a fall in the domestic interest rate providing other things remain equal.

Because capital flows depend at least partly on the domestic interest rate, what determines the domestic interest rate becomes an important question. Essentially, the interest rate is determined by the **money/income ratio** or by the supply of money relative to its demand. Since the money supply is controlled by the central bank, it is usually considered a given. Attention, therefore, is focused not on *who* but on *what* determines the demand for money.

The primary determinants of the demand for money are income and the interest rate itself. The demand for money is *positively* related to the level of real income and *negatively* correlated with the interest rate. As income expands, individuals demand more money in order to carry out a higher level of transactions. In contrast, the demand for money declines as interest rates climb. Higher interest rates mean that it is possible to obtain a relatively higher return on wealth by placing it in financial assets such as bonds, rather than holding it in the form of money. (It is normally assumed that money balances do not earn interest or only a negligible return at best.) Therefore as interest rates rise, individuals demand less money because the return on bond investments increases while the cost of holding wealth in the form of money becomes more expensive in terms of interest forgone.

These relationships are shown in Figure 12.2a. The interest rate depends on the money/real-income ratio. The larger the ratio, the lower the interest rate. Given a certain level of real income, suppose the central bank increases the money supply causing an increase in the money/income ratio from, say, .5 to 1. (The figures in this example are purely illustrative. Money/real-income ratios do not double except in cases of hyperinflation.) The interest rate falls from 6 to 4 percent, or money market equilibrium moves from point b to point c in Figure 12.2a. How much the interest rate actually declines depends on the slope of the money demand or L curve. If the demand for money is interest elastic—meaning that a small change in the interest rate will lead to a large change in the demand for money given the level of income—the L curve is flat and an increase in the money supply will cause only a small decrease in the interest rate. When the demand for money is interest inelastic, the L curve is steep and any change in the money supply or the money/income ratio has a marked effect on the interest rate.

BOX 12.1   Money, Inflation, and Interest Rates

The main thread of the analysis has avoided one complication so far. It has assumed implicitly that the domestic price level remains constant. Because of this assumption, we could assume that an increase in the money/real-income ratio would bring interest rates down with a thump. But an inflationary expansion of the money supply will not lead to lower interest rates even though it will increase the money/real-income ratio. Instead, it will lead to higher interest rates. Moreover, the resulting high interest rates will not lead to a capital inflow into the inflating country. In the fall of 1995, short-term interest rates were roughly 180 percent in Russia and 44 percent in Venezuela, but there was no sign that international money managers were moving funds into ruble- and bolivar-denominated assets.

How does our framework explain this phenomenon? If the domestic price level rises, the L schedule will shift to the right and a given money/real GDP ratio will be associated with a higher interest rate. How and why this occurs is explained by Figure 12.3.

Imagine an economy is operating at or close to its potential level of income so that any increase in aggregate demand will lead to an increase in the general price level. Assume as well that the money/real income ratio is .5 and the interest rate is 6 percent. Under these conditions an increase in the money supply may initially cause interest rates to drop or move the money supply/money demand equilibrium point from b to c along L_0 in Figure 12.3a. The ensuing expansion in aggregate demand will raise the price level and, perhaps, real

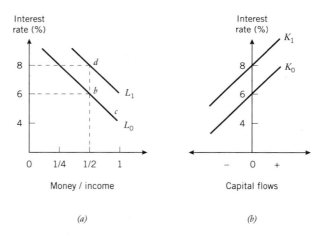

(a)   (b)

FIGURE 12.3   Price levels, interest rates, and capital flows.

If an economy is operating close to full capacity, an increase in the money-to-real-GDP ratio will not necessarily lead to lower interest rates. Under such conditions, an increase in the money supply will probably raise the price level, or generate inflationary expectations. Inflation or rising inflationary expectations will shift the L schedule in panel (a) from L_0 to L_1—assuming the anticipated rate of inflation is 2 percent. The increase in the money/income ratio will, under these conditions, raise the interest rate from, say, 6 percent to 8 percent. The higher interest rate will not lead to a capital inflow since the capital flow schedule will shift from K_0 to K_1. Money managers will anticipate that the domestic currency will depreciate by 2 percent. Thus, to prevent an outflow of capital, the domestic interest rate must equal the foreign interest rate, assumed to be 6 percent, plus the anticipated depreciation of the domestic currency. This means that the position of the capital flow schedule depends not only on the foreign interest rate, but on the expected depreciation or appreciation of the domestic currency as well.

income. Any increase in real income will move the economy back toward point b on L_0 and lead to a higher interest rate. The important point here is that the increase in the money supply will lead to a higher price level. In turn, the higher price level will shift the L schedule up to L_1 so that interest rates will be higher at all money/real income ratios. Assume that due to the increase in the price level and real income, the economy settles at point d on schedule L_1. The nation, therefore, ends up with a higher, not lower, interest rate following monetary expansion.

The higher interest rate, 8 percent in the example, will not lead to a positive capital flow even if the foreign interest rate remains at 6 percent. The higher domestic price level causes the capital flow schedule to shift from K_0 to K_1. Why? If the domestic inflation rate is 2 percent higher than the foreign rate, domestic interest rates must be 2 percent higher than foreign interest rates if capital flows are to be nil. It is assumed that a 2 percent higher rate of inflation implies that the domestic currency will depreciate by 2 percent. Thus the nation's real international rate of interest equals its nominal interest minus the expected rate of domestic currency depreciation, or 6 percent, not 8 percent, in this example.

To return to the Russian and Venezuelan examples, in the fall of 1995, rates of inflation in these two countries were 215 percent and 52 percent respectively. If these rates of inflation accurately reflected the future depreciation of the ruble and the bolivar against a basket of currencies, an international money manager would take a hefty loss if she purchased ruble- and bolivar-denominated assets despite the high interest rates prevailing in the two countries.

Monetary Policy and the Balance of Payments

We can see, then, how monetary policy affects capital flows and the balance of payments. Assume that the aggregate supply and demand curves intersect at P_0Q_0 in Figure 12.4c. Because the economy is positioned to the right of the trade balance curve, TB_0, it is running a trade deficit. If it is also assumed that domestic and foreign interest rates are both 6 percent, capital flows are zero and the nation's balance of payments position is identical to its trade balance position.

Now suppose the central bank reduces the money supply and that the money/income ratio falls to .25 and the interest rate rises from 6 to 8 percent. The higher domestic interest rate leads to a capital inflow, which finances the nation's trade deficit. In Figure 12.4c, the balance of payments curve shifts from BP_0 to BP_1.

Capital Flows and Economic Policy

The model just discussed has practical policy implications. Suppose a nation is faced with both unemployment and a trade deficit. Currency depreciation would be the preferred policy tool in this case. But if a nation does not want to pay the costs associated with a depreciation, what should it do? Robert Mundell posed and answered that question.

Following the lead of Jan Tinbergen, Mundell argued that if there are two targets—internal and external equilibrium in this example—the nation should employ two policy tools and each one should be devoted to hitting one of the two objectives. Since the

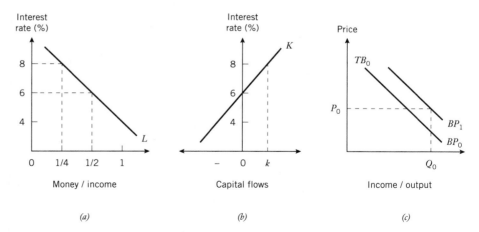

FIGURE 12.4 Interest rates, capital flows, and the balance of payments: II.

If a country faces unemployment, but its trade balance equals zero, an expansionary fiscal policy may allow it to return to full employment and still balance its external accounts. An expansionary fiscal policy will raise GDP, which will reduce the money/income ratio in panel (a). The domestic interest rate will rise from, say, 6 percent to 8 percent. Given the higher interest rate, capital will flow into the country, panel (b). The capital inflow will shift the balance of payments curve from BP_0 to BP_1. Since a higher income will mean higher imports, the economy will move to the right of the TB curve in panel (c). But in this example, the trade imbalance is "covered" by the capital inflow brought about by the higher interest rate. If the economy ends up with an income of Q_0 at the price level P_0, it will have a trade deficit, but its balance of payments will be balanced.

Effective market classification. Given multiple economic targets, such as internal and external balance, the process of matching the appropriate policy tool with a specific target. For example, given fixed exchange rates and capital mobility, monetary policy is more effective in correcting an external imbalance than fiscal policy.

choice of policy tools is constrained by the desire to maintain the exchange rate, the nation is limited to expenditure-reducing or expenditure-increasing policies, or to monetary and fiscal policy.

The question is: *Which tool* should be used to attain each of the objectives? Mundell used the principle of **effective market classification** to answer the question. One tool, say monetary policy, may be more effective in hitting *both* targets. But its comparative advantage may be in the external sector rather than the internal sector.

Mundell argued that monetary policy affects income and the trade balance; but since monetary policy helps determine interest rates, it affects the capital account as well. In comparison, some economists believe that while fiscal policy affects income and, consequently, the trade account, it has no direct impact on the capital account. Fiscal policy, it is argued, should be used to maintain internal equilibrium.

Monetary-Fiscal Mix

The results of the monetary-fiscal mix can be sketched out briefly. Again, imagine that the economy has a trade deficit in addition to high unemployment. Fiscal expansion raises real income and employment but leads also to an increase in imports and a worsening trade deficit. However, the increase in real income causes the money/income ratio to drop, which raises the interest rate. If the easy fiscal policy is combined with a tight monetary policy, interest rates will rise even higher. In turn, higher domestic interest rates lead to a capital inflow and, if all goes as planned, the capital account surplus equals the trade deficit and the balance of payments is balanced.

The policy mix will be even more effective if fiscal policy concentrates on reducing investment taxes, rather than raising government expenditures or reducing consumption taxes. Such a tax package by itself may shift the capital flow schedule to the right, further stimulating the capital inflow.

It may appear that economics is pure Newtonian mechanics—as easy as balancing a mobile over a baby's crib—but carrying out an economic policy is never this simple. Monetary-fiscal policy will balance the external accounts *only if* the rest of the world is willing to follow a low-interest policy even to the point where the home country raises its interest rates. If foreign countries balk at this effort and raise their interest rates to match the increase in home country interest rates, the domestic policy is doomed.

It happens that the United States followed the above policy mix in the early 1980s, and it worked—at first. Unemployment fell as the U.S. economy expanded; and, although the United States ran a trade deficit, it was more than adequately financed by capital inflows as evidenced by the appreciation of the dollar during the early 1980s.

Constraints on the Monetary-Fiscal Mix

The post-1985 experience of the United States and of other nations as well, however, suggests that such a monetary-fiscal mix can be only a short-run policy. First, the nation will find it increasingly difficult to rely on continual capital flows to cover its trade deficit at a constant domestic interest rate. Instead, the nation will be compelled to raise its interest rate ever higher in order to attract the yearly capital inflow required to maintain external equilibrium. In other words, like a bad drug habit, the interest differential necessary to induce a positive capital flow becomes ever larger as a nation's external debt expands.

Portfolio theory describes why individuals will spread their wealth among various assets depending upon relative rates of interest (returns) on the assets and the perceived risk associated with holding the various assets. An individual will increase her holdings of a risky asset only if the asset yields a higher rate of return.

Aspects of **portfolio theory** help explain why an ever-rising interest rate is required. Portfolio theory asserts that individuals are willing to hold a greater proportion of their wealth in risky financial assets providing they are amply rewarded for it. Suppose J.P. Fatcat wants to obtain the highest possible rate of return on his wealth but also wants to avoid undue risk. If J.P.'s choice is limited to holding just two common stocks, he will consider the average rates of return on each stock plus the historic variation in their rates of return before deciding on the overall composition of his portfolio.

If one asset yields a steady 8 percent while the other stock returns an unvarying 6 percent rate of return, J.P. will purchase the first stock. But if the return on the first stock gyrates to such a degree that days of feast are followed by days of famine, he may select the less capricious, more dependable stock. While the first stock pays a higher rate of return on average, its return is variable and, hence, risky compared with the return of the second stock.

The composition of J.P.'s portfolio will depend on his appetite for risk. If it is high, his portfolio holdings will be skewed toward the first stock. Given different preferences, he may hold his wealth in the second stock exclusively or split his holdings of the two stocks into various proportions.

What happens if the rate of return on the first stock jumps to 10 percent while the return on the second stock remains constant? J.P. will change the composition of his portfolio, selling some of his holdings of the second stock and purchasing more of the first stock even though this step will increase the risk to his total portfolio. But J.P. calculates that the higher risk is more than offset by an increase in the anticipated rate of return. This illustrates once again the major point of portfolio theory: People will take risks if they are rewarded for doing so.

We use this example of stock-selection as an analogy for how investors in international capital markets weigh opportunities against risks. We are concerned with the question of why an individual who holds a portfolio of short-term assets denominated in marks, pounds, dollars, and other currencies would switch from holding mark-denominated Treasury bills to holding dollar-denominated Treasury bills. Part of the answer is interest differentials. But this does not explain why the spread between American and German interest rates must continue to widen in order to induce international investors to hold an increasing proportion of their wealth in dollar-denominated assets.

The explanation for the need for widening interest-rate spread is *risk*—specifically, the *risk of dollar depreciation*. Suppose J.P. holds DM200 of German Treasury bills and $100 of American Treasury bills, the exchange rate is DM2/$, and the interest rate is 10 percent in both nations. Given the exchange rate, J.P.'s annual total yield measured in dollars is $20, a $10 return on the U.S. bills and a DM20 or $10 return on the German Treasury bills. By similar calculations, his total yield measured in marks is DM40. If the mark appreciates and the new exchange rate is DM1/$, his yield in dollars increases to $30, a $10 return on U.S. bonds, the same as previously, and a DM20 or $20 return, when converted into dollars, on German bonds. J.P.'s yield measured in marks, however, falls from DM40 to DM30 since his $10 return on U.S. bonds is now worth only DM10. It turns out that after exchange-rate adjustment, J.P. is trading dollars for marks at the current exchange rate or at a one-to-one ratio. J.P. is neither better nor worse off. Measured in terms of dollars, his interest income rises; measured in terms of marks, he loses. The gains and losses offset each other. The standoff was the result of the initial assumptions: namely that there were only two currencies and that wealth is divided equally between them.

Imagine now that J.P. places $150 in U.S. bonds and purchases DM100 of German bonds, a 75/25 split in favor of dollar assets when measured in dollars. Now if the mark appreciates as it did before, J.P.'s yield in dollars will rise to $25, or $5 less than previously, and his yield measured in marks will fall to DM25, a drop of DM15. In a sense, he "trades" DM15 to obtain $5, an exchange rate not only lower than the initial exchange rate but also inferior to the present one. J.P.'s loss in marks at both the present and initial exchange rates exceeds his gains in dollars, and, thus, he is worse off. If J.P. places all his funds in dollars and the mark appreciates, his yield in dollars will remain constant at $20 but will fall from DM40 to DM20 when expressed in marks. He gives up DM20 for nothing.

The lesson is clear. As a greater proportion of funds is placed in a single currency, the potential loss due to the currency's depreciation increases. Therefore, to induce an individual to hold an increasing proportion of dollar assets and fewer yen and mark assets, the return on dollar assets must rise relative to the yield on the other assets.

By placing more of his wealth in dollar assets, J.P. is taking a bigger risk. But individuals *can* be induced to take such a risk if they are amply rewarded for it. If J.P. is to be encouraged to hold 60 percent of his wealth in dollar assets, the interest differential in favor of such assets may well have to be 2 percent. To persuade him to hold 70 percent

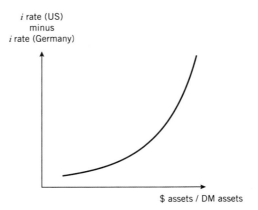

FIGURE 12.5 Interest rate differentials and portfolio composition.

When money managers place an increasing proportion of their funds in dollar-denominated assets, the impact of dollar depreciation on the interest income and purchasing power of their portfolio when expressed in marks will fall. Thus, to induce money managers to take this risk, the interest differential between U.S. and German interest rates will have to widen.

of his portfolio in dollar assets, the interest differential might have to rise to 4 percent or more. In sum, to induce J.P. to hold increasing proportions of dollar assets, the U.S. interest rate will have to keep rising, assuming other national interest rates are constant. And one can imagine that a point will arrive where the risk involved in holding greater proportions of his portfolio in dollar assets becomes so great that he will not switch from mark or yen assets to dollar assets *regardless* of the interest differential.

Although devoid of specific numerical values on either axis, Figure 12.5 summarizes the argument. The American and German interest rate differential is placed on the vertical axis and the proportion of dollar-denominated assets relative to German assets is placed on the horizontal axis. The individual's preference schedule is drawn sloping up from left to right. It shows that in order to induce an individual to place a greater proportion of his or her wealth in dollar assets, the differential between U.S. and German interest rates must rise. But ever-increasing U.S. interest rates will probably damp down expansion in the U.S. economy so that one of the goals of the initial policy will be hindered.

Throughout our discussion, we have assumed that foreign governments will follow policies that accommodate the monetary-fiscal needs of the deficit nation. And in this case, an accommodating policy does not mean a hands-off or laissez-faire attitude. If Germans switch out of mark assets in order to obtain dollar-denominated assets because of higher U.S. interest rates, German interest rates could also rise. But higher German interest rates would have the effect of frustrating the American policy. The German central bank, therefore, might have to expand the German money supply to keep German interest rates constant. It is not enough that the German government sits still and does not attempt to rock the boat; the boat will be rocked and the German policy makers must use domestic economic policy to assure the success of a foreigner's economic policy. Politically, economic cooperation between governments can be a tall order indeed.

Summary

Any explanation of balance of payments adjustment must include a discussion of capital flows. In this chapter we have described a framework—the balance of payments curve, the capital flow curve, and how the interest rate is determined—that permits us to include capital flows in the balance of payments adjustment process. We have also described situations in which capital flows can be influenced in order to offset trade deficits and surpluses. Such a strategy is at best a short-run policy, since a capital flow represents a change in capital stock positions, and the ability of interest differentials and ever-increasing differentials to induce individuals to change their asset or portfolio positions is limited. In the example, suppose high U.S. interest rates ran up against a growing American external deficit and expectations of a future dollar depreciation. At some point, even if individuals can cover themselves in the forward market, the forward discount on the dollar could become so great and the necessary interest differential so large that the policy could become ineffectual. High U.S. interest rates would be seen as a sign of a weak dollar, and all investors who had not covered themselves in the forward market would run for cover and unload dollars. The policy would end up crashing like a plane without wings.

Key Concepts and Terms

balance of payments schedule and curve

capital flow schedule and curve

effective market classification

monetary/fiscal mix

money/income ratio and interest rates

portfolio theory

risk and return trade-off

trade balance schedule and curve

Review Questions

1. Derive the trade balance curve. Explain what will happen to the curve and why if the following events take place:

(a) Foreign income rises.

(b) Domestic government expenditures go up.

(c) The rate of domestic inflation doubles.

(d) The rate of foreign inflation doubles, while the domestic rate of inflation declines.

2. What is the *BP* curve? What is its relation to the *TB* curve?

3. Draw a capital flow curve. Explain what will happen to the curve if the following events take place, other things remaining constant:

(a) Foreign interest rates decline.

(b) The interest rate elasticity of capital flows increases.

(c) Economic expansion takes place abroad.

(d) Domestic capital taxes are reduced.

(e) A radical government is elected.

4. What forces determine domestic interest rates? How might the determination of domestic interest rates be affected if the domestic capital market becomes integrated with foreign capital markets?

5. Explain the principle of effective market classification.

6. Suppose an individual holds 50 percent of her financial assets in dollars and 50 percent in marks. If she is to be induced to hold a greater proportion of her portfolio in dollars, what must happen?

References and Suggested Readings

Robert Mundell's classic article on "The Appropriate Use of Monetary and Fiscal Policy" is reprinted in his *International Economics* (New York: Macmillan, 1968). He extended the analysis to domestic economic problems in *The Dollar and the Policy Mix: 1971*, Essays in International Finance 85 (Princeton, NJ: International Finance Section, Princeton University, 1971).

Michael Melvin discusses portfolio theory and international investment in *International Money and Finance*, 4th edition (New York: HarperCollins, 1995); Chapter 7.

Chapter 13

Money and the Balance of Payments

In the early 1970s, following the collapse of the **Smithsonian agreement,** most major nations embraced flexible exchange rates. At the same time, and not coincidentally, **monetarism** became the lens through which most economists looked at international monetary affairs. While monetarism no longer has the cachet it once had, it remains a powerful framework for the analysis of the balance of payments and the adjustment mechanism.

The Path Ahead

In this chapter, we investigate the monetarist approach to the balance of payments in four steps:

- First, we ask: What is monetarism?
- Next we discuss how the money supply is determined.
- Then we look at the demand for money from a monetarist perspective.
- Finally, we describe how money supply and demand interact to determine the level of income and the balance of payments, and the policy implications derived from the monetarist approach.

What Is Monetarism?

Monetarists argue that the primary determinant of changes in the level of nominal income or aggregate demand is an *increase or decrease in the money supply*. Monetarists concede that the money supply is not the *only* determinant of income, but assert it is simply the most important and consistent one.

Monetary Expansion and Contraction

In December 1971, the Group of Ten countries met at the Smithsonian Institute, Washington, DC, and hammered out an agreement—the **Smithsonian Agreement**—to realign currencies in order to maintain a system of fixed exchange rates. Hailed "as the greatest monetary agreement in the history of the world" at the time, the agreement lasted for roughly one year.

Monetarists contend that changes in the money supply are the single most important variable that explains changes in aggregate demand and, thus, changes in the rate of inflation and the level of unemployment.

Bank reserves are those funds which a bank holds as a reserve against its deposit liabilities. The proportion or the bank's **reserve ratio** is normally prescribed by the central bank.

We turn next to the question of how the money supply is increased or decreased. The money supply, narrowly defined, equals currency plus checking deposit accounts at various financial institutions. Imagine an economy in which there is no currency and all checking accounts are held at banks. The total money supply, therefore, equals the deposit liabilities of the banks. In the example that follows, bank deposit liabilities are initially $200. Since these deposits equal the money supply, they are listed as "money" rather than as deposits.

The money supply also equals some multiple of commercial **bank reserves** or the **monetary base.** The monetary base, which is crucial in the monetarist framework, equals the sum of bank reserves and currency in circulation (since the following example assumes that there is no currency in circulation, the monetary base and bank reserves are one and the same). Bank reserves, in turn, are funds which banks must hold as a reserve against deposit liabilities, and are computed by multiplying banks' deposit liabilities by the **reserve ratio.** The reserve ratio equals the proportion of deposits that the central bank requires commercial banks to hold as a reserve against deposit liabilities. In this example, the ratio is 10 percent. Since the banks' deposit liabilities, or money, initially equal $200, bank reserves equal $20.

Why is the money supply tied to a multiple of bank reserves? If a bank receives a $20 deposit, and if the reserve ratio is 10 percent, it will have to hold $2 of it as a reserve deposit with the central bank. In order to make a profit, the bank will loan the remaining $18 to some borrower. It is safe to assume that if John Q. borrows $18, he will spend it. When John Q. spends the $18, Johnna Q. will receive it and, it is assumed, deposit the money at her bank—what is called the "second generation" bank. The second bank will place 10 percent of the $18, or $1.80, on reserve, and loan out $16.20. Notice what is taking place: At the first generation or stage, bank deposits increase by $20; at the second generation, bank deposits (or money) increase by $18; at the third generation or stage, the money supply increases by $16.20. The multiple-deposit expansion continues through the fourth and on to the nth stage. In the end, the money supply expands by 10 times the initial deposit or increase in bank reserves; in other words, we can say that the increase in the money supply equals the increase in bank reserves times the **money multiplier.** The money multiplier, therefore, equals the *reciprocal of the reserve ratio.*[1]

If the money supply equals bank reserves times the money multiplier, what determines the initial level of bank reserves? Bank reserves are a *liability* of the central bank, since commercial banks are required by law to deposit their reserves with the central bank. But if bank reserves are a liability of the central bank, what are the central bank's corresponding assets or what backs the monetary base? Monetarists divide such assets

---

[1]The increase in the money supply equals the sum of a geometric expansion, or $\Delta MS = \Delta$Bank Res$(1 + .9 + .9^2 + .9^3 + ... + .9^n)$, which equals $\Delta MS = \Delta$Bank Res$(1/1 - .9)$. In the end, $\Delta MS = \Delta$Bank Res$(1/.1)$, where .1 equals the reserve ratio.

The **monetary base** can be computed by looking at either the central bank's assets or liabilities. On the asset side, the base is the sum of **international reserves** plus the domestic component of the monetary base, primarily central bank holdings of government bonds. On the liability side of the central bank's balance sheet, the monetary base equals bank reserves plus currency in circulation.

How much an increase in the monetary base leads to an increase in the money supply depends on the **money multiplier.**

into **international reserves,** the foreign component of the monetary base, and the domestic component. The domestic component primarily consists of central bank holdings of domestic government bonds.

The commercial banks' liability, money, has been described. For assets, banks hold loans plus bank reserves. *Bank reserves are vital.* These reserves are the conduit connecting central bank policy to the commercial banks and, ultimately, to the money supply. Table 13.1 shows the assets and liabilities of both the central bank and the private banks at a given moment.

Now assume that the central bank decides to increase the money supply, as shown in Table 13.2. The central bank purchases a $10 government bond in the government bond market and pays the seller with its own check. This step has two effects. First, it increases the central bank's holding of government bonds by $10. Second, since the bond seller deposits the check at her bank, her deposit account rises by $10. Her bank, in turn, presents the check to the central bank for payment. The central bank honors the check by adding $10 to the bank's reserves. Through the process previously described, the initial $10 deposit or $10 increase in the commercial bank's reserves is multiplied by 10, the value of the money supply multiplier, and the money supply increases by $100 to $300. In summary, central bank holdings of government bonds are

TABLE 13.1 Central Bank's and Commercial Banks' Assets and Liabilities

Central Bank

Assets		Liabilities	
International Reserves	$10	Bank Reserves	$20
Government Bonds	$10		

Commercial Banks

Assets		Liabilities	
Bank Reserves	$20	Money	$200
Loans	$180		

TABLE 13.2 Monetary Expansion

Central Bank

Assets		Liabilities	
International Reserves	$10	Bank Reserves	$30
Government Bonds	$20		

Commercial Banks

Assets		Liabilities	
Bank Reserves	$30	Money	$300
Loans	$270		

TABLE 13.3 Monetary Contraction

Central Bank

Assets		Liabilities	
International Reserves	$0	Bank Reserves	$20
Government Bonds	$20		

Commercial Banks

Assets		Liabilities	
Bank Reserves	$20	Money	$200
Loans	$180		

up by $10, bank reserves increase by $10, and its loans by $90, and the money supply rises by $100.

Now let's assume that individuals spend $10 on foreign goods or to acquire $10 of foreign financial assets. In order to purchase foreign commodities or financial assets, they need to obtain foreign currency, say marks. To acquire marks, they go to their banks and sell dollars in exchange for marks. It is unlikely, however, that U.S. banks will hold an unlimited supply of marks, so they will have to purchase marks from the central bank. To complete this transaction, the banks "sell" some of their reserves to the central bank in exchange for marks. The transaction reduces both the central bank's holdings of international reserves by $10 and the commercial banks' reserves by $10. By the multiplier process just discussed, the $10 decline in reserves leads to a $100 reduction in the money supply, which drops back to $200.

Table 13.3 shows that the nation's monetary balance sheet returns to its initial position except that the assets of the central bank—which equal $20 as before—are now composed entirely of the domestic component of the monetary base or government bonds. Where have the international reserves gone? They are now safely tucked away in the bank account of a foreigner or some foreign central bank. If foreigners, however, are willing to sell either goods or financial assets for dollars because they want to build up their dollar balances in the United States, the U.S. money will remain at $300 as in Table 13.2. The only difference would be that foreigners would own a proportion of U.S. bank deposits.

The Demand for Money

Since the money supply is ultimately controlled by the central bank and, therefore, is considered given, the major thrust of monetarism describes what governs the demand for money and how it interacts with the money supply to establish the level of nominal income or aggregate demand.

According to monetarists, the demand for money depends upon *permanent income*, which is some yearly level of income people expect to enjoy over an *extended period*. In addition to income, the demand for money depends on the interest rate and the price level or, more precisely, the expected rate of inflation.

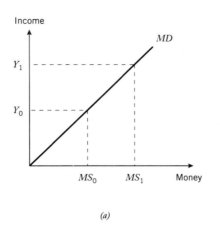
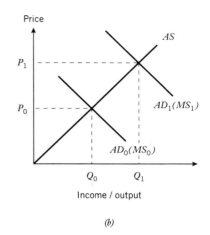

(a)

(b)

FIGURE 13.1 Money and income.

Panel (a) shows the nominal level of income on the vertical axis and the money
supply and the demand for money on the horizontal axis. The demand for money
is assumed to be a constant proportion of nominal income, and, therefore, is drawn
as the diagonal line, MD. The money supply is controlled by the central bank and,
as a result, is considered given. The equilibrium level of income is arrived at when
the money supply equals the demand for money. If the money supply is MS_0, the
equilibrium level of nominal income or aggregate demand is Y_0; when the money
supply is MS_1, the equilibrium level of income is Y_1. The price level and the level
of real income depend on the interplay of aggregate demand and aggregate supply.
The relationship is shown in panel (b). Given the money supply MS_0, the
aggregate demand curve is AD_0. Given the aggregate supply curve AS, the price
level is P_0 and the level of real GDP is Q_0. If the money supply rises to MS_1, the
aggregate demand curve shifts to the right to AD_1. The price level rises to P_1, and,
in this example, real GDP rises to Q_1.

For purposes of our discussion let's simply imagine that the demand for money is
proportional to the price level and to the level of real income, which means that it is
proportional to nominal income as well. Symbolically, we will suppose that the demand
for money, MD, equals a constant proportion of nominal income, PQ, or that $MD =
kPQ$, where k equals the proportion of nominal income that individuals desire to hold
in the form of money. Since many monetarist studies conclude that the interest rate
elasticity of the demand for money is quite low (that is, it takes a hefty change in the
interest rate to affect the demand for money) we will also assume that the demand for
money is not affected by the interest rate.

Given the above assumptions, we can now employ the *real balance equation* of
Chapter 2 both to show the demand for money and to demonstrate how a change in
the money supply affects the level of nominal income.[2] We do this in Figure 13.1.
Figure 13.1a shows the relationship between nominal income, Y, money demand, MD,
and money supply, MS. Nominal income is measured on the vertical axis and money

---

[2]There is an important difference between the way the real balance equation was employed in Chapter 2 and
how it is employed here. In Chapter 2, we looked at the equation $MS = kPQ$ and asked: Given the money
supply (MS) and k, how much will a change in the *price level (P)* change the *level of real aggregate demand (Q)?*
Here we look at the equation and ask: Given k, how much will a change in the *money supply (MS)* change the
level of *nominal aggregate demand (PQ)?*

supply and demand are measured on the horizontal axis. The demand for money, which is a constant proportion of nominal income, equals the diagonal line *MD*. As can be seen, an increase in the money supply from MS_0 to MS_1 raises the level of nominal income from Y_0 to Y_1. Why does this happen?

To see the connection between the money supply and nominal income, let's imagine a simple economy in which the desired money-to-income ratio, *k*, equals 1; the money supply is $100; and 100 units of output are produced and sell for $1 each. Nominal income, therefore, equals $100. Now imagine that the money supply is doubled so that the money/income ratio rises from 1 to 2. Because individuals do not desire to maintain such a high money/income ratio, they *spend* their excess money balances, or an additional $100. The additional expenditures, in turn, raise the level of nominal income to $200.

The relationship between the money supply and nominal income does *not* tell us how much of an increase (or decrease) in nominal income/aggregate demand shows up as a change in output and how much shows up as a change in the price level. Because equilibrium price and output levels are determined by the interaction of aggregate demand and aggregate supply, one must know the *elasticity* of the aggregate supply schedule to arrive at the answer. If it is unit elastic, as is assumed here, greater demand leads to both higher prices and greater output, as shown in Figure 13.1b.

If initially the money supply equals MS_0, aggregate demand at all price and output levels equals AD_0. Assuming the aggregate supply curve equals *AS*, the price and real income levels are P_0 and Q_0. If the money supply expands to MS_1, pushing the aggregate demand curve out to AD_1, the price level and real output rise to P_1 and Q_1.

Changes in Money, Output, and Prices

A change in the money supply, therefore, may lead to simultaneous changes in real income and prices in the short run. But if the economy is operating at or close to its potential—a monetarist assumption—the long-run effect of excessive monetary expansion is purely inflationary. The long-run relationship between money, prices, and output can be expressed by adjusting the demand for money equation and by recalling that money supply equals money demand in equilibrium. The equilibrium condition, $MS = kPQ$, can be transformed to equal[3]:

$$\%P = \%MS - \%Q$$

The equation states that the rate of inflation equals the rate of monetary growth minus the growth in real income, or inflation is the result of too much money chasing too few goods. The growth of real income, *Q*, depends on the expansion of the labor force, increases in productivity, entrepreneurial ability, the business climate, and so forth.

---

[3]$MS = kPQ$ can be transformed into logarithms; $\ln MS = \ln k + \ln P + \ln Q$. The expression can be first differenced, which eliminates *k* since it is a constant. As a result, $\ln MS(t) - \ln MS(t-1) = \ln P(t) - \ln P(t-1) + \ln Q(t) - \ln Q(t-1)$, or $\%MS = \%P + \%Q$, which means that $\%P = \%MS - \%Q$.

These variables can and do change, but are assumed to change at a constant rate so that the rate of growth of real output is steady.

The correlations between money, real income, and prices in a nation's economy motivates the **fixed-rate rule** of monetary theory—specifically, that monetary policymakers should set and then *stick with* a given rate of monetary growth since variable rates of monetary growth can cause economic instability. The rule is applicable to both open and closed economies. For this reason—the desirability of a steady rate of monetary growth—mainstream monetarism argues that all countries should adopt flexible exchange rates. Only a system of *flexible exchange rates* permits a nation to carry out an independent monetary policy and be able to follow the fixed-rate monetary rule.

Some monetarists disagree with the mainstream approach and all monetarists agree that a nation can, even if unwisely, adopt *fixed exchange rates*. Thus, the monetarist approach to the balance of payments can be investigated first under the assumption that fixed exchange rates are in fashion.

The **fixed-rate rule** argues that the money supply should be increased at a *constant rate*, regardless of the rate selected.

Money and the Balance of Payments under Fixed Exchange Rates

If we suppose that an open economy is in internal and external equilibrium, what happens to the economy if the domestic money supply expands at a faster than normal rate? Individuals will end up with excess money balances and will raise their expenditures in the attempt to push their money/income ratio back down to its desired level. At first, they will do this by purchasing domestic goods and services, but this will drive up domestic prices. Confronted with higher domestic prices, individuals will buy foreign goods and services, which leads to a trade deficit.

The same sequence takes place in financial markets. Initially, individuals use their excess money balances to purchase domestic financial assets, but this drives up domestic financial asset prices and reduces their yield (or effective return). Confronted with lower yields on domestic financial assets, individuals turn away from domestic sources and buy *foreign* financial assets, which causes the nation's capital account to turn negative.

Monetarists emphasize that neither the current nor the capital account is paramount. An excess money balance may be used to purchase foreign financial assets, foreign goods, or some mix of the two. Therefore, concentrating on balancing the trade account should not be the priority for policymakers. Nor should policymakers treat the capital account as a balancing item. The crucial element is the *initial monetary disequilibrium*, not how it is recorded in the external accounts.

The impact of an increase in the money supply in an open economy can be explained through the aggregate supply and demand framework, which utilizes all the tools associated with aggregate supply and demand analysis, plus one more: the **world aggregate supply curve,** *ASw*. This curve shows the quantity of some composite good that will be supplied by all the world's producers at various price levels.

Viewed from a country's perspective, the elasticity of the *ASw* curve depends on the size of its economy. If the country is small, the elasticity of the *ASw* curve is infinite; if the country is large, the *ASw* curve is elastic but not infinitely elastic. Nevertheless, regardless of the size of the nation, the elasticity of the world's aggregate supply schedule will *exceed* the elasticity of an individual nation's aggregate supply schedule. In the

The **world aggregate supply curve** shows the quantity of some composite good that will be supplied by all the world's suppliers (nations) at various *domestic* price levels providing everything else remains constant.

example, it is assumed that the nation in question is small and that its economy is operating at its full potential. Therefore, the *ASw* curve is horizontal and the *AS* curve is vertical.

The assumptions have important implications. In a closed economy, aggregate demand equals absorption, so that any increase in the money supply shifts the combined $A = AD$ curve to the right and leads to pure inflation. The result is different in an open economy, where an increase in the money supply shifts the absorption curve to the right. Whether the aggregate demand curve shifts depends on how much of the new or additional money is spent on domestic goods. In the example, since all additional money is spent on foreign goods, the *AD* curve does not shift.

As shown in Figure 13.2, the money supply advances from MS_0 to MS_1 and the absorption curve shifts from A_0 to A_1. As individuals start spending their excess money balances, they also start noticing that domestic prices are higher than world prices. As a result, they spend all of their excess money balances on imports. The *AD* curve remains constant and the difference between A_1 and *AD* at the price level *Pw*, or *Qn* to *Q* on the horizontal axis, equals the trade deficit. The trade deficit permits the nation to absorb more goods than it produces, and eliminates or reduces the inflationary effects of excessive monetary expansion.

But there is a catch. In order to purchase foreign goods, domestic citizens have to ship domestic money out of the country. As previously described, this will decrease the domestic money supply, and the absorption curve will shift back to its original position. Thus, a one-time rapid increase in the money supply may cause a temporary payments imbalance, but not a permanent one.

This review of the impact of monetary expansion in closed and open economies leads us to some major propositions of monetarism. In a closed economy, excessive

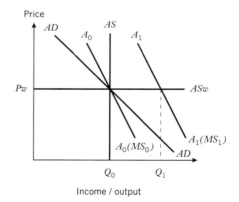

Price

Income / output

FIGURE 13.2 Monetary expansion in a small, open economy.

If a closed economy is operating at its potential so that its aggregate supply curve is a vertical line, such as *AS*, an increase in the money supply will shift the *AD* curve, which also equals the absorption curve in a closed economy, to the right. The economy will end up with pure inflation. In a small, open economy—one whose production and consumption does not affect the world price level—an increase in the money supply will push the absorption schedule to the right from, say, A_0 to A_1. Rather than pure inflation, the economy will run a balance of payments deficit, and both its trade account and its capital account will be in the red. This analysis assumes that exchange rates are fixed. If exchange rates are flexible, the nation's currency will depreciate.

monetary expansion leads to *pure inflation;* in an open economy, excessive monetary expansion generates a balance of payments deficit that may *temporarily* repress the domestic inflationary consequences of excessive monetary expansion.

Money and the World Price Level

Seigniorage. Originally, it was the fee that rulers charged for turning metals into coins. Today, the term refers to the ability of certain countries to pay for goods by issuing money that exporting countries are willing to hold as international reserves.

The relevance of monetarism is not limited to policies of individual countries; it has worldwide implications. Monetarism explains the relation between domestic monetary expansion in a large country and worldwide inflation. Assume, for example, that the U.S. money supply constitutes 50 percent of the world's money supply and that the Fed increases the U.S. money supply by 10 percent. Given their new cash balances, Americans purchase foreign goods and financial assets and pay for them by shipping dollars overseas. The German who, it is assumed, sells Americans either goods or financial assets will not, under normal circumstances, want to hold dollars since he will need marks to hire labor or purchase goods in Germany. Using his bank as an intermediary, the German will sell the dollars for marks at the Bundesbank. He ends up with fewer German financial assets and goods, which have been sold to Americans, but with more marks. The Bundesbank now holds more dollars, but most important, the German money supply has increased.

Excessive monetary expansion in the United States, therefore, has short- and long-run implications for both national and world welfare. In the short run, and this can be very short indeed, the U.S. gains what is called *seigniorage.* It pays for goods and financial assets by printing up dollars—an inexpensive exercise. Other nations give up commodities in return for green pieces of paper. As long as the rest of the world is willing to carry on with this exchange, the United States benefits at the rest of the world's expense. However, the probability that the rest of the world will indeed carry on with such an exchange is remote. When the Bundesbank purchases dollars in exchange for marks, it is unlikely to hold so many pieces of green paper or a non–interest-bearing deposit. It will use the dollars to purchase U.S. Treasury bonds in order to earn interest on its dollar holdings. At this point, seigniorage, the "free lunch" for Americans, either comes to an end or is markedly reduced.

However, the consequences of excessive U.S. monetary expansion are not limited to questions of seigniorage. In a closed economy, a 10 percent increase in the U.S. money supply will raise the U.S. price level by 10 percent or more, assuming output is constant. In an open economy, Americans can purchase foreign-made as well domestically produced products. If domestic prices begin to rise when Americans start to spend their new money balances, Americans will purchase foreign products in their place. Given the assumption that the American money supply equaled 50 percent of the world's money supply, the world's money supply will increase by 5 percent given the 10 percent increase in the U.S. money supply and the ensuing American expenditures on world products. If world output is constant, the monetarist formula says that world and U.S. inflation rates will rise by 5 percent. The United States thus is able to pass one-half of its potential inflation on to the rest of the world. Even though the United States pays for its excessive monetary expansion through a larger external debt and correspondingly larger interest payments, the rest of the world pays as well. The worldwide rate of inflation is higher and foreign nations have, willingly or not, become U.S. creditors.

Monetary Sterilization

An inflow of foreign money into a country will, if not offset, raise the country's money supply. **Sterilization** is the act of offsetting this monetary inflow, thereby keeping the domestic money supply constant.

How can a foreign nation avoid stepping into this trap? If the foreign nation adopts a flexible exchange rate, it can avoid inflation and also escape becoming an unwilling U.S. creditor. Let's suppose, though, that the nation is *willing* to be a U.S. creditor, but that it wants to avoid the inflationary consequences of the U.S. monetary expansion and does not want to adopt a flexible exchange rate. What should that country do?

A central bank has the ability, within limits, to offset or **sterilize** an inflow of foreign money, thus keeping the domestic money supply constant and circumventing domestic inflation. Sterilization is explained with the help of Table 13.4, which is the German counterpart to the previous example regarding the U.S. money supply. As before, central bank assets consist of international reserves and government securities. Also, as before, the assets of the central bank must rise and boost bank reserves if the money supply is to increase.

Table 13.4a shows the initial balance sheets of the central banks and the commercial banks. Now, suppose a $5 increase in the U.S. money supply is used to purchase a German good. The German exporter receives the $5, which she sells to her bank in exchange for a DM10 deposit, assuming the exchange rate is DM2/$. Her bank in turn sells the dollars to the Bundesbank in exchange for a DM10 increase in its reserve deposit at the central bank. In the end, as shown in Table 13.4b, the Bundesbank's international reserves rise to DM20 and commercial bank reserves go up to DM30, and, potentially, the German money supply increases to DM300.

The Bundesbank can, by sterilizing or offsetting the increase in the German monetary base, keep the German money supply constant. By selling government bonds to the public, the Bundesbank can hold bank reserves and the monetary base to DM20 and, thereby, keep the money supply constant. The results of the sterilization policy are shown in Table 13.4c.

The ability of a central bank to carry out the policy just described depends on the mix of assets it holds. At first, in stage a, the Bundesbank is in a position to sterilize a capital inflow since 50 percent of its assets are in government bonds. But by stage c it is unable to sterilize or offset any additional dollar inflows by **open market operations** because its holdings of government bonds have dropped to zero. Thus, any additional dollar inflows must increase the German money supply.

When the central bank buys or sells government securities in the government securities market, it is conducting **open market operations.** When the central bank purchases securities in the market, it expands the monetary base and the money supply. When the central bank sells securities in the government bond securities, the monetary base and the money supply contract.

There is an alternative available to the central bank. The Bundesbank could raise the required bank reserve ratio from 10 percent to 15 percent, thus offsetting or sterilizing the $5 or DM10 monetary inflow from the United States. Imagine the Bundesbank takes this step (not shown in the table). Although the money is deposited at a bank, which should lead to the multiple-deposit expansion previously described and increase the German money supply by DM100, the banks will have to increase their deposits at the Bundesbank by DM10. The Bundesbank ends up holding DM30 in international reserves against DM30 in bank reserves. But given the new 15 percent reserve ratio, banks are compelled to hold DM30 in reserves against DM200 in bank deposits or money. In order for the banks to build up their reserves to DM30, they must contract their loans by DM10, or decrease them from DM180 to DM170.

Ultimately, the higher reserve requirements do sterilize the capital inflow and do keep the German money constant. But they also put a squeeze on German banks and borrowers, hardly a policy designed to win popularity within Germany.

TABLE 13.4 Monetary Sterilization
[a]

Central Bank

Assets		Liabilities	
International Reserves	DM10	Bank Reserves	DM20
Government Bonds	DM10		

Banks

Assets		Liabilities	
Bank Reserves	DM20	Money	DM200
Loans	DM180		

[b]

Central Bank

Assets		Liabilities	
International Reserves	DM20	Bank Reserves	DM30
Government Bonds	DM10		

Banks

Assets		Liabilities	
Bank Reserves	DM30	Money	DM300
Loans	DM270		

[c]

Central Bank

Assets		Liabilities	
International Reserves	DM20	Bank Reserves	DM20
Government Bonds	DM0		

Banks

Assets		Liabilities	
Bank Reserves	DM20	Money	DM200
Loans	DM180		

Flexible Exchange Rates

Even if sterilization is possible, monetarists argue that it is easier for Germany to avoid the inflationary consequences of excessive U.S. monetary expansion if it adopts a flexible exchange rate. Suppose there are only two countries, Germany and the United States. The German money supply is DM200 and the U.S. money supply equals $100. Given the exchange rate of DM2/$, the world money supply is $200 or

DM400. If, as before, the U.S. money supply increases by 10 percent or by $10, the world money supply rises from $200 to $210 (or to DM420), providing the exchange rate is fixed. But suppose the dollar depreciates by 10 percent to DM1.8/$. The world money supply still rises when expressed in dollars, but it remains constant when expressed in marks.

In the example, worldwide inflation is averted. Dollar expansion leads to dollar depreciation and frustrates any attempt by the United States to pass a portion of its domestic inflation on to the rest of the world. Under a flexible exchange rate, the Bundesbank does not buy dollars and boost its international reserves and the German monetary base. Germany, therefore, is able to isolate its money supply and economy from U.S. monetary policy. This capability is hardly revolutionary. It is exactly what happens when the supply of Mexican pesos runs ahead of the demand for pesos: The peso depreciates and Mexican monetary expansion has no impact on the world money supply.

Thus we have the foundations for the monetarist case for flexible exchange rates. A country needs a flexible exchange rate in order to protect its economy from external shocks and enhance its capacity to carry out an independent domestic economic policy.

Purchasing Power Parity

Purchasing power parity (PPP) is a theory that nominal exchange rates will adjust for inflation differentials over the long run. Thus, PPP exchange rates, the nominal exchange rate adjusted for inflation differentials, will remain constant over the long run, but not necessarily in the short run.

The **law of one price** argues that the price of tradable goods—minus any transportation costs—should be the same throughout the world.

But even flexible exchange rates should follow a predictable path. If they bob up and down, external events will very likely push the economy into a pattern of oscillating economic growth and inflation despite heroic attempts to follow a stable domestic economic policy. The majority of monetarists believe that exchange rates are determined by **purchasing power parity (PPP)** over the long run, although *in the short run* they may deviate from PPP values.

Purchasing power parity is closely tied to the **law of one price.** That law argues that the price of an internationally traded product should be the same in every country. If a mountain bike costs $1,000 in the United States and the mark/dollar exchange rate is DM2/$, it should cost DM2000 in Germany. If instead it costs DM4000 in Germany, traders will take advantage of the price disparity. Bikes will be shipped from America to Germany and parity will be restored by some combination of higher prices in America, lower prices in Germany, and dollar appreciation.

Purchasing power parity is not so much concerned with the price of a given commodity as it is with prices in general, or how national price levels move over time. What PPP says is that if the general price level doubles in the United States while remaining constant in Germany, the exchange rate will adjust to reflect the disparity between the relative rates of inflation. Imagine the Federal Reserve doubles the U.S. money supply. As dollar prices double, Americans will rush to purchase German products. This will increase both the supply of dollars and the demand for marks on the foreign exchanges and cause the dollar to depreciate.

The new exchange rate, DM/$(t), according to PPP, will equal the old exchange rate, DM/$(t − 1), adjusted for changes in relative price levels, $\%\Delta P_G/\%\Delta P_{US}$, or:

$$DM/\$(t) = [DM/\$(t-1)][\%\Delta P_G/\%\Delta P_{US}]$$

BOX 13.1 Purchasing Power Parity and the Big Mac Index

The Economist devised a clever way to measure purchasing power parity. Rather than using a conventional price index, *The Economist* compares the price of a McDonald's Big Mac across a number of countries. Presumably, if the law of one price holds, the exchange-rate-adjusted price of a Big Mac should be roughly similar in all countries. For example, the average price of a Big Mac in the United States was $2.32 in April 1995, and at the same time the DM/$ exchange rate stood at DM1.38 per dollar; according to PPP, the price of a Big Mac in Germany should have been 2.32 times 1.38 or DM3.20.

However, the price of a Big Mac in Germany in April 1995 was DM4.80. Therefore, something was wrong. Either the American price of a Big Mac was too low, the German price too high, or the mark was overvalued. According to the monetarist version of PPP, exchange rates are supposed to adjust to equalize prices, not prices to equalize exchange rates. (If prices adjust to equalize exchange rates, there is no need for flexible exchange rates.)

How much was the mark overvalued? Using the Big Mac index, we find that the DM/$ exchange rate should have equaled the price of a Big Mac in Germany divided by the price of a Big Mac in the United States or DM4.8/$2.32 or DM2.07/$. This means that at DM1.38/$, the mark was 50 percent overvalued against the dollar—(DM2.07 − DM1.38)/DM1.38.

Table 13.5 presents *The Economist*'s Big Mac index calculations of the PPP exchange rates in April 1995 for America's five major trading partners. The total index, not printed here, shows that the dollar was undervalued against developed country currencies—for example, the Swiss Franc was overvalued some 124 percent against the dollar—and undervalued against most less developed country currencies—for example, the Chinese yuan was undervalued by 55 percent against the dollar.

The Big Mac index does not commend PPP. On average, the absolute-percentage deviation of the 32 actual exchange rates from their PPP exchange rates was 39 percent.[*] As *The Economist* points out, the Big Mac index may not be a fair measure of purchasing power parity. First, Big Macs are not an internationally traded good—an American does not hop on the Concorde and jet over to Paris in order to purchase a Big Mac. Second, the price of a Big Mac includes rents and local taxes, which can be a hefty proportion of the price of the hamburger and vary greatly between locations. Finally, PPP is a long-run theory of exchange rate determination. It does not claim to explain every twist and turn in an exchange rate.

---

[*]"Economic Focus: Big Mac Index." *The Economist*, April 15, 1995, p. 74.

TABLE 13.5 The Big Mac Index
[April 7, 1995]

	Big Mac Prices (local)	(in $)	Exchange Rate (implied)	Exchange Rate (actual)	Over- or under-valuation (percent)
United States	$2.32	$2.32	—	—	—
Canada	C$2.77	$1.99	1.19	1.39	−14
Japan	¥391.00	$4.65	169.00	84.00	+100
Mexico	P10.90	$1.71	4.70	6.37	−26
Britain	£1.74	$2.80	.75[1]	.62	+21
Germany	DM4.80	$3.48	2.07	1.38	+50

[1]*The Economist* quotes the exchange rate as $/£; here the exchange rate is £/$

Source: "Economic Focus: Big Mac Index." *The Economist*, April 15, 1995, p. 74.

Assuming the price indices equal 100 initially, a doubling of the U.S. price level boosts its price index to 200 while the German index remains constant. According to PPP, the difference in the relative rates of inflation will double the price of the mark in terms of dollars. Or if the initial exchange rate was DM2/$, the new rate will be DM/$.

Computing Purchasing Power Parity

Computing PPP requires two choices: (1) the base year for the indices and (2) which price index to use. If an incorrect base year is selected, the distortion will become obvious fairly quickly since some nations will run continual trade deficits and others will run trade surpluses. Presumably, base-year exchange rates can be adjusted in light of this behavior.

Selecting, or even creating, the price index which works best can also pose difficulties. Most economists reject the consumer price index as a measure for PPP, since it includes prices of many nontraded services. The most popular candidates are the wholesale price index and an index based on labor costs per unit of output in manufacturing, the assumption being that all manufactured goods are potential exports or imports. Some monetarists believe that since inflation is a monetary phenomenon and that sooner or later any monetary expansion raises all price indices, a good index to use is the rate of growth of the money supply *minus* the trend rate of growth of real output.

One can overemphasize the difficulties associated with computing an ideal price index. The important question is whether exchange rates, however measured, tend to move with PPP, or if they deviate from PPP exchange rates for long periods and by substantial amounts. If they do, PPP determined exchange rates will be a poor compass by which to guide economic policy.

Recent history has not been kind to PPP. Table 3.2 shows that it is very difficult to explain the ¥/$ exchange rate over the last decade on the basis of inflation differentials alone. A broader measure also casts doubt on the PPP hypothesis. Table 13.6 presents the real effective or real multilateral exchange rate index of several countries as com-

TABLE 13.6 Real Effective Exchange Rate Indexes
(1990 = 100)

Year	Germany	Japan	UK	US
1982	80.6	79.9	116.1	139.4
1984	82.5	86.7	102.8	149.9
1986	90.0	108.1	96.2	124.6
1988	96.1	119.1	106.0	101.5
1990	100.0	100.0	100.0	100.0
1992	102.1	127.6	103.5	96.3
1994	112.2	136.2	97.1	97.4

Source: Relevant country pages in International Monetary Fund, *International Financial Statistics Yearbook*, 1995, and in International Monetary Fund, *International Financial Statistics*, January, 1996.

BOX 13.2 Real versus Purchasing Power Exchange Rates

It is difficult to keep close tabs on the various types of exchange rates and remember how they differ from one another. This seems especially true in the case of real exchange rates and purchasing power exchange rates. They both look at the nominal exchange rate and adjust it by some measure of relative rates of inflation to obtain some "correct" exchange rate. Essentially, the real exchange rate looks at the nominal exchange rate, adjusts it, and states what it actually is. The purchasing power exchange rate looks at the nominal exchange rate, modifies it, and argues that this is what it should be.

To better understand the difference between these measures, look first at the real exchange rate. The real rate equals the spot rate times the price index of the reference country divided by the price index of the second country. Using the United States as the reference country and Germany as the second country, the real rate, $(DM/\$)_R$, equals the spot rate, $DM/\$$, times (PI_{US}/PI_G). Suppose that in 1980 the spot rate was $DM4/\$$ and that the price indices in both Germany and the United States were 100. Now imagine that it is ten years later and the spot rate is $DM6/\$$. The spot rate indicates that the mark depreciated 50 percent against the dollar in nominal terms. But suppose prices had doubled in Germany but remained constant in the United States during the 10 years. In light of this evidence, has the mark appreciated or depreciated in real terms? The formula, given here, tells us that the mark has actually appreciated in real terms: $DM/(100/200) = DM3$.

$$(DM/\$)_R = (DM/\$)_{90} (PI_{US}/PI_G)$$

The PPP exchange rate equals the initial spot rate times the price index of the second country divided by the price index of the reference country, or:

$$(DM/\$)_{PPP} = (DM/\$)_{80} (PI_G/PI_{US})$$

Employing the previous figures, we find that in 1990 the $(DM/\$)_{PPP}$ equals $(DM4/\$)(200/100)$ or $DM8/\$$. What this figure tells us is that if Germany is to maintain its competitiveness, the nominal rate should be $DM8/\$$. Since the nominal rate is $DM6/\$$, the mark is overvalued, which is the same as saying that the mark has appreciated in real terms.

These numbers may appear confusing. So let's assume that the nominal rate in 1990 actually goes to $DM8/\$$. In this case, the nominal rate and the purchasing power rate are equal and, therefore, the mark is neither overvalued nor undervalued according to this criterion. What about the real exchange rate? Employing the formula for the real rate, we discover that it has remained constant at $DM4/\$$. Thus, by this measure as well, the mark is neither overvalued nor undervalued.

What can we conclude? According to this illustration, if Germany is to *maintain* its competitive position, the *real* exchange rate of the mark must remain constant or the mark should always equal $DM4/\$$. But this will only occur if the nominal exchange rate adjusts to relative rates of inflation. And this is what the *PPP* exchange rate measures: to what extent the nominal rate reflects changes in relative rates of inflation.

Table 13.7 shows the nominal, real, and purchasing power exchange rates of America's major-trading-partner currencies against the dollar from 1985 to 1994. Except in the case of the Canadian dollar, exchange rates went slightly bonkers. According to the figures, the U.S. dollar was undervalued against all the other currencies except the Mexican peso and the Canadian dollar. The rather surprising record of the £/$ exchange rates is no doubt due to the selection of a bad year as the base for comparisons. The rate of British inflation, measured by producer prices, was faster than the U.S. rate; nevertheless, the pound appreciated against the dollar.

TABLE 13.7 Real and Purchasing Power Exchange Rates
(Domestic currency per dollar)

		Nominal Exchange Rate	Price Index	Real Exchange Rate	PPP Exchange Rate
Canada	1985	1.37	100	1.37	—
(C$)	1994	1.37	120	1.34	1.40
Japan	1985	239.00	100	239.00	—
(yen)	1994	102.00	84	142.10	171.60
Mexico	1985	0.34	100	0.34	—
(peso) *	1994	3.33	2091	0.19	6.01
Britain	1985	0.78	100	0.78	—
(pound)	1994	0.65	140	0.56	0.91
Germany	1985	2.94	100	2.94	—
(mark)	1994	1.61	105	1.79	2.64
US	1985		100		
	1994		117		

*dollars per pound.

Source: Computed from data on the relevant country pages in International Monetary Fund, *International Financial Statistics Yearbook*, 1995.

puted by the IMF. The index is computed by adjusting nominal exchange rates for changes in wholesale prices. If PPP holds, the resulting real exchange rates should be uniform. Clearly, they were not.

What might account for the deviation? PPP is designed only to explain the impact of inflation differentials on exchange rates—it says little about rates of capital formation, economic growth, and other real variables that may affect a nation's competitive position and, therefore, its exchange rate.

Summary

The monetarist approach to the balance of payments emphasizes the total balance of payments. Monetary expansion can lead to either a trade deficit, a capital account deficit, or both. Balance of payments theories have traditionally focused on the balance of trade or the current account. The trade account received primary attention because it was felt that it helped determine, and was determined by, output and employment, the major stuff of macroeconomics. Monetarists do not diminish the importance of the trade balance, although some contend that in certain instances trade surpluses and deficits balance capital flows and not the other way around. In any event, monetarists claim it is a waste of time to analyze ex-

actly how a monetary imbalance shows up in the balance of payments since both trade and capital account deficits and surpluses reflect an underlying monetary imbalance. And it is the monetary imbalance that must be corrected if a nation is to attain external and internal equilibrium.

The monetarist advocacy of flexible exchange rates is not a matter of doctrine. They believe that it is simply *too difficult* for a nation to carry out an effective economic policy if it is constrained by the need to maintain a fixed exchange rate. Fixed exchange rates, in their opinion, leave a nation open to the vagaries of foreign economic policy. Given fixed exchange rates, policymakers are forced to look not only at the domestic implications of their policy proposals, but also at how they will affect foreign economies and how foreigners may react to them.

Key Concepts and Terms

bank reserves

bank's required reserve ratio

Big Mac index

fixed-rate rule for monetary expansion

foreign and domestic components of the monetary base

international incidence of domestic inflation

law of one price

monetarism

monetary base

monetary sterilization

money supply multiplier

open market operations

purchasing power parity

seigniorage

world aggregate supply curve

Review Questions

1. According to monetarists, what is the most likely result of rapid expansion in the money supply in a closed economy, in an open economy?

2. What is the so-called fixed-rate rule for conducting monetary policy? Why is it advocated?

3. Explain how a central bank can hold the domestic money supply constant despite an inflow of foreign capital.

4. Why do most monetarists advocate flexible exchange rates?

5. What is meant by purchasing power parity? How would one compute it?

6. Explain the difference between the real and the purchasing power parity exchange rate.

References and Suggested Readings

Michael Melvin describes the monetarist approach to the balance of payments in his book *International Money and Finance*, 4th edition (New York: HarperCollins, 1995); pp. 167–176.

Harry D. Johnson explains the differences between the Keynesian and the monetarist approach to the balance of payments in *Money, Balance of Payments: Theory and the International Monetary Problem*, Essays in International Finance no. 124 (Princeton, NJ: International Finance Section, Princeton University, November 1977). This is a classic essay on the subject.

The Economist calculates and presents its Big Mac index every year. Michael T. Belongia discusses the recent experience of U.S. exchange-rate intervention in his article, "Foreign Exchange Intervention by the United States: A Review and Assessment of 1985–89," published in the Federal Reserve Bank of St. Louis *Review* 74 (May/June 1992): pp. 32–51.

Milton Friedman, the father of modern monetarism, devotes the majority of his work to an analysis and defense of the monetarist approach. Friedman, however, is concerned with much more than statistical relationships. He is concerned with issues affecting policy at all levels in addition to controlling the money supply. An excellent general introduction into his thinking is contained in a book he wrote with his wife, Rose, entitled *Free to Choose* (New York: Harcourt Brace Jovanovich, 1980). His Public TV series of the same name is available on videocassette.

Exchange Rate Systems, International Reserves, and Economic Policy

Chapter 14

Exchange Rate Systems

The **Bretton Woods** conference was held at Bretton Woods, NH, in 1944. At that conference, the world's major economic power set the foundations for the creation of the International Monetary Fund and established a system of fixed exchange rates for the world economy.

Since 1973, when the **Bretton Woods** agreement collapsed, every country in the world has been faced with the problem of deciding its own exchange rate policy or system. Selecting an exchange rate system should be straightforward. In Chapter 11 we compared the costs of income adjustment with the costs of depreciation, and concluded that a *flexible* exchange rate is preferable if the costs of income adjustment are greater than the costs of depreciation. If the reverse holds, a *fixed* exchange rate is a nation's best option. But then, besides costs, there is the question of benefits—what an exchange rate system does for a country. Obviously, in picking an exchange rate system, a country needs to compare the costs and benefits of each alternative.

The Path Ahead

In this chapter, we investigate the pros and cons of various exchange rate systems in light of the following policy issues:

- How does an exchange rate regime affect the ability of a nation to maintain an independent economic policy, one that is dedicated primarily to solving domestic economic problems?
- How and to what degree is international trade influenced by various exchange rate regimes?
- Will the choice of either a fixed or flexible exchange rate regime help a nation combat inflation and maintain price stability?
- Does or should the economic structure of a nation determine its exchange rate regime?

Fixed versus Floating Exchange Rates: A First Look

An **adjustable peg** is a fixed exchange rate which can be adjusted (devalued or revalued) from time to time as economic fundamentals dictate. If a new exchange rate is deemed necessary, it is established by government decree and not, at least directly, by market forces.

Under a **managed float,** exchange rates are primarily determined by market forces. However, under a managed float, governments attempt to control the speed at which exchange rates change and the magnitude of the change in a given time period. Under a *free float,* exchange rates are determined hour-by-hour by market forces and the government does not try to influence the exchange rate. The market reigns supreme.

As we have already indicated, a nation can choose either a fixed or flexible exchange rate system. But there is a debate about what is meant by "fixed" or "pegged" and how one defines the term "flexible." Many individuals claim that there is no such thing as a fixed exchange rate, over the long run at least. International economic relations are buffeted by winds of change, and what may be an equilibrium exchange rate under certain conditions will be sadly dated in other circumstances. Changing economic conditions have forced even the most devoted fixed-rate advocates to adjust their exchange rates from time to time. It is, therefore, more accurate to describe a fixed exchange rate system as an **adjustable peg,** one in which exchange rates are set in the short-to-medium run but are raised or lowered over time. Even under the Bretton Woods agreement, which established a system of fixed exchange rates after World War II, nations were allowed, and even urged, to depreciate their currency if their balance of payments was in *fundamental disequilibrium*—meaning that a nation would be hard put to maintain an existing exchange rate given its export-import picture.

So the meaning of "fixed" exchange rates is relative indeed. It is just as difficult to talk of "free" or market-determined exchange rates. Well-intentioned government officials find it impossible to avoid meddling with exchange rates despite their claim that they intend to stand aside and allow market forces alone to determine the rate. In the early 1990s, U.S. government officials on several occasions attempted to "talk down" the value of the dollar, especially relative to the yen. Other countries have also tried to influence the drift of exchange rates. Based on this history, many economists have concluded that "flexible exchange rates" are more accurately described as a **managed float,** in which the exchange rate is primarily determined by market forces but is *nudged* up or down—not always successfully—by government interventions.

There are, nevertheless, distinct differences between fixed and free systems. A fixed exchange is established when a government declares that its currency will exchange for a *specific number* of yen, dollars, marks, and so forth. Of course, any government can do this. But the big question is: Is any government wise enough to know what is the *proper international price* of the domestic currency? In other words, will the government set the right price? If one accepts that the government could do so, there is a second question. When the exchange rate moves into fundamental disequilibrium, will the government know when and by how much an exchange rate should be adjusted? Fixed-exchange-rate advocates believe that the answer to both questions is *yes.*

In contrast, flexible-rate advocates believe that market forces are the best judge of what is an equilibrium exchange rate. Further, they feel that when the economic environment makes the existing exchange rate no longer tenable, the foreign exchange markets will quickly ascertain what the new equilibrium exchange rate is and the present exchange rate will quickly move toward it.

Thus, underlying the *technical* debate regarding the pros and cons of various exchange-rate systems there is a *political* debate over the wisdom of the government and the smooth functioning of markets. If an individual believes that foreign exchange markets are too volatile or cause too much damage (real or potential) to the domestic economy, she or he will probably opt for a fixed exchange rate system. And if one believes that government intervention is inefficient at best and harmful at worst, she or he will most likely advocate flexible exchange rates.

What Is an Equilibrium Exchange Rate?

What, then, is an "equilibrium exchange rate"? In a world without capital flows, an equilibrium exchange rate would balance a nation's exports and imports over the medium-to-long run. But one must take care here. If a nation is willing to depress domestic demand and accept the resulting rates of unemployment, external equilibrium can be obtained at many different exchange rates. Likewise, a nation can attain external balance at a given exchange rate by employing trade restrictions and artificially holding down imports. But few economists believe that external balance should be attained by restricting trade and it is unlikely that a nation will accept long-run unemployment in order to preserve a particular exchange rate. Thus, the equilibrium exchange should balance exports and imports at the full employment (or potential) level of output under conditions of free trade.

Today, however, we live in a world with large and rapid international capital flows that must be counted when determining an equilibrium exchange rate. The difficulty is that economists disagree over which capital movements should be counted. One school believes that short-term capital movements are not tied to the international division of labor and should not be considered when calculating the equilibrium exchange rate. Long-term capital flows are different since they represent saving and investment decisions, production and absorption judgments that need to be taken into account. Hence, the crucial external balance is the basic balance of payments as defined in Chapter 4. Therefore, the equilibrium exchange rate comes down to that rate which balances the basic balance of payments at the full employment level of output under conditions of free trade.

There is a high probability that an equilibrium exchange rate will vary over time. Obviously, the exchange rate will rise or fall if trade patterns change or if national investment and savings patterns are modified. Suppose that Argentina borrows funds overseas to finance an expansion in its productive capacity. At first, when it is importing capital or borrowing, Argentina requires a sufficiently "high" exchange rate so that it can run the import surplus needed to transfer resources from the rest of the world to Argentina. When it begins to repay its external obligations, Argentina will in all likelihood need a lower exchange rate that will increase its exports and reduce its imports, enabling it to run the trade surplus required to repay its loans.

If long-term capital flows do not change radically in the short run, a fixed exchange rate may be preferable. Market forces might drive the exchange rate of the borrowing nation too high in the first stage just described and generate a massive trade deficit and a large external debt. As a result, an equally drastic fall in the exchange rate would then be required in the second stage. According to fixed-rate advocates, these wide gyrations in exchange rates damage international trade and investment. Naturally, if long-term capital flows vary and exchange rates need to be adjusted to maintain external equilibrium, there appears to be a case in favor of flexible rates.

Economists have come to strikingly different conclusions on the advantages and disadvantages of fixed and flexible exchange rates. Disagreements among economists have created the impression that exchange rate policy analysis is wooly and that economists waffle and weave back and forth, supporting first one system and then another. In fact, except for diehards in each camp, economists have generally been open to contradictory evidence and have been hospitable to wide disagreement on the meaning of that evidence.

Exchange Rates and Policy Independence

A claimed advantage of flexible exchange rates is that they **insulate** an economy from external developments. Thus, if a flexible exchange rate prevents an external bout of inflation from affecting the domestic price level, flexible exchange rates are said to insulate the domestic economy.

A major bone of disagreement among economists is whether flexible exchange rates **insulate** a domestic economy from external developments, thereby permitting policy-makers to concentrate on the domestic economy. For example, the pound and the mark were tied together at a fixed rate for most of 1992. But Germany raised its interest rates during the year in order to nip any inflationary pressures in the bud. Rising German interest rates put Britain in a bind. In order to maintain the fixed DM/£ exchange rate, the Bank of England had to raise British interest rates. Failure to do so would have led to an interest differential between German and British financial centers, and a flow of capital from Britain to Germany that would have put the exchange rate in peril. Yet the British economy was in recession in the fall of 1992, so higher interest rates were not the proper medicine from the British point of view. Britain had a dilemma: Boost domestic interest rates, maintain the exchange rate, and permit the economy to slip into recession; or concentrate on improving the domestic economy even if it meant discarding the exchange rate parity. In the end, Britain chose the latter course.

The dilemma facing the British authorities is illustrated in Figure 14.1, which shows the capital flow curve, the market for pounds, and Britain's aggregate demand and supply. Assume that the initial capital flow curve is K_0, in Figure 14.1a, and that German

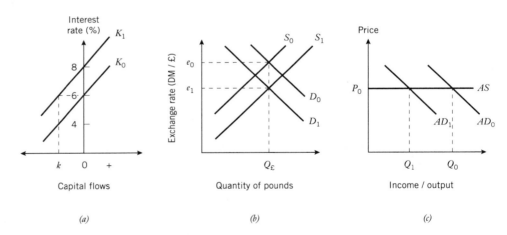

FIGURE 14.1 Capital flows, exchange rates, and aggregate demand.

Suppose that initially interest rates are 6 percent in both Britain and Germany, and that Germany raises its interest rate to 8 percent. The higher German interest rate raises the capital flow schedule from K_0 to K_1. If Britain does not raise its interest rate in step with Germany, capital will flow out of Britain toward Germany, panel (a). The capital flow will cause the demand curve for pounds to shift to the left from D_0 to D_1, and the supply curve of pounds to shift to the right from S_0 to S_1. As a result, the exchange rate will fall from e_0 to e_1, panel (b). The depreciation of the pound should reduce Britain's imports, raise its exports, and shift the British aggregate demand curve from AD_1 to AD_0. In the end, assuming the price level is constant, British income and employment will expand, as in panel (c). On the other hand, if Britain decides to defend the exchange rate, it will have to raise its interest rate in step with the Germans. However, the higher interest rate will shift the aggregate demand curve from AD_0 to AD_1 in panel (c). Britain will pay a heavy price for maintaining the international value of the pound.

and British interest rates are 6 percent. Also assume that the initial exchange rate, e_0, is determined by the supply, S_0, and the demand, D_0, for pounds (Figure 14.1b); and that aggregate demand equals AD_0 so that British output equals Q_0, (Figure 14.1c).

Now imagine that the German interest rate climbs from 6 to 8 percent. The higher German interest rate shifts the capital flow curve from K_0 to K_1 in Figure 14.1a. If the British interest rate remains at 6 percent, capital will flow from Britain to Germany and place the DM/£ exchange rate, e_0, in jeopardy. The capital flow from Britain to Germany will cause the supply curve of pounds to shift to the right, to S_1, as British investors sell pounds in order to purchase German treasury bills. In addition, the combination of downward pressure on the pound and relatively lower British interest rates will cause the demand for pounds to shift from D_0 to D_1. Unchecked, the pound will fall to e_1.

If the British want to maintain the value of the pound at e_0, they will have to match the Germans and raise *their* interest rate to 8 percent. This step will plug the capital drain and take the downward pressure off the pound. But Britain's new tight monetary policy will reduce Britain's aggregate demand and the AD curve will shift from AD_0 to AD_1 in Figure 14.1c, causing British income to drop. The exchange rate will be maintained, but at a cost to the British standard of living.

By comparison, if the British authorities do not attempt to defend the pound by raising domestic interest rates, the capital flow out of the country will lead to a depreciation of the pound which, by stimulating exports and reducing imports, will push the British aggregate demand curve to the right of AD_0, and raise British income.

The key point is not which option the British authorities actually selected when faced with this dilemma back in 1992. The key point is that, given a fixed exchange rate plus the actions of an international partner, British economic policy options were severely constrained. When the British authorities chose to stop defending the exchange rate and actually permitted the pound to float on the foreign exchanges, they freed themselves from the box they were in and were able thenceforth to focus their attention on improving the domestic British economy. Flexible exchange rate advocates claim that Britain would not have faced such a choice if it had not pegged the pound in the first place. In short, a flexible exchange rate would have insulated Britain from the effects of German economic policy.

Other economists question the ability of flexible exchange rates to insulate one economy from the infectious "germs" of a neighboring big economy as it "sneezes" and catches cold. These economists argue that it is quite possible that German economic policy will affect Britain even under flexible exchange rates. Higher German interest rates will cause capital to flow to Germany and lead to a depreciation of the pound. Pound depreciation will then help the British economy come out of the doldrums. But if the British economy was facing inflation instead of recession, an increase in German interest rates followed by pound depreciation would make things worse for Britain. The major point is that the British economy *is* affected by the German economic policy *even if* the pound floats.

Insulation is not the same thing as **policy independence.** Even if a flexible exchange rate arrangement does not insulate an economy from all external developments, the arrangement may permit a country to follow economic policies that will counteract any negative effects. (Of course, if the external effects have a positive impact on the domestic economy, the home economy will not want to offset them.)

Take the case of Britain again. With a fixed exchange rate in place during early 1992, British monetary policy was obliged to defend the exchange rate. If Britain had a floating rate, British monetary policy could have worked partly to offset the impact

One of the claimed attributes of flexible exchange rates is that they permit a nation to follow a monetary policy exclusively aimed at domestic targets. Domestic monetary policy, is, therefore, considered **policy independent;** it is not constrained by external factors or forces.

BOX 14.1 Exchange Rates and Insulation _____

Have flexible exchange rates insulated nations from external developments? Table 14.1 is a rudimentary attempt to find out. It compares rates of real GNP growth in four countries, all of which had bilateral flexible exchange rates. Rates of economic growth differ across nations for many reasons, since growth depends on many variables, such as the investment/GNP ratio, entrepreneurial ability, and labor productivity.

Now, if flexible exchange rates *do* in fact insulate national economies, one would not expect national rates of economic growth to rise and fall together. And yet the growth rates of the four major nations profiled here tended to do *exactly that;* only the expansion in the United States in 1975–79 bucks the trend. The figures give the impression that the level of economic activity among countries tends to rise and fall in tandem *regardless* of the exchange rate system in vogue.

TABLE 14.1 Average Rates of Economic Growth
[average rates of growth of real GNP]

Nation	*1970–74*	*1975–79*	*1980–84*	*1985–89*	*1990–94*
Germany	3.4%	2.8%	1.1%	2.9%	2.9%
Japan	6.0	4.7	3.9	4.8	2.3
UK	2.7	2.1	0.8	3.3	0.7
US	2.4	3.2	1.9	2.9	2.0

Source: Computed from Organization for Economic Cooperation and Development, *Economic Outlook,* © OECD, various issues.

---

of external developments but more importantly to solve Britain's internal economic problems. Britain would have been able to follow an easy, steady, or tight monetary policy depending on its needs, regardless of German economic policy.

What should we then conclude? The consensus view among economists is that individual countries are never completely isolated from external developments and, therefore, full policy independence is not possible in the sense of not having to react to external developments. But the consensus also holds that flexible exchange rates do *a far better job* in insulating an economy from external developments than do fixed rates and, more important, they enable a nation to carry out a *more independent* economic policy.

Exchange Rate Variation and Trade

We reported in the introduction to this volume that trade and economic growth were higher in the late 1960s, prior to the adoption of flexible exchange rates, than in the 1970s and early 1980s, when flexible rates were in fashion. Moreover, trade restrictions became a growth industry in the late 1970s and 1980s. Fixed-exchange-rate proponents jumped on these coincidences and claimed that they prove that flexible exchange rates inhibit international trade.

Why should exchange rate variation reduce trade? The argument is that exchange rate variation heightens the risk and uncertainty (and therefore the costs) associated with conducting international trade. Assuming that all exports are priced in German marks, an importer in the United States can never be sure what her domestic currency cost will be if the DM/$ exchange rate jumps about. Or, if an order for German-made BMWs is placed at one exchange rate, say DM2/$, an American importer of BMWs could find herself strapped for funds if the exchange rate stands at DM1/$ when the bill comes due. Although she can cover herself against the consequences of exchange rate variation in the options and forward exchange markets, the cost of such coverage raises the transactions cost of trade and, presumably, hampers it.

The counterargument that there is just as much chance that the dollar will rise to DM3/$ rather than falling to DM1/$ does not diminish the negative effect of exchange rate variation on trade. The equal probability of gaining or losing an economic windfall still increases the risk associated with international trade and investment. And, given that risk, individuals will demand a higher rate of return before engaging in international trade.

The decline in the rate of trade expansion in the 1970s and early 1980s, however, may not have been caused by variations in exchange rates. Paul De Grauwe found that slower income growth was the major explanation of the decrease in the rate of trade expansion of the 10 largest industrial countries between 1973 and 1984, although 20 percent of the decline in the *growth* of trade could in fact be attributed to fluctuations in real exchange rates.

Thus, on balance, if everything else is equal (an important qualifier), one might argue that *fixed* rather than flexible exchange rates are probably best for trade. But the evidence is by no means clear-cut. Hali J. Edison and Michael Melvin sifted through several empirical studies and concluded that "it is clearly inappropriate to claim that floating rates have depressed the volume of international trade below what would have existed in the presence of fixed exchange rates."[*]

Memberwide fixed exchange rates from the middle-to-late 1980s on may have helped foster intra-EU trade. Yet the yen bounced around quite a bit with no apparent ill-effects on Japan's export performance; although it appears that the steady *appreciation*, not the *variation*, in the international value of the yen started to affect the Japanese export-import balance in the middle 1990s. In addition, Canadian-U.S. trade has grown over the years even though the Canadian dollar/U.S. dollar exchange rate has floated for decades. It should be stressed that what is being discussed here is the relationship between exchange rate variation and total or worldwide trade, not the relation between secular or long-run movements in the exchange rate and the export performance of a particular nation.

Exchange Rates and Inflation

Worldwide rates of inflation accelerated after the world's major economic powers adopted flexible exchange rates in the early 1970s. This experience led some economists to con-

---

[*]Hali J. Edison and Michael Melvin, "The Determinants and Implications of the Choice of an Exchange Rate System," in *Monetary Policy for a Volatile Global Economy*, edited by William S. Haraf and Thomas D. Willett (Washington, D.C.: AEI Press, 1990); p. 41.

clude that flexible exchange rates have an inflationary bias while fixed exchange rates provide an anchor for noninflationary monetary policies and attendant price stability.

The argument connecting flexible exchange rates to accelerating inflation is based on the following logic. When a government sets or fixes the value of its currency in terms of marks or yen, it takes on the obligation to maintain it. An excessively easy monetary policy will lead to inflation and make it difficult (some say impossible) for a government to fulfill this obligation. But since the prestige and reelection chances of the government are tied to the international value of the currency, they will slide with the value of the currency. Thus, a government pledged to maintain a certain exchange rate will not inflate. By contrast, if the exchange rate is determined by so-called impersonal market forces, a government *can* inflate and blame the resulting fall in the value of the currency on unscrupulous currency speculators and manipulations by bankers and foreign agents.

French and Italian experience is often cited to support this latter proposition. Both countries had high rates of inflation during most of the post–World War II era when the franc and the lira were two of the weaker Western European currencies. But when France and Italy joined the exchange rate mechanism of the European Monetary System (described in Chapter 16), they were forced to maintain the value of their currencies relative to the currencies of the other ERM members, particularly the German mark. Having made a pledge to maintain the values of their currencies within a narrow range or "band," they were compelled to follow noninflationary monetary policies. France did in fact follow such policies, and, despite the currency turmoil of 1992 and 1993, the franc has remained strong. But in the fall of 1992, the lira ran into trouble, partly because of Italy's high rate of inflation, and consequently dropped out of the exchange rate mechanism.

Despite the unhappy Italian experience, more and more people believe that the lack of an "anchor" is a major reason for the persistence of hyperinflation in Russia. Russia adopted a flexible exchange rate in the early 1990s. Freed from the need to maintain a stated ruble/mark parity, Russia increased its money supply at inflationary rates. As a result, inflation soared and the international value of the ruble virtually melted away. By comparison, Estonia pegged its currency, the krooni, to the German mark at the exchange rate of 8 krooni per mark in 1992 after its rate of inflation began to accelerate. In mid-1995, the Russian rate of inflation—over 200 percent per year—was more than 10 times the Estonian rate of inflation. And generally speaking, transitional and developing countries that pegged or tied their currencies either to one currency or to a basket of currencies rather than allowing them to float have had a better record in controlling inflation.

What is the response of floating-rate advocates to this evidence? They reply that inflation is caused by *excessive monetary expansion*, not the exchange rate system. If a government is bent on expanding the money supply at an inflationary rate, an exchange rate system, whether fixed or free, will not prevent it. In contrast, if a government follows a noninflationary monetary policy, inflation will be mild regardless of the exchange rate policy adopted. Floaters see no reason why a central bank dedicated to maintaining price stability will necessarily behave one way under a fixed-rate regime and another way under floating rates.

Table 14.2 attempts to shed some light on this question, although admittedly it is a rather dim light. The seven countries listed can be placed into two groups: the continental Europeans and the UK plus others. First, look at the records of the continental European countries. In 1979, the first four countries together with other members of the European Union banded together in an attempt to tie their currencies together under the Exchange Rate Mechanism (ERM). As members of the ERM, Belgium, the Netherlands, and France were compelled to stabilize their currencies in terms of the

TABLE 14.2 Average Rates of Inflation
(average increase in the consumer price deflator)

Country	1970–75	1975–79	1980–84	1985–89	1990–94
Germany	6.2%	4.2%	4.5%	1.5%	3.5%
Belgium	7.3	6.4	7.2	2.7	2.9
Netherlands	8.2	7.7	4.7	1.0	2.9
France	8.1	7.9	11.0	3.4	3.1
UK	10.4	15.4	9.3	4.0	4.7
Japan	11.3	7.5	3.9	1.1	2.1
USA	6.2	8.0	7.5	3.6	3.7

Sources: Computed from Organization for Economic Cooperation and Development, *Economic Outlook*, © *OECD*, (June 1995); p. A18, and June, 1994, p. A18.

mark, the key currency, and, by implication, were forced to follow the anti-inflationary policy of the Bundesbank, the German central bank. According to fixed-rate proponents, fixed exchange rates helped these ERM countries to combat inflation. Granted, it took some countries time to adjust down to the German rate of inflation—France did not adopt a serious anti-inflation stance until the 1985–89 period—but their inflation performance was superior post-ERM compared with pre-ERM. This was no fluke, according to the fixed-rate camp. By tying their currencies to the mark and their monetary policies to the Bundesbank, their anti-inflation polices became **credible,** which is another way of saying they became believable.

An economic policy is judged **credible** if the society believes that it will be carried out. For example, an anti-inflation policy will not be considered credible if the public believes the government will back off the policy if it causes some pain, such as higher unemployment. An anti-inflation policy is credible if the public believes that the government will stick to its guns even if combatting inflation leads to an increase in the rate of unemployment.

Britain was the odd one out. It did not join the ERM until late 1990, and then left it in late 1992. But during most of the period covered by Table 14.2, Britain had higher rates of inflation than its European neighbors—proof, according to fixed-rate proponents, that exchange rate systems make a difference.

But then consider the cases of Japan and the United States, whose exchange rates floated from 1974 on. Similar to the experience in Belgium, the Netherlands, and France, the U.S. rate of inflation declined during the 1980s and edged up slightly during the early 1990s. Overall, the American rate of inflation was higher than the Belgian and Dutch rates throughout the period and higher than the French rate of inflation from 1985 on. But, quite frankly, the differences were minuscule except for the Dutch and American rates of inflation in the 1980s.

The Japanese record does not lend weight to the argument that a nation operating under a fixed exchange rate system will have a lower rate of inflation than a country adopting a flexible exchange rate. The evidence, therefore, is decidedly mixed. Fixed-rate advocates are right, perhaps, when they claim that ERM discipline forced the Belgian, French, and Dutch governments to follow a German-based anti-inflation policy and that, but for this linkage, rates of inflation would have been *much higher* in these countries and that Britain's record would have been *much better* if it had joined the ERM earlier. Yet the Japanese record indicates that a country does not have to adopt a fixed exchange rate in order to attain price stability.

Whether flexible exchange rates have an inflationary bias depends on the rates of inflation in *all* countries, not a selected few. For example, major bilateral exchange rates were fixed during most of the 1970–74 period, but were flexible between 1985 and 1993, a period of lower worldwide inflation. Yet most countries had hefty rates of inflation during the 1975–85 period when flexible rates were predominant. Most observers, however, believe that much of the inflation in these two periods can be attributed not to the exchange rate systems, but to two OPEC oil shocks plus a worldwide boom in the late 1970s.

Attempts to select an exchange rate system on the basis of policy independence, the level and growth of trade, and inflation can be frustrating. Individual economists look at the same historical evidence and come to different conclusions. Even if the evidence appears clear-cut, one can always find other evidence which invalidates it. Due to this confusion, some economists believe that a nation's economic structure should play the primary role in determining whether it should opt for a fixed or for a flexible exchange rate.

Economic Structure and Exchange Rates

What structural variables determine whether a nation should float or fix (peg) its currency? A short list includes the *size and openness* (trade as a percentage of GDP) of the economy, the degree of *export diversification* measured by both products and markets, the rate of domestic inflation relative to the pace of inflation among major trading partners, and the *degree of capital mobility* (the elasticity of the capital flow schedule described in Chapter 12).

It is unlikely that a nation's choice between exchange rate systems will be clear cut. Based on some criteria, it should let its currency float; based on others, it should peg it to, say, the currency of its major trading partner or peg to some currencies and float against others.

The U.S. dollar should float, according to the criteria set forth in Table 14.3. The United States is a large nation with a relatively closed economy, has a low marginal propensity to import, and its exports are diversified. Because of its low propensity to import, the United States would need a hefty change in income in order to attain external equilibrium under a fixed exchange rate. In addition, because its exports are diversified by product and destination, the demand elasticity of its exports is likely to be high, especially compared to the export demand elasticities of a nation whose exports are concentrated. Given diversified exports and high elasticities, a small depreciation should right a trade imbalance. High elasticities also assure that the terms-of-trade cost of a depreciation will be low.

In addition, because the United States is a *financially* open economy (high capital mobility), it would probably be impossible for it to maintain a fixed exchange rate

TABLE 14.3 Economic Characteristics and Exchange Rate System

Peggers	*Floaters*
small nation	large nation
open economy	closed economy
concentrated trade	diversified trade
product concentration	product diversification
low capital mobility	high capital mobility
low inflation differential	high inflation differential

unless it introduced capital controls or dedicated its monetary policy exclusively to preserving the exchange rate.

The guidelines in Table 14.3 indicate that most LDCs should employ fixed exchange rates. Their exports tend to be concentrated in terms of both products and markets and, in addition, face low demand price elasticities. As a result, large depreciations or appreciations will be required to restore trade balance equilibrium. Moreover, low price elasticities point to a high terms-of-trade cost of exchange rate adjustment. But not all of the criteria indicate that fixed exchange rates are best for LDCs. Many LDCs suffer from hyperinflation, and, under such conditions, it is impossible to fix or set an exchange rate.

For some nations, a *mixed system* may be superior. The Austrian schilling, according to the criteria, should be pegged to the German mark. Austria is a small nation that primarily trades with Germany. Because of its strong trading relations with Germany, a depreciation of the Austrian schilling against the mark (or even the threat of one) would lead to a mass exit from the schilling as Austrians built up mark balances. The schilling would go into a tailspin. For this reason alone, Austria should peg to the mark. By comparison, Austria's trade with the United States is modest—in fact, Austria could very easily be classified as a "closed economy" vis-à-vis the United States. The best approach for Austria then might be to peg its currency to the mark and let the DM/$ rate establish the ASch/$ rate.

Evidence also suggests that the costs of depreciation are high for small, open countries. Jacques Artus and Anne Kenny McGuirk estimated that, given weak feedbacks, a 10 percent depreciation would raise the GDP deflator, or price level, 3.0 percent in the Netherlands, an open economy, and 1.4 percent in the United States, a closed economy; given strong feedbacks, the figures are 6.8 percent and 4.4 percent respectively.

Exchange Rate Systems and Capital Mobility

While the majority of the structural characteristics are easily understood, the relationship between the degree of capital mobility and exchange rate systems requires greater discussion. Advanced texts in international economics demonstrate that given various degrees of capital mobility, the exchange rate system determines whether a government can successfully use fiscal or monetary policy. We ignore that discussion here. Although we did demonstrate in Chapter 12 that if a country faced unemployment and a trade deficit and wanted to maintain a fixed exchange, it could employ a monetary-fiscal mix and restore internal and external equilibrium. However, we were also quick to point out that such a policy would at best provide only a short-run solution.

Our point of departure for analyzing the relation between policy instruments, capital mobility, and exchange rate systems is Britain's experience in the fall of 1992 cited at the beginning of this chapter. In that case, we found that Britain was able to carry out an independent monetary policy and boost the British economy only when it switched from pegging the pound to the mark and allowed the pound to float. That experience leads to our central conclusion: Given capital mobility, monetary policy will be effective only if exchange rates are flexible.

Suppose a nation faces unemployment and is operating under a system of fixed exchange rates. If the central bank expands the money supply in an attempt to raise the level of aggregate demand and generate more jobs, the policy will not work.

Consider Figure 14.2. An easy monetary policy will increase the money/GDP ratio from .5 to 1— panel (a). As a result, the interest rate drops to 4 percent and capital flows out of the country— panel (b). In the foreign exchange market, panel (c), the supply of pounds shifts from S to S_1, putting downward pressure on the pound. The central bank, then, is forced to reverse its policy in order to protect the value of the pound.

Now assume that the exchange rate is flexible. Monetary expansion leads to lower interest rates, a capital outflow, and pound depreciation just as before. However, rather than attempting to defend the pound, the Bank of England lets it depreciate. As a result, not shown, Britain's exports climb, its autonomous imports drop, and the British economy expands.

The conclusion seems clear. Given capital mobility, monetary policy cannot maintain an exchange rate and external and internal equilibrium at the same time if exchange rates are fixed. Thus, the case for maintaining a fixed exchange rate in a world of large and often unforeseen capital flows rests on the ability of fiscal policy to offset such capital flows and maintain the exchange rate, internal equilibrium, and external

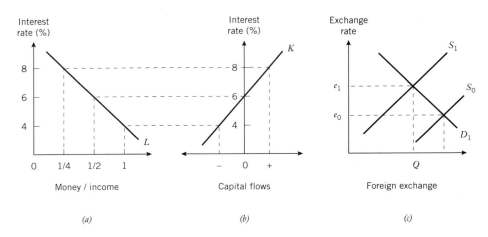

FIGURE 14.2 Flexible exchange rates and capital mobility.

If capital is mobile and exchange rates are flexible, monetary policy is an effective policy tool. Consider a country that faces unemployment. An easy monetary policy will lower the domestic interest rate, lead to a capital outflow, and, on the foreign exchange market, shift the supply curve of the domestic currency from S_1 to S_0. Currency depreciation will raise exports, reduce imports, and raise aggregate demand. On the other hand, if exchange rates are fixed, the policy will not work. As before, monetary expansion will drop the domestic interest rate and lead to a capital outflow. Once again the exchange rate will come under pressure. However, since the central bank must maintain the initial exchange rate, e_1, it will have to reduce the domestic money supply and raise interest rates so as to discourage capital outflows in order to maintain the exchange rate. The economy ends up at its initial position. Given flexible exchange rates, the results of fiscal expansion are even worse. An increase in, say, government expenditures will raise income, but this will drop the money/GDP ratio, from, say, one-half to one-quarter, and raise the domestic interest rate from 6 percent to 8 percent. As a result, capital will flow toward the country, which means that the demand for the domestic currency will increase (not shown) and raise the exchange rate. Currency appreciation will drop exports, increase autonomous imports, and drop the level of aggregate demand.

BOX 14.2 **Current Exchange Rate Arrangements**

Table 14.4 represents an abbreviated summary of existing exchange rate arrangements and their relative popularity. The classifications range from pegged to independently floating currencies. A number of currencies, due to reasons of either location or tradition, are tied or pegged to the French franc, Australian dollar, German mark, Indian rupee, Russian ruble, and South African rand. Three nations peg to the SDR today (see Chapter 15), down from 12 in 1985 and another four currencies, those of Bahrain, Qatar, Saudi Arabia, and the United Arab Emirates fluctuate, within limits, against the U.S. dollar. And an additional three currencies are frequently adjusted according to a set of indicators determined by the country in question.

The number of currencies pegged to the dollar has markedly declined since 1988 and today no major currency is tied to the dollar. Likewise, the number of currencies pegged to some composite of currencies has also sharply declined. The big growth has been in the number of currencies operating under a managed float or an independent float. The managed float category consists primarily of LDC currencies. The number of independently floating currencies, including the Canadian dollar, the U.S. dollar, the yen, and many Eastern European currencies, has expanded most rapidly in the last seven years. But an independently floating currency is not necessarily a *freely floating* currency. The United States, Japan, and other countries have attempted to move or maintain the values of their currencies at various times.

TABLE 14.4 **Exchange Rate Arrangements**
(end of period*)

Category	1988	1990	1992	1994	1995
Pegged to:					
Dollar	36	25	24	23	23
Other Currencies	26	25	31	26	25
Composite	31	35	29	26	20
EMS	8	9	9	10	10
Managed Float	22	23	23	33	35
Independent Float	17	25	44	58	59

*1995 = end of 1st quarter.

Source: Calculated from International Monetary Fund, *International Financial Statistics,* June, 1995, p. 8.

equilibrium simultaneously. This is indeed a tall order. And there is no evidence that it can be accomplished. Fiscal policy cannot be turned on a dime. Witness the inability of most OECD nations to turn budget deficits into budget surpluses, something that would be required if a nation was to maintain an exchange rate and internal and external equilibrium at the same time.

It is worth recalling that the structural approach to selecting an exchange rate system consists of several criteria. A large, relatively closed, financially developed country may, for reasons outlined, find that a flexible exchange rate best serves its interests. But not all economies fit into these categories. For them, a fixed or quasi-fixed exchange rate system may be preferable, especially if the immediate cause of a trade deficit is recession in trading-partner economies. In such a case, a policy that seeks to reduce the international value of the domestic currency may have to be reversed once economic activity picks up in trading-partner economies.

Nevertheless, theoretical arguments appear to come down in favor of *flexible* exchange rates and, as indicated in Box 14.2, floating or flexible exchange rates have definitely become more popular in the last decade. This does not mean that fixed exchange rates are ready for the dust bin. If one takes a broad view of post–World War II period economic developments, one is struck by the close association between the move toward free trade and a system of pegged exchange rates. Certainly, the GATT and the IMF seemed to move in tandem, the success of one organization appearing to be related to the success of the other.

Was it sheer coincidence that the growth of trade restrictions seems to have taken off right after the breakdown of the Bretton Woods system of fixed exchange rates? If it was not coincidence, will the successful conclusion of the Uruguay Round lead to the reemergence of a pegged exchange rate system? Any answer at this time would be speculative at best. Yet one can note that the move toward economic unification or regional free trade in Europe has been associated with an attempt to establish a fixed exchange rate system within Europe.

Summary

In this chapter, we have looked at various criteria which can serve as guides to selecting an exchange rate system: policy independence, impact on trade, the ability to control inflation, and the structure of an economy. Flexible exchange rates do give a country a ration of policy independence which is lacking under a system of fixed exchange rates. This does not mean that a country can, in a sense, shut itself off from the rest of the world and never be affected by external developments simply because it adopts a flexible exchange rate. It does mean, however, that it can follow a more independent monetary policy as the British case cited at the beginning of this chapter illustrated.

A fixed exchange rate, if it can be maintained without recourse to controls and unemployment, appears to be more pro-trade than a flexible exchange rate system—at least theoretically. Recently, individuals have also argued that a fixed exchange rate can serve as an anchor to combat inflation. But here it is important to remember that an exchange rate system does not stand alone. Its success or failure depends on the economic environment in which it operates, and, as that environment changes, its effectiveness can slip or improve. There is little doubt that if an exchange rate regime is adopted in an unstable world, it will not perform as expected. Such may have been the case of flexible exchange rates in the middle-to-late 1970s. The world's major players adopted flexible exchange rates in the early 1970s in the aftermath of the first oil shock. After that, the world economy went through another oil shock and a period of rapid inflation followed by a steep recession. It is unlikely that any exchange rate system would have been effective in such an economic environment.

In 1973, the world's monetary authorities did not sit down together in a calm atmosphere and discuss the merits and shortcomings of various exchange rate systems and come to the conclusion that flexible rates were superior to fixed exchange rates. Floating rates were introduced in a panic. It is fair to suggest that when the international monetary system was falling apart, the world's economic leaders decided it was time to give the market a chance. Therefore, any judgment regarding the performance of the flexible exchange rate system must take the economic and political environment into account.

In fact, today's case for a fixed or managed exchange rate is based on the wide swings in exchange rates that have occurred under the floating system and the assumed relationship between these swings and the recent growth in trade restrictions. Moreover, it is not just the wide swings in exchange rates that led many observers to conclude that flexible rates are detrimental to international trade. When America ran large trade deficits in the early-to-middle 1980s, the dollar actually appreciated so that, in the opinion of many observers, market forces actually pushed the exchange rate in the wrong direction and that, in turn, fostered and sustained global imbalances. Therefore, experience, not theory, argues that exchange rates must be fixed or at least be kept within limits according to this perspective.

Recent exchange rate experience highlights two facts. In a world of capital flows, it is impossible to insulate an economy from external developments regardless of the exchange rate system adopted. In addition, any system will have a tough time of it if the economic policies of trading partners diverge. One nation cannot introduce an expansionary domestic policy and attain internal and external equilibrium if the rest of the world decides to follow restrictive policies. Likewise, a nation will not be able to maintain its exchange rate through a high-interest policy if all nations raise their interest rates at the same time.

All exchange rate systems yield benefits, but they can be attained only by paying the required costs, which means, among other things, that countries must play by the rules of the game. A fixed exchange rate system and even a floating system which limits the degree of the float, either explicitly or implicitly, places a premium on international cooperation and the provision of international liquidity, and, in today's world, arrangements whereby nations with consistently higher- than-average inflation rates can keep their currencies tied to others at a realistic, although ever-changing, exchange rate. These rules of the game are taken up in the next chapter.

Key Concepts and Terms

adjustable peg

domestic insulation

equilibrium full employment exchange rate

fixed exchange rate

flexible exchange rate

managed float

policy independence

Review Questions

1. Why is it factually incorrect to talk of completely fixed or freely flexible exchange rates?

2. If a nation wants to follow an independent policy, which type of exchange system should it adopt, and which type of exchange rate system should it avoid?

3. Which type of exchange system would you advocate for a Latin American nation whose exports consist of one or two primary products?

4. Should the United States adopt fixed or flexible exchange rates? Why? What type of exchange rate system should Canada adopt?

5. If a country's capital market is integrated with the world capital market, or capital is mobile, should the nation opt for fixed or flexible exchange rates?

References and Suggested Readings

Brief and lively description of various exchange rate proposals are found in "Economic Focus: An Exchange Rate Map, Part 1," *The Economist* (May 21 1988); p. 77, and "Economic Focus: An Exchange Rate Map, Part 2," *The Economist* (May 28, 1988); p. 65.

Paul De Grauwe's estimate of the impact of flexible exchange rates on international trade is contained in his article "Exchange Rate Variability and the Slowdown in Growth of International Tarde," *International Monetary Fund Staff Papers* 35 (March 1988); pp. 63–84. As previously noted, Hali J. Edison and Michael Melvin review the empirical literature on trade and flexible exchange rates in their article, "The Determinants and Implications of the Choice of an Exchange Rate System," in *Monetary Policy for a Volatile Global Economy*, edited by William S. Haraf and Thomas D. Willett (Washington, D.C.: AEI Press 1990). Jacques R. Artus and Anne Kenny McGuirk estimated the effect of a depreciation on the domestic price level in their article, "A Revised Version of the Multilateral Exchange Rate Model," *International Monetary Fund Staff Papers* 28 (June 1981); p. 295ff.

The classic pro-flexible exchange rates article is Milton Friedman's "The Case for Flexible Exchange Rates," reprinted in *AEA Readings in International Economics*, edited by Richard Caves and Harry G. Johnson (Homewood, IL: Richard D. Irwin, 1968). Although originally published in 1955, the Friedman piece is still worth reading. Another classic article on flexible exchange rates is Harry G. Johnson, "The Case for Flexible Exchange Rates," Federal Reserve Bank of St. Louis *Review* 51 (June 1969); pp. 12–24.

On the recent debate over flexible exchange rates, see Robert M. Dunn, Jr., *The Many Disappointments of the Flexible Exchange Rates*, Essays in International Finance no. 154 (Princeton, NJ: International Finance Section, Princeton University, 1983); and Morris Goldstein, *Have Flexible Exchange Rates Handicapped Macroeconomic Policy?*, Special Papers in International Finance 14 (Princeton, NJ: International Finance Section, Princeton University, 1980).

Finally, H. Robert Heller discusses the choice of an exchange rate system in "Determinants of Exchange Rate Practices," *Journal of Money, Credit, and Banking* 10 (August 1978); pp. 308–321. This is one of the classic articles that discusses the relationship between exchange rates and national economic structures.

Three more current articles on exchange rates are: "Economic Focus: Time to Fix?," *The Economist* (July 30, 1994); p. 65; "Economic Focus: Fixed and Floating Voters," *The Economist* (April 1, 1995); p. 64; and Paul Krugman, "Monetary Virtue Leads Two-Peso Tussle," *Financial Times* (July 13, 1995); p. 17. *The Economist*, the *Financial Times*, the *New York Times*, and the *Wall Street Journal* regularly publish articles on international monetary policy.

Chapter 15

International Liquidity and International Monetary Cooperation

It is one thing to set an exchange rate and another to maintain it. This chapter addresses the second question, namely what a nation must do in order to keep the value of its currency within a target range such as DM1.6/$ to DM1.4/$. Even in a relatively calm environment, exchange rates can move rapidly up or down due to market pressures and a rash of selling could threaten to push a currency below its lower bound, or the dollar below DM1.4/$ in this example.

What can the Fed do to counter or offset such pressures and maintain the value of the dollar? Two options were discussed in Chapter 3. The Fed can raise U.S. interest rates and hope to reverse the flight out of dollars despite the potentially damaging effects of higher U.S. interest rates on the level of economic activity, or the Fed can sell marks and buy dollars on the foreign exchanges. The increase in the supply of marks will reduce its price, while a greater demand for the dollar will raise its price.

In order to carry out this policy, the Fed must have sufficient **international reserves.** Clearly, if its international reserves are inadequate for the job, the Fed will face an insurmountable task and will be forced to abandon its attempt to hold the exchange rate within prescribed limits. Thus, from America's point of view, an abundant, even an infinite, supply of international reserves is optimum.

Yet when the world is awash in liquid assets, debtor nations can run continuous trade deficits financing their excess of imports over exports by drawing down their reserves. But when one nation uses reserves to finance its deficits, other nations must accept them as compensation. A "surplus" nation is unlikely to accept payments in international reserves indefinitely, thereby extending an infinite amount of credit. It is more probable that before long, surplus nations will opt out of an international monetary system in which they must play the role of "creditor" to the world's big spenders. The conclusion is that either *too much* or *too little* international liquidity will impair attempts to preserve a system of fixed or semifixed exchange rates.

International reserves are a sum of funds that a country sets aside to finance trade imbalances or intervene in the foreign exchanges to strengthen its currency when it comes under pressure. In most cases, a country's international reserves consist of its holdings of major foreign currencies plus its line of credit at the IMF plus its holding of *special drawing rights.*

The Path Ahead

This chapter addresses three issues:

- What determines the demand for international reserves?
- How have international reserves been supplied in the past, what are the current arrangements for providing international reserves, and what plans have been proposed for supplying them in the future?
- Notwithstanding that an effective international monetary system requires international monetary cooperation, why might such cooperation not be forthcoming?

In what follows, we assume that participating nations want to establish and maintain a system of fixed exchange rates, an objective, it must be stressed, that can be attained only if the participating nations follow noninflationary monetary policies. But even assuming noninflationary monetary policies, *international liquidity* is essential if fixed exchange rates are to be maintained. Even if nations opt for a managed float (which we have already defined as a cross between fixed and fluctuating exchange rates), international reserves will be required. By contrast, if exchange rates are set by market forces alone, there is no need for international money.

The Demand for a Precautionary Cash Reserve

Individuals, firms, and countries hold a **precautionary cash reserve** so that they can bridge the gap between expenditures and income.

A nation's demand for international reserves is similar to an individual's demand for a **precautionary cash reserve,** a reserve fund that will tide the individual over if her income falls short of her planned expenditures. As long as her income and expenditures move in unison, she will never need a cash reserve. If she receives and spends $100 per month, she will not need a reserve. But if she suffers a transitory decline in income—say from $100 to $90, a cash reserve will enable her to bridge the gap and maintain her expenditures at $100 per month until her income climbs back to its normal level.

How much of a cash reserve should she hold? The quick answer is $10. But this answer ignores two facts: First, holding a cash reserve involves costs, and, second, it does not make much sense to hold a $10 reserve if the probability that her income will fall by $10 is very small. With this in mind, one can argue that if the probability of her having a $10 gap is 40 percent, her optimum cash reserve, other things considered equal, is $4, not $10. If we assume, in addition, that the probability of her having a $20 shortfall is 5 percent, her optimum cash reserve would be $5—$4 for the $10 probable gap and $1 for the $20 probable gap. As can be seen in Table 15.1, since the probability of her having wider and wider gaps declines, her demand for *additional* reserves will decline the greater the probable gap. To compute her total demand reserves, one would sum up each possible gap times the probability that it will occur. Considering the data in Table 15.1, the individual will want to hold or will demand a $6.70 reserve.

Now if the probability of a $10 gap is .45, the probability of a $20 gap is .05, and the probabilities of a $30 or a $40 gap are zero, the individual's demand for a precautionary balance will equal $5.50. Assuming the probability of having a surplus equals 50

TABLE 15.1 The Demand for a Precautionary Cash Reserve

Potential Excess of Expenditures over Income	Probability that the Potential Excess Will Occur	Demand for Reserves at each Potential Gap
$10	.40	$4.0
$20	.05	$1.0
$30	.03	$0.9
$40	.02	$0.8

percent, the probability of expenditures exceeding receipts will also equal 50 percent. *However,* an individual does not need a reserve if her income exceeds her expenditures.

The Costs and Benefits of International Reserves

A nation's demand for international reserves can be computed in a similar, though more complicated manner. The potential gap between a nation's imports and its exports, and the probability that the gap will occur, is the important measure.

The benefits of holding a cash reserve can be measured by the adjustment costs the nation would incur if it had to correct a trade deficit. For example, suppose a nation's full-employment level of income is $100, and at that level of income, exports and imports equal $20 each. Imagine foreign income contracts and cuts domestic exports by $10, but the nation is able, via domestic economic policy, to maintain its income at $100. While a success on the home front, the policy will lead to a $10 trade deficit. If the nation does not have any international reserves and wants to maintain a given exchange rate, it will have to contract its income to bring exports and imports into equilibrium.

How much will the nation have to contract its income in order to balance its imports and its exports? If its marginal propensity to import equals .2, its income must decline by $50 to balance its exports and imports. The annual benefit of the reserves, therefore, is $50 times the probability that the $10 deficit will occur. If we assume, as in Table 15.1, that the probability of a $10 deficit is .4, the benefit of holding a $10 reserve is $20. Following the same procedure for other possible trade deficits, we can compute the benefit the nation derives from holding $40 in reserves, which is $33.50 in this example.

International reserves, however, are not a "free good" since any sum of money has alternative uses. For example, the funds could be used for investment. And if the return on domestic investment is 20 percent, the cost of holding $10 in reserve would equal $2. In this example, it is quite clear that the nation would want to hold the $10 reserve since the benefit of holding the reserve is $20, which swamps the $2 cost of holding the reserve.

Additional complications must be considered. First, if the nation holds its $10 reserve in an interest-bearing asset that yields 10 percent or $1 per year, the cost of holding reserves is cut in half, or almost in half since any reserves actually used to finance a trade deficit will not earn interest. Second, a country may be able to borrow the required funds on the international capital market or from its trading partners. This option is

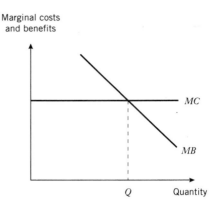

FIGURE 15.1 The demand for international reserves.

The demand for international reserves depends on the benefits and costs of holding international reserves. A nation will demand reserves up to the point at which the marginal benefit of holding an additional unit of reserves equals the marginal cost of holding it. In the graph, it is assumed that benefits derived from holding an additional unit of reserves decline, while the costs involved in holding an additional unit of reserves are constant.

superior in certain circumstances. Suppose as before that the return on domestic investment is 20 percent and that the country receives 5 percent on any reserves that it holds. Therefore, the opportunity cost of holding reserves is 15 percent. If the nation can borrow reserves as needed at 15 percent or less, borrowing reserves is its best option.

Figure 15.1 shows the costs and benefits of holding international reserves and summarizes this section of the discussion. The benefits of holding and thus the demand for reserves slopes down from left to right under the assumption that the probability of a trade deficit declines as its possible magnitude increases; that is, the probability of a $10 deficit is higher than the probability of a $20 deficit. The optimum quantity of reserves equals that amount at which the benefit of holding an extra dollar of reserves equals the cost of holding an extra dollar of reserves, or the quantity Q_0 in Figure 15.1. (It is assumed that the cost of holding reserves is constant.)*

International Reserves and Creditor Countries

Up to this point, we have ignored the question of whether surplus nations should want the debtor nations' demand for international reserves to be satisfied. Basically, the answer is *yes*—at least within limits. Suppose Mexico's exports decrease due to a cyclical

---

*The analysis just given applies only to cases in which capital is immobile. Major currencies, and even some minor currencies on occasion, are apt to be buffeted by short-term capital flows. As a result, key currency countries will require more international reserves than most nations, and more than suggested here. Exactly how much greater their reserves must be is more difficult to calculate. Given the target exchange rate, say DM2/$, one would have to calculate the excess supply of dollars at various exchange rates, such as DM1.8/$ and so on, times the probability that the dollar would fall to such a level. For example, if the probability that the dollar would fall to DM1.8/$ is 10 percent, and that the excess supply of dollars would equal $100 at that rate while the U.S. mpm is .2, the benefit for the United States of holding $100 in reserves would be $50.

BOX 15.1 International Reserves and Imports

Because it is assumed that a nation will want to maintain its level of reserves in the face of a transitory decline in exports, a nation's reserves are most often measured as a percentage of their imports, or how many months' worth of imports the reserves will buy.

Table 15.2 shows that the ratio of the world's international reserves relative to weeks of worldwide imports has remained relatively constant over the last decade. Individual countries, of course, have different reserve to import ratios as shown in Table 15.3.

TABLE 15.2 International Reserves and Weeks of Imports (billions of SDRs or percent)

Year	Reserves	Reserves/Imports (weeks)
1982	327.9	10.4%
1984	407.0	11.1
1986	418.6	12.8
1988	542.6	13.6
1990	637.6	13.8
1992	692.9	13.3
1994	812.7	12.8

Source: International Monetary Fund, *International Financial Statistics Yearbook*, 1995; p. 51. The figures for international reserves do not include gold.

TABLE 15.3 Reserves/Import Ratios for Selected Countries: 1994 (percent)

Country	Ratio	Country	Ratio
Taiwan	108.7	Germany	22.8
Singapore	57.0	UK	18.2
Japan	44.0	France	11.5
China	31.6	Mexico	10.3
Korea	25.0	United States	9.5

Source: Calculated from data presented in the relevant country pages in International Monetary Fund, *International Financial Statistics*, August 1995. International reserves were converted from SDRs into dollars to make the calculations.

decline in economic activity in the United States. If Mexico is forced to squeeze its level of economic activity in order to decrease its imports and balance its trade accounts, U.S. exports will fall, which will further dampen the level of economic activity in the United States. Both Mexico and the United States, therefore, will be better off if Mexico maintains its level of imports despite the decline in its exports and the resulting Mexican trade deficit. This suggests that, at least to some limit, creditors should ensure that there is sufficient international liquidity in the world. The question is what is meant by "sufficient" reserves and what is defined as "excessive" reserves.

International Reserves and the Timing of Devaluation/Revaluation

Regardless of the stock of international reserves and the desires of surplus and deficit nations, there is a high probability that real exchange rates will need to be adjusted at some time. It is difficult to know exactly when this should occur, but the ability to measure the costs and benefits of international reserves can provide a clue. If a nation is operating at full capacity and runs continuous trade surpluses, the benefits it will obtain from an additional dollar of international reserves will be marginal at best even though it will receive interest on its reserve holdings. If the interest rate on held reserves is less than the rate of return on domestic investment, the costs of holding reserves will exceed their potential benefits. The currency, therefore, should be revalued.

Currency revaluation will involve transitory costs as labor and capital move from contracting to expanding sectors, but such costs will be easier to bear since currency revaluation or appreciation will move the terms of trade in the nation's favor. The nation, in other words, will make the adjustments in an environment of *expanding*, not contracting, income.

Cost-benefit analysis leads to the conclusion that a country should never devalue its currency as long as it can borrow the funds required to finance its trade deficit on reasonable terms. In the previous example, we assumed that the nation in question ran a $10 trade deficit. If export supply elasticities are infinite and the sum of the import demand elasticities equals 1.5, the terms-of-trade cost of correcting the deficit by depreciation would be $20, which in this case measures the benefits of holding or borrowing reserves. If the nation can borrow $10 at a 20 percent interest rate, the cost of borrowing reserves would be $2, substantially less than $20. In this example, the cost of borrowing reserves would have to rise to 200 percent before it would make sense for the nation to devalue its currency.

If one looked at the choice over time, one might think that the country might want to devalue its currency once the cost of financing past and present imbalances exceeded the terms-of-trade costs of the devaluation. For example, using simple figures, if the nation ran a $10 deficit for 10 years, its annual cost of financing past deficits would equal $20—the cost of currency devaluation. But a depreciation in the tenth year will not reduce the cost of financing past imbalances; in fact, assuming the foreign debt is quoted in terms of a foreign currency, devaluation will raise the domestic currency cost of financing the external debt.

The important point is that at the margin, it is always cheaper for a country to borrow the needed reserves than to depreciate its currency—unless the interest rate soars to astronomical levels. This is one reason why debtor nations continue to add to their debts and why creditor countries are loathe to endorse an unlimited increase in the supply of international reserves.

International Money

IMF **drawing rights** define how much an individual country can borrow from the IMF.

Having described the demand for international reserves, we can now outline the supply of international reserves. Defining international money was simpler prior to the breakdown of the Bretton Woods system in the early 1970s. One simply added up a nation's gold and dollar holdings plus a portion of its IMF **drawing rights** and its allo-

TABLE 15.4 International Reserves: 1982—1994 (billions of SDRs)

Year	Total	Foreign Exchange	IMF	SDRs
1982	327.9	284.7	25.4	17.7
1984	407.0	349.0	41.6	16.5
1986	418.6	363.8	35.3	19.2
1988	542.6	494.2	28.3	20.2
1990	637.6	593.5	23.7	20.3
1992	692.9	646.2	33.9	12.9
1994	812.7	765.0	31.7	15.8

Source: International Monetary Fund, *International Financial Statistics Yearbook,* 1995, pp. 55, 59, 63. IMF-provided international reserves represent the reserve position of member states at the Fund. It is close to the gold tranche of the member states, which is discussed later in this chapter, but it does not equal the total borrowing rights of the member states, which are also discussed later in this chapter. The decline in IMF provided reserves between 1984 and 1990 indicates that member nations used an increasing proportion of their gold tranche during these years.

Special drawing rights (SDRs), sometimes referred to as paper gold, were conceived at the IMF annual meeting at Rio de Janeiro in 1967. Upon approval of its members, the IMF issues SDRs to its member countries who can use them as international reserves to settle international debts. There is a limit on the amount of SDRs a creditor nation must accept in settling debts.

cation of **special drawing rights (SDRs)** to obtain its international reserves. Gold, while still held by central banks, is not used as an international reserve at the present time and dollar holdings have been supplemented by mark and yen holdings. For the nations of the European Union, one would add their holdings of European currency units (ECUs) to the sum just mentioned to compute their international reserves. Table 15.4 provides a brief summary of the present-day composition of international reserves. As can be seen, foreign exchange holdings constitute the majority of international reserves. In fact, it is fair to say that other sources of international reserves are minuscule.

There is no universal agreement on which currencies should count as international reserves. But if a particular currency meets two criteria, popularity and convertibility, it is generally regarded as a reserve currency. If a currency is widely used in conducting international trade, it passes the first test. Since world trade is dominated by the United States, Japan, and Germany, the *dollar, mark,* and *yen* are regarded as major reserve currencies at the present time. The second criteria, and in many ways the acid test, is whether a currency is convertible. In other words, can individuals convert an unlimited amount of the particular currency into marks, yen, and dollars at a relatively constant price? If this is possible, foreign holdings of the currency will normally be counted as international reserves. (If Swiss francs are readily convertible into one or all of the three major world currencies, a Belgian will probably count his or her holdings of Swiss francs as international reserves.)

The Dilemma of Reserve Currency

There is a logic in using national currencies as international reserves. If a number of nations want to embrace fixed exchange rates but are unable to reach agreement on how international reserves should be created, it makes sense to employ the currency of the major nation or nations as international reserves. At the end of World War II, the United States was the world's economic powerhouse and the dollar became the dominant currency. But as other countries recovered from the effects of war and regained economic strength, the economic position of the United States relatively declined, and the dollar dwindled as the lone source of international liquidity.

Despite this fragmentation, the world or a group of nations may actually benefit more if only one currency is used as international reserves. Assuming that the reserve currency country follows a noninflationary policy, other nations are able to adopt its economic stability and make their anti-inflationary policies credible by tying their currencies to the reserve currency—consider the role of the mark and German monetary policy in fostering European-wide price stability. Thus if instilling monetary credibility is paramount in the eyes of the policymakers, the benefits derived from joining a currency zone, such as a dollar or mark zone, may exceed the costs associated with losing policy independence.

The reserve currency country also obtains benefits and incurs costs from such a setup. If the world is on a dollar standard, other nations must be able to obtain dollars in order to increase their international reserves, and, to do this, they will need to run trade surpluses with the United States. The United States, therefore, will be able to exchange pieces of paper for goods and services—although as suggested earlier the gain will be limited, since foreign nations will hold their dollar exchange reserves in short-term interest-bearing assets such as U.S. Treasury bills. Nevertheless, if the return on domestic investment in the United States exceeds the U.S. Treasury bill rate, the United States will obtain investment funds at a cheap rate.

The U.S. financial community will profit as well if the world adopts a dollar standard since a sizable portion of international trade will be financed in dollars. If the dollar serves as a **vehicle currency,** foreign firms could very well build up dollar deposits in American banks. Assuming such funds can be invested at a higher interest rate than the deposit rate, the reserve currency's financial institutions and the host country itself will gain.

The U.S. dollar is an example of a **vehicle currency.** Often, nonmajor currency countries will denominate their exports in U.S. dollars rather than in their own currency. Most trades on international commodity exchanges are denominated or priced in terms of U.S. dollars or pounds sterling.

All is not rosy however; being the world banker entails costs. The world will remain on a dollar standard only if it is confident that the dollar will be stable over the long run. Generating such assurance will constrain the conduct of U.S. monetary policy since the Fed will have to keep an eye on foreign attitudes and concerns when it conducts U.S. monetary policy. Rapid monetary expansion or a low interest rate policy, perhaps justified by the state of the U.S. economy, could generate fears of dollar depreciation and would have to be avoided. Moreover, if the dollar is the reserve currency, the United States will be unable to correct or modify its external position via currency depreciation. To the extent that depreciation promotes internal and external equilibrium, the freedom of action of the reserve currency country is restricted. It is not surprising, then, that today no country seems eager to play the role of banker.

From the world point of view, the real dilemma of a dollar (or mark or yen) standard is that in order to acquire international reserves, a nation must run a trade surplus with the United States or sell domestic financial assets in exchange for dollars. This means that the U.S. must run balance of payments deficits on an official reserve basis in order to expand the volume of international reserves. But if the United States rings up continual deficits, it will become a debtor nation, which may very well engender fears of an impending dollar depreciation. In such a setting, it is hard to believe that any country would either want to build up its dollar reserves or maintain its dollar holdings.

History bears this out. Despite heroic attempts to preserve it, the dollar standard collapsed in the early 1970s. There naturally followed a plethora of explanations of the collapse. Robert Triffin, however, had pointed out roughly 20 years prior to its collapse that any reserve system based on a particular currency would fail for reasons just cited.

Centrally Created Reserves

A country's **subscription** is the amount of money it pays into the International Monetary Fund when it joins the organization. Based on its subscription, a country is granted a **quota** which defines how much money it can borrow from the IMF.

The **General Arrangement to Borrow** is a line of credit provided to the International Monetary Fund by its major members.

The **gold tranche** is the proportion of a member's line of credit at the IMF that can be automatically borrowed. It equals 25 percent of the country's subscription to the IMF. The remaining portions of a country's line of credit, called **credit tranches,** are more difficult to obtain.

Normally, if a country wants to borrow more than 50 percent of its drawing rights, it must submit a letter, the so-called **letter of intent,** describing the policies it plans to follow to overcome the difficulties which led to its request for funds.

The internal contradiction inherent in utilizing national currencies as international reserves has been recognized for a long time. Indeed, the need for centrally created international reserves was a paramount concern when the IMF was established in 1944.

The IMF provides international liquidity by two routes. First, member states, roughly 150 nations, can borrow from the Fund based on their **subscription** or **quota;** second, the IMF creates paper gold or SDRs (special drawing rights), which nations can use as international money. The major difference is that SDRs are owned by the nation and can be used at its discretion. Quotas and subscription rights are a line of credit and can be employed only with the permission of the IMF.

On becoming a member, a nation pays or subscribes a certain sum of money, valued in SDRs, to the Fund. Suppose, neglecting SDR conversion, a nation's subscription equals 100 pesos. Of this amount, 25 percent is paid to the Fund either in SDRs or dollars and the remaining amount in pesos or the national currency.

This means that a large chunk of the IMF's resources, roughly 50 percent, is fairly useless. Countries want to borrow dollars, yen, and marks—not pesos and bolivianos. The Fund, however, can supplement its holdings of major currencies by borrowing them from major countries (some $26 billion as of mid-1995, but due to be expanded) under the **General Arrangement to Borrow** and also under the provisions of the Enhanced Structural Adjustment Facility, which is described in Box 15.2.

Based on its subscription, a nation has certain borrowing rights. It can borrow the first 25 percent of its quota, what is called the **gold tranche,** at will. In addition, a member state can borrow an additional 100 percent of its quota in the form of four **credit tranches.** The first credit tranche can be quite readily obtained, but further requests for funds must normally be accompanied by a plan designed to get the borrowing nation's economic house in order. The content of the plan—which usually includes fiscal, monetary, and exchange-rate policies—is spelled out in the **letter of intent** that the borrowing nation submits to the Fund.

As is evident, the majority of IMF drawing rights cannot be considered international reserves. With the exception of the gold tranche, a member state must agree to abide with selected policies when it borrows from the Fund. There is nothing unique about such a requirement; nations must satisfy certain conditions when they raise funds on private markets. The important difference is that the IMF is more likely to lend to its member states when they are in financial distress than are private institutions. In fact, private lenders often wait until a nation agrees to carry out an IMF-sponsored stabilization program before extending it credit.

Special Drawing Rights

Special drawing rights (SDRs), created by the IMF in 1970, is a composite currency whose value is computed from the weighted value of five currencies that make it up: the dollar (with a weight of 42%), yen (15%), D-mark (19%), French franc (12%), and the pound (12%), the weights of which are reviewed and, if necessary, revised every five years. To the extent that trade and financial transactions are carried out in SDRs,

The **Extended Fund Facility,** established in 1974, allows members to borrow up to 140 percent of their quotas for three to four years to help them overcome structural imbalances.

The **Compensatory and Contingency Financing Facility (CCFF)** was set up in 1963. Its objective is to help members overcome the impact of a fall in export earnings or a rise in the price of cereal imports which are beyond its control. Under its provisions, a member can borrow up to 100 percent of its quota. The *Buffer Stock Financing Facility*, established in 1969, which helps nations finance their contributions to approved international buffer stock schemes, is part of the compensatory and contingency financing facility.

The **Structural Adjustment Facility (SAF)** was created in 1986. Under its provisions, the IMF provides a line of credit to a member nation to help them finance structural reforms, such as financial reform to encourage greater domestic savings. Under the SAF and the **Enhanced Structural Adjustment Facility (ESAF),** which was established in 1988, the IMF extends loans, primarily to LDCs and Eastern European countries, for periods of up to 10 years at subsidized or below market rates of interest.

BOX 15.2 · Current Provisions of the IMF

The International Monetary Fund's facilities have expanded over the years. The **Extended Fund Facility,** established in 1974, increased the size of the credit tranche relative to a member's quota and lengthened the duration of IMF loans. Under it and other new arrangements, a member can borrow approximately 450 percent of its quota for up to seven years in certain instances compared with the normal repayment period of three to five years. Two new facilities of special interest to raw material producers were instituted in the 1960s: the *Compensatory Financing Facility* and the *Buffer Stock Financing Facility* which, for accounting purposes, have been merged into the **Compensatory and Contingency Financing Facility (CCFF).** The facility assists member nations in offsetting variations in foreign exchange earnings caused by cyclical swings in the price and volume of raw material exports or unforeseen increases in import prices. During the first OPEC crisis of 1973–74, when the price of oil quadrupled, a special facility was established to help LDCs cope with resulting balance-of-payments difficulties. In 1990, on the heels of the Gulf War, an oil facility was created or added to the CCFF which was designed to assist LDCs to maintain oil imports in the face of higher oil prices. The facility was suspended at the end of 1991.

The IMF established two new facilities in 1986 and 1988: the **Structural Adjustment Facility (SAF)** and the **Enhanced Structural Adjustment Facility (ESAF).** Their creation signaled a broadening of IMF concerns and interests. During its first 40 years, Fund policy was devoted almost exclusively to providing countries a line of credit when they faced a temporary shortfall of international reserves; the IMF was not in the business of lending funds for development or structural adjustment. The Fund, however, became convinced that structural adjustment was an essential prerequisite for economic stability in many LDCs and in most Eastern European nations. The SAF and the ESAF attempt to help nations overcome structural problems, such as reforming the domestic financial system in order to create more efficient financial markets and to encourage greater savings. Under the programs, which are spelled out in **Policy Framework Papers (PFP),** a nation can borrow between 70 percent and 250 percent, 350 percent in exceptional circumstances, of its quota at a .5 percent interest rate. Moreover, loan repayment does not begin until 5.5 years after disbursement and is amortized over 10 years. This signaled a break with IMF traditions. Yet, it is fair to say that notwithstanding the SAF and ESAF arrangements, which equaled roughly 13.5 percent of IMF disbursements at the end of 1993, most IMF programs are designed to provide short-term international liquidity. In 1992 the IMF established the **Systemic Transformation Facility** to provide modest assistance to hard-pressed transitional economies of the former communist bloc.

---

traders avoid the consequences of a sharp drop in one particular currency. If the dollar declines 10 percent while the mark rises 10 percent, the value of the SDR remains constant (the unequal weighting of the currencies throws this off a bit).

SDRs are markedly different from IMF drawing or borrowing rights. Unlike drawing rights, which require an initial deposit, SDRs are created by the stroke of a pen when 85 percent of IMF members vote to create them. (IMF voting is weighted so that big nations have more clout than small ones.) Once the decision to create SDRs has been made, the IMF credits each nation's account with its allocation, which is based on its importance in the world economy. A nation can use its SDRs as it sees fit and all IMF members are obligated to accept SDR payments up to 3 times their allocation. So if Mexico and Germany are each allocated SDR10 and Mexico has an SDR10 trade deficit with Germany, it can use its SDRs to finance the deficit since Germany has to accept an additional SDR20 as payment for its exports.

Policy Framework Papers (PFP) spell out the policies a nation plans to follow when it borrows funds from the IMF under the Structural Adjustment Facility or the Enhanced Structural Adjustment Facility.

The **Systemic Transformation Facility** (1992) provides modest assistance to hard-pressed transitional economies of the former communist bloc.

It is readily understandable why creditor nations are wary of endorsing a rapid expansion in the supply of SDRs despite the interest they receive on their holdings of SDRs. (The interest rate equals a weighted average of Treasury bill rates prevailing in the five nations whose currencies make up the SDR.) SDRs, like any form of international liquidity, primarily benefit nations with balance-of-payments deficits. Some economists argue this is all to the good and that SDR creation could be one way for the rich to help the poor. Under what has been called **project link,** all newly created SDRs would be allocated to LDCs so that international reserve expansion would be coupled with economic assistance for the most needy.

Given the logic of basing international liquidity on centrally created reserves, SDRs could replace foreign exchange as the major source of international liquidity in the future. But the figures presented in Table 15.4 suggest that this is a long way off. The possibility of creating a **currency substitution account** under IMF auspices was bandied about in the late 1970s when there was a worldwide excess supply of dollars. According to the plan, nations would sell unwanted dollars to the IMF for SDRs at a predetermined exchange rate. Such a conversion would have been a striking step toward international monetary reform. Nations would have received an interest-paying asset with an exchange rate guarantee in place of unwanted dollars. The plan did not find support and failed for two reasons. The United States opposed the plan since it would have dethroned the dollar; at the same time, the dollar gained strength on foreign exchange markets, and central banks reconsidered the wisdom of selling off their dollars. Today, the possible need or demand for a substitution account is remote since major currencies float against each other.

The Crawling Peg

Project link. A proposal to relate the creation of international reserves to economic assistance to the most needy. For example, under a link project, all new SDRs would go to less-developed countries. As they spent the SDRs, worldwide international reserves would increase.

Currency substitution account. An idea of the late 1970s. Under the proposal, countries would convert any unwanted dollar reserves into SDRs or some type of IMF deposit. The plan never got off the ground.

Often, nations with close economic relationships are better served if they tie their exchange rates together rather than let them float. This supposition has led some economists to predict that the world will evolve into **currency zones** in which individual currencies are pegged to the dominant member's currency. Latin American currencies would peg to the dollar, for example, and European currencies to the mark, and Asian currencies to the yen. It is possible (though developments in 1992 and 1993 cast doubt) that intrazone bilateral exchange rate stability could be maintained in Europe. Such stability is highly unlikely in the Americas since the countries of the Western hemisphere historically have had widely divergent rates of inflation and it is impossible to peg currencies under such conditions.

Some economists believe the **crawling peg** (which was briefly described in Chapter 14) might be the best option when exchange rate stability is not possible. Under a crawling peg, a nation agrees to depreciate its currency against a major currency by a stated amount at regular (monthly or weekly) intervals. Imagine that the Mexican peso is tied to the U.S. dollar, but that Mexico's annual rate of inflation is 6 percent higher than the U.S. rate of inflation. Under a crawling peg, Mexico would "institutionalize" a monthly .5 percent depreciation of the peso.

What are the advantages of such an arrangement? If the peso were pegged to the dollar, it would quickly become overvalued, given the divergent rates of inflation between Mexico and the United States. An overvalued peso harms Mexico's export industries and can lead to a massive capital flight as firms and individuals attempt to protect the

Currency zones. An area or economic zone in which all countries tie their currencies to the currency of the major area economic power. For example, all European currencies would be tied to or set in terms of the German mark.

Under a **crawling peg**, a nation pegs its currency to another currency, such as the Mexican peso to the U.S. dollar. But the exchange rate—pesos per dollar—is adjusted, normally depreciated, by a specified amount at regular intervals, such as weekly or monthly.

international purchasing power of their assets by selling pesos. A crawling peg, it is claimed, eliminates the first problem by initiating a program of continuous depreciation. Second, capital flights normally occur when individuals fear that a currency is about to be devalued or that a government will introduce exchange controls in order to avoid or postpone such action. Under the crawling peg, the rate of depreciation is known and this knowledge reduces uncertainty and eliminates the need for exchange controls.

What are the crawling peg's drawbacks? If Mexico states that the peso is going to depreciate 6 percent a year against the dollar, Mexican interest rates will have to be sufficiently high to deter liquid assets from migrating overseas—in this case 6 percent above those in the United States. This appears to be a large differential. But in the typical inflationary situation, interest-rate differentials tend to equal or surpass the expected rate of depreciation of one currency against another. If people anticipate that the peso will depreciate 6 percent against the dollar, Mexican interest rates will most likely be at least 6 percent higher than comparable U.S. interest rates.

A second criticism of the crawling peg is that it makes it easier for a nation to follow inflationary policies. Under a fixed-rate regime, a government is compelled to follow a noninflationary monetary policy in order to preserve the exchange rate. Under the crawling peg, there is no such constraint. A built-in 6 percent peso depreciation against the dollar allows Mexico to inflate by at least this rate or even more if the United States has a positive rate of inflation. Nor does a crawling peg guarantee that the Mexican rate of inflation will be only 6 percent above the U.S. rate of inflation. If the Mexican rate of inflation picks up, the crawl could be adjusted upward.

Crawl proponents assert that if the crawl is continuously raised, it will lose credibility. In a word, the crawling peg does not eliminate the need for monetary discipline. Indeed, proponents view the crawl as a first step toward reducing the rate of inflation. If the crawl and the monetary policy upon which it is based become credible, the crawl and the rate of inflation could be reduced to ever-lower levels.

A major criticism of the crawling peg is that it is too simplistic. Mexico introduced a crawling peg of 2 percent against the dollar in the early 1990s, but later changed it to 4 percent. However, the peso depreciated by some *50 percent* against the dollar at the end of 1994 even though, on the face of it, the crawl appeared to be working reasonably well. The Mexican rate of inflation was only 4 to 5 percent higher than the rate of inflation in the United States, and Mexican short-term interest rates were roughly 10 percent higher than comparable U.S. interest rates. Perhaps the crawl should have been adjusted upward by some 1 percent, but the statistics did not portend a collapse of the peso.

As described in Box 4.2, the Mexican current-account deficit grew from 1990 on. This meant that to maintain the value of the peso, Mexico had to rely on capital inflows and spend its international reserves. When the capital stopped flowing into Mexico and instead started to flow out, the Mexican government had to throw increasing quantities of its international reserves into the foreign exchanges in order to bolster the peso. But the reserves ran out and Mexico had to allow the peso to depreciate.

What does Mexico's calamity mean for the utility of the crawling peg? We conclude that simply maintaining inflation and interest differentials is not sufficient to maintain a fixed exchange rate. If the trade balance were determined by price differentials alone and the capital account depended solely on interest differentials, a crawling peg would have a chance at succeeding. But if the trade balance and capital flows depend upon more than inflation and interest differentials, a crawling peg can work only if a government takes all economic factors, both monetary and real, into account.

BOX 15.3 Currency Boards

Under a **currency board,** a nation ties its money supply or its **monetary base** to its holdings of foreign exchange reserves. For example, under its currency board arrangement, Argentina can expand its monetary base only if the nation's dollar reserves increase.

The Mexican peso crisis reduced the allure of the crawling peg and sparked a renewed interest in **currency boards.** Under a currency board, such as practiced in Argentina, the exchange rate is fixed at a certain parity such as one peso per dollar, and all citizens have the right to convert pesos into dollars at this exchange rate. A currency board can be called a fixed exchange rate with teeth. It does more than simply declare that a nation will maintain a fixed exchange rate; it establishes a monetary structure which presumably guarantees it.

Under a pure currency board, the domestic money supply, Argentine pesos for example, is fully backed by a foreign currency, such as U.S. dollars. The domestic money supply, therefore, expands and contracts as dollar reserves expand and contract. (Actually Argentina's currency board is not a pure one. The dollar backing is limited to the *monetary base,* a term defined in Chapter 13. Since the Argentine money supply is a multiple of the monetary base, it is not fully backed by official holdings of dollars.)

What does a currency board arrangement achieve? Since the supply of Argentine pesos is limited by the supply of dollars held by the Argentine central bank, it is claimed there can never be an excess supply of pesos, implying that the Argentine peso will never come under selling pressure. Suppose that the Argentine central bank decides to expand the supply of pesos even though the nation's holdings of international reserves is constant. The increase in the supply of pesos will cause the peso/dollar exchange rate to drop. Since under the arrangement Argentine citizens can convert pesos into dollars on demand at a set price, they will do so. As a result, the central bank will end up holding pesos and the citizens holding dollars, and the Argentine economy will become *dollarized.* (Of course, if the central bank decides to plunge ahead with peso creation, the currency board system would collapse.)

Assuming that Argentina sticks to a currency board, Argentina's monetary policy will be credible. And given that credibility, it is claimed that the peso will never come under a speculative attack. Thus, even though the Argentine stock market took a hit when the Mexican peso depreciated in December 1995, the Argentine peso maintained its parity with the dollar.

What are the potential drawbacks of a currency board? Critics argue that the theoretical foundations of the currency board are basically monetarist, in other words, that payments imbalances reflect an imbalance between the supply and demand for money. But suppose the U.S. economy goes into a recession and U.S. imports from Argentina decline leading to a potential full employment trade deficit in Argentina. In that case, the United States would "sneeze" and Argentina could very well "catch pneumonia." And Argentina's ability to offset the effects of external developments would be seriously constrained.

Obviously, it would be impossible to devalue the peso without giving up on the currency board. But the greater drawback is that it would be almost impossible for Argentina to use its dollar holdings as international reserves, since if in the attempt to maintain its national income it used its dollar holdings to finance a trade deficit, the Argentine money supply would decline, which would impart downward pressure on the Argentine economy.

The hope is that if Argentina maintained its interest rates while interest rates dropped in the United States, and individuals were convinced that the peso/dollar exchange rate would not move, foreign funds would flow into Argentina. The inflow of capital would increase Argentina's international reserves and give it flexibility in conducting its monetary policy. This may be a lot to hope for.

Sources: "Economic Focus: Pegging Currencies," *The Economist* (January 14, 1995); p. 68; Paul Krugman, "Monetary Virtue Leads Two-Peso Tussle," *Financial Times* (July 13, 1995); p. 17.

Target Zones

Under the **target zone** proposal currencies would be allowed to fluctuate within a broad band. If, for example, the *fundamental equilibrium exchange rate* is DM1.5/$, the exchange rate might be allowed to fluctuate between DM1.65/$ and DM1.35/$, or within a 10 percent band on each side of the target exchange rate. The zone would, therefore, be a 20 percent zone.

The **fundamental equilibrium exchange rate (FEER)** is the exchange rate which balances exports and imports plus or minus underlying long-term capital flows at the full employment level of income. In turn, underlying capital flows are determined by underlying savings and investment patterns in various countries.

If intrazone exchange rate stability can be maintained, how then should exchange rates between the dominant currencies be determined? In other words, how are the DM/$, ¥/$, and DM/¥ rates determined? The usual answer is to let the major currencies *float* against each other. But we assume policymakers want to establish and maintain fixed exchange rates.

Nearly everyone agrees that it would be difficult, if not impossible, to maintain the ¥/$ rate within a narrow band. But some economists believe that it is possible to avoid wide swings in that exchange rate. To that end, John Williamson offered his **target zone** proposal. Under his plan, the three major exchange rates would be allowed to fluctuate within a broad band. The first step in the process would be for Germany, Japan, and the United States to establish what he calls **fundamental equilibrium exchange rates (FEERs),** rates that balance imports and exports plus or minus underlying long-term capital flows at full employment levels of income.

Underlying long-term capital flows are based on underlying savings and investment decisions in the various countries. For example, if the level of savings exceeds the level of investment in Japan, Japan will or should run a trade surplus. And if the level of investment exceeds the level of savings in the United States, the United States should run a trade deficit. In fact, if despite the existence of excess investment the United States runs a trade surplus, the current exchange rate will not be a fundamental equilibrium rate.

This means that fundamental exchange rates cannot be fixed in stone. A change in underlying capital flows, for example, may require exchange rate adjustment. In addition, if German productivity grows at twice the rate of U.S. productivity, it is difficult to see how a given exchange rate can be maintained. However, since the target zone proposal assumes that the nations will follow similar long-run monetary policies, exchange rates would not have to be adjusted for inflation differentials.

Given fundamental exchange rates, the next step is to establish exchange rate targets and attempt to maintain them. The target, however, would not be a set rate such as DM2/$, but rather a band around the central or fundamental rate. The exchange rate would be permitted to oscillate above and below its central rate by a predetermined margin. For example, given a 10 percent margin on each side of parity or a 20 percent band, the German and American authorities would attempt to keep the mark/dollar rate within the DM2.2/$ and DM1.8/$ range, assuming a fundamental rate of DM2/$. A 20 percent band is quite wide. However, target zone proponents contend it would be foolhardy to institute exchange rate targets with narrow bands at the outset.

A narrow band, such as the 1.5 percent band that existed under the Bretton Woods system, would be difficult to defend. Prior to 1971, speculators had a field day because of the narrow (.75 percent) margins on each side of parity. If the official rate stood at DM4/$, and an individual suspected that the mark was going to rise, she would sell dollars and purchase marks. In carrying out this transaction, she would not have to pay more than DM4.03/$ when she bought marks since the German government was committed to purchasing all dollars offered at this price. If the mark appreciated by at least 1.5 percent, the speculator was home free. If the dollar strengthened and the speculator had to unwind her deal, her greatest possible loss would be 1.5 percent because the mark could not fall below DM3.97/$. At this price, the U.S. government was compelled to purchase all marks offered for sale in order to keep the exchange rate within permissible margins.

With a 20 percent rather than 1.5 percent band, a speculator would have more to lose if he made the wrong decision. For example, he could sell the dollar at close to its lower limit and watch in horror as the dollar rose to its upper limit. Presumably, the fear of such potential losses would damp down speculative capital movements.

Even if there were a need to adjust the central or fundamental rate, a wide band would help. If it became necessary to depreciate the dollar by 10 percent from DM2/$ to DM1.8/$, the new upper limit of the dollar, DM2/$, would exceed its old lower limit, DM1.8/$. Thus despite the depreciation, the dollar could still rise. Speculators would still be denied the possibility of one-way speculation. Figure 15.2 charts out this situation. The solid lines represent the band and the dotted line shows the movement of the actual exchange rate.

Some target zone proponents take comfort in the relative stability of intra-European exchange rates that occurred following the restructuring of the European Union's exchange rate mechanism (ERM) in the fall of 1993. At that time, ERM exchange rates were permitted to float within a 30 percent band. However, with the exception of the Spanish peseta, rather than moving up or down toward the band limits, the spread between the currency with the largest upward deviation from its central rate and the currency with the largest downward deviation from its central rate hardly ever exceeded 6 percent.

Skeptics point out that intra-European exchange rate stability is different from maintaining ¥/$ stability. For one thing, exchange rate stability within the ERM occurred only after many central exchange rates were adjusted and some nations had opted out of the ERM. Moreover, given the growth of international capital markets, skeptics are convinced that central banks will never have sufficient international reserves to stem a concerted sell-off of a particular currency and hence will never again be able to maintain exchange rates within a target zone. In fact, the proposed widened band is an admission that a narrow band cannot be sustained. This raises the question: Can a *wider* band be maintained?

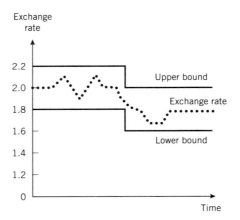

FIGURE 15.2 Change in the exchange rate band.

Under the band proposal, an exchange rate is permitted to fluctuate between certain limits. As the exchange rate threatens to breech one of these limits, the band is adjusted. Ostensibly, adjusting the band will reduce or eliminate the possibility of one-way currency speculation, since after the band is adjusted the exchange rate can go up as well as down.

Coordinating Economic Policies

The foundation of the target zone proposal—what ultimately will make it work—is policy coordination and convergence, and international monetary cooperation. If the economic policies of Germany, Japan, and the United States fly off in different directions, no power on earth will be able to maintain key currency exchange rates. But international monetary cooperation requires more than harmonizing monetary policies among key currency nations. It requires central banks to take into account the external as well as the internal consequences of their actions.

Consider the following example, based on the work of Professor Ronald McKinnon. Suppose there is a worldwide increase in the demand for dollars such as occurred in the early 1980s when the dollar soared on the foreign exchanges. In order to maintain exchange rates, the Fed must increase the U.S. money supply to satisfy the increased demand for dollars. Since the increase in the demand for dollars implies a relative reduction in the demand for marks and yen, Germany and Japan, in turn must reduce their money supplies. These steps would have two beneficial results: They would maintain exchange rates and would maintain the world money supply, which would avoid the possible inflationary/deflationary consequences of the increase or decrease in the world money supply.

If the central banks were to simply maintain their respective money supplies given the relative increase in the demand for dollars, the higher demand for dollars would cause U.S. interest rates to rise and would lead to a capital flow that would cause the dollar to appreciate and the mark and yen to depreciate. In the end, Germany and Japan would become more competitive with expected consequences. The bright side is that since the world money supply would remain constant, the increased demand for dollars would not have a worldwide inflationary effect.

On the other hand, if the United States increased its money supply in line with the increased demand for dollars, and both Germany and Japan held their money supplies constant, the results would be different. Exchange rates would move in the same direction as before, although not as much as in the first case. However, the world money supply and potential inflation would increase.

The key point is that international monetary cooperation requires central banks to adopt new perceptions of how monetary policy should be conducted. For example, a 5 percent annual increase in the money supply could represent either a "loose," "tight," or "neutral" monetary policy depending on what is happening on the foreign exchanges. If the dollar appreciated even though the U.S. money supply was increasing at 5 percent, we would conclude that the demand for dollars exceeded the supply of dollars and that U.S. monetary policy was tight; if the dollar was depreciating, it would signal that monetary policy was too loose.

This does not mean that the Federal Reserve, for example, can or should take its eyes off the domestic economy. Its long-run objective, according to Professor McKinnon, should be to stabilize the wholesale prices of America's potential exports. If the central banks of Germany, Japan, and the United States can do this, they will be able to maintain constant purchasing power exchange rates. Maintaining purchasing power parity exchange rates will go a long way toward eliminating the need to raise and lower rates of monetary growth in order to accommodate shifts in the international demand for a particular currency.

Policy Coordination: A Pessimistic View

Much of the skepticism concerning international policy coordination is not a criticism of the concept, but rather a concern that it may be unattainable. Nations may not be willing to coordinate their policies or may be willing to do so only up to a point due to different national preferences or because they face different economic problems.

Figure 15.3 shows a hypothetical short-run aggregate supply curve that is similar for Germany and the United States. Imagine that at least over the short-to-medium run it is possible for either nation to position its aggregate demand curve anywhere along this supply curve. What position will each nation select? Greater output means lower unemployment, but also higher prices. If we assume the countries are the same size and have the same propensities to import, same elasticities, and so forth, external equilibrium requires that both nations have similar aggregate demand schedules.

If Germans prefer low inflation over low unemployment, they will want to be at point *G* on the aggregate supply schedule. The United States, however, may prefer the point *US*, since it is willing to accept higher inflation if it can reduce unemployment. Given these differences, when will the nations cooperate, and when will their preferences cause conflict? If both economies happen to *lie below* the point *G* or *above* the point *US*, they will cooperate, since both will move to either eliminate recession or to stamp out inflation. But between points *G* and *US*, there is a *conflict* over which economic policy should be followed.

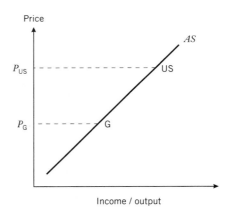

FIGURE 15.3 Cooperation or conflict: I.

Figure 15.3 shows a short-run aggregate supply schedule that is similar for Germany and the United States. In order to balance their bilateral trade position at a fixed exchange rate, their price levels must be similar, or their aggregate demand schedules must intersect the *AS* curve at the same point. But if Germany prefers low inflation, P_G, while the United States prefers a higher rate of inflation in order to generate a higher level of output and lower unemployment, P_{US}, a conflict can arise. When the price level is below P_G, both nations will want to stimulate aggregate demand; and when the price level is above P_{US}, both nations will want to repress aggregate demand. But when the price level lies between P_{US} and P_G, the nations will be in conflict. Germany will want to repress aggregate demand, while the United States will want to stimulate it.

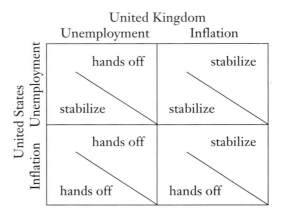

FIGURE 15.4 Cooperation or conflict: II.

Suppose the pound comes under pressure and starts to fall. Will the UK and the United States cooperate in stabilizing the pound on the foreign exchanges? The pay-off matrix shows that in only two cases will the countries agree on what should be done. And in only one case, when the UK faces inflation and the United States faces unemployment, will they agree to cooperate in stabilizing the international value of the pound.

Figure 15.4 shows an additional scenario of potential conflict. Even if the countries have similar preferences between inflation and unemployment, they may face different economic predicaments. Imagine, for example, that the pound drops by 10 percent. Will the countries cooperate to stabilize the value of the pound? The answer depends on whether the nations face unemployment or inflation.

Each nation can choose either to stabilize the pound or to follow a hands-off policy. The UK will attempt to stabilize the pound if it faces inflation and follows a hands-off policy and allows the pound to depreciate when it is confronted with unemployment. (The British choice is shown at the top of each cell.) American officials will select exactly the opposite combination as do their British counterparts. If the United States faces unemployment, it will want the pound to rise or the dollar to depreciate; but if domestic inflation is the major concern, pound depreciation (dollar appreciation) is the best option for the United States. As the grid shows, cooperation will take place in only *half* of the possible cases—in those cases in which Britain and America face opposite problems. And in one of them—when Britain faces unemployment and America faces inflation, the nations will attempt to push the value of the pound lower. Granted, pound depreciation is no doubt best for both nations in these circumstances. But in this case, economic cooperation will not push the pound toward the assumed target exchange rate.

Criticisms of Target Zones

The target zone proposal has been criticized on practical as well as analytical grounds. Target zones, at least in a weak form, were adopted when the **Louvre Accord** was signed in early 1987. At that time, the finance ministers of the large OECD nations— Canada, France, Germany, Italy, Japan, the UK, and the United States—claimed that bilateral exchange rates were at or close to their equilibrium values as dictated by eco-

The **Louvre Accord.** An agreement "signed" by major countries in the spring of 1987. Under the agreement, the major countries agreed to attempt to halt the slide in the dollar that was taking place at that time.

nomic fundamentals, and implied that intergovernmental cooperation would help to maintain them. Obviously, the policy was either not forthcoming, ineffective, or both since exchange rates have gyrated since the signing of the Accord.

The Louvre Accord, however, was and remains a far cry from target zones. There are differences between the proposals embodied in the Accord and the target zone concept, which, while important, are not the stuff of violent schisms. For example, one difference involves the tendency to refer to and perhaps concentrate on bilateral nominal exchange rates under the Accord rather than real multilateral exchange rates as under the target zone proposal. Such differences are minor compared with the major one: There is little indication that the agreement ushered in an era of economic policy convergence that is the keystone for a target zone proposal. If the Louvre Accord was the first step toward target zones, it was at best a halting one.

Target zone critics believe that the degree of policy coordination and national self-sacrifice required to make a target zone viable is so large that the proposal is not practicable. Moreover, they feel that the plan is unrealistic. If exchange rates can vary no more than 10 percent on either side of the target rate, they can realistically never be allowed to vary that much. For if an exchange rate should approach one of its limits, unstoppable market pressures could quickly drive the rate beyond such a boundary.

Target zone proponents do not dismiss these criticisms. And it is for this reason that they suggest that only three exchange rates be targeted. But they are persuaded that the global economic environment will improve and erratic exchange rate fluctuations will be damped down if a small measure of policy coordination can be attained. Finally, target zone proponents are quick to point out that the crawling peg and target zones did not spring from theoretical dreaming. They evolved from historical experience and the hard lesson that the current international monetary regime is flawed. If steps are taken to improve it, it will encourage rather than hinder international trade.

Summary

Traditionally, the operation of a system of fixed exchange rates was thought to entail only two features: (1) a firm commitment on the part of governments *not* to follow inflationary policies and (2) a stock of international reserves to help nations finance temporary deficits. Since it was assumed that governments would follow noninflationary policies if they wanted a system of fixed exchange rates, much of the analysis of a fixed exchange rate system concentrated on how international reserves would be provided or created. However, by stressing the possible need for a crawling peg, fixed-rate advocates recognize that in certain cases only a *moving* fixed rate is possible. Moreover, they are aware that, given the growth of international capital markets, international reserves by themselves may not be sufficient to maintain a system of fixed rates at least within a narrow band. Something more, namely international monetary cooperation, is required.

Key Concepts and Terms

benefits of international reserves

compensatory and contingency financing facility

costs of international reserves

crawling peg

credit tranche

currency board

currency substitution account

currency zones

drawing rights

enlarged access policy

extended fund facility

fundamental equilibrium exchange rates

general arrangement to borrow

gold tranche

IMF subscriptions and quotas

international reserves

letter of intent

policy framework papers

precautionary cash reserve

reserves/imports ratios

special drawing rights (SDRs)

structural adjustment facility and the enhanced structural adjustment facility

target zones

Review Questions

1. Analyze the costs and benefits of holding international reserves. What determines the benefits of holding reserves?

2. Briefly describe the following:
   (a) Special drawing rights
   (b) Key currencies
   (c) Gold tranche
   (d) Letter of intent
   (e) Widened band

3. What difficulties arise when one national currency is used as international reserves?

4. Describe the costs and benefits associated with being a reserve currency nation.

5. What is the major problem that must be overcome if a system of centrally created reserves is to be established?

6. What are currency zones? Are they the same as target zones?

References and Suggested Readings

Brian Tew, *The Evolution of the International Monetary System: 1945–85*, 3rd edition (London: Hutchinson, 1985), is an excellent historical survey of the international monetary system. One of the first economists to point out the inadequacies of the Bretton Woods system was Robert Triffin. His analysis is contained in his book, *Gold and the Dollar Crisis* (New Haven: Yale University Press, 1960). The *Annual Report* of the International Monetary Fund contains a yearly appraisal of the international economy and a description of the uses of the Fund's facilities by member states.

The crawling peg was first proposed by John Williamson, *The Crawling Peg*, Essays in International Finance no. 50 (Princeton, NJ: International Finance Section, Princeton University, December 1965). A brief book on currency boards is John Williamson, *What Role for Currency Boards?* (Washington, DC: Institute for International Economics, 1995). Williamson's proposal for target zones is contained in his book, *The Exchange Rate System*, 2nd edition (Washington, DC: Institute for International Economics, 1985). Briefer descriptions of the concept can be found in John Williamson, "Exchange Rate Management: The Role of Target Zones," *American Economic Review, Papers, and Proceedings* 77 (May 1987); pp. 200–204; "Economic Focus: European Currencies," *The Economist* (May 8, 1993); p. 83; and Lars E.O. Svensson, "An Interpretation of Recent Research on Exchange Rate Target Zones," *Journal of Economic Perspectives* 6 (Fall 1992).

Ronald I. McKinnon's original argument for policy coordination is contained in his *An International Standard for Monetary Stabilization* (Washington, DC: Institute for International Economics, 1984). While still fundamentally the same, his more recent proposal is explained in his article "Monetary and Exchange Rate Policies for International Financial Stability: A Proposal," *Journal of Economic Perspectives* 2 (Winter 1988): pp. 83–103. Also see the comments on his proposal by John Williamson, "Comments on McKinnon's Monetary Rule," and by Rudiger Dornbusch, "Doubts About the McKinnon Standard," in the same issue of the *Journal of Economic Perspectives*.

George A. Kahn wrote a very readable article on "International Policy Coordination in an Interdependent World," Federal Reserve Bank of Kansas City *Economic Review* 77 (March 1987): pp. 14–32. Yoichi Funabashi reviews international monetary policy in his book, *Managing the Dollar: From the Plaza to the Louvre* (Washington, DC: Institute for International Economics, 1988).

PART 6

Current Economic Issues

Chapter 16

Economic Integration

A **free trade area** is a group of nations that abolishes intragroup trade restrictions, but permits each nation to maintain its own, and perhaps different, trade restrictions vis-à-vis nonmembers.

A **customs union** consists of a group of countries that abolish intraregional trade restrictions and *also* erect a common tariff on trade with nonmembers.

A **common market** is a customs union which attempts to develop common policies in matters other than international trade. For example, the European Union has introduced unionwide policies in agriculture, international monetary policy, social legislation, and so on.

Just as courtship involves several steps before a perfect union is achieved, there are several steps on the path toward full or complete economic integration. The first step is to form a **free trade area.** A free trade area, such as the former European Free Trade Association (EFTA) and the North American Free Trade Agreement (NAFTA), abolishes trade barriers between member countries, but permits each country to set its own tariffs and quotas with nonmember nations. Thus if Denmark, Norway, and Sweden formed a free trade area, a Volvo could enter Denmark and Norway duty free, while a Volkswagen that might enter Denmark duty free could confront a 100 percent tariff at the Norwegian and Swedish frontiers.

A **customs union** takes economic integration a step further. It eliminates trade restrictions within the region and establishes a common external tariff applicable to all members. If a Volkswagen faced a 50 percent tariff at the Swedish border, it would face the same tariff at the Danish and Norwegian borders.

A **common market** goes even further than a customs union. Besides abolishing trade barriers between member states and instituting a common external tariff, it seeks the full economic integration of its members. In the European Union (EU), then called the European Economic Community (EEC), the move toward full integration led to the establishment of the Common Agricultural Policy (CAP), the European Monetary System (EMS), plus a number of measures designed to promote labor and capital mobility within the area, harmonize national codes in order to eliminate nontariff barriers to trade, and promote competition. These latter steps were summarized in the **Single European Act of 1987,** more commonly known as the single market act or *1992,* the date when the provisions of the Single European Act were introduced across the European Union.

The final step toward full economic integration is the creation of an **economic union.** At this stage, as envisioned under the provisions of the **Maastricht Treaty,** the European Union will adopt a single currency and create a European central bank charged with carrying out a unionwide monetary policy. British pounds, Dutch guilder, German marks, and so on will be replaced by a European currency, and the Bank of England, the Bundesbank, and other European central banks will fade away.

The **Single European Act of 1987** set out to abolish all nontariff barriers to trade within the EU, and to eliminate all restrictions on capital and labor mobility within the region. The act came into force on January 1, 1993.

Economic integration poses its share of problems. On the one hand, regional economic integration will increase intraregional trade and expand its members' economic welfare. But by erecting a common external tariff, regional integration may contract trade between member and nonmember countries and reduce the members' economic welfare. Since a customs union can both expand and reduce its members' economic welfare, the question is whether the net welfare effect is positive or negative.

In addition, by reducing internal trade barriers, to say nothing of creating a common external tariff, regional integration may diminish the level of trade between the region and the rest of the world and, as a consequence, leave the rest of the world worse off. Thus regional economic integration can leave both the region and the world worse off; the region better off, but the world worse off; or both the region and the world better off.

The Path Ahead

This chapter reviews the effects of economic integration by investigating several topics:

- The difference between trade creation and trade diversion.
- The difference between the static and dynamic gains from economic integration.
- Trade relations between member and nonmember nations of the economic union.
- The move toward monetary integration within the European Union.

Trade Creation and Trade Diversion

An **economic union** is the final step toward full economic integration. An economic union is a common market plus. It involves the harmonization of tax codes, labor standards, the creation of a common currency, and the establishment of an areawide central bank to conduct areawide monetary policy.

Whether economic integration helps or hurts a nation can be determined by calculating the static and dynamic effects of economic integration. Since it is almost always assumed that any dynamic effect enhances a nation's and a region's welfare, it would seem that the only possible way that economic integration could hurt a nation would be if the static effects of forming a customs union somehow reduced the nation's economic welfare. Jacob Viner demonstrated many years ago that this was indeed possible. Whether the static effects of forming a customs union are positive or negative depends on what Viner called the **trade-creating** and **trade-diverting** effects of a customs union.

Trade creation and trade diversion are explained with the help of Figure 16.1. (Note that Figure 16.1a is strikingly similar to Figure 7.1, which explained the microeconomic effects of a tariff.) Figure 16.1a represents the Belgian textile market both prior to and after the creation of the union. The world supply curve is the horizontal line labeled Sw, but this curve moves to Sw_t if Belgium imposes a tariff equal to $Sw\text{-}Sw_t$ on imports. Given the tariff, domestic textile production equals Q_2, domestic consumption equals Q_3, and imports total Q_2 to Q_3.

Now suppose Belgium joins a customs union whose common external tariff equals Belgium's preunion tariff. Suppose further that there is a union member, Ireland, whose production costs are lower than Belgium's but higher than the world's most ef-

The **Maastricht Treaty** is the formal document which, among other things, clears the way for the creation of the Economic and Monetary Union (EMU). The Maastricht meeting was held in 1991 and since that time most members of the European Union have ratified it.

By dropping intraregional tariffs, economic integration normally leads to **trade creation.** Trade creation measures the increased trade among the bloc countries and is one measure of the benefits of forming a free trade area or a customs union.

Following the formation of a customs union, member countries often pay more when they purchase goods from member countries than they used to pay for the same goods when they purchased them from nonunion members. Trade is thus **diverted** from cheaper external sources to more expensive intraunion sources.

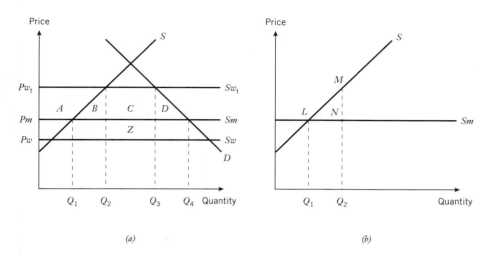

FIGURE 16.1 Trade creation and trade diversion.

Prior to the formation of a customs union, Belgium imposes a tariff equal to Pw_t-P_w on imports of textiles. Given the tariff, Belgium produces Q_2 units of textiles and consumes Q_3 units of textiles, which means that it imports Q_2-Q_3 units as shown in panel (a). If Belgium and Ireland form a customs union, Irish textiles, assumed less expensive than Belgian textiles, are allowed to enter the Belgian market duty free. If the Irish price of textiles equals Pm, the following will take place. Belgium's production of textiles will fall to Q_1 units and its consumption of textiles will rise to Q_4 units of textiles. Belgium will, then, import Q_1-Q_4 units of textiles from Ireland. As the price of textiles falls from Pw_t to Pm, consumer surplus increases by the areas A, B, C, D in panel (a). Part of the gain in consumer surplus is offset by the loss in producer surplus, A, and part by a loss in government revenue, C. That means that net gain in consumer surplus equals the triangles B and D, parts of the former dead-weight loss of the tariff. This net gain in consumer surplus is called *trade creation*, and measures the static benefits a nation derives from forming a customs union. However, there are costs involved in forming a customs union. Prior to union, Belgium imported Q_2-Q_3 units of textiles and taxed them at a rate of Pw_t-Pw. The government, therefore, obtained revenue equal to areas C plus Z in panel (a). With the formation of the customs union, consumers gain the area C, but not the area Z. This area, which is lost by the government, measures the degree of *trade diversion* and equals the static loss involved in forming the customs union. Panel (b) shows the domestic resources Belgium saves by importing textiles rather than domestically producing them. Prior to the union, Belgium used resources equal to the area Q_1LMQ_2 to obtain Q_1-Q_2 units of textiles. With a union, Belgium obtains the same number of units of textiles at a cost of Q_1LNQ_2 measured in terms of domestic inputs, a saving of LMN.

ficient producers. This assumption is shown in Figure 16.1a. Let's say that Ireland's textile supply curve, Sm, lies above the world supply curve, Sw, at every level of output. But since Irish textiles enter Belgium duty-free, the relevant world supply curve, Sw_t, is higher than the Irish supply curve, Sm, at every level of output.

Under these circumstances, economic integration will lead to greater trade between Belgium and Ireland. Belgium's consumption of textiles will rise from Q_3 to Q_4, its production of textiles will drop from Q_2 to Q_1, and its imports of textiles will increase to Q_1-Q_4. Belgians' consumer surplus will expand by the sum of the areas of the rectangles A and C and the triangles B and D. (Areas A and C also represent the *loss* in producer surplus and the *decline* in government revenue. But because the increase in consumer surplus exceeds the combined loss in producer surplus and government revenue, Belgium gains more than it loses.)

The net gain in consumer surplus, triangles B and D, equals the *trade-creating* effects of a customs union. The increase in welfare associated with triangle D is straightforward, but the gain associated with triangle B requires a fuller explanation. With trade, Belgium obtains the imports Q_1–Q_2 at the average price of Pm per textile. In terms of domestic production costs, this is equivalent to the area Q_1LNQ_2 in Figure 16.1b. If textiles are domestically produced, the resource cost equals Q_1LMQ_2 which exceeds Q_1LNQ_2 by the area of the triangle B. In other words, it is cheaper, in terms of domestic inputs, for Belgium to *import* textiles than to produce them domestically.

However, Ireland exports textiles to Belgium because it is the *union's* most efficient producer, not because it is the *world's* most efficient producer. Consequently, Belgium pays more for its imports of textiles under a customs union than under free trade. Prior to economic integration, Belgium imported Q_2–Q_3 textiles at an average price of Pw. After integration, Belgium pays Pm per textile imported, which means that it pays more for the quantity Q_2–Q_3 than it previously did. Graphically, the additional cost equals the area Z, which represents the amount of *trade diversion* and, therefore, Belgium's cost of joining the union. (Cast differently, the Belgium government obtained tariff revenue equal to area C plus area Z prior to economic integration. After integration, Belgium consumers gain area C, but Irish producers obtain area Z.)

We need to ask ourselves: In the example, does Belgium *gain* or *lose* by joining the union? If the degree of trade creation exceeds the degree of trade diversion (or if $B + D > Z$), Belgium's economic welfare will increase when it joins the union. Of course, it is possible that Belgium's economic welfare may decline when it joins the union. Suppose that, prior to joining the EU, Belgium imported 10 textiles at a cost of ECU10 per unit. (The **European Currency Unit (ECU),** which is more formally described later, is a composite currency used by the European Union.) In addition, imagine that the Belgian authorities received ECU2 in tariff revenue for each textile imported for a total of ECU20.

After the formation of the union, Belgium imports 12 textiles, but now at Ireland's production costs or ECU11 per unit. Belgian consumers now pay less for textiles—previously they paid SDR12 for a textile—but one of Belgium's new imports replaces a textile that was domestically produced at a cost of ECU12; so Belgium saves one ECU on that unit. Belgium also consumes one additional textile, and given the assumptions regarding initial prices and tariff rates, the gain in consumer surplus associated with the consumption of one additional textile is also ECU1. In the final analysis, the cost of trade diversion, ECU10 (or the loss in tariff revenue, ECU20, minus the amount Belgian consumers save due to the lower price of Belgium's *initial* imports, ECU10) exceeds the value of trade creation, ECU2, and Belgium's economic welfare declines.

The **European Currency Unit (ECU)** is a basket of European currencies and is used in all the official transactions of the European Monetary System.

What Determines the Gains of Economic Integration?

The example contradicts most empirical studies which conclude that the gains derived from trade creation usually exceed the costs associated with trade diversion. And one does not need a graph to verify this finding. The more than doubling of EU membership proves that economic integration pays. No nation will join an organization that reduces its economic well-being.

How much a nation may gain from joining a customs union depends on several factors. Trade creation will be larger if the domestic demand for textiles is highly elastic. In that event, a lower price will precipitate a robust increase in demand and lead to a large consumption gain. Of course, the higher a country's preunion tariff, the more the price may drop. On the other side of the coin, trade diversion will be low if the cost differential between the world's most efficient producer(s) and the member supplier(s) is low and the member producer's supply curve is highly elastic. The net welfare effect, therefore, comes down mainly to the question of existing price differentials and elasticities. The *lower* the price differential and the *larger* the elasticities, the greater the gain.

Trade theory also suggests that smaller nations will gain more from the creation of a customs union than will large nations. However, tariff theory also asserts that a small nation should have low tariffs in any event. But then how can a small, tariff-free nation possibly hope to increase its economic welfare if it joins an organization that erects a common external tariff? At least in theory, the answer is that it *cannot*, since the resulting trade diversion will probably swamp the resulting trade creation. Clearly, the nation's best option is to join a free trade area instead of a customs union. However, if a customs union, or its members, is its major export market, it will probably have to join the union in order to maintain the market for its exports, especially if the common external tariff is high.

Dynamic Gains from Economic Union

The **static gains (losses)** from economic integration equal the gains from trade creation minus the losses from trade diversion.

If economic integration leads to economies of scale, more rapid technological change, and the diffusion of productive techniques across a common market, it is said to generate **dynamic gains.**

Static gains and losses (or how economic integration changes production, consumption, and trade patterns given existing resources) are important. But it is the **dynamic gains** from economic integration that are most important in the opinion of many observers, for they will ultimately prove the worth or detriment of economic integration to a nation's economy. And dynamic gains (or losses) are relevant not only to the union members, but to the rest of the world as well.

What are the dynamic gains that presumably flow from economic integration? Proponents of integration argue that free trade will generate faster economic growth both by widening internal markets and by providing firms with the opportunity to expand production and enjoy economies of scale. An integrated market, it is claimed, will also enhance the diffusion of efficient production techniques throughout the community and lead to external economies. Economic union will foster labor and capital mobility within the community and boost factor productivity. And economic integration, through more open regional trade, promises to promote competition that will tend to break or reduce the power of local monopolies. Formerly protected industries will be forced to adopt the most efficient technologies and management practices or else face the threat of bankruptcy. The bracing effects of competition were stressed, for example, by common market proponents when Britain was debating the pros and cons of European Union membership.

Essentially, the arguments outlined so far affect the supply side. In a nutshell, free-trade proponents believe that economies of scale, diffusion of technology, factor mobility, and so on will shift the community's aggregate supply curve—and those of each member—to the right. The payoff for members is greater output, lower prices, and faster rates of economic growth.

The Single European Act of 1987

It was the prospect of *dynamic gains* from economic union that led the European Union to adopt the Single European Act of 1987—what is popularly known as the "1992 Initiative." The single-market proposal, entitled "Completing the Internal Market" and containing roughly 300 provisions, was supposed to raise members' rates of economic growth and reduce their rates of inflation through several microeconomic reforms. Specifically, the White Paper called for the abolition of restraints on capital mobility and the elimination of nontariff barriers such as border controls and discriminatory technical standards, and for the liberalization of government procurement policies so as to break down domestic monopolies in member countries.

The **Treaty of Rome** was signed by Belgium, France, Italy, Luxembourg, the Netherlands, and West Germany in 1957. The treaty established the European Economic Community, a customs union consisting of the six countries.

Why were the 1992 initiatives needed? Some trade liberalization came with the signing of the **Treaty of Rome** in 1957, but remaining trade restrictions within the community continued to hamper intra-EU trade. The lack of European-wide product standards effectively discouraged foreign (including EU) goods from crossing national frontiers. Moreover, differing national product standards had the effect of raising costs since firms were forced to produce several versions of the same good in order to meet a *multitude* rather than a single set of requirements. Such requirements hindered the ability of EU firms to achieve economies of scale and contributed to the inefficiency of the system.

Another example of NTBs in Europe were border controls—the hours required for a load of goods to receive clearance to cross from, say, Germany into France. Richard Cooper pointed out: "Despite the absence of internal tariffs, commercial traffic in Europe still must endure an average 80 minute delay at European borders, while it takes only 1 second for a truck to roll from Massachusetts to Connecticut."* Even though the costs of 80-minute tie-ups are not overwhelming, when added to other costs, such as product standards, health and safety standards, and so on, they cumulatively became sufficient to discourage a significant amount of potential trade and reduce the static and dynamic gains associated with economic integration.

Not everyone is convinced that economic integration is the "magic pill" to cure all ills. For example, EU skeptics pointed out that economies of scale are often a *plant*, not a company, phenomenon; and, given the multitude of EU plants producing similar products, optimum-size plants had already been built. If so, how could one hope to wring out even greater economies of scale? Integration proponents argued that potential economies of scale in the production of specialized inputs had been frustrated by border controls, the lack of capital mobility, and national standards. A single market would, it was claimed, enable firms to capture these still-elusive economies of scale.

The Dynamic Effects of Economic Integration and Trade Creation/Diversion

Suppose that the EU's member states are indeed able to attain economies of scale following economic integration. These economies will then feed back and affect the ini-

---

*Richard Cooper, "Europe without Borders," *Brookings Papers on Economic Activity* 2 (1989); p. 326.

BOX 16.1 The Estimated Benefits of the Single European Act

Michael Emerson conducted a massive study to estimate the benefits of the 1992 initiatives. According to Emerson, eliminating intra-EU trade barriers would increase the European Union's GDP by 2.2 percent (Table 16.1). Economies of scale in the single market would raise the EU's GDP by 2 percent and greater levels of competition would raise it an additional 1.6 percent. (Employing a different variant, Emerson estimated that the microeconomic gains from the creation of a single market would total 6.4 percent rather than 5.8 percent of GDP.)

The microeconomic gains, Emerson demonstrated, would engender a sizable increase in real economic growth, a decrease in the rate of inflation, and an increase in the number of jobs throughout the EU.

TABLE 16.1 Potential Gains from 1992

Microeconomic Efficiency (percent of GDP)	
Removing Trade Barriers	2.2
Economies of Scale	2.0
Competitive Effects	1.6
Macroeconomic Gains (percent after 6 years)	
Increase in GDP	4.5
Decline in Consumer Prices	6.1
Increase in Employment	1.8 (millions)

Source: Michael Emerson and others, *The Economics of 1992, The EC Commission's Assessment of the Economic Effects of Completing the Internal Market* (New York: Oxford University Press, 1988), Table 10.1.1, p. 203, and Table 10.2.1, p. 208. Reprinted by permission of Oxford University Press.

---

tial static gains and losses associated with economic integration. Figure 16.2 shows how this occurs.

In this example, imagine that prior to the formation of the customs union, Sweden imposes a tariff equal to the vertical distance between Pw and Pw_t. Due to the tariff, Sweden's imports are restricted to the quantity Q_3-Q_4. Now imagine that Sweden joins a customs union in which the common external tariff equals Sweden's preunion tariff. Also suppose that Denmark is the low-cost producer in the union. Due to economic integration, the price of video cassettes in Sweden falls from Pw_t to Pm_0. As a result, Sweden's imports increase from Q_3-Q_4 to Q_2-Q_5. The gains from trade creation equal the triangles B and D. But the costs of trade diversion equal the sum of the rectangles Z_1 and Z_2. Clearly, Sweden's net economic welfare declines.

But now assume that the formation of the customs union leads to all the dynamic gains envisioned in the Single European Act of 1987. Denmark's production costs decline and the price of Danish video cassettes falls to Pm_1 as its supply curve drops from Sm_0 to Sm_1. Given the lower price of cassettes, Sweden's imports now increase to Q_1-Q_6. It turns out that the additional trade-creating effects caused by the lower price equal the sum of the areas of e, f, g, and h, while the loss due to trade diversion falls

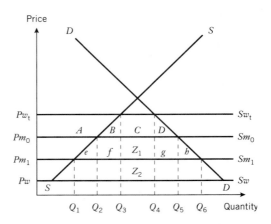

FIGURE 16.2 Trade creation and trade diversion: II.

The dynamic effects of economic union may increase the efficiency of union producers. If this occurs, it will modify the static gains and losses associated with economic union. Although not drawn to scale, Figure 16.2 is a replica of Figure 16.1a. There is, however, one notable exception. Due to the dynamic gains from union, Denmark's cost of producing video cassettes drops from Sm_0 per unit to Sm_1 per unit. When the union is first formed, Sweden's static gains from the union equal B plus D, and trade diversion equals the sum of Z_1 and Z_2. Given Denmark's lower production costs, Sweden's static gains increase by e, f, g, and h, and its static losses fall to Z_2. Thus, the dynamic effects of the union will increase the static gains and reduce the static losses associated with economic union.

from Z_1 plus Z_2 to Z_2 alone. The union's now-lower costs of production transform what formally had been a negative net welfare effect into a positive net welfare effect.

Hence, if the static gains from economic integration are *positive*, the dynamic effects of integration will reinforce them. This also means that even if the static gains are negative *at first*, the dynamic gains may so affect markets that static losses will be turned into static gains.

Economic Union and External Trade Relations

The rest of the world has watched the evolution of the European Union with some apprehension. A common external tariff may not only block the rest of the world's exports to the EU, but it may even be used to swing the commodity terms of trade in its favor. The union could attempt to erect an optimum tariff.

But *implementing* an optimum tariff is far more difficult than talking about it. In cases where EU members are important consumers, the union does not seem to have exercised monopoly buyer power in order to obtain a better deal. (See Box 16.2.) Nor did the EU confront OPEC oil producers during the oil crises of the 1970s with massive buying power and force them to grant EU members special discounts. In fact, the evidence suggests that Britain and Norway (a member of EFTA) rode high oil prices and North Sea oil discoveries to domestic prosperity, not to EU or EFTA prosperity.

Potentially, the EU might have been able to obtain a better deal on food imports since it is a large market and there are many potential food suppliers in the world. But even if the EU had decided to impose or had attempted to impose an optimum tariff, it would have faced the dilemma that all nations confront when attempting to force down the price of a particular import via a tariff. First, they need an acceptable substitute in order to make the policy stick. But the development of a substitute industry creates a dilemma as the union or country must decide whether to push for an optimum import duty or to protect the substitute industry. In most cases, the union or country will select the latter course of action as the experience of the common agricultural policy (CAP) indicates. That policy has made the EU *more than* self-sufficient in a number of agricultural products, but it has not decreased food prices within the EU nor has it raised much money for the union. In fact, the CAP has been quite expensive—the total CAP budget was approximately $48 billion in 1994.

This does not mean that the EU's policies have not harmed nonmembers. For example, the oil seeds dispute between the EU and the United States would not have occurred unless the EU's policy had adversely affected the United States. However, it was not an optimum tariff that caused the turmoil, but rather questions of subsidized production and closed markets that caused the turbulence.

It is possible that a common external tariff may yield benefits even if it is not employed as an optimum tariff. Foreign firms, faced with the loss of an important market due to the common external tariff may "hurdle" the common external tariff by setting up operations and producing goods *within* the community. The net effect of such a move would be to transfer production and employment from the rest of the world to member nations. Of course, not every proposed economic union can count on such a large inflow of foreign firms seeking to bypass a common external tariff. Firms will "leap over" a tariff only if a lucrative or promising market exists on the other side.

External Trade and Disharmony within the EU

An economic union may not always present a united front toward the rest of the world. Disagreements among union members are bound to occur as different countries may have treated various imports differently. In the case of the European Union, for example, prior to the creation of the single market, France and Italy restricted the import of Japanese cars while Germany did not; and Britain had promoted the construction of Japanese car manufacturing facilities to sites within the UK—the transplants then sold their output throughout the EU. An economic area has an obvious dilemma: it cannot simultaneously *permit imports* and *restrict imports*. It so happens that this impasse regarding the treatment of Japanese car exports to the EU was surmounted when Japan, through a voluntary export restraint (VER) agreement, agreed to limit its car sales within the European Union. (The VER included cars produced at transplants, but the agreement is scheduled to be eliminated by the year 2000.)

Tensions within the European Union have cropped up in other areas as well. Ireland and Greece, unlike other EU members, do not impose quotas on Chinese-made athletic shoes. The whole community must consider what course of action should be taken if Nike and Reebok were to ship their Chinese-made footwear to Greece and Ireland for *re-export* to the rest of the EU. Obviously, harmonization among these conflicting practices must be achieved.

BOX 16.2 **The Banana Feud of 1995**

The single market act of 1993 set the stage for the three-sided banana feud of 1995. As the name indicates, the feud has to do with bananas and more specifically, *who* can sell this tropical fruit in the European Union. One might wonder why EU officialdom did not simply permit citizens to buy bananas from the cheapest source and smile complacently as they consumed their daily dose of potassium.

Such was not the case. EU regulations insist that Europeans should consume lots of ACP-grown bananas. ACP stands for the African, Caribbean, and Pacific countries that are signatories of the **Lomé Convention.** For the most part these nations are former colonies of leading European nations, and under the terms of the convention, ACP manufacturers and most ACP tropical fruit products have duty-free access to the EU.

The hangup is that Latin American bananas are far cheaper than ACP-grown bananas. Thus, to protect the former colonies' market share, quotas had been imposed on the sale of Latin American bananas in the EU. In 1993, Latin America's export quota to the EU was cut from to 2.4 million to 2 million tons; but in 1994, the quota was raised to 2.2 million tons. Then, after the European Union expanded to include Austria, Finland, and Sweden, a proposal was put forward to increase the Latin American quota from 2.4 million tons to 2.6 million tons. Good for consumers, but bad for ACP banana producers.

The other battle has taken place in South America. Under the arrangement, each producing country has a specific quota. Naturally, countries disagree over who should get what quota. But there is also a disagreement over how the quota should be allocated among various producers within a given nation. At present, the government issues export licenses to would-be exporters. Exporters have complained that the Colombian and Costa Rican governments have used the allocation of export licenses to drive the price of EU-destined bananas up to EU prices. That means that either the government or the original banana producers get the quota rent.

Some Latin American banana exporters—for example, Chiquita, a U.S.-owned company—have complained both about the unfair trade practices and how governments in producing countries have grabbed the quota rent. Europeans, especially Germans, want to see the quota system scrapped or radically reformed.

Sources: Canute James, "U.S. Probe into EU Banana Trade," *Financial Times* (December 15, 1994); p. 6; Nancy Dunne, "Belize Irked Over U.S. Banana Regime," *Financial Times* (March 28, 1995); p. 7; and Caroline Southey, "EU Draws Up Plans on Banana Regime," *Financial Times* (April 5, 1995); p. 6.

The **Lomé Convention** is a trade and aid agreement between the European Union and various developing countries—primarily ex-colonies of European nations. The agreement was signed in Lomé, the capital to Togo, in 1975, and has been renewed several times.

Economic Integration and the Aggregate Economy

Members of any economic union, including the EU, will measure the success or failure of economic integration by its effect on the *aggregate* or total economy. Michael Emerson predicted that, after six years, the Single European Act would raise the EU's GDP by an additional 4.5 percent, that consumer prices would be 6 percent lower than otherwise, that roughly 2 million additional jobs would be created, and that the EU's current account would improve by 1 percent.

Figure 16.3 shows how the Single European Act may affect the EU as a whole. Assume the microeconomic measures of the act cut unit costs of production. Lower production costs would shift the EU's aggregate supply curve to the right, from AS_0 to AS_1 in Figure 16.3b, and reduce the general price level.

By itself, a lower price level will increase exports and decrease imports. But, in addition, lower production costs will also improve the community's international com-

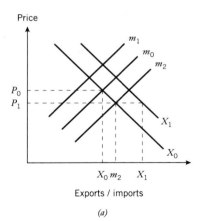
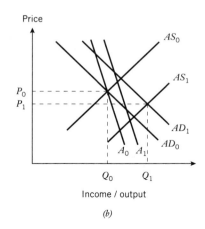

(a)　　　　　　　　　　　　　　　　(b)

FIGURE 16.3 The macroeconomics of economic integration.

If economic union leads to greater efficiency and lower production costs, the union's aggregate supply curve will shift to the right from AS_0 to AS_1 in panel (a). Increased competitiveness should shift the union's export curve from X_0 to X_1 and its import curve from m_0 to m_1 in panel (b). The union's exports will be higher at every price level and its imports lower at every price level. The improved trade balance will shift the union's aggregate demand curve from AD_0 to AD_1. If absorption grows at a slower rate than output, the union will run a trade surplus, equal to the difference between AD_1 and A_1 at the price level P_1. In panel (a), the increase in aggregate demand shifts the import schedule from m_1 to m_2; but as can be seen, exports, X_1, exceed imports, m_2, at the price level P_1. In the end, the union's price level is lower, its income is higher, and its trade balance moves into a surplus.

petitiveness and shift its export curve from X_0 to X_1 and its import curve from m_0 to m_1, as in Figure 16.3a. The competitively induced shifts in the export and import curves will move the aggregate demand curve to the right from AD_0 to AD_1. If the community's marginal propensity to absorb is less than unity, the shift of the absorption curve to the right, A_0 to A_1, will be less than the shift in the AD curve. Moreover, the net gap between the AD and A curves will be larger at the new and lower price level than it was at the initial and higher price level. Therefore, even though the import curve shifts to the right, from m_1 to m_2, due to greater absorption, the EU ends up with greater output, higher employment, a higher potential level of output, and a trade surplus. This is precisely what Michael Emerson predicts.

The European Union and the World Economy

Many nations are worried that the single market scheme and economic integration in general will lead to a "fortress Europe" mentality and, as a result, foreign goods will be shut out of the European market. For example, on January 1, 1993, the EU adopted local-content rules and domestic-preference rules in public procurement contracts. The Utilities Directive gives EU firms preference over foreign firms when bidding for public utility contracts, particularly in the areas of power-generating and telecommunications equipment. Specifically, the region's utilities may reject foreign bids if the foreign product contains less than a 50 percent EU content. In cases in which the EU content of the foreign product *exceeds* 50 percent, EU utilities can give community firms a 3 percent price preference. While the directive loosens the access to thousands of government projects that formerly were exclusively limited to local companies, the "playing field" is not yet level. Foreign companies are justifiably concerned since government procurement equals 15 percent of the EU's GDP.

In defending the guidelines, EU officials have emphasized the market-opening character of the directive and have countered U.S. criticism by citing various **Buy American Acts** which discriminate against non-American companies. The EU has charged that detractors in the United States have been comparing apples and oranges. Within the EU, public procurement covers purchases by central and local governments plus private firms in government-regulated industries such as mass transit, airports, and ports. In the United States, public procurement is defined as purchases by the central government and publicly owned utilities only; it excludes state and local government purchases—exactly the level at which Buy American preferences bite.

American-EU disputes in telecommunications, in aircraft construction (over the Airbus subsidy), and over agricultural exports does not mean that the European Union is destined to follow restrictive trade policies in the future. The consensus view of economists is that the EU will be more assertive in trade disputes and will pursue *regional* rather than national interests in the area of international trade and finance. A regional bias does not imply that the EU will turn its back on the rest of the world. While intra-European trade is *most important* to EU members, external trade is also vital since it comprises close to 10 percent of Europe's GDP. It is hard to imagine that the EU will move to build up its internal market and, at the same time, take other steps (such as restricting trade) that would tear it down.

European economic integration may have positive effects on the rest of the world. If economic integration leads to faster economic growth within the European Union, an expanding EU market will stimulate the demand for the rest of the world's exports, and intra-European cost-cutting measures will lead to cheaper European commodities to the benefit of consumers worldwide.

> As the name implies, **Buy American Acts** are a series of acts and practices, adopted at all levels of government in the United States, which give preference to American-made relative to foreign-made products.

Intraregional Assistance and the Social Charter

From the beginning, the European Union has recognized that free trade combined with capital mobility—and especially with internally fixed exchange rates—can cause economic dislocations, and that some parts of the community may be left behind or may not progress as rapidly as the rest of the EU.

The **European Regional Development Fund (ERDF)** was created to help overcome such transitional problems. Funded by the Union's budget, the ERDF finances projects in economically depressed regions throughout the community. Initially the grants were allocated on a per-country basis, with *so much* for France, *so much* for Germany, and so on. But today, grants are exclusively based on need regardless of country.

Besides giving aid to economically depressed areas, the EU has moved to protect workers' rights. The **European Social Charter** was enacted to engender social harmony within the EU by compelling all member states to safeguard workers' rights. These

> The **European Regional Development Fund (ERDF)** is an agency of the European Union which helps fund economic development projects in economically deprived regions within the union.

A relatively new institution, the **European Social Charter** is a vehicle for establishing certain minimum standards and safeguards regarding wages, labor standards, health insurance, and so on for all workers within the European Union.

assurances go beyond the promise of equal pay and benefits for similar work in any country. The social charter is intended to establish a *social compact* that will provide universal health care, occupational safety, unemployment and redundancy benefits, maternity benefits, and the like to all workers, whether foreigners or citizens in all countries of the EU. In addition, some members of the EU are pushing for worker representation on the boards of directors of private companies, while others want rules requiring that trade unions be consulted before a firm undertakes any radical restructuring of its activities.

The degree of social harmonization envisioned and the added costs of social benefits proposed have pitted the wealthier Northern tier of the EU against the poorer Southern rim. If benefits were fixed at or close to Northern levels, firms might locate in Germany, France, and the Benelux (Belgium, the Netherlands, and Luxembourg) in order to be close to potential markets. But if minimal labor or social standards were established, firms might locate in Spain and Portugal to take advantage of low labor costs.

European Monetary Arrangements

The **European Payments Union (EPU)** (described further in the glossary) was set up in 1950. It was the first European-wide monetary arrangement in the post–World War II era.

The **snake in the tunnel** (1972–73) was a shortlived European exchange rate system under which cross-exchange rates between European currencies were allowed to vary no more than 2.25 percent against each other, and only 4.5 percent against the dollar.

The European Union has attempted to push economic integration further than any other regional trading bloc in the world. This is especially true with respect to *monetary policy*. Beginning with the **European Payments Union (EPU)** in 1950, European nations have sought to maintain fixed exchange rates among European currencies in the belief that stable exchange rates would stimulate trade and growth among all participants. In 1972, the original six members of the EU (the Benelux nations, France, Germany, and Italy) plus Britain, Denmark, Ireland, and Norway created the **snake in the tunnel.** Under the arrangement, intra-European bilateral exchange rates were permitted to move only 2.25 percent against each other. In turn, this band of exchange rates, the "snake," was allowed to float 4.5 percent, the "tunnel," against the dollar. The scheme broke down very quickly as Italy and Britain pulled out almost immediately and France quit, rejoined, and quit the system for good in 1973. The snake was transformed into a German mark area or zone, in which the Benelux currencies were pegged to the mark which in turn floated against the American dollar. Despite this limited success, the dream of a unified currency area with fixed exchange rates persisted and ultimately led to the creation of the *European Monetary System* described later in this chapter.

The EU's desire for intraregional fixed exchanged rates is based on the European conviction that fixed or quasi-fixed exchange rates are good for trade. EU countries are open economies, trade amounts on average to 50 percent of their GDP, and regional trade is a large proportion of their total trade. The fear is that the free trade area could be placed in jeopardy if currencies can be depreciated at will. Depreciation may improve a particular member's trade balance, but it will lead to at least *transitory* adjustment costs in other member countries. These costs may be minimal for the depreciating country, whose income will probably expand with the depreciation, but *major* for a country whose currency *appreciates*. If wild swings in exchange rates lead to sharp surges in imports and adversely affect domestic employment, a nation may have to quit the free trade area. There are positive attractions in fixed exchange rates, in addition to the desire to avoid the painful swings of flexible exchange rates. For example, certain EU programs, the common agricultural policy for one, are easier to administer under fixed rather than flexible exchange rates (See Box 16.3).

BOX 16.3 The Common Agricultural Policy and Exchange Rates

The Common Agricultural Policy is dedicated to maintaining farm income within the EU. Initially, the CAP sought to achieve this through a system of guaranteed price supports. Wheat, for example, would be guaranteed a set price regardless of supply and demand conditions. But the CAP is unlike so many other national agricultural price support schemes. The CAP attempts to maintain agricultural prices at the same level in *several nations* at once rather than in just one country. Commodity support prices are quoted in ECUs. If, for example, the German mark and the ECU exchange at a 1:1 rate and the wheat support price is ECU10 per bushel, a German farmer who produces 10 bushels of wheat would have an income of ECU100 or DM100.

So, in practice everything ran smoothly as long as the ECU/DM exchange rate remained stable. But difficulties were guaranteed to emerge if the mark doubled in value relative to the ECU. At the new exchange rate, ECU2/DM, the German farmer's ECU income would remain constant, but his mark income, the important one from his perspective, would drop to DM50, since ECU100 would now equal DM50. How then could his mark income be preserved?

This anxiety created the need for **green money,** a synonym for the agricultural exchange rates that were designed to protect farm income from the effects of appreciation. Let's suppose the German government sets the green rate at ECU1/DM. Then, if the mark appreciates to ECU2/DM while the ECU price of wheat remains constant, the German mark price of a bushel of wheat would fall to DM5 (since 10 ECUs would equal 5 marks) and, with it, the farmer's income. But if the "green rate" was kept constant at ECU1/DM, the German farmer would still earn DM10 per bushel of wheat and his income would remain constant.

The farmer would be content but the German government would face the cost of adjustment. Having kept the green rate constant, the government would have to raise DM50 to pay the farmer the difference between the green rate and the market-exchange-rate price of wheat. In the beginning, these funds were derived from **monetary compensatory amounts (MCAs),** basically a system of export and import taxes. Under that scheme, the German authorities would impose a positive MCA that would subsidize exports of wheat and tax imports of wheat.

If the mark fell on the foreign exchanges and the green rate was kept constant, the German farmer's income would remain constant in terms of ECUs and rise in terms of marks. The German government would then have to introduce a negative MCA that would tax exports and subsidize imports. Or it could just depreciate its green rate in line with the market exchange rate.

In recent years, the CAP has evolved. Farm income is maintained today by a system of support prices plus direct payments to farmers. Prices and payments are still totaled up in ECUs, however, which means that if the mark appreciates, German farmers would still be hit. Adjustments are still needed, and so, in the spring of 1995, the EU adopted a dual system of green rates—one to cover support prices and another to cover direct payments to farmers.

The real point is not whether the EU has a system of green rates, but rather that fixed instead of variable intraregional exchange rates will allow the CAP to run smoothly.

Sources: Caroline Southey, "EU Farm Currency Clash Looms," *Financial Times* (May 3, 1995): p. 3; and "Dual Green Currency Wins the Night," *Financial Times* (June 23, 1995), p. 2; and "Capping the Farm Budget," *Financial Times* (June 26, 1995): p. 15.

Green money is actually the exchange rate applied to farm products under the Common Agricultural Policy. Since farm prices are quoted in ECUs, if the mark appreciates against the ECU, a German farmer's income would fall in terms of marks. But if the "green" mark, which is set by decree, is kept constant relative to the ECU, the farmer's mark income would remain constant.

Monetary compensatory amounts (MCAs) is a system of taxes and subsidies which finances any difference between an EU member's ECU exchange rate and its "green" rate.

Optimum Currency Areas

Within the United States, the U.S. dollar is the **common currency.** Within Belgium and Luxembourg, the Belgian franc is the common currency. Under the Maastricht Treaty, the European Union is projected to create and adopt a common currency.

An **optimum currency area** is a region, not necessarily a country, where it makes sense to employ one currency. Such an area may include more than one country, in which case the countries may adopt a common currency or national currencies that are tied together under a system of fixed exchange rates. The study of optimum currency areas concentrates on analyzing those conditions necessary to make a region optimum.

Under the Maastricht Treaty, which Margaret Thatcher called a vision of yesterday, the EU set up a timetable to move toward a **common currency.** Given a common currency, all national currencies—such as the mark, franc, guilder, pound, and so on—would be eliminated and replaced by the Euro. Critics of the proposal complained and still contend today that it does not make much sense for the EU to adopt a common currency unless the EU is an **optimum currency area.**

What is an optimum currency area? Essentially it is a region of considerable intraregional trade and factor mobility. Robert Mundell, an economist who has explored this topic, asked the following question: Suppose, due to a change in tastes or some other noncyclical factor, that France runs a trade deficit with Germany, what can be done to eliminate it?

The analysis in Chapter 10 tells us that the franc should *depreciate* relative to the mark. But if both France and Germany want to maintain a constant FFr/DM exchange rate, depreciation is not an option. The only way to restore France's external accounts is to depress income and price levels in France and expand them in Germany. It is unlikely that market forces alone will cause this to happen to the degree required to balance France's external accounts—except perhaps over many years' time.

The inability of market forces alone to restore external equilibrium to France and Germany can be explained with the help of Figure 16.4. Initially, price and output levels equal P_1 and Q_1, respectively, in the two countries. As can be seen, absorption equals

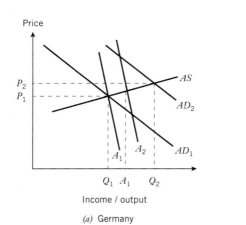

(a) Germany

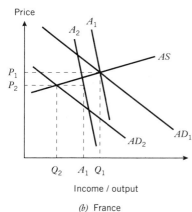

(b) France

FIGURE 16.4   Change in relative demand and the trade balance.

A switch in demand away from French goods toward German goods will shift the German aggregate demand curve from AD_1 to AD_2 in panel (a), and the French aggregate demand curve from AD_1 to AD_2 in panel (b). As discussed in Chapter 10, an increase in exports (Germany) or an increase in autonomous imports (France) will shift the absorption curve by less than the shift in the aggregate demand curve. Thus, Germany will run a trade surplus and France will run a trade deficit. Because we have assumed that aggregate supply curves are not infinitely elastic, a change in aggregate demand will lead to a change in the price level. In this case, the price · level rises in Germany and falls in France. However, the real appreciation of the mark is not sufficient to wipe out Germany's trade surplus or France's trade deficit.

aggregate demand at these price and income levels, so that each nation's trade account is balanced. An increase in the demand for German products and a decrease in the demand for French commodities will cause the German aggregate demand and absorption curves to shift to the right while the French curves shift to the left. Germany ends up with a trade surplus and France with a trade deficit despite the rise in the German price and income levels and the corresponding fall in the French price and income levels. (The trade surplus or deficit equals the difference between Q_2 and A_2.)

Since market forces alone will not eliminate the trade imbalances, the German government must push German income and price levels *even higher* and the French government must depress French income and deflate the French price level to an *even lower* level. But while such policies may equilibrate the external accounts, they will cause unemployment in France and inflation in Germany.

Clearly, rising unemployment and inflation are unacceptable to both countries. What other options are open? Optimum currency area theory points out two additional ways to attain external and internal equilibrium: first, wage-price flexibility; and second, labor mobility. Let's see how they would work.

At the outset, we see that the initial shift in demand reduces the level of employment in France. If wages and prices are *flexible*, unemployed French workers will accept *lower wages* in order to retain their jobs. The lower wage rate shifts the French aggregate supply curve to right, improves France's competitiveness, and leads to a greater demand for French products. In Germany, the opposite occurs. The initial shift in aggregate demand produces a *greater demand* for workers, *higher wages*, and a *leftward shift* of the German aggregate supply curve with predictable results.

Besides flexible wages, a second option is labor mobility. Suppose that unemployed French workers migrate from France, where the demand for labor is low, to Germany, where the demand for labor is high. How does this labor migration improve the French trade balance? In a modern industrial society, with unemployment compensation and the like, unemployed workers will continue to absorb even when they are not producing. Therefore, the migration of unemployed workers from France will cut French absorption more than it cuts French production. So, if absorption declines while output remains constant, the French trade balance should improve.

Thus, given both wage-price flexibility and labor mobility, the initial trade imbalance should be corrected without France having to suffer unemployment or Germany having to endure inflation. Now, while labor mobility may be sufficient to restore external equilibrium regardless of other conditions, the same cannot be said for wage-price flexibility. If the foreign-trade sector is a small proportion of the economy, greater unemployment in the foreign trade sector will probably not lead to much, if any, fall in money wages throughout the economy. If only 10 percent of the work force is employed in the foreign trade sector, a 10 percent increase in unemployment in that sector will lead to just a 1 percent decrease in total employment—hardly enough to initiate a decrease in wages and a shift in the aggregate supply curve to the right.

So, whether two nations constitute an optimum currency area depends on four things: the degree of wage-price flexibility, the degree of labor mobility, the degree of bilateral trade, and the openness of the economies. The members of the EU satisfy two of the criteria: They are open and intraregional trade is large. But wages and prices are not flexible and intra-EU labor mobility is low, which implies that the EU is not an optimum currency at the present time. Nevertheless, even though it is not an optimum currency area according to the previously listed criteria, the EU has created a monetary framework designed to lead to a common currency.

The European Monetary System

The precursor to the Maastricht Treaty was the European Monetary System established in 1979. The brainchild of Chancellor Helmut Schmidt of West Germany and President Giscard d'Estaing of France, the EMS was designed to create a zone of monetary stability within Europe. The desire for such a zone was partly engendered by what appeared to European eyes as erratic monetary behavior in the United States at that time. Given that turbulence, Schmidt and d'Estaing believed that the EU would find itself in an international monetary sea of troubles if it remained passive. They felt that an active policy—a European solution—would create the monetary stability deemed essential for Europe's economic progress.

The EMS is similar to the snake in the tunnel. Like its predecessor, the EMS aimed to maintain fixed exchange rates between EU members. To accomplish this, the architects of the EMS envisioned closer monetary cooperation between member states and a harmonization of economic policies. To add substance to the vision, the EMS created a new monetary unit, the European currency unit (ECU), and developed a two-part approach to stabilizing exchange rates.

The ECU is a composite of ten currencies. The weight of each currency in determining the ECU's value depends on the nation's gross domestic product and its importance in intra-EU trade—the four more important weights are, roughly, D-mark (37%), French franc (17%), British pound (15%), and Dutch guilder (10%). ECUs are created when EMS members deposit foreign exchange reserves—dollars and gold—with the **European Monetary Cooperation Fund (EMCF).** At the inception of the EMS, members were required to deposit 20 percent of their international reserves with the EMCF (officially FECOM by its French initials) in return for ECU deposits. The deposits or accounts are used to settle foreign exchange intervention debts between the central banks, and the ECU itself is employed as the unit of account in totaling up intra-EU central bank credits and debits.

> The **European Monetary Cooperation Fund (EMCF)** is the International Monetary Fund of the European Monetary System.

Computing Intra-EU Cross-Exchange Rates: The Parity Grid

At present, the chief importance of the ECU is that each currency's central rate is set in terms of ECUs. Because all members' central currency rates are set in terms of ECUs, it is a quick step to derive cross-exchange rates. For example, if three francs, two guilders, and one mark respectively equal one ECU, cross-exchange rates would be FFr3/DM, G2/DM, and FFr1.5/G. The resulting cross-exchange rates are used, in turn, to establish the **parity grid** for each currency against all other currencies in the EMS.

Despite efforts to maintain it, the parity grid had to be realigned *twelve times* between 1979 and 1993 even though realignment was always considered the policy of *last resort*. The general consensus was that, given the parity grid and divergence thresholds, the system would face few problems if the monetary and fiscal policies of the members converged or moved in tandem. If a member's economic fundamentals were sound, it could count on EMS assistance through the EMCF to help it keep its currency within desired bounds.

> Under the European Monetary System, each currency has a central rate against the ECU. Given these central rates, it is a quick step to establish cross-exchange rates for each pair of currencies. The **parity grid** summarizes the resulting cross-exchange rates.

BOX 16.4 The Exchange Rate Mechanism

A part of the European Monetary System, the **exchange rate mechanism** established the permissible band of fluctuations for bilateral or cross-exchange rates within the system. Until 1993, the permitted fluctuation was 2.25 percent on either side of central rates—or a band of 4.5 percent. Since 1993, the permitted band has been 30 percent, or 15 percent on each side of central rates.

The **divergence indicator** is designed to alert a country when its currency has moved 75 percent of its permitted divergence from its central ECU rate. When the alarm goes off, a country is supposed to take steps to bring its currency back closer to its central ECU rate.

Prior to the summer of 1993, intra-European exchange rates were maintained within a narrow band. Under the guidelines of the **exchange rate mechanism (ERM),** each currency was permitted to move no more than 2.25 percent on either side of its central rate, except that the Spanish peseta and the Portuguese escudo were permitted to move 6 percent on either side of their central rates.

Let's illustrate by supposing the French franc comes under pressure and falls against the mark. According to conventional wisdom, France is responsible for preserving the FFr/DM rate. But if the franc is falling, the mark is rising and, under the rules of the EMS, it becomes the *joint* responsibility of both nations to stabilize the exchange rate.

Joint stabilization may make sense on paper but will become impossible to carry out in fact if the two countries' fiscal and monetary policies are out of line. If the rate of monetary expansion in France is *double* the German rate, for example, the countries' inflation rates will soon diverge and purchasing power parity exchange rates will deviate by increasing amounts.

To prevent such disparities from emerging, the EMS adopted the second of its two-prong approach to exchange-rate stability: the **divergence indicator.** The divergence indicator in this case measures the deviation of the present, say, DM/ECU currency rate from its central rate. The degree of permissible divergence varied from currency to currency and was based on their weights in determining the value of the ECU. Nations with greater weights were permitted less divergence because a movement in their currency had a greater impact on the value of the ECU. The permissible divergence of a currency was computed as follows: .0225 (1 − currency's weight in ECU). Thus, if a currency's weight in the ECU was 20 percent, the permissible deviation of its current ECU rate from its central ECU rate was 1.8 percent.

Under EMS rules, when a currency diverges from its central rate by more than 75 percent of its allowable deviation, the nation is supposed to take steps to bring the actual rate back closer to the central rate. Suppose in terms of the illustration France pumps up its money supply at *twice* the rate of monetary expansion in other EMS countries. This will cause the French franc to fall against all other EMS currencies, but also to fall against its ECU central rate. If the permitted divergence from central rates is 10 percent and the franc's central ECU rate is FFr10/ECU, the franc can only rise to FFr9/ECU or fall to FFr11/ECU. If the franc falls 10 percent against all currencies, its current ECU rate will be 10 percent lower than its central rate and the franc will have moved 100 percent of its allowable divergence. As the franc slides to FFr10.75/ECU, it will hit its divergence indicator or threshold and, as some have put it, "set off the alarm." France will then have to reduce its rate of monetary expansion and bring its rate of inflation into line with the ERM norm. Short of this, the financial authorities of EMS countries would have to meet and hammer out a new system of central rates.

The importance of divergence indicators cannot be overemphasized. All nations are responsible for maintaining the parity grid; but if the grid is ruptured by the economic conduct of one nation, which shows up as its currency hits or passes the divergence indicator, that nation is obliged to make things right.

On the other hand, if the rules of the game required that all participating nations intervene to maintain the grid regardless of circumstances, the system would quickly fall apart. Suppose, for example, that an inflationary French economic policy led to a fall in the franc. If Germany was forced to stabilize the FFr/DM rate, the Bundesbank would have to intervene in the foreign exchange market and sell marks and purchase francs. But this policy might expand the German money supply and push up the German price level and, in the process, enable France to pass some of its inflation over to Germany. Obviously, if this happened, Germany would soon quit the system.

Under the European Monetary System, when actual exchange rates—expressed as the ECU rate of a given currency—had moved so far from their central exchange rates that it appeared it would be impossible to maintain the existing parity grid, central rates were **realigned.** Realignment, in turn, led to a new parity grid.

The **very short-term credit facility** is an arrangement under which one EU central bank will lend another EU central bank funds for up to three months so that the second central bank can attempt to maintain the international value of its currency when it comes under pressure.

> A second example shows the importance of the divergence indicator. Suppose individuals flee the dollar and purchase marks. The mark will rise against the dollar and also against other EMS currencies. EMS governments would then either have to use international reserves or raise domestic interest rates in order to maintain the value of their currencies relative to the mark and to preserve the parity grid. But here's where the divergence indicator comes into play. The mark would cross its divergence threshold and Germany would either have to attempt to push the mark down or exchange rates within the EMS would need to be **realigned.**

The European Monetary Cooperation Fund can extend credit to a member nation for periods of 45 days to five years. Like IMF credits, borrowing conditions for EMCF credits become more stringent as the amount and duration of the credits increase.

Notwithstanding the good work of the EMCF, central bank cooperation is *most* important in maintaining the parity grid. EMS central banks may lend each other funds for periods up to three months under the **very short-term credit facility.** Of course, the willingness of one central bank to extend credit to another depends on the economic environment and the degree of their confidence in each other. So, in the final analysis, the most important asset of the EMS is the region's desire to maintain a zone of monetary stability in Europe. If the goal becomes unimportant, all the funds, indicators, and facilities in the world will not save the system.

This political reality is reflected in the short history of the EMS. Its initial success was credited in no small part to the convergent economic policies in Germany and France. For example, when French economic policy diverged from the EMS norm in 1981, the EMS did not perform up to expectations. But after France modified its economic policy in 1983 and kept it more in line with the EMS norm, intra-EMS policy convergence grew and the system enjoyed greater success until the fall of 1992.

September 1992

The EU was quite pleased, perhaps even smug, regarding the EMS at the beginning of 1992. After central rate realignment in 1987, membership had expanded and plans were being made to evolve from fixed exchange rates to a common currency. The exchange rate crises of September 1992 and August 1993, however, forced the plans to be put on hold and raised the question of whether the exchange rate mechanism itself would survive. It did survive, but in a far weaker, less inclusive form.

The immediate cause of the mayhem in 1992 has been attributed to the increase in German interest rates and decrease in U.S. interest rates during that year. In the United States, the Fed pushed short-term interest rates down to approximately 3 percent in an attempt to spur American economic recovery. In Germany, the Bundesbank raised short-term interest rates to close to 9.5 percent in an attempt to counter the potentially inflationary costs of German unification.

As the short-term interest rate differential between Germany and the United States widened, funds moved out of dollars and into marks and the mark appreciated. To prevent their currencies from falling relative to the mark, EMS members were compelled to raise *their* interest rates. In certain cases, higher interest rates exacerbated underlying economic conditions, and, in other cases, problems that might have been easily handled in less strained circumstances quickly blew into a firestorm.

Oddly enough, the first currencies to come under pressure in September 1992 were the Finish markkaa and the Swedish krona. Neither Finland nor Sweden was a member of the ERM at the time, although both nations were attempting to keep their currencies at par with the ECU in anticipation of joining the EMS at a later date. After heroic attempts to maintain the krona/DM exchange rate, the krona together with the markkaa and the Norwegian krone, had to be allowed to float against the German mark.

The Irish punt, Italian lira, Portuguese escudo, and Spanish peseta were also battered in the fall of 1992. The punt, peseta, and escudo were devalued—the latter two on several occasions, even though all three currencies remained within the ERM. The lira depreciated by 7 percent in the early days of the crisis; a short time later, the lira dropped out of the EMS and was permitted to float. Although the Italian rate of inflation exceeded the EU average, observers were in nearly universal agreement that it was the Italian government's budget deficit—more than 11 percent of GDP in 1992—that scared international investors and caused them to flee the lira.

Major attention was focused on the impact of the currency maelstrom on the British pound and the French franc. On September 16, 1992, Britain withdrew sterling from the ERM and, following the lira, allowed the pound to float. In the following days, sterling depreciated approximately 20 percent against the mark and the dollar. The British government had vainly attempted to maintain sterling at its ERM central exchange rate. British short-term interest rates had been raised first from 10 percent to 12 percent and later to 15 percent, although the second hike was rescinded on September 16 when the pound was set free to float. It is estimated that the British government spent as much as $30 billion in the foreign exchange markets attempting to prop up the sagging value of the pound.

Why was the British government frustrated in its attempt to maintain the international value of the pound? Critics charge that the Bank of England waited too long to raise interest rates, and, when it did, the magnitude of the increase was too timid. A 5 percent interest premium in favor of London compared to Frankfurt will not sustain the DM/£ rate if market players believe that the rate will fall by *more* than 5 percent. The question is, why did market players believe that the pound would fall by more than 5 percent? The UK and Germany had roughly similar rates of inflation at that time—3.6 percent and 3.5 percent respectively—and both countries' current accounts were in the red.

However, the British economy, in contrast to Germany's, was mired in a recession with negative economic growth. Money managers concluded that if Britain was unable to run a trade surplus with a negative rate of economic growth, it certainly could not run a surplus if aggregate demand picked up. Money managers, therefore, sold pounds in order to avoid taking a loss—and given the probability of pound depreciation—to make a profit.

Having made their money betting on sterling depreciation, currency speculators turned east and attacked the French franc. The franc, however, stood firm, but not without costs. The Bank of France raised the overnight interest rate from 10.5 percent to 13 percent, and spent between $30 billion and $50 billion buying francs on the foreign exchange markets to bolster the franc's value. Germany stood beside France in the battle to preserve the FFr/DM rate by loaning France marks and intervening in the foreign exchange market to prop up the franc. The two governments then issued a joint statement signaling their intent to maintain the exchange rate.

The franc withstood the speculative pressures; a month and a half later, the Bank of France declared victory, cut interest rates, and claimed that it had recovered all international reserves spent to defend the franc and had, in addition, actually made a profit of FFr1.2 billion on its stabilization operations. (This victory was shortlived: France spent some $50 billion attempting to stabilize the franc the following year.)

August 1993

Recriminations were rampant following the currency turmoil. The Bundesbank and its high-interest-rate policy was faulted. The Germans, it was said, had been selfish and indifferent to the welfare of other EMS members. Other observers, including Carlo Ciampi, then governor of the Bank of Italy, were not so hard on the Bundesbank, asserting that the crisis could have been avoided if policymakers had just opened their eyes and realigned the currencies in early 1992.

At the time, Germany was running a large budget deficit in order to finance its reunification with the former East Germany. Regardless of German monetary policy, the budget deficit would have raised German interest rates. Given unrestricted capital mobility, funds would have flown toward Germany and raised the international value of the mark. Since mark appreciation was a foregone conclusion, exchange rates should have been realigned.

In what may now seem surprising—especially with 20-20 hindsight—several commentators said that the less-inclusive ERM would now run more smoothly. The currencies that had been forced to either adjust their central rates or drop out of the system were, for the most part, the newer members of the institution or were currencies outside the system that were attempting to track the mark. Having, so to speak, cleared the decks, the ERM was ready to plow ahead.

Events were not kind to such optimism. Throughout the early summer of 1993, speculative pressures built up against the Danish krone, the Belgian franc, and the French franc. Speculators believed that the FFr/DM rate was being maintained by high French interest rates even though the French rate of inflation was 2.5 percent lower than the German rate. This meant that France had lofty real interest rates even though its unemployment rate stood close to 12 percent. In light of the high level of unemployment, the market bet that France would be unable to maintain high interest rates and preserve the franc. In the wake of the 1992 calamities, speculators also knew that bilateral ERM exchange rates were no longer invincible, and, given the narrow band, felt they could attack a currency with impunity. And they did just that.

After a crisis meeting, EU authorities introduced a new ERM on August 1, 1993. A new 15 percent level of fluctuations above or below the central exchange rate replaced the old 2.25 percent level. The new level meant that the FFr/DM rate, and any other bilateral exchange rate, could vary by 30 percent and still remain within prescribed limits.

BOX 16.5 Capital Controls and the ERM

The experiences of 1992 and 1993 led many people to conclude that it is impossible to maintain fixed exchange rates even within a common market comprised of similar nations. But a number of economists disagree. Barry Eichengreen and Charles Wyplosz argue that, with the exception of Italy, Britain, and Spain, the competitive positions of ERM countries had not deteriorated relative to Germany prior to September 1992. Hence, there was no need for currency realignments and, therefore, no need for the widened band in 1993. If economic fundamentals did not cause the crises, what precipitated the mayhem? In their view, large short-term speculative capital flows were the major culprit, and it follows that if such flows can be reduced, a system of fixed exchange rates is possible.

A **special deposit** is a sum of money that a bank must deposit interest free at the central bank for, say, one year whenever it purchases a foreign currency. The idea behind a special deposit is to increase the costs of speculating against the domestic currency. Special deposits would be employed only when exchange rates come under speculative pressure.

How can such capital movements be curtailed? Eichengreen and Wyplosz suggest a **special deposit** requirement. Under their proposal, central banks would require domestic financial institutions to make a one-year non-interest-bearing domestic currency deposit, a special deposit at the central bank whenever they purchase foreign currency, either on their own account or when acting on behalf of clients. If the value of the deposit is set equal to 100 percent of the value of the foreign exchange purchased, a French bank that purchases DM100 will, assuming the exchange rate is FFr3/DM, have to deposit FFr300 at the Bank of France for one year. Obviously, such funds cannot be loaned out. Thus the cost of the deposit to a French bank will depend on the interest rate. If it is 10 percent, the bank will have to forgo FFr30 in interest income when it purchases DM100. The costs of purchasing foreign exchange will rise and the controls will have a stronger bite as interest rates rise. Moreover, it would always be possible to raise and lower the deposit requirement. The rate could be raised to, say, 1000 percent in times of currency turmoil and drop back to zero when the foreign exchanges are calm.

A **foreign exchange transaction tax,** a tax on the buying and selling of foreign exchange, is designed to raise the cost and thus reduce the volume of speculative capital flows. Proponents of the proposal claim, and the mathematics agree, that the tax would severely penalize short-term capital movements but not seriously affect long-term capital flows.

Another option, originally proposed by James Tobin, is to place a 1 percent **foreign exchange transactions tax** on all transactions. Assuming a round trip—that is, moving from dollars to pounds and back to dollars—the annualized cost of a foreign exchange transaction would be nearly *8,000 percent* on a one-day shift, but *only .2 percent* for a 10-year round trip. The difference is important. Short-term and presumably speculative capital movements would be heavily taxed, but the tax on long-term capital flows would be negligible. The tax, therefore, would impede short-term capital flows and reduce speculation, but it would not obstruct long-term capital flows nor would it affect the long-term allocation of resources.

Eichengreen and Wyplosz do not claim that capital controls, or greater government controls, are ends in themselves. They argue that short-term capital flows are *so large* that they can destabilize the foreign exchanges even when currencies are in fundamental equilibrium. If the need to realign some exchange rates should ever arise, speculative capital flows may put undue pressure on all currencies within the parity grid and may transmit false signals. What is required is some policy—like a circuit breaker on Wall Street—that will damp down the flows and permit the authorities to get on with the task of realigning currencies in a calmer environment.

Critics of the foreign exchange tax and the special deposit scheme believe that both measures represent backsliding, especially in the case of the EU. Phase one on the road toward Maastricht was devoted to eliminating, not bolstering, capital controls. Second, critics claim that the measures would ultimately be futile. In a world of foreign or offshore banking, it is difficult for one country to impose capital controls for a long period. One can count on financial markets to test the boundaries and to discover ways to avoid the intent of the controls. Such innovations would then compel governments to fight ongoing battles to save the system, to impose even more controls in order to make the original controls work.

Sources: Barry Eichengreen and Charles Wyplosz, "The Unstable EMS," *Brookings Papers on Economic Activity* 1 (1993):pp. 51–124; James Tobin, "Tax on Speculators," *Financial Times* (December 2, 1992); and James Tobin, "A Proposal for International Monetary Reform," *The Eastern Economic Journal* 4 (July-October 1978): pp. 153–159.

Economic and Monetary Union

Economic and Monetary Union (EMU) is not an institution; rather it is an objective spelled out in the Maastricht Treaty. In a sense, it spells out the timetable and the steps that must be taken to attain currency unification, and the institution (the European Central Bank) that will carry out European-wide monetary policy once a common currency is in place.

The currency upheavals of 1992 and 1993 put a damper on the plans for **Economic and Monetary Union (EMU),** although currency unification still appears to be on the horizon. The target date for monetary unification, however, which had been considered possible by 1997, has been pushed back to at least 1999 and, perhaps, to 2002.

But one can ask: If the EU can install a system of immutable exchange rates, why should it want to go further and create a single currency? What is to be gained? For one thing, a common currency will reduce intra-European transaction costs since firms will not have to pay fees to convert one EU currency into another. While such costs are far more expensive for a tourist than for a business firm, it has been estimated that transaction fees soak up roughly 1/2 percent of the EU's GDP. But since the costs of currency conversion generate income for bankers, the creation of common currency would not yield a net gain of 1/2 percent of GDP.

A second motive for a common currency is that it eliminates the foreign exchange risk associated with trade. But if exchange rates are "permanently fixed," where is the risk? The answer is that even if all governments proclaim that the existing exchange rate parity grid is set for all time, a substantial number of people will not believe them. Government promises to maintain exchange rates have been broken before, so that, unless the exchange rate remains fixed for a prolonged period, people will be dubious of government commitments. And even though a firm can cover its foreign exchange risks in the forward exchange and options markets, such steps cost time and money. Moreover, it is either impossible or expensive for a firm to cover the perceived foreign exchange risk associated with building a plant in another EU country. The creation of a single communitywide currency would eliminate both these risks.

The Stages of Monetary Unification

Founded in 1994, the **European Monetary Institute (EMI)** is, supposedly, the forerunner of the European Central Bank. At the present time, it is charged with attempting to further coordinate national monetary policies within the European Union. This is the institution that will decide whether a nation should be permitted to join the European Monetary Union.

Under the Maastricht Treaty, the move toward a common currency will have three stages. Stage one, which began in 1990, was supposed to eliminate capital controls and promote unrestricted capital mobility throughout the European Union and, by promoting economic policy convergence, narrow the rates of inflation among member countries. Stage two began in January 1994, when the **European Monetary Institute (EMI)** was created. As a forerunner of the proposed **European Central Bank,** the EMI's immediate task is to further coordinate national monetary policies which, presumably, will lead to greater economic convergence and greater intra-European exchange rate stability. The EMI will also decide whether the economic performance of EU members has converged sufficiently that the final stage, tentatively set to begin in 1999, can be initiated. In stage three, the common currency will be adopted and the European Central Bank will replace the EMI and begin to conduct communitywide monetary policy.

Who Will Be Admitted to the EMU?

The **European Central Bank** is still on the drawing board. Presumably, it will begin operations when European currencies are replaced by a common currency sometime in the future. Given monetary union, the European Central Bank will displace all existing national central banks and will be in charge of Europe's monetary policy.

The **convergence indicators** are a list of macroeconomic targets which a nation must attain before it will be permitted to join the European Common Currency. The targets relate to interest and inflation rates, and the budget and national debt position of a country.

The general consensus is that policy convergence is a prerequisite for monetary unification. If all countries are following similar macroeconomic policies, then the move toward currency union will be an easy passage. Accordingly, a nation will be allowed to join the EMU if it meets the following conditions:

- Its central ERM exchange rate has not been revalued in the last two years.
- Its rate of inflation is not more than 1.5 percent higher than the average of the three lowest national rates of inflation within the EMS.
- Its long-term government bond interest rate is not more than 2 percent higher than the average interest rate prevailing in the three members with the lowest rates of inflation.
- Its central government budget deficit is 3 percent or less of GDP.
- Central government debt is no more than 60 percent of GDP.

Table 16.2 shows how countries stood relative to the **convergence indicators** just described in 1994.

As can be seen, four countries—Greece, Italy, Portugal and Spain—did not meet the inflation and interest rate criteria. Sweden met the inflation criteria but not the interest rate standard. All countries fared much worse on the deficit and debt criteria. In only four countries—Germany, Ireland, Luxembourg, and the Netherlands—was the

TABLE 16.2 Convergence Indicators in 1994

	ΔP/P	Interest Rate	Budget (% of GDP)	Debt (% of GDP)
Austria	3.0%	7.1%	−4.0	64.5
Belgium	2.4	7.6	−5.3	136.1
Denmark	2.0	8.7	−3.9	75.6
Finland	1.1	8.9	−5.5	60.1
France	1.7	7.3	−6.0	48.5
Germany	3.0	7.0	−2.5	50.1
Greece	10.9		−12.5	113.6
Ireland	2.3	8.2	−2.5	90.9
Italy	3.9	11.4	−6.9	125.4
Luxembourg	2.2	6.4	+2.3	7.0
Netherlands	2.8	7.0	−3.0	78.3
Portugal	5.2	10.8	−5.7	69.5
Spain	4.7	11.0	−6.6	62.6
Sweden	2.6	11.9	−10.4	79.1
UK	2.5	8.2	−6.5	52.5
Criteria	3.1	10.3	−3.0	60.0

Sources: Budget and debt ratios are from Organization for Economic Cooperation and Development, *Economic Outlook,* © OECD, June, 1995, pp. A33, A69. Reproduced by permission of the OECD; interest rates and inflation were computed from the relevant country pages of International Monetary Fund, *International Financial Statistics,* July, 1995. Inflation, ΔP/P, is measured by the increase in the consumer price index.

Under the **two-speed approach** to currency unification those nations that have met the convergence criteria can form a currency union at a certain date without having to wait for all members of the European Union to satisfy entrance requirements. Members who do not initially meet the criteria will be allowed to join the EMU at a later date, providing they have met the criteria.

budget deficit 3 percent or less of GDP, and only 5 of the 15 countries had debt/GDP ratios of 60.1 percent or less. Based on the convergence criteria, only Germany and Luxembourg would have been eligible to adopt a common currency in 1994.

Clearly, it will be impossible for most of the countries to drop their public debt/GDP ratio to 60 percent by 1999 or by 2002. But if a country can hold its budget deficit/GDP ratio to 3 percent or less, and if one assumes that nominal GDP grows by 5 percent per annum, the debt/GDP ratio will decline steadily over time. Thus, the important criteria will be the *current* budget position of a member country.

A country's budget position will also be important after currency unification. Given a European central bank conducting a European-wide monetary policy, one can assume that national interest rates and national inflation rates will converge. But members will still set their own budgets. What will prevent a member from running a budget deficit in excess of 3 percent of its GDP? In late 1995, the Germans, backed by the French, proposed a "stability pact for Europe." Under the proposal, a country whose budget deficit exceeds 3 percent of its GDP would have to set aside a non-interest-rate-bearing deposit with the ECB amounting to .25 percent of GDP for each percentage point of a budget deficit in excess of 3 percent of GDP. If, after two years, the country's budget deficit still exceeds 3 percent of GDP, the deposit would be converted into a fine and paid into the EU's budget.

A Two-Speed Approach Toward Currency Unification

What happens if some European Union members qualify for EMU membership, but other members do not? One proposal is that the EU should follow a **two-speed approach** toward currency union. Under such a scheme, currencies in fundamental equilibrium—such as the German mark, the French, Belgian and Luxembourg francs, the Dutch guilder, and Austrian schilling—would form a currency union, and other members would be admitted into the union as their economic vital signs improved. The argument is that currency unification, and its assumed benefits, should not depend on *all countries* attaining fundamental equilibrium at the same time and that stragglers should not be able to hold up the progress of the pacesetters.

A country's relative competitive position improves following a real devaluation. **Devaluation dumping** is a name given to instances when a country devalues its currency in order to obtain a competitive advantage—at least in the eyes of its competitors.

The two-speed approach suffers from a potentially major difficulty. Suppose Britain and Italy either do not join or are not permitted to join the restricted common currency. Imagine as well that the pound and the lira depreciate against the Euro in real terms. Britain and Italy would gain a competitive advantage that could unbalance trade within Western Europe. (France, for example, accused Britain, Italy, and Spain of **devaluation dumping** after their currencies depreciated against the franc following the turmoil of the summer of 1992.) In order to offset this competitive advantage, the common currency countries might have to introduce at least temporary import duties on British and Italian goods. Thus, the monetary arrangement would have to be maintained by *controls* rather than by *cooperation*.

To date, the passage toward monetary union has been tempestuous. Perhaps, the storm is behind the European Union; but, then, perhaps it is gathering strength.

Summary

Economic integration comes in several forms. In a free-trade area, members abolish trade barriers for intraregional trade, but each member sets its own tariff rates and quotas with the rest of the world. A customs union also abolishes intraregional trade restrictions, but it establishes a common external tariff with the rest of the world. With respect to trade, there is little difference between a customs union and a common market. But a common market takes economic integration a step beyond a customs union, by attempting to promote the free flow of capital and labor in addition to goods within the region. In the case of the European Union, member nations are attempting to form a common currency and initiate a unionwide monetary policy.

Economic integration may lead to both static and dynamic gains. The static gains or losses of economic integration are measured by the degree of trade creation relative to the degree of trade diversion. Dynamic gains can result from economies of scale, regionwide diffusion of technology, externalities, and the breakdown of local monopolies through an increase in competition. In addition, dynamic gains may be enhanced by the free movement of capital and labor throughout the market.

Regional economic integration may hurt the rest of the world. If economic integration leads to a high level of trade diversion, the rest of the world may be pinched. If their exports to the region are shut out or sharply reduced by a regionwide common external tariff, they will be injured. However, if economic integration leads to faster regional growth, the rest of the world may benefit from the increased demand for imports in the region. There is also the possibility that, through multilateral negotiations, the common external tariff will be reduced. In that case, the rest of the world should gain over the long haul. Assuming the dynamic effects of economic integration raise the region's GDP, the rest of the world may enjoy an expanding market. In addition, and just as important, if economic integration leads to hefty dynamic effects, the region's export supply curve may shift to the right and the rest of the world may be able to obtain the area's products at a lower price.

The EU has always felt that economic integration can be furthered by instituting a system of fixed intraregional exchange rates. This desire was manifest in the creation of the exchange rate mechanism and the Maastricht Treaty. The ERM went through tough times in the fall of 1992 and the summer of 1993, perhaps a foretaste of difficulties to come. Nevertheless, the EU is still groping, attempting to find common ground in order to create a European-wide central bank and institute a common currency for *political* if not necessarily economic reasons.

Key Terms and Concepts

Buy American Acts

common currency

common external tariff

common market

convergence criteria

customs union

devaluation dumping

divergence indicator

dynamic gains from economic integration

Economics and Monetary Union

European Currency Unit

European Monetary Cooperation Fund

European Monetary Institute

European Monetary System

European Regional Development Bank

exchange rate mechanism

free-trade area

foreign exchange transaction tax

green money

Maastricht Treaty

monetary compensatory amounts

optimum currency areas

parity grid

Single European Act of 1987

snake in the tunnel

social charter

social dumping

special deposits

trade creation

trade diversion

two-speed approach toward monetary unification

very short-term credit facility

Review Questions

1. Describe the differences between a free-trade area and a common market.

2. What is meant by trade divergence? Under what conditions is it most likely to be high?

3. Imagine that, upon establishing a common market, it is discovered that the degree of trade divergence exceeds the degree of trade creation. Does this mean that the common market should be disbanded?

4. Optimists claim that the formation of the European Union benefits the rest of the world, while pessimists hold the opposite position. What reasons do these groups put forward to support their opposite opinions?

5. What are the characteristics of an optimum currency area? If two areas form a currency union, will the union be an optimum currency area?

6. Outline the convergence criteria for the EMU. Which of these criteria do most observers believe will have to be waived if a common currency is to be created by the end of the century?

References and Suggested Readings

Many books describe the mechanics of the European Union. Two of them are: S.F. Goodman, *The European Community*, 2nd edition (London: Macmillan, 1993), and Dennis Swann, *The Economics of the Common Market*, 7th edition (London: Penguin, 1992). The classic work on trade creation versus trade diversion is Jacob Viner, *The Customs Union Issue* (New York: Carnegie Endowment for International Peace, 1950). The Federal Reserve Bank of Kansas City published the papers of a symposium it held in 1991 titled *Policy Implications of Trade and Currency Zones*. The volume contains a wealth of readable and lively papers by top economists. See especially the articles in the collection by Paul Krugman and Martin Feldstein. A collection of articles on the European Union is contained in *Reviving the European Union*, C. Randall Henning, Eduard Hochreiter, and Gary Clyde Hufbauer, editors (Washington, DC: Institute for International Economics, 1994).

As indicated in the chapter, a major work on the planned expansion of Europe's internal market is Michael Emerson and others, *The Economics of 1992: The EC Commission's Assessment of the Economic Effects of Completing the Internal Market* (New York: Oxford University Press, 1988). The *Brookings Papers on Economic Activity 2* (1989) contains a symposium on Europe 1992. Two articles especially worth noting are: Richard Cooper, "Europe without Borders," and Rudiger Dornbusch, "Europe 1992: Macroeconomic Implications."

The Economist publishes excellent survey articles on the European Union about every two years. The last two are: "Family Frictions," October 22, 1994; and "A Rude Awakening," July 3, 1993.

The two classical articles on optimum currency areas are Robert Mundell, "A Theory of Optimum Currency Areas," reprinted in his *International Economics* (New York: Macmillan, 1968); and Ronald I. McKinnon, "Optimum Currency Areas," *American Economic Review* 63 (September 1963): pp. 15–30.

Paul De Grauwe, *The Economics of Monetary Integration*, 2nd revised edition (New York: Oxford University Press, 1994), is probably the best work on monetary integration. It is a highly readable and accessible text, and only about 200 pages long. The last four chapters of De Grauwe's book discuss the EMS and the Maastricht Treaty. Geoffrey M. B. Tootell, "Central Bank Flexibility and the Drawbacks of Currency Unification," Federal Reserve Bank of Boston, *New England Economic Review* (May/June 1990): pp. 3–18, presents a different viewpoint regarding currency unification, and thus the

EMS, by discussing optimum currency areas within the United States. Although it covers more than the EMS and the ERM, "Exchange Rate Regimes and Volatility," Federal Reserve Bank of Kansas City, *Economic Review* (Third Quarter 1993) by Charles Engel and Craig S. Hakkio is particularly pertinent. The case against the EMU is cogently presented by Martin Feldstein, "Europe's Monetary Union," *The Economist* (June 13, 1992); pp. 23ff.

David Hale sketched out alternative scenarios regarding the ERM crisis before it actually came to a head. See his article, "The Pain of Monetary Reform," *International Economic Insights* (September/October 1992): pp. 22–23. As pointed out, Barry Eichengreen and Charles Wyplosz present their case for capital controls in their article, "The Unstable EMS," *Brookings Papers on Economic Activity* 1 (1993): pp. 51–124. Although parts of it are difficult, this article presents an excellent review of events leading up to the currency mayhem of 1992. The comments on this article by William H. Branson and Rudiger Dornbusch in the same issue of the *Brookings Papers on Economic Activity* are also well worth reading. Eichengreen and Wyplosz presented a synopsis of their article in a letter to *The Economist*, published June 5, 1993, p. 89, as "Economic Focus: ERM Again."

Chapter 17

The North American Free Trade Agreement

The **North American Free Trade Agreement (NAFTA),** which was ratified in 1994, established a free trade area among Canada, Mexico, and the United States.

In 1994, Canada, Mexico, and the United States ratified the **North American Free Trade Agreement (NAFTA),** establishing a free trade area among the three North American nations. Unlike the EU, NAFTA is neither a customs union nor a common market—there are, for example, no plans to create a North American monetary system or a common agricultural policy. In addition, there are some fundamental differences between the fifteen-nation EU and the three-nation NAFTA. The EU economies are more open than the NAFTA economies. This means that the costs and benefits of economic integration bear more heavily on its members than they do on the NAFTA countries. But an even more striking difference between the two trading blocs is that EU nations have *roughly similar* incomes per capita, while within NAFTA, the first regional trading agreement composed of both developed and developing countries, income per capita is *far higher* in Canada and the United States than in Mexico.

Thus, the theoretical basis for trade with one's regional partners is different between the EU and NAFTA. Much intra-EU trade derives from intraindustry trade and economies of scale, while intra-NAFTA trade can be explained by factor endowment, factor mobility, and the product cycle. Intra-EU trade, therefore, tends to be based on *similarities* while intra-NAFTA trade is rooted to a larger extent on *differences.* And, because a portion of intra-NAFTA trade may be based on the amended product cycle theory of trade (see Chapter 6), there is more chance of conflict within NAFTA than within the EU.

Yet, far from being revolutionary, NAFTA simply recognizes the existing and growing interdependence of the three North American economies. Mexican trade with the United States between 1990 and 1994 equaled roughly 74.5 percent of its total exports and 67.3 percent of its total imports. Canadian trade with the United States during the same period averaged 78 percent of its exports and 63.9 percent of its imports. Even prior to NAFTA, trade among the three countries was, for the most part, "free;" when tariffs were applied, they averaged between 5 percent and 10 percent in most cases. Of course, there were exceptions: Mexico imposed import licenses on cars and pharmaceuticals, and Canada and the United States maintained quotas on textiles (Table 17.1).

TABLE 17.1 Canadian and Mexican Exports to and Imports from the United States: 1990—94 (percentage of total exports and imports)

Year	Canada		Mexico	
	Exports	Imports	Exports	Imports
1990	75.4	62.8	70.1	64.8
1991	75.7	62.3	74.6	70.8
1992	75.6	63.5	69.0	62.8
1993	81.3	65.1	78.4	68.2
1994	82.1	65.7	80.4	69.8

Source: Computed from data in International Monetary Fund, *Direction of Trade Statistics Yearbook*, 1995, pp. 145, 273. The figures are for merchandise exports and imports.

TABLE 17.2 U.S. Exports and Imports (billions of $ and percent of total U.S. exports and imports)

	1990	*1991*	*1992*	*1993*	*1994*
Canada					
Exports	$99.1	$103.0	$109.7	$117.8	$132.3
	18.4%	17.8%	17.6%	18.3%	18.9%
Imports	$101.1	$101.0	$109.1	$124.2	$143.0
	16.5%	16.6%	16.6%	17.4%	17.7%
Mexico					
Exports	$35.8	$41.4	$49.5	$50.1	$59.8
	6.5%	7.1%	8.0%	7.8%	8.5%
Imports	$38.1	$39.4	$43.3	$48.9	$58.6
	6.2%	6.5%	6.6%	6.9%	7.3%

Source: U.S. Department of Commerce, *Survey of Current Business*, various issues. The figures have been rounded.

The **Canada–US Free Trade Agreement (FTA)** went into effect on January 1, 1989. Under the provisions of the agreement, all bilateral tariffs between the two nations will be eliminated by 1999.

Since Canadian–Mexican trade is minuscule, Canada's only advantage in signing the NAFTA pact was to protect the preferences it had obtained under the **Canada–United States Free Trade Agreement (FTA)** of 1988. NAFTA, in many respects, is an extension of the FTA and the Mexican government evidently felt it could not exclude Canada in signing a trade pact with the United States. For the United States, the pact recognizes and confirms reality: Canada is America's largest customer and Mexico is the third-largest and most-rapidly-expanding market for U.S. exports measured in percentage terms (Table 17.2).

The Path Ahead

In this chapter, we look at topics that directly concern NAFTA and some issues that took center stage during the debate over its passage:

- The major features of the trade agreement.
- The bitter debate that was sparked by NAFTA negotiations when some people within the United States hailed it as a logical step in the right direction, while others claimed that its adoption would seriously impair the U.S. economy.
- Some peripheral issues raised in the debate over its passage: trade and the environment, and labor standards.

Major Features of NAFTA

Export performance requirements can mean many things. In the context of foreign direct investment, performance requirements state that a foreign firm must export a certain percentage of its output.

Under **domestic content** or **local content rules,** a firm must purchase a specified amount of the inputs needed to produce a product from domestic or local sources.

Under NAFTA, the **snap-back** provision permits tariff rates to be set at a pre-NAFTA level for three to four years when an industry is imperiled by a surge of imports.

Rules of origin specify how much of the value of a product must be added locally or, in the case of free trade agreements, regionally in order for the product to receive preferential tariff treatment.

Under the provisions of the agreement, Canada, Mexico, and the United States agreed to eliminate tariffs on trade with each other for a 10-year period (15 years in the case of a few import-sensitive products). The NAFTA treaty broke ground in two ways. First, the accord phases in free trade in agricultural products between Mexico and the United States over 15 years, although in side agreements, a substantial portion of citrus fruit production in the United States was effectively exempted for the time being.

Second, the NAFTA agreement established regional free trade in textiles and apparel, albeit with origin requirements that must be met if a product is to attain duty-free status. NAFTA thus marks the first time that Canada and the United States have opened up their markets in textiles and apparel to a developing country, at least on such an unrestricted scale.

Unlike the EU, the NAFTA accord does not institute a common external tariff. Mexico's external tariffs, however, will gradually be brought down to the most-favored-nation tariff levels prevailing in Canada and the United States. This step is the culmination of the free trade policy initiated by Mexico in the 1980s.

NAFTA also liberalizes cross-border investment. Foreign companies are no longer subject to **export performance requirements** that compel them to export a certain percentage of their output or to **domestic or local content** rules that force companies to purchase inputs from local or domestic sources. In addition, U.S., Canadian, and Mexican investors are free to invest in most sectors of all three countries. The provision opens up foreign investment opportunities in previously restricted areas of Mexico including petrochemicals and financial services. The notable exception to the rule is primary energy.

In line with the FTA, NAFTA creates a number of independent panels to adjudicate trade disputes among the three partners. The expectation is that such panels can prevent minor disputes from escalating into a full-scale trade war. In addition, the agreement provides a safety net for industries imperiled by a surge of imports. Under the **snap-back** provision, tariffs equal to pre-NAFTA levels can be reimposed for three to four years to offset import surges.

One of the most restrictive aspects of NAFTA is that it imposes steep **rules of origin** requirements that must be adhered to if a product is to receive preferential treatment. Under the FTA, for example, Honda does not pay an import duty on a car made and sold in Canada or the United States if 50 percent of the car's value is added in either country. If only 40 percent of the value of the car is added in Canada or the United States, the car is subject to import duties in both countries. In the case of cars, the regional value-added requirement under NAFTA is set at 62 percent. NAFTA, therefore, *raises* rather than lowers the origin requirement for cars. NAFTA requires products generally to undergo "substantial transformation" within the region in order to qualify for preferential treatment.

Export platform. The construction of productive facilities in one country, say, Mexico, for the export of goods to another country, say, the United States. By setting up operations in Mexico, a non–North American firm can meet NAFTA's **rules of origin** requirements.

There are two drawbacks to rules of origin requirements. They can compel domestic producers to purchase *more expensive* regional inputs in place of cheaper external ones, a burden that may harm the ability of regional producers to compete in world markets. Second, rules of origin requirements set an expensive precedent that could be copied elsewhere when other regional trading blocks are established.

Why did the three nations agree to such a trade-diverting measure? No doubt, FTA precedence had something to do with it. But, in addition, there was concern that foreign firms might set up **export platforms** in Mexico to take advantage of low-cost labor as well as preferential access to North American markets, with dire consequences for Canadian and U.S. manufacturers. Such fears were greatest in the case of cars, although critics of rules of origin say they have been applied too liberally in other areas, for example, textiles.

The Consequences of NAFTA

Social dumping consists of a claim that a country obtains an unfair competitive advantage by skimping on workers' working conditions and benefits. **Environmental dumping** consists of the claim that a country obtains an unfair competitive advantage by skimping on environmental standards and their enforcement.

Because NAFTA includes both developed and developing countries, it has raised the specter of both **social** and **environmental dumping.** "Social dumping" is based on the assertion that a country obtains an unfair competitive advantage by skimping on workers' health insurance, disability benefits, and the like. The question of social dumping also arose when Portugal and Spain entered the EU, and it has been raised on other occasions as well. The same claim is applied to environmental standards. If one country turns a blind eye toward pollution, firms operating in that nation may gain a cost advantage over firms operating under stricter, costlier standards in other countries.

NAFTA opponents argued that U.S. and foreign firms would shift their operations to Mexico to take advantage of lower labor costs and less-stringent and less-costly environmental standards. Not only would jobs migrate from the north to the south, but regionwide environmental standards would suffer in the process.

NAFTA proponents concede that, since hourly labor compensation in manufacturing in Mexico is roughly 15 percent of Canadian and U.S. levels, some U.S. and Canadian jobs will be shifted to Mexico. If unit costs of production are lower in Mexico than in the United States and Canada, some firms (foreign transplants) will inevitably switch their manufacturing operations to Mexico. But jobs may move in the other direction as well. Gary Hufbauer and Jeffrey Schott note, that although the average hourly compensation per worker in manufacturing in the United States was 8 times higher than in Mexico, value added per employee in the United States was 8.2 times higher than value added per worker in Mexico's *maquiladoras*. Since the ratios of wages and value added nearly equal each other, the mix of wages, productivity, infrastructure, and proximity to major markets could cause some firms to move from Mexico to one of its northern neighbors.

The Economic Impact of NAFTA

Projections of NAFTA's impact on the American economy suffer from one fact. Quite correctly, they were made *prior* to the signing of the accord in order to estimate its im-

BOX 17.1 The Maquiladoras

A **maquiladora** is the name given to industrial parks made up of primarily foreign firms in Northern Mexico. Such firms, *maquilas*, can import inputs duty free into Mexico, but the final product must be exported.

The **maquiladora** program was initiated in 1965 after the United States canceled the *bracero* program, which had permitted Mexican workers to cross the border in order to do seasonal work in the United States. Cut off from a source of foreign exchange, the Mexican government initiated the maquiladora program (roughly translated, an industrial park comprised of foreign-owned plants), under which foreign-owned firms could set up operations in Mexico and import inputs duty-free as long as the *final products* were exported out of Mexico. Thus, a maquila (the foreign-owned firm) could import capital equipment from the United States into Mexico without paying any tariff. In addition, the maquila could import raw materials (sugar, let's say) from the Caribbean without paying any duty providing the final product (such as candy) was not sold in Mexico.

The maquiladora program has been a success, at least when measured by conventional economic yardsticks. Between 1980 and 1994, employment grew at an annual rate of 12 percent and the net exports of maquiladoras expanded at a 15.8 percent annual rate (Table 17.3). In 1994, maquiladoras exported $26 billion worth of goods to the United States, roughly 43 percent of Mexico's total exports to the United States. In addition, maquiladora products represented 52 percent of Mexico's total manufactured exports.

There is a downside to the maquiladora program. The rush of people to find jobs within a concentrated area has led to problems with water supplies and public sanitation. In addition, steps have not been taken to adequately dispose of toxic wastes resulting from the increased production.

TABLE 17.3 Maquiladoras: Employment and Net Exports

Year	Number of Plants	Employment (thousands)	Net Exports (millions of dollars)
1980	578	119.5	772
1982	585	127.0	851
1984	722	199.7	1,155
1986	844	249.8	1,295
1988	1,441	369.5	2,337
1990	1,938	460.3	3,611
1992	2,075	505.0	4,808
1994	2,085	579.4	6,000

Source: Gary C. Hufbauer and Jeffrey J. Schott, *NAFTA: An Assessment*, revised edition (Washington, DC: Institute for International Economics, 1993), Copyright © 1993 by the Institute for International Economics. All rights reserved. Table A3, p. 172. Lucinda Vargas, "Beyond the Border, Marquiladoras: Mexico's Bright Spot," Federal Reserve Bank of Dallas, *The Southwest Economy* 5 (1995); pp. 9–10.

pact on the U.S. economy. But that means they were made *prior* to the peso crisis and the resulting marked decline—some 10 percent in 1995—in the level of economic activity in Mexico. Since we have seen that a sharp fall in economic activity in any country will reduce that country's imports, we would expect that Mexico's imports would decline following the depreciation of the peso and the fall in Mexico's GDP. In other words, unforeseen developments played havoc with some aspects of the projections.

Projections of NAFTA's impact on U.S. wages and employment differ radically. Timothy Koechlin and Mehrene Larudee estimated that by the year 2000, in the wake of NAFTA, U.S. firms would redirect between $31 billion and $52 billion of investment from the United States to Mexico. According to Koechlin and Larudee, the redirected investment would create between 400,000 and 680,000 jobs in Mexico at the cost of some 290,000 to 490,000 jobs in the United States.

In addition, Koechlin and Larudee predicted that the migration of U.S. capital to Mexico and the resulting job loss in the United States would impact the U.S. labor market by dropping the rate of growth of the demand for labor and that the threat of potential job migration would place a damper on wage increases in the United States. Koechlin and Larudee estimated that the loss in real wages in the United States due to the agreement would be some 1.2 percent to 2 percent by the year 2000.

While Koechlin and Larudee painted a bleak picture, their projections seemed almost like a ray of sunshine when compared with the projection of Ross Perot and Pat Choate, who estimated that NAFTA threatened some 6 million jobs in the United States. How did Perot and Choate arrive at this astounding figure? They added up all the manufacturing jobs at all U.S. firms where labor costs exceeded 20 percent of costs. They included both high-skill and low-skill jobs in both high-tech and low-tech industries. Professional economists were underwhelmed with their study and the majority of economists rejected their conclusion. Gary Hufbauer and Jeffrey Schott, for example, cracked that (Perot and Choate) "use analytic methods that bear a closer kinship to astrology than to economics."[1]

Koechlin's and Larudee's forecasts have been attacked on several fronts. First, their projections assume that all capital transfers to Mexico will come from preexisting or already planned investment in the United States. But some observers contend that the passage of NAFTA will inspire *totally new* investment in Mexico independent of planned investment in the United States. And while Koechlin and Larudee tend to minimize potential capital and job transfers if NAFTA had been rejected, their critics believe that today's Mexico-bound firms would have moved their operations anyway, say to Asia. Hence, NAFTA did not necessarily change the *magnitude* of the capital transfer, only its *destination*.

Gary Hufbauer and Jeffrey Schott offered a less-pessimistic prediction about the impact of NAFTA on the U.S. economy. They predicted that by 1995, an additional 316,000 jobs would be created in the United States due to NAFTA. So even though some 145,000 jobs would be lost to Mexico, NAFTA would create 171,000 net additional jobs in the United States. Bear in mind that, since total employment in the United States was 123 million in 1994, the total employment contribution of NAFTA would be .14 percent—or "a drop in the bucket."

Hufbauer and Schott also estimated that U.S. exports to Mexico would climb an additional $17 billion per year by 1995 as a result of the trade accord. And since Mexican exports to the United States due to the trade pact were projected to rise by $8 billion per year, the U.S. trade balance with Mexico would improve by $9 billion per year by 1995. (In fact, due to the depreciation of the peso and the drop in Mexican income, the U.S. trade balance with Mexico showed an $8 billion deficit for the first six months of 1995.)

Of course, NAFTA's projected positive effects on employment must be balanced against various social dislocations, such as when workers move from contracting to ex-

---

[1]Gary Clyde Hufbauer and Jeffrey J. Schott, *op. cit.*, p. 177.

panding industries. Hufbauer and Schott do not believe that this sort of dislocation will be a serious problem, and, in fact, they estimate that NAFTA will cause only 2 percent of all job dislocations in the United States over the five years following the enactment of the treaty. Even Koechlin and Larudee put the figure at a relatively low 6 percent. So even in the worst case, NAFTA-caused dislocations are expected to be mild. Hufbauer and Schott argue further that employment and unemployment effects of NAFTA will be spread across all industries and all job classifications, both skilled and unskilled. Job losses were expected in farming, textiles, and bulk steel production, while employment gains were expected in processed foods, plastics, pharmaceuticals, capital goods, and high-grade steel.

Hufbauer and Schott emphasized that the trade pact would lead to greater efficiency and higher economic growth, and generate $15 billion additional yearly benefits to be divided between Mexico and the United States. Assuming a 20 percent return on investment, this is similar to adding $75 billion to the public capital stock of both nations—a windfall for both, if these estimates are correct.

NAFTA and the Environment

President Bush signed the NAFTA accord in the final months of his administration, and President Clinton shepherded it through the Congress. Prior to presenting NAFTA for ratification by the Congress, President Clinton negotiated "side agreements" on labor standards, environmental issues, and measures to protect industries harmed by a sudden surge of imports.

Of these side issues, those concerning the environment have probably raised the biggest storm. Even though NAFTA has been hailed in some circles as the "greenest trade" accord ever negotiated, it is still not green enough to satisfy some critics who fear that NAFTA will encourage foreign firms to set up operations in Mexico so as to benefit from its relatively low environmental standards and its slack enforcement. Since environmental standards add to the cost of production costs (the more stringent they are, the higher the costs), firms will tend to locate where environmental standards are lowest. Hence, one would expect firms to migrate from Canada and the United States to Mexico.

To environmentalists a big question is whether the NAFTA agreements encourage firms to **internalize** their full costs of production or encourage them to avoid internalizing full costs. When a firm internalizes its full costs of production, it covers all its costs of production *including* any environmental mess caused by the production process. If a firm is not compelled to internalize its full costs of production, it can **externalize** or pass some of its production costs on to someone else. The costs may be passed on as poorer air quality, toxic waste, and so on. Or the costs of cleaning up the environment may be passed on to the society as a whole in the form of taxes.

Consider a firm that locates in Mexico due to low environmental standards. The firm's production should raise the level of income in the community by some multiple. Given the higher income, the Mexican government could tax a portion of it and use the tax receipts to clean up the environment. If that occurs, the area would end up with a higher income and the same level of environmental protection. However, even if it did, the program would involve a firm specific subsidy.

If a firm **internalizes** its full costs of production, it will cost-out the environmental impacts of its production. This will raise the firm's production costs. If a firm does not have to internalize or pay for the environmental havoc it wreaks upon the community, it is able to **externalize** some of its social costs of production. The community pays for a portion of the firm's total costs of production in the form of pollution or in the form of the taxes required to fund a cleanup of the firm-created pollution.

A less-developed country could argue that an environmental subsidy is no different than the subsidies given to firms by developed countries in the form of tax breaks, construction of access roads to major highways, funds for worker training programs, and so on in order to induce them to locate their operations in a developed region, especially if the increased production funds the resources necessary to maintain environmental standards. Environmentalists believe that this argument is too clever by half, and that by ignoring externalities caused by accepting lower environmental standards, NAFTA is not promoting the efficient use of resources. Thus not only will NAFTA increase pollution, but also it is not based on an efficient allocation of resources.

Plant location decisions, however, depend on myriad factors, only one of which is the cost of complying with environmental standards. If compliance costs are a small percentage of total costs, they will probably not figure prominently when a firm selects a plant site. In this regard, a 1992 World Bank study concluded that only small savings are derived by most industries which exploit lax environmental standards, and that these savings are outweighed by relocation costs and by risks associated with political instability. (The World Bank found that pollution abatement costs are less than 3 percent of operating costs in 86 percent of U.S. industries.)

However, while the cost of compliance may be minor *across* industries, they can be major for a *particular* industry. Environmentalists argue that "dirty" industries—those that face high environmental-standard compliance costs—will move to Mexico. If such migration does take place, it would, as pointed out, only change the *source* of pollution in the Northern hemisphere, not its level. But environmentalists also fear that non–North American foreign transplants will set up operations in Mexico due to NAFTA's rules of origin and tariff preferences. Thus, environmentalists contend that NAFTA-inspired relocation will actually *raise* the level of pollution in the Northern hemisphere, especially if the trade accord leads to a higher rate of economic growth within the region. Given a constant ratio of pollutants per unit of output, greater output equals a higher level of pollution. And if production is diverted from areas with high pollution standards to areas with lower standards, environmental degradation will rise even if total output remains constant.

Environmentalists have other concerns. Under the maquiladora program, many firms set up operations on the Mexican-U.S. border. Naturally, this development led to an influx of workers into the area. But many cities and towns along the border lacked the public infrastructure required to guarantee healthy sanitation and water quality. As a result, Mexican public health standards deteriorated along the border and, in addition, pollution generated in Mexico spilled over into the United States. A long-running concern in California, for example, was untreated or poorly treated waste water flowing into the Pacific Ocean from Tiajuana and, from there, up to San Diego and to cities, suburbs, and beaches beyond. Environmentalists dread that further economic development along the border will increase pollution on both sides of it, and especially in the United States.

However, some economists have looked at NAFTA and concluded that a potential side benefit of the trade pact could be a reduction in the level of pollution in Mexico. Why? Gene M. Grossman and Alan B. Krueger argue that Mexico's comparative advantage is in agricultural products and labor-intensive manufacturers, a mix of activities that on the whole are cleaner than average. That means that if NAFTA leads to greater specialization, Mexico could end up with a cleaner environment, although, by the same reasoning, Canada and the United States would end up with a slightly dirtier environment because they would specialize in pollution-generating capital-intensive activities.[2]

Even prior to the side agreement, Mexico and the United States established a joint fund to finance pollution abatement along the border. The initial aim was to maintain but not necessarily improve environmental standards. But President Clinton, by negotiating the side agreement on pollution, attempted to improve rather than just maintain environmental standards along the border. Mexico itself spent 1 percent of its GDP on improving the environment—a very high proportion for an LDC or an NIC. In addition, Mexico strengthened its environmental laws, raised its expenditures on environmental protection, hired more inspectors, and closed down some 200 plants that violated environmental quality standards.

Green taxes are a tax on pollution. Under a system of green taxes, a firm would be charged a certain sum of money per unit of pollutant emitted. The revenues generated by the taxes could be used to help clean up the environment.

To encourage environmental protection, a trilateral commission was established by the three countries to monitor pollution standards throughout the region and advise member countries on environmental issues. It is conceivable that the commission eventually could be given the authority to impose **green taxes** on regional exports of a member country whose producers violate environmental quality standards. Since green taxes are still in the proposal stage, the question of whether they would be used to help sustain and clean up the environment is still open.

GATT/WTO and the "Greens"

Environmentalist attitudes toward the GATT/WTO are not ambivalent: They range from "mad" to "very mad." Some greens are categorically antigrowth; since trade is an engine of growth, they want to curtail it or roll it back. Because the WTO is specifically designed to promote international trade, it is pure anathema to these environmentalists.

The greens' bitter attack on the WTO surprised some people. It is hard to relate the level of pollution in the United States to its level of international trade. Cars may cause pollution, but there is little evidence, given regulations, that a Volkswagen causes more pollution than a Chevrolet. Nor is there any evidence that closed economies have lower degrees of pollution than open economies. The ecological performance of the closed economies of Eastern Europe was pretty dismal despite the propaganda that showed or described how socialist heros of labor worked in harmony with the environment.

There is, in addition, a paradox associated with this extreme "green" position. If worldwide economic growth comes to an end, the majority of the world's population will be doomed to poverty unless some supranational organization finds a way to redistribute world income. The chance of this occurring is at best remote. And there is scant evidence that environmentalists have seriously considered applying the compensation principle to attain their objectives, except in rare instances (see Box 18.3), and, in one case, the compensation has been financed with other people's money.

---

[2]Gene M. Grossman and Alan B. Krueger, "Environmental Impacts of a North American Free Trade Agreement," in *The Mexico-U.S. Free Trade Agreement*, edited by Peter M. Garber (Cambridge, MA: MIT Press, 1993), pp. 47–48.

Net economic welfare is a measure designed to show the true economic welfare of a country. It is computed by adding such things as leisure brought about by a shorter work week to *Gross Domestic Product (GDP)*, and subtracting such items as the cost of pollution and congestion from GDP.

When antipollution laws are enacted, a firm will attempt to find cleaner ways to produce a product and innovate to make the final product itself cleaner. These are called **innovation offsets**, and, according to some economists, will actually reduce the firm's costs of production.

First mover. If a country is first to enact strong environmental measures, it will be the first nation to spawn an environmental cleanup industry. Then when the rest of the world raises its environmental standards, the already developed domestic cleanup industry will have a worldwide comparative advantage. Thus pollution control will create a new industry.

The normal assumption is that there is a trade-off between protecting the environment and economic growth. The assumed trade-off does not imply that a society will necessarily be worse off if it selects some environmental protection in place of a modicum of growth. Presumably the number of goods available to a society will decline, or not grow as rapidly, but the quality of life will improve. This is an old battle between quantity versus quality or between gross domestic product and **net economic welfare**—a measure which adds such things as more leisure brought about by a shorter working week and better health standards to the GDP, and subtracts such things as traffic congestion and environmental damage from the GDP.

Recently, however, a new thesis has emerged that argues that a clean environment is good for growth. One can obtain a cleaner environment plus a higher GDP. Because quantity and quality are complements rather than substitutes, there is no trade-off.

There are three threads to the argument. First, it is claimed that environmental controls will create more jobs than they destroy because higher environmental standards will spawn firms to clean up the pollution and create jobs in those firms which specialize in producing antipollution devices such as catalytic converters. Certainly, the cleanup industry has grown at a rapid clip, and the OECD estimates that it will be a $300 billion industry by the end of the decade. But even if the cleanup industry adds jobs to the economy and improves the quality of life, it is difficult to see how this will increase the quantity of goods available to the society. If resources are shifted away from producing widgets to cleaning up the environmental mess created by producing them, the society will end up with fewer widgets.

Thus, the ability of environmental regulations to generate economic growth depends on the second strand of the argument: namely, that such regulations will lead firms to produce the same level of output using fewer resources, an efficiency gain which will obviously raise standards of living as normally defined. Put another way, given environmental regulations, firms will use fewer resources to produce a widget. This liberates resources from widget production and permits a society to produce greater quantities of other goods.

Michael Porter, Professor of Management at Harvard University, has been a keen advocate of this strand of the argument. He believes that environmental regulations lead to what he calls **innovation offsets** either through product offsets or process offsets. Given regulations, a firm will seek to minimize their impact on production costs, or look to offset them. In looking for such offsets, Porter contends firms will learn how to recycle materials, reduce the number of inputs per unit of output, reduce their consumption of energy, and so on. In addition, Porter also believes that the products themselves can be improved as a result of environmental regulation. Hitachi, for example, responded to a Japanese recycling law by making it easier to recycle washing machines and vacuum cleaners. In so doing, it reduced the number of parts in a washing machine by 16 percent and the number of parts in a vacuum cleaner by 30 percent. Product redesign led to fewer parts and, thus, easier assembly and lower production costs.

Since many economists find this strand of the argument hard to take, it is the third part of the argument, what is called the **first mover** idea, that most impresses them. If the United States imposes strict environmental guidelines, it will create an efficient cleanup industry. Since the demand for a cleaner environment expands as income per capita rises, the U.S. firms will be well placed to meet the demand for cleanup services as income per capita rises throughout the world. The United States, in short, will have a comparative advantage in the cleanup industry. Thus, the nation that first imposes strict environmental rules will gain a competitive advantage in a burgeoning industry.

To some observers this seems too good to be true. Government regulations will create employment, enhance economic efficiency, and generate a comparative advantage.

Sources: Michael E. Porter and Claas van der Linde, "Toward a New Conception of the Environment-Competitiveness Relationship," *Journal of Economic Perspectives* 9 (Fall 1995): pp. 97–118; and "How to Make Lots of Money and Save the Planet Too," *The Economist* (June 3, 1995); pp. 57–58.

In the field of environmental studies, **product standards** refer to the environmental quality of a particular product, such as DDT causes so much harm. **Process (production) standards** refer to the environmental damage caused by the production of a particular product. An environmentally "clean" product can be produced by clean methods in one country and by "dirty" methods in another. For example, a product can be produced in plants where power is generated by burning coal. The acid test: Which plant is equipped with scrubbers?

The majority of environmentalists, however, do not favor zero economic growth, although most greens believe that economic growth as we have known it since World War II is not sustainable over the long run. Nevertheless, they are convinced that the GATT/WTO is antigreen. What are their complaints?

First, the GATT specifies that domestic and foreign goods must be treated equally regardless of *how* they are produced. That is, the WTO permits the **product standard** (the what) to override the **process standard** (the how). A country with high environmental standards cannot impose an import duty on a foreign good (the product standard) even when it is produced under what the country considers subpar environmental standards (the process standard). Trade restrictions, therefore, cannot be based on environmental standards under the rules of the WTO, which greens believe is another way of saying that the environment does not matter.

Such rules, according to environmentalists, encourage pollution since there are costs to meeting environmental standards, and the higher the standards, the higher the costs. In fact, some analysts believe that the costs of meeting higher standards rises exponentially with each turn of the "ratchet." If this is the case, goods produced under "dirty" conditions will enjoy a growing cost advantage compared with goods produced under "clean" conditions. The natural reaction of firms producing in countries with high environmental standards will be either to move their operations to a country where standards are less rigorous, or to petition the government to relax its environmental rules on grounds that they reduce domestic competitiveness and ultimately will cost the country jobs. Both steps will increase pollution and bring environmental standards down to the lowest common denominator.

A country with high environmental standards might be able to solve the dilemma by subsidizing its export industries, enabling them to meet national standards and still remain competitive in world markets. However, even if a country is willing to take such an initiative, it could still run afoul of the WTO, which discourages subsidies, though not very effectively.

The greens have additional reservations regarding the WTO. Under the WTO, a country cannot restrict trade in one or more products in order to enforce its regulations on other products. The United States, for example, cannot impose duties or restrict Japanese exports of, say, consumer electronics because it is unhappy with Japan's whaling practices. Nor can a nation ban the export of goods, for example, pesticides, that violate its environmental standards but pass muster in other countries.

Greens find little comfort in the tone of the proposed technical standards adopted at the Uruguay Round, which argue that, even if environmental standards are applied equally to domestic and foreign goods, they can still be challenged if they are not the *least trade-restrictive* way of meeting the objective. In addition, greens are upset by WTO's health standards—human, animal, and plant. Under the revisions, countries have to base domestic standards on international standards if they exist, or set their standards so they do not discriminate against countries in similar conditions. According to environmentalists, this means that even if the United States establishes a rule limiting the amount of pesticide residue permitted on food sold in America regardless of source, foreign or domestic, it may not be able to bar imports with double the permitted amount of residue if the world standard for permitted pesticide residue is double the American standard.

The LDCs' Viewpoint

It is not surprising, therefore, that environmentalists are disturbed with the WTO and with the present international trading system. However, it is also not surprising that many LDCs believe that the present emphasis on environmental concerns is a smoke-screen, perhaps unintentional in the case of the greens, designed to keep LDC exports out of developed-country markets.[3] Since developed countries are richer, they can afford environmental regulations that are beyond the reach of most LDCs. Given growth, they argue, they too will be able to meet the environmental standards of the North. (Gene M. Grossman and Alan B. Krueger found that the level of sulfur dioxide pollution in cities around the world with a per-capita income in excess of $4,000 to $5,000 has fallen with the rise in per-capita income.) In fact, as people become richer they tend to demand more public goods, *including* a cleaner environment.

LDCs also question the way environmental rules are established. Environmentalists, they say, view pollution as a byproduct of *marginal* or additional production just as economic theory says they should. In such a framework, a flat tax on pollutants emitted per unit of output would affect the *most dirty* production first. If the amount of pollutants emitted per ton of a phosphate is 10 units in Australia and 20 units in Bolivia, Bolivia is the high *marginal* polluter and the total number of pollutants will decline if phosphate is produced only in Australia. However, if Australia produces 100 tons of phosphate while Bolivia produces only 20 tons, Australia, not Bolivia, is the big polluter (1000 units of pollution in Australia versus 400 units in Bolivia).

In summary, the LDCs contend that pollution standards are stacked against them. Rich developed nations have the ability to finance expensive environmental cleanup programs and to impose stiff standards. LDCs have a tougher time meeting such standards because they are poorer and do not have the resources required to mount a strong environmental program. In addition, the elimination of pollution is not such a pressing issue for them at the present time. If a country is so poor that it cannot afford to maintain a clean water supply, most likely it will not worry very much about the use of agricultural pesticides. Even given the resources required to follow through on a strong environmental policy, there is little doubt that the priorities of the LDCs will be different from those of the developed world. Jagdish Bhagwati observes that "Mexico has a greater social incentive than does the U.S. to spend an extra dollar preventing dysentery than reducing lead in gasoline."[4] Mexico is probably more concerned about the level of pollution in Mexico City than it is about pollution along the U.S.-Mexican border, while the United States is no doubt more exercised over pollution along the frontier than it is about pollution in Mexico City.

---

[3]LDCs are also suspicious that developed countries use labor standards as a pretext for restricting their exports. Everyone understands that, because LDCs are poorer, exchange rate–adjusted direct wages will continue to be higher in developed countries than in LDCs. Proponents of labor standards, including the AFL-CIO, do not concern themselves with direct wages alone, but instead talk about raising *working conditions* throughout the world. Their objective is to create minimum standards as regards hours worked, occupational safety, vacations, health care, pensions, and other worker benefits and protection. Even though apparently well-intended, such rules seem hypocritical and even hostile to the LDCs. Under the guise of helping humankind, they actually *raise* production costs in LDCs, rendering them less competitive and, as a result, making them poorer.

[4]Jagdish Bhagwati, "The Case for Free Trade," *Scientific American* 269 (November 1993): p. 44.

Environmental concerns will become more and more pressing in the next century. Global warming, the depletion of natural resources, air and water quality, the impact of a larger population, and other issues cannot be ignored. And even though it is foolish to argue that the degree of worldwide pollution is going to rest on the environmental

---

BOX 17.3 Ecoimperialism

The **Marine Mammal Protection Act (MMPA)** was enacted in 1972 in the United States. Among other things, it requires the U.S. government to reduce the incidental killing of marine mammals by policing commercial fishers.

The North has introduced environmental standards which the South considers discriminatory. Here are four examples. The Netherlands proposed a ban on tropical timber imports, while still permitting imports of temperature-climate timber. The intent is to save the rain forests by reducing the rapid pace of timber harvesting in tropical areas. Such a policy, however, would cramp the timber industry of LDCs and give a boost to timber exports of the temperate, more-developed countries.

Another North-South dispute arose in the early 1990s when environmentalists in the United States won a lawsuit under the **Marine Mammal Protection Act (MMPA)**, effectively banning the import of Mexican tuna into the United States, a ruling later overturned by a GATT dispute panel. The MMPA prohibits importation of tuna from any country that has a lax dolphin policy (defined as any country whose fishermen destroy more than 1.5 times as many dolphins as the American fishing fleet did in the same year). The Mexicans complained to GATT that they could not know before the fact how many dolphins the American fishing fleet was going to destroy in a given year, and, besides, dolphins were not on anyone's endangered species list.

A third example of North-South conflict came about when Germany passed a law requiring wholesalers and producers to take back from consumers all packing and shipping materials used in marketing a product. The requirement burdens foreign producers most heavily—such as Kenyan flower growers, since foreign firms either have to ship the materials back home or hire private German firms to recycle the packing and shipping materials. German firms, by contrast, either already have disposal systems in place or can establish them quickly and relatively cheaply. LDCs contend that their exports are restricted by an "environmental" measure which in the scheme of things produces little environmental gain.

The final example concerns U.S. regulations on the environmental quality of reformulated oil sold in the United States. Under the Clean Air Act, reformulated oil sold in the United States cannot be any dirtier than reformulated oil sold in the United States in 1990. (Oil sold in heavily polluted urban areas in the United States must meet stiffer requirements regarding levels of toxic and smog-causing contaminants than oil sold in other parts of the country.) However, when enforcing the regulations, the U.S. Environmental Protection Agency allowed domestic oil refineries to use their actual 1990 quality levels as the baseline while imported oil had to meet a baseline based on the average level of purity found in the United States in 1990. In other words, imports had to meet the average level of 1990, while selected domestic refineries were only required to meet their own level purity of 1990, not the national average. Venezuela and Brazil complained to the World Trade Organization that the U.S. regulations amounted to discrimination against non-U.S. oil. A WTO dispute panel found in favor of those two countries and concluded that while the United States had every right to maintain whatever oil standards it desired, domestic-produced and foreign-produced reformulated oil should be treated equally, or be held to the same standard.

In summary, LDCs contend that such environmental measures, perhaps enacted for the best possible reasons, had the side effect of discriminating against the sale of their products in the developed world.

Sources: The Economist, "Trade and the Environment" (February 27, 1993); pp. 25–28; Daniel C. Esty, *Greening the GATT* (Washington, DC: Institute for International Economics, 1994); pp. 185–188; Frances Williams, "US May Appeal Against WTO Ruling," *Financial Times* (January 19, 1996); p. 4.

qualities of international trade, it is highly probable that the WTO will be faced with the problem of meeting legitimate environmental demands while preventing environmental standards from becoming a tool of trade discrimination.

To this end, many observers, including free traders, feel that the WTO should be less secretive in its affairs and more open to greater public scrutiny. The majority of environmentalists are voicing broadly held public concerns, and the WTO, which claims that it is not antienvironmental, should be encouraged to pay attention to them.

Summary

We have outlined the basic provisions of the NAFTA accord, and have seen why some people believe it is simply a continuation and extension of existing trading relations among Canada, Mexico, and the United States. We have also seen why some individuals believe that NAFTA is good while others believe it is bad for the United States.

The NAFTA negotiations raised questions concerning trade and both labor standards and environmental standards. We have seen why environmentalists are critical of the GATT/WTO and why some LDCs feel that, to some degree, environmentalists' concerns are a smokescreen behind which developed countries are trying to restrict LDC exports.

Key Concepts and Terms

Canada–United States Free Trade Agreement

Domestic or local content rules

Environmental dumping

Export platforms

Externalizing costs

First mover

Green taxes

Innovation offsets

Internalizing costs

Maquiladora

Net economic welfare

North American Free Trade Agreement

Process standard

Product standard

Rules of origin

Snap-back provisions

Social dumping

Review Questions

1. Why do some people believe that NAFTA is just a logical step forward in the evolution of Canadian–Mexican–United States trade relations?

2. Why were some people so vehemently opposed to the passage of NAFTA?

3. What, in the eyes of an economist, are the essential differences between NAFTA and the EU?

4. Why are environmentalists discouraged by the WTO's attitude toward the environment?

5. Explain why LDCs sometimes feel that developed-country environmental standards are discriminatory?

6. Distinguish between social and environmental dumping.

References and Suggested Readings

Gary Clyde Hufbauer and Jeffrey J. Schott, *NAFTA: An Assessment*, revised edition (Washington, DC: Institute for International Economics, 1993), is the best introduction to the NAFTA and its implications. The addendum to this book contains a discussion of the NAFTA side agreements and a comparison of the various estimates of the impact of the NAFTA on jobs in Mexico and the United States. Timothy Koechlin and Mehrene Larudee, "The High Cost of NAFTA," *Challenge* (September/October 1992): pp. 19–26, present a more pessimistic view of the proposed free trade area. But their pessimism is tame compared to the pessimism of Ross Perot and Pat Choate, *Save Your Job, Save Our Country* (New York: Hyperion, 1993). The World Bank's estimates of the gains a firm derives from moving its operations from an area with strict environmental guidelines to an area with lax environmental standards are from their *World Development Report: 1992* (Washington, DC: International Bank for Reconstruction and Development, 1993), p. 28.

Linda M. Aguilar, "NAFTA: A Review of the Issues," *Economic Perspectives*, Federal Reserve Bank of Chicago (January/February 1993): pp. 12–20, presents a brief, readable discussion of the issues raised by NAFTA. The November/December 1993 issue of *Foreign Affairs* contains two articles on NAFTA: "Myth versus Facts: The Whole Truth about the Half-Truths," by William A. Orme, Jr., and "The Uncomfortable Truth about NAFTA: It's Foreign Policy, Stupid," by Paul Krugman. Sheldon Friedman, "NAFTA as Social Dumping," *Challenge* (September/October 1992): pp. 27–32 presents a critical assessment of NAFTA.

Daniel C. Esty, *Greening the GATT: Trade, Environment and the Future* (Washington, DC: Institute for International Economics, 1994), is a major work on trade and the environment. Gene M. Grossman and Alan B. Krueger, "Environmental Impacts of a North American Free Trade Agreement," in *The Mexico-U.S. Free Trade Agreement*, edited by Peter M. Garber (Cambridge: MIT Press, 1993), pp. 13–56 is a reasoned evaluation of the potential environmental impacts of the NAFTA. Jagdish Bhagwati, "The Case for Free Trade," and Herman E. Daly, "The Perils of Free Trade," debated the pros and cons of trade and the environment. Both articles appeared in *Scientific American* 269 (November 1993): pp. 42–57. A brief but informative discussion on the GATT and the environment can be found in "Trade and the Environment," *The Economist* (February 27, 1993): pp. 25–28. Roberto Salinas-Leon discusses environmental concerns in his article, "Green Herrings: NAFTA and the Environment," *Regulation* (Winter 1993): pp. 29–34. The GATT itself discusses the question of trade and the environment in Chapter 3, Volume 1 of *International Trade 1990–91* (Geneva: General Agreement on Tariffs and Trade). *The Economist*, "The Tragedy of the Oceans" (March 19, 1994): pp. 27–30, is a short article on the use and exploitation of renewable resources.

Michael E. Porter's and Claas van der Linde's article was cited in the text (Box 17.2). A counterargument is presented by Karen Palmer, Wallace E. Oates, and Paul R. Portney, "Tightening Environmental Standards: The Benefit–Cost or the No-Cost Paradigm?" *Journal of Economic Perspectives* 9 (Fall 1995): pp. 119–132.

Chapter 18

The International Debt Crisis

The international debt crisis was the major international financial problem of the 1980s. The crisis came to a head in 1982 when Mexico was unable to service its external debt and an international rescue operation had to be mounted to help Mexico meet its obligations. A decade later, in a spirit of self-congratulation, the financial community declared victory and claimed that the crisis was over. Less euphoric observers say that the debt problem still remains, although it is far less pressing.

Victory has not been achieved in reducing the international debts of most African nations, especially those south of the Sahara. Indeed, the only triumph has been the recognition that, barring an economic miracle, these nations will not be able to pay off or service their international obligations. In addition, the external debts of some Eastern European countries still hand heavy. Victory, therefore, is limited to the improved international financial positions of several Latin American nations, especially Argentina, Chile, Mexico, and Venezuela, although the Mexican peso crisis in 1994–95 threw new fuel on the fire.

The Path Ahead

This chapter examines three aspects of the debt crisis:

- The external debt figures of the major Latin American debtors.
- What is meant by a sustainable debt-to-GDP ratio.
- The various measures that were undertaken to solve the debt problem.

Why the World Was Concerned

At the height of the debt crisis, there were two major concerns. The primary worry was the potential effect of debt repayment on the economies of the debtor countries. The question was: How does a debtor run the required trade surplus in order to repay its debts without depressing its economy to such a degree that the debtor nation would decide that repudiating its external debts was its best option? If the debtor nations had actually repudiated their external debts, the second concern would have surfaced: the impact of debt repudiation on private creditors. Assuming debtor nations were unable to service their loans, their creditors, the international banking community, would have ended up with a large number of nonperforming or worthless loans on their books. That, in turn, could have caused the collapse of some major international banks and reduced international lending to a trickle.

The statistics in Table 18.1 show why this catastrophe is no longer probable. At the end of 1993, the *long-term* external debts of Argentina, Brazil, Mexico, and

TABLE 18.1 Long-Term Debt (LT Debt), Long-Term Debt Owed Commercial Banks (Banks), and Total Debt/GNP: Selected Years (billions of dollars and percent)

	1980	*1987*	*1990*	*1993*
Argentina				
LT Debt	$17	$51	$49	$61
Due Banks	$6	$29	$23	0
Banks/LT Debt	35%	57%	47%	0
Total Debt/GNP	36%	56%	46%	30%
Brazil				
LT Debt	$57	$106	$90	$105
Due Banks	$24	$56	$46	$45
Banks/LT Debt	42%	53%	51%	43%
Total Debt/GNP	31%	44%	30%	18%
Mexico				
LT Debt	$41	$98	$83	$74
Due Banks	$26	$60	$8	$7
Banks/LT Debt	63%	61%	10%	9%
Total Debt/GNP	30%	82%	45%	36%
Venezuela				
LT Debt	$14	$29	$28	$30
Due Banks	$8	$21	0	0
Banks/LT Debt	57%	72%	0	0
Total Debt/GNP	42%	74%	70%	64%

Source: World Bank, *World Debt Tables: 1994–95*, Vol. 2, (Washington, DC: World Bank 1995); pp. 14–15, 58–59, 314–315, 518–519.

Venezuela were an estimated $61, $105, $74, and $30 billion respectively; but, except for Brazil, the banks' exposure in the countries was minimal. For the nine largest U.S. commercial banks, loan exposure relative to capital fell from 194 percent to 50 percent between 1982 and 1992. And the exposure relative to capital of all U.S. banks in 17 highly indebted countries fell from 130 percent in 1982 to 27 percent in 1992. Some of the improvement was due to an increase in the banks' loan-loss reserves, but a large amount was due to the decrease in bank loans to highly indebted countries between 1987 and 1993. The position of the debtor nations was improved, but not without a hefty sacrifice on their part in terms of unemployment and stagnant income.

International Debt, Investment, and Repayment

Given the adjustment costs the debtors had to pay to get their financial houses back in order, one might conclude that international borrowing is bad for borrowers. This is not the case. Even the claim that borrowing externally and creating an external debt is markedly different from borrowing at home and adding to national debt is not valid. What is unique about international borrowing is that the debt is owed to foreign creditors and not to domestic creditors. The "man on the street" typically assumes that the economic impact of repaying money owed domestic citizens is different from and better than the economic effects resulting from repaying money owed foreigners. Money owed domestic citizens is viewed as "family" debts since interest and principal repayments remain at home—one taxes Petra to pay Paula. In contrast, external debt is viewed as money owed to "nonfamily"; and in that way, foreigners obtain control over domestic resources, since what is absorbed abroad cannot be domestically consumed.

What is wrong with this analysis? If a government borrows from its own citizens, the pool of resources it can tap are limited to those within its own borders. When the same government borrows abroad, it gains command over foreign resources. Therefore, although a nation loses control over domestic resources when it repays a loan, it obtains the use of foreign resources when it issues the loan or goes into debt in the first place.

However, since foreigners must be repaid the face value of the loan plus interest, the fundamental question turns on how a nation utilizes the borrowed funds. If the borrowed resources are productively used, the loan will pay for itself. This fact is illustrated in Figure 18.1, which shows the effects of a successful borrowing policy. Figure 18.1a depicts the economy prior to external borrowing. Aggregate supply and demand intersect at a point where the price level equals P and real income equals Qn, the potential level of output. If aggregate demand equals absorption, the nation has neither a trade surplus nor a trade deficit.

Now imagine the country borrows abroad, shown in Figure 18.1b. The absorption curve shifts to the right and the nation runs a trade deficit. The domestic price level remains constant since it is assumed that any excess of absorption over domestic production—the difference between AD and A_1 at the price level P—is supplied by foreign nations at a constant price level. At this stage, the debtor absorbs more than it produces and runs up its international debt.

Figure 18.1c depicts the situation after the loan is spent. Suppose the funds are used to expand the economy's potential output. The aggregate supply curve shifts to the right together with the potential income curve. AS_1 intersects AD_1 at a point where the price level is still P but the level of real income is now Qn_1. What must occur, either

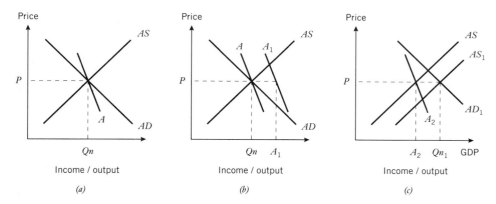

FIGURE 18.1 International debt-repayment cycle.

Prior to borrowing from the rest of the world, the nation's *AD*, *AS*, and *A* curves intersect at the price level *P* in panel (a). Therefore, the nation's external accounts are in equilibrium. In panel (b), the nation borrows funds from the rest of the world and runs an import surplus since its absorption curve, A_1, lies to the right of its *AD* curve at the price level *P*. Assuming the nation employs the borrowed resources productively, its aggregate supply curve shifts from *AS* to AS_1 in panel (c), and its potential level of income rises from *Qn* to Qn_1. Its aggregate demand curve is now AD_1, but its new absorption curve, A_2, lies to the left of the *AD* curve. The economy runs a trade surplus, and repays its external obligations out of *additional* production.

automatically or via government policy, is that the absorption curve, A_2, must lie to the left of the aggregate demand curve, AD_1, in order to create an export surplus. The excess of production relative to absorption at the price level *P* equals the export surplus that is used to pay off the debt.

Is this borrowing-expanding-repaying cycle worth it? If the expansion in income due to borrowing abroad exceeds the interest and principal repayments on the loan, the loan itself and external borrowing turns out to be a wise policy. However, if a nation borrows overseas and uses the proceeds either to boost consumption, raise the level of nonproductive government expenditures, or to line the pockets of various government officials, then the cycle just described will not take place. In terms of Figure 18.c, potential income will remain constant, equaling *Qn*, and the *AS* curve will not shift. The country, however, will still require an export surplus in order to repay the debt, which means that the absorption curve must lie to the left of the *AD* curve. The nation will have to tighten its belt and reduce absorption below its preborrowing level in order to honor its external obligations.

Sustainable Debt Ratio

If the borrowing-expanding-repaying cycle is potentially beneficial, are there any limits to the amount of funds a nation should borrow? The answer appears to be *no*, providing the funds are productively used. But lenders want to be assured that funds lent will be paid back, and so they require guidelines when making loans.

TABLE 18.2 Sustainable Debt Ratio: I

Period	GDP	Debt	Imports
1	$100	$50	$5
2	$110	$55	$5.5
3	$121	$60.5	$6.05

TABLE 18.3 Sustainable Debt Ratio: II

Period	GDP	Debt	Imports	Interest	Exports
1	$100	$50	$5	$5	$5
2	$110	$55	$5.50	$5.50	$5.50
3	$121	$60.5	$6.05	$6.05	$6.05

A **sustainable debt ratio** *(sustainable debt)* is the debt-to-income ratio that will remain constant given output, absorption, real interest rates, the growth in real income, and the current debt/GDP ratio. If absorption exceeds output and/or the real rate of interest on the debt exceeds the rate of growth of real output, the nation's debt/GDP ratio will rise and the past debt-to-income ratio will be unsustainable.

One such guideline is the notion of **sustainable debt,** which in this context is a judgment regarding the amount of external debt that a nation can carry and service (repay the principal and interest on the debt). A nation's sustainable debt is not a number such as $50 billion; rather, it is a relative figure and is most often calculated as the ratio of debt to income. Sustainable debt ratios are influenced by economic events, so that a given debt/GDP ratio can be considered "sustainable" or "nonsustainable" under different conditions.

Table 18.2 depicts an economy whose external debt equals 50 percent of its income. Imagine that this debt/GDP level is considered sustainable by foreign lenders, or that foreigners will lend the country resources providing the debt/GDP ratio does not rise above 50 percent. Can the country take on more debt? The answer is *yes.* As long as its GDP grows at the same rate as its debt, the debt/GDP ratio will remain constant. In the first period, the nation's income is $100, its debt is $50, and its trade deficit (imports in this example) equals $5. The debt in any period equals the debt of the previous period plus the trade account deficit of the previous period. Debt in period 2 equals $55 or $50 plus $5—an increase of 10 percent. If the nation's income grows by 10 percent to $110, the debt/GNP ratio will still be 50 percent. Thus, if imports and income grow at the same rate, the assumed sustainable debt ratio will be maintained.

The previous example neglected exports and interest payments on the debt. Assume the interest rate is 10 percent. A quick glance at Table 18.2 will tell us that, at a 10 percent interest rate, the nation will have to borrow funds just to pay the interest on its outstanding debt. Suppose, however, that the country starts out with $5 of exports that grow 10 percent per period. Table 18.3 shows that the nation is able to finance increasing amounts of imports, since exports, in a sense, cover interest payments. Therefore, the nation can borrow additional funds to pay for additional imports without breaching the targeted debt/income ratio.

Now consider Tables 18.4 and 18.5, which add further complications. In Table 18.4, the interest rate rises to 20 percent in the second period. In order to maintain the debt/GDP ratio of 50 percent, the level of imports must drop to zero. Exports now are used exclusively to pay higher interest charges. In Table 18.5, exports fall to zero in the second period and, once again, the nation is forced to borrow in order to pay interest on its debt. In both these cases, the nation borrows funds in order to pay interest on its external debt—not to add to its productive capacity.

TABLE 18.4 Sustainable Debt Ratio: III

Period	GDP	Debt	Imports	Interest	Exports
1	$100	$50	$5	$5	$5
2	$110	$55	$0	$11	$5.50
3	$121	$60.5	$0	$12.1	$6.05

TABLE 18.5 Sustainable Debt Ratio: IV

Period	GDP	Debt	Imports	Interest	Exports
1	$100	$50	$5	$5	$5
2	$110	$55	$0	$5.50	$0
3	$121	$60.5	$0	$6.05	$0

We can see how a debt crisis, defined as a debt/income ratio that exceeds some sustainable level, can arise. (Because a decline in exports will normally lead to a fall in income and cause the debt/income ratio to rise above its sustainable level, the fourth example is not realistic.)

The following formula shows how we can render the relationship symbolically.*

$$\dot{d} = -(1-a) + d(r - \dot{y})$$

where

$\dot{d}$ = the rate of growth of the debt/income ratio

a = absorption/output ratio

d = the debt/income ratio

r = the real interest rate on the debt

$\dot{y}$ = the rate of growth of real income

The equation tells us that the *debt-to-income* ratio will rise if the absorption/income ratio exceeds 1, the real interest rate rises, or the rate of growth of domestic output declines. It is possible, of course, that some variables will move in one direction while others move in the opposite direction. In such a case, how the *debt/income* ratio moves cannot be

---

*The formula is derived from the following relationships. The growth in the debt over time, dD/dt, depends on the trade balance and the interest payable on any existing debt, rD, where r equals the interest rate and D the level of debt. A trade deficit or surplus equals the difference between the levels of imports and exports which, in turn, equals the difference between the levels of absorption, A, and output, Y. This means that the increase or decrease in the level of debt over time, or its rate of growth, can be written as follows:

$$dD/dt = A - Y + rD$$

The debt/income ratio, d, equals (D/Y), or $D = dY$. It follows that $\dot{D} = \dot{d}Y + \dot{Y}d$, where $\dot{D}$, $\dot{d}$ and $\dot{Y}$ are the time derivatives of D, d, and Y respectively. Substituting into the original equation yields:

$$\dot{d}Y + \dot{Y}d = A - Y + rD$$

calculated by looking at only one variable. For example, the normal assumption is that if output exceeds absorption—which implies that exports exceed imports—the external *debt/income* ratio will fall; but this may not happen if the interest rate on the existing debt rises by a significant amount.

The advantage of the formula is that it illustrates the important variables in determining changes in the *debt/income* ratio, or why a debt crisis may occur and what must be done to reduce or eliminate it. The formula does not specifically tell us what will happen to the *level* of the external debt—although it can be computed. The *level* of the debt may rise while the *debt/income* ratio falls. It is assumed that it is the *ratio* of debt to income rather than the level of the debt that matters in determining whether a nation's external debt position is becoming unmanageable.

---

and dividing by Y and rearranging yields:

$$\dot{d} = (a - 1) + d(r - \dot{y}), \text{ or}$$

$$\dot{d} = -(1 - a) + d(r - \dot{y})$$

where a equals A/Y, $d = D/Y$, and $\dot{y} = \Delta Y/Y$, or the rate of growth of real GDP. The last equation, in either form, is the important one.

BOX 18.1 **The Debt/Income Ratio and the Tequila Effect**

The embers of the Latin American debt crisis of the 1980s roared back into an inferno again when the Mexican peso was devalued at the end of 1994. The blaze was not confined to Mexico. Although it had been expected that the Mexican stock market would tumble given the peso's weakness, not everyone anticipated that the decline in the Mexican stock market would spread to other markets throughout South America. Yet that is what happened. Stock markets in Argentina, Brazil, and Peru declined by roughly 30 percent in the first months of 1995, and markets in other emerging markets outside of Latin American were affected as well.

According to Carlos E. Zarazaga of the Federal Reserve Bank of Dallas, the peso crisis could or should have been anticipated. First, World Bank figures showed the Mexico's short-term debt had increased from $9 to $27 billion between 1989 and 1993. As a result, Mexico's short-term debt as a percent of its total debt jumped from 9 percent to 23 percent. In addition, Mexico's current account deficit and its trade balance deficit as a percentage of GDP had risen in the years prior to 1994.

Was Mexico's external debt rising above a sustainable level? The answer is *yes* and an amended version of the formula given in this section will tell us why—even though the formula is principally used to explain long-term trends.

Now in the case of Mexico, we use the export/GDP and the import/GDP ratios rather than employing the absorption/output ratio or absorption/real GDP ratio as in the previous model. The equation, therefore, becomes:

$$\dot{d} = (m - x) + d(r - \dot{y})$$

In 1993, the Mexican trade balance deficit as a percentage of GDP, $(m - x)$, equaled 4.35 percent, and Mexico's rate of economic growth was a sluggish .4 percent. In 1992, its debt/GDP ratio, or d, stood at 35.5 percent. In the example, the real rate of interest is assumed to be 2.7 percent.

Placing these figures into the equation, we get the following result:

$$.052 = .0435 + .355(.027 - .004)$$

Thus, according to the formula, we would expect the Mexican debt/income ratio to rise by 5.2 percent in 1993. One could argue that the anticipated increase in the Mexican debt/GDP ratio raised the specter of currency depreciation and this was sufficient to cause people to flee the peso, thus bringing on the peso crisis. Moreover, U.S. interest rates rose during 1994, which made it even more probable that the Mexican debt/GDP ratio would rise in the future if the Mexican rate of economic growth remained sluggish and its trade deficit remained negative.

The Mexican peso crisis can be viewed in a different light. We can normalize the equation, that is, set d equal to zero, meaning that the debt/GDP ratio will neither *rise* nor *fall* if certain conditions are met. Here are the conditions:

$$(x - m) = d(r - \dot{y})$$

The trade balance as a proportion of GDP must equal the real interest rate minus the rate of economic growth times the debt/GDP ratio. Given the figures for the interest rate, growth in GDP, and the debt/GDP ratio, we get the following result:

$$(x - m) = .0077$$

The equation tells us that Mexico needed to run a trade balance/GDP surplus of .77 percent if it was to maintain its debt/GDP ratio. Since it did not, the Mexican debt/GDP ratio rose.

The peso crisis spilled over to Argentina. Not only did the Argentine stock market take a large loss at the beginning of the year, but the Argentine government was forced to introduce a strong stabilization package in order to maintain economic stability and the international value of the peso.

Stabilization did not come cheap to Argentina. By the summer of 1995, the rate of unemployment in the country had topped 19 percent. Does the equation tell us that Argentina was heading toward trouble in 1993? We find that, according to the last equation, Argentina could have run a trade deficit equal to 1 percent of GDP and still have maintained its external debt/GDP ratio, primarily because its rate of economic growth was running at 6 percent.

$$-.01 = .3(.028 - .06)$$

Actually, the Argentine trade deficit equaled 1.8 percent of GDP, which tells us that its debt/GDP ratio should have increased by roughly 1 percent.

There is, of course, a big difference between 5 percent (Mexico) and 1 percent (Argentina). Therefore, based on the equation, Argentina should not have run into the degree of economic turmoil it did. But the equation is a long-run description. Moreover, as stressed before, a *sustainable* debt ratio may not be an *acceptable* debt ratio in the eyes of international money managers, nor is an acceptable debt/income ratio constant. In buoyant times, a particular debt ratio may be acceptable, but the same ratio may be viewed as too high at other times.

Even though economic conditions in Argentina and Mexico were markedly different, the fall in the Mexican peso raised doubt regarding the safety of foreign investments in Argentina and concerns on the part of Argentine citizens themselves as to the safety of keeping their funds in Argentinean pesos.

Sources: Relevant country pages of International Monetary Fund, *International Financial Statistics*, August, 1995; World Bank, *World Debt Tables: 1994–95*, Volume 2; and Carlos F. Zarazaga, "Beyond the Border: The Tequila Effect," Federal Reserve Bank of Dallas, *The Southwest Economy* 2 (1995); p. 7.

Debt Service and Interest Service Ratios

The **debt service ratio** equals **debt service**, annual interest payments on debt, plus scheduled repayments of principal on the debt, divided by export earnings.

The **interest service ratio** equals the annual interest payments on external debt divided by exports.

An external debt can also be analyzed in terms of the **debt service ratio** and the **interest service ratio.** The interest service ratio equals interest payments due on the debt divided by exports, and the debt service ratio equals interest and principal payments divided by exports.

An important difference between these measures compared with the previous formula is the prominence given directly to exports. Exports are felt to be the key, since they are the vehicle by which a nation can earn the foreign exchange either to service or reduce its debt. The previous equation, by contrast, emphasizes the absorption/GDP ratio. However if this ratio is less than one, then exports exceed imports by definition. Indeed, one advantage of the equation is that it looks at the total economic performance of a nation rather than just its level of exports. High exports by themselves will not enable a nation to reduce its debt if its absorption is high.

Table 18.6 presents long-term debt figures and important ratios for the **severely indebted countries (SICs)** in selected years.

Funding the Debt

A country is classified as **severely indebted** by the World Bank when the present value of its total debt service exceeds either 220 percent of its exports or 80 percent of its GDP.

The debt service ratio depends on three variables: the level of exports, interest rates, and the maturity of the debt. The maturity of the debt is important since it determines yearly principal repayments. For example, if the maturity of a $100 loan is 5 years, annual principal repayments are $20 per year. If the maturity of a loan is extended from 5 years to 10 years and the loan is repaid in equal installments, annual principal repayments would drop from $20 to $10 per year.

TABLE 18.6 Debt and Debt Ratios for Severely Indebted Countries (billions of dollars or percent)

Middle-Income Countries			
	1980	*1987*	*1990*	*1993*
Total Debt	$170	$384	$412	$445
Debt/GNP	32%	61%	48%	42%
Debt Service/Exports	24%	31%	25%	27%
Interest/Exports	12%	17%	9%	12%

Low-Income Countries			
	1980	*1987*	*1990*	*1993*
Total Debt	$55	$141	$191	$202
Debt/GNP	30%	90%	130%	117%
Debt Service/Exports	12%	26%	25%	18%
Interests/Exports	6%	11%	12%	9%

Source: World Bank, *World Debt Tables: 1994–95*, Volume 1, pp. 220, 224.

If a debt that consists of one-year bonds is converted into a debt composed of 10-year bonds, the debt is said to have been **funded**.

Stretching out or **funding** the debt reduces principal repayments and, assuming exports remain constant, reduces the debt service ratio. The downside to funding the debt is that total interest payments will rise. For example, assume the nation has $100 debt and that the debt is repaid in equal installments regardless of maturity. If the maturity is 5 years, the debt is repaid in installments of $20 per year; if the maturity is 10 years, repayments equal $10 per year. Thus, on average, regardless of maturity, the average outstanding debt equals $50. If the interest rate is 6 percent and the majority of the loan is 5 years, total interest payments on the debt will be roughly $17 or $3.4 per year. The total **debt service,** not the debt service ratio, will be roughly $23.4 per annum since it equals annual interest payments plus principal repayments. If the maturity of the loan is extended to 10 years, total interest rate payments will equal $39, but the debt service will decline to $13.9 per year. Extending the maturity of the debt will involve higher costs over the long run but will reduce the annual costs of servicing the debt in the short run. In short, funding the debt may reduce debt service, but it will not reduce the debt.

Economic Shocks and International Debt

A nagging question is, how did SICs build up such large external debts in the first place? The major culprit, according to some observers, was economic mismanagement in the debtor nations. But it is difficult to place much credence in the idea that the external debt problems of many developing nations are solely the result of economic mismanagement. One could hardly talk of an international debt crisis unless it could be demonstrated that all indebted countries woke up one morning and decided to pursue economic policies that would land them in debt. If that were the case, why did prudent bankers loan such vast amounts of money to these "spendthrifts"?

William Cline, who has followed the debt crisis from the beginning, attributes 80 percent of the $500 billion rise in the external debt of non–oil developing countries between 1973 and 1982 to three forces: the rise in oil prices (52 percent); world recession in 1981–82 (20 percent); and the rise in real interest rates (8 percent).

TABLE 18.7 Current Accounts and External Debt: 1978–1983 (billions of dollars)

Year	*Current Account LDCs: Oil Producers*	*Current Account LDCs: Non-oil Producers*	*Current Account Industrial Countries*	*External Debt* LDCs Total	*External Debt* LDCs Non-Oil Producers
1978	−$0.7	−$35.5	$31.9	$398.3	$342.6
1979	$54.0	−$53.8	−$5.6	$470.9	$406.3
1980	$100.1	−$77.5	−$38.8	$565.0	$489.5
1981	$34.7	−$91.0	$3.1	$660.5	$578.3
1982	−$23.4	−$76.2	$1.2	$747.0	$655.0
1983	−$17.0	−$53.6	$2.2	$790.7	$693.5

Source: International Monetary Fund, *World Economic Outlook,* April, 1985; pp. 236, 261, 265.

Table 18.7 shows the impact of the second oil shock on LDC debt. In 1979, the price of oil rose from $12 to $32 per barrel and led to massive swings in the current account positions of oil exporters, non-oil LDCs, and industrial countries. The current account position of oil exporters improved by $189 billion between 1979 and 1981, while the current account deficits of non–oil-producing LDCs, hit by both the increase in the price of oil and recession in the industrial world, totaled approximately $222 billion between 1979 and 1982. Given these deficits, the external debts of non–oil-producing LDCs rose $236 billion during the period.

Recycling Petrodollars

The international debt crisis would never have arisen if oil producers had increased and oil-importing countries decreased their respective absorption/GDP ratios. But oil exporters were unwilling to expand their absorption in line with their export earnings, just as oil importers were unwilling to contract their absorption to avoid running current account imbalances.

The oil producer's surpluses, consequently, were deposited with international banks. The banks, heavy with funds on which they were paying interest, searched for customers and found them in oil importers with trade deficits. The solution suited almost everyone. Oil exporters built up their short-term deposits and earned interest. Oil exporters had to pay interest on the funds they borrowed, but, evidently, calculated that the costs of borrowing, which enabled them to maintain their absorption/income ratios, were less than the political costs of depressing absorption. The banks were happy, since they borrowed at **LIBOR (London Interbank Offer Rate)** and loaned at LIBOR plus, in addition to earning substantial fees for arranging the loans. Despite the volume of loans, banks felt secure because the majority of the loans were made to sovereign governments and it was assumed that governments could not go broke.

LIBOR (London Interbank Offer Rate) is the interest rate banks charge each other for loans or interbank borrowing on the eurodollar and eurocurrency markets.

Today, it is easy to criticize the way the second oil shock was handled. With perfect hindsight, we can see that oil-importing LDCs should have depressed their absorption at the outset rather than attempting to avoid the effects of higher oil prices. However, economic analysis suggests that it may be less costly for an individual to adjust slowly to an adverse shock rather than rapidly—this is obviously the case if the shock is temporary and reversible. Indeed, nations hold and borrow international reserves just to avoid such painful adjustments. Even if the shock is permanent, there is much to be said for a slow but steady adjustment. If each additional dollar spent on absorption gives less and less pleasure, then it would make sense to cut absorption by $10 per year over five years rather than by $50 in one whack.

Moreover, the world had financed the first oil shock successfully and held down the potential economic fallout by recycling **petro dollars** from oil producers to oil consumers. And, although international debt had grown between 1973 and 1977, the debt service ratio of international debtors increased by only half a percentage point in that period from 10.3 to 10.8 percent.

Because oil was priced in dollars, **petrodollars** was the name given to the export surpluses of OPEC countries during the two oil crises. These funds were recycled from oil exporters to oil importers, permitting the latter to pay the higher oil prices, through the *eurodollar market*—an offshore market for dollars.

This analysis does little to explain the external indebtedness of oil exporters such as Mexico and Venezuela. According to the preceding analysis, these countries should have been building up international *assets*, not international *debts*. But if an individual anticipates that her income is going to rise in the future, she very likely will consume some of the expected increase today by borrowing against her future earnings. Similarly, if a country feels its exports and future income growth have taken a permanent turn for the better, there is no reason why it cannot absorb some of this potential immediately. Because permanently higher oil prices were considered a fact of life in the 1970s, Mexico and Venezuela borrowed and absorbed some of their anticipated future income.

Strategies for Debt Reduction

The **Baker Plan,** named for Secretary of Treasury James Baker and initiated in 1986, was an attempt to reduce the deleterious effects of external debt on debtor countries and create the economic conditions that would allow them to service their debts. The plan called for funding the debt, new loans by creditors to debtors, and stabilization programs in the debtor countries.

The world responded to the debt crisis in two ways. Initially, many observers, especially those with clout, assumed that the crisis would be temporary since they felt that the world economy would pick up and would expand the demand for SIC's exports. At the same time, internal economic reform within the SICs would make it possible for these countries to take advantage of expanding markets, run trade surpluses, and reduce their international indebtedness. In terms of the formula previously given, revamped internal economic policies combined with economic growth would reduce the absorption/output ratio and, in turn, the debt/GDP ratio. Because this process would take time to unfold, its success depended on the willingness of creditors to extend to SICs additional assistance, essentially loans to pay interest on outstanding loans. This was the essence of the **Baker Plan.**

The second debt-reduction strategy, the **Brady Plan,** took a different tack. Economic growth and absorption ratios were still considered important, but the plan also involved writing off a portion of a troubled nation's external debt. Obviously, such a policy would reduce the debt/GNP ratio and, if carried to the limit, would eradicate all external debts. (The initial formula is repeated here so that the arguments can be more easily interpreted.)

$$\dot{d} = -(1 - a) + d(r - \dot{y})$$

The Baker Plan, then, concentrated on economic stabilization in order to boost the growth of real GDP ($\dot{y}$) and to contract the absorption/GDP ratio (a) in order to reduce the debt to GDP ratio (d), while the Brady Plan attempted to reduce the debt/GDP ratio by reducing the outstanding debt itself and the interest rate (r) paid on it.

The Baker Plan

Capital flight refers to a large and sudden outflow of capital from a country due to fears of an imminent devaluation or impending exchange controls.

Introduced in 1985, the Baker Plan stressed internal stabilization within debtor countries and external assistance via debt restructuring and new loans. Domestic stabilization efforts were designed to increase the troubled nation's competitiveness and also to reverse **capital flight**—the tendency of domestic and foreign citizen to sell off the domestic currency before it depreciates in order to make a profit or, in the case of foreigners, to avoid taking a loss.

The **Brady Plan,** named after Secretary of the Treasury Nicholas Brady, was initiated in 1989. Unlike the Baker Plan, the Brady Plan was based on the premise that debtor nations would be able to repay a portion of their external obligations only if creditors were willing to forgive, or write off, a portion of the debts.

The Baker Plan also called for banks to extend more loans to the debtor nations and to restructure existing loans by stretching out their maturity. Such steps would provide debtor nations with needed investment funds and would, it was argued, help bankers over the long run. If debt restructuring and additional loans generated greater investment and exports in the debtor nations, there would be a greater probability that all bank loans, both new and old, would be repaid. In contrast, if the steps were not taken, the debtor countries would be unable to service their existing loans to the detriment of the bankers.

The Baker Plan never really got off the ground. Bankers were not persuaded by its logic and had no desire to expand their loans to debtor nations. For example, Mexico's public and **publicly guaranteed** long-term debt stood at $66.8 billion in 1983. Of this amount, $60 billion, roughly 90 percent, came from private creditors. In 1990 the debt equaled $76.2 billion, of which $53.5 billion, or roughly 70 percent of the total, was owed to private creditors. These figures illustrate the unwillingness of private creditors to maintain, to say nothing of expanding, their loans to debtor nations. Mexico received some $16 billion in new loans from official institutions, but private banks reduced their exposure in Mexico by $6.5 billion.

Debt Overhang and the Brady Plan

Publicly guaranteed loans are loans made to private firms whose repayment is guaranteed by the government. Thus, if a Mexican firm borrows money overseas and is unable to repay it, the government of Mexico, which has guaranteed the loan, must repay it.

The Mexican experience was not unique. The unwillingness of private banks to extend additional credits to the SICs gave rise to the Brady Plan, named after Nicholas Brady, then Secretary of the Treasury. Unlike the Baker Plan, the Brady Plan assumed that the central problem was the size of the debt. And unless the debt was reduced, debtor nations would never be able to pay off even a portion of their debts. For the banks, there was a crucial difference between the Baker and Brady plans. The Baker Plan advised banks to lend more in order to be repaid in full; the Brady Plan told the banks that repayment in full would not occur. They might receive, say, 50 cents on the dollar, but if they were stubborn and did not write down a portion of their outstanding loans, they might not receive even a penny on the dollar.

The debt overhang thesis is a close relative of the **Laffer curve,** which asserted that a cut in tax rates would reduce the penalty on work and raise the price of leisure and, as a consequence, stimulate work efforts and raise income. Higher income, in turn, would generate additional tax revenue, meaning that a tax cut would actually *increase* the total tax revenue collected.

The logic of the debt-related Laffer curve runs along the following lines. Imagine a firm goes bankrupt and files to protect itself from its creditors. Although the firm is effectively defunct, imagine its owners see a golden investment opportunity that will return a hefty sum of money if it is carried out. The owners, however, might not undertake the investment because all the hard-earned cash would go to their creditors. In a very real sense, they face a 100 percent marginal tax rate. What should the creditors do in this case? Suppose they reach an agreement with the owners to take 50 percent of the profits on the investment, the investment is undertaken, and all goes well. The creditors end up with half of the profits, fulfilling the old adage that half a loaf is better than none at all.

A country confronted with debt-servicing problems may find itself in a similar position. If it invests and its exports expand, a major portion of its increased export earn-

The **Laffer curve** was the brain-child of economist Arthur Laffer. What the curve claims to show is that if tax *rates* are reduced, tax *revenues* will increase. Why? Lower taxes will encourage greater work and thus raise the tax base and tax revenue by more than the lower tax rate will reduce it. The thesis of the Laffer curve is not accepted by most economists.

ings will be used to service its external debt and the country will gain nothing—except that its international credit rating may jump up a notch. So when given the choice between an economic policy that favors either investment or consumption, the government will opt to encourage or at least not restrict consumption.

If the external debt is owed by the government but the investing and exporting is done by private firms, a public external debt will hinder the private sector because the government may tax the private sector in order to service its external debt. Yet if a large proportion of the returns on investment are destined to be siphoned off via taxes, investment will be discouraged and capital flight encouraged. Therefore, even in this case, foreign creditors may benefit if they write off or excuse some of the debtor nation's obligations.

International Debt Discount Corporation

The **International Debt Discount Corporation (IDDC)** was an institution proposed by Peter Kenen. If embraced, it would have publicized private loans and, hopefully, have reduced the debt crisis. Under Kenen's proposal, the IDDC would purchase a bank's loans to an LDC at a discount and give the bank a long-term bond issued by the IDDC. The IDDC would then renegotiate the loan with the debtor country, stretching out the repayment period and reducing the interest rate. The IDDC was never created.

Assuming that both creditors and debtors accept the debt overhand thesis, how do they go about writing down a portion of the SIC's external debts? Since the external debt of each SIC is held by a multitude of creditors, it would be difficult for each country and its creditors to hammer out a debt-reduction package. Conflicts of interest between creditors are bound to arise. Some banks might favor a 50 percent writeoff, while others might push for a 25 percent discount.

To surmount such barriers to debt reduction, several arrangements were advanced that would have taken the loans public. Peter Kenen proposed the creation of an **International Debt Discount Corporation (IDDC),** modeled along the lines of the Reconstruction Finance Corporation of the Great Depression. The IDDC would offer to purchase a bank's loans at a 10 percent discount—this discount would give the organization a cash reserve. Thus, if a bank sold a $100 loan with a 3-year maturity and a 10 percent interest rate to the organization, it would receive $90. Payment, however, would not be made in cash, but instead through a $90 bond—with, say, a 10-year maturity and an 8 percent interest rate—issued by the IDDC to the bank. The bond would be guaranteed by the IDDC and, presumably, by the OECD nations that set it up. Banks, therefore, would exchange short-term risky assets for more secure long-term bonds, although at a price.

The IDDC, in conjunction with debtor countries, would reschedule the loans at full value, stretching out their maturity and reducing the applicable interest rate to, say, 8.5 percent. Various options could be added to the rescheduling plans: Repayment could be tied to the country's export earnings, the loan might be denominated in SDRs instead of a particular currency, and so on. The major points are the stretch-out and the lower interest rate.

The Brady Initiative

The Brady Plan was more modest than Professor Kenen's proposal, which, despite revisions, was never adopted. The Brady Plan did not, for example, propose a suprainternational organization. But even if it was more modest, the Brady Plan can claim the prize for being most effective: By 1995, over a dozen countries had renegotiated their external debts under Brady guidelines.

The Mexican plan, introduced in the summer of 1989, included an array of instruments such as funding, writeoffs, interest rate reductions, buy-backs, and debt-for-equity swaps. The agreement covered $54 billion of the $69 billion owed banks, so it did not encompass the total long-term Mexican external debt, which, at the time, exceeded $80 billion.

Under the plan, banks were given a menu. First, they could have exchanged their loans for a 30-year bond bearing a 6.25 percent interest rate with a recapture clause permitting banks to tack on an additional 3 percent interest if, after July 1996, the price of oil exceeded $14 a barrel. Second, banks could have converted their old loans into 30-year bonds carrying a LIBOR plus slightly less than 1 percent interest rate. The catch was that the loans had to be discounted 35 percent, that is, a $100 loan had to be exchanged for a $65 bond. Thus, if banks exchanged loans for what are called **exit bonds,** they either had to accept a discount on the value of old loans or a lower interest rate. Third, banks were permitted to maintain their existing loans providing they agreed to loan Mexico additional funds or to recycle interest payments on outstanding loans back to Mexico.

Mexico was the clear winner in these negotiations. Does this mean bankers were the losers? From their perspective, yes. Aside from their natural complaint about letting debtors off the hook, some bankers felt that they could have obtained a better deal and, in any event, they should not have been forced to carry the major burden of the initiative.

Given their concerns, why did bankers sign on to the Brady agreement? Basically, they had no choice. The new bonds are senior bonds, which in essence means that interest will be paid on these bonds prior to payment on any other Mexican debt obligations. Seniority was essential so as to eliminate free riders, since every bank had an incentive to let other banks write down the value of their loans to Mexico, thus enhancing that country's ability to service its debt. If the program worked and Mexico began to service its debt, the nonsigners' loans as well as the signers' loans might be serviced in full. Nonsigners, therefore, would obtain a free ride and prove that it is far better for a bank to stand firm on its loan contract. Without seniority, few banks would have agreed to the Brady Plan. With it, bankers faced a stark choice: Get on the bandwagon or get run over.

An **exit bond** is the bond a bank receives in exchange for writing off a loan made to a debtor country. In all cases, the value of the bond is only a portion of the value of the loan. In some cases, the bond is guaranteed by an organization such as the World Bank.

Buy-Backs

Under a **buy-back,** a country purchases its external obligations on the secondary market. The country saves money by this step since its obligations usually sell at a discount on the secondary market, and when the obligations are repurchased and retired, the country no longer has to pay interest on them.

Buy-backs are another feature of the Brady Plan. The idea of a buy-back is simple. A secondary market for Latin American debt emerged when some banks with a small exposure in Latin America decided their best policy was to sell off their loans at almost any price, accept a loss, and get on with their major business. The loans were sold at heavily discounted prices to speculators who bet that debtor nations would start servicing their debts in the future. If this occurred, the secondary market price of the loans would rise, enabling the speculators to sell off their holdings and make a profit.

Under a buy-back, a debtor country uses its hard currency holdings or borrows funds from, say, the IMF, and purchases its external obligations on the secondary market. For example, if Mexico received a $3.5 billion loan from the IMF and its debt instruments were selling at 30 cents on the dollar (a 70 percent discount), it could buy back and retire $10.5 billion of its external debt, although it would owe the IMF $3.5 billion.

BOX 18.2 Peru Goes it Alone

Buy-backs have not been without controversy. The usual assumption is that under the Brady Plan, creditors and debtors will negotiate together and reach some common ground for reducing the debtors' external debt even if the package includes buy-backs.

This harmony went flat when Peru, according to estimates, spent $600 million in the summer of 1995 to purchase some $1.2 to $1.4 billion of its $8 billion public debt on the secondary debt market. Peru's major saving comes from the interest charges it will not have to pay on this debt because of the buy-back. Normally, under a Brady arrangement, countries restructure their debt by issuing Brady bonds under which they agree to pay back not only the principal at a fixed, although discounted, value but also any interest owed. Thus, by purchasing its debt in the secondary market, Peru avoids paying these interest charges.

Peru's move angered some of its creditors, such as Citibank and Chase Manhattan, who felt that Peru should have used the $600 million to pay the interest charges on other portions of its outstanding public external debt. (In 1983, Peru had stopped paying interest on its external debt to commercial banks and was estimated to owe $8 billion in principal and unpaid interest.)

Peru appears to have purchased the loans at the right time: Peru's external debt, which had been selling at 60 cents on the dollar in the secondary market in September 1994, fell to 45 cents on the dollar in 1995 in the wake of the Mexican peso crisis. At the time, some economists doubted the wisdom of Peru's action. Peru was the only major Latin American debtor nation that had not negotiated a Brady Plan and these economists felt that Peru's action might jeopardize its chances of negotiating such an accord. These fears, however, were proven unfounded. In late 1995, Peru agreed, in principle, with its private creditors on a debt reduction scheme which will cover some $10 billion in debt principal repayments and interest payments arrears. The package includes a novel feature: The Peruvian government will tender, by **Dutch auction**, as much as $1.4 billion of the debt it secretly purchased. This step will "legitimize" Peru's undercover buy-back.

Sources: Sally Bowen, Lisa Bransten, and Stephan Fidler, "Peru May Tender Debt It Bought Back Last Year," *Financial Times* (October 10, 1995); p. 5; Lisa Bransten and Sally Bowen, "Peru Urged to End Doubt on Debt Buy-back," *Financial Times* (September 11, 1995); p. 4; and Sally Bowen and Lisa Bransten, "Peru Saves $1.2bn Buying Back Par of Debt Mountain," *Financial Times* (August 1, 1995); p. 1.

A **Dutch auction** is an upside-down auction. In a normal auction, the price of a Van Gogh may start at $1mn and be bid up to $4mn. Under a Dutch auction, the Van Gogh is first offered at, say, $6mn. If there are no buyers at that price, the price is dropped continuously until someone is willing to purchase the Van Gogh at that price.

Debt-for-Equity Swaps

Although more complicated, a **debt-for-equity swap** is the exchange of LDC external debt for equity investment. For the debtor country, the plus is the reduction in its external debt. For the business firm, the plus is the ability to purchase the *domestic* currency at what amounts to a favorable exchange rate provided the funds are used to expand investment in the debtor country.

Some nations, especially Argentina and Chile, used **debt-for-equity swaps** to reduce their external debts. A swap allows holders of, say, Chilean dollar-denominated debt to exchange it for Chilean pesos at a favorable exchange rate (or at a low price) providing the funds are invested in Chile. How does this type of swap work? Suppose a U.S. bank believes that its loan to Chile will never be repaid and, to cut its potential losses, sells its $10 million loan to a broker in the secondary market for $4 million. In turn, the broker sells the loan for $4.5 million to a business firm that wants to expand its operations in Chile. The firm then goes to the Chilean central bank and converts the *$10 million* into pesos, invests the pesos, and expands its production.

The business firm definitely gains, and so does the broker. The bank loses although it might feel that a sure 40 cents on the dollar is the best deal it can make. The Chilean government gains in several respects in that its external debt and future interest payments are reduced. And if we take a longer view, we can see that Chile does very well indeed. It borrowed and absorbed $10 million worth of goods and paid $4.5 million plus interest for them.

The importance of debt-for-equity swaps should not be over- or underestimated. According to World Bank figures, the biggest relative "swapper," Chile, reduced its debt by close to 50 percent in 1986 by utilizing them ($10 billion in swaps relative to a total external debt of $21 billion in 1986), and Argentina cut its debt by $12 billion employing debt-for-equity swaps. But the relative importance of debt-for-equity swaps has declined in recent years. The price of some debtors' obligations on the secondary market rose, partly due to debt-for-equity swaps, and reduced the potential profit margins for brokers and business firms in this market.

BOX 18.3   Debt-for-Development Swaps

A **debt-for-nature swap** is a close cousin to a debt-for-equity swap. In a debt-for-nature swap, the debtor country reduces its debts and the equity is used to fund environmental improvements within the debtor country. Thus, the debtor country reduces its debt and gets a better environment to boot. A **debt-for-development swap** essentially does the same thing as a debt-for-nature swap except that instead of financing environmental efforts, the equity is used to finance development projects in the debtor country.

The world does not live on debt-for-equity swaps alone. Other types of swaps, including **debt-for-nature** and **debt-for-development** swaps, have been used to reduce LDC's external debts. Under a debt-for-nature swap, for example, an environmental group purchases the debt of an LDC on the secondary market, normally at a steep discount. (In fact, the debt is often donated to the group by a private bank.) The agency then "sells" the debt at a pre-arranged price to the government of the debtor nation, which, in turn, issues an environmental bond denominated in the local currency. The interest on this bond is then employed to fund local environmental projects.

For example, the World Wildlife Fund purchased $1.87 million of Madagascar's external debt for $.91 million, roughly a 51 percent discount, in 1993. The World Wildlife Fund then "sold" the funds to the government of Madagascar for a bond of equal value—expressed in Madagascar francs. Interest payments on the bond will be used to fund environmental projects in Madagascar. It so happens that at a minimum, the government of Madagascar gains $.96 million, since it was able to absorb $1.87 of foreign goods and only had to pay $.91 million for them. In addition, Madagascar reaps the benefit of a better environment.

Besides nature or environment swaps, UNICEF has instituted debt-for-child-development swaps in order to fund (primarily) water and health programs. The Debt for Development Coalition, a private, nonprofit organization, has used debt-for-development swaps to finance programs in health, low-income housing, community development, ecotourism, agriculture, education, and other areas. In addition, governments have used debt forgiveness as a tool for initiating health, education, and environmental programs in LDCs.

According to the World Bank, the LDCs' external debt has been cut by roughly $350 million due to these swaps. Since the long-term debt of the SICs was $500 billion in 1993, $350 million of debt reduction is not a very sizable amount, although the $350 million figure excludes bilateral government debt forgiveness, which, in certain cases, has been more substantial.

Source: World Bank, *World Debt Tables:* 1994–95, Volume 1; pp. 163–169; Hilary de Boerr, "Swapping Foreign Debt for Nature." *Financial Times* (June 2, 1993); p. 12.

Summary

There are signs that the debt crisis is winding down, but the signs were far better prior to the recent peso crisis. This chapter reviewed certain aspects of external debt as well as the debt crisis.

First, we saw that an external debt is not necessarily bad. Whether a foreign debt is "good" or "bad" depends upon how the borrowed funds are used. If they are employed productively, external borrowing can make eminent good sense. But if the borrowed funds are wasted (spent to boost consumption), the consequences can be grim. Large borrowing left Mexico with a large external debt in the early 1980s. Mexico reduced its external debts and restored its international solvency, but Mexican citizens paid a high price. Between 1982 and 1986, Mexico's real GDP fell by 2 percent, while its population grew by 8.8 percent. As a result, real per-capita GDP in Mexico fell by almost 11 percent in four years. And unfortunately, Mexico had little to show for this sacrifice. It was only after many years and much more hardship that Mexico's external financial position began to improve.

Second, we looked at what constitutes a sustainable debt ratio and the importance of the debt service ratio in judging whether a country's external borrowing was "excessive."

Third, we looked at the reasons behind the emergence of the debt crisis and some of the policies that were adopted to alleviate the crisis.

Key Concepts and Terms

Baker Plan

Borrowing-expanding-repaying cycle

Brady Plan

Buy-backs

Capital flight

Debt-for-development swaps

Debt-for-equity swaps

Debt-for-nature swaps

Debt Laffer curve

Debt service

Debt service ratio

Funding or stretching out the debt

Interest service ratio

LIBOR

Petrodollars

Recycling funds

Sustainable debt/income ratio

Review Questions

1. Explain why a nation may benefit if it incurs an external debt.

2. In light of your answer to the previous question, why is there a debt problem?

3. "Because several countries owe vast sums of money to private Western banks, the Western banking system is in just as much trouble as the debtor countries." Comment on this statement.

4. What forces determine whether a country can maintain its debt/GDP ratio at some sustainable level? For example, how would a rise in real interest rates affect a country's international debt and its debt/GDP ratio? What would the nation have to do to maintain its debt/GDP ratio under these conditions?

5. "One could have expected Brazil to have debt problems, but it is incomprehensible that Mexico should have built up such a large external debt in the 1980s." Comment on this statement.

6. Explain what is meant by the debt-relief Laffer curve.

7. What are the essential differences between the Baker Plan and the Brady Plan?

References and Suggested Readings

This chapter covered only selected highlights of the debt "problem" or "crisis," therefore additional reading is strongly recommended. A good place to start is volume 1 of the World Bank's *World Debt Tables*, which presents a yearly analysis of debt problems and summary tables. Country tables are in volume 2.

The classic exposition on the international debt crisis is William R. Cline's *International Debt Reexamined* (Washington, DC: Institute for International Economics, 1995). The statistics on U.S. banks' exposure in highly indebted countries are found on pages 72–75 of this book. The reference to Cline's estimates of the effects of oil prices, recessions, and high real interest rates on the international debt of non-oil-producing LDCs are from his article "International Debt: From Crisis to Recovery?" *American Economic Review, Papers and Proceedings* 75 (May 1985): pp. 185–190. Cline also wrote a brief summary of the lessons learned from the debt crisis: "Managing International Debt: How One Big Battle Was Won," *The Economist* (February 18, 1995): pp. 17–19.

Paul Krugman analyzes the debt-relief Laffer curve and other topics in "Market-Based-Debt-Reduction Schemes," in *Analytical Issues in Debt*, edited by Jacob A. Frenkel, Michael P. Dooley, and Peter Wickham (Washington, DC: International Monetary Fund, 1989).

Peter B. Kenen's first proposal for an IDDC is in his article, "Third-World Debt: Sharing the Burden—A Bailout Plan for the Banks," *New York Times* (March 6, 1983). His more recent views are in "Organizing Debt Relief: The Need for a New Institution," *Journal of Economic Perspective* 4 (Winter 1990): pp. 7–18. There are three additional articles in the same issue of the *Journal of Economic Perspectives* worth looking at: Jeffrey D. Sachs, "A Strategy for Efficient Debt Reduction," pp. 19–30; Jeremy Bulow and Kenneth Rogoff, "Cleaning up Third World Debt Without Getting Taken to the Cleaners," pp. 31–42; and Jonathan Eaton, "Debt Relief and the International Enforcement of Loan Contracts," pp. 43–56. The four articles present different perspectives. Kenen and Sachs are very much in favor of an IDDC, while Bulow, Rogoff, and Eaton have reservations.

The Brady debt-reduction initiative is discussed by Jeffrey D. Sachs, "Making the Brady Plan Work," *Foreign Affairs* 68 (Summer 1989): pp. 87–104. Debt-for-equity swaps are discussed by Felipe Larrain and Andres Velasco, *Can Swaps Solve the Debt Crisis? Lessons from the Chilean Experience*, Studies in International Finance 69 (Princeton, NJ: International Finance Section, Princeton University, November 1990).

Now that the Latin American debt crisis has been declared dead, what can be learned from it? Masood Ahmed and Lawrence H. Summers give some answers in their article, "Ten Lessons of the Debt Crisis," *International Economic Insights* III (July/August 1992): pp. 15–20.

Glossary

Absolute advantage. A country has an absolute advantage in the production of a particular commodity if it can produce the commodity with fewer inputs than any other nation.

Absorption. The total level of expenditures on goods and services produced both at home and abroad for use within the domestic economy. In an open economy, absorption may be greater, equal, or less than national output. If absorption exceeds domestic production, imports will be greater than exports. The **absorption curve** shows the level of absorption at various domestic price levels, assuming everything else remains constant.

Adjustable peg. A fixed exchange rate which is devalued or revalued from time to time as dictated by economic fundamentals.

Adjustment costs. The costs involved when, for example, a country reduces trade restrictions. Some workers may face unemployment as imports displace formerly domestically produced goods. Adjustment costs can be temporary or permanent.

Aggregate demand. Total expenditures on consumption, investment, and government purchases of goods and services plus exports minus imports. In an open economy, aggregate demand, which equals domestic output, may be greater than, less than, or equal to **absorption.** By contrast, aggregate demand equals ab-

sorption in a closed economy. The **aggregate demand curve** shows the quantity of output demanded at various national price levels, assuming all other economic variables are constant.

Aggregate supply. The total supply of domestically produced goods and services at various price levels.

Alternative trading organizations. See **fair trade.**

Appreciation. An increase in the value of one currency in terms of one or several other currencies. For example, the dollar appreciates when it exchanges for 4 rather than 2 marks. Floating exchange rates appreciate while fixed exchanged rates are **revalued.**

Autarky. An autarkic country is completely independent of other nations and does not engage in international trade.

Autonomous. If an American purchases more British goods given a constant income and set prices (including the exchange rate), her expenditures are said to be autonomous. However, if the American's income rises or the relative price of British goods declines or the pound **depreciates** and she buys more British goods, her expenditures are **induced.**

Baker Plan. The Baker Plan, named after Secretary of the Treasury James Baker and initiated in 1986, attempted to reduce the deleterious effects of external debts on indebted countries while fostering economic conditions that would allow such countries to service their debts. The plan called for **funding** the debt, new loans by creditors to debtors, and stabilization programs in the debtor countries.

Balance of indebtedness. The international financial position of a country at a point in time. A nation's net **direct foreign investment** is excluded in computing its balance of indebtedness.

Balance of payments. A record of a nation's international transactions with the rest of the world. The **balance of payments curve (BP)** shows the domestic price and income levels at which the balance of payments is balanced on an **official reserve basis.**

Bank for International Settlements. The central banks' bank. The BIS is where the world's major central bankers meet on a regular basis at its offices in Basel, Switzerland. It is a vehicle for both central bank cooperation and for disseminating the central bankers' views on the world economy.

Bank reserves. Funds that a bank holds as a reserve against their deposit liabilities. The quantity of reserves an individual bank must hold, or a bank's **reserve ratio,** is normally prescribed by the central bank.

Barter. The exchange of one commodity for another—for example, of wheat for textiles rather than the sale of wheat for money.

Basic balance of payments. One method of measuring whether a country has a balance of payments surplus or deficit. The basic balance is computed by adding together the **current account** and the **long-term capital account.** If credits exceed debits, the nation has a basic balance surplus.

Beggar thy neighbor. A country may **devaluate** or allow its currency to **depreciate** with the primary aim of expanding its exports in order to reduce domestic unemployment even though this creates unemployment in other countries. In other words, the country attempts to export its unemployment to its trading partners or to the rest of the world. (Trade restrictions are also a vehicle for beggaring one's neighbor.) The policy is usually not successful since other countries can play the same game: Country A devalues or depre-

ciates its currency, and country B responds by doing the same thing.

Benign deficit. A trade deficit that occurs when domestic investment exceeds domestic saving. Unlike a **malign deficit,** many economists believe that this type of deficit does not pose long-run problems.

Brady Plan. Named after Secretary of the Treasury Nicholas Brady, the Brady Plan was first proposed in 1989. Unlike the **Baker Plan,** the Brady Plan was based on the premise that debtor nations would be able to repay only a portion of their external obligations, which meant that creditors would have to write off a portion of the debts if they were to receive partial repayment.

Bretton Woods. Bretton Woods is a small town in New Hampshire that hosted a conference in 1944 at which the **International Monetary Fund** and the post–World War II exchange rate system was created. The fixed exchange rate regime that resulted from this conference became known as the *Bretton Woods system.*

Buffer stock. A stock of a commodity, which, if everything goes as planned, rises and falls with the production and the demand for the commodity and, thus, stabilizes the commodity's price. In a recession, when supply exceeds demand at the target price, the manager of the buffer stock arrangement buys the commodity and stores it. Thoeretically, the greater demand will raise the price of the commodity and all member nations of the arrangement will be pleased. When the demand for the commodity in question runs ahead of current production and the price of the commodity rises above its target price, the manager of the buffer stock sells from his stockpile, which brings the price of the commodity back down toward the target level.

Bundesbank. The German central bank.

Buy American Acts. A series of acts and practices, adopted at all levels of government in the United States, which give preference to American-made products over foreign-made products.

Buy-backs. A buy-back takes place when a nation purchases or buys-back its external obligations on the secondary international debt market. The country saves money through such operations since its external obligations usually sell at a discount on the secondary market.

Canada–United States Free Trade Agreement. A free trade agreement between Canada and the United States that went into effect on January 1, 1989. Under the provisions of the agreement, all bilateral tariffs between the two nations are to be eliminated by 1999.

Capital account. A record of a nation's international capital transactions with the rest of the world. The capital account is divided into long- and short-term capital flows. The long-term capital account is further subdivided into **direct investment, portfolio investment,** and long-term loans.

Capital flight. A sudden and large outward flow of capital from a nation due to fears of an impending currency **depreciation** or the imposition of **exchange controls.**

Capital flows. The transfer of capital from one nation to another. The **capital flow curve** shows the flow of capital either *to* or *from* a nation at various national interest rates, assuming everything else remains constant.

Capital intensive. If a good is said to be produced by capital-intensive methods of production, it is produced with relatively more capital and less labor compared to other goods. For example, electrical power generation is capital intensive while hand-made sweaters are labor intensive.

Capital stock. The quantity of capital in a given economy at a certain point in time. It is normally measured as the value of machines, equipment, and structures.

Central bank intervention. Central banks often intervene in foreign exchange markets by buying or selling foreign exchange in the attempt to stabilize or influence foreign exchange rates. In order to carry out such a policy, central banks usually require **international reserves.**

Common agricultural policy (CAP). The expensive agricultural policy of the **European Union (EU).** By guaranteeing farm prices, the CAP initially encouraged excess production. To prevent cheaper foreign

agricultural products from entering the EU, a series of import levies were introduced which boosted the price of imports up to or beyond EU levels. In order to get rid of its excess production, the EU relied on export subsidies, much to the consternation of the United States and other food-exporting countries. Today, the CAP maintains farm income through a system of direct payments to farmers and export subsidies have been curtailed. The CAP soaks up roughly one-half of the EU's total budget.

Common currency. The dollar is the common currency in the United States and the Belgian franc is the common currency in Belgium and Luxembourg. Under the **Maastricht Treaty,** the **European Union** is supposed to adopt a common currency, officially the **Euro,** by 2002.

Common market. A customs union which also attempts to develop a common policy in matters other than international trade. For example, the **European Union** has initiated communitywide policies in agriculture, exchange rates, labor legislation, and so on.

Comparative advantage. A measure that describes what a country can do most efficiently relative to another country or relative to the world. Assume the United States needs 5 inputs to produce wheat and 10 inputs to manufacture textiles. If Canada requires 10 and 30 inputs, respectively, to make wheat and textiles, the United States has a comparative advantage in producing textiles.

Compensatory and Contingency Financing Facility (CCFF). A financing facility established by the **International Monetary Fund** in 1963. If a country's export receipts fall dramatically due to a worldwide dip in economic activity, the nation can borrow funds from the IMF to ease the impact of the worldwide recession on its economy. Likewise, a nation can borrow funds to offset the impact of a sharp rise in the price of vital imports such as cereals. The **Buffer Stock Financing Facility (BSFF),** which helps nations finance contributions to buffer stocks, is a part of the CCFF.

Consumer surplus. The difference between what a consumer is willing to pay for a good versus what she actually pays for it. Because the consumer would be willing to pay more for the first yo-yo than for the *n*th yo-yo, she will end up with a surplus since the price of yo-yos will equal the value of the last yo-yo purchased.

Consumption possibility line. A line that shows the various combinations of two goods that can be consumed at a given terms of trade or international exchange ratio.

Convertibility. The ability to convert a currency into other currencies upon demand at the official or market-determined exchange rate.

Countervailing duties. Import duties imposed to offset the impact of foreign subsidies on domestic industries. For example, if Germany decides to subsidize its beer stein industry and if, in turn, German-made steins displace domestically produced goblets in the American market, the U.S. government may impose a countervailing duty. The subsidy does not need to be granted to the beer stein industry itself in order to trigger countervailing duties. An upstream subsidy, one granted to a component required in the manufacture of a beer stein, is sufficient.

Covered interest arbitrage. The closest thing in international finance to both having your cake and eating it. For example, an American money manager may purchase pounds on the **spot** market in order to buy a three-month British Treasury bill which pays a higher interest rate than a comparable U.S. Treasury bill. At the same time, the money manager sells British pounds or purchases U.S. dollars in the **forward** market to avoid the risk associated with possible exchange rate variation.

Crawling peg. A fixed or pegged exchange rate which is adjusted, normally depreciated relative to a major currency, by small specified amounts at regular intervals, such as weekly or monthly. Thus, prior to the Mexican peso crisis of late 1994, the peso was allowed to depreciate at the preannounced rate of 4 percent per year.

Credibility. An economic policy will be *credible* if the society believes that the policy will be carried out. For example, an anti-inflation policy will not be considered credible if the public believes that the government will back off if the policy causes some pain, such as unemployment.

Credit tranche. See **gold tranche.**

Crowding out. What may occur when a government runs a budget deficit. In order to finance the deficit, a government must borrow funds on the capital market. This step may raise domestic interest rates and reduce private borrowing and investment. Hence, the budget deficit is effectively financed by a reduction in private investment.

Currency band. Under a fixed exchange rate system, exchange rates are permitted to fluctuate within a prescribed band. If the official exchange rate is DM2/$, under a 2 percent band on either side to the central rate, the exchange rate is allowed to vary between DM2.04/$ and DM1.96/$. Under the **Bretton Woods** system, exchange rates were permitted to fluctuate only 1.5 percent on either side of parity or the official rate. Under a **widened band,** the range of permissible fluctuations is enlarged, such as 15 percent under the present guidelines of the **exchange rate mechanism** of the **European Monetary System.**

Currency board. Under a currency board, a nation ties its money supply or **monetary base** to its holdings of **foreign exchange reserves.** For example, under its currency board arrangement, Argentina can increase its monetary base only if its foreign exchange reserves (dollars) increase.

Currency substitution account. In the 1970s, some individuals suggested that countries which held an excess supply of U.S. dollars should ship them to the IMF in exchange for SDRs. Such an exchange would have been a substantial step toward establishing a system of centrally created international reserves. Due to U.S. opposition and a rise in the international value of the dollar, the plan never got off the ground.

Currency zone. A group of nations who tie their currencies to the currency of the major country of the area. For example, many European currencies are tied to the German mark in practice if not in law. In Africa, many former members of the French Empire use the French franc as their official currency.

Current account. That part of the **balance of payments** which measures what are called current transactions. The current account includes exports and imports of goods and services, dividend and interest payments, plus private and public transfers. Private transfers include foreign workers sending money home, while official transfers include payments on official debts, contributions to international institutions, and foreign aid.

Customs union. A group of countries that eliminates trade barriers among members, but maintains a common external tariff on trade with nonmember countries.

Dead-weight loss. When a **tariff** or **quota** is imposed, consumer surplus contracts and consumers lose. Some of this loss, but not all of it, is "offset" by a gain in **producer surplus** and an increase in government revenue. That portion of the loss which is *not* so offset is the dead-weight loss associated with the trade restriction. (Unlike a tariff, a quota may not lead to an increase in government revenue. If the revenue goes to foreign producers rather than to the government or domestic producers, the national dead-weight loss of a quota will exceed the dead-weight loss of a tariff.)

Debt-for-development swaps. See **debt-for-nature swaps.**

Debt-for-equity swaps. Although more complicated than this, basically it involves the swap of LDC external debt-for-equity investment. For an LDC, the advantage is the reduction in its external debt. To some, the downside of a debt-for-equity swap is the increase of foreign ownership of productive facilities within the LDC.

Debt-for-nature swaps. A close cousin to a debt-for-equity swap. In a debt-for-nature swap, the country reduces its debt and the equity is used is to finance environmental improvements within the country. A **debt-for-development swap** is essentially the same as a debt-for-nature swap, except that, rather than financing environmental efforts, the "equity" is used to finance development projects within the country.

Debt service. The annual payment of interest on and repayment of principal on money borrowed overseas (or domestically). Normally, the yearly repayment of principal is only a portion of the sum initially borrowed.

Debt service ratio. Debt service divided by the value of exports.

Decreasing costs. Production costs decrease as output expands. Although not exactly the same, decreasing costs are often associated with economies of scale. See **increasing returns to scale.**

Depreciation. The dollar has depreciated if today it exchanges for 2 marks when yesterday it was worth 4 marks.

Derived demand. The demand for a commodity, service, or factor that depends on the demand for some other product. The demand for tonic depends on the demand for gin; the demand for ship-builders is based on the demand for ships.

Devaluation. See **depreciation.** Fixed exchange rates are devaluated; flexible rates depreciate.

Devaluation dumping. The name given to instances when a country devalues its currency in order to obtain a competitive advantage—at least in the eyes of its competitors. (See **beggar thy neighbor.**) **Environmental dumping** occurs when a country obtains a competitive advantage from low environmental standards or lax enforcement. **Social dumping** is the argument that a country obtains a competitive advantage from low labor standards.

Direct investment. Either the construction of new facilities in a foreign country or the purchase in a foreign country of existing physical assets, or the financial assets required to control them.

Divergence indicator. See **European Monetary System.**

Domestic or local content rules. Under domestic or local content rules, a firm must purchase from domestic sources a specified amount, normally a percent of the total value of the product, of the inputs needed to produce the product. It is a policy designed to increase the demand for local products and services.

Drawing rights. A nation's line of credit at the **IMF.** The conditions for using this line of credit become more stringent as a greater proportion of it is used. See **letter of intent.**

Dumping. Selling a good below production costs (including a return on investment) or below a "fair" price. See **price discrimination**.

Dutch auction. An upside-down auction. In a normal auction, the price of a Van Gogh may start at $1mn and be bid up to $4mn. Under a Dutch auction, the Van Gogh is first offered at, say, $6mn. If there are no buyers at that price, the price is dropped continuously until someone is willing to purchase the Van Gogh at that price.

Dutch disease. Occurs when the demand for a particular export rises to such dizzying heights that production costs increase throughout the economy. As a result of Dutch disease, export expansion in one sector of the economy hinders or harms exports in other sectors.

Dynamic gains from economic integration. If economic integration leads to economies of scale, more rapid technological change, and the diffusion of productive techniques throughout the common market, it is said to generate dynamic gains.

Economic and monetary union. A three-phase plan which aims to introduce a single currency within the **EU** by the year 2002. If successful, the creation of a single currency will lead to the demise of individual European currencies such as the pound, French franc, and so on. The single currency will be managed by the European Central Bank. (Sometimes referred to as the European Monetary Union.)

Economic union. The final step toward full economic integration. An economic union is a **common market** plus. It involves the harmonization of national tax codes, labor standards, the creation of a common currency, and the establishment of an areawide central bank to conduct monetary policy.

Effective market classification. Given multiple targets, such as internal and external balance, the process of matching the appropriate policy tool with a specific target.

Effective protection. The rate of protection actually given to domestic resources, such as labor, by a tariff. In the majority of cases, the rate of effective protection exceeds the nominal rate of protection since an input,

such as leather, is either allowed into the country duty-free or at a reduced tariff rate, while the finished product, such as leather bags or shoes, pays a hefty import duty.

Elasticity. A method for measuring the change in one variable given a change in another. For example, the price elasticity of demand for CDs is computed by dividing the percentage change in the quantity of CDs purchased by the percentage change in their price—or $\%\Delta Q/\%\Delta P$. By a similar approach, one can measure the price elasticity of the supply of CDs. The **income elasticity** of demand for CDs is computed by dividing the percentage change in quantity demanded by the percentage change in income.

Elasticity pessimism. The belief that import demand price elasticities are so low that a depreciation will not improve a country's balance of trade. See **Marshall-Lerner-Robinson Conditions**.

Environmental dumping. See **devaluation dumping**.

Equilibrium exchange rate. In some circles, the equilibrium exchange rate is defined as the exchange rate which balances the current plus long-term capital accounts at the full employment or potential level of income providing international trade is not restricted. Most often, it is defined as the exchange rate which balances the supply and demand for one currency relative to another.

Escape clause provision. Section 201 of the Tariff Act of 1974 grants an industry *temporary* protection from imports when it is judged that imports have caused serious injury to the industry.

Euro. The proposed **common currency** of the **European Union**. According to a timetable established in late 1995, the Euro will be introduced in 1999 and will become the official and exclusive currency of the EU by 2002.

Eurodollar market. The supply and demand for eurodollars. A eurodollar is a dollar deposited outside the United States. Although it is the major individual offshore market, it is part of the **eurocurrency market**. A eurocurrency is any major currency that is deposited outside its country of origin.

European Bank for Reconstruction and Development (EBRD). Established in 1991, the EBRD is designed to channel resources and managerial talent from the West to the former Communist countries of the East. Up until 1995, many observers felt that the EBRD was most noteworthy for its posh headquarters in London. In 1994, Vaclav Klaus, then prime minister of the Czech Republic, viewed foreign advisors as "purveyors of soft advice for hard currency."

European Currency Unit (ECU). A composite currency composed of, or weighted by, elements of the currencies of all members of the **European Monetary System (EMS).** Weights depend on a nation's share of intra-EU trade. The ECU is used in all the official transactions of the EMS.

European Free Trade Association (EFTA). A now mostly defunct free trade area that was originally composed of Austria, Britain, Denmark, Norway, Portugal, Sweden, and Switzerland. All of these charter members, except Norway and Switzerland, are now members of the **European Union.** Today, in addition to Norway and Sweden, Iceland and Liechtenstein are members of EFTA.

European Monetary Cooperation Fund (EMCF). A part of the **European Monetary System.** Member-country central banks deposit 20 percent of their international reserves with the EMCF, and in turn, the EMCF is then employed to clear intra-central bank imbalances. More important, the EMCF is a source of short-term credit for nations that need assistance in maintaining the value of their currency within the **parity grid.** From its inception, the EMCF was expected to evolve into the **European Monetary Fund,** which would, in turn, evolve into the European central bank. See **European Monetary Institute.**

European Monetary Institute (EMI). The embryonic form of the European Central Bank that opened its doors in 1994. The EMI is charged with coordinating monetary policy within the EU and preparing the way for phase three of the **EMU,** at which time the EMI will become the European Central Bank and conduct monetary policy for the whole region.

European Monetary System (EMS). Born in 1979, the EMS initially set out to establish a system of European-wide fixed-exchange rates. Until the summer of 1993, the most important component of the system was the **exchange rate mechanism** which consisted of two elements: the **parity grid** and the **divergence indicator.** Under the ERM, each currency has a fixed value expressed in **european currency units (ECUs),** called its central rate. Given central rates, it is a quick step to establish cross exchange rates or what is called the parity grid for all currencies within the system. Under EMS guidelines, all nations are responsible for maintaining the parity grid. When a currency moves away from its initial central value, the divergence indicator indicates that the country should take steps to bring its currency back to the norm. Prior to 1993, a currency's value was permitted to swing 2.25 percent on either side of its central rate; today, a currency can swing 15 percent on either side of the central rate. Thus, the present ERM is a wispy ghost of times past.

European Payments Union (EPU). A clearing arrangement set up in 1950 and administered by the **Bank for International Settlements** which was designed to promote intra–Western European trade. Nations received credit and debits at the BIS depending on the magnitude of their exports and imports to other member nations. At the end of each accounting period, debtors would ship the BIS gold to settle their debts, while creditors would receive gold from the institution. The EPU also provided a limited amount of credit to debtor nations. For example, at the end of an accounting period, a debtor nation might have to pay only half of its outstanding balance and be permitted to finance the remainder by receiving short-term credit. A surplus country, therefore, might receive only 50 percent of its surplus immediately. This provision meant that surplus countries would, in the short run, finance debtor countries.

European Regional Development Fund. An agency of the **European Union** which helps fund economic development in economically deprived regions within the union.

European Social Charter. Sometimes called the humane face of the **European Union,** the social charter is the vehicle for establishing minimum safeguards and standards regarding wages, labor standards, health benefits, and so on for all who work within the EU.

European Union (EU). A common market which consisted of six Western European nations in 1957—Belgium, France, Germany, Italy, Luxembourg, and the Netherlands; by 1995, the EU had more than doubled to 15 members.

Exchange controls. Government regulations which prohibit or limit the ability of a citizen to acquire foreign exchange or money. In some cases, citizens may purchase foreign currencies, but only for government-approved uses.

Exchange rate. The price of one currency in terms of another, such as FFr5/$, Y100/$, and $1.50/£.

Exchange rate stabilization. Government attempts to stabilize an exchange rate, either within certain limits or around a trend value, by buying and selling currencies on the foreign exchanges. In order to carry out stabilization, a government needs **international reserves.** Exchange rate stabilization is a close cousin to **official intervention.** The difference is that the goal of intervention may be to push the international value of a currency up or down, not to stabilize it.

Exchange ratio. The rate at which two commodities exchange or trade.

Exit bond. Under the **Brady Plan,** for example, several Mexican creditors traded or exchanged loans of various maturities for longer-term bonds. By accepting this conversion, even if grudgingly, the creditors could not be called upon to refinance their existing loans to Mexico or make new ones. The bonds, which sometimes are guaranteed by the **World Bank,** permit creditors, so to speak, to exit.

Expenditure reducing. A policy, such as higher taxes, which reduces expenditures. Since the taxes can be reduced as well as increased, the policy can be **expenditure increasing** if taxes are cut.

Expenditure switching. An economic policy such as exchange rate depreciation which, by raising the price of foreign goods relative to the price of domestic goods, causes domestic citizens to switch their expenditures away from foreign-produced toward domestically produced commodities.

Export curve or schedule. A curve which shows the quantity of a nation's exports at various national price levels, assuming other economic variables remain constant.

Export performance requirements. Stipulations that a firm must export a certain minimum amount of its output or a proportion of its output.

Export platforms. The construction of a plant in one country, such as in Mexico, in order to produce goods that are then exported to another country, such as the United States. By setting up operations in Mexico, a Japanese firm, for example, can meet NAFTA's **rules of origin** requirements.

Extended Structural Adjustment Facility. See **Structural Adjustment Facility.**

External economies. A development *external* to the firm which reduces the firm's costs of production. For example, a new and improved transportation system may reduce production costs regardless of the firm's managerial capacities. The firm's actions, in contrast, result in **internal economies.** One firm's internal economies may generate external economies for another firm.

Factors of production. The inputs of land, labor, and capital that a nation can utilize to produce goods and services. Business schools cite management as the fourth, and most important, factor of production.

Fair trade. Advocates of fair trade believe that certain individuals, especially farmers in less-developed countries, do not receive a fair price for their products and, thus, their efforts. **Alternative trading organizations** are associations which attempt to see that such individuals receive a just or socially ethical return on their labor.

Federal Reserve System. Better known as the *Fed,* the Federal Reserve is the central bank of the United States.

First mover. If a country is first to enact strong environmental measures, it will be the first nation to spawn an environmental cleanup industry. Then when the rest of the world raises its environmental standards, the already developed domestic cleanup industry will have a worldwide comparative advantage. Thus pollution control will create a new industry.

Fisher Effect. Named after Irving Fisher, this theory describes how a change in the money supply may ultimately lead to an increase in the general price level and cause nominal interest rates to climb.

Fixed exchange rates. Exchange rates set by the government, often called "pegged exchange rates."

Fixed rate rule. This rule argues that the money supply should be increased at a *constant* rate, regardless of the rate selected.

Flexible exchange rates. Exchange rates that are determined *primarily* by market forces. **Freely flexible exchange rates** are determined *solely* by market forces.

Foreign exchange transactions tax. A tax on the buying and selling of foreign exchange. It is designed to raise the costs of such transactions and thereby reduce the volume of speculative capital flows. In turn, a reduction in speculative capital flows makes it easier for a central bank to maintain a target exchange rate.

Foreign repercussions. Foreign repercussions measure the impact of a change in economic activity in one country on the level of economic activity in another country or on the rest of the world, and how the change in economic activity in the second country, in turn, affects economic activity in the first country.

Foreign trade multiplier. The income multiplier in an open economy. Due to external relations, the value of the foreign trade multiplier is less than the value of the closed economy multiplier. It is equal to the reciprocal of the sum of the marginal propensity to save and the marginal propensity to import.

Forward exchange market. The market where currencies are bought and sold for delivery at a given point in the future. Active forward exchange markets are limited to major international currencies, and forward contracts seldom exceed a year.

Forward premium (discount). The difference between the **forward** and **spot** rate of a currency. Often, the forward rate is quoted as a percentage of the spot.

Forward pricing. Setting today's price in light of possible future markets. Suppose a company introduces a product whose demand, given a price incentive, may expand dramatically. Imagine as well that the product is produced under conditions of **decreasing costs.** Thus, it makes sense for the firm to price today as if the market had expanded and decreasing costs had been attained.

Free trade area. A group of countries that promote free trade between member nations, but permit each nation to maintain its own, and perhaps different, trade restrictions vis-à-vis nonmembers. For example, the **North American Free Trade Agreement.**

Full adjustment. The total adjustment of an economy to a shock or stimuli. For example, an **appreciation (depreciation)** will first hit the export and import markets of an economy, then it will ripple through the entire economy. When the entire economy has adjusted to the shock or stimuli, the adjustment is complete or full.

Fundamental equilibrium exchange rate. An exchange rate which balances exports and imports and long-term capital flows, as determined by underlying savings and investment patterns, at the full employment level of income.

Funding. Converting short-term into long-term debt. Funding the debt has been advocated as a partial solution to the international debt problem of some LDCs.

General Agreement on Tariffs and Trade (GATT). Founded in 1947, the GATT was an organization of more than 100 countries which attempted to promote free trade by eliminating or reducing barriers to trade. The GATT evolved into the **World Trade Organization (WTO)** at the conclusion of the **Uruguay Round** trade negotiations in 1994, and officially wrapped up its operations at the end of 1995.

General Arrangement to Borrow. A line of credit for the **International Monetary Fund** provided primarily by major countries and Saudi Arabia. It was set up in 1962. For example, if there is a strong demand for marks on the part of IMF members and the Fund does not have sufficient marks on hand to satisfy the demand, the IMF can borrow marks from Germany.

Generalized System of Preferences (GSP). Preferences extended to selected **LDC** and **NIC** exports in the form of lower **tariffs** by developed countries.

Gold standard. The world's monetary standard from roughly 1850 to 1914, and briefly again in the 1920s and early 1930s. In order to be on the gold standard, a government must agree to buy and sell gold at a particular price. If the governments of all major trading countries guarantee the gold convertibility of their currencies, then the world is said to be on a gold standard.

Gold tranche. The proportion of an **IMF** member's line of credit at the Fund that can be borrowed automatically. It equals 25 percent of the member country's paid-in quota or subscription to the IMF. The remaining portions of a country's line of credit, called **credit tranches,** can be utilized only if certain conditions are met.

Green money. A part of the **common agricultural policy,** green money is actually an exchange rate for agricultural goods. Since European farm prices are quoted in **ECUs,** an appreciation of the mark relative to the ECU would cause German farm income expressed in marks to drop. To overcome this problem, a special exchange rate is established so that ECUs earned producing agricultural products can be converted into marks at a favorable rate. To bridge the gap between the value of sales at the actual exchange rate and the receipt of income at the green rate, **monetary compensatory amounts** are used.

Green taxes. Under a system of green taxes, a firm is charged a certain sum of money per unit of pollutant emitted. The revenue generated by such taxes is then used to help clean up the environment.

Gross domestic product (GDP). A measure of total economic activity within a nation, equal to the value of goods and services produced. Since output equals **aggregate demand,** GDP can be computed by adding together consumption, investment, and government expenditures on goods and services plus exports of goods and services and subtracting imports of goods and services. GDP also equals the level of **absorption** plus the **trade balance** (which can be negative). **Nominal GDP** equals the total value of goods and services produced in an economy measured in current market prices. **Real GDP** equals nominal GDP divided by the **GDP price deflator.** Real GDP strips away the effects of changes in the general price level and allows one to measure the level and changes in the level of real output and income.

Gross national product (GNP). Officially, the value of goods and services produced by domestic citizens both at home and abroad. GNP also equals the sum of consumption, investment, government expenditures on goods and services, and exports minus imports of goods and services, plus what domestic citizens earn abroad minus the corresponding earnings of nonresidents in the home country. GNP equals the level of **absorption** plus the **current account.** GNP, therefore, does differ from **GDP,** but this difference is inconsequential in the United States.

Heckscher-Ohlin (H-O) Theorem. According to the H-O theorem, international trade takes place because different countries have different relative factor proportions. Canada has *relatively* more land than Denmark, which has *relatively* more labor than Canada. One of the more important ideas in international economics, the H-O theorem was developed by Swedish economists Eli Heckscher and Bertil Ohlin.

Hedging. Playing it safe by avoiding taking an open or **uncovered** position in the foreign exchange market. For example, assume a U.S. importer of Mercedes-Benz automobiles knows that he will have to remit DM200 to the German company in, say, three months. To cover or hedge himself, he could buy DM200 on the **spot** market or the **forward** market, or purchase an **option** to buy marks. Regardless of the route he takes, the importer is protected from the effects of an appreciation of the mark during the next three months.

Import curve or schedule. A curve which shows the level of imports at various domestic price levels, assuming everything else is constant.

Import substitution. A development policy based on building up domestic industries, usually behind tariff walls and quotas, to displace imports. This is an inward-looking policy which, by and large, has been a colossal failure.

Incidence. Normally, the ultimate distribution of the burden of a tax. For example, an import duty on a given good may be paid partly by consumers and partly by producers who are afraid that passing all the tax onto consumers in the form of higher prices may adversely affect their sales. In such a case, the producers do not raise their price by the full extent of the duty, but absorb or pay a portion of it.

Increasing returns to scale. If all inputs are doubled and output more than doubles, increasing returns to scale have occurred. If inputs and output both double, **constant returns to scale** hold; and if output does not increase in step with an increase in inputs, but grows more slowly, **decreasing returns to scale** exist.

Indicative planning. Attempts by a government to encourage business firms to expand output in selected areas. The government provides a forecast showing the projected growth of demand in the target areas and hopes that this will encourage business firms to expand their activities in the area. Often, indicative planning is supplemented by government grants or subsidies as well as preferential tax treatment to firms doing business or planning to do business in the target areas.

Induced. See **Autonomous.**

Industrial policy. An economic policy designed to promote selected strategic or leading-edge industries through the judicious use of tax breaks, subsidies, import protection and the like.

Infant industry. A classic argument for tariff protection. Under conditions of **decreasing costs,** a newly established domestic industry that faces a limited market will be unable to compete with a foreign firm producing in a developed market. But, given protection today, the domestic firm will become profitable in the future as the domestic market expands.

Innovation offsets. When antipollution laws are enacted, a firm will attempt to find cleaner ways to produce a product and innovate to make the final product itself cleaner. These innovation offsets, according to some economists, will actually reduce the firm's production costs.

Interest rate parity. The **forward premium** or **discount** on, say, the dollar relative to the mark will equal the difference between interest rates in New York and Frankfurt.

Interest service ratio. Interest rate payments on external debt as a proportion of export earnings.

Internalizing costs. If a firm **internalizes** its full costs of production, it will cost-out the environmental impacts of its production. This will raise the firm's production costs. If a firm does not have to internalize or pay for the environmental havoc it wreaks upon the community, it is able to **externalize** some of its social costs of production. The community pays for a portion of the firm's total costs of production in the form of pollution or in the form of the taxes required to fund a cleanup of the firm-created pollution.

International investment position. The **direct investment** and international financial position of a country at a given point in time.

International Monetary Fund (IMF). Established in 1944, the IMF initially attempted to maintain fixed exchange rates by loaning funds to a nation when its currency came under pressure. Each of its more than 150 members pays subscriptions or quotas to the Fund when they join it—25 percent in dollars or **special drawing rights,** and 75 percent in their domestic currency. Based on their quotas, members have specified drawing rights **(gold and credit tranches),** and, in addition, they can obtain assistance from the several special facilities that have been established, such as the **Compensatory and Contingency Financing Facility.** With the breakdown of the fixed exchange rate system in the early 1970s, the IMF has devoted its efforts to helping nations in dire economic straits by giving them advice and financial assistance: for example, the severely indebted countries and the Eastern European nations.

International reserves. The sum of a nation's foreign exchange reserves of major currencies, its allotment of **SDRs,** plus its **gold tranche** at the **International Monetary Fund.**

Intraindustry trade. The simultaneous export and import of a given commodity. The United States, for example, both exports and imports telecommunications equipment. See **representative demand.**

J curve. An explanation of why a country's trade balance (graphed in the shape of a capital "J") will often deteriorate before it improves following a devaluation or depreciation.

Keynesians-Keynesianism. The term for economists who follow the lead of John Maynard Keynes in analyzing the economy and macroeconomic problems.

Labor costs per unit of output (LCUO). The labor cost involved in producing, say, a bicycle. Often, LCUO is computed by dividing total wage payments by the number of bicycles produced.

Labor intensive. See **capital intensive**.

Law of diminishing returns. If all inputs except one are fixed, output will increase, but at a decreasing rate as additional units of the variable input are employed.

Learning curve. Learning by doing. As production expands over time, unit costs drop due to an increase in the knowledge gained from repeatedly carrying out an operation. At the firm or industry level, learning by doing can show up when, given the capital stock, production increases even though direct labor inputs are reduced.

Least cost combination. The combination of capital and labor, given their wages or prices, that will produce a given amount of a particular commodity at minimum costs.

Leontief Paradox. A study by Wassily Leontief which demonstrated that the production of U.S. imports, when manufactured in the United States, was more capital intensive than the production of U.S. exports, the opposite of what the **Heckscher-Ohlin Theorem** would lead one to expect.

Less-developed Countries (LDCs). A difficult definition to pin down, although most economists generally know which countries they are talking about. Basically an LDC is a nonindustrialized country that has yet to achieve a sufficiently high level of national income that would permit it to finance economic growth solely from domestic sources.

Letter of intent. As a member state borrows increasing amounts from its line of credit at the **International Monetary Fund,** the conditions attached to the borrowing become more stringent. Normally, if a member state wants to borrow more than 50 percent of its **drawing rights,** it must submit a letter outlining its plans for overcoming the economic difficulties which led to the request for funds in the first place.

Liquidity effect. The change in the interest rate due to a change in the nominal money supply relative to the level of real income. By contrast, the **income effect** explains the change in the interest rate resulting from a change in real income given the nominal money supply.

Lomé Convention. The Lomé Convention was signed in Lomé, the capital of Togo, in 1975, and has been renewed several times. It is a trade and aid agreement between the **European Union** and various developing countries, primarily former colonies of European nations.

London Club. The location where debtor countries and their private creditors meet to negotiate terms of debt repayment. It is the private version of the **Paris Club.**

London Interbank Offer Rate (LIBOR). Best known by its acronym (LIBOR), it is the interest rate banks charge each other for loans on the **eurodollar** and **eurocurrency markets.** The LIBOR is also the basic interest rate in these markets.

Louvre Accord. An agreement by major countries signed in early 1987 that attempted to halt the slide in the value of the dollar at the time. The accord was later criticized by many economists for attempting to hold the dollar at unsustainable levels.

Maastricht Treaty. The 1991 agreement that outlined the steps to be taken to attain **Economic and Monetary Union.** The treaty has been ratified by most members of the EU, although Britain and Denmark have kept their options open.

Malign deficit. A trade deficit resulting from excessive absorption, normally in the form of a government budget deficit. See **benign deficit.**

Managed float. Under a managed float, exchange rates are determined primarily by market forces. However, governments attempt to control the speed at which exchange rates change and the magnitude of the change in a given time period.

Marginal propensity to consume (mpc). The increase in consumption given an increase in income. Similarly, the **marginal propensity to import (mpm)**

and the **marginal propensity to save (mps)**, respectively, measure the increase in imports and the increase in savings given an increase in income.

Marine Mammal Protection Act (MMPA). Enacted in 1972, the act requires the U.S. government to reduce the incidental killing of marine mammals by commercial fishers. Thus, when it was discovered that Mexican fishers were killing more than 1.5 times as many dolphins as U.S. fishers, the United States banned the importation of Mexican-caught tuna. (A GATT panel later ruled that the U.S. action was illegal.)

Market demand. The demand for an individual commodity or service such as TVs or nurses. The **market demand curve** shows the demand for TVs, for example, at various prices, other forces remaining constant.

Market supply. The supply of an individual commodity or service. The **market supply curve** displays the quantity supplied at various prices when other economic variables are constant.

Marshall-Lerner-Robinson Conditions. The necessary (although not sufficient) conditions for a successful depreciation-devaluation. In its simplest form, the argument states that the sum of import-demand elasticities, domestic and foreign, must exceed unity if depreciation-devaluation is to improve the trade balance.

Ministry of International Trade and Industry (MITI). An important Japanese institution which, together with private firms, works to promote Japanese exports. To some Japan-bashers, MITI is the devil incarnate.

Monetarists-monetarism. Economists who believe that changes in the money supply are the single most important determinant of changes in the level of aggregate demand, and, thus, the most important variable in explaining the rate of inflation and changes in the level of unemployment.

Monetary base. The foundation of the money supply. It can be measured by looking at either central bank assets or liabilities. On the asset side, the base is the sum of international reserves plus the domestic component of the monetary base, primarily central

bank holdings of government bonds. On the liability side, the base equals member bank reserves plus currency in circulation.

Monetary compensatory amounts (MCAs). A system of taxes and subsidies which finance the gap between a European community member's central **ECU** exchange rate and its green or agricultural exchange rate. See **green money.**

Monetary reform. Exchanging old money for new money. For example, East Germans traded in Ost marks for marks after the collapse of East Germany. Some of the old money, usually so much per firm or family, is exchanged for new money at a rate of, say, one to one, while additional amounts of the old money may be exchanged at increasingly unfavorable rates.

Money-income curve. The money-income curve shows the interest rate that prevails given the ratio of the money supply to real GDP, providing everything else remains constant. A rise in the general price level, for example, will lead to a higher interest rate, even though the money-to-real-GDP ratio may remain constant.

Money multiplier. In the simplest case, the reciprocal of the banks' **required reserve** ratio. The **monetary base** times the money multiplier equals the money supply.

Most favored nation (MFN). A most favored nation receives the best deal possible on trade relations with another nation. For example, if the United States were to grant Russia MFN status, Russian exports to the United States would face the same tariff rates imposed on the exports of existing most favored nations. Usually, the granting of MFN status is **reciprocal.** If the United States grants Russia most-favored-nation status, Russia bestows MFN on U.S. exports.

Multifiber arrangement (MFA). An international arrangement designed to limit exports of textiles from **LDCs** and **NICs** to developed countries. Under the **Uruguay Round** agreements, the multifiber arrangement is supposed to be phased out over 10 years.

Multilateral exchange rate. See **trade-weighted exchange rate.**

Net economic welfare. A measure designed to show the true economic welfare of a country. It is computed by adding such things as leisure brought about by a shorter work week to **gross domestic product,** and subtracting such items as the cost of pollution and congestion from **GDP.**

Newly industrializing countries (NICs). As in the case of **LDCs,** a precise definition of a NIC is difficult. Yet again, everyone knows the countries so classified. While not yet rich, NICs such as Korea and Taiwan are far from poor and their economies are rapidly advancing. Given present trends, they should be very wealthy in the next century.

Nontariff barriers (NTBs). Since **quotas** are outlawed by the rules of the **GATT,** and **tariffs** have been steadily cut in the post–World War II period, governments have used NTBs to protect selected domestic industries from foreign competition. The fruit of this work has been the development of such imaginative measures as **voluntary export restraints, product standards** and the like, all of which can and do restrict trade.

North American Free Trade Agreement (NAFTA). A free-trade area consisting of Canada, Mexico, and the United States instituted in 1994.

Official intervention. See **exchange rate stabilization.**

Official reserve balance. A method of measuring a nation's **balance of payments** position. A nation has a balance of payments surplus if, on a *net* basis, its central bank acquires international reserves. Thus, if foreign central bank holdings of dollars rise by $20 but the **Fed** holdings for foreign exchange reserves rise by $25, the United States has an official reserve balance surplus of $5.

Optimum currency area. A geographic region, not necessarily a country, in which it is advantageous to employ a single currency. Such an area may comprise more than one country, such as Russia and Belarus, in which case the nations may adopt a common currency or fixed exchange rates. Whether two or more countries constitute an optimum currency area depends on several things: the degree of wage-price flexibility within the area, the degree of labor mobility within the region, the degree of intraregional trade and the openness of the economies. If all these measures are high or large, the countries comprise an optimum currency area.

Optimum tariff. A country with a monopoly buyer position may be able to impose a tariff that, although it will cut the quantity of imports, will lead to such a drastic cut in the price of the commodity that the nation will be better off. Nations with a monopoly seller position may be able to impose an **optimum export duty.** Although this will lead to a drop in the quantity of goods exported, the resulting increase in the price will more than offset such a drop and the nation will actually end up earning more foreign exchange.

Options. The right, but not the obligation, to buy or sell foreign exchange (and other financial assets) at a set price at some specified time in the future.

Orderly Marketing Agreement (OMA). A trade agreement negotiated by several nations, both exporters and importers, and permitted under the rules of the **GATT.** The **multifiber arrangement** is an example.

Organization for Economic Cooperation and Development (OECD). The rich nations' economic club. Its 24 members are primarily Western European countries plus Australia, Canada, Japan, New Zealand, and the United States. Many **NICs** are joining the club, however, and it is reasonable to assume that more will join it in the future.

Overvalued currency. A currency whose nominal exchange rate is too high given relative rates of inflation. Imagine that the mark/dollar exchange rate stands initially at DM2/$1. Then suppose that the U.S. price level doubles. The nominal exchange rate should move to DM1/$ in order to maintain the real exchange rate. If the nominal exchange rate remains at DM2/$, the dollar is said to be overvalued and, most likely, U.S. exports will decline and its imports will increase. Some economists contend that overvaluation and undervaluation should also be related to changes in labor productivity. Thus, if German labor productivity doubles while U.S. labor productivity remains constant, the exchange rate should move from DM2/$ to DM1/$, or the dollar will be overvalued if the exchange rate remains constant.

Paris Club. Meetings held in Paris at which a group of creditor countries negotiate the scheduling or rescheduling of payments on government (but not private) loans. See **London Club.**

Parity Grid. See **European Monetary System.**

Pass-through effect. Often called the **pass-through coefficient,** it measures the extent to which a depreciation-devaluation is passed through to domestic prices. Especially in the case of imperfect competitors, foreign suppliers may absorb a portion of the depreciation and, as a result, a 10 percent depreciation may only lead to a 5 percent increase in the domestic price of imports. If that happens, half the cost of the depreciation is passed through to domestic consumers and half is absorbed by foreign suppliers.

Petrodollars. At the time of both the first and second oil shocks (1974 and 1979, respectively), oil was priced in dollars. Because the rapid rise in petroleum prices generated large dollar earnings, oil exporters were unable to spend all their dollar earnings. They deposited excess funds in the **eurodollar market,** which led to the name "petrodollars."

Plaza Accord. In the fall of 1985, representatives of the governments of Germany, France, Japan, the UK, and the United States met to discuss the international position of the dollar. They concluded that the dollar had appreciated too much against other currencies during the 1980s and recommended, for the sake of the world economy, that the dollar should fall even if this required **official intervention** in the foreign exchange markets. The dollar did depreciate markedly in 1986, but since it had been depreciating slightly prior to the Plaza Accord, there is a debate as to how much the accord had to do with the dollar's subsequent decline.

Policy framework papers (PFP). These papers spell out the policies that a nation plans to adopt when it borrows funds from the IMF under the **Structural Adjustment Facility.**

Policy independence. Under a flexible exchange rate, the monetary authority does not need to worry about the exchange rate, but can follow a monetary policy dedicated solely to solving domestic problems. Under a fixed exchange rate, the monetary authority does not have such independence, since it must keep an eye on external events and the possible impact of domestic policies on the exchange rate.

Portfolio investment. The purchase of stocks of a foreign company. The purchase of a controlling interest, 10 percent or more, is classified as **direct investment,** not as portfolio investment.

Portfolio theory. A description of why an individual will spread her wealth among various financial assets depending upon relative rates of return and the perceived risk associated with holding the various assets. She will increase her holdings of a risky asset only if it yields a higher-than-average rate of return.

Potential gross national product. The level of real output that an economy can produce if all its resources, labor and capital, are fully employed.

Precautionary cash reserve. A cash reserve that an individual holds to bridge an unforeseen but potential gap between expenditures and income. On the international scene, countries hold **international reserves** in order to bridge a gap between expenditures on imports and earnings from exports.

Price discrimination. Selling a commodity at different prices in different markets. It is associated with **dumping** in international trade.

Pricing to market. Firms set prices at different levels in different markets in order to maintain or expand their market shares. See **price discrimination.**

Process (production) standards. A measure of the environmental damage caused by the production of a particular commodity. A product can be produced by environmentally "clean" standards in one country, but by "dirty" methods in another. See **devaluation dumping.**

Producer surplus. What the producer obtains from the sale of an item minus what it costs him to produce it. An increase in the price of the item will increase his surplus.

Product cycle. The theory, initially formulated by Raymond Vernon, that products go through a life cycle. In their early stages, they are manufactured in developed nations. With the passage of time, production is moved to **LDCs** and **NICs.**

Product standard. In the field of environmental studies, product standard refers to the environmental quality of a particular product, such as DDT causes so much harm.

Production possibility curve. A chart or diagram which shows the alternative combinations of two commodities—traditionally guns and butter—that can be produced in a given economy at a particular moment of time.

Productivity. The wellspring of national well being. Labor productivity can be measured by output per worker or output per worker-hour.

Project Link. A proposal to link the creation of **special drawing rights** with economic assistance to LDCs. Thus, under Project Link, all new SDRs would be allocated to LDCs. As the LDCs spend the SDRs, the worldwide supply of **international reserves** would increase. In other words, the LDCs would get the **seignorage** associated with the expansion of international reserves.

Protective tariff. A tariff designed to restrict imports and encourage domestic production of either the commodity in question or a substitute commodity. Most tariffs have a **protective effect** regardless of their purpose.

Publically guaranteed loans. When a bank makes a loan, for example, to a private Mexican company and the government of Mexico guarantees the repayment of the loan, the loan is said to be publically guaranteed. In some instances, a public guarantee is required if a private firm is to borrow on international capital markets.

Purchasing power parity (PPP). PPP argues that nominal exchange rates should be adjusted for inflation differentials so that real exchange rates remain constant. Purchasing power or some variant is often employed to see whether a currency is either **overvalued** or **undervalued.**

Quota. A physical limit on the number of foreign goods that may be imported into a country.

Real balance. A money balance with constant purchasing power.

Real balance effect. The impact of a change in real money balances on the economy. Suppose the domestic price level and the wage level double. In real terms, wages are constant so real consumption should remain constant. However, inflation drops the purchasing power of money balances and this causes real consumption to decline as people use some of their income to rebuild their real balances. A decrease in the general price level, which increases the purchasing power or value of money balances, will lead to an increase in real expenditures since individuals will spend their excess real money balances.

Real rate. The change or level of the nominal rate minus the change or level of the general price level. The term is used, for example, with the **real rate of interest,** the **real exchange rate, real GNP,** and so on. The real exchange rate, $(DM/\$)_R$, equals the nominal exchange rate, $(DM/\$)$, times any change in domestic price indices, (PI_{US}/PI_G). Thus, if the exchange rate was DM2/$ in 1994, and U.S. prices doubled while German prices remained constant, and the nominal exchange rate did not change, the real exchange rate in 1995 would be DM4/$, or a real appreciation of the dollar. (DM2/$ times 200/100 equals DM4/$).

Relative price. The price of one good or service in terms of another.

Representative demand. Basically income per capita. The concept, introduced by Steffan Linder, has been employed to explain the growth of **intraindustry trade** between countries with similar incomes per capita.

Repressed inflation. A situation in which an inflationary increase in the money supply does not lead to the expected increase in the domestic price level. An inflation can be repressed by price controls or by an import surplus.

Revealed comparative advantage. An attempt to measure a country's relative comparative advantage over a number of products. Revealed comparative advantage is determined, for example, in PCs by computing a country's share of worldwide exports of PCs and dividing that number by the country's share of *total* worldwide exports. The higher the resulting quotient compared to other such quotients, the greater the country's revealed comparative advantage in personal computers.

Revenue tariff. A tariff designed to raise revenue, not to restrict imports. Most tariffs have a **revenue effect** even if their primary objective is to protect a domestic industry, not to raise revenue.

Rules of origin. Rules of origin specify how much of the value of a product must be added locally, or regionally, in the case of free-trade arrangements, for the product to receive preferential tariff treatment. Under NAFTA, for example, 60 percent of the value of a car must be added in Canada, Mexico, and/or the United States for the car to receive preferential tariff treatment.

Seignorage. In today's context, the income one obtains by issuing money. If the dollar were the sole internationally acceptable currency, for example, the United States would receive income if foreigners held dollars as international reserves, especially if they did not hold the dollars in interest-earning obligations of the U.S. government. If the gold standard were reintroduced, the two largest gold producers, Russia and the Union of South Africa, would receive most of the seignorage.

Severely indebted country (SIC). A country is classified as "severely indebted" by the **World Bank** if the present value of its debt service exceeds 220 percent of its exports or 80 percent of its GDP.

Single European Act. The 1987 act which set out to abolish all nontariff barriers to trade within the **EU,** and to eliminate all restrictions on capital and labor mobility within the region. The target date for achieving these objectives was December 31, 1992.

Smithsonian Agreement. The last futile attempt to preserve the **Bretton Woods** system of fixed exchange rates. In 1971, President Nixon had the bad timing to declare the Smithsonian Agreement "the greatest monetary agreement in the history of the world." Less

than two years later, the agreement was dead as a door-nail.

Snake in the tunnel. An exchange rate system employed by a group of European nations between 1972 and 1973. Under it, cross-exchange rates between European currencies were allowed to vary ±2.25 percent against each other and ±4.5 percent against the dollar. Under the **European Monetary System,** the snake still lives, but the tunnel has been abandoned. Until 1993, European currencies that were members of the **Exchange Rate Mechanism** could move only ±2.25 percent against each other but without limit against the dollar. Since August 1993, ERM currencies can move ±15 percent against each other, and freely against the dollar.

Snap-back provision. Under NAFTA, a country is permitted to raise its tariffs to pre-NAFTA levels for three to four years when an industry is imperiled by a surge of imports.

Social dumping. See **devaluation dumping.**

Special deposit. Under a system of special deposits, a bank is required to deposit a certain sum of money interest-free for a specified period whenever it purchases foreign exchange. The special deposit could be for a year and equal 100 percent of the value of the foreign exchange purchased. The idea behind the concept is to raise the cost of purchasing foreign exchange—the bank loses the interest it could have received on the funds—and to reduce speculation.

Special drawing rights (SDRs). Sometimes called paper gold, SDRs were conceived at the **IMF** meeting at Rio de Janeiro in 1967. Upon approval of its members, the IMF issues **SDRs** to member countries who can then use them as **international reserves.**

Speculative bubble. The **appreciation** or **depreciation** of a currency based on the belief, not on economic fundamentals, that it will rise or fall in value.

Spot market. The current market for a currency as distinguished from the **forward market.**

Static gains and losses. Normally associated with economic integration. The static net gain or loss from economic integration equals the gain from **trade creation** minus the loss resulting from **trade diversion**.

Sterilization. The attempt by a central bank to offset the impact of international trade or capital flows on the domestic money supply. For example, a **trade balance** surplus will increase the central bank's holdings of **international reserves** and, as a result, the **monetary base** in most cases. By selling off some of its holdings of government bonds, the central bank can reduce the **domestic component** of the monetary base and keep the money supply constant. Sterilization, or attempts at it, can also be used to maintain the money supply in the face of a trade deficit.

Strategic trade policy. A theory which shows how, under special conditions, a nation may gain at the expense of its trading partners by employing subsidies and trade restrictions.

Structural Adjustment Facility (SAF). An account or line of credit at the **IMF** that member nations may utilize to finance structural reforms such as changing the banking system in order to encourage greater private savings. Under the **SAF** and the **Extended Structural Adjustment Facility (ESAF)**, the IMF extends loans, primarily to LDCs and Eastern European countries, for periods of up to 10 years at subsidized (below market) rates of interest.

Subsidies. A government cash grant per unit produced. As a result, domestic goods are priced below production costs. This may enable a country to keep out imports or to expand exports. See **countervailing duties**.

Super 301. A section of the U.S. Trade Act of 1988 which requires the U.S. Trade Representative to impose restrictions on U.S.-destined exports of countries whose economic policies are judged to discourage or restrict potential U.S. exports.

Sustainable debt ratio. The debt-to-income ratio depends on output, absorption, real interest rates, the growth in real income, and the current debt/GDP ratio. If absorption exceeds output (that is, if imports exceed exports), or even if absorption equals output, while the real rate of interest on the debt exceeds the real rate of growth of GDP, the nation's debt/GDP ratio will rise, or the present debt/GDP ratio will not be sustainable.

Swap agreement. In the present context, an agreement between central banks to exchange domestic currencies. For example, the Bundesbank and the Fed swap marks for dollars and agree to reverse the swap at a specified date at a certain exchange rate. It is a technique that permits central banks to increase their **international reserves** in the short run.

Systemic Transformation Facility. A recently created IMF facility which gives assistance to hard-pressed transitional economies such as Russia. It is designed to help former communist states in their passage toward market-based economies.

Target zones. A target range of permitted exchange rate fluctuations. Similar to a **currency band**.

Tariffs. A tax on imports. Many tariffs are percentage or **ad valorem** taxes.

Terms of trade. In its simplest form, the price of exports divided by the price of imports. This is called the **commodity terms of trade**. The **income terms of trade** is calculated by multiplying the commodity terms of trade by the quantity of exports.

Trade balance. In the press, defined as the difference between exports and imports of goods or merchandise exclusively. In the calculation of national income, the trade balance is defined as the exports of goods and services minus imports of goods and services. The **trade balance curve** shows the levels of national income and national prices at which exports equal imports providing other variables are constant.

Trade balance multiplier. The change in the trade balance equals the change in some variable—such as investment or government expenditures or exports—times the trade balance multiplier. The trade balance multiplier tells us how much a change in the autonomous variable will change the trade balance.

Trade creation. The increase in trade which results from the elimination of intraunion tariffs when a **customs union** is created.

Trade diversion. Often referred to as the costs of a customs union—at least in static terms. More specifically, it is the welfare cost incurred when a country stops purchasing a good from the world's most efficient producer and buys it from the custom union's most efficient producer following the erection of the common external tariff.

Trade effect. The impact of a change in the general price level on the **trade balance** and, as a result, on **aggregate demand** and **GDP.** A decline in the general price level will stimulate exports, reduce imports, and increase aggregate demand.

Trade-weighted exchange rate. A trade-weighted exchange rate is an index number that tells us what has happened to the value of the dollar relative to the currencies of all its major trading partners. Often, a trade-weighted exchange rate is called a **multilateral exchange rate.**

Transitory adjustment. If there is an increase, for example, in the demand for PCs, the price of PCs will rise. As a result, PC producers will make greater profits and will produce more PCs. However, higher profits will induce other firms to start producing PCs, further increasing the supply of PCs and driving down their price and the profits of all PC producers. The temporary rise in the price of PCs and the profits of the producers are the transitory adjustment.

Treaty of Rome. The agreement signed by Belgium, France, Germany, Italy, Luxembourg, and the Netherlands at Rome in 1957, which established the European Economic Community which, in turn, evolved into the **European Union.**

Uncovered Interest Rate Parity Theorem. The rate of the rise or fall in the DM/$ rate, for example, depends on the difference between nominal interest rates in Germany and the United States since, according to the theorem, that difference reflects the difference in the relative rates of inflation in Germany and the United States. And it is assumed that nominal exchange rates will adjust to inflation differentials.

Uncovered (open) position. See **hedging.**

Undervalued currency. See **overvalued currency.**

Uruguay Round. The latest round of **GATT** talks, which were completed in 1994.

Value-added tax (VAT). A tax on the value added at each stage of production. For example, if a firm buys $20 of materials and then makes a yo-yo which it sells for $50, the value added is $30. If the VAT is 10 percent, the firm pays a $3 tax on the $30 value which is added. VATs are a major source of tax revenue within the nations of the **European Union.** Value-added taxes have been introduced in Eastern Europe as part of the reform packages.

Vehicle currency. Only a few currencies are used in conducting international trade, that is, for pricing goods and services and financial assets. Such currencies are called vehicle currencies.

Very-Short-Term Credit Facility. An arrangement under which the central banks of the EU lend each other funds for up to three months in order to help stabilize exchange rates. For example, during the European currency mayhem in the fall of 1992, it is estimated that the Bundesbank lent some $100 billion to other European central banks in an attempt to maintain the **parity grid** of the **European Monetary System.**

Vicious circle. A vicious circle occurs when one event leads to another which offsets the positive effects of the first. A depreciation, introduced to improve the trade balance, may lead to domestic inflation which negates the trade-improving effect of the depreciation and leads to the need for another depreciation which leads to more inflation and so on. In a **virtuous circle,** one positive event leads to another.

Voluntary Export Agreement (VER). An accord under which an exporter agrees to limit his exports of a particular commodity to a specific country. The VER covering Japanese automobile exports to the United States is an example.

Voluntary Import Expansion Agreement (VIE). Under a VIE, a nation agrees to import a certain number or value of, say, auto parts by a certain date or in a particular period.

Widened band. See **currency band.**

World aggregate supply. The world aggregate supply curve shows the quantity of some composite good supplied by all the world's producers at various **domestic** price levels.

World Bank. Officially, the **International Bank for Reconstruction and Development.** The World Bank helps to finance development in LDCs by raising funds on private capital markets and loaning the proceeds to third world countries.

World Trade Organization (WTO). The successor to the **GATT.** Conceived at the **Uruguay Round** of trade talks, it was born in 1994.

Index